William Keddie

Anecdotes literary and scientific

Illustrative of the characters, habits, and conversation of men of letters and science. Third Edition

William Keddie

Anecdotes literary and scientific
Illustrative of the characters, habits, and conversation of men of letters and science. Third Edition

ISBN/EAN: 9783337108519

Printed in Europe, USA, Canada, Australia, Japan

Cover: Foto ©Suzi / pixelio.de

More available books at **www.hansebooks.com**

ANECDOTES

LITERARY AND SCIENTIFIC

ILLUSTRATIVE OF THE

CHARACTERS, HABITS, AND CONVERSATION OF
MEN OF LETTERS AND SCIENCE

EDITED BY

WILLIAM KEDDIE,
SECRETARY TO THE PHILOSOPHICAL SOCIETY OF GLASGOW

Third Edition

LONDON
CHARLES GRIFFIN AND COMPANY
STATIONERS' HALL COURT
1863

PREFACE.

The contents of the following pages have been culled from many sources, and embrace a great diversity of subjects. It has been the purpose of the compiler to combine useful information with innocent entertainment; to invite to the cultivation of literature and of science; to minister to refined tastes, and foster large intellectual sympathies. Whilst the volume aims at the gratification of a general class of readers, the interests of the young have been constantly kept in view in the selection, which, it is hoped, contains nothing, either in sentiment or expression, adverse to their moral and intellectual improvement.

The paucity of anecdotes, in the annals of science, possessed of personal interest, will account for the meagreness of this department of the collection, as compared with the amplitude and variety of the literary portion.

The subject of Art and Artists is deferred for another of the Cyclopædias projected by the Publishers.

CONTENTS.

	PAGE
Abernethy, Dr., and Curran,	99
" A Class Illustration,	100
" Integrity and Honour,	104
" Generosity,	104
" Wit and Eccentricity,	103
Actors and Preachers,	123
Addison and the Poetaster,	157
Addison's Companions,	172
" Diffidence,	184
" Gravity,	184
" Timidity,	222
"Admiral Hosier's Ghost,"	182
Aërolites in British Museum,	350
Agassiz, M., on the Alps,	20
Age, Literary and Scientific pursuits of,	211
Ainsworth's Dicitionary burnt by his Wife,	24
Akenside and Rolt,	251
Akenside's "Pleasures of Imagination,"	44
Albert, Prince, Experiments with Gun-Cotton,	89
Alchymists, Common lot of,	224
Aldrich's Love of Music,	254
Alfieri and his Assistant Translators,	367
Alfred the Great Learning to Read,	196
Alibi, Proving an,	297
Almanac, First English,	48
Almanac Weather Wisdom,	48
Amanuenses,	34
American Goethe,	180
Anæsthetic Agents,	105
Anagrams,	252
" and Puns,	194
Anatomists and Anatomy,	1
"Anatomy of Melancholy,"	18
Anderson, Dr. W., a Ponderous Author,	187
Animals, Footprints of, on Ancient Rocks,	299
Animals, Playfulness of,	296
Animosity, Judicial,	110
Antiquarian Enthusiasm,	293
Antiquarianism,	32
Antiquary Described,	33
"Apprentices," Hogarth's,	246

	PAGE
Arachnoid Garment,	241
Archimedes and the Lever,	31
Army, Literature in the,	288
Arnauld and Spelman,	211
Art Criticism,	275
Art of Printing, Origin of,	188
Asinine Bishopric,	108
"Asses and Savans," Napoleon's, in Egypt,	209
Astronomer, Female,	68
Astronomers and Astronomy,	5
Atomic Theory of Dalton, La Place's Opinions of,	207
Attainments of Dr. Whewell,	209
Atterbury's, Bishop, Oratory,	119
Author, a Mad,	31
" a Mendicant,	15
Authoress, American, and Sir Walter Scott,	115
Authors, Amanuenses of,	34
" Conversation of,	33
" Deceptions of,	27
" Dull,	225
" Favourite Dishes of,	36
" Honours and Rewards of,	14
" Irritability and Vanity of,	31
" Learning and Labours of,	22
" Miscellaneous Anecdotes of,	35
" Not the Best Judges of their own Writings,	32
" Peculiarities and Eccentricities of,	18
" Precocity of,	7
" Tenderness and Affection of,	28
" Trials and Miseries of,	17
" Whims and Caprices of,	31
" Wit and Humour of,	24
Authorship, Profits of Recent,	218
Autographs in British Museum,	341
Babbage's Calculating Machine,	280
Bacon, Lady,	366
" Founder of the Inductive Philosophy,	73
Bacon's, Lord, Name and Memory,	111
" Inconsistencies,	270
Baillie, Joanna,	137
Bainbridge, Dr., Epigram on,	253

CONTENTS.

	PAGE
Ballantyne, John, Amanuensis to Scott,	34
Balzac's, M., Romantic Marriage,	95
Bank Note for a Million Pounds,	167
Bank of England's Weighing Machine,	87
Banks, Sir Joseph, and Dr. Solander,	12
Bards, Honour to the,	16
Bargain-Hunters of Books,	47
Barton and Nash,	281
Bateman's, Dr., Economy of Time,	97
Bautru, M. de,	271
Bayle's Pyrrhonism,	11
Beecher's Chemical Enthusiasm,	56
Bee in the Crystal Palace,	315
Beecher, Dr. Lyman, Sermon to a Small Audience,	109
Bells,	340
" What they said to the Widow,	233
Berthollet the Chemist,	207
Berzelius the Chemist,	227
Bettesworth and Swift,	163
Bible, Early Translations of,	40
" Present Translation of,	40
" Lost Books Mentioned in,	40
" the " Vinegar,"	266
Bibles, English, Inaccuracies of,	189
Bibliomania,	262
Binding of Books,	46
Bindings, Preservation of,	46
Bishop, Madame A., Singing in Ten Languages,	126
Black, Dr., and the Hydrogen Gas Balloon,	54
Black and Hutton's Snail-Dinner,	224
" Mrs., the "Maid of Athens," Visit of N. P. Willis to,	130
Black-Letter Books,	42
" Hunters,	42
Blacklock and David Hume,	154
Blood, Transfusion of, in Royal Society,	206
Blue Stockings, Origin of the Name,	87
Boerhaave, Old Age of,	103
Boileau and Racine,	155
Bolingbroke, Lord,	231
Book Auctions,	45
" Trade of Leipsig,	45
" Attempt to Print a Perfect,	190
" the first Printed,	190
" Collectors,	347
" Making,	346
Books, Ancient Value of,	346
" Hood the Humourist on,	198
Bookseller and Author,	44

	PAGE
Booksellers and Printers,	192
" the Patrons of Literature,	44
Booksellers, Books, and Bibliomaniacs,	41
" Manœuvres of,	290
Bossuet,	267
Boswell, James, and Johnson,	218
" and the Writ of " Quare adhæsit pavimento,"	90
" Bear-Leading Rewarded,	224
Botanical Satire,	314
Botanist, the, and the Irish Mail-Coach Driver,	49
Botanists and Botany,	49
Bourdonne, Madame de,	275
Bowles, Caroline,	148
Bowles and Moore,	233
Bowles', Canon, Absence of Mind,	144
Boyse, Samuel, a Poor Fag Author,	152
Boxhorn's Smoking and Reading,	250
Brain, How to Turn the,	240
Bramble's, Matthew, " Vimonda,"	19
Brandt, the Indian Chief, and Campbell the Poet,	169
Breakfast at Rogers',	165
Brebeuf,	250
Brevity,	267
Bristol Milkwoman's Poetry,	275
Brougham and Lyndhurst,	121
Brougham's, Lord, Chancellorship,	92
" Labours,	121
" Natural Portraits,	92
Buchanan, George, and Henry VIII.,	152
Buchanan's " Scotland,"	23
Buckland's, Dr., Alligator and Dinner Party,	2
Buffon, the Naturalist,	242
Buffon's Son,	286
Bumper, Origin of the Word,	38
Bunbury, Selina, and the Norwegian Fairy Legend-Hunter.	212
Bunker Hill Monument, Effect of Heat,	363
Bunyan and the "Book of Martyrs,"	226
Burke, Edmund, at Hastings' Trial,	124
" and the Riot Act,	280
" put to Flight in the Commons,	121
Burke's Conversation,	216
" Melodramatic Trick and Sheridan's Sarcasm,	122
Burnet, the Judge and the Bishop,	220
Burnet's Absence of Mind,	297
Burney, Dr., and Johnson,	236
" Miss (Madame D'Arblay),	118

	PAGE
Burney's Anagram on Nelson,	195
Burning of Shelley's Remains,	180
Burn's "Justice,"	231
Burns in a Printing Office,	191
Burns', Robert, "Chloris," her Unhappy Fate,	132
" Early Reading,	146
Burritt, Elihu, the Learned Blacksmith,	127
Burton's "Anatomy of Melancholy,"	18
Burton, Author of "Anatomy of Melancholy,"	253
Butler's "Hudibras,"	35
" Pride,	155
Byron and Peel,	153
Byron's "Maid of Athens,"	130
" Heartless Mother,	174
" Writings, Characteristics of,	258
Cacoethes Scribendi, incurable case of,	187
Calendar, Roman,	239
Camoens and his Black Servant,	155
Camoens' "Lusiad,"	154
Campbell, The Lord Rector,	9
" at Hohenlinden,	182
" and the Queen,	147
" and Hooke,	163
" and Turner the Painter,	159
" and Wilson at Paisley Races,	136
" and Son of the Indian Chief,	169
Campbell's, Thomas, University Spree,	24
" Reminiscence of James Grahame,	35
" "Gertrude," and the "Pleasures of Hope,"	153
" "Lochiel's Warning,"	108
" Lyrics,	143
" Death,	164
"Can she spin?"	127
Candour,	267
Canning on Grattan's Eloquence,	123
Canning's Rhyme for Julianna,	148
Caprices and Contradictions,	32
Carey's, Henry, Ballads,	19
Carlos', Don, Travels of King Philip,	260
Carlyle's, T., Advice to the Poets,	176
Carmeline the Dentist,	252
Casaubon,	270
Cato,	232
Cause and Effect, Charles Lamb,	26
Cavendish, Hon. Henry, the Chemist, his Oddities	52
Cavendish's Disregard of Money,	216

	PAGE
Caxton, William, the first English Printer,	183
Cellini's, Benvenuto, History,	13
Cervantes, Magnanimity of,	117
Chalmers'. Dr. Thos., Literary Habits,	219
" Pulpit Oratory in London,	122
" Simplicity and Tenderness,	28
" Estimate of Butler's "Analogy,"	252
Chapelain and the Spider,	241
Charles V., Saying of,	266
Chatham, Lord,	281
Chatterton's Misery,	136
Chaucer in the Tower,	177
Chaucer's Dream of a Crystal Palace,	86
Cheeryble, Brothers,	115
Chemical Experimenting,	222
Chemists and Chemistry,	52
Chemist's Dream,	56
" Power over Matter,	343
Chesterfield, Lord, and Johnson,	235
Chillingworth,	254
Chloroform and Ether,	105
Christianity, Sir H. Davy on,	227
Churchill's, "Rosciad,"	153
Clairvoyance,	328
Clarkson the Philanthropist,	107
Classical Application,	234
" Glory,	127
" Spots in,	322
Club, The Roxburgh,	108
Coal, Steam, and Iron,	83
Cobbett's Early Recollections,	281
Coffee-Houses, Literary,	283
Coleridge as a Horseman,	164
" as a Soldier,	140
" at Rogers',	166
" Wordsworth, and Cottle,	151
Coleridge's Youth,	159
" Opium-eating,	159
" " Remorse for	160
" Absence of mind,	161
" Mistake of Silence for Wisdom,	110
" "Watchman,"	228
Collins the Poet,	255
Collodion and Gun-cotton,	88
Colman's, the Younger, Recollections of Goldsmith,	248
"Coming Events cast their Shadows before,"	108
Commerce and Science,	213

CONTENTS

	PAGE
Comptroller of Stamps and Wordsworth,	168
Conchology and Collectors,	295
Consonants, Doing Justice to the,	123
Contentment of Boerhaave,	103
Controversy, Scholastic,	266
Conversation,	275
" of Birch,	217
" Burke,	216
" Coleridge,	217
" Descartes, La Fontaine, Butler, Addison, Milton, &c.,	33
" Johnson,	216
" Literary Men,	110
Copyrights, American,	272
Corneille,	252
"Corsair," Byron's,	224
"Cotter's Saturday Night,"	272
Cottle's, Jos., Anecdotes of Coleridge,	140
" Anecdotes of Wordsworth,	142
Courtly Complaisance, D'Usez,	234
Cowley and his Misfortunes,	171
Cowper and his Critic,	225
Cowper's, William, Letters,	138
" Schoolboy Tormentor,	138
" Amusements,	147
" "John Gilpin,"	178
" Habits of Composition,	143
" Poems at first unsaleable,	43
" "Task,"	144
Crabbe and Lord-Chancellor Thurlow,	147
Cranmer and Henry VIII.,	325
Critic, a true, defined by Swift,	60
" Royal,	60
Critical Dictionary of Bayle,	11
Criticism, Dying of,	216
" of a Hatter's Sign,	269
Criticized Poet,	227
Critics and Criticism,	60
Crusoe, Robinson, Manuscript of,	107
Crystal Palace and Victoria Regia,	291
" Poetical Prediction of,	86
" Statistics of,	86
Curran, Judicial Animosity against,	110
" and Abernethy,	99
Curran's Rebuke to Lord Clare on the Bench,	111
" Opinion of Byron's Sorrows,	133
Cuvier, Baron,	206
Cuvier's Literature and Science,	71
" Childhood,	71
" Reconstruction of Organic Remains,	72
Czar and Monk,	368

	PAGE
Dale, Dr., and Queen Elizabeth,	319
Dalrymple, Sir J., and Burns,	191
Dalton's Atomic Theory and La Place,	207
Dante's "Comedia,"	23
Darwin's Prediction of Railways and Steam-boats,	88
Davies, Eleanor, and the Anagram,	194
Davy, Sir Humphry, on Christianity,	227
" Geologizing in Sicily,	71
" Scott, and the Tyrolese Patriot,	228
" and Wordsworth,	150
" and the French Savans,	207
Davy's, Sir Humphry, Industry and Devotedness,	55
" Disinterested Humanity,	73
Dawes', Sir W., Fondness of a Pun,	255
Day in the Crystal Palace,	299
Day, Author of "Sandford and Merton,"	287
Decimals,	249
Dedications,	213, 262
De Lolme's Treatment in England,	21
"De Mortuis nil nisi Bonum,"	246
Defoe, Daniel,	118
" and the Ghost,	27
" and the Union,	18
Denon and Madame Talleyrand,	16
Deodati and Dumonlin,	260
Derby, Lord, and Brougham,	246
Dermody and Chatterton,	7
Descartes,	242, 262
"Deserted Village," Goldsmith's,	158
Devil and Dr. Faustus,	190
Diary, Moore's, Notes of a Speech in,	149
Dibdin's Poems,	16
Dickens, Charles, and Squeers,	116
" and the Brothers Cheeryble,	115
Diet, Singular,	299
Dinner, Poetical invitation to, by Moore,	230
" at Haydon's Painting-Room,	167
" Literary,	214
Diplomatists, Singing and Dancing,	185
Dipping Charles Lamb,	135
Diversion, Literary,	92
Diving-bell, Descent in,	82
Doctors, Female,	102
Dollar, Origin of the Word,	289
Don Quixote,	26
Douglas', David, Botanical Ardour and Hapless Fate,	40

CONTENTS.

	PAGE
Dream, the Chemist's,	56
Drelincourt upon Death,	27
Drummond,	81
Dryden at Westminster School,	145
Dryden's Poverty and Toils,	152
Ducking-Stool,	313
Dungeon Compositions,	177
Duns Scotus,	25
Dutch, the,	242
Dwight's Theology Dictated to an Amanuensis,	34
"Edinburgh Review,"	279
Edward VI., the Gifted,	243
Eldon, Lord, Travelling to London, when a Boy,	89
Electioneering Epigram,	324
Electric Spark,	80
,, Telegraph, Comic,	75
,, ,, Early Ideas of,	75
,, ,, Marriage by,	78
,, ,, Origin of,	76
,, ,, Parliamentary,	78
,, ,, Romance of,	74
,, ,, Storm of,	74
Electricity, Velocity of,	79
Eliot and the Indians,	367
Eloquence in Wine,	39
Engineering, the Pyramids and the Railways,	83
English and German,	242
English Wife on Saturday Night,	297
Epitaph, Progress of an,	63
Erasmus' "Colloquies,"	260
Errata, Intentional,	193
Errors of the Press,	190, 192, 193
Erskine's, Lord, Points,	91
,, ,, Debut at the Bar,	122
"Essay on Man," Pope's,	176
Ether and Chloroform,	105
Ettrick Shepherd and Scott,	277
Euripides' Three Verses,	182
"Exegi Monumentum,"	367
Experiments on the Lower Animals,	1
Explorers of Africa, Early,	66
Extempore Preaching,	240
Falstaff's Buckram-men,	220
Fans,	312
Faraday, Michael, as a Lecturer,	121
Faraday's Perseverance,	55
Faustus, Dr., and the Devil,	190
Favourite Authors, Predilection for,	37
Female Promoters of Science and Philosophy,	67
Fenelon, a Saying of,	11
Ferula of the Ancients,	342

	PAGE
Fielding's "Amelia,"	221
"Fife and Drum,"	24
Filicaia's Sonnets,	38
Fitzgibbon and Curran,	110
Forbes, Professor, in the Alps,	208
Foulises of Glasgow, their Editions of Classics,	191
Fox, Charles J., at Hastings' Trial,	122
France, Savans of,	206
Francis I.,	266
Franklin, Benjamin, as a Bookseller,	41
Franklin's, Benjamin, Discoveries,	88
,, ,, Knowledge of Languages,	128
French Academy,	293
,, Blunders, in translation,	367
,, and English,	297
,, Mrs., a Female Doctor,	102
Friend-hunter, a Disappointed,	363
Froissart's Antiquarianism,	23
Fuseli on Small Talk,	228
Galileo's Blindness,	6
,, Youthful Pursuits,	210
,, Abjuration,	210
Gallery of the House of Commons, Scene in,	120
Galvanic Experiments on a Murderer,	3
Galvanism, Discovery of,	346
Galvanizing an Indian,	324
Gardiner, W., in the Gallery of the House of Commons,	120
Gassendi,	241
Gay-Lussac,	207
Gay's Wealth and Improvidence,	185
,, Portrait,	186
,, Appetite at Table,	186
Geological Allegory,	69
,, Discovery,	349
Geology and Natural History,	69
Geometry of Newton,	5
German Student,	339
"Gertrude of Wyoming," and Son of Brandt,	169
Gibbon and Lord North,	15
Gibbon's Roman Empire,	22
,, Rule for Reading,	198
Gladiatorship, Intellectual,	261
Glazing of Ancient Windows,	348
Glover, Dr., and the Tulips,	182
"God Save the King," authorship of,	19
,, ,, origin of,	178
Goethe's Novel,	118
,, Facility of Composition,	146
Goldsmith at Green Arbor Court,	215
,, and the Dog,	170

CONTENTS

	PAGE
Goldsmith's Blossom-coloured Coat,	238
,, Death and Debts,	17
,, "Deserted Village,"	156
,, Domestic Habits,	180
,, Playfulness,	248
,, Trial of an Amanuensis,	34
Good Company,	327
Gottingen, Celebration at,	276
Graham, Dr. Robert, the Botanist,	49
Grahame's, James, Singing,	35
,, "Sabbath,"	139
Grattan's Expression of Contempt,	121
Gray and the Duchess,	228
,, and Mason, Progress of an Epitaph,	63
Gray's "Elegy," quasi Johnsonian Criticism of,	186
,, ,, Manuscript of,	161
Great Plague and Great Fire in London,	359
Greatness, Symptoms of,	273
Grub Street,	221
Guadaloupe Fossil Skeleton,	306
Guizot, Precocity of,	243
Gun-Cotton and Collodion,	88
Gutta Percha, its Discovery and Uses,	85
Hale, Sir Matthew,	241
Haller's, Baron, Opinion of his own Poetry,	161
Hall's, Robert, Precocity,	244
Handel's "Messiah,"	37
Harpers, the New York Publishers,	193
Harrington's Extravagance,	274
,, "Oceana,"	39
Harvey Ridiculed for his Discovery of the Circulation,	96
Harvey's Examination of the Living Heart,	4
Hastings, Mrs., a Female Doctor,	102
Hawkesworth and Bishop Newton,	215
Haydon and Clarkson the Philanthropist,	107
,, at Sir Joshua Reynold's,	12
Hazlitt and Gifford,	173
Heart, Examination of in Motion, by Harvey,	4
Heights and Depths,	354
Helen,	252
Hemans, Felicia, Visit to,	138
,, Described by an American,	139
,, Described by Miss Jewsbury,	171
Henry, Patrick, the American Statesman,	298

	PAGE
Heroines, Poetical,	130
Herschel, Miss Caroline L.,	68
Hervey, Lord, and Pope,	10
Hieroglyphics, a Poet's,	144
Historical Omissions of Goldsmith,	227
Hoax, Etymology of the Word,	38
Hogg, James,	277, 349
"Hohenlinden," Campbell's,	182
Holy Writ, Illustrations of,	344
"Home, Sweet Home," Fate of its Author,	143
Hood, Thomas,	257
Hook's, Theodore E., Extempore Versifying,	162
Hope, Dr. J., and the Stethoscope,	105
Hough, Bishop,	229
House of Commons, Applause in Gallery of,	120
House of Commons, Speaker's Mace,	334
,, of Lords,	351
"Hudibras," Elaboration of,	35
,, Pride of Author of,	155
Human Skeleton, Fossil, in British Museum,	306
Humboldt, Baron, and the French Savans in Egypt,	209
Hume, David,	249
Hume's Generosity to Blacklock,	154
,, Habits of Composition,	8
Hunt, Leigh, and Thos. Campbell,	168
Hunt's, Leigh, Description of Moore,	170
Hunter and Cullen, Drs.,	223
Hunter's, John, Operation for Aneurism,	1
Hutton and Black's Snail-Dinner,	224
,, W., the Bookseller,	193
Hutton's, Dr., Geological Enthusiasm,	71
Ibrahim Pasha's Autograph,	364
Ignorance,	274
,, in Translators,	368
Illuminators,	42
Illustration, Equivocal, in Law,	91
Imagination, Force of,	25
Immortality,	270
Impromptu,	270
Improvisatori of Italy,	186
"In Hoc Signo Vinces,"	38
Information, the Latest,	270
Ingenious Trifling in Latin,	93
Inoculation Introduced by Lady M. W. Montagu,	99
Inquisition and Galileo,	210
Insanity and Book-hunting,	289
Inventions and Discoveries,	73

	PAGE
Invitations,	272
Iron, Coal, and Steam,	83
Irving, Edward,	227
James I. and Archie Armstrong,	320
" in Lancashire,	300
Jaw Dislocated,	100
Jebb's, Sir R., Rapacity as a Physician,	101
Jeffrey, Francis, "Ultimus Romanorum,"	61
Jeffrey's Duel with Moore,	62
" Marriage,	61
" Presentation Speech to Kemble,	122
" Playfulness and Affection,	29
Jenner, Dr., and the Foreign Potentates,	100
Jenner's, Dr., Discovery of Vaccination,	97
" Discouragement, Honour, and Influence,	98
"Jerusalem Delivered," Tasso's,	172
Jesuit in a Storm,	234
"Joan of Arc," Southey's,	177
"John Gilpin," Origin of,	178
Johnson, Dr., on Milton's Sonnets,	156
" and Goldsmith,	16, 237
" and his "Beauties,"	17
" and Dr. Parr,	105
" and Voltaire,	237
" and Burney,	236
" and Lord Elibank,	224
" and Osborne the Bookseller,	106
" and the Philologist,	126
" and the Poetess,	269
" on Robertson's "Scotland,"	238
" on John Bunyan,	238
Johnson's, Dr. Samuel, Rudeness,	12
" Conversation,	216
" Dictionary and Millar the Bookseller,	44
" a Parliamentary Reporter,	204
" Sermons,	27
" Style,	288
" Treatment of Boswell,	218
Johnsoniana,	235
Jones', Sir William, Learning,	125
" and his Mother,	198
Julian "the Apostle,"	91
Junker, Professor, and the Revived Criminal,	1
Kay, John, the First Poet-Laureate,	165

	PAGE
Keats, Wordsworth, and Lamb,	167
Keith, Mrs. M., and Waverley,	119
Kemble, John, and Jeffrey's Presentation Speech,	122
Kenyon's Lord, Lapsus Linguæ,	91
Kepler's, John, Enthusiasm,	6
Kew, Royal Botanic Garden,	344
Knocking out an *i*,	218
Knowing and Judging Books,	198
Knowledge, Mode of Acquiring,	214
Knox, John,	242
La Place,	207
" and his English Translator and Expositor,	68
Laconic Lady, and Dr. Abernethy,	104
Laidlaw, Wm., Amanuensis to Scott,	35
Lalande and the French Revolutionists,	6
"Lalla Rookh,"	93
Lamartine's, M., Marriage,	96
Lamb, Charles, and the Comptroller of Stamps,	167
" Dipping at Hastings,	135
" and the Poetaster,	135
Lamb's Wit and Eccentricity,	134
" Stammering Wit,	230
Lamb, Lady Caroline,	249
Lamp, the Davy,	73
Landon, Letitia (L. E. L.),	148
Language, English,	290
Laud, Archbishop, and Archie Armstrong	321
"Laudamny and Calamy,"	276
Lavoisier's Discoveries and Fate,	84
Law and Lawyers,	89
Ledyard and Lucas, African Discovery,	66
Legislator from the Plough,	336
Leighton, Archbishop,	250
"Less than no time,"	77
Leti the Historian, and Charles II.,	227
Letters, Cowper's, Elegance of,	138
Letter-Writing,	225
Leyden's, Dr. John, Early Studies,	11
" "Complaynt of Scotland,"	23
"Liberty, a Plant,"	111
Libraries, Frederick the Great,	197
" Arrangement of Books in Ancient,	46
" Early English,	46
Library, a Dictionary,	266
" of British Museum,	300
Lightning Steed,	78
Linguist, Female,	128
Linnæus's Herbarium, Visit to, in London,	50

CONTENTS.

	PAGE
Literary and Scientific Pursuits of Age,	211
,, Cautiousness,	155
,, Diversion,	92
,, Labour,	298
,, Men, Conversation of,	110
,, Property,	47
,, Property and Remuneration,	93
,, Residences,	14
,, Works, Cheapness of,	94
Literature, its Pleasures and Toils,	129
,, as a Profession,	284
,, and the Card-Playing Lady,	230
Locke, J., on acquiring Knowledge,	214
Lodi's, Marco de, Sonnet,	235
London, Classical Spots in,	322
,, Docks and Warehouses,	355
,, Old, Recollections of,	246
Longfellow, Henry W.,	157
Lonsdale's Parliamentary "Ninepins,"	246
Lord, a Whimsical,	284
Loughborough, Lord, and the Reporters,	205
Lubricating Business,	89
Lunatic and Sportsman,	295
Lycoperdon, or Puff-Ball,	105
Lyndhurst and Brougham,	121
Lyons, Archbishop of,	275
Lyrical Writer, Fate of a,	143
Macdiarmid's, J., Trials and Death,	20
Mace of the Royal Society,	205
Machiavel and "Old Nick,"	38
Machine, Calculating,	280
Mackintosh and Madame de Stael,	287
Mackintosh's, Sir J., Humour,	227
Madman's Art,	364
Magazine, The Gentleman's,	94
Magazines,	94
,, The First,	95
Magnet, Sir I. Newton's,	88
Mammoth Cave of Martinique,	348
Manner, Effect of, in Speaking,	124
Manuscript of Gray's "Elegy,"	161
Marlborough's, Duchess of, Apology,	10
Marriages of Men of Genius,	95
"Marseillaise," Origin of,	181
Martineau, Miss, and the Pyramids,	83
Mary Queen of Scots, her Letters,	36
Mather, two Drs. of Boston,	244
Mechanical Triumphs,	96
Medical Men,	96
Medicinal Anecdote,	230

	PAGE
Medicis, Mary de,	234
Menage,	262
Milton and James II.,	158
Milton's Daughters, his Amanuenses,	34
,, Domestic Habits,	179
,, Literary Habits,	17
,, "Paradise Lost,"	144
,, "Paradise Regained,"	145
,, Sonnets,	156
Mithridates and Cleopatra,	126
Monologues of Coleridge,	217
Monomaniac in Chancery,	91
Montagu's, Lady Mary W., Letters,	37
,, Latinity,	24
,, Edward Wortley, Literary Stratagem,	27
Montgomery, James, the Poet,	183
,, and the Robber,	158
Monumental Conceit, a,	194
Moore, Thos., Bowles, and Crabbe,	149
,, and Leigh Hunt,	170
Moore's Diary, Extracts from,	232
,, Duel with Jeffrey,	62
,, Invitation to the Marquis of Lansdowne,	230
,, Singing,	35
More, Hannah, and the Bristol Milkwoman,	175
,, True and False Sympathy,	220
More, Sir Thomas,	39, 251
More, Sir T., and Henry VIII.,	347
Museum, British, Founded by Sir H. Sloane,	102
Mythology of Science,	81
Namby-Pamby,	79
Names Latinized,	255
Napoleon, Anagram on,	195
,, Shooting a Bookseller,	155
Napoleon's Savans in Egypt,	209
National Characteristics,	234
Nationality, French,	291
Natural Compass,	341
Necker and Le Veger,	212
Necker's, Madame, Table-Talk,	214
Newspapers,	347
Newton, Bishop, and Hawkesworth,	215
,, Sir Isaac, and the Royal Academy,	5
Newton's Experiments on Soap Bubbles,	6
,, Methods,	5
,, Absence of Mind,	347
Niagara Safety Bridge,	341

	PAGE		PAGE
Niebuhr on Baiæ and Avernus,	338	Physiognomy,	283
"Night Thoughts," Young's,	172	Piracy in the Pulpit,	128
Nineveh, Rapid Decay of,	328	Pitcairne and Dutch Degrees,	281
" Sculptures in British Museum,	309	Pitt and the Duke of Newcastle,	290
		Pitt, Fox, and Sheridan, in Debate,	123
Norton's, Sir F., "Two Little Manors,"	91	Planet-watchers at Greenwich,	340
		Plants, British,	365
Novels and Novelists,	111	Pleasures and Toils of Literature,	129
" of Defoe, Goethe, and Miss Burney,	118	Plundering a Crystal Grotto,	335
" Botanical Classification of,	239	Poe, Edgar Allen, the American Poet,	134
		" " " Retort upon a Critic,	158
O'Carroll, The,	330		
Ocean Volcano,	361	Poet Laureate, the First,	165
Ogilvie, Dr. Johnson's Sarcasm to,	11	Poetic Effusion, First in America,	173
Old Names with New Faces,	333	" Inspiration, Goldsmith's,	169
Oldys, W., and his Anagram,	195	Poetry and Poets,	133
Oracles,	234	" and Practice,	251
Oratory and Elocution,	119	Poets at Breakfast,	133
Organic Remains, Superstitions Respecting,	70	" Extempore, of Italy,	186
		" Unharnessing a Horse,	151
Origines,	261	Pollok, Robert, as a Divinity Student,	163
Orthography, Foreign,	341		
Ossian's Poems,	39	Polyglot Housekeeper,	336
O'Sullivan the Reporter, and Wilberforce,	200	Pompeian Drawing-room,	365
		Ponderous Erudition,	187
Otranto, Castle of,	297	Pope Innocent XI.,	267
Otway's Death and Debts,	18	Pope no Public Speaker,	9
Over-Poetic Poet,	182	Pope's Accuracy,	136
Overtasking the Mind,	330	" "Dunciad" and Enemies,	156
		" Early Popularity,	156
"Pamela," Richardson's,	284	" Feud with Voltaire,	154
Paper-Making Machinery,	80	" Sarcasms on Lord Hervey,	10
"Paradise Lost,"	144	Popularity of Poets,	143, 161
" French Translation of,	367	Porson, Professor, Anecdotes of,	22
Parliamentary Electric Telegraph,	78	" and the Oxonian in a Stage Coach,	126
" Reprimand,	91		
" Repartee,	318	" and Gillies on Greek Metres,	127
Parr, Dr., and Samuel Johnson,	105		
" and Thos. Moore,	232	" at School,	286
" Erudition,	24	Porson's Humour,	265
Pascal,	287, 288, 289	" Memory,	285
Paselikin, a Russian Poet,	156	" Retort not Courteous,	126
Pastimes of Poets,	93	Portland Vase in the British Museum,	331
Patronage, an Author Soliciting,	273	Port-Royal Society,	240
Pedagogue and Pig-iron,	328	Postscripts to Ladies' Letters,	245
Peel and Byron,	153	Poulet's, Lord W., Ignorance,	288
Pennant's Eccentricities,	289	Preacher, a Gascon,	268
Percival, the American Poet,	172	Preachers and Actors,	123
Perfumed Gloves at Oxford,	221	Preaching, Extempore,	240
Perils of the Alps,	208	Precocity of Authors,	7
Peter the Great a Surgeon,	223	Priestly, Dr., not an Analyst,	56
"Peveril of the Peak,"	278	Printing and Printers,	188
Philology and Linguists,	125	" of Tindal's New Testament,	189
Philosophy, Inductive—Bacon its Founder,	73		
		" Press, first English,	190

	PAGE
Prior, Matthew, Poet and Diplomatist,	185
Proby, John, the Parliamentary Reporter,	203
Pronunciation, American,	214
,, Vulgar,	280
Property, Literary,	93
Prynne, William,	241
Psalmody,	362
Publishers,	42, 193
Pulpit Climaxes,	315
,, Piracy in,	128
,, the,	124
Pun on a Tea-Chest,	195
Punctuation,	188, 287
Punning in French,	195
,, in Latin,	196, 255
,, Text,	315
Puns, Translatable,	318
,, and Anagrams,	194
Pursuits of Johnson, Chaucer, Cellini, and Franklin, in advanced Life,	211
,, of Dryden, Angelo, Wren, and Accorso, in advanced Life,	211
Quantity and Quality,	267
Queen Elizabeth's Manuscripts,	244
Quid Pro Quo,	252
Rabelais' Opinion of the World,	152
Racan,	235
Racine and Boileau,	155
Railway System,	83
Railways and Steamboats, Poetical Prediction of,	88
Raleigh's History of the World,	9
Readers, Book-Stall,	280
Reading,	196
,, Elegant and Expressive,	123
,, Hood the Humourist on,	198
,, Methodical,	198
Receipt for Payment of "Paradise Lost,"	167
Reid's, Dr. John, Heroism,	4
Relics,	300
Religion and Law,	94
Reporting and Reporters,	200
,, from Memory,	205
Reports, the First Parliamentary,	203
Retort, Courteous,	271
Reward of Poetical Composition,	156
Richard I.,	270
Richelieu, Cardinal,	272
Ritson the Antiquary, and Leyden,	23

	PAGE
Rival Remembrance,	173
Robber and Restitution to a Poet,	158
Rogers', Samuel, Wealth and Taste,	165
Rolinus' Sermons,	233
Rome,	266
Romilly's Affection,	90
"Rosciad," Churchill's,	153
Rousseau's Account of Himself,	12
,, Quarrel with David Hume,	31
Rowe, Mrs., and Dr. Watts,	155
Roxburgh Club,	108
,, Library, Sale of,	41
Royal Society of London, Mace of,	205
Sale of Literary Works,	93
Santeuil and the Devil,	267
"Sat Cito, Si Sat Bene,"	90
Satire, How to Circulate a,	260
Saussure and the Arran Mineralogist,	69
Savans in Egypt, their Joint Work,	209
,, of France, Napoleon's, in Egypt,	206, 209
Scaliger, Julius,	240
Scarron and the Hiccup,	234
Scepticism,	252
Schiller's True Nobility,	222
Schœffer, Peter, Inventor of Movable Types,	188
Scholar, a Scarred,	331
Schönbein, Professor, Inventor of Gun-Cotton,	88
"Schoolmaster Abroad,"	245
Science and Commerce,	213
,, Royal Problem in,	279
,, and Superstition,	206
,, its Triumphs,	207
Scientific Adventure,	
,, and Literary Pursuits of Age,	211
,, Men,	209
Scot and Sot,	25
Scott, Sir Walter, Sir H. Davy, and the Tyrolese Patriot,	228
,, on Acquiring Knowledge,	214
,, and the American Authoress,	115
Scott's, Sir Walter, Amanuenses,	34
,, Breakfasts,	283
,, Early Life,	112
,, First Verses,	146
,, Habits,	113
,, Habits of Composition,	111
,, Reverses,	114
Scott, Sir William, his Wit, and Dislike to Novelty,	89
Scottish Prospects, Johnson on,	11

	PAGE		PAGE
Scribe, Indian, in the Field of Battle,	364	Southey's Visit to Sidney Smith,	256
"Seasons," Thomson's,	173	,, "Joan of Arc,"	177
Sedan Chairs,	333	,, Sonnet to Miss Bowles,	149
Sedgwick's, Miss, Visit to Joanna Baillie,	132	South's, Dr., Stolen Sermon,	128
Servants,	280	Spaniards in Spanish Town,	328
Sex, the Fair,	273	Speaking, Evil,	272
Shakspeare,	267	Speaking a Foreign Language,	212
,, and the Climate of Scotland,	108	Speckbacker the Tyrolese Patriot, Sir W. Scott, and Sir H. Davy,	228
Shelley's Amusements,	282	Speeches, Long, and Gray Hairs,	235
,, Death and Funeral,	180	Spinola and Louis XIV.,	235
,, Library,	245	Squeers and the Yorkshire School,	116
Sheridan and Richardson,	25	Staël, Madame,	67
,, Parliamentary Retort of,	120	Stammering Wit, Lamb's,	230
Sheridan's Critical Formula for New Books,	60	Stationers' Company,	192
		Statues to Great Men,	322
,, Debts and Evasions,	26	Steam-Horse,	83
,, Potions,	124	Sterne Rebuked for Profanity,	229
,, in Bellamy's, and "up" in the House,	125	Sterne's Death,	249
		,, Hard-Heartedness,	117
Shirt Tree,	362	,, Maudlin Sensibility,	247
Shooting a Bookseller,	155	,, Sermons (Yorick's),	11
Sketches in the Great Exhibition,	329	Stethoscope,	105
Silence not the Indication of Wisdom,	110	Stewart, Scott, Chalmers, and Jeffrey,	61
		Stories, Stupid,	289
Sloane's, Sir H., Liberality,	102	Stowe the Antiquary,	15
Smellie, William, the Edinburgh Printer, and Burns,	191	Stowell's, Lord, Aversion to Changes,	89
		Study,	341
Smith, James, Author of "Rejected Addresses,"	220	Sugar Plums in Henry III.'s time,	220
		Sun, Spots on,	267
,, Sidney, and Brougham,	214	Superstition and Science,	206
,, ,, and Landseer the Painter,	214	Supple, Mark, the Parliamentary Reporter,	202
,, ,, and Southey,	256	Surgery, Ancient State of, in Scotland,	103
,, Sir Harry, the Caffres, and the Voltaic Battery,	80	Swift and Bettesworth,	163
		Swift's, Jonathan, Conversation,	184
Smith's, Adam, Absence of Mind,	215	,, Eccentricity,	145
,, ,, Amusements of Age,	212	,, Latin Puns,	196
,, ,, Habits of Composition,	8	,, Mental Malady,	183
,, ,, Taciturnity,	8	,, Personal Character,	264
,, Sidney, Memory,	287	,, Power of Invective,	263
,, Sir J. E., Purchase of Linnæus's Herbarium,	50	,, Religion,	184
		,, Rudeness to Lady Burlington,	183
Smoker, the First,	271		
Smollett's, Tobias, Struggles,	20	Table-Talk and Varieties,	212
,, "England,"	44	Talmud, Jewish,	241
Snail-Dinner,	224	"Task," Cowper's,	144
Snail-eating, Modern,	295	Tasso and Ariosto,	63
Solander, Dr., and Sir Joseph Banks,	12	,, and his Critics,	172
Sounding Line,	364	Teaching, Popular,	265
Sounds,	320	"Teetotal," Origin of the Word,	288
Southey and Campbell, Altercation with a Shop-keeper,	9	Telegraphic Blunder,	79
		,, Office, Storm in,	79
,, Mrs.,	148	,, Reporting in America,	77

	PAGE
Thames Tunnel,	86
Things to be Done at Once,	242
Thomson and Quin,	173
Time, Loss of,	266
Tindal's New Testament,	189
Title, a Curious,	165
Tobacco,	216, 363
Tonson the Elder and Dryden,	43, 93
Townley the Antiquarian,	293
Townley's Translation of "Hudibras,"	366
Transfusion of Blood,	206
Translations and Translators,	366
Travelling Library, Porson's,	126
"Tu Doces,"	195
Turner and Campbell,	159
Tyndale's Translation of the New Testament,	366
Typographical Errors,	190, 192
Ure's, Dr., Experiments on a Murderer's Corpse,	3
Vaccination, Discovery of,	97
Vandalism of Gregory VII.,	241
Versifying Extemporaneously, Hook's,	162
Versifying Extemporaneously in Italian,	186
"Vicar of Wakefield,"	119
" in French	368
Victoria Regia and Crystal Palace	291
Voltaire and Montesquieu,	268
" and the Englishman,	270
" Description of,	8
" His Cup, and his Petulance,	250
" and Johnson,	237
Voltaire's Eagle,	263
" Feud with Pope,	154
" Genius,	270
" Marianne,	268
Walpole's Opinion of Johnson,	291
Walton, Izaak,	164
" and Reid,	212
Warburton and Pope,	176
Watering-Places, Ancient Roman,	338
Watts, Dr., and Mrs. Rowe,	155
Waverly, Authorship of,	119
"We,"	218
Weighing Machine of Bank of England,	87
Welsh Curate and Tillotson's Sermons,	366
"Wet the Ropes,"	82

	PAGE
Whewell, Dr., and the College "Dons,"	209
White, Professor,	265
White's, Henry K., Love of Fame,	150
" Youthful Genius,	178
Whitefield's "Oh!"	124
Widow, and the Curé,	253
Wig Riot,	317
Wilberforce and the Irish Reporter,	200
Wilberforce's Practical Views Dictated to an Amanuensis,	34
Wilkin's Proposed Voyage to the Moon,	245
Williams', Rev. J., and the Rarotongan,	197
Wilson, Professor, and Campbell, at Paisley Races,	136
"Winter," Thomson's, in the Bookseller's,	182
Wit and Wisdom,	289
Wolsey, Cardinal,	220
Words, Corruptions of,	288
" Misapplication of, by Foreigners,	108
Wordsworth and Haydon,	10
" and Sir H. Davy,	150
" Coleridge, and Cottle,	151
" Lamb, and Keats at Haydon's Dinner,	167
" Mrs. the Farmer's Wife, and the Stock-dove,	14
" Suspected by the Country People,	142
Wordsworth's Farewell Visit to Scott,	278
" Literary Talk,	133
" Lyrical Ballads,	94
" Want of Smell,	162
Writing, Characters in,	259
" for the Present,	176
" History,	227
" South Sea Islanders' Notion of,	197
" Worthless,	290
Yearsley, Ann, the Poetic Milkwoman,	175
Young, Dr., Epigram,	346
" and Tonson and Lintot the Publishers,	42
Young's, Dr., Lamp for Tragedy,	17
" "Night Thoughts,"	172
" Satire on Sir Hans Sloane,	102
Zimmerman's Retort to Frederic the Great,	133

LITERARY AND SCIENTIFIC ANECDOTES.

ANATOMISTS AND ANATOMY.

EXPERIMENTS ON THE LOWER ANIMALS.

Dr. George Wilson, in his Life of Dr. John Reid, shows by the following instance, that there are occasions on which the infliction of suffering on the lower animals may, so far from being intentionally cruel, be the fruit of an enlightened and profound humanity. Till late in the last century, aneurism in the arteries was treated by cutting off the limb. The great physiologist, John Hunter, was led by his intimate knowledge of anatomy to think it probable, that by the simple device of tying a silk thread round the artery in a certain part of its course, he should be able to cure the disease, and save both life and limb. He made trial on living dogs, and succeeded; he proceeded to do the same with the human sufferer from aneurism, and, at the expense of a small amount of pain, effected a cure. No one in his senses (says the writer) will say that the infliction of a little transient pain on a dog some eighty years ago, has not been amply compensated by the untold sum of human agony which it has since prevented; or deny that he who tortured the living dog, did not merely a lawful, but also a meritorious act. One could almost imagine the dog proud of the service it had rendered to mankind. The operation introduced by Hunter is now universally practised in surgery.

PROFESSOR JUNKER.

Many who were personally acquainted with the celebrated Junker, professor of the University of Halle, have frequently heard him relate the following anecdote:—

Being professor of anatomy, he once procured, for dissection, the bodies of two criminals who had been hanged. The key of the dissecting-room not being immediately at hand, when they were brought home to him, he ordered them to be laid down in an apartment which opened into his bed-chamber. The evening came, and Junker, according to custom, proceeded to resume his literary labours before he retired to rest. It was now near midnight, and all his family were fast asleep, when he heard a rumbling noise in his closet. Thinking that, by some mistake, the cat had been shut up with the dead bodies, he arose, and taking the candle, went to see what had happened. But what must have been his astonishment, or rather his panic, on perceiving that the sack, which contained the two bodies, was rent through the middle? He approached, and found that one of them was gone!

The doors and windows were well secured, and that the body could have been stolen he thought impossible. He tremblingly looked round the closet, and found the *dead* man seated in a corner. Junker stood for a moment motionless; the dead man seemed to look towards him; he moved both to the right and to the left, but the dead man still kept his eyes fixed on him. The professor then retired, step by step, with his eye still fixed upon the object of alarm, and holding the candle in his hand until he reached the door. The dead man instantly started up and followed him. A figure of so hideous an appearance, naked, and in motion, the lateness of the hour, the deep silence which prevailed, everything concurred to overwhelm him with confusion. He let fall the only candle which was burning, and all was darkness! He made his escape to his apartment, and threw himself on his bed; thither, however, he was followed; and he soon found the dead man embracing his legs, and loudly sobbing.

Repeated cries of "Leave me! leave me!" released Junker from the grasp of the dead man, who now exclaimed, "Ah! good executioner! good executioner! have mercy upon me!"

Junker soon perceived the cause of what had happened, and resumed his fortitude. He informed the reanimated sufferer whom he really was, and made a motion in order to call up some of his family. "You then wish to destroy me," exclaimed the criminal. "If you call up any one, my adventure will become public, and I shall be executed a second time. In the name of humanity I implore you to save my life."

The physician struck a light, decorated his guest with an old night-gown, and having made him drink a cordial, requested to know what had brought him to the gibbet? "It would have been truly a singular exhibition," observed Junker, "to have seen me, at that late hour, engaged in a *tête-à-tête* with a *dead* man, decked out in an old night-gown."

The poor wretch informed him, that he had enlisted as a soldier, but that, having no great attachment to the profession, he had determined to desert; that he had intrusted his secret to a kind of crimp, a fellow of no principle, who recommended him to a woman, in whose house he was to remain concealed; that this woman had discovered his retreat to the officers of police, &c.

Junker was extremely perplexed how to save the poor man. It was impossible to retain him in his own house; and to turn him out of doors was to expose him to certain destruction. He resolved to conduct him out of the city, in order that he might get him into a foreign jurisdiction; but it was necessary to pass the gates, which were strictly guarded. To accomplish this point, he dressed him in some of his old clothes, covered him with a cloak, and, at an early hour, set out for the country, with his *protégé* behind him. On arriving at the city-gate, where he was well known, he said, in a hurried tone, that he had been sent for to visit a sick person in the suburbs, who was dying. He was permitted to pass. Having both got into the fields, the deserter threw himself at the feet of his deliverer, to whom he vowed eternal gratitude; and, after receiving some pecuniary assistance, departed, offering up prayers for his happiness. Twelve years after, Junker, having occasion to go to Amsterdam, was accosted on the Exchange by a man well dressed, and of the first appearance, who, he had been informed, was one of the most respectable merchants of that city. The merchant, in a polite tone, inquired whether he was not Professor Junker, of Halle? and, being answered in the affirmative, he requested, in an earnest manner, his company to dinner. The professor consented. Having reached the merchant's house, he was shown into an elegant apartment, where he found a beautiful wife, and two fine healthy children; but he could scarcely suppress his astonishment at meeting so cordial a reception from a family, with whom he thought he was entirely unacquainted.

After dinner, the merchant, taking him into his counting-room, said, "You do not recollect me?"—"Not at all." "But I will recollect you, and never shall your features be effaced from my remembrance: you are my benefactor: I am the person who came to life in your closet, and to whom you paid so much attention. On parting from you, I took the road to Holland; I wrote a good hand; was tolerably good at accounts; my figure was somewhat interesting, and I soon obtained employment as a merchant's clerk. My good conduct, and my zeal for the interests of my patron, procured me his confidence, and his daughter's love. On his retiring from business I succeeded him, and became his son-in-law. But for you, however, I should not have lived to experience all these enjoyments. Henceforth, look upon my house, my fortune, and myself, as at your disposal." Those who possess the smallest portion of sensibility can easily represent to themselves the feelings of Junker.

SINGULAR GALVANIC EXPERIMENTS.

The galvanic experiments which have hitherto been made by philosophers upon animal bodies, may be reduced nearly to a single point; the statement of which will suffice to give the reader a general idea of the subject. Lay bare any principal nerve, which leads immediately to some great limb or muscle; when this is done, let that part of the nerve which is exposed, and which is farthest from the limb or muscle, be brought into contact with a piece of zinc. While in this state, let the zinc be touched by a piece of silver, while another part of the silver touches the naked nerve, if not dry, or the muscle to which it leads, whether dry or not. In this state, violent contractions will be produced in the limb or muscle, but not in any muscle on the other side of the zinc.

Among the numerous experiments which have lately been made, very few have been more singular in their effects than those which were produced by Dr. Ure, in Glasgow, on the body of a man named Clydesdale, who had been executed for murder. These effects were produced by a voltaic battery of 270 pair of four-inch plates, of which the results were terrible. In the first experiment, on moving the rod from the thigh to the heel, the leg was thrown forward with so much violence as nearly to overturn one of the assistants. In the second experiment, the rod was applied to the phrenic nerve in the neck, when laborious breathing commenced; the chest heaved and fell; the belly was protruded and collapsed with the relaxing and retiring diaphragm; and it was thought that nothing but the loss of blood prevented pulsation from being restored. In the third experiment, the supra-orbital nerve was touched, when the muscles of the face were thrown into frightful actions and contortions. The scene was hideous, and many spectators left the room; and one gentleman nearly fainted, either from terror, or from the momentary sickness which the scene occasioned. In the fourth experiment, from meeting the electric power, from the spinal marrow to the elbow, the fingers were put in motion, and the arm was agitated in such a manner, that it seemed to point to some spectators, who were dreadfully terrified, from an apprehension that the body was actually coming to life. From these experiments Dr. Ure seemed to be of opinion, that had not incisions been made in the blood-vessels of the neck, and the spinal marrow been lacerated, the body of the criminal might have been restored to life.

HARVEY'S EXAMINATION OF THE HEART.

In the time of Charles I., a young nobleman of the Montgomery family had an abscess in the side of his chest, in consequence of a fall. The wound healed, but an opening was left in his side of such a size that the heart and lungs were still visible, and could be handled. On the return of the young man from his travels, the King heard of the circumstance, and requested Dr. Harvey to examine his heart. The following is Harvey's own account of the examination:—"When I had paid my respects to this young nobleman and conveyed to him the King's request, he made no concealment, but exposed the left side of his breast, where I saw a cavity into which I could introduce my finger and thumb. Astonished with the novelty, again and again I explored the wound, and, first marvelling at the extraordinary nature of the case, I set about the examination of the heart. Taking it in one hand, and placing the finger of the other on the pulse of the wrist, I satisfied myself that it was indeed the heart which I grasped. I then brought him to the King, that he might behold and touch so extraordinary a thing, and that he might perceive, as I did, that unless when we touched the outer skin, or when he saw our fingers in the cavity, this young nobleman knew not that we touched the heart."

DR. JOHN REID—HIS HEROISM.

The late Dr. Reid was afflicted with cancer in the tongue, which ultimately extended to the throat, causing his death. He was twice operated upon, and directed the surgeon's knife on both occasions, the parts affected being those on which he had thrown fresh light by his physiological researches. In his memoir by Dr. George Wilson, an admirable piece of scientific and religious biography, the following particulars are given:—"There were unusual elements of piety in Dr. Reid's case. The physician was for the time the patient; the public speaker was struck inarticulate and dumb; and it was a surgeon who was under the knife of the surgeons. But this was by no means all. The surgeons were the attached friends of the patient. They did not gather round him, with cold professional eye, to discharge an official duty. Fellow-lecturers, fellow-students, or fellow-scholars, and old playmates, they all were, and now they were assembled to perform, with grieved hearts, a cruel and painful task. For doctors so circumstanced there is no sympathy in the unprofessional public heart. The surgeon who can lift his knife upon his friend, is looked upon as little better than an assassin in spirit. Yet among the medical men who were with Dr. Reid on that painful day, were hearts as tender, affectionate, and gentle, as we need wish or may hope to find. Sorely reluctant had they been to undertake the unwelcome duty to which they were now called. Only the conviction that there was no other way of serving him whom they loved so deeply, gave them courage to go on; and no one understood this better than he who was the object of all this sympathy. On his side there was corresponding courage, and he showed entire submission to their guidance. The operation he had to undergo was not one which admitted of alleviation of its pains by the administration of anæsthetics. It required not merely endurance, but firmness and active fortitude; and the *patient* was expected to be something more than that negative term implies. Nor was the expectation disappointed. His face wore even a smile, as before putting himself in Mr. Fergusson's hands, he recognized an old school-fellow among the non-medical attendants, and saluted him with a sobriquet of the play-ground. Throughout the operation he rendered every assistance, by deliberate acts implying real heroism. Chloroform was purposely withheld, that the sufferer, with every sensation and faculty alive, might assist, and literally become an operator upon himself." The wound had scarcely healed, when the disease returned, and another operation was performed; on this occasion under the effects of chloroform. When he partially awoke from the state of insensibility thus induced, his resolute firmness was strangely mingled with gleams of his native humour. He remembered afterwards that whilst his friends were anxiously applying a ligature to a divided artery, he was seized with a strong desire to let it "spout" on the white neckcloth of one of them. This genial man and ingenious physiologist, sank under a third recurrence of the fatal disease.

ASTRONOMERS AND ASTRONOMY.

SIR ISAAC NEWTON AND THE ROYAL SOCIETY.

In 1671, Mr. Isaac Newton, Professor of Mathematics at Cambridge, was proposed as a Fellow of the Royal Society by Seth Ward, Bishop of Sarum. Newton, then in his thirtieth year, had made several of his greatest discoveries. He had discovered the different refrangibility of light. He had invented the reflecting telescope. He had deduced the law of gravity from Kepler's theorem; and he had discovered the method of fluxions. When he heard of his being proposed as a Fellow, he expressed to Oldenburg, the secretary, his hope that he would be elected, and added, that "he would endeavour to testify his gratitude by communicating what his poor and solitary endeavours could effect towards the promoting their philosophical design."

The communications which Newton made to the Society, excited the deepest interest in every part of Europe. His little reflecting telescope, the germ of the colossal instruments of Herschel and Lord Rosse, was deemed one of the wonders of the age.—(Brewster, North British Review.)

NEWTON'S METHODS.

The doctrine of universal gravitation is one of the greatest of human discoveries. The following remarks by Mr. Whewell tend to enhance the admiration and wonder with which the immortal discoverer will always be regarded. "No one for sixty years after the publication of the *Principia*, and, with Newton's methods, no one up to the present day, has added anything of any value to his deductions. We know that he calculated all the principal lunar inequalities; in many of the cases he has given us his processes, in others only his results. But who has presented in his beautiful geometry, or deduced from his simple principles, any of the inequalities which he left untouched? The ponderous instrument of synthesis, so effective in his hand, has never since been grasped by one who could use it for such purposes; and we gaze at it with admiring curiosity, as on some gigantic implement of war, which stands idle among the memorials of ancient days, and makes us wonder what manner of man he was who could wield as a weapon what we can hardly lift as a burden."

SIR ISAAC NEWTON'S EXPERIMENTS.

When Sir Isaac Newton changed his residence, and went to live in Leicester Place, his next-door neighbour was a widow lady, who was much puzzled by the little she had observed of the philosopher. One of the Fellows of the Royal Society of London called upon her one day, when, among other domestic news, she mentioned that some one had come to reside in the adjoining house, who she felt certain was a poor crazy gentleman, "because," she continued, "he diverts himself in the oddest ways imaginable. Every morning, when the sun shines so brightly that we are obliged to draw the window-blinds, he takes his seat in front of a tub of soap-suds, and occupies himself for hours blowing soap-bubbles through a common clay pipe, and intently watches them till they burst. He is doubtless now at his favourite amusement," she added; "do come and look at him." The gentleman smiled, and then went up stairs, when, after looking through the window into the adjoining yard, he turned round and said, "My dear madam, the person whom you suppose to be a poor lunatic is no other than the great Sir Isaac Newton, studying the refraction of light upon thin plates, a phenomenon which is beautifully exhibited upon the surface of a common soap-bubble." This anecdote serves as an excellent moral not to ridicule what we do not understand, but gently and industriously to gather wisdom from every circumstance around us.

JOHN KEPLER—HIS ENTHUSIASM.

When John Kepler discovered, after seventeen years of incessant investigation, the third of his laws, namely, that relating to the connection between the periodic times and the distances of the planets, his delight knew no bounds. "Nothing holds me," says he; "I will indulge in my sacred fury; I will triumph over mankind by the honest confession, that I have stolen the golden vases of the Egyptians, to build up a tabernacle for my God, far away from the confines of Egypt. If you forgive me, I rejoice; if you are angry, I can bear it. The die is cast; the book is written, to be read either now or by posterity,—I care not which. It may well wait a century for a reader, as God has waited six thousand years for an observer."

LALANDE.

Lalande, the French astronomer, when the Revolution broke out, only paid the more attention to the revolutions of the heavenly bodies; and when he found, at the end, that he had escaped the fury of Robespierre and his fellow-ruffians, he gratefully remarked, "I may thank my stars for it."

GALILEO'S BLINDNESS.

The last telescopic observations of Galileo resulted in the discovery of the diurnal libration of the moon. Although his right eye had for some years lost its power (says Sir David Brewster), yet his general vision was sufficiently perfect to enable him to carry on his usual researches. In 1636, however, this affection of the eye became more serious; and, in 1637, his left eye was attacked with the same disease. His medical friends at first supposed that cataracts were formed in the crystalline lens, and anticipated a cure from the operation of couching. These hopes were fallacious. The disease turned out to be in the cornea, and every attempt to restore its transparency was fruitless. In a few months the white cloud covered the whole aperture of the pupil, and Galileo became totally blind. This sudden and severe calamity had almost overwhelmed Galileo and his friends. In writing to a correspondent he exclaims, "Alas! your dear friend and servant has become totally and irreparably blind. These heavens, this earth, this universe, which by wonderful observation I had enlarged a thousand times beyond the belief of past ages, are henceforth shrunk into the narrow space which I occupy myself. So it pleases God; it shall, therefore, please me also."

AUTHORS.
PRECOCITY.

DERMODY, CHATTERTON, ETC.

Cowley received the applauses of the great at eleven, Pope at twelve, and Milton at sixteen. The meed of distinguished praise, therefore, cannot be denied this wonderful boy [Dermody], when it is related that at ten years old he had written as much genuine poetry as either of these great men had produced at nearly double that age. Reared in the metropolis of a great nation, where genius finds many excitements, their early effusions were blazoned forth with admiration. Very different at this time was the fate of our extraordinary youth; with no pattern of prudence before his eyes, no stimulus to exertion, no protecting hand to cherish the opening bud of genius; but, like the unhappy Chatterton, slumbering in obscurity, neglected and unknown. —(Life by Raymond.)

Dermody died at the age of twenty-seven years and six months. In the cast of his mind he resembled the unfortunate Chatterton, and in his propensities the eccentric Savage, but in precocity of talent and of classical information, excelled both them and every other rival, having in the first fourteen years of his life acquired a competent knowledge of the Greek, the Latin, the French, and Italian languages, and a little of the Spanish. Like Savage, he would participate in the pleasures of the lowest company, but had not the same eagerness after money, nor the same effrontery in demanding it of his friends. And notwithstanding Dermody's insatiate desire for liquor kept him in perpetual poverty, yet his applications (though full of lamentations) were never degraded by meanness or fulsome adulation; nor did ingratitude, in his worst excesses, ever sully his character through life.... Had he qualified those errors which hurt only himself; had his ambition kept pace with the encouragement which he received; had he studied and pursued moral with the same ardour as poetical; had his regard for character and decorum equalled his poverty and his love of dissipation; he might have lived to be the admiration of the great, the wonder of the learned, and the ornament of society: science might have smiled upon his labours, fame might have proclaimed his excellence, and posterity with delight would record his name. But mistaking the way to happiness he plunged into misery, and fell an early victim to imprudence.—(Life by Raymond.)

PECULIARITIES AND ECCENTRICITIES.

ADAM SMITH AND DAVID HUME.

Mr. Smith observed to me, not long before his death, "that after all his practice in writing, he composed as slowly, and with as great difficulty, as at first." He added, at the same time, that Mr. Hume had acquired so great a facility in this respect, that the last volume of his *History* was printed from the original copy, with a few marginal corrections. Mr. Smith, when he was employed in composition, generally walked up and down his apartment, dictating to a secretary. All Mr. Hume's works (it has been said) were written with his own hand.—(Stewart.)

ADAM SMITH.

The comprehensive speculations with which Mr. Smith had always been occupied, and the variety of materials which his own invention continually supplied to his thoughts, rendered him habitually inattentive to familiar objects, and to common occurrences. On this account, he was remarkable, throughout the whole of life, for speaking to himself when alone, and for being so absent in company, as, on some occasions, to exceed almost what the fancy of a Bruyere could imagine In company, he was apt to be engrossed by his studies; and appeared, at times, by the motion of his lips, as well as by his looks and gestures, to be in the fervour of composition. It was observed, that he rarely started a topic himself, or even fell in easily with the common dialogue of conversation. When he did speak, however, he was somewhat apt to convey his ideas in the form of a lecture; but this never proceeded from a wish to engross the discourse, or to gratify his vanity. His own inclination disposed him so strongly to enjoy, in silence, the gaiety of those around him, that his friends were often led to concert little schemes, in order to bring on the subjects most likely to interest him.—(Life.)

VOLTAIRE.

This extraordinary person has contrived to excite more curiosity, and to retain the attention of Europe for a longer space of time, than any other man this age has produced, monarchs and heroes included. His person is that of a skeleton; but this skeleton, this composition of skin and bone, has a look of more spirit and vivacity than is generally produced by flesh and blood, however blooming and youthful. The most piercing eyes I ever beheld are those of Voltaire, now in his eightieth year. His whole countenance is expressive of genius, observation, and extreme sensibility. An air of irony never entirely forsakes his face, but may always be observed lurking in his features, whether he frowns or smiles. By far the greatest part of his time is spent in his study, and whether he reads himself, or listens to another, he always has a pen in his hand, to take down notes or make remarks. Composition is his principal amusement. No author who writes for daily bread, no young poet ardent for distinction, is more assiduous with his pen, or more anxious for fresh fame, than the wealthy and applauded Seigneur Ferney. Happy if this extraordinary man had confined his genius to its native home, to the walks which the muses love; and that he had never deviated from these into the thorny paths of impiety!—(Dr. John Moore.)

POPE NO PUBLIC SPEAKER.

I never could speak in public; and I do not believe that if it was a set thing, I could give an account of any story to twelve friends together; though I could tell it to any three of them with a great deal of pleasure. When I was to appear for the Bishop of Rochester on his trial, though I had but ten words to say, and that on a plain easy point (how that bishop spent his time whilst I was with him at Bromley), I made two or three blunders in it; and that, notwithstanding the first row of Lords (which were all I could see), were mostly of my acquaintance.—(Pope.)

RALEIGH'S HISTORY.

Raleigh's *History of the World* was composed during his imprisonment in the Tower. Only a small portion of the work was published, owing to the following singular circumstance:—One afternoon looking through his window into one of the courts in the Tower, Sir Walter saw two men quarrel, when the one actually murdered the other; and shortly after two gentlemen, friends to Sir Walter, coming into his room, after expressing what had happened, they disagreed in their manner of relating the story; and Sir Walter, who had seen it himself, concurred that neither was accurate, but related it with another variation. The three eye-witnesses disagreeing about an act so recently committed put Sir Walter in a rage, when he took up the volumes of manuscript which lay by, containing his *History of the World*, and threw them on a large fire that was in the room, exclaiming, that "it was not for him to write the history of the world, if he could not relate what he saw a quarter of an hour before." One of his friends saved two of the volumes from the flames, but the rest were consumed. The world laments that so strange an accident should have mutilated the work of so extraordinary a man.—(Granger's Wonderful Magazine.)

THOS. CAMPBELL, THE LORD RECTOR.

Southey tells the following story of the poet Campbell:—

Taking a walk with Campbell, one day, up Regent Street, we were accosted by a wretched-looking woman, with a sick infant in her arms, and another starved little thing at her mother's side. The woman begged for a copper. I had no change, and Campbell had nothing but a sovereign. The woman stuck fast to the poet, as if she read his heart in his face, and I could feel his arm beginning to tremble. At length, saying something about it being his duty to assist poor creatures, he told the woman to wait; and, hastening into a mercer's shop, asked, rather impatiently, for change. You know what an excitable person he was, and how he fancied all business must give way till the change was supplied. The shopman thought otherwise; the poet insisted; an altercation ensued; and in a minute or two the master jumped over the counter and collared him, telling us he would turn us both out; that he believed we came there to kick up a row for some dishonest purpose. So here was a pretty dilemma. We defied him, but said we would go out instantly, on his apologising for his gross insult. All was uproar. Campbell called out,

"Thrash the fellow! thrash him!"

"You will not go out, then?" said the mercer.

"No, never, till you apologise."

"Well, we shall soon see. John, go to Vine Street, and fetch the police."

In a few minutes two policemen appeared; one went close up to Mr. Campbell, the other to myself. The poet was now in such breathless indignation, that he could not articulate a sentence. I told the policemen the object he had in asking change; and that the shopman had most unwarrantably insulted us. "This gentleman," I added, by way of a climax, "is Mr. Thomas Campbell, the distinguished poet, a man who would not hurt a fly, much less act with the dishonest intention that person has insinuated." The moment I uttered the name, the policeman backed away two or three paces, as if awe-struck, and said,

"Guidness, mon, is that Maister Cammell, the Lord Rector o' Glasgow?"

"Yes, my friend, he is, as this card may convince you," handing it to him; "all this commotion has been caused by a mistake."

By this time the mercer had cooled down to a moderate temperature, and in the end made every reparation in his power, saying he was very busy at the time, and had he but known the gentleman, "he would have changed fifty sovereigns for him."

"My dear fellow," said the poet, who had recovered his speech, "I am not at all offended," and it was really laughable to see them shaking hands long and vigorously, each with perfect sincerity and mutual forgiveness.

SARAH, DUCHESS-DOWAGER OF MARLBOROUGH.

This favourite duchess, who, like the proud Duke of Espernon, lived to brave the successors in a court where she had domineered, wound up her *capricious* life with an apology for her conduct. The piece, though weakened by the prudence of those who were to correct it, though maimed by her grace's own corrections, and though great part of it is rather the annals of a wardrobe than of a reign, yet it has still curious anecdotes, and a few of those sallies of wit, which fourscore years of *arrogance* could not fail to produce in so fantastic an understanding.—(Walpole's R. & N. Authors.)

LORD HERVEY AND POPE.

Lord Hervey, having felt some attacks of the epilepsy, entered upon and persisted in a very strict regimen, and thus stopped the progress and prevented the effects of that dreadful disease. His daily food was a small quantity of asses' milk and a flour biscuit: once a-week he indulged himself with eating an apple: he used emetics daily. Mr. Pope and he were once friends; but they quarrelled; and persecuted each other with virulent satire. Pope, knowing the abstemious regimen which Lord Hervey observed, was so ungenerous as to call him "a mere cheese-curd of asses' milk." Lord Hervey used paint to soften his ghastly appearance. Mr. Pope must have known *this* also, and therefore it was unpardonable in him to introduce it into his celebrated portrait. That satirist had the art of laying hold on detached circumstances, and of applying them to his purpose, without much regard for historical accuracy. Thus, to his hemistic, "Endow a college or *a cat*," he adds this note, that "*a* Duchess of Richmond left annuities to her cats." The lady, as to whom he seems so uncertain, was *La Belle Stuart* of the Comte de Grammont. She left annuities to certain female friends, with the burden of maintaining some of her cats; a delicate way of providing for poor, and, probably, proud gentlewomen, without making them feel that they owed their livelihood to her mere liberality.—(Lord Hailes.)

FENELON.

Monsieur Fenelon, the author of *Telemachus*, and Archbishop of Cambray, used to say, that he loved his family better than himself, his country better than his family, and mankind better than his country; for I am more a Frenchman, added he, than a Fenelon, and more a man than a Frenchman.—(Chevalier Ramsay.)

BAYLE'S DICTIONARY.

His *Critical Dictionary* is a vast repository of facts and opinions; and he balances the *false* religions in his sceptical scales, till the opposite quantities (if I may use the language of algebra) annihilate each other. The wonderful power which he so boldly exercised, of assembling doubts and objections, had tempted him jocosely to assume the title of the νεφεληγερετα Ζευς, the cloud-compelling Jove; and in a conversation with the ingenious Abbé (afterwards cardinal) de Polignac, he freely disclosed his universal Pyrrhonism. "I am most truly," said Bayle, "a Protestant; for I protest indifferently against all systems and all sects."—(Gibbon.)

STERNE'S SERMONS.

Mr. Sterne, it may be supposed, was no great favourite with Dr. Johnson; and a lady once ventured to ask the grave doctor how he liked Yorick's *Sermons*. "I know nothing about them, madam," was his reply. But sometime afterwards, forgetting himself, he severely censured them; and the lady very aptly retorted, "I understood you to say, sir, that you had never read them." "No, madam; I did read them, but it was in a stage coach. I should not have even deigned to have looked at them had I been at large."—(Cradock's Literary Memoirs.)

DR. JOHN LEYDEN.

His chief place of retirement was the small parish church, a gloomy and ancient building, generally believed in the neighbourhood to be haunted. To this chosen place of study, usually locked during weekdays, Leyden made entrance by means of a window, read there for many hours in the day, and deposited his books and specimens in a retired pew. It was a well-chosen spot of seclusion, for the kirk (except during divine service) is rather a place of terror to the Scottish rustic, and that of Cavers was rendered more so by many a tale of ghosts and witchcraft, of which it was the supposed scene; and to which Leyden, partly to indulge his humour, and partly to secure his retirement, contrived to make some modern additions. The nature of his abstruse studies, some specimens of natural history, as toads and adders, left exposed in their spirit-vials, and one or two practical jests played off upon the more curious of the peasantry, rendered his gloomy haunt not only venerated by the wise, but feared by the simple of the parish.—(Memoirs by Sir Walter Scott.)

DR. OGILVIE

Was one of the few Scotsmen of whom Dr. Johnson entertained a favourable opinion. The sanctity of the character of Ogilvie, the religious tendency of his writings, in some measure abated the fierce antipathy with which the great English critic regarded the nation whose literary efforts have raised them to so high a rank in the intellectual history of mankind. It was to Dr. Ogilvie that the unreasonable Johnson uttered the sarcasm relative to Scotch prospects. When in London, Ogilvie one day, in Johnson's company, observed, in speaking of grand scenery, that Scotland had a great many wild prospects. "Yes, sir," said Johnson, "I believe you have a great many. Norway, too, has noble wild prospects, and Lapland is remarkable for prodigious noble wild prospects. But, sir, let me tell you, the noblest prospect which a Scotsman ever sees is the high road that leads him to London." "I admit," rejoined Ogilvie, "that the last prospect is a very *noble* one, but I deny that it is *as wild* as any of those we have enumerated."—(Scotsman's Library.)

DR. SAMUEL JOHNSON—URSA MAJOR.

Oct. 13, 1845.—On the 7th I left town by express train to visit Mrs. Gwatkin at Plymouth, to examine Sir Joshua's private memorandum concerning the Academy quarrel. Mrs. Gwatkin was Miss Palmer, sister to the Marchioness of Thomond, and niece to Sir Joshua. . . At twelve I called. Mr. Reynolds Gwatkin came down and introduced me. I went up with him, and found on a sofa, leaning on pillows, a venerable aged lady, holding an ear-trumpet, like Sir Joshua, showing in her face great remains of regular beauty, and evidently the model of Sir Joshua in his Christian virtues (a notion of mine which she afterwards confirmed). After a few minutes' chat, we entered on the purport of my visit, which was to examine Sir Joshua's private papers relating to the Academy dispute which produced his resignation. Mrs. Gwatkin rose to give orders; her figure was fine and elastic, upright as a dart, with nothing of decrepitude; certainly extraordinary for a woman in her eighty-ninth year. . . . We had a delightful chat about Burke, Johnson, Goldsmith, Garrick, and Reynolds. She said she came to Sir Joshua quite a little girl, and at the first grand party Dr. Johnson staid, as he always did, after all were gone; and that she, being afraid of hurting her new frock, went up stairs, and put on another, and came down to sit with Dr. J. and Sir Joshua. Johnson thundered out at her, scolded her for her disrespect to him, in supposing he was not as worthy of her best frock as fine folks. He sent her crying to bed, and took a dislike to her ever after. She had a goldfinch, which she had left at home. Her brother and sister dropped water on it from a great height, for fun. The bird died from fright, and turned black. She told Goldsmith, who was writing his *Animated Nature*. Goldsmith begged her to get the facts, and he would allude to it. "Sir," roared out Johnson, "if you do, you'll ruin your work, for, depend upon it, it's a lie." She said that after Sir Joseph Banks and Dr. Solander came from their voyage, at a grand dinner at Sir Joshua's, Solander was relating that in Iceland he had seen a fowl boiled in a few minutes in the hot springs. Johnson broke up the whole party by roaring out, "Sir, unless I saw it with my own eyes I would not believe it." Nobody spoke after, and Banks and Solander rose and left the dining-room.—(Taylor's Life of Haydon.)

J. J. ROUSSEAU.

When obliged to exert myself I am ignorant what to do! when forced to speak I am at a loss for words; and if any one looks at me I am instantly out of countenance. If animated with my subject I express my thoughts with ease, but in ordinary conversations I can say nothing—absolutely nothing; and, being obliged to speak, renders *them* insupportable. . . The timidity common to my age was heightened by a natural benevolence, which made me dread the idea of giving pain. Though my mind had received some cultivation, having seen nothing of the world, I was an absolute stranger to polite address, and my mental acquisitions, so far from supplying this defect, served to increase my embarrassment by making me sensible of every deficiency.

When I write, my ideas are arranged with the utmost difficulty. They glance on my imagination, and ferment till they discompose, heat, and bring on a palpitation: during this state of agitation I see nothing properly, cannot write a single word, and must wait till it is over. Insensibly the agitation subsides, the chaos acquires form, and each circumstance takes its proper place. Had I always waited till that confusion was past, and then painted, in their natural beauties, the objects that had presented themselves, few authors would have surpassed me.—(Confessions.)

BENVENUTO CELLINI.

I have been reading lately a most extraordinary work, which I did read once before, but had totally forgotten, *The History of Benvenuto Cellini*, a Florentine goldsmith and designer, translated from the Italian by Thomas Nugent. There is something in it so singularly characteristical, that it is impossible to reject the whole as fabulous, and yet it is equally impossible not to reject a great part of it as such. To reconcile this I would suppose, what the work itself strongly evinces, that the author must have been an ingenious, hot-headed, vain, audacious man, and that the violence of his passions, the strength of his superstition, and the disasters into which he plunged himself, made him mad in the end. We know that the Italians of the sixteenth century were very ingenious in everything that relates to drawing and designing; but it cannot be believed that popes, emperors, and kings were so totally engrossed with those matters as Signior Cellini represents them. If you have never seen the book I would recommend it as a curiosity, from which I promise that you will receive amusement. Nay, in regard to the manner of those times, there is even some instruction in it.—(Dr. Beattie.)

WORDSWORTH AND HAYDON THE PAINTER.

"May 22.—Wordsworth called to-day, and we went to church together. There was no seat to be got at the chapel near us belonging to the rectory of Paddington, and we sat among publicans and sinners. I determined to try him, so advised our staying, as we could hear more easily. He agreed like a Christian; and I was much interested in seeing his venerable white head close to a servant in livery, and on the same level. The servant in livery fell asleep, and so did Wordsworth. I jogged him at the Gospel, and he opened his eyes and read well. A preacher preached when we expected another, so it was a disappointment. We afterwards walked to Rogers's, across the park. He had a party to lunch, so I went into the pictures, and sucked Rembrandt, Reynolds, Veronese, Raffael, Bassan, and Tintoretto. Wordsworth said, 'Haydon is down stairs.' —'Ah,' said Rogers, 'he is better employed than chattering nonsense up stairs.' As Wordsworth and I crossed the park, we said, 'Scott, Wilkie, Keats, Hazlitt, Beaumont, Jackson, Charles Lamb are all gone —we only are left.' He said, 'How old are you?'—'Fifty-six,' I replied. 'How old are you?'—'Seventy-three,' he said; 'in my seventy-third year. I was born in 1770.' —'And I in 1786.'—'You have many years before you.'—'I trust I have; and you, too, I hope. Let us cut out Titian, who was ninety-nine.'—'Was he ninety-nine?' said Wordsworth.—'Yes,' said I, 'and his death was a moral; for as he lay dying of the plague, he was plundered, and could not help himself.'—We got on Wakley's abuse,

We laughed at him. I quoted his own beautiful address to the stock-dove. He said, once in a wood Mrs. Wordsworth and a lady were walking, when the stock-dove was cooing. A farmer's wife coming by said to herself, 'O, I do like stock-doves.' Mrs. Wordsworth, in all her enthusiasm for Wordsworth's poetry, took the old woman to her heart. 'But,' continued the old woman, 'some like them in a pie; for my part, there's nothing like 'em stewed in onions.'' (Haydon's Diary.)

HONOURS AND REWARDS.

LITERARY RESIDENCES.

Men of genius have usually been condemned to compose their finest works, which are usually their earliest, under the roof of a garret; and few literary characters have lived, like Pliny and Voltaire, in a villa or *chateau* of their own. It has not therefore often happened, that a man of genius could raise local emotions by his own intellectual suggestions. Ariosto, who built a palace in his verse, lodged himself in a small house, and found that stanzas and stones were not put together at the same rate: old Montaigne has left a description of his library—"over the entrance of my house where I view my court-yards and garden, and at once survey all the operations of my family." A literary friend, whom a hint of mine had induced to visit the old tower in the garden of Buffon, where that sage retired every morning to compose, passed so long a time in that lonely apartment, as to have raised some solicitude among the honest folks of Montbar, who, having seen "the Englishman" enter, but not return, during a heavy thunder-storm which had occurred in the interval, informed the good mayor, who came in due form to notify the ambiguous state of the stranger. My friend is, as is well known, a genius of that cast who could pass two hours in the *Tower of Buffon*, without being aware that he had been all that time occupied by suggestions of ideas and reveries, which such a locality may excite in some minds. He was also busied by his hand; for he has favoured me with two drawings of the interior and the exterior of this *old tower in the garden;* the nakedness within can only be compared to the solitude without. Such was the studying room of Buffon, where his eye, resting on no object, never interrupted the unity of his meditations on nature. Pope, who had far more enthusiasm in his poetical disposition than is generally understood, was extremely susceptible of those literary associations with localities: one of the volumes of his *Homer* was begun and finished in an old tower over the chapel at Stanton Harcourt; and he has perpetuated the event, if not consecrated the place, by scratching with a diamond on a pane of stained glass this inscription:—

In the year 1718,
Alexander Pope
Finished HERE
The fifth volume of Homer.

It was the same feeling which induced him one day, when taking his usual walk with Harte in the Haymarket, to desire Harte to enter a little shop, where going up three pair of stairs into a small room, Pope said, "In this garret Addison wrote his *Campaign!*" Nothing less than a strong feeling impelled the poet to ascend this garret—it was a consecrated spot to his eye; and certainly a curious instance of the power of genius contrasted with its miserable locality! Addison, whose mind had fought through "a campaign" in a garret, could ho have called about him "the pleasures of imagination," had probably planned a house of literary repose, where all parts would have been in harmony with his mind. Such residences of men of genius have been enjoyed by some; and the vivid descriptions which they have left us, convey something of the delightfulness which charmed their studious repose.—(D'Israeli's Curiosities.)

GIBBON AND LORD NORTH.

Mr. Gibbon, in the general preface to the three last volumes of his history, has the following passage, which we consider worthy of notice, not less on account of its elegance, than for the striking contrast it exhibits between Mr. Gibbon's original enmity of spirit to Lord North, and his subsequent expressions of friendship for that nobleman:—"Were I ambitious of any other patron than the public (says Mr. Gibbon), I would inscribe this work to a statesman, who, in a long, a stormy, and at length an unfortunate administration, had many political opponents, almost without a personal enemy; who has retained, in his fall from power, many faithful and disinterested friends; and who, under the pressure of severe infirmity, enjoys the lively vigour of his mind, and the felicity of his incomparable temper. Lord North will permit me to express the feelings of friendship in the language of truth; but even truth and friendship should be silent, if he still dispensed the favours of the crown." For the sake of contrast, one anecdote may be added. In June, 1781, Mr. Fox's library came to be sold. Amongst his other books, the first volume of Mr. Gibbon's history was brought to the hammer. In the blank leaf of this was a note, in the handwriting of Mr. Fox, stating a remarkable declaration of our historian at a well-known tavern in Pall-Mall, and contrasting it with Mr. Gibbon's political conduct afterwards. "The author (it observed) at Brookes's said, That *there was no salvation for this country, until six heads of the principal persons in administration* (Lord North being then prime minister) *were laid upon the table.* Yet (as the observation added) *eleven days afterwards, this same gentleman accepted a place of a lord of trade* under those very ministers, and *has acted with them ever since.*" This extraordinary anecdote, thus recorded, very naturally excited the attention of the purchasers. Numbers wished to have in their own possession such an *honourable* testimony from Mr. Fox in *favour* of Mr. Gibbon. The contention for it rose to a considerable height, and the volume by the aid of this manuscript addition to it, was sold for three guineas.—(English Review. 1788.)

A MENDICANT AUTHOR.

Even in the reign of the literary James, great authors were reduced to a state of mendicity, and lived on alms, although their lives and their fortunes had been consumed in forming national labours. The antiquary Stowe exhibits a striking example of the reward conferred on such valued authors. Stowe had devoted his life, and exhausted his patrimony, in the study of English antiquities; he had travelled on foot throughout the kingdom, inspecting all monuments of antiquity, and rescuing what he could from the dispersed libraries of the monasteries. His stupendous collections, in his own handwriting, still exist, to provoke the feeble industry of literary loiterers. It was in his eightieth year that Stowe at length received a public acknowledgment of his services which will appear to us of a very extraordinary nature. He was so reduced in his circumstances that he petitioned James I. for *a license to collect alms* for himself! "as a recompense for his labour and travel of *forty-five years* in setting forth *the chronicles of England*, and *eight years* taken up in the *survey of the cities of London and Westminster*, towards his relief now in his old age; having left his former means of living, and only employing himself for the service and good of his country." Letters patent under the great seal were granted. After no penurious commendation of Stowe's labours, he is permitted "to gather the benevolence of well-disposed people within this realm of England: to ask, gather, and take the alms of all our loving subjects." These letters patent were to be published by the clergy from their pulpits; they produced so little that they were renewed for another twelvemonth; one entire parish in the city, gave seven shillings and sixpence! Such then was the patronage received by Stowe, to be a licensed beggar throughout the kingdom for one twelvemonth! Such was the public remuneration of a man who had been useful to his nation, but not to himself.—(D'Israeli.)

HONOUR TO THE BARDS.

At a court held at Icolmkill, August 23, 1609, by Andrew, Bishop of the Isles, at which most of the gentry of the neighbouring isles were present, amongst other good resolutions for reformation is the following:—

"The which day it being considered, that amongst the remanent abuses which, without reformation, has defiled the whole isles, has been the entertainment and bearing with idle bellies, special vagabonds, *bards*, idle and sturdy beggars, express contrare the laws and laudable acts of Parliament; for the remedy whereof it is likewise enacted, by common consent, that no vagabond, bard, nor profest pleasant (fool by profession), pretending liberty to bard and flatter, be received within the bounds of the said isles, by any of said special barons and gentlemen, or any other inhabitants thereof, or entertained by them, or any of them, in any sort; but in case any vagabond, bard, juggler, or such like, be apprehended by them, or any of them, he is to be taken, and put in sure seizement and keeping in the stocks, and thereafter to be debarred forth of the country with all goodly expedition.—(Scotsman's Library.)

DIBDIN'S POEMS.

I have not the smallest pretensions to the "rhyming art," although in former times I did venture to dabble with it. About twelve years ago I was rash enough to publish a small volume of poems, with my name affixed. They were the productions of my juvenile years; and I need hardly say, at this period, how ashamed I am of their authorship. The *Monthly* and *Analytical Reviews* did me the kindness of just tolerating them, and of warning me not to commit any future trespass upon the premises of Parnassus. I struck off 500 copies, and was glad to get rid of half of them as waste paper; the remaining half has been partly destroyed by my own hands, and has partly mouldered away in oblivion amidst the dust of booksellers' shelves. My only consolation is, that the volume is *exceedingly rare!*—(Rev. T. F. Dibdin.)

DENON AND MADAME TALLEYRAND.

It is told of Madame Talleyrand, that one day her husband having told her that Denon, the French savan, was coming to dinner, bid her read a little of his book on

Egypt, just published, in order that she might be enabled to say something civil to him upon it, adding that he would leave the volume for her on his study-table. He forgot this, however, and madame, upon going into the study, found a volume of *Robinson Crusoe* on the table instead, which having read very attentively, she was not long in opening upon Denon after dinner about the desert island, his manner of living, &c., to the great astonishment of poor Denon, who could not make head or tail of what she meant. At last, upon her saying, "*Eh puis, ce cher Vendredi!*" he perceived she took him for no less a person than Robinson Crusoe.—(Moore.)

DR. YOUNG.

When Dr. Young was deeply engaged in writing one of his tragedies, the Duke of Wharton, who had presented him with £2000 on the publication of his *Universal Passion*, made him a gift of a different kind. He procured a human skull, and fixed a candle in it, and gave it to the doctor, as the most proper lamp for him to write tragedy by.—(Rawlinson.)

JOHNSON AND HIS BEAUTIES.

"The Beauties of Johnson" are said to have got money to the collector; if the "Deformities" have the same success, I shall be still a more extensive benefactor.—(Dr. Johnson.)

TRIALS AND MISERIES.

OLIVER GOLDSMITH.

Of poor, dear Dr. Goldsmith, there is little to be told more than the papers have made public. He died of a fever, made, I am afraid, more violent by uneasiness of mind. His debts began to be heavy, and all his resources were exhausted. He had raised money and squandered it by every acquisition and folly of expense. Sir Joshua [Reynolds] is of opinion, that he owed not less than two thousand pounds. Was ever poet so trusted before?—(Dr. Johnson.)

MILTON.

After Milton was driven from all public stations, he was still too great not to be traced by curiosity to his retirement, where he has been found by Mr. Richardson, the fondest of his admirers, sitting before his door in a grey coat of coarse cloth, in warm, sultry weather, to enjoy the fresh air; and so, as in his own room, receiving the visits of a few of distinguished parts as well as quality. According to another account, he was seen in a small house, neatly enough dressed in black clothes, sitting in a room hung with rusty green; pale, but not cadaverous, with chalk-stones in his hand. He said that, if it were not for the gout, his blindness would be tolerable. In the intervals of his pain, being made unable to use the common exercises, he used to swing in a chair, and sometimes played upon an organ. He was at this time employed upon his *Paradise Lost*. His domestic habits, so far as they are known, were those of a severe student. He drank little strong drink of any kind, and fed without excess in quantity, and in his earlier years, without delicacy of choice. In his youth, he studied late at night; but afterwards changed his hours, and rested in bed from nine to four in the summer, and five in the winter. The course of his day was best known after he was blind. When he first rose, he heard a chapter in the Hebrew Bible, and then studied till twelve; then took some exercise for an hour; then dined, then played on the organ, and sang, or heard another sing; then studied to six; then entertained his visitors till eight; then supped, and after a pipe of tobacco and a glass of water, went to bed. Milton has the reputation of having been in his youth eminently beautiful, so as to have been called the lady of his college. His hair, which was of a light brown, parted at the fore-top, and hung down upon his shoulders, according to the picture which he has given of Adam. He was, however, not of the heroic stature, but rather below the middle size, though both vigorous and active. His eyes, which are said never to have been good, were much weakened by study, and are believed to have been of little service to him after writing his *Defence of the People*, in answer to the *Defensio Regis* of Salmasius; and as Salmasius reproached Milton with losing his eyes in this quarrel, Milton delighted himself with the belief that he had shortened Salmasius' life; but both, perhaps, with more malignity than reason. Salmasius, however, died at the Spa about two years after; and as controversists are commonly said to be killed by their last dispute, Milton was flattered with the credit of destroying him.—(Johnson's Lives.)

DEATH OF OTWAY.

Otway died in his thirty-third year, in a manner which I am unwilling to mention. Having been compelled by his necessities to contract debts, and hunted, as is supposed, by the terriers of the law, he retired to a public-house on Tower Hill, where he is said to have died of want; or, as it is related by one of his biographers, by swallowing, after a long fast, a piece of bread which charity had supplied. He went out, as is reported, almost naked in the rage of hunger, and, finding a gentleman in a neighbouring coffee-house, asked him for a shilling. The gentleman gave him a guinea; and Otway going away, bought a roll, and was choked with the first mouthful. All this, I hope, is not true; and there is ground of better hope that Pope, who lived near enough to be well informed, relates, in Spence's *Memorials*, that he died of a fever, caught by violent pursuit of a thief that had robbed him of his funds. But that indigence, and its concomitants, sorrow and despondency, pressed hard upon him, has never been denied, whatever immediate cause might bring him to the grave.—(Johnson's Lives.)

BURTON'S ANATOMY OF MELANCHOLY.

The first edition of this book was published in 1621, in 4to. The author is said to have composed it with a view of relieving his own melancholy, but increased it to such a degree, that nothing could make him laugh, but going to the bridge-foot and hearing the ribaldry of the bargemen, which rarely failed to throw him into a violent fit of laughter. Before he was overcome with this horrid disorder, he, in the intervals of his vapours, was esteemed one of the most facetious companions in the university [Christ's Church College, where he died at or very near the time he had some years before foretold, from the calculation of his own nativity, and which, says Wood, being exact, several of the students did not forbear to whisper among themselves, that rather than there should be a mistake in the calculation, he sent up his soul to heaven through a slip about his neck.]—(Granger.)

DE FOE AND THE UNION.

He appears to have been no great favourite in Scotland, although, while there, he published *Caledonia*, a poem in honour of the nation. He mentions many hair-breadth 'scapes, which, by "his own prudence and God's providence," he effected; and it is not wonderful, that where almost the whole nation was decidedly averse to the Union, a character like De Foe, sent thither to promote it by all means, direct and indirect, should be regarded with dislike, and even exposed to the danger of assassination. The act for the Union was passed by the Scotch Parliament in January, and De Foe returned to London in February, 1707, to write a history of that great international treaty. It is believed that his services were rewarded by a pension from Queen Anne.—(Memoirs by Mr. John Ballantyne.)

MATTHEW BRAMBLE.

About twenty years ago, the town was amused almost every morning by a series of humorous burlesque poems by a writer under the assumed name of *Matthew Bramble*—he was at that very moment one of the most moving spectacles of human melancholy I have ever witnessed. It was one evening I saw a tall, famished, melancholy man enter a bookseller's shop, his hat flapped over his eyes, and his whole frame evidently feeble from exhaustion and utter misery. The bookseller inquired how he proceeded in his new tragedy? "Do not talk to me about my tragedy! Do not talk to me about my tragedy! I have indeed more tragedy than I can bear at home!" was the reply, as the voice faltered as he spoke. This man was Matthew Bramble, or rather M'Donald, the author of the tragedy of *Vimonda*, at that moment the writer of comic poetry; his tragedy was indeed a domestic one, in which he himself was the greatest actor among a wife and seven children—he shortly afterwards perished. I heard at the time, that M'Donald had walked from Scotland with no other fortune than the novel of *The Independent* in one pocket, and the tragedy of *Vimonda* in the other. Yet he lived some time in all the bloom and flush of poetical confidence. *Vimonda* was even performed several nights, but not with the success the romantic poet, among his native rocks, had conceived was to crown his anxious labours—the theatre disappointed him — and afterwards, to his feelings, all the world.—(D'Israeli's Calamities of Authors.)

HENRY CAREY—NAMBY-PAMBY.

Henry Carey was a true son of the Muses. He is the author of several little national poems. In early life he successfully burlesqued the affected versification of Ambrose Phillips, in his baby poems; to which he gave the fortunate appellation of "*Namby-Pamby*, a panegyric on the new versification;" a term descriptive in sound of these chiming follies, and now adopted in the style of criticism. Carey's *Namby-Pamby* was at first considered by Swift as the satirical effusion of Pope, and by Pope as the humorous ridicule of Swift. His ballad of *Sally in our Alley* was more than once commended for its nature by Addison, and is sung to this day. Of the national song, *God Save the King*, he was the author, both of the words and the music. He was very successful on the stage, and wrote admirable burlesques of the Italian opera, in *The Dragon of Wantley*, and *The Dragoness;* and the mock tragedy of *Chrononhotonthologos* is not forgotten. Among his poems lie still concealed several original pieces; those which have a political turn are particularly good, for the politics of Carey were those of a poet and a patriot. Yet poor Carey, the delight of the Muses, and delighting with the Muses, experienced all their trials and all their treacheries. At the time that this poet could neither walk the streets, nor be seated at the convivial board, without listening to his own songs and his own music—for in truth, the whole nation was echoing his verse, and crowded theatres were clapping to his wit and honour—while this very man himself, urged by his strong humanity, had founded a "Fund for decayed musicians"— at this moment was poor Carey himself so broken-hearted, and his own common comforts so utterly neglected, that, in despair, not waiting for nature to relieve him from the burthen of existence, he laid violent hands on himself; and when found dead, had only a half-penny in his pocket! Such was the fate of the author of some of the most popular pieces in our language! He left a son who inherited his misery and a gleam of his genius.—(D'Israeli's Calamities.)

JOHN MACDIARMID.

Was one of those Scotch students whom the golden fame of Hume and Robertson attracted to the metropolis. He mounted the first step of literary adventure with credit; and passed through the probation of editor and reviewer, till he strove for more heroic adventures. He published some volumes, whose subjects display the aspirings of his genius: "An inquiry into the nature of civil and military subordination;" another into "the system of military defence." It was during these labours I beheld this inquirer, of a tender frame, emaciated, and study-worn, with hollow eyes, where the mind dimly shone like a lamp in a tomb. With keen ardour he opened a new plan of biographical politics. When, by one who wished the author and his style were in better condition, the dangers of excess of study were brought to his recollection—he smiled, and, with something of a mysterious air, talked of unalterable confidence in the powers of his mind—of the indefinite improvement in our faculties; and, although his frame was not athletic, he considered himself capable of trying it to the extremity—his whole life indeed was one melancholy trial—often the day cheerfully passed without its meal, but never without its page. The new system of political biography was advancing, when our young author felt a paralytic stroke. He afterwards resumed his pen, and a second one proved fatal. He lived just to pass through the press his *Lives of British Statesmen*, a splendid quarto, whose publication he owed to the generous temper of a friend, who, when the author could not readily procure a publisher, would not see even the dying author's last hopes disappointed. Some research and reflection are combined in this literary and civil history of the sixteenth and seventeenth centuries—but it was written with the blood of the author, for Macdiarmid died of over-study. —(D'Israeli's Calamities.)

TOBIAS SMOLLETT.

Of most authors by profession— who has displayed a more fruitful genius, and exercised more intense industry, with a loftier sense of his independence, than Smollett? But look into his life and enter into his feelings, and you will be shocked at the disparity of his situation with the genius of the man. His life was a succession of struggles, vexations, and disappointments, yet of success in his writings. Smollett, who is a great poet though he has written little in verse, and whose rich genius had composed the most original pictures of human life, was compelled by his wants to debase his name by selling it to voyages and translations, which he never could have read. When he had worn himself down in the service of the public or the booksellers, there remained not, of all his slender remunerations, in the last stage of life, sufficient to convey him to a cheap country and a restorative air on the Continent. Smollett gradually perishing in a foreign land, neglected by an admiring public, and without fresh resources from the booksellers, who were receiving the income of his works—threw out his injured feelings in the character of *Bramble;* the warm generosity of his temper, but not his genius, seemed fleeting with his breath. Yet when Smollet died, and his widow in a foreign land was raising a plain monument over his dust, her love and her piety but "made the little less." She perished in friendless solitude! Yet Smollett dead—soon an ornamented column it raised at the place of his birth, while the grave of the author seemed to multiply the editions of his works. There are indeed grateful feelings in the public at large for a favourite author; but the awful testimony of those feelings by its gradual progress, must appear beyond the grave! They visit the column consecrated by his name, and his features are most loved, most venerated, in the bust.—(D'Israeli's Calamities.)

DE LOLME.

I do not know an example in our literary history that so loudly accuses our tardy and phlegmatic feeling respecting authors, as the treatment De Lolme experienced in this country. His book on our constitution still enters into the studies of an English patriot, and is not the worse for flattering and elevating the imagination, painting everything beautiful, to encourage our love as well as our reverence for the most perfect system of governments. It was a noble as well as an ingenious effort in a foreigner—but could not obtain even individual patronage. The fact is mortifying to record, that the author, who wanted every aid, received less encouragement than if he had solicited subscriptions for a raving novel, or an idle poem. De Lolme was compelled to traffic with booksellers for this work; and, as he was a theoretical rather than a practical politician, he was a bad trader, and acquired the smallest remuneration. He lived, in the country to which he had rendered a national service, in extreme obscurity and decay; and the walls of the Fleet too often inclosed the English Montesquieu. He never appears to have received a solitary attention (except from the hand of literary charity, having been more than once relieved by the Literary Fund), and became so disgusted with authorship, that he preferred silently to endure its poverty, rather than its other vexations. He ceased almost to write. Of De Lolme I have heard little recorded, but his high-mindedness; a strong sense that he stood degraded beneath that rank in society which his book entitled him to enjoy. The cloud of poverty that covered him, only veiled without concealing its object; with the manners and dress of a decayed gentleman, he still showed the few who met him, that he cherished a spirit perpetually at variance with the adversity of his circumstances.—(D'Israeli.)

LEARNING AND LABOURS.

PROFESSOR PORSON.

Porson by no means excelled in conversation; he neither wrote nor spoke with facility. His elocution was perplexed and embarrassed, except where he was exceedingly intimate, but there was strong indication of intellect in his countenance, and whatever he said was manifestly founded on judgment, sense, and knowledge. Composition was no less difficult to him. Upon one occasion he undertook to write a dozen lines upon a subject which he had much turned in his mind, and with which he was exceedingly familiar. But the number of erasures and interlineations was so great as to render it hardly legible; yet, when completed, it was, and is, a memorial of his sagacity, acuteness, and erudition.

It is sufficiently notorious that our friend was not remarkably attentive to the decoration of his person; indeed, he was at times disagreeably negligent. On one occasion he went to visit a learned friend, afterwards a judge, where a gentleman, who did not know Porson, was waiting in anxious and impatient expectation of the barber. On Porson's entering the library, where the gentleman was sitting, he started up and hastily said to Porson, "Are you the barber?" "No, sir," replied Porson, "but I am a cunning shaver, much at your service."

His peculiarities and failings have been by some too harshly pointed out and commented upon, without due consideration of how exceedingly they were counterbalanced by the most extraordinary and most valuable endowments. Of what importance is it, that when he shaved himself he would walk up and down his room, conversing with whomsoever might happen to be present; that he knew the precise number of steps from his apartment to the houses of those of his friends with whom he was the most intimate, which, by the way, in the metropolis, must have been strongly indicative of a mind not easily made to swerve from its purpose; that at one period he was remarkably fond of the theatre, and all at once, as it were, ceased to frequent it? The circumstance most remarkable concerning his habits and propensities is, that he latterly became a hoarder of money, and, when he died, had not less than two thousand pounds in the funds. All these, however, are minor subjects of reflection. In him criticism lost the most able, most expert, most accomplished support of her sceptre; learning one of its greatest ornaments. His knowledge was far more extensive than was generally understood, or imagined, or believed. There are very few languages with which he had not some acquaintance. His discernment and acuteness in correcting what was corrupt, and explaining what was difficult and perplexed, were almost intuitive; and, in addition to all this, his taste was elegant and correct. His recitations and repetitions were, it must be confessed, sometimes tedious and irksome, which would not, however, have been the case, unless they had been too often heard before, for he never repeated anything that was not characterized by excellence of some kind or other.—(Beloe's Sexagenarian.)

GIBBON'S ROMAN EMPIRE.

It was at Rome, on the 15th of October, 1764, as I sat musing amidst the ruins of the capitol, while the bare-footed friars were singing vespers in the temple of Jupiter, that the idea of writing the Decline and Fall of the city first started to my mind. But my original plan was circumscribed to the decay of the city rather than of the empire: and, though my reading and reflections began to point towards that object, some years elapsed, and several avocations intervened, before I was seriously engaged in the execution of that laborious work.—(Gibbon.)

BUCHANAN'S SCOTLAND.

If Buchanan's history had been written on a subject far enough back, all the world might have mistaken it for a piece writ in the Augustan age! It is not only his words that are so pure, but his entire manner of writing is of that age.—(Dean Lockier.)

LEYDEN—"COMPLAYNT OF SCOTLAND."

A new edition of an ancient and singularly rare tract, bearing this title, written by an uncertain author, about the year 1548, was published in 1801, by Dr. Leyden. As the tract was itself of a diffuse and comprehensive nature, touching upon many unconnected topics, both of public policy and private life, as well as treating of the learning, the poetry, the music, and the arts of that early period; it gave Leyden an opportunity of pouring forth such a profusion of antiquarian knowledge in the preliminary dissertation, notes, and glossary, as one would have thought could hardly have been accumulated during so short a life, dedicated, too, to so many and varied studies. The intimate acquaintance which he has displayed with Scottish antiquities of every kind, from manuscript histories and rare chronicles down to the tradition of the peasant, and the rhymes even of the nursery, evince an extent of research, power of arrangement, and facility of recollection, which have never been equalled in this department. This singular work was the means of introducing Leyden to the notice and correspondence of Mr. Ritson, the celebrated antiquary, who, in a journey to Scotland, in the next summer, found nothing which delighted him so much as the conversation of the editor of the *Complaynt of Scotland*, in whose favour he smoothed down and softened the natural asperity of his own disposition. The friendship, however, between these two authors was broken off by Leyden's running his Border hobby-horse a full tilt against the Pythagorean palfrey of the English antiquary. Ritson, it must be well remembered, had written a work against the use of animal food; Leyden, on the other hand, maintained it was a part of a masculine character to eat whatever came to hand, whether the substance was vegetable or animal, cooked or uncooked; and he concluded a tirade to this purpose, by eating a raw beef-steak before the terrified antiquary, who never afterwards could be prevailed upon to regard him, except as a kind of learned ogre.—(Memoirs by Sir Walter Scott.)

DANTE'S COMEDIA.

Dante wrote before we began at all to be refined; and, of course, his celebrated poem is a sort of Gothic work. He is very singular and very beautiful in his similes, and more like Homer than any of our poets since. He was prodigiously learned for the time he lived in, and knew all that a man could then know. His poem got the name of *Comedia* after his death. He, in that piece, had called Virgil's works tragedies (or sublime poetry), and, in deference to him, called his own comedy (or low); and hence was that word used afterwards by mistake, for the title of his poem.—(Ficoroni.)

DR. SAMUEL PARR.

It may very reasonably be questioned whether the services which Dr. Parr has done to the world have been adequate to his ability or his knowledge. Much is to be allowed, however, for that want of leisure and opportunity which every man of letters must feel whose constant and necessary occupation is the instruction of youth. To the character of a profound scholar, though the printed testimonies he has afforded us may have been slender, none shall dare to dispute his claim; and were our remaining possessions of Greek and Latin authors to share the fate of the celebrated Alexandrian Library, we believe that this gigantic proficient could afford us, from recollection, a very tolerable idea of Grecian and Roman literature. Of the English style of Dr. Parr it has been said that it unites the strength of Johnson with the richness of Burke.—(Literary Memoirs, 1798.)

AINSWORTH'S DICTIONARY.

When Mr. Ainsworth was engaged in the laborious work of his Dictionary of the Latin language, his wife made heavy complaints at enjoying so little of his society. When he had reached the letter S of his work, the patience of his helpmeet was completely exhausted; and, in a fit of ill-nature, she revenged herself for the loss of his company, by committing the whole manuscript to the flames! Such an accident would have deterred most men from prosecuting the undertaking; but the persevering industry of Ainsworth repaired the loss of his manuscript by the most assiduous application.

LADY M. WORTLEY MONTAGU.

When I was young I was a vast admirer of Ovid's Metamorphoses, and that was one of the chief reasons that set me upon the thoughts of stealing the Latin language. Mr. Wortley was the only person to whom I communicated my design; and he encouraged me in it. I used to study five or six hours a-day for two years in my father's library, and so got that language, whilst everybody thought I was reading nothing but novels and romances.—(Lady Mary Wortley Montagu.)

WIT AND HUMOUR.

THOMAS CAMPBELL.—UNIVERSITY SPREE.

A respectable apothecary named Fife had a shop in the Trongate of Glasgow (when Campbell, at the age of seventeen, was attending the University of that city in 1795, with this notice in his window, printed in large letters, "*Ears pierced by A. Fife;*" meaning the operation to which young ladies submit for the sake of wearing earrings. Mr. Fife's next door neighbour was a citizen of the name of *Drum*, a spirit-dealer, whose windows exhibited various samples of the liquors which he sold. The worthy shopkeepers having become alienated by jealousy in trade, Thomas Campbell and two trusty college chums fell upon the following expedient for reconciling them. During the darkness of night, long before the streets of Glasgow were lighted with gas, Campbell and his two associates having procured a long fir-deal, had it extended from window to window of the two contiguous shops, with this inscription from Othello, which it fell to the youthful poet, as his share of the practical joke, to paint in flaming capitals:—

"THE SPIRIT-STIRRING DRUM, THE EAR-PIERCING FIFE."

Hitherto (observes Campbell's biographer) the two neighbours had pursued very distinct callings; but, to their utter surprise, a sudden co-partnership had been struck during the night, and Fife and Drum were now united in the same martial line. A great sensation was produced in the morning, when, of course, the new co-partnery was suddenly dissolved. Campbell was, after some inquiry, found to have been the sign-painter, and threatened with pains and penalties, which were, however, commuted into a severe reprimand, suggesting to the poet the words of Parolles—

"I'll no more drumming: a plague of all Drums."

SHERIDAN AND RICHARDSON.

Lord John Russell told us a good trick of Sheridan's upon Richardson. Sheridan had been driving out three or four hours in a hackney coach, when, seeing Richardson pass, he hailed him and made him get in. He instantly contrived to introduce a topic upon which Richardson (who was the very soul of disputatiousness) always differed with him; and at last, affecting to be mortified at Richardson's arguments, said, "You really are too bad, I cannot bear to listen to such things; I will not stay in the same coach with you." And accordingly got down and left him, Richardson hallooing out triumphantly, "Ah, you're beat, you're beat!" Nor was it till the heat of his victory had a little cooled, that he found out he was left in the lurch to pay for Sheridan's three hours' coaching.— (Diary of Thomas Moore.)

DUNS SCOTUS.

This eminent theologian and scholar of the ninth century, known as the "subtle doctor," combined with his philosophic genius a cordial love of pleasantry. Charles the Bald, when seated opposite to him at table, asked him archly, "What is the distance between a *Scot* and a *sot*?" "The width of the table," was the ready answer, which drew a smile from the king.

SYDNEY SMITH AND THOS. CAMPBELL.

I met Sydney Smith (wrote Campbell) the other day. "Campbell," he said, "we met last, two years ago, in Fleet Street; and, as you may remember, we got into a violent argument, but were separated by a waggon, and have never met since. Let us have out that argument now. Do you recollect the subject?" "No," I said, "I have clean forgotten the subject; but I remember that I was in the *right*, and that you were violent, and in the wrong!" I had scarcely uttered these words, when a violent shower came on. I took refuge in a shop, and he in a cab. He parted with a proud threat that he would renew the argument the next time we met. "Very well," I said, "but you shan't get off again, either in a waggon or a cab."

DR. BUCKLAND—FORCE OF IMAGINATION.

This distinguished geologist one day gave a dinner, after dissecting a Mississippi alligator, having asked a good many of the most distinguished of his classes to dine with him. His house and all his establishment were in good style and taste. His guests congregated; the dinner table showed splendidly, with glass, china and plate, and the meal commenced with excellent soup.

"How do you like the soup?" asked the Doctor, after having finished his own plate, addressing a famous *gourmand* of the day.

"Very good, indeed," answered the other. "Turtle, is it not? I only ask because I do not find any green fat."

The Doctor shook his head.

"I think it has somewhat of a

musky taste," said another; "not unpleasant, but peculiar."

"All alligators have," replied Buckland; "the cayman peculiarly so. The fellow whom I dissected this morning, and whom you have just been eating—"

There was a general rout of the whole guests. Every one turned pale. Half a dozen started up from the table. Two or three of them ran out of the room and vomited; and only those who had stout stomachs remained to the close of an excellent entertainment.

"See what imagination is," said Buckland. "If I told them it was turtle, or terrapin, or bird's-nest soup—salt water amphibia or fresh, or the gluten of a fish from the maw of a sea-bird, they would have pronounced it excellent, and their digestion been none the worse. Such is prejudice."

"But was it really an alligator?" asked a lady.

"As good a calf's head as ever wore a coronet," answered Buckland.

SHERIDAN.

Shaw, having lent Sheridan near £500, used to dun him very considerably for it; and one day, when he had been rating S. about the debt, and insisting that he must be paid, the latter, having played off some of his plausible wheedling upon him, ended by saying that he was very much in want of £25 to pay the expenses of a journey he was about to take, and he knew Shaw would be good-natured enough to lend it to him. "'Pon my word," says Shaw, "this is too bad; after keeping me out of my money in so shameful a manner, you now have the face to ask me for more; but it won't do; I must be paid my money, and it is most disgraceful," &c., &c. "My dear fellow," says Sheridan, "hear reason; the sum you ask me for is a very considerable one; whereas I only ask you for five-and-twenty pounds."

CAUSE AND EFFECT.

Charles Lamb tells a story of a rencontre with a fellow-traveller, which illustrates his peculiar humour. "We travelled," says he, "with one of those troublesome fellow-passengers in a stage coach that is called a well-informed man. For twenty miles we discoursed about the properties of steam, probabilities of carriage by ditto, till all my science, and more than all, was exhausted, and I was thinking of escaping my torment by getting up on the outside, when getting into Bishop's Stortford, my gentleman, spying some farming land, put an unlucky question to me—'What sort of a crop of turnips I thought we should have this year.' Emma's eyes turned to me, to know what in the world I could have to say; and she burst out into a violent fit of laughter, maugre her pale, serious cheeks, when, with the greatest gravity, I replied, that 'it depended, I believed, upon boiled legs of mutton.'"

DON QUIXOTE.

We are here presented with an instance of that species of partial madness, which occours not unfrequently in real life. A worthy man, in other respects of a sound judgment, has his head so turned by reading books of chivalry, that he sees nothing in nature but castles and palaces, giants and enchanters. Into these he transforms everything he meets with; and the author has very happily chosen the meanest objects of common life for the subject of this metamorphosis. The striking contrasts which are thus produced, the monstrous mistakes and ludicrous distresses of the hero, are painted in so lively a manner as to render this the most laughable performance perhaps that the wit of man ever produced.—(Murray's Morality of Fiction.)

DE FOE AND THE GHOST THAT MADE THE BOOK SELL.

An adventurous bookseller had ventured to print a considerable edition of Drelincourt's *Book of Consolation against the Fears of Death*, translated by M. D'Assigny. But, however certain the prospect of death, it is not so agreeable (unfortunately) as to invite the eager contemplation of the public, and the book, being neglected, lay a dead stock on the hands of the publisher. In this emergency he applied to De Foe to assist him in rescuing the unfortunate book from the literary death to which general neglect seemed about to consign it. De Foe's genius and audacity devised a plan, which, for assurance and ingenuity, defied even the powers of Mr. Puff in the *Critic;* for who but himself would have thought of summoning up a ghost from the grave to bear witness in favour of a halting body of divinity? There is a matter-of-fact, business like style in the whole account of the transaction, which bespeaks ineffable powers of self-possession. The apparition of Mrs. Veal is represented as appearing to a Mrs. Bargrave, her intimate friend, as she sat in her own house in deep contemplation of certain distresses of her own. After the ghostly visitor had announced herself as prepared for a distant journey, her friend and she began to talk in the homely style of middle-aged ladies, and Mrs. Veal proses concerning the conversations they had formerly held, and the books they had read together. Her very recent experience probably led Mrs. Veal to talk of death and the books written on the subject, and she pronounced, *ex cathedra*, as a dead person was best entitled to do, that "Drelincourt's book on death was the best book on the subject ever written." She also mentioned Dr. Sherlock, two Dutch books which had been translated, and several others; but Drelincourt, she said, had the clearest notions of death and the future state of any who had handled that subject. She then asked for the work, and lectured on it with great eloquence and affection. Dr. Kenrick's *Ascetick* was also mentioned with approbation by this critical spectre (the Doctor's work was no doubt a tenant of the shelf in some favourite publisher's shop), and Mr. Norris' poem on *Friendship*, a work which, I doubt, though honoured with the ghost's approbation, we may now seek for as vainly as Corelli tormented his memory to recover the sonata which the devil played to him in a dream. The whole account is so distinctly circumstantial, that, were it not for the impossibility, or extreme improbability at least, of such an occurrence, the evidence could not but support the story.

The effect was most wonderful. Drelincourt *upon Death*, attested by one who could speak from experience, took an unequalled run. The copies had hung on the bookseller's hands as heavy as a pile of bullets. They now traversed the town in every direction, like the same balls discharged from a field-piece. In short, the object of Mrs. Veal's apparition was perfectly attained.—(Scott's Memoir of De Foe.)

EDWARD WORTLEY MONTAGU.

Mr. Foster had, in the early part of his life, been selected by old Edward Wortley Montagu (husband of the celebrated Lady Mary), to superintend the education of that very eccentric character, the late Edward Wortley Montagu. Young Montagu, after thrice running away from his tutor, and being discovered by his father's valet crying flounders about the streets of Deptford, was sent to the West Indies, whither Foster accompanied him. On their return to England a good-natured stratagem was practised to obtain a temporary supply of money from old Montagu, and, at the same time, to give him a favourable opinion of his son's attention to a particular species of erudition. The stratagem was this:—Foster wrote a book which he entitled, *The Rise and Fall of the Roman Republics.* To this he subjoined the name of Edward Wortley Montagu, jun., Esq. Old Wortley seeing the book advertised, sent for his son, and gave him a bank note of one hundred pounds, promising him a similar present for every new edition which the book should pass through. It was well received, and therefore a second edition occasioned a second supply. It is now in libraries with the name of Wortley Montagu prefixed as the author, although he did not write a line of it.—(L. T. Rede's Anecdotes. London. 1799.)

DR. JOHNSON'S SERMONS, ETC.

The papers in the *Adventurer*, signed with the letter T., are commonly attributed to one of Mr. Johnson's earliest and most intimate friends, Mr. Bathurst the bookseller; but there is reason to believe they were written by Johnson, and by him given to his friend. At that time Johnson was himself engaged in writing the *Rambler*, and could ill afford to make a present of his labours. The various other pieces he gave away have conferred fame, and probably fortune, on several persons, to the great disgrace of some of his *clerical friends;* forty sermons, which he himself tells us he wrote, have not yet been *deterré.*—(L. T. Rede's Anecdotes. London. 1799.) [Query: Are the sermons here alluded to those left for publication by John Taylor, LL.D., which have long been recognized as the genuine production of the learned lexicographer?]—(See a letter of Dr. Beattie's, of date October 31, published in his life by Sir W. Forbes.)

TENDERNESS AND AFFECTION.

DR. CHALMERS.

The simplicity and tenderness of Dr. Chalmers's character have never been better illustrated than in the details given in the following passage from the *Memoir* by Dr. Hanna:—

"In the spring of 1845, Dr. Chalmers visited his native village. It almost looked as if he came to take farewell, and as if that peculiarity of old age which sends it back to the days of childhood for its last earthly reminiscences, had for a time, and prematurely, taken hold of him. His special object seemed to be to revive the recollections of his boyhood — gathering Johnny-Groats by the sea-beach of the Billowness, and lilacs from an ancient hedge, taking both away to be laid up in his repositories at Edinburgh. Not a place or person familiar to him in earlier years was left unvisited. On his way to the church-yard, he went up the very road along which he had gone of old to the parish school. Slipping into a poor-looking dwelling by the way, he said to his companion, Dr. Williamson, 'I would just like to see the place where Lizzy Geen's water-bucket used to stand,'—the said water-bucket having been a favourite haunt of the over-heated ball-players, and Lizzy a great favourite for the free access she allowed to it. He called on two contemporaries of his boyhood, one of whom he had not seen for forty-five, the other for fifty-two years, and took the most boyish delight in recognizing how the 'mould of antiquity had gathered upon their features,' and in recounting stories of his school-boy days. 'James,' said he to the oldest of the two, a tailor, now upwards of eighty, who in those days had astonished the children, and himself among the number, with displays of superior knowledge, 'you were the first man that ever gave me something like a correct notion of the form of the earth. I knew that it was round, but I thought always that it was round like a shilling, till you told me that it was round like a marble.' 'Well, John,' said he to the other, whose face, like his own, had suffered severely from small-pox in his childhood; 'you and I have had one advantage over folk with finer faces—theirs have been aye getting the waur, but ours have been aye getting the better o' the wear!' The dining-room of his grandfather's house had a fireplace fitted up behind with Dutch tiles, adorned with various quaint devices, upon which he had used to feast his eyes in boyish wonder and delight. These he now sought out most diligently, but was grieved to find them all so blackened and begrimed by the smoke of half-a-century, that not one of his old windmills or burgomasters was visible. To one apartment he felt a peculiar tie, as having been appropriated exclusively to his use in his college days, when the love of solitary study was at times a passion. But the most interesting visit of all was to Barnsmuir, a place a few miles from Anstruther, on the way to Crail. In his school-boy days it had been occupied by Capt. R——, whose eldest daughter rode in daily on a little pony to the school at Anstruther. Dr. Chalmers was then a boy of from twelve to fourteen years of age, but he was not too young for an attachment of a singularly tenacious hold. Miss R—— was married (I believe while he was yet at college) to Mr. F——, and his opportunities of seeing her in after-life were few, but that early impression never faded from his heart. At the time of his visit to Anstruther in 1845, she had been dead for many years, but, at Dr. Chalmers's particular request, her younger sister met him at Barnsmuir. Having made the most affectionate inquiries about Mrs. F—— and her family, he inquired particularly about her death, receiving with deep emotion the intelligence that she had died in the full Christian hope, and that some of his own letters to her sister had served to soothe and comfort her latest hours. "Mrs. W——," said he eagerly, "is there a portrait of your sister anywhere in this house?" She took him to a room, and pointed to a profile which hung upon the wall. He planted himself before it—gazed on it with intense earnestness — took down the picture, took out his card, and, by two wafers fixed it firmly on the back of the portrait, exactly opposite to the face. Having replaced the likeness, he stood before it and burst into a flood of tears, accompanied by the warmest expressions of attachment. After leaving the house, he sauntered in silence round the garden, buried in old recollections, heaving a sigh occasionally, and muttering to himself—"More than forty years ago!"

JEFFREY'S PLAYFULNESS AND AFFECTION.

The gentle and playful disposition of the distinguished reviewer of the *Edinburgh*, is finely illustrated in the following letter to his grandchild:—

"My sonsy Nancy!—I love you very much, and think very often of your dimples and your pimples, and your funny little plays, and all your pretty ways; and I send you my blessing, and wish I were kissing your sweet rosy lips, or your fat finger tips; and that you were here so that I could hear your stammering words, from a mouthful of curds; and a great purple tongue (as broad as it's long); and see your round eyes open wide with surprise, and your wondering look to find yourself at Craigcrook! To-morrow is Maggie's birthday, and we have built up a great bonfire in honour of it; and Maggie Rutherfurd (do you remember her at all?) is coming out to dance round it; and all the servants are to drink her health, and wish her many happy days with you and Frankie; and all the mammas and papas, whether grand or not grand. We are very glad to hear she and you love each other so well, and are happy in making each other happy, and that you do not forget dear Tarley or Frankie when they are out of sight, nor Granny either, or even old Granny pa, who is in most danger of being forgotten, he thinks."

Here is another exquisite letter to one of his grandchildren, when its writer was in his seventy-fifth year:—

"Craigcrook, June 21, 1847.

"A high day! and a holiday! the longest and the brightest of the year; the very middle day of the summer, and the very day when Maggie first opened her sweet eyes on the light! Bless you ever, my darling and bonny bairn. You have now blossomed beside us for six pleasant years, and been all that time the light of our eyes and the love of our hearts; at first the cause of some tender fears from your weakness and delicacy, then of some little provocation from your too great love, as we thought, of your own will and amusement, but now only of love and admiration for your gentle obedience to your parents, and your sweet yielding to the wishes of your younger sister and brother. God bless and keep you then for ever, my delightful and ever-improving child, and make you not only gay and happy as an angel without sin and sorrow, but meek and mild like that heavenly Child, who was once sent down to earth for our example. Well, the sun is shining brightly on our towers and trees, and the great bonfire is all piled up and ready to be lighted, when we come out after drinking your health at dinner; and we have got a great blue and yellow flag hung out on the tower, waving proudly in the wind, and telling all the country around that this is a day of rejoicing and thanksgiving, and wishes of happiness, with all who live under its shadow. And the servants are all to have a fine dinner, and wine and whisky to drink to your health, and all the young Christies (that is, the new gardener's children) will be taught to repeat your name with blessings; and when they are drawn up round the bonfire will wonder a little, I dare say, what sort of a creature this Miss Maggie can be, that we are making all this fuss about! and so you must take care, when you come, to be good enough and pretty enough, to make them understand why we all so love and honour you. Frankie and Tarley have been talking a great deal about you this morning already, and Granny is going to take them, and Mary Rutherfurd and her brother, down to the sea at Cramond, that they may tell the fishes and the distant shores what a happy and a hopeful day it is to them, and to us all. And so bless you again, my sweet one, for this and all future years. Think kindly of one who thinks always of you, and believe, that of all who love you there is none who has loved you better or longer, or more constantly, than your loving Grandpa."—(Life of Lord Jeffrey.)

IRRITABILITY AND VANITY.

ROUSSEAU AND DAVID HUME.

In 1762, the Parliament of Paris issued an *arret* against Jean Jacques Rousseau, on account of his opinions, and the good offices of David Hume were engaged to find him a retreat in England. He was established comfortably in the mansion of Mr. Davenport, at Wooton, in Derbyshire. This vain man appeared in public in London wearing an Armenian dress, which of course attracted much notice; and so long as he was an object of curiosity, his vanity found ample gratification. But being irritable as he was vain, whenever the interest of his first appearance in England began to subside, and he found himself exposed to the animadversions of the press, he became dissatisfied and jealous, and quarrelled with his benefactor, Hume, whom he accused of conceiving horrible designs against him. Rousseau has related an amusing interview with Hume at the time when he entertained this morbid suspicion of the historian's sincerity. The contrast betwixt the phlegmatic reserve of Hume, and the violent effervescence of the Genevese philosopher is highly characteristic. The scene arose out of a dispute about the payment of a return chaise:—" As we were sitting one evening, after supper, silently by the fireside, I caught his eye intently fixed on mine, as indeed happened very often; and that in a manner of which it is very difficult to give an idea. At that time he gave me a steadfast, piercing look, mixed with a sneer, which greatly disturbed me. To get rid of the embarrassment I lay under, I endeavoured to look full at him in my turn; but in fixing my eyes against his, I felt the most inexpressible terror, and was obliged soon to turn them away. The speech and physiognomy of the good David is that of an honest man; but where, great God! did this good man borrow those eyes he fixes so sternly and unaccountably on those of his friends? The impression of this look remained with me, and gave me much uneasiness. My trouble increased even to a degree of fainting; and if I had not been relieved by an effusion of tears I had been suffocated. Presently after this I was seized with the most violent remorse; I even despised myself; till at length, in a transport, which I still remember with delight, I sprang on his neck, embraced him eagerly, while almost choked with sobbing, and bathed in tears, I cried out in broken accents, No, no, David Hume cannot be treacherous. If he be not the best of men, he must be the basest of mankind. David Hume politely returned my embraces, and, gently tapping me on the back, repeated several times, in a good-natured and easy tone, Why, what, my dear sir! nay, my dear sir! O, my dear sir! He said nothing more. I felt my heart yearn within me. We went to bed; and I set out the next day for the country."

WHIMS AND CAPRICES.

A MAD AUTHOR.

An insane author, once placed in confinement, employed most of his time in writing. One night, being thus engaged by aid of a bright moon, a slight cloud passed over the luminary, when, in an impetuous manner, he called out—" Arise,

Jupiter, and snuff the moon." The cloud became thicker, and he exclaimed—"The stupid! he has snuffed it out."

AUTHORS NOT THE BEST JUDGES OF THEIR OWN WRITINGS.

It is known that Milton preferred his *Paradise Regained* to his divine poem of *Paradise Lost.* Virgil is recorded to have ordered, on his deathbed, that the *Æneid* should be burnt, because he did not think it sufficiently finished for publication; and it is to the disobedience of his executors that we are indebted for the possession of that exquisite performance. Tasso new-modelled and injured his *Gierusalemme Liberata.* And it may reasonably be doubted, from the specimen which Akenside has left of the manner in which he intended to alter his *Pleasures of Imagination,* whether that beautiful poem would have been improved by the experiment, had he lived to finish it. Sir William Forbes, in his *Life of Dr. Beattie,* adduces his omitting, in the late editions of his poems, of several beautiful pieces published in his first collection, and reprinting others of inferior poetical merit, as another of the many instances of authors differing from the general opinion.

RABELAIS.

Rabelais had writ some sensible pieces, which the world did not regard at all. "I will write something," says he, "that they shall take notice of;" and so sat down to write nonsense. Everybody allows that there are several things without any manner of meaning in his Pantagruel. Dr. Swift likes it much, and thinks there are more good things in it than I do.—(Pope.)

CAPRICES AND CONTRADICTIONS.

A More, fiercely persecuting for opinion while writing in favour of the rights of thought; a Bacon, teaching morals and taking bribes; a La Fontaine, writing intrigues while avoiding, in his own person, a single amour; a Young, making wretched puns and writing *Night Thoughts;* a Sterne, beating his wife and crying over a dead ass; a melancholy Cowper, gasping out the laughter-moving story of *John Gilpin:* truly that chapter which shall have to deal with all the oddities and anomalies of the literary life must be long and curious, infinitely various in its illustrations, and deep in its insight and its philosophy.—(Athenæum.)

ANTIQUARIANISM.

FROISSART.

I rejoice you have met with Froissart, he is the Herodotus of a barbarous age; had he but had the luck of writing in as good language, he might have been immortal! His locomotive disposition (for then there was no other way of learning things); his simple curiosity, his religious credulity, were much like those of the old Grecian.—(Thomas Gray to Mr. Nicholls.) [In a letter to Dr. Wharton more than ten years before this, he says] Froissart is a favourite book of mine (though I have not attentively read them, but only dipped here and there); and it is strange to me that people, who would give thousands for a dozen portraits (originals of that time) to furnish a gallery, should never cast an eye on so many moving pictures of the life, actions, manners, and thoughts of their ancestors, done on the spot, and in strong, though simple colours. In the succeeding century Froissart, I find, was read with great satisfaction by everybody that could read; and on the same footing with King

Arthur, Sir Tristram, and Archbishop Turpin: not because they thought him a fabulous writer, but because they took them all for true and authentic historians; to so little purpose was it in that age for a man to be at the pains of writing truth.

AN ANTIQUARY.

He is a man strangely thrifty of time past, and an enemy indeed to his maw, whence he fetches out many things when they are now all rotten and stinking. He is one that hath that unnatural disease to be enamoured of old age and wrinkles, and loves all things (as Dutchmen do cheese) the better for being mouldy and worm-eaten. He is of our religion, because we say it is most ancient; and yet a broken statue would almost make him an idolater. A great admirer he is of the rust of old monuments, and reads only those characters, where time hath eaten out the letters. He will go with you forty miles to see a saint's well or a ruined abbey; and there be but a cross or stone footstool in the way, he'll be considering it so long, till he forget his journey.—(Bishop Earle.)

CONVERSATION.

DESCARTES, LA FONTAINE, MARMONTEL, CORNEILLE, BUTLER, ADDISON, ROUSSEAU, MILTON, ETC.

Descartes, the famous mathematician and philosopher; La Fontaine, celebrated for his witty fables; and Buffon, the great naturalist, were all singularly deficient in the powers of conversation. Marmontel, the novelist, was so dull in society that his friend said of him, after an interview, "I must go and read his tales to recompense myself for the weariness of hearing him." As to Corneille, the greatest dramatist of France, he was completely lost in society—so absent and embarrassed that he wrote of himself a witty couplet, importing that he was never intelligible but through the mouth of another. Wit on paper seems to be something widely different from that play of words in conversation, which, while it sparkles, dies; for Charles II., the wittiest monarch that ever sat on the English throne, was so charmed with the humour of *Hudibras*, that he caused himself to be introduced, in the character of a private gentleman, to Butler, its author. The witty king found the author a very dull companion, and was of opinion, with many others, that so stupid a fellow could never have written so clever a book. Addison, whose classic elegance has long been considered the model of style, was shy and absent in society, preserving, even before a single stranger, stiff and dignified silence. . . . In conversation Dante was taciturn or satirical. Gray and Alfieri seldom talked or smiled. Rousseau was remarkably trite in conversation; not a word of fancy or eloquence warmed him. Milton was unsocial, and even irritable, when much pressed by talk of others. Dryden has very honestly told us, "My conversation is dull and slow, my humour is saturnine and reserved; in short, I am not one of those who endeavour to break jest in company, or make repartees."—(Salad for the Solitary.)

c

AMANUENSES OF AUTHORS.

MILTON'S PARADISE LOST.

Milton was blind when he composed that immortal work, the "Paradise Lost." His daughters were his amanuenses. Nor did they merely write what he dictated; but they read to him from day to day whatever classical or other authors he might wish to consult in the way of reference, or to relax or invigorate his mind. But reading to their father the Greek and Latin authors must have been very tedious to them, as it is said they were quite ignorant of both those ancient languages.

GOLDSMITH'S TRIAL.

A voluminous author was one day expatiating on the advantages of employing an amanuensis, and thus saving time and the trouble of writing. "How do you manage it?" said Goldsmith. "Why, I walk about the room, and dictate to a clever man, who puts down very correctly all that I tell him, so that I have nothing to do more than just to look over the manuscript, and then send it to the press."

Goldsmith was delighted with the information, and desired his friend to send the amanuensis the next morning. The scribe accordingly waited upon the Doctor, with the implements of pens, ink, and paper placed in order before him, ready to catch the oracle. Goldsmith paced the room with great solemnity, several times, for some time; but, after racking his brains to no purpose, he put his hand into his pocket, and, presenting the amanuensis with a guinea, said, "It won't do, my friend, I find that my head and hand must go together."

DWIGHT'S THEOLOGY.

Dr. Timothy Dwight, of Newhaven, prepared his *System of Theology* for the press in his old age, when his defective sight no longer enabled him to use the pen. He dictated to an amanuensis that long and eloquent course of sermons on the various doctrines of religion, which will carry down his name through coming time, and spread his influence over the world.

WILBERFORCE.

The style of Wilberforce's *Practical View of the Prevailing Religious System*, on the appearance of that elegant essay, was characterized as possessing all the fluency, ease, and grace of an unwritten address, and all the author's skill in debate and Parliamentary tact. It turned out that the work had not been written, but dictated to an amanuensis while the author walked backward and forward in his study.

SIR WALTER SCOTT'S AMANUENSIS.

William Laidlaw (author of the beautiful song of "Lucy's Flittin'"), and John Ballantyne the printer, were Scott's amanuenses, when, suffering from extreme bodily pain, he was composing the "Bride of Lammermoor." He preferred the latter, says Lockhart, on account of the superior rapidity of his pen; and also because John kept his pen to the paper without interruption, and, though with many an arch twinkle in his eyes, and now and then an audible smack of his lips, had resolution to work on like a well-trained clerk; whereas good Laidlaw entered with such keen zest into the interest of the story as it flowed from the author's lips, that he could not suppress exclamations of surprise and delight—"Gude keep us a'!—the like o' that!—eh sirs! eh sirs!" and so forth—which did not promote despatch. I have often, however, in the sequel, heard both these secretaries describe the astonishment with which they were equally affected when Scott began this experiment. The affectionate Laidlaw beseeching him to stop dictating, when his audible suffering filled every pause, "Nay, Willie," he answered, "only see that the doors are fast. I would fain keep all the cry as well as all the wool to ourselves; but as to giving over work, that can only be when I am in woollen." John Ballantyne told me, that after the first day, he always took care to have a dozen of pens made before he seated himself opposite to the sofa on which Scott lay, and that though he often turned himself on his pillow with a groan of torment, he usually continued the sentence in the same breath. But when dialogue of peculiar animation was in progress, spirit seemed to triumph altogether over matter—he arose from his couch and walked up and down the room, raising and lowering his voice, and as it were acting the parts. It was in this fashion that Scott produced the far greater portion of *The Bride of Lammermoor* —the whole of the *Legend of Montrose*—and almost the whole of *Ivanhoe*.—(Scott's Life, p. 397.)

MISCELLANEOUS ANECDOTES.

THOMAS MOORE—HIS SINGING.

Thomas Moore sung his songs into popularity. We have this entry in his diary:—

"Dined with the Fieldings: sung in the evening to him, her, Montgomery, and the governess—all four weeping. This is the true tribute to my singing." Similar entries are common in his diary, in which all who shed tears at his singing invariably found a place.

"No one believes how much I am sometimes affected in singing, partly from being touched myself, and partly from an anxiety to touch others."

JAMES GRAHAME—HIS SINGING.

Thomas Campbell preserved the following reminiscence of the devotional feeling of James Grahame, author of *The Sabbath*, with whom he was on a familiar footing when both were young men residing in Edinburgh:—

"One of the most endearing circumstances which I remember of Grahame was his singing. I shall never forget one summer evening that we agreed to sit up all night, and go together to Arthur's Seat to see the sun rise. We sat, accordingly, all night in his delightful parlour, the seat of so many happy remembrances! We then went and saw a beautiful sunrise. I returned home with him, for I was living in his house at the time. He was unreserved in all his devoutest feelings before me; and from the beauty of the morning scenery, and the recent death of his sister, our conversation took a serious turn on the proofs of Infinite Benevolence in the creation, and the goodness of God. As I retired to my own bed I overheard his devotions—not his prayer, but a hymn which he sung, and with a power and inspiration beyond himself, and beyond anything else. At that time he was a strong-voiced, and commanding-looking man. The remembrance of his large expressive features when he climbed the hill, and of his organ-like voice in praising God, is yet fresh, and ever pleasing, in my mind."

BUTLER'S HUDIBRAS.

Hudibras was not a hasty effusion; it was not produced by a sudden tumult of imagination, or a short paroxysm of violent labour. To accumulate such a mass of sentiments at the call of accidental desire, or of sudden necessity, is beyond the reach and power of the most active and comprehensive mind. I am informed by Mr. Thyer of Manchester, that excellent editor of this author's reliques, that he could show something of *Hudibras* in prose. He has in his possession the commonplace book, in which Butler reposited, not such events and precepts as are gathered by reading, but such remarks, similitudes, allusions, assemblages, or inferences, as occasion prompted, or meditation produced, those thoughts that were generated in his own mind, and might be usefully applied to some future purpose. Such is the labour of those who write for immortality.—(Dr. Johnson.)

FAVOURITE DISHES.

Dr. Rondelet, an ancient writer on fishes, was so fond of figs, that he died in 1566, of a surfeit occasioned by eating them to excess. In a letter to a friend, Dr. Parr confesses his love of "hot boiled lobsters, with a profusion of shrimp sauce." Pope, who was an epicure, would lie in bed for days at Lord Bolingbroke's, unless he were told that there were stewed lampreys for dinner, when he arose instantly, and came down to table. A gentleman treated Dr. Johnson to new honey and clouted cream, of which he ate so largely, that his entertainer became alarmed. All his lifetime Dr. Johnson had a voracious attachment for a leg of mutton. "At my aunt Ford's," says he, "I ate so much of a boiled leg of mutton, that she used to talk of it. My mother, who was affected by little things, told me seriously that it would hardly ever be forgotten." Dryden, writing in 1699 to a lady, declining her invitation to a handsome supper, says, "If beggars might be choosers, a chine of honest bacon would please my appetite more than all the marrow puddings, for I like them better plain, having a very vulgar stomach." Dr. George Fordyce contended that as one meal a day was enough for a lion, it ought to suffice for a man. Accordingly, for more than twenty years, the Doctor used to eat only a dinner in the whole course of the day. This solitary meal he took regularly at four o'clock, at Dolly's chop-house. A pound and a-half of rump steak, half a broiled chicken, a plate of fish, a bottle of port, a quarter of a pint of brandy, and a tankard of strong ale, satisfied the Doctor's moderate wants till four o'clock next day, and regularly engaged one hour and a-half of his time. Dinner over, he returned to his home in Essex Street, Strand, to deliver his six o'clock lecture on anatomy and chemistry. Baron Maseres, who lived nearly to the age of ninety, used to go home one day in every week without any dinner, eating only a round of dry toast at tea. Aristotle, like a true poet, seems to have literally feasted on fancy. Few could live more frugally; in one of his poems, he says of himself, "that he was a fit person to have lived in the world when acorns were the food of men."—(Salad for the Solitary.)

MARY QUEEN OF SCOTS.

At Paris, you may be sure, we met with entertainment enough: at the Scotch Jesuits there, I fancy either you or Mr. Baker would have willingly took a peep with us. There was a folio volume of letters of Mary Queen of Scots and her husband, and King James I. and his Queen, &c., all originals: but most were Queen Mary's to the Archbishop of Glasgow, who gave the Society this book, and many other papers. At the end of the book was Queen Mary's will in her own writing, the day before her being beheaded; all in French. I read many parts of it; and last of all a sort of a codicil in her own hand (disposing of four or five other particulars), dated in her own words, "Le Matin de ma Mort."—(Rev. J. Church to Dr. Z. Grey, 1736.)

ORIGIN OF THE NAME BLUE STOCKINGS.

It is well known that Mrs. Montagu's house was at that time (1771) the chosen resort of many of those of both sexes most distinguished for rank, as well as classical taste and literary talent, in London. This society of eminent friends consisted, originally, of Mrs. Montagu, Mrs. Vesey, Miss Boscawen, and Mrs. Carter, Lord Lyttelton, Mr. Pulteney, Horace Walpole, and Mr. Stillingfleet. To the latter gentleman, a man of great piety and worth, and author of some works in natural history, &c., this constellation of talents owed that whimsical appellation of "Bas Bleu." Mr. Stillingfleet being somewhat of an humorist in his habits and manners, and a little negligent in his dress, literally wore gray stockings; from which circumstance Admiral Boscawen used, by way of pleasantry, to call them "The Blue Stocking Society," as if to intimate that when these brilliant friends met, it was not for the purpose of forming a dressed assembly. A foreigner of distinction hearing the expression, translated it literally "Bas Bleu," by which these meetings came to be afterwards distinguished. — (Forbes' Life of Beattie.)

A FAVOURITE AUTHOR.

A predilection for some great author, among the vast number which must transiently occupy our attention, seems to be the happiest preservative for our taste. Accustomed to that excellent author whom we have chosen for our favourite, we may possibly resemble him in this intimacy. It is to be feared that if we do not form such a permanent attachment, we may be acquiring knowledge while our enervated taste becomes less and less lively. Taste embalms the knowledge which otherwise cannot preserve itself. He who has long been intimate with one great author, will always be found to be a formidable antagonist; he has saturated his mind with the excellencies of genius; he has shaped his faculties, insensibly to himself, by his model; and he is like a man who ever sleeps in armour, ready at a moment! The old Latin proverb reminds us of this fact, *Cave ab homine unius libri*—be cautious of the man of one book.—(D'Israeli in Curiosities of Literature.)

LADY M. W. MONTAGU'S LETTERS FROM THE LEVANT.

The publication of these letters will be an immortal monument to the memory of Lady Mary Wortley Montagu, and will show, as long as the English language endures, the sprightliness of her wit, the solidity of her judgment, the elegance of her taste, and the excellence of her real character. These letters are so bewitchingly entertaining, that we defy the most phlegmatic man on earth to read one without going through them, or, after finishing the third volume, not to wish there were twenty *more of them*.—(Dr. Smollett.)

HANDEL'S MESSIAH.

When Handel's *Messiah* was first performed, the audience were exceedingly struck and affected by the music in general; but when that chorus struck up, "For the Lord God omnipotent reigneth," they were so transported, that they all, together with the king (who happened to be present), started up, and remained standing till the chorus ended: and hence it became the fashion in England for the audience to stand while that part of the music is performing. Some days after the first exhibition of the same divine oratorio, Mr. Handel came to pay his respects to Lord Kinnoul, with whom he was particularly acquainted. His Lordship, as was natural, paid him some compliments on the noble entertainment which he had lately given the town. "My Lord," said Handel, "I should be sorry if I only entertained them; I wish to make them better." These two anecdotes I had from Lord Kinnoul himself. You will agree with me, that the first does great honour to Handel, to music, and to the English nation: the second tends to confirm my theory, and Sir John Hawkins' testimony, that Handel, in spite of all that has been said to the contrary, must have been a pious man.—(Dr. Beattie to Rev. Dr. Laing.)

ETYMOLOGY—HOAX.

This word is now very common in our language. Dr. Johnson has not introduced it into his Dictionary, although it was employed long before his time, but disguised by its orthography. In Richard Head's *Art of Wheedling*, 12mo, 1634, p. 254, it is thus used—"The mercer cries, Was ever a man so hocus'd?" So that *hoax*, or, as it was originally written, *hocus*, is any species of dexterous imposition—similar to the tricks of the juggler, whose art was termed *hocus pocus*, which is generally admitted to be a corruption of *Hoc est corpus*.

MACHIAVEL AND OLD NICK.

As cunning as *Old Nick*, and as wicked as *Old Nick*, were originally meant of our Nicolas Machiavel; and so came afterwards to be perverted to the devil.—(Dr. Cocchi, Florence.)

Machiavel has been generally called so wicked from people mistaking the design of his writings. In his "Prince," his design, at bottom, was to make a despotic government odious. "A despotic prince," he says, "to secure himself, must kill such and such people." He must so; and therefore no wise people would suffer such a prince. This is the natural consequence; and not that Machiavel seriously advises princes to be wicked.—(Dr. Cocchi, Florence.)

ORIGIN OF BUMPER.

When the English were good Catholics, they usually drank the Pope's health in a full glass, every day after dinner—*au bon pere:* whence your word *bumper*.—(Dr. Cocchi, Florence.)

IN HOC SIGNO VINCES.

When Henry the Fourth of France was reconciled to the church of Rome, it was expected that he should give some remarkable testimonial of his sincerity in returning to the true faith. He accordingly ordered a cross to be erected at Rome, near the church of Santa Maria Maggiore, with this inscription, *In hoc signo vinces*, on the principal part of it. This passed at first as very Catholic, till it was observed that the part in which the inscription is put is shaped in the form of a cannon, and that he had really attributed only to his artillery what they had taken to be addressed to heaven.—(Ficaroni.)

FILICAIA'S SONNETS.

Filicaia, in his sonnets, makes use of many expressions borrowed from the Psalms, and consequently not generally understood among us. A gentleman of Florence, on reading some of the passages in him, which were literally taken from David, cried out, "O! are you there again with your barbarisms?" and flung away the book, as not worth his reading.—(Crudeli of Florence.)

HARRINGTON'S OCEANA.

It is strange that Harrington, so little while ago, should be the first man to find out so evident and demonstrable a truth, as that of property being the true basis of power. His *Oceana*, allowing for the different situations of things (as the less number of Lords then, those Lords having no share in the Parliament, and the like), is certainly one of the best founded political pieces that ever was writ.—(Dean Lockier.)

ELOQUENCE IN WINE.

Sir Thomas More was sent by Henry VIII. on an embassy to the emperor of Germany, where, before he delivered it, he commanded one of his servants to fill him a beer-glass of wine, which he drank off; and afterwards repeated, and at the same time directing his servant to bring him a third; the servant knowing his master's usual temperance, at first refused to fill him another, being under a concern for his behaviour, but on a second command of Sir Thomas, he did it; which being drank, he then made his immediate address to the emperor, and delivered his oration in Latin like one inspired, to the very great admiration of all the auditors. This I mention to show the influence of wine!—(Life of Sir T. Moore.)

OSSIAN'S POEMS.

That there never existed poems exactly in the form in which *Fingal* and *Temone* were published by Macpherson, seems now to be the opinion generally entertained. But it is still maintained by many, with the strongest appearance of reason, that there certainly were poetical compositions, consisting of songs and ballads, and other pieces, existing in the Highlands many years before Macpherson was born, of which sufficient traces are even yet to be found in various parts of that country, some in a more, some in a less perfect form. From these scattered fragments it probably was, that Macpherson, by imitations and additions of his own, wrought his work into a whole, and thus gave it the appearance, in some degree, of a regular epic poem. Nor is it difficult, perhaps, to conceive how these fragments may have been handed down from father to son, even without the use of writing, among a people, who, with scarcely any knowledge of agriculture, commerce, or the useful arts, filled up the vacancies of a pastoral life, by the recital of those popular songs and ballads. This is a practice not peculiar to the Highlands of Scotland, but to be found in all nations, who, by their local situation in the midst of hills and fastnesses, are cut off from any great degree of intercourse with neighbouring countries, farther advanced in the arts of polished life. Nor will it appear so very wonderful if, in this manner, that poetry may have been preserved, which is believed by many to have existed in the Highlands, when the powers of the memory are considered, and the strength it acquired by the perpetual exercise of listening to the bards, who were an appendage of the state and magnificence of a Highland chieftain.—(Sir William Forbes.)

BIBLE.

EARLY TRANSLATIONS OF THE BIBLE.

The translation of the Bible was begun very early in this kingdom. Some part of it was done by king Alfred. Adelmus translated the Psalms into Saxon in 709. Other parts were done by Edfrid, or Egbert, 750; the whole by Bede. In 1357 Trevisa published the whole in English. Tindall's translation appeared in 1334, was revised and altered in 1538, published with a preface of Cranmer's in 1549, and allowed to be read in churches. In 1551 another translation was published, which, being revised by several bishops, was printed with their alterations in 1560. In 1613 a new translation was published by authority, which is that in present use. There was not any translation of it into the Irish language till 1685. The pope did not give his permission for the translation of it into any language till 1759.—(Jenoway's Notes.)

PRESENT TRANSLATION OF THE BIBLE.

This translation was made at the command of King James I.; the translators were fifty-four of the most learned men of that time, who were divided into five bodies, of which each was to labour on a particular part of the Bible, which was thus divided:— The Pentateuch, and the Books of Judges, Ruth, Samuel, and Kings, to the Deans of Westminster and St. Paul's, Doctors Saravia, Clark, Layfield, Leigh, Messrs. Stretford, Sussex, Clare, Bedwell. From the Chronicles to Ecclesiastes, to Dr. Richardson, and Messrs. Sirley, Chadderton, Dillingham, Harrison, Andrews, Spalding, Binge. All the Prophets and Lamentations to Dr. Harding, Reinolds, Holland, Kilby, Messrs. Hereford, Brett, Fareclowe. All the Epistles to the Dean of Chester, Dr. Hutchinson, Spencer, Messrs. Fenton, Rabbit, Sanderson, Dakins. The Gospels, Acts, and Apocalypse, to the Deans of Christchurch, Winchester, Worcester, Windsor, Drs. Perin, Ravins, Messrs. Savile, Harmer. And the Apocrypha, to Drs. Duport, Braithwaite, Ratcliffe, Messrs. Ward, Downes, Boyse, Warde. They met at Westminster, Oxford, and Cambridge, as it was convenient for each body. The method in which they proceeded was thus:—Several translations of each part were drawn up by the members of that body to which it was allotted, who then, in a joint consultation, selected three of the best, or compiled them out of the whole number. Thus in three years three translations of the whole were sent to London; then six deputies, two from each place, were appointed to extract one translation out of the three, which was finished and printed in the year 1611.

BOOKS MENTIONED IN THE BIBLE, NOW LOST OR UNKNOWN.

At your request, I have copied out, from the collection I have made, the ten underwritten (I think) lost books; but should be glad to be set to rights by better information:—

I. "The Prophecy of Enoch." See Epistle to Jude 14.

II. "The Book of the Wars of the Lord." See Numb. xxi. 14.

III. "The Prophetical Gospel of Eve, which relates to the Amours of the Sons of God with the Daughters of Men." See Origen Cont. Celsum, Tertul. &c.

IV. "The Book of Jeshur." See Joshua x. 13; and 2 Sam. i. 18.

V. "The Book of Iddo the Seer." See 2 Chron. ix. 29; and xii. 15.

VI. "The Book of Nathan the Prophet." See as above.

VII. "The Prophecies of Ahijah the Shilonite." See as above.

VIII. "The Acts of Rehoboam, in the Book of Shemaiah." See 2 Chron. xii. 15.

IX. "The Book of Jehu the son of Hanani." See 2 Chron. xx. 34.

X. "The Five Books of Solomon, treating on the nature of trees, beasts, fowl, serpents, and fishes." See 1 Kings iv. 33.

XI. You may add the 151st Psalm. I have it somewhere in the house, but cannot at present find it.—(Mr. Ames to Mr. Da Costa.)

BOOKS, BOOKSELLERS, AND BIBLIOMANIACS.

FRANKLIN AS A BOOKSELLER.

One fine morning when Franklin was busy preparing his newspaper for the press, a lounger stepped into the store, and spent an hour or more looking over the books, &c., and finally taking one in his hand, asked the shop-boy the price.

"One dollar," was the answer.

"One dollar," said the lounger, "can't you take less than that?"

"No, indeed; one dollar is the price."

Another hour had nearly passed, when the lounger said—

"Is Mr. Franklin at home?"

"Yes, he is in the printing-office."

"I want to see him," said the lounger.

The shop-boy immediately informed Mr. Franklin that a gentleman was in the store, waiting to see him. Franklin was soon behind the counter, when the lounger, with book in hand, addressed him thus:

"Mr. Franklin, what is the lowest you can take for that book?"

"One dollar and a quarter," was the ready answer.

"One dollar and a quarter! Why, your young man asked me only a dollar."

"True," said Franklin, "and I could have better afforded to have taken a dollar then, than to have been taken out of the office."

The lounger seemed surprised, and wishing to end the parley of his own making, said—

"Come, Mr. Franklin, tell me what is the lowest you can take for it?"

"One dollar and a half."

"A dollar and a half! Why, you offered it yourself for a dollar and a quarter."

"Yes," said Franklin, "and I had better have taken that price then, than a dollar and a half now."

The lounger paid down the price, and went about his business—if he had any—and Franklin returned into the printing-office.

SALE OF ROXBURGH'S LIBRARY.

Unlike most other species of property, books, in some instances, advance in value in proportion to their age. Many cases might be cited to prove this; the most remarkable on record is that of the great sale of Lord Roxburgh's library, in 1812, which occupied forty-five days at auction, and which cost its founder, fifty years before, less than £5000, but which actually realized on the occasion referred to the enormous sum of £23,341. One book, the folio (first) edition of Boccaccio, printed by Valdarfer, of which it is believed this was the only copy extant, brought £2260. Its original price was something like ten shillings. Bibliomania was at this time, certainly, at its extreme height.

BLACK-LETTER BOOKS.

It was in the period of Scott's early manhood that the mania for black-letter books began to manifest itself in the land, and, like the once notable tulip madness in Holland, proved an important source of emolument to those who had even a small capital to embark in the purchase of rare specimens. It was quite possible for such traders occasionally to purchase for a trifling sum an entire library from some improvident or illiterate representative of an old family, by whom the books were looked upon as mere lumber. From these the fortunate purchaser well knew how to select the gems inestimable in the eyes of a collector, any one of which, being properly set and adorned in its fragrant binding of Russia leather, would sometimes bring nearly as much money as had been given for the whole lot. It was, indeed, on this basis principally that Mr. Constable, who had the honour of publishing the *Lay of the last Minstrel*, and *Marmion*, contrived to accumulate that wealth, or acquire that credit, which, if more prudently managed, might have insured him stability and reputation for life. Mr. Scott was one of the very few among Constable's patrons who could turn this mania to good account; for, whilst he seemed to the uninitiated to have an indiscriminate appetite for old books of every description, the truth was, that he seldom made a purchase of one without some rational and special object in view.

RIVAL PUBLISHERS.

Both Tonson and Lintot were rivals for publishing a work of Dr. Young's. The poet answered both their letters the same morning, but unfortunately misdirected them. In these epistles, he complained of the rascally cupidity of each. In the one he intended for Tonson, he said that Lintot was so great a scoundrel, that printing with him was out of the question; and writing to Lintot, he declared that Tonson was an old rascal, with many other epithets equally opprobrious.

BLACK-LETTER HUNTERS.

"Others, like Kemble, on black-letter pore,
And what they do not understand, adore;
Buy at vast sums the *trash* of ancient days,
And draw on prodigality for praise.
These when some lucky hit, or lucky price,
Has blessed them with "*The Boke of gode advice*,"
For *ekes* and *algates only* deign to seek,
And live upon a *whilome* for a week."

Though no great catalogue-hunter, I love to look into such marked ones as now and then fall in my way. That of poor Dodd's books amused me not a little. It exhibited many instances of BLACK-LETTER mania; and what is more to my purpose, a transfer of much valuable "*trash of ancient days*," to the fortunate Mr. Kemble. For example:—

	£	s.	d.
"First part of the tragicall reigne of Selimus Emperor of the Turks	1	11	6
Jacob and Esau, a Mery and Whittie Comedie	3	5	0
Look about You, a Comedie,	5	7	6
The Tragedie of T. Nero, Rome's Greatest Tyraunte, &c., &c."	1	4	0

"How are we ruined!"—(Gifford, in Baviad.)

ILLUMINATORS.

As to the word *Alluminor* in the "Richard III.," I take it that, even before the invention of printing, when, as well as afterwards, it was the custom to illuminate the initial letters, such had the privilege of being members, and were entitled to the privileges of universities, whereof you will find some memorandums in the history of Bullens, or that of Paris; and if you will inspect the present Judge Fortescue's edition of Fortescue's work of Supreme Power (or some such title), you will find a pleasant dispute about the import of the word *Illuminators*, in the case of the University of Oxford, among the wise judges of the Common Pleas. . . . . In the early printed books the initial letter was generally a small one, with a large room left for the illuminator to make a larger letter, and to adorn or illuminate it either with colours or metals. I take it that among those who enjoy the privilege of the universities, are illuminators. The word is used figuratively in our liturgy,—"illuminate all bishops, priests, and deacons," though with relation to spiritual gifts.—(Mr. Austis to Mr. Ames.)

THE ELDER TONSON.

The elder Tonson's portrait represents him in his gown and cap, holding in his right hand a volume lettered *Paradise Lost*—such a favourite object was Milton and copyright. Jacob Tonson was the founder of a race who long honoured literature. His rise in life is curious. He was at first unable to pay twenty pounds for a play by Dryden, and joined with another bookseller to advance that sum; the play sold, and Tonson was afterwards enabled to purchase the succeeding ones. He and his nephew died worth two hundred thousand pounds.

Much old Tonson owed to his industry; but he was a mere trader. He and Dryden had frequent bickerings; he insisted on receiving ten thousand verses for two hundred and sixty-eight pounds, and poor Dryden threw in the finest ode in the language towards that number. He would pay in the base coin which was then current, which was a loss to the poet.

Tonson once complained to Dryden, that he had only received fourteen hundred and forty-six lines of his translations of *Ovid* for his Miscellany for fifty guineas, when he had calculated at the rate of fifteen hundred and eighteen lines for forty guineas; he gives the poet a piece of critical reasoning, that he considered he had a better bargain with *Juvenal*, which is reckoned not so easy to translate as *Ovid*. In these times such a mere trader in literature has disappeared.

COWPER'S POEMS.

Mr. Johnson, the bookseller in St. Paul's Churchyard, obtained the copyright of Cowper's *Poems*, which proved a source of great profit to him, in the following manner:— A relation of Cowper called one evening, at dusk, on Johnson, with a bundle of these poems, which he offered to him for publication, provided he would print them on his own risk, and let the author have a few copies to give to his friends. Johnson perused, and approved of them, and accordingly printed and published them. Soon after they had appeared before the public, there was not a review which did not load them with the most scurrilous abuse, and condemn them to the butter-shops. In consequence of the public taste being thus terrified, or misled, these charming effusions lay in a corner of the bookseller's shop as an unsaleable pile for a long period. Some time afterwards, the same person appeared, with another bundle of manuscripts from the same author; which were offered and accepted upon the same terms. In this fresh collection was the inimitable poem of *The Task*. Not alarmed at the fate of the former publication, and thoroughly assured, as he was, of their great merit, Mr. Johnson resolved to publish them. Soon after they had appeared, the tone of the reviewers instantly changed; and Cowper was hailed as the first poet of his age. The success of this second publication set the first in motion, and Johnson immediately reaped the fruits of his undaunted judgment.

BOOKSELLER AND AUTHOR.

Un libraire et un auteur sont deux especes de filoux, qui ne peuvent l'un sans l'autre attraper l'argent du public.—(Lesage.)

BOOKSELLERS THE PATRONS OF LITERATURE.

Johnson has dignified the booksellers as "the patrons of literature," which was generous in that great author, who had written well and lived but ill all his life on that patronage. Eminent booksellers, in their constant intercourse with the most enlightened class of the community, that is, with the best authors and the best readers, partake of the intelligence around them; their great capitals, too, are productive of good and evil in literature; useful, when they carry on great works; and pernicious, when they sanction indifferent ones. Yet are they but commercial men. A trader can never be deemed a patron, for it would be romantic to purchase what is not saleable; but where no favour is conferred, there is no patronage. Authors continue poor, and booksellers become opulent; an extraordinary result! Booksellers are not agents for authors, but proprietors of their works; so that the perpetual revenues of literature are solely in the possession of the trade.—(D'Isr.) Tonson, and all his family and assignees, rode in their carriages with the profits of Milton's *five-pound* Epic.

SMOLLETT'S ENGLAND.

Smollett never wrote a continuation to *Hume's History*, but the booksellers, wanting a continuation of *Hume*, took that portion of Smollett's history from the Revolution to the death of George II., and printing it in five volumes in 1791, called it Smollett's *Continuation of Hume*. Mr. Dibdin says it was first published in 1763, but that was the continuation of Smollett's own history from 1748, which was brought down to the end of 1765, and the last volume not being reprinted in the bookseller's edition gave occasion to the report that it was suppressed by authority, because it contained the only mention of the first appearance of the late king's malady in 1765.—(Gent. Mag. Nov. 1824.)

JOHNSON'S DICTIONARY.

Mr. Andrew Millar, bookseller in the Strand, took the principal charge in conducting the publication of Johnson's *Dictionary;* and as the patience of the proprietors was repeatedly tried, and almost exhausted, by their expecting that the work would be completed within the time which Johnson had sanguinely supposed, the learned author was often obliged to despatch, more especially as he had received all the copy-money by different drafts, a considerable time before he had finished his task. When the messenger who carried the last sheet to Millar returned, Johnson asked him, "Well, what did he say?" "Sir," answered the messenger, "he said, 'Thank God, I have done with him.'" "I am glad," replied Johnson with a smile, "that he thanks God for anything." —(Boswell's Life of Johnson.)

AKENSIDE'S PLEASURES OF IMAGINATION.

In 1744 appeared before the public Akenside's *Pleasures of Imagination*, which so long as genius holds an admirer, will ever be valued for chasteness of design, purity of morals, and all that pleasing witchery which marks the healthful offspring of genuine poetry. It was welcomed as a work of such intrinsic worth ought to be welcomed. From its sale the author's finances were improved and his fame established. Dr. Johnson mentions, that he has heard Dodsley (by whom it was published) say, that when the copy was offered him, the price demanded for it, which was a hundred and twenty pounds, being such as he was not inclined to give precipitately, he carried the work to Pope, who having looked into it, advised him not to make a niggardly offer, for "this was no every day writer." —(Hutchinson's Biog. Medica.)

BOOK AUCTIONS.

The first book-auction in England, of which there is any record, was in 1676, when the library of Dr. Scarnan was brought to the hammer. Prefixed to the catalogue there is an address to the reader, saying, "Though it has been unusual in England to make sale of books by auction, yet it hath been practised in other countries to advantage." For general purposes this mode of sale was scarcely known till 1700. —(Jenoway's Notes.)

BOOK TRADE OF LEIPSIG.

As Frankfort monopolizes the trade in wine, so Leipsig monopolizes the trade in books. It is here that every German author (and in no country are authors so numerous) wishes to produce the children of his brain, and that, too, only during the Easter fair. He will submit to any degree of exertion that his work may be ready for publication by that important season, when the whole brotherhood is in labour, from the Rhine to the Vistula. If the auspicious moment pass away, he willingly bears his burden twelve months longer, till the next advent of the bibliopolical Lucina. This periodical littering at Leipsig does not at all arise, as is sometimes supposed, from all or most of the books being printed there; Leipsig has only its own proportion of printers and publishers. It arises from the manner in which this branch of trade is carried on in Germany. Every bookseller of any eminence, throughout the confederation, has an agent or commissioner in Leipsig, to whom he applies for whatever books he may want, whether published there or elsewhere. The whole book trade of Germany thus centres in Leipsig. Wherever books may be printed, it is there they must be bought; it is there that the trade is supplied.

Before the end of the sixteenth century the book-fair was established. It prospered so rapidly that, in 1600, the Easter catalogue, which has been annually printed ever since, was printed for the first time. It now presents every year, in a thick octavo volume, a collection of new books and new editions to which there is no parallel in Europe. At the fair all the brethren of the trade flock together in Leipsig, not only from every part of Germany, but from every European country where German books are sold, to settle accounts and examine the harvest of the year. The number always amounts to several hundreds, and they have built an exchange for themselves.

Yet a German publisher has less chance of making great profits, and a German author has fewer prospects of turning his manuscript to good account, than the same classes of persons in any other country that knows the value of intellectual labour. Each state of the confederation has its own law of copyright, and an author is secured against piracy only in the state where he prints. If the book be worth anything it is immediately reprinted in some neighbouring state, and as the pirate pays nothing for the copyright, he can obviously afford to undersell the original publisher. Such a system almost annihilates the value of literary labour. The unpleasing exterior of ordinary German printing, the coarse watery paper, and worn-out types, must be referred, in some measure, to the same cause. The publisher, or author, naturally risks as little capital as possible in the hazardous speculation. Besides, it is his interest to diminish the temptation to reprint, by making his own edition as cheap as may be. The system has shown its effects, too, in keeping up the frequency of publication by subscription, even among authors of the most settled and popular reputation. Klopstock, after the *Messiah* had fixed his name, published in this way. There has been no more successful publisher than Cotta, and no German writer has been so well repaid as Göthe, yet the last Tübingen edition of Göthe himself is adorned with a long list of subscribers. What would we think of Byron or Campbell, of Scott or Moore, publishing a new poem by subscription?—(Russell's Tour in Germany.)

BINDING OF BOOKS.

King Alphonsus, about to lay the foundation of a castle at Naples, called for *Vitruvius*, his booke of architecture; the booke was brought in very bad case, all dustie and without covers; which the king observing said, "Hee that must cover us all, must not goe uncovered himselfe;" then commanded the booke to bee fairely bound and brought unto him. "So say I, suffer them not to lie neglected, who must make you regarded; and goe in torne coates, who must apparell your minde with the ornaments of knowledge, above the roabes and riches of the most magnificent princes. — (Peacham's Compleat Gentleman, 1627.)

PRESERVATION OF BINDINGS.

It was supposed that a binding of Russian leather secured books against insects, but the contrary was recently demonstrated at Paris by two volumes pierced in every direction. The first bookbinder in Paris, Bozerian, told me he knew of no remedy except to steep the blank leaves in muriatic acid.— (Pinkerton's Recoll. of Paris.)

MODE OF PLACING BOOKS IN ANCIENT LIBRARIES.

It may not be known to those who are not accustomed to meet with old books in their original bindings, or of seeing public libraries of antiquity, that the volumes were formerly placed on the shelves with the *leaves*, not the *back*, in front; and that the two sides of the binding were joined together with neat silk or other strings, and in some instances, where the books were of greater value and curiosity than common, even fastened with gold or silver chains.—(Philip Bliss, Oxen.)

EARLY ENGLISH LIBRARIES.

Never had we been offended for the loss of our libraries, being so many in number, and in so desolate places for the most part, if the chief monuments and most notable works of our excellent writers had been reserved. If there had been in every shire of England but one *Solempne Library*, to the preservation of those noble works, and preferment of good learning in our posterity, it had been yet somewhat. But to destroy all without consideration is, and will be, unto England for ever, a most horrible infamy among the grave seniors of other nations. A great number of them which purchased those superstitious mansions, reserved of those library-books, some to serve the jakes, some to scour their candlesticks, and some to rub their boots. Some they sold to the grocers and soap-sellers; some they sent over sea to the bookbinders, not in small number, but at times whole ships full, to the wondering of the foreign nations. Yea, the universities of this realm are not all clear of this detestable fact. But, cursed is that belly which seeketh to be fed with such ungodly gains, and shameth his natural country. I know a merchantman, which shall at this time be nameless, that bought the contents of two noble libraries for forty shillings price; a shame it is to be spoken! This stuff hath he occupied in the stead of gray paper, by the space of more than ten years, and yet he hath store enough for as many years to come!—(Bale's Preface to the Laboryouse Journey of Leland.)

LITERARY PROPERTY.

Mr. Alexander Donaldson, bookseller, of Edinburgh, had for some time opened a shop in London and sold his cheap editions of the most popular English books, in defiance of the supposed common-law right of literary property. Dr. Johnson, though he concurred in the opinion which was afterwards sanctioned by a judgment of the House of Lords, that there was no such right, was at this time very angry that the booksellers of London, for whom he uniformly professed much regard, should suffer from an invasion of what they had ever considered to be secure, and he was loud and violent against Mr. Donaldson. "He is a fellow who takes advantage of the law to injure his brethren; for notwithstanding that the statute secures only fourteen years of exclusive right, it has always been understood by *the trade* that he who buys the copyright of a book from the author obtains a perpetual property; and, upon that belief, numberless bargains are made to transfer that property after the expiration of the statutory term. Now Donaldson, I say, takes advantage here of people who have really an equitable title from usage; and if we consider how few of the books of which they buy the property succeed so well as to bring profit, we should be of opinion that the term of fourteen years is too short; it should be sixty years." *Dempster:*—"Donaldson, sir, is anxious for the encouragement of literature. He reduces the price of books so that poor students may buy them." *Johnson* (laughing):—"Well, sir, allowing that to be his motive, he is no better than Robin Hood, who robbed the rich in order to give to the poor."—(Boswell's Life of Johnson.)

BARGAIN-HUNTERS.

You will perhaps be surprised when I inform you that there are in London (and, I suppose, in other populous places), persons who purchase every article which they have occasion for (and also many articles which they have no occasion for, nor ever will) at stalls, beggarly shops, pawnbrokers, &c., under the idea of purchasing cheaper than they could at respectable shops, and of men of property. A considerable number of these customers I had in the beginning, who forsook my shop as soon as I began to appear more respectable, by introducing better order, possessing more valuable books, and having acquired a better judgment, &c. Notwithstanding which, I declare to you upon my honour, that these very bargain-hunters have given me double the price that I now charge for thousands and tens of thousands of volumes. For, as a tradesman increases in respectability and opulence, his opportunities of purchasing increase proportionably, and the more he buys and sells the more he becomes a judge of the real value of his goods. It was for want of the experience and judgment, stock, &c., that for several years I was in the habit of charging more than double the price I do for many thousand articles. But professed bargain-hunters often purchase old locks at the stalls in Moorfields, when half the wards are rusted off, or taken out, and give more for them than they would have paid for new ones to any reputable ironmonger. And what numerous instances of this infatuation do we meet with daily at sales by auction, not of books only, but of many other articles, of which I could here adduce a variety of glaring instances. At the sale of Mr. Rigby's books at Mr. Christie's, Martin's *Dictionary of Natural History* sold for fifteen guineas, which then stood in my catalogue at four pounds fifteen shillings; Pilkington's *Dictionary of Painters* at seven guineas, usually sold at three; Francis' *Horace*, two pounds eleven shillings; and many others in the same manner. At Sir George Colebrook's sale the octavo edition of the *Tatler* sold for two guineas and a half. At a sale a few weeks since Rapin's *History* in folio, the two first volumes only (instead of five) sold for upwards of five pounds! I charge for the same from ten shillings and sixpence to one pound ten shillings. I sell great numbers of books to pawnbrokers, who sell them out of their windows at much higher prices, the purchasers believing that they are buying bargains, and that such articles have been pawned. And it is not only books that pawnbrokers purchase, but various other matters, and they always purchase the worst kind of every article they sell. I will even add, that many shops which are called pawnbrokers never take in any pawn, yet can live by selling things which are supposed to be kept overtime.—(Lackington's Memoirs.)

FIRST ENGLISH ALMANAC.

The first almanac in England was printed in Oxford, in 1673. "There were," says Wood, "near thirty thousand of them printed, besides a sheet almanac for twopence, that was printed for that year; and because of the novelty of the said almanac, and its title, they were all vended. Its sale was so great, that the Society of Booksellers in London bought off the copy for the future, in order to engross the profits in their own hands."

ALMANAC WEATHER WISDOM.

An English paper tells a pleasant anecdote of Partridge, the celebrated almanac maker, about one hundred years since. In travelling on horseback into the country, he stopped for his dinner at an inn, and afterwards called for his horse, that he might reach the next town, where he intended to sleep.

"If you will take my advice, sir," said the hostler, as he was about to mount his horse, "you will stay where you are for the night, as you will surely be overtaken by a pelting rain."

"Nonsense, nonsense," exclaimed the almanac maker; "there is a sixpence for you, my honest fellow, and good afternoon to you."

He proceeded on his journey, and sure enough he was well drenched in a heavy shower. Partridge was struck by the man's prediction, and being always intent on the interest of his almanac, he rode back on the instant, and was received by the hostler with a broad grin.

"Well, sir, you see I was right after all."

"Yes, my lad, you have been so, and here is a crown for you; but I give it to you on condition that you tell me how you knew of this rain."

"To be sure, sir," replied the man; "why, the truth is, we have an almanac at our house called Partridge's *Almanac*, and the fellow is such a notorious liar, that whenever he promises us a fine day, we always know that it will be the direct contrary. Now, your honour, this day, the 21st of June, is put down in our almanac in-doors as 'settled fine weather; no rain.' I looked at that before I brought your honour's horse out, and so was enabled to put you on your guard."

BOTANISTS AND BOTANY.

DAVID DOUGLAS—HIS ARDOUR AND DEVOTEDNESS.

The introduction of ornamental plants from abroad was effected, in former days, by diplomatic persons, merchants, or travellers, who interested themselves about such things, and forwarded or took them home. Afterwards travelling botanists, especially those accompanied by skilful gardeners, were the chief promoters of such importations. More recently our shrubberies and pleasure-grounds have been enriched by scientific gardeners sent abroad expressly for that purpose. Among the latter class no one deserves greater credit than David Douglas. Being sent out by the Horticultural Society of London to the northern states of America, and its north-west coast, especially the banks of the river Columbia, he introduced into England a greater number of hardy trees, shrubs, and animals, than any one had done before him; namely, 53 woods and 145 herbaceous plants, making, altogether, 198 species, for the most part quite new. These plants being hardy enough to bear the climate of Europe, have multiplied to an incredible extent in England, as well as on the Continent, so that one scarcely ever sees a garden, however humble, that is without some of these ornaments. Having done so much in America, Douglas went to the Sandwich Islands, where he fell a sacrifice to his ardent zeal, being gored to death by a wild bull, caught in a pit dug by the natives, and into which the unfortunate traveller fell. He was only thirty-six years old. If we consider the powerful moral influence which floriculture exerts on mankind, we may assuredly rank that young man among those who have honourably sacrificed their lives in the performance of their duty, not less than the soldier who dies on the field of battle.

DR. ROBERT GRAHAM OF EDINBURGH.

Dr. Ransford, in a biographical sketch read before the Harveian Society of Edinburgh of the late Dr. Graham, relates that when that ardent botanist was on an excursion in Ireland, in order to obtain a desired specimen he had recourse to a stratagem, which, for the benefit of future tourists, it may be useful to mention. The incident was related to Dr. R. by an eye-witness. When travelling from Galway to Ballinasloe on Bianconi's mail car, Dr. Graham noticed *Nepeta Cataria* at the side of the road. This being a plant which had not been gathered during the trip, he was anxious to get some of it. To have asked the driver of her Majesty's mail to stop for such a purpose would have been deemed Quixotic; he therefore *intentionally* dropped his hat, and immediately his companions, previously made aware of the trick, shouted loudly to Paddy, whose politeness induced him instantly to pull up. Dr. Grahame's anxiety to get at the plant was so great, that he jumped from the car before it had fully stopped, and received a very severe abrasion of his arm. In spite of

D

this, however, he and the rest of the party rushed to the spot where the *Nepeta* was growing, and, to the no small surprise of their fellow-passengers, proceeded to pull large quantities of it, the hat being, of course, a minor object of consideration, though it was not left behind. Having thus detained the mail for a few minutes, the party resumed their seats, highly pleased with their successful botanical adventure.

SIR J. E. SMITH—LINNÆUS'S HERBARIUM.

The stranger whose predilections are botanical will not be long in London till he turns aside from the heady current and distracting turmoil of its great thoroughfares, into the comparative seclusion and tranquillity of Soho Square, to pay a pilgrim's homage at a shrine which commands the veneration of botanists from all quarters of the world. In a quiet nook of the square is the suite of rooms occupied by the Linnæan Society. The house formerly belonged to Sir Joseph Banks, and was for many years the rendezvous of the savans of England, and the resort of scientific foreigners visiting the metropolis. It is now the repository of the herbarium of Linnæus, that collection of plants which furnished the illustrious Swede with the materials for the construction of the artificial method of classification, with an ultimate view to the establishment of the more philosophical system which has since taken its place, founded on the natural alliances of plants. It was in this collection that Linnæus studied the characters of individual plants, and accumulated the observations which have enabled succeeding botanists to group them into families.

There is a little history connected with the herbarium, which may prove interesting to other than botanical readers. Sir James Edward Smith, the eminent English botanist, was, when a young man, a constant visitor at Sir Joseph Banks's, to whom he had recommended himself by his taste for natural history. It was in this house, in 1783, that he learned from his patron that the library and natural history collections of Linnæus had been offered to him for a thousand guineas. After a life of labour and vicissitude, Linnæus had died at Upsal, full of honours and even of wealth, in 1778, in the seventy-first year of his age. He had twenty years before been elevated to the nobility, and assumed the title of Von Linné. Still greater honours were paid to his memory after his death. His remains were borne to their resting-place in the cathedral of Upsal by members of his university, sixteen doctors of medicine, his former pupils, supporting the funeral pall. A general mourning of the citizens showed that his death was felt to be a public loss. King Gustavus II. caused a medal to be struck in commemoration of his name; and attended a meeting of the Royal Academy of Sciences at Stockholm, held in honour of the memory of the great naturalist. In his speech from the throne, Gustavus lamented the death of Linnæus as a public calamity. It seems strange that in so brief a period as five years after these national tributes were paid to his memory, a portion of his property so identified with his scientific fame as his books and collections in natural history, should have been offered for sale in England. But although Linnæus, while he lived, had enjoyed the esteem both of his countrymen and of foreigners, and, after his death, was embalmed in their remembrances, his honour and happiness had been betrayed by the relative who, of all others, should have most dearly cherished them ; whose tyrannical disposition and unnatural treatment of her own offspring had deprived his home of all that should have constituted it the sanctuary of his affections; and whose sordid parsimony was now eager to convert his collections into money, and send away for ever, from the country which claimed him as the most distinguished of her sons, the priceless inheritance of his scientific treasures. The eldest son of Linnæus, who was sedulously following in the footsteps of his father, and had already proved himself not unworthy to share in his renown, was, in consequence of the mercenary conduct of his mother, obliged to purchase, at her own price, the books and collections, including the herbarium, which were his own by birthright. He died in 1783, and his books, plants, &c., reverted to his mother and sisters. The offer of sale made to Sir Joseph Banks was at the instance of the mother, who was thus making merchandise a second time of the collections of the great naturalist. Sir Joseph declined to avail himself of the offer, but recommended the purchase to Smith, then a student of medicine. He made the purchase, and the possession of Linnæus's collections determined his future pursuit as a botanist. "Though enthusiasm and a love of fame," remarks Lady Smith in his memoirs, "had perhaps some influence, a love of science and of truth had greater still. He said to others, 'The fairest flower in the garden of creation is a young mind, offering and unfolding itself to the influence of Divine wisdom, as the heliotrope turns its sweet blossoms to the sun;' and may it not be said of him that taste and virtue fixed his choice?" The number of volumes was upwards of 2000, including some valuable manuscripts; there were 3198 insects; 1564 shells; 2424 minerals; and 19,000 plants. Deducting a small herbarium which belonged to young Linnæus, and contained no species that were not included in the great collection, Smith obtained the whole for 900 guineas: but the entire cost, including the freight, ultimately amounted to £1088. Through the intervention of Sir John Jervis, afterwards Earl St. Vincent, and at this period one of the members for Great Yarmouth, an order was obtained from the Treasury passing the whole collection, except the books, free of Custom-house duty. It was in October, 1784, that a ship, named *The Appearance*, was freighted with the precious treasures. The vessel had just left the shores of Sweden, when King Gustavus III., who had been absent in France, returned to his dominions, and on learning that the herbarium and other monuments of the labours of the illustrious naturalist had been sent out of his native kingdom, he despatched a frigate to the Sound to intercept the voyage of *The Appearance* to England. But the latter vessel distanced her pursuer, and the valuable cargo was safely landed at the Custom-house of London. This singular race between the two vessels has been commemorated in a pictorial representation. The event is still remembered in Sweden, as we learned from a botanist of that country whom we found employed upon the herbaria of the Linnæan Society. Sir James Smith's own views of the conduct of the Swedish nation in allowing the herbarium and other collections to be sold to a foreigner, were expressed in the following terms, in a letter to Dr. Acrel, who had negotiated the bargain with him:—"Between ourselves, it is certainly a disgrace to the university (of Upsal) that they suffered such a treasure to leave them; but if those who ought most to have loved and protected the immortal name of Linné failed in their duty, he shall not want a friend or an asylum while I live or have any power, though ever so small, to do him honour." After the death of Smith, the herbarium was purchased by the Linnæan Society of London, of which he was the founder.

The herbarium of Linnæus contains only 10,000 species, which, along with duplicate specimens, are fixed upon 14,000 sheets of paper. At Kew, Sir William Hooker kindly showed us his herbarium, containing about 140,000 species of flowering plants alone, being the largest and completest collection in the world. The difference between the two collections shows the progress which has been made in descriptive botany since the days of Linnæus. The Swedish herbarium is contained in three plain wooden cases or presses, the doors of which still retain impressions of a series of illustrations of the forms of leaves, which were cut in tin, and fastened upon the wood, and employed by Linnæus in lecturing to his class. A royal Swedish physician, M. Pontin, has described the country residence and lecture-room of Linnæus, at Hammarby, near Upsal, which he visited in 1834:—"The building containing Linnæus's dwelling-house consists of two houses, and is situated at the foot of a stony height, surrounded by large rocks, as if an earthquake had thrown the granite rocks around it. It was only here and there that a tree could find space enough to spring up among these rocky ruins; and yet the lecture-room of Linnæus, so well known to the world, is found at the summit of a majestic uptowering pyramid, formed of them." It was here where he established his collections in every department of natural history, and, during the academical vacations, lectured eight hours a-day, communicating his discoveries "to a select audience, who lodged with the neighbouring peasantry, so as to be always present at these lectures, which were venerated as the sayings of an oracle." The pious and grateful spirit of the illustrious naturalist was shown in the inscription over the entrance to his parlour — "Dum faveat Cœlum,"— "While it pleases Heaven."

We took advantage of the obliging offer of the Curator to show us some of the more remarkable plants in the herbarium, and the simple style in which they were fastened upon very unpretending paper, with the names written on the back of the sheet. Of all the collection, which plant could we select for examination so appropriate as the modest and beautiful *Linnæa borealis!* Sir James Smith, in the *English Botany*, observes that "Linnæus has traced a pretty fanciful analogy between his own early fate, and this 'little northern plant, long overlooked, depressed, abject, flowering early,'—and we may now add, more honoured in its name than any other." It was the favourite plant of Linnæus, who had it painted on his China vases and tea service.

CHEMISTS AND CHEMISTRY.

CAVENDISH—HIS ODDITIES.

The following anecdotes of this eccentric chemist, betwixt whom and Watt lies the merit of the discovery of the nature of water, are from the *Life of the Hon. Henry Cavendish*, by Dr. George Wilson:—"At this period (1785) Cavendish's reputation was widespread, in spite of his solicitous endeavours to prevent himself becoming famous. It may be well, therefore, to refer here to his position in London between the years 1783 and 1785, when his most remarkable chemical researches were either made or published. His town residence was close to the British Museum, at the corner of Montague Place and Gower Street. Few visitors were admitted, but some found their way across the threshold, and have reported that books and apparatus formed its chief furniture. For the former, however, Cavendish set apart a separate mansion in Dean Street, Soho. Here he had collected a large and carefully chosen library of works on science, which he threw open to all engaged in research, and to this house he went for his own books as one would go to a circulating library, signing a formal receipt for such of the volumes as he took with him.

"His favourite residence was a beautiful suburban villa at Clapham, which, as well as a street or row of houses in the neighbourhood, now bears his name. 'The whole of the house at Clapham was occupied as workshops and laboratory.' 'It was stuck about with thermometers, rain-gauges, &c. A registering thermometer of Cavendish's own construction, served as a sort of landmark to his house. It is now in Professor Brande's possession.' A small portion only of the villa was set apart for personal comfort. The upper rooms constituted an astronomical observatory. What is now the drawing-room was the laboratory. In an adjoining room a forge was placed. The lawn was invaded by a wooden stage, from which access could be had to a large tree, to the top of which Cavendish, in the course of his astronomical, meteorological, electrical, or other researches occasionally ascended.

"The hospitalities of such a house are not likely to have been overflowing. Cavendish lived comfortably, but made no display. His few guests were treated, on all occasions, to the same fare, and it was not very sumptuous. A Fellow of the Royal Society reports, 'that if any one dined with Cavendish he invariably gave them a leg of mutton, and nothing else.' Another Fellow states that Cavendish 'seldom had company at his house, but on one occasion three or four scientific men were to dine with him, and when his housekeeper came to ask what was to be got to dinner, he said, 'a leg of mutton!' 'Sir, that will not be enough for five.' 'Well, then, get two,' was the reply.'"

Dr. Thomas Thomson states of Cavendish:—" He was shy and bashful to a degree bordering on disease; he could not bear to have any person introduced to him, or to be pointed out in any way as a remarkable man. One Sunday evening he was standing at Sir Joseph Banks', in a crowded room, conversing with Mr. Hatchett, when Dr. Ingenhousz, who had a good deal of pomposity of manner, came up with an Austrian gentleman in his hand, and introduced him formally to Mr. Cavendish. He mentioned the titles and qualifications of his friend at great length, and said that he had been peculiarly anxious to be introduced to a philosopher so profound and so universally known and celebrated as Mr. Cavendish. As soon as Dr. Ingenhousz had finished, the Austrian gentleman began, and assured Mr. Cavendish that his principal reason for coming to London was to see and converse with one of the greatest ornaments of the age, and one of the most illustrious philosophers that ever existed. To all these high-flown speeches Mr. Cavendish answered not a word, but stood with his eyes cast down, quite abashed and confounded. At last, spying an opening in the crowd, he darted through it with all the speed of which he was master, nor did he stop till he reached his carriage, which drove him directly home."

Sir Humphry Davy, in addition to the eloquent eulogium passed on Cavendish, soon after his death, left this less studied but more graphic sketch of the philosopher amongst his papers:—"Cavendish was a great man, with extraordinary singularities. His voice was squeaking, his manner nervous, he was afraid of strangers, and seemed, when embarrassed, even to articulate with difficulty. He wore the costume of our grandfathers; was enormously rich, but made no use of his wealth. He gave me once some bits of platinum, for my experiments, and came to see my results on the decomposition of the alkalis, and seemed to take an interest in them; but he encouraged no intimacy with any one. . . . . He lived latterly the life of a solitary, came to the club dinner, and to the Royal Society, but received nobody at his own house. He was acute, sagacious, and profound, and, I think, the most accomplished British philosopher of his time."

J. G. Children, Esq., was often in the company of Cavendish, and thus refers to his interviews with him: "I am now the father of the Royal Society Club. I remember Cavendish well, and have often dined at the Crown and Anchor with him. When I first became a member of the club I recollect seeing Cavendish on one occasion talking very earnestly to Marsden, Davy, and Hatchett. I went up and joined the group, my eye caught that of Cavendish, and he instantly became silent; he did not say a word. The fact is he saw in me a strange face, and of a strange face he had a perfect horror. . . . He was thus, to appearance, a misanthrope, and still more a misogynist. He was reported among his contemporaries indeed to have a positive dislike of women. Lord Burlington informs me, on the authority of Mr. Allnutt, an old inhabitant of Clapham, 'that Cavendish would never see a female servant; and if an *unfortunate maid* ever showed herself she was immediately dismissed.' Lord Brougham tells us that Cavendish ' ordered his dinner daily by a note, which he left at a certain hour on the hall table, where the housekeeper was to take it, for he held no communication with his female domestics from his morbid shyness.'" Dr. George Wilson, who has ably written the life of Cavendish, says, "He did not love, he did not hate, he did not hope, he did not fear, he did not worship as others do." He lived and died an almost passionless man. He communed with nature, and elicited many of her hidden truths. "His brain seems to have been a calculating engine; his eyes inlets of vision, not fountains of tears; his hands instruments of manipulation which never trembled with emotion, or were clasped together in adoration, thanksgiving, or despair; his heart only an anatomical organ necessary for the circulation of the blood."

DR. BLACK AND THE HYDROGEN GAS BALLOON.

Dr. Thomson relates the following anecdote of Dr. Black, the discoverer of carbonic acid gas and latent heat, in proof of his indifference to his personal reputation:—"There is an anecdote of Black which I was told by the late Mr. Benjamin Bell, of Edinburgh, author of a well-known system of surgery, and he assured me that he had it from the late Sir George Clark, of Pennicuik, who was a witness of the circumstance related. Soon after the appearance of Mr. Cavendish's paper on hydrogen gas, in which he made an approximation to the specific gravity of that body, showing that it was at least ten times lighter than common air,

Dr. Black invited a party of his friends to supper, informing them that he had a curiosity to show them. Dr. Hutton, Mr. Clark, of Eldin, and Sir George Clark, of Pennicuik, were of the number. When the company invited had assembled, he took them into a room. He had the allentois of a calf filled with hydrogen gas, and upon setting it at liberty, it immediately ascended, and adhered to the ceiling. The phenomenon was easily accounted for: it was taken for granted that a small black thread had been attached to the allentois, that this thread passed through the ceiling, and that some one in the apartment above, by pulling the thread, elevated it to the ceiling, and kept it in this position. This explanation was so probable, that it was acceded to by the whole company: though, like many other plausible theories, it turned out wholly unfounded; for when the allentois was brought down no thread whatever was found attached to it. Dr. Black explained the cause of the ascent to his admiring friends; but such was his carelessness of his own reputation, and of the information of the public, that he never gave the least account of this curious experiment even to his class; and more than twelve years elapsed before this obvious property of hydrogen gas was applied to the elevation of air-balloons, by M. Charles, in Paris."

SIR HUMPHRY DAVY—HIS INDUSTRY.

The unwonted honours paid to Davy as a lecturer, never relaxed the intensity with which he devoted himself to his laboratory. Writing in 1809 to his mother, he says,—

"At present, except when I resolve to be *idle* for health's sake, I devote every moment to labours which I hope will not be wholly ineffectual in benefiting society, and which will not be wholly inglorious for my country hereafter; and the feeling of this is the *reward* which will continue to keep me employed."

Cuvier, in his eloge of him officially made to the Institute, as a foreign member, referring to this period of his life, to his discoveries and reputation, said,—

"Davy, not yet thirty-two, in the opinion of all who could judge of such labours, held the first rank among the chemists of this or of any other age."

Sir Humphry Davy, when experimenting on the inhalation of gases, inspired a large quantity of carburetted hydrogen (the fire-damp of the coal-miners). Cottle records that the first inspiration produced numbness and loss of feeling in the chest. After the second, he lost all power of perceiving external things, except a terrible oppression on his chest, and he seemed sinking fast to death. He just had consciousness enough to remove the mouthpiece from his unclosed lips, when he became wholly insensible. After breathing the common air for some time, consciousness was restored, and Davy faintly uttered, as a consolation to his attendant, "I don't think I shall die."

MICHAEL FARADAY—HIS PERSEVERANCE.

Michael Faraday, England's most eminent chemist, was born in 1794, the son of a poor blacksmith. He was early apprenticed to one Ribeau, a bookbinder, in Blandford Street, and worked at the craft until he was twenty-two years of age. Whilst an apprentice his master called the attention of one of his customers (Mr. Dance, of Manchester Street) to an electrical machine and other things which the young man had made; and Mr. Dance, who was one of the old members of the Royal Institution, took him to hear the four last lectures which Sir Humphry Davy gave there as professor. Faraday attended, and seating himself in the gallery, took notes of the lectures, and at a future time sent his manuscript to Davy, with a short and modest account of himself, and a request, if it were possible, for scientific employment in the labours of the laboratory. Davy, struck with the clearness and accuracy of the memoranda, and confiding in the talents and perseverance of the writer, offered him, upon the occurrence of a vacancy in the laboratory, in the beginning of 1813, the post of assistant, which he accepted. At the end of the year he accompanied Davy and his lady over the Continent, as secretary and assistant, and in 1815 returned to his duties in the laboratory, and ultimately became Fullerian Professor. Mr. Faraday's researches and discoveries have raised him to the highest rank among European philosophers, while his high faculty of expounding, to a general audience, the result of recondite investigations, makes him one of the most attractive lecturers of the age. He has selected the most difficult and perplexing departments of physical science, the investigation of the reciprocal relations of heat, light, magnetism, and electricity; and by many years of patient and profound study, has tended greatly to simplify our ideas on these subjects. It is the hope of this philosopher that, should life and health be spared, he will be able to show that the imponderable agencies just mentioned are so many manifestations of one and the same force. Mr. Faraday's great achievements are recognized by the learned societies of every country in Europe; and the University of Oxford, in 1832, did itself the honour of enrolling him among the Doctors of Law. In private life he is beloved for the piety, simplicity, and truthfulness of his character, and the kindliness of his disposition.

J. J. BECCHER—HIS ENTHUSIASM.

John Joachim Beccher, a German professor, may be quoted as an example of the buoyant and enthusiastic spirit which was evoked at the call of chemistry, in the infancy of that science, and as contrasting favourably with the grovelling experimenters of the previous age, that of the alchemists. In a work entitled "Physica Subterranea," he describes chemists as a strange class of mortals, impelled by an almost insane impulse to seek their pleasure amongst smoke and vapour, soot and flame, poisons and poverty. "Yet amongst all these evils," says he, "I seem to myself to live so sweetly, that may I die if I would change places with the Persian king. I trust that I have got hold of my pitcher by the right handle —the true method of treating this study. For the pseudo-chemists seek gold; but the true philosophers science, which is more precious than gold!"

DR. PRIESTLEY.

Although Dr. Priestley made known a great number of new gaseous bodies, he was never (says Dr. Thomson), strictly speaking, entitled to the name of chemist, as he was never able to make a chemical analysis.

THE CHEMIST'S DREAM.

Methought I was exploring the hidden recesses of an extensive cave, whose winding passages had never before echoed to the tread of human foot. With ever-fresh admiration and delight, I was gazing at the thousand wonders which the flashing torch-light revealed on every side at each step of my progress, when a strange sound, as of the hum of many voices, fell upon my ear. What such a sound could mean in such a place was more than I could divine.

Curiosity led me on in the direction whence it came. The buzz of conversation, cheerful as it would seem from the occasional bursts of merriment that were heard, grew more and more distinct, until the dark and narrow passage I had been following suddenly opened upon one of those magnificent rock-parlours, of whose grandeur and beauty description can convey but a faint idea. A flood of light illuminated the arching roof with the vast columns of stalactite sparkling with crystals that supported it, and was reflected with imposing effect from the huge sheets of the same material, of the purest white, that hung from the ceiling in graceful but substantial drapery. I stood in one of nature's noblest halls—but not alone.

A strange company had gathered there. "Black spirits and white, blue spirits and gray," were before me. A festive occasion had assembled in joyous mood and in holiday attire the first-born of creation, the ELEMENTS of things.

In dreams nothing ever surprises us. It seemed perfectly natural to see those fairy forms in that strange grotto; so, accosting without hesitation the one nearest to me, I apologized for my intrusion, and was about to withdraw. From my new acquaintance, however, I received so cordial a welcome, and so earnest an invitation to become a partaker in the festivities, that I could not deny myself the pleasure of accepting the hospitality so kindly proffered.

I was soon informed that some of the leading characters among the elements had resolved some weeks before upon having a general pic-nic dinner party. Fifty-six family invitations had accordingly been sent out, one to each of the brotherhood; and preparations for the feast made upon a most extensive scale. Sea and land had been ransacked for delicacies, and everything was put in requisition that could minister to the splendour of the entertainment or to the enjoyment of the occasion.

At the hour I so unexpectedly came upon them, nearly all the guests with their families had assembled in the strange drawing-room I have described, awaiting the summons to the banquet. Spacious as that drawing-room was, it was nearly filled with these interesting children of nature. And here they were seen, not as in the chemist's laboratory, writhing in the heated crucible, or pent-up in glassy prisons; or peering out of gas-holders and Florence flasks, but arrayed in their native beauty; each free as air, and acting as impulse prompted. There were those present of every hue, every style of dress, every variety of appearance. The metals, the gases, the salts, the acids, the oxides, the alkalies—all were there. From the mine, from the shop of the artizan, from the mint, from the depths of ocean even, they had come; and a gayer assemblage, a more animated scene, my eyes had never beheld.

Many of the ladies of the party were most tastefully attired. Chlorine wore a beautiful greenish-yellow robe, that displayed her queen-like form to good advantage. The fair daughters of Chromium particularly attracted my attention, with their gay dresses of the liveliest golden-yellow and orange-red. Iodine had but just arrived, and was not yet disencumbered of an unpretending outer garment of steel-gray that enveloped her person; but the warmth of the apartment soon compelled her to throw this aside; when she appeared arrayed in a vesture of thin gauze, of the most splendid violet colour imaginable. Carbonic Acid was there, but not clad in the airy robes in which I expected to see her. The pressure of the iron hand of adversity had been upon her, and now her attire was plain, simply a dress of snowy white; the best which the straitened circumstances to which she had been reduced allowed her to assume. Quite a contrast to her was her mother Carbon, whom you would have supposed to be a widow in deep mourning, or a nun who had taken the black veil, so sable were her garments, so gloomy her countenance, had not her earrings of polished jet, and a circlet of diamonds that glittered on her brow, evinced that she had not yet altogether renounced the vanities of the world. The belle of the room appeared to be Nitrous Acid, the graceful daughter of Nitrogen; airy in all her movements, and with dress of deepest crimson, that corresponded well with a lip and cheek rivalling the ruby in their redness.

Among the lady metals too, there were many of bright faces and resplendent charms; but I must pass on to a description of the gentlemen of the party. Sulphur wore a suit of modest yellow-plush, while Phosphorus quite disconcerted some of the most decorous matrons present, by making his appearance in a pair of flesh-coloured tights. Phosphuretted Hydrogen, or, as he is nicknamed "Will of the Wisp," startled me by flitting by in a robe of living flame, the dress in which the graceless youngster is said to haunt church-yards and marshy places, playing his pranks upon poor benighted travellers.

The king of the metals, Gold, was arrayed in truly gorgeous apparel; though it must be confessed there was a glitter and an air of haughtiness about him, from which you would turn with pleasure to the mild sweet face of his royal sister, Silver, who leaned upon his arm; a bright-eyed, unassuming creature, of sterling worth.

Mercury was there, as lively and versatile as ever; a most restless being; now by the thermometer, noting the subterranean temperature; now by the barometer, predicting a storm in the regions overhead; now arm-in-arm with this metal, then with that; and they all, by the way, save stern old Iron, had hard work to shake him off. A strange character surely was he; a philosopher of uncommon powers of reflection; the veriest busy-body in the world; well versed in the art of healing; a practical amalgamationist; in short, a complete factotum. Potassium, though a decidedly brilliant-looking fellow, manifested too much levity in his deportment to win respect, and was pronounced by those who knew him best, to be rather soft. In gravity, Platinum, surpassed all the company; in natural brightness, Tin was outshone by few.

When Oxygen arrived, and his light, elastic tread was heard, and his clear, transparent countenance was seen among them, a murmur of congratulation ran round the drawing-room, and involuntarily all assembled arose to do him homage. He was a patriarch indeed among them; literally a father to many of the younger guests. His arrival was the signal for adjournment to the banqueting-room, where of right he took his seat at the head of the table.

Touching the apartment we had now entered, I can only say that it was grand beyond description! It was lighted up with the radiance of noon-day, by an arch of flame intensely dazzling, produced by a curious apparatus which Galvanism, who excels in these matters, had contrived for the occasion, out of some materials with which his friends Zinc and Copper had furnished him. Festoons of evergreens and wreaths of roses encircled the alabaster columns, and made the whole look like Fairy Land.

But I must describe the table and its paraphernalia. The preparation of the viands, I mean the baking, boiling, roasting, stewing, and the like—had been committed to Caloric, who has had long experience in that department. The nobler of the metals had generously lent their costly services of plate, while Carbon united with Iron to furnish the elegant steel cutlery used on the occasion. Alumina provided the fine set of china that graced the table; and Silex and Potash, without solicitation, sent, as their joint contribution, cut-glass pitchers and tumblers, of superior pattern and transparency.

As among these sons of nature there is no craving for artificial excitement, Oxygen and Hydrogen (who, by the way, have done more for the cold water societies than DELEVAN or FATHER MATHEW), were commissioned to provide the drinkables; and what beverage *they* furnished may easily be conjectured. Carbon, with Oxygen and Hydrogen, found most of the vegetables; and Nitrogen, whose assistance as commissary here was indispensable, joined them in procuring the meats, under which the table groaned. No taste but would be satisfied with the variety; no appetite but would be cloyed with the profusion of good things.

Though the liberality of the four who have been named, left but little for their associates to contribute, still some individual offerings to the feast deserve to be noticed. Thus the oysters, Carbonate of Lime had sent in the shell; the pyramids of ice-cream for the dessert were provided by the daughter of Chlorine and Sodium, who was out several hours in the snow, engaged in freezing them; and the almonds and peaches came from the conservatory of Hydrocyanic Acid, the druggist.

After grace had been said by Affinity, who is a sort of chaplain to the elements, having officiated at the weddings of all the married ones of the company, a vigorous onset was made upon the good things before them. At first all were too much engaged for conversation; but the dessert appearing at last, as they cracked the nuts the jest too was cracked; toast and song were called for, and wit and innocent hilarity became the order of the day. Even Oxygen, who had presided with such an air of dignity, relaxed from his sternness, and entertained the younger ones at the table with many a tale of his mischievous pranks in the days of old Father Chaos, when time and himself were young. Strange tales they were, too, of earthquakes with which Hydrogen and he would now and then frighten the Icthyosauri and Megatheria of the ancient world; and of conflagrations comical, as old Vulcan's tongs and anvil, kindling them before his eyes with the very bolt he was forging. "This, however," he added, with a sly glance at his staid partner Nitrogen, who sat near, "was before marriage had sobered down his spirits, and tamed his impetuosity."

I have no space to chronicle more of these freaks of Oxygen's early youth, nor any of the sayings and doings of others of the party on this memorable night. Else would I give the marvellous story Nickel had to relate, of a *falling out* he once had with the Man in the Moon, and of a journey he was consequently under the necessity of making in hot haste to the earth for refuge. I would tell too of the drolleries of Nitrous Oxide, that funniest, queerest, craziest of youngsters; and how Phosphorus made a flaming speech, and Potash a caustic one; and how Mercury proposed as a toast, "The medical profession: to whom we say, 'Use us, but do not abuse us.'" I must speak however of a curious little by-scene I chanced to witness; it was a flirtation that Platinum was carrying on with Hydrogen, whom, much to my surprise, I found seated among the Metals, and quite at home among them, too. There was quite a contrast between Platinum, gray, heavy, and dull as he was, and the light and buoyant creature by his side: but there soon seemed to be evidence of some mutual attraction. Platinum grew warm in his attentions, and ere long quite a flame was kindled between them. So passed the evening: all went "merry as a marriage-bell," with nothing to mar the good humour that prevailed; till, in an evil hour, Sulphuretted Hydrogen, a disagreeable fellow, against whose appearance at the banquet most of the company had protested, entered the apartment with a very offensive air. In an instant the whole family of Metals, to whom he was particularly obnoxious, changed colour; Lead fairly grew black in the face with indignation; Arsenic and Antimony seemed to be jaundiced with rage; Ammonia, to whom his presence recalled very unpleasant associations, in trying to avoid him, precipitated several Metallic Oxides to the floor; while Chlorine, with more self-command than the rest, advanced with a firm step to expel the intruder, looking as if she were about to annihilate him on the spot.

How the scene might have terminated I know not; for just at that moment a strange sound, of awful import, like the tramping of a mighty host, came to my ears: I felt sure it was "an earthquake's voice," and that now my fate was sealed! My knees tottered under me; the arching grotto and the festive board gradually vanished from before my eyes, which —— *opened* upon the class, as they were leaving the laboratory of our worthy professor of chemistry, where it seemed, much to my confusion, I had fallen asleep during lecture, and

" Dreamed a dream in the midst of my slumbers."

—(Dr. House, in Knickerbocker, an American publication.)

CRITICS AND CRITICISM.

A TRUE CRITIC,

In the perusal of a book, is like a dog at a feast, whose thoughts and stomach are wholly set upon what the guests fling away, and consequently is apt to snarl most when there are the fewest bones.—(Dean Swift, Tale of a Tub.)

SHERIDAN.

Sheridan had a very convenient formula for acknowledging all the new publications that were constantly sent him:—"Dear sir, I have received your exquisite work, and I have no doubt I shall be highly delighted *after* I have read it."

A ROYAL CRITIC—KING JAMES THE FIRST.

As I remember some years since, there was a very abusive satyr in verse brought to our king; and as the passages were a-reading before him, he often said, "That if there were no more men in England, the rogue should hang for it." At last being come to the conclusion, which was (after all his railing)—

" Now God preserve the king, the queen, the peers,
And grant the author long may wear his ears."

This pleased his majesty so well, that he broke into a laughter, and said, "By my soul, so thou shalt for me. Thou art a bitter, but thou art a witty knave."—(Howel's Letters, 1621.)

FRANCIS JEFFREY—ULTIMUS ROMANORUM.

He prepared himself for what he did by judicious early industry. He then chose the most difficult spheres in which talent can be exerted, and excelled in them all; rising from obscurity and dependence to affluence and renown. His splendour as an advocate was exceeded by his eminence as a judge. He was the founder of a new system of criticism, and this a higher one than had ever existed. As an editor, and as a writer, he did as much to improve his country and the world as can almost ever be done, by discussion, by a single man. He was the last of four pre-eminent Scotchmen, who, living in their own country, raised its character and extended its reputation during the period of his career. The other three were Dugald Stewart, Walter Scott, and Thomas Chalmers; each of whom, in literature, philosophy, or policy, caused great changes; and each left upon his age the impression of the mind that produced them. Jeffrey, though surpassed in genius certainly by Scott, and perhaps by Chalmers, was inferior to none of them in public usefulness, or in the beauty of the means by which he achieved it, or in its probable duration. The elevation of the public mind was his peculiar glory. In one respect alone he was unfortunate. The assaults which he led against error were efforts in which the value of his personal services can never be duly seen. His position required him to dissipate, in detached and nameless exertions, as much philosophy and beautiful composition as would have sustained avowed and important original works. He has raised a great monument, but it is one on which his own name is too faintly engraved.—(Life by Lord Cockburn.)

JEFFREY'S MARRIAGE.

The marriage took place on November 1, 1801. It had all the recommendations of poverty. His father, who was in humble circumstances, assisted them a very little; but Miss Wilson had no fortune, and Jeffrey had told his brother, only six months before, that "*my profession has never yet brought me £100 a-year*, yet have I determined to venture upon this new state. It shows a reliance on Providence scarcely to be equalled in this degenerate age, and indicates such resolutions of economy as would terrify any less magnanimous adventurer." His brother having asked him to describe his wife, he did so, as I think, who came to know her well, with great accuracy. "You ask me to describe my Catherine to you; but I have no talent for description, and put but little faith in full-drawn characters; besides, the original is now so much a part of myself, that it would not be decent to enlarge very much, either upon her excellencies or her imperfections. It is proper, however, to tell you, in sober earnest, that she is not a showy or remarkable girl, either in person or character. She has good sense, good manners, good temper, and good hands, and above all, I am perfectly sure, that she has a good heart, and that it is mine without reluctance or division." She soon secured the respect and esteem of all his friends, and made her house, and its society, very agreeable. Their first home was in Buccleuch Place, one of the new parts of the old town, not in either the eighth or the ninth stories, neither of which ever existed, but in the third story, of what is now

No. 18 of the street. His domestic arrangements were set about with that honourable economy which always enabled him to practise great generosity. There is a sheet of paper containing an inventory, in his own writing, of every article of furniture that he went the length of getting, with the prices. His own study was only made comfortable at the cost of £7, 18s.; the banqueting-hall rose to £13, 8s., and the drawing-room actually amounted to £22, 19s.—(Life by Lord Cockburn.)

MOORE'S DUEL WITH JEFFREY.

Francis Jeffrey having, in 1806, attacked Thomas Moore's *Odes and Epistles*, for their immorality, in the *Edinburgh Review*, the poet resolved to challenge the critic to mortal combat. Preliminaries were accordingly arranged for a hostile meeting at Chalk Farm. Moore borrowed his pistols from the poet Spencer, who sent the Bow Street officers to prevent the two little men from killing each other. The sequel is narrated by Moore in his diary:—

"I must have slept pretty well; for Hume, I remember, had to wake me in the morning, and the chaise being in readiness, we set off for Chalk Farm. Hume had also taken the precaution of providing a surgeon to be within call. On reaching the ground we found Jeffrey and his party already arrived. I say his 'party,' for although Horner only was with him, there were, as we afterwards found, two or three of his attached friends (and no man, I believe, could ever boast of a greater number) who, in their anxiety for his safety, had accompanied him and were hovering about the spot. And then was it that, for the first time, my excellent friend Jeffrey and I met face to face. He was standing with the bag, which contained the pistols, in his hand, while Horner was looking anxiously around. It was agreed that the spot where we found them, which was screened on one side by large trees, would be as good for our purpose as any we could select; and Horner, after expressing some anxiety respecting some men whom he had seen suspiciously hovering about, but who now appeared to have departed, retired with Hume behind the trees, for the purpose of loading the pistols, leaving Jeffrey and myself together. All this had occupied but a very few minutes. We, of course, had bowed to each other at meeting; but the first words I recollect to have passed between us was Jeffrey's saying, on our being left together, 'What a beautiful morning it is!'—'Yes,' I answered with a slight smile, a 'morning made for better purposes;' to which his only response was a sort of assenting sigh. As our assistants were not, any more than ourselves, very expert at warlike matters, they were rather slow in their proceedings; and as Jeffrey and I walked up and down together, we came once in sight of their operations: upon which I related to him, as rather *a propos* to the purpose, that Billy Egan, the Irish barrister, once said, when, as he was sauntering about in like manner while the pistols were loading, his antagonist, a fiery little fellow called out to him angrily to keep his ground. 'Don't make yourself unaisy, my dear fellow,' said Egan, 'sure, isn't it bad enough to take the dose, without being by at the mixing up?' Jeffrey had scarcely time to smile at this story, when our two friends, issuing from behind the trees, placed us at our respective posts (the distance, I suppose, having been previously measured by them), and put the pistols into our hands. They then retired to a little distance; the pistols were on both sides raised; and we waited but the signal to fire, when some police-officers, whose approach none of us had noticed, and who were within a second of being too late, rushed out from a hedge behind Jeffrey; and one of them, striking at Jeffrey's pistol with his staff, knocked it to some distance into the field, while another running over to me, took possession also of mine. We were then replaced in our respective carriages, and conveyed crest-fallen to Bow Street."— It is known that Moore and Jeffrey afterwards became cordial friends.

TASSO AND ARIOSTO.

Menzine, in his Poetics, gives the truest idea of Ariosto's and Tasso's rival poems of any of our writers. The poem of the former, says he, is like a vast palace, very richly furnished, but built without the rules of architecture; whereas, that of Tasso is like a neat palace, very regular and beautiful.—(Crudeli.)

GRAY AND MASON—PROGRESS OF AN EPITAPH.

The poet of the *English Garden* and the *Heroic Epistle* was proud to obtain the critical judgment of the author of the *Elegy* ;—and Gray, it must be said, was a fastidious critic, who dwelt on words and expressions with a fine sense of the delicacy and strength of the English language. Gray composed slowly—weighing every word in a sovereign scale.—Mason, on the other hand, was a rapid writer—seldom attending to the subtle distinctions to be met with in words. Words, indeed—to use his own expression to the contrary about Gray—digested easily with him. Gray has hit off this defect in his friend in one of his letters:—"Why, you make no more, dear Mason," he says, "of writing an ode, and throwing it into the fire, than of buckling and unbuckling your shoe." To which the other replies, as we now learn for the first time—"Pray, Mr. Gray, why won't you make your muse do now and then a friendly turn? An idle slut as she is! if she was to throw out her ideas never so carelessly, it would satisfy some folks that I know, but I won't name names." Yet Mason was afraid of what, after Pope, he calls "the desperate hook" of Gray:— and Gray, when he heard that Mason was concocting *An Elegy in the Garden of a Friend,* writes by way of postscript—"Send me the Elegy,—my *hoe* is sharp."

Another instance in which we obtain the critical judgment of Gray relates to Mason's Epitaph on the daughter of Archbishop Drummond:—

"I dined lately at Bishopthorpe, when the archbishop took me into his closet, and, with many tears, begged me to write an epitaph on his daughter. In our conversation he touched so many unison strings of my heart (for we both of us wept like children), that I could not help promising him that I would try, if possible, to oblige him. The result you have on the opposite page. If it either is or can be made a decent thing, assist me with your judgment immediately, for what I do about it I would do quickly, and I can do nothing neither, if this will not do with correction. It cannot be expected, neither would I wish it, to be equal to what I have written from my heart upon my heart's heart. Give me, I beg, your own sentiments upon it as soon as possible. To conclude, I wish heartily to be with you, but cannot fix a time, for I was obliged to invite Mr. Robinson and the Wadsworths hither, and I have not received their answer. In my next perhaps I can speak more determinately. My best compliments to Dr. and Mrs. Wharton, and best wishes for the continuance of Mr. Brown's beatifications.—Yours cordially,

W. MASON."

Epitaph on Miss Drummond.

Hence, stoic apathy to hearts of stone:
  A Christian sage with dignity can weep.
See mitred Drummond heave the heart-felt groan,
  Where the cold ashes of his daughter sleep.
Here sleeps what once was beauty, once was grace,
  Grace that express'd in each benignant smile,
That dearest harmony of soul and face,
  When beauty glories to be virtue's foil.

Or thus,—

That sweetest sympathy of soul and face,
  When beauty only blooms as virtue's foil.
Such was the maid, that, in the noon of youth,
  In virgin innocence, in nature's pride
Grac'd with each liberal art and crown'd with truth,
  Sunk in her father's fond embrace, and died.
He weeps. O venerate the holy tear!
  Faith soothes his sorrows, lightens all their load;
Patient he spreads his child upon her bier,
  And humbly yields an angel to his God.

Gray's reply is, as usual, to the point:—

"Old Park, Sunday, July 19, 1767.

"DEAR MASON,—I come forthwith to the epitaph which you have had the charity to write at the Archbishop's request. It will certainly do (for it is both touching and new), but yet will require much finishing. I like not the first three lines: it is the party most nearly concerned, at least some one closely connected, and bearing a part of the loss, that is usually supposed to speak on these occasions, but these lines appear to be written by the chaplain, and have an air of flattery to his patron. All that is good in them is better expressed in the four last verses; "where the cold ashes," &c. These five verses are well, except the word 'benignant,' and the thought (which is not clear to me, besides that it is somewhat *hardly* expressed) of 'when beauty only blooms,' &c. In gems that want colour and perfection, *a foil* is put under them to add to their lustre. In others, as in diamonds, the foil is black; and in this sense, when a pretty woman chooses to appear in public with a homely one, we say she uses her *as a foil*. This puzzles me, as you neither mean that beauty sets off virtue by its contrast and opposition to it, nor that her virtue was so imperfect as to stand in need of beauty to heighten its lustre. For the rest I read, 'that sweetest harmony of soul,' &c.; 'such was the maid,' &c. All this to the end I much approve, except 'crowned with truth,' and 'lightens all their load.' The first is not precise; in the latter you say too much. 'Spreads his child,' too, is not the word. When you have corrected all these faults it will be excellent."

A week later, this was followed by another letter:—

"Old Park, 26th July, 1767.

"DEAR MASON,—You are very perverse. I do desire you would not think of dropping the design you had of obliging the Archbishop. I submitted my criticisms to your own conscience, and I allowed the latter half to be excellent, two or three little words excepted. If this will not do, for the future I must say (whatever you send me), that the whole is the most perfect thing in nature, which is easy to do when one knows it will be acceptable. Seriously, I should be sorry if you did not correct these lines, and am interested enough for the party (only upon your narrative) to wish he were satisfied in it, for I am edified when I hear of so mundane a man, that yet he has a tear for pity. By the way, I ventured to show the other epitaph [on Mason's wife] to Dr. Wharton, and sent him brimful into the next room to cry. I believe he did not hear it quite through, nor has he ever asked to see it again; and now will you not come and see him?".

Mason's rejoinder will repay attentive perusal:—

"Had you given me any hint, any *lueur*, how the three first lines might have been altered, it would have been charitable indeed; but you say nothing, only that I must alter them. Now, in my conscience, to which you appeal, I cannot find fault with the sentiment which they contain; and yet, in despite of my conscience, if I thought that they implied the least shadow of flattery to the Archbishop, I would wipe them out with a sponge dipped in the mud of the kennel. But I cannot think they do. I think, on the contrary, they give the composition that unity of thought which ought always to run through compositions of this kind; for in my mind a *perfect epitaph is a perfect epigram without a sting*. N.B. This sentence in our Epistolæ familiares cum notis variorum, will be explained in a note of Dr. Balguy's, to the contentation of every reader; in the meantime, if you do not understand it yourself, console yourself with the pleasing idea that posterity will, and that is enough in reason. However, to show you my complacency, and in dread that you should ever do as you threaten, and call whatever I send you the most perfect things in nature, I will sacrifice the first stanza on your critical altar, and let it consume either in flame or smudge as it choose. Then we begin, 'here sleeps,' a very poetical sort of *ci git*, or 'here lies,' and which I hope will not lead the reader to imagine a sentence lost.

1. Here sleeps what once was beauty, once was grace,
2. Grace that with native sentiment combined
3. To form that harmony of soul and face,
4. Where beauty shines the mirror of the mind.
5. Such was the maid, that, in the noon of youth,
6. In virgin innocence, in nature's pride,
7. Blest with each art that taste supplies or truth,
8. Sunk in her father's fond embrace and died.
9. He weeps. O! venerate the holy tear;
10 Faith lends her aid to ease affliction's load:
11. The parent mourns the child upon her bier,
12. The Christian yields an angel to his God.

—Various sections, pick and choose. 2. 'Inborn sentiment.' 3. 'Displayed (or diffused) that harmony,' &c. 7. 'That springs from taste or truth;' 'derived from taste or truth;' 'that charms with taste and truth.' But, after all, I do not know that she was a metaphysician, 'blest with each art that owes its charms to truth,' which painting does, as well as logic and metaphysics. 10. 'Faith lends her lenient aid to sorrow's load;' 'Faith lends her aid, and eases (or lightens) sorrow's load.' 11. 'Pensive he mourns,' or 'he views' or 'gives.' 12. 'Yet humbly yields,' or 'but humbly.' Now, if from all this you can pick out twelve ostensible lines, do, and I will father them; or if you will out of that lukewarm corner of your heart where you hoard up your poetical charity throw out a poor mite to my distresses, I shall take it kind indeed; but, if not, *stat prior sententia*, for I will give myself no farther trouble about it; I cannot in this uncomfortable place, where my *opus magnum sive didacticum* has not advanced ten lines since I saw you."

Gray again appears with his "hook" and "hoe:"—

"I exceedingly approve the epitaph in its present shape. Even what I best liked before is altered for the better. The various readings I do not mind, only, perhaps, I should read the 2nd line:

Grace that with tenderness and sense combined,
To form, &c.

for I hate 'sentiment' in verse. I will say nothing to 'taste' and 'truth,' for perhaps the Archbishop may fancy they are fine things; but, to my palate, they are wormwood. All the rest is just as it should be, and what he ought to admire."

—After this knocking about and bitter digestion of words, the Epitaph assumes the shape in which we now know it:—

Here sleeps what once was beauty, once was grace,
Grace that with tenderness and sense combined,
To form that harmony of soul and face,
Where beauty shines the mirror of the mind.
Such was the maid, that, in the morn of youth,
In virgin innocence, in nature's pride,
Blest with each art that owes its charm to truth,
Sunk in her father's fond embrace, and died.
He weeps. O! venerate the holy tear!
Faith lends her aid to ease affliction's load:
The parent mourns his child upon its bier,
The Christian yields an angel to his God.

—A young poet may read an instructive lesson in the changes which took place in *twelve* lines ere they took their present appearance.—(Athenæum, review of Correspondence of Thomas Gray and William Mason.)

EARLY EXPLORERS OF AFRICA.

LEDYARD AND LUCAS.

In 1788 a society of English gentlemen, among whom were the then Bishop of Llandaff and Sir Joseph Banks, was instituted for the purpose of having the interior districts of Africa explored by agents of the society. Fortune instantly helped the promoters of the scheme to a couple of men than whom it is hardly possible to conceive better geographical missionaries. One of these was Ledyard, a name not yet forgotten. This daring American, whose earlier life had been partially spent in the wigwams of the Indians, who had made the voyage of the world with Captain Cook, and who had gone through the most terrible privations and dangers in a gallant effort of his own to traverse the continent of America from the Pacific to the Atlantic, offered himself to Sir Joseph Banks for the African expedition. Being asked when he would set out, he replied, "To-morrow morning." That was the sort of man for the purpose, and Ledyard started, arriving at Cairo on the 19th of August, 1788, the journey, which can now be performed in fifteen days, having occupied him about fifty. He wrote home to his employers that his next letter would be dated from Sennar, but he fell a victim, as was generally supposed, to the climate, and his restless heart was quieted for ever. The other emissary of the society was Lucas, whose name is less familiar to readers of the present day than that of Ledyard, whose affectionate tribute to the character of woman, and whose untimely end, have, thanks to versification, been kept in the remembrance of young students of geography. Lucas had, when a boy, been sent to Spain for education, but on his return was captured by a "Salee rover," and taken to Morocco as a slave. After three years he was released, and was subsequently nominated the English vice-consul in the country into which he had originally been brought as a captive. Sixteen years later he came to England again, and was appointed Oriental interpreter to the British Court. When in this capacity, he undertook the African expedition, and embarked for Tripoli in 1788, intending to proceed, over the great desert, to Gambia, but he was prevented from fulfilling his purpose, and his researches were brought to a speedy termination. He appears to have obtained, however, a good deal of information, and though much of it was hearsay, and though many of his informants, like those of Ledyard, told him absurd fables, he made respectable progress in the objects of the society.

These were amongst the earliest explorers of the enormous region concerning which, more than half a century later, we have so much to learn. But no one who has trodden in the steps of Ledyard or Lucas, or who has ventured on the task of making his way through the inhospitable deserts of Africa, has entered on his work in a more chivalrous spirit, or told his tale more unaffectedly than that of this young and distinguished traveller. His journey, like that of his predecessors, ended in sickness and discomfiture, but he undertook it with the noblest motives, went through it, so long as his physical power permitted, with unflagging resolution, and recorded it in an earnest and manly narrative, which, we write the words in all sincerity, no one can read without admiration and esteem for its author.

FEMALE PROMOTERS OF SCIENCE AND PHILOSOPHY.

MADAME DE STAËL.

Madame de Staël, with all her splendid talents and extraordinary vivacity, had little or no relish for the beauties of nature. "Oh for the rivulet in the Rue du Bac!" she exclaimed, when some one pointed out to her the glorious Lake of Geneva. Many years later, she said to M. Molé,—"Si ce n'était le respect humain, je n'ouvrirais pas ma fenêtre pour voir la baie de Naples; tandis que je ferais cinq cents lieues pour aller causer avec un homme d'esprit." The reader will be reminded of Charles Lamb, invited down to the Lakes by Wordsworth, sighing for the silversmiths' shop-windows in Cheapside, and "the sweet shady side of Pall Mall."

At the age of twenty, this lady had attained a dangerous reputation as a wit and a prodigy. She was passionately proud of the brilliant society in which she lived, but set at nought its restraints, and trampled upon its conventionalities, in a style which the men forgave in consideration of her genius, and the women in consideration of her ugliness. Her vivacity was excessive, and her talk interminable. But her influence in Paris was so great, that Napoleon banished her from France. During her wanderings, she made the friendship of Schiller in Germany, who, writing to Goethe a description of her extraordinary intellectual capacity, was under the necessity of qualifying his praise by saying,—"One's only grievance is the *altogether unprecedented glibness of her tongue.*" In England, Byron celebrated her virtues and attractions in a pompous note to *Childe Harold*, but in his diary and correspondence recorded his genuine impressions.—" I saw Curran," he says, "presented to Madame de Staël, at Mackintosh's; it was the grand confluence of the Rhone and the Saône; they were both so —— ugly that I could not help wondering how the best intellects of France and Ireland could have taken up respectively such residences."

Mr. Jerdan, in his autobiography, mentions his acquaintanceship with Madame de Staël, remarking that she was far from handsome or attractive, and an almost incessant talker. He adds, by way of apology, that in London society, everybody endeavoured to "draw her out."

LAPLACE AND HIS ENGLISH TRANSLATOR AND EXPOSITOR.

Nathaniel Bowditch, the translator of Laplace's *Mécanique Céleste*, was cheered on in his arduous labours by his wife, who not only relieved him from domestic cares, but offered to submit to any degree of self-denial necessary to his publishing the work at his own risk. In grateful acknowledgment of her support and sympathy, he dedicated the book to her memory. An idea of the difficulty of the task of translation and exposition is conveyed by a remark of Dr. Bowditch, who used to say—" I never come across one of Laplace's *Thus it plainly appears*, without feeling sure that I have got hours of hard study before me to fill up the chasm, and find out and show *how* it plainly appears." It is highly honourable to the sex, that the only exposition of Laplace's work that has appeared in England, is from the pen of a female — the accomplished Mary Somerville, wife of Dr. Somerville, of Chelsea Hospital. This is published under the title of the *Mechanism of the Heavens*, of which it is observed in the *Edinburgh Review*, " this, unquestionably, is one of the most remarkable works that female intellect ever produced in any age or country; and, with respect to the present day, we hazard little in saying that Mrs. Somerville is the only individual of her sex in the world who could have written it." For this signal service to science a pension of £300 per annum was bestowed upon the authoress, on the recommendation of the late Sir Robert Peel.

MISS CAROLINE LUCRETIA HERSCHEL.

This very interesting lady died at Hanover on the 9th of January, 1848, in the 98th year of her age. She was the sister of Sir William Herschel; and, consequently, aunt to Sir John Herschel, the present representative of this truly scientific family.

Miss Herschel was the constant companion of her brother, and sole assistant of his astronomical labours, to the success of which her indefatigable zeal, diligence, and singular accuracy of calculation, not a little contributed. For the performance of these duties, his Majesty King George the Third was pleased to place her in the receipt of a salary sufficient for her singularly moderate wants and retired habits. In the intervals, she found time both for astronomical observations of her own, and for the execution of more than one work of great extent and utility. The observations she made with a small Newtonian sweeper, constructed for her by her brother, with which she found no less than eight comets; and on five of these occasions her claim to the *first* discovery is admitted. These sweeps also proved productive of the detection of several remarkable nebulæ and clusters of stars, previously unobserved.

On her brother's death, in 1822, Miss Herschel returned to Hanover, which she never again quitted; passing the last twenty-six years of her life in repose—enjoying the society and cherished by the regard of her remaining relatives and friends; gratified by the occasional visits of eminent astronomers, and honoured with many marks of favour and distinction on the part of the King of Hanover, the Crown Prince, and his amiable and illustrious consort.—(Athenæum.)

GEOLOGY AND NATURAL HISTORY.

SAUSSURE AND THE ARRAN MINERALOGIST.

Having arrived at Lochranza we saw a house of good appearance, which was said to be the inn. The host was previously announced to us as a man remarkable for his originality; he had cultivated, no one knew how, a taste for geology; he composed verses, was a musician, a composer, even, without neglecting the labours which his small farm required, and fishing, which occupied a part of his time. We were eager to enter into the house; but the interior was far from corresponding with the outside; everything was dirty and in the greatest disorder. The room we were introduced into was, at the same time, a sleeping and a drinking room; the stone flags were all loose and full of holes, half of the window was broken, and currents of freezing air penetrated from all parts. It was there, however, we found Mr. Cowie, our host, busy in drinking a bottle of whisky with the doctor of the Isle, who was making the tour of his patients. The latter, whom we had already seen at Brodick, had informed Cowie of our arrival; thus, the moment he saw us he arose, and came with eyes sparkling with joy to invite us to see his minerals, and without even thinking of preparing a fire, or any refreshment for us, he had already commenced a geological dissertation.

There was nothing in the house, and it was necessary to send a considerable way off to gather turf for fuel. An old woman, who wished to entertain us with distinction, gave herself an incredible movement, mounted and descended the staircase, spoke without ceasing, and brought us—nothing. It was a frightful noise, and notwithstanding so much eagerness, we could not obtain what we demanded. In fine, fatigued with so much bustle, we left the inn, begging Mr. Cowie to show us what the environs possessed as most interesting. But this great man, who would not permit his philosophical pursuits to encroach upon his rustic duties, begged us to allow him to repair a cart before giving himself up to the study of mineralogy. We did not wait long; he conducted us a route as interesting for the phenomena of natural history which it presented, as for the beauty of its scenery.—(Sauss.)

GEOLOGICAL ALLEGORY OF THE THIRTEENTH CENTURY.

The Arabian writers of the middle ages cultivated with some success the study of mineralogy, but no geological discoveries were elicited by their labours. Sir Charles Lyell quotes an Arabian allegory connected with this era, which anticipates, in a beautiful and remarkable manner, some of the conclusions evolved by the modern geology. It is contained in a manuscript work, entitled the "Wonders of Nature," preserved in the Royal Library at Paris, by an Arabian author, Mohammed Kazwini, who flourished in the 17th century of the Hegira, or at the close of the 13th century of our era. It is as follows:—"I passed one day," an allegorical personage is represented as saying, "by a very ancient and wonderfully populous city, and asked one of its inhabitants how long it had been founded? 'It is, indeed, a mighty city,' replied he, 'we know not how long it has existed, and our ancestry were on this subject as ignorant as ourselves.' Five centuries afterwards, as I passed by the same place, I could not perceive the slightest vestige of the city. I demanded of a peasant, who was gathering herbs upon its former site, how long it had been destroyed? 'In sooth, a strange question!' replied he. 'The ground here has never been different from what you now behold it.' 'Was there not of old,' said I, 'a splendid city here?' 'Never,' answered he, 'so far as we have seen, and never did our fathers speak to us of any such. On my return there 500 years afterwards, *I found the sea in the same place,* and on its shores were a party of fishermen, of whom I inquired how long the land had been covered by the waters? 'Is this a question,' said they, 'for a man like you?—this spot has always been what it is now.' I again returned, 500 years afterwards, and the sea had disappeared; I inquired of a man, who stood alone upon the spot, how long this change had taken place; and he gave me the same answer as I had received before. Lastly, on coming back again, after an equal lapse of time, I found there a flourishing city, more populous, and more rich in beautiful buildings than the city I had seen the first time, and when I would fain have informed myself concerning its origin, the inhabitants answered me, 'Its rise is lost in remote antiquity; we are ignorant how long it has existed, and our fathers were on this subject as ignorant as ourselves.'"

SUPERSTITIONS RESPECTING ORGANIC REMAINS.

There are still people credulous enough to believe that fossils are freaks of nature, having no relation whatever to the organisms of a previous condition of our planet. There is less room, therefore, to wonder at the popular belief of former days, that the shells of ammonites, found in the series of rocks beginning with the lias and ending with the chalk, were petrified snakes. A legend bore, that St. Hilda, a female devotee at Whitby, in Yorkshire, where they abound, destroyed the living serpents by praying their heads off, and then praying them into stone. It is to this legend that Sir Walter Scott refers in *Marmion:*—

"And how the nuns of Whitby told
How, of countless snakes, each one
Was changed into a coil of stone,
When holy Hilda pray'd;
Themselves within their sacred bound
Their stony folds had often found."

This superstition prevailed till a recent period. Mr. Sowerby mentions that a dealer was requested by his customers to supply them with some of the creatures which had escaped decapitation; and being anxious to gratify his patrons by providing them with snakes with their heads on, he contrived, with the aid of plaster of Paris, to produce the entire animal. In fact, he drove a brisk trade in the restored specimens, until some remorseless geologist, on visiting the place, beheaded the luckless reptiles with his hammer, and reduced them to their original condition of ammonite shells. In the same poem, Sir Walter celebrates the beads of St. Cuthbert, the fragments of the stems of crinoidea, or stone lilies, common in the older deposits, and which, being hollow, were frequently strung together, and used as rosaries in former times. The remains of the elephant and mastodon, in superficial deposits, have, in like manner, been invested with superstitious fancies, and assigned to giants of a remote age. Sir Roderick Murchison relates, that when travelling along the eastern flanks of the Ural mountains, it was his lot to visit many accumulations of gold alluvia, in which bones of the mammoth and other extinct quadrupeds were found. For these remains the poor Bashkirs, the original inhabitants of the tract, preserved so deep a veneration that, in freely permitting the search after the true wealth of their country, which they were incapable of extracting, their sole appeal to the Russian miners was—" Take from us our gold, but, for God's sake, leave us our ancestors!"

SIR HUMPHRY DAVY.

When Davy was in Sicily he was studying geology, and the rap and clatter of his hammer among the rocks astonished the Catanian peasants, who accounted him mad. They told their priest of the danger from the maniac, but Davy had seen the priest before them ; his reverence quietly intimated to the peasants that it was a foreign gentleman from a far-off land, who was practising a penance ! Davy was then regarded by the Catanians as a saint.

DR. HUTTON.

When the founder of the Huttonian theory first observed in Glentilt veins of red granite traversing the black micaceous schist, he uttered a shout of exultation, which his guides ascribed to nothing less important than the discovery of a vein of gold or silver.

CUVIER.

When the Count de Seze replied to an eloquent discourse of Cuvier, he stated that, since the Restoration, Cuvier was the second example of fortunate combination of literature and science, and that he had been preceded only by that illustrious geometer (the Marquis de Laplace), whom we may call " the *Newton* of France." In referring to the European reputation of Cuvier, and to the vast extent and variety of his knowledge, he applied to him the happy observation which Fontenelle made respecting Leibnitz—that while the ancients made one Hercules out of several, we might out of one Cuvier make several philosophers.

CHILDHOOD OF CUVIER.

Cuvier, like Sir Isaac Newton, was born with such a feeble and sickly constitution, that he was scarcely expected to reach the years of manhood. His affectionate mother watched over his varying health, instilled into his mind the first lessons of religion, and had taught him to read fluently before he had completed his fourth year. She made him repeat to her his Latin lessons, though ignorant herself of the language; she conducted him every morning to school ; made him practise drawing under her own superintendence, and supplied him with the best works on history and literature. His father had destined him for the army. In the library of the Gymnasium, where he stood at the head of the classes of history, geography, and mathematics, he lighted upon a copy of Gesner's *History of Animals and Serpents*, with coloured plates ; and, about the same time, he had discovered a complete copy of Buffon among the books of one of his relatives. His taste for natural history now became a passion. He copied the figures which these works contained, and coloured them in conformity with the descriptions; whilst he did not overlook the intellectual beauties of his author.

In the fourteenth year of his age he was appointed president of a society of his school-fellows, which he was the means of organizing, and of which he drew up the rules; and seated on the foot of his bed, which was the president's chair, he first showed his oratorical powers in the discussion of various questions, suggested by the reading of books of natural history and travels, which was the principal object of the society.

When at the age of nineteen, the casual dissection of a colmar, a species of cuttle-fish, induced Cuvier to study the anatomy of the mollusca; and the examination of some fossil terebratulæ, which had been dug up near Fécamp, in June, 1791, suggested to him the idea of comparing fossil with living animals; and thus, as he himself said, "the germ of his two most important labours—the comparison of fossil with living species, and the reform of the classification of the animal kingdom—had their origin at this epoch."

CUVIER'S RECONSTRUCTION OF ORGANIC REMAINS.

This philosopher achieved his greatest discoveries by following the guidance of the principle of design in the structure of animal bodies. The following singularly interesting account, by himself, of the application of this principle to the reconstruction of the fossil remains of extinct animals, is without a parallel in the history of science:—
"When the sight of some bones of the bear and the elephant, twelve years ago, inspired me with the idea of applying the general laws of comparative anatomy to the reconstruction and the discovery of fossil species—when I began to perceive that these species were not perfectly represented by those of our day which resembled them the most, I did not suspect that I was every day treading upon a soil filled with remains more extraordinary than any that I had yet seen; nor that I was destined to bring to light whole genera of animals unknown to the present world, and buried for (incalculable) ages at vast depths under the earth. It was to M. Veurin that I owed the first indications of these bones furnished by our quarries. Some fragments which he brought me one day having struck me with astonishment, I made inquiries respecting the persons to whom this industrious collector had sent any formerly. What I saw in these collections served to excite my hopes and increase my curiosity. Causing search to be made at that time for such bones in all the quarries, and offering rewards, to arouse the attention of the workmen, I collected a greater number than any person who had preceded me. After some years, I was sufficiently rich in materials to have nothing further to desire; but it was otherwise with respect to their arrangement and the construction of the skeletons, which alone could conduct me to a just knowledge of the species. From the first moment, I perceived that there were many different species in our quarries, and soon afterwards that they belonged to various genera, and that the species of the different genera were often of the same size; so that the size alone rather confused than assisted my arrangement. I was in the situation of a man who had given to him, pêle mêle, the mutilated and incomplete fragments of a hundred skeletons, belonging to twenty sorts of animals; and it was required that each bone should be joined to that which it belonged to. It was a resurrection in miniature; but the immutable laws prescribed to living beings were my directors. At the voice of comparative anatomy,

each bone, each fragment, regained its place. I have no expressions to describe the pleasure experienced in perceiving that, as I discovered one character, all the consequences, more or less foreseen of this character, were successively developed. The feet were conformable to what the teeth had announced, and the teeth to the feet; the bones of the legs and the thighs, and everything that ought to unite these parts, were conformable to each other. In one word, each of the species sprung up from one of its elements. Those," he adds, "who will have the patience to follow me in these memoirs, may form some idea of the sensations which I experienced in thus restoring, by degrees, those ancient monuments of mighty revolutions."

INVENTIONS AND DISCOVERIES.

INDUCTIVE PHILOSOPHY—ROGER BACON ITS FOUNDER.

Roger Bacon was the true founder of the inductive philosophy. He taught the scientific world, that truth could not be obtained without experiment and observation, and that no reasonings, however ingenious, and no arguments, however sound, could of themselves satisfy a mind anxiously seeking for what is true. Nearly two centuries afterwards, Leonardo da Vinci taught and practised the same truth. It sprung up, heaven-born, in the minds of Copernicus, Galileo, Tycho, Pascal, Huygens, and Gilbert; and Sir Isaac Newton may be considered as having carried to perfection the true method of investigating truth by observation and experiment. The great doctrine, thus innate in some minds, was taught with peculiar eloquence and success by Lord Bacon.—(Sir D. Brewster.)

THE DAVY LAMP.

Sir H. Davy spoke of the desire for knowledge being powerfully enhanced, when that knowledge is felt to be practical power, and when that power may be applied to lessen the miseries or increase the comforts of our fellow-creatures. It was in this spirit that he prosecuted the discovery of the safety-lamp.

In August, 1815, his attention was first particularly directed to the subject of fire-damp. He was then in the Highlands of Scotland on a shooting excursion. On his way back he stopped at Newcastle, and made minute inquiries into the circumstances of the mines in connection with the destructive agent. At his request, specimens of fire-damp were forwarded to him in London. He then entered, in his laboratory, on the experimental investigation. On the 9th of November, the results of his inquiry were read to the Royal Society, and the principle of the safety-lamp was announced; and the lamp itself was perfected in December.

For this great service done to science and humanity, Sir Humphry received votes of thanks from the entire coal trade in the north of England, together with a service of plate valued at £2500. The late Emperor Alexander of Russia sent him a silver-gilt vase, and the honour of a baronetcy was conferred upon the chemist by his own Sovereign. When urged by his friends, including Mr. Buddle, to take out a patent for his discovery, "No, my good friend," he said to that gentleman, "I never thought of such a thing; my sole object was to serve the cause of humanity, and if I have succeeded, I am amply rewarded in the gratifying reflection of having done so. More wealth," he added, "could not increase either my fame or my happiness."

ROMANCE OF THE ELECTRIC TELEGRAPH.

A newspaper paragraph relates, that a Liverpool citizen, touring in Holland, suddenly found himself in want of £100; instead of writing from Amsterdam to Liverpool and waiting the return of post, an operation of five or six days, he walks into the telegraph office and sends a few words by lightning to state his need. This was at twelve o'clock. A turn or two on the quays, round the square of the Palace, would bring him to the hour of dinner. Six o'clock found him at his wine. A tap at the door, a stranger is introduced:—" Have I the honour to address M. ——?"—" Yes."—" Our London correspondent desires us to place in your hands a cheque for £100."—The *Athenæum* relates an anecdote which has a different interest. The scene is the Prague railway-station in Vienna; the time, six in the morning, on the arrival of the great train from Dresden, Prague, and Brunn. An Englishman, who has lost his passport, is on his way to a guard-house, conducted by a Croat soldier, on suspicion of being a refugee and a conspirator. He has about him letters to various persons in Hungary and in Italy, chiefly patriots—and, knowing the Austrians, he is altogether conscious that his case is bad. Arrived at the guard-house, he is asked to tell the story of his life, those of the lives of his father, mother, friends, and acquaintances. He is cross-questioned, doubted, threatened. Of course, he lets them know that he is a free-born Briton, and he plainly hints that they had better mind what they are about. His words are disbelieved, and put down as evidence against him. He is without a passport, and every man without a passport is a vagabond. A thought strikes him:—when he entered Austria at Bodenbach, he remembers that he was detained a couple of hours while the police looked into his passport and copied it into their books. That entry must still be there. He appeals to it, and suggests an inquiry by telegraph if his story be not true. The Croats, with their long guns and baker-boy faces, stare in bewilderment: they were probably thinking of the glacis and a short range. But the official could not refuse the appeal, especially as the prisoner offered to pay the expenses of the inquiry. Away flashed the lightning along the plains of Moravia, by the Moldau and the Elbe, through the mountains of Bohemia to the heart of the Saxon Switzerland; the book was opened, the story found, and the reply sent back. By ten o'clock the answer was at the gates of Vienna, the Croats gave up their spoil, and in less than an hour afterwards the tourist was enjoying a Viennese breakfast at the Herz-Erzhog Karl. In such anecdotes we see how science has tended to lengthen life by superseding the necessity for intervals of waste, and assisted to disarm the despotisms of the world, by atoning for accidents and offering a ready means for innocence to vindicate itself—as it does, in other cases, for the circumventing and overtaking of guilt.

ELECTRO-TELEGRAPHIC STORM.

M. Breguet, in a letter to M. Arago, records the following remarkable instance of the electric telegraph being interrupted by atmospheric electricity:—

It appears that one afternoon, at five o'clock, during a heavy fall of rain, the bells of the electric telegraph, placed in a small shed at one end of the St. Germain's Atmospheric Railway, began to ring, which led the attendant to suppose that he was about to receive a communication. Several letters then made their appearance; but finding they conveyed no meaning, he was about to make the signal "Not understood," when suddenly he heard an explosion, similar to a loud pistol-shot, and at the same time a vivid flash of light was seen to run along the conductors placed against the sides of the shed. The conductors were broken into fragments, which were so hot as to scorch the wooden tables on which they fell, and their edges presented evident traces of fusion. The wires of several electro-magnets, belonging to the apparatus placed in the shed, were also broken; and at the same instant the attendant experienced a violent concussion, which shook his whole frame. The shed is placed in connection with the Paris station by wires supported on posts; yet at Paris nothing was broken, nothing remarkable occurred, except that several of the bells were heard to ring. But at a short distance from the shed, the top of one of the posts which support the wire was split; and where the wires were bent from a vertical into a horizontal direction at the corners of the angles, three branches (*aigrettes*) of light were observed several seconds after the explosion.

At the time of the explosion, an attendant, who was holding a handle which moves a needle at a short distance from the extremity of the railway, sustained all over the body a violent concussion; and several workmen, standing about him, also experienced severe shocks.

In M. Breguet's opinion, the explosion came from the railway; for, on account of the immense quantity of metal employed in its construction, and the extent of its surface, it is very probable that, during a thunder-storm, it may be the seat of an intense electric tension; and that the fluid thus attracted may discharge itself on the telegraphic wires, which are near the iron rails, tubes, needles, &c.

COMIC ELECTRIC TELEGRAPH.

Mr. G. S. Richmond has made a plaything of the lightning, by inventing a "comic electric telegraph and key-board, which consists of a mahogany case, having in front a comic face, and three signs concealed by shutters, the features of the face and the shutters being capable of simultaneous motion by an electric current, which also rings a bell placed inside." This instrument was shown in the Great Exhibition.

IDEA OF THE ELECTRIC TELEGRAPH.

Akenside, in the *Pleasures of Imagination*, compares the tendency of ideas to suggest each other, to the mutual influence of two sympathetic needles, which Strada, in one of his Prolusions, availing himself of a supposed fact, which was then believed, makes the subject of verses, supposed to be recited by Cardinal Bembo, in the character of Lucretius. The needles were fabled to have been magnetized together, and suspended over different circles, so as to be capable of moving along an alphabet. In these circumstances, by the remaining influence of their original kindred magnetism, they were supposed, at whatever distance, to follow each other's motions, and pause accordingly at the same point; so that, by watching them at concerted hours, the friends who possessed this happy telegraph, were supposed to be able to communicate to each other their feelings, with the same accuracy and confidence as when they were together.

The above description, which is literally realized in the wonderful discovery of the electric telegraph, introduces, in Dr. Thomas Brown's *Philosophy of the Human Mind*, the passage referred to in Akenside's poem, of which the following are the lines alluding to Strada's fanciful idea of the sympathetic needles:—

"For when the different images of things
By chance combined, have struck the attentive soul
With deeper impulse, or, connected long,
Have drawn her frequent eye; howe'er distinct
The external scenes, yet oft the ideas gain
From that conjunction an eternal tie
And sympathy unbroken. Let the mind
Recal one partner of the various league,
Immediate, lo! the firm confederates rise.
'Twas thus, if ancient fame the truth unfold,
Two faithful needles, from the informing touch
Of the same parent-stone, together drew
Its mystic virtue, and at first conspired
With fatal impulse quivering to the pole.
Then, though disjoined by kingdoms—though the main
Rolled its broad surge betwixt—and different stars
Beheld their wakeful motions—yet preserved
The former friendship, and remembered still
The alliance of their birth. Whate'er the line
Which one possessed, nor pause nor quiet knew
The sure associate, ere, with trembling speed,
He found its path, and fixed unerring there."

Addison, in one of his elegant papers in the *Spectator*, also refers to Strada's fancy, and in a playful strain observes—"If ever this invention should be revived, or put in practice, I would propose that upon the lovers dial-plate there should be written, not only the twenty-four letters, but several entire words which have always a place in passionate epistles; as, flames, darts, die, language, absence, Cupid, heart, eyes, hang, drown,—and the like. This would very much abridge the lover's pains in this way of writing a letter, as it would enable him to express the most useful and significant words with a single turn of the needle."

ORIGIN OF THE TELEGRAPH.

Upwards of sixty years ago (or, in 1787–89), when Arthur Young was travelling in France, he met with a Monsieur Lomond, "a very ingenious and inventing mechanic," who had made a remarkable discovery in electricity. "You write two or three words on a paper," says Young: "he takes it with him into a room, and turns a machine inclosed in a cylindrical case at the top of which is an electrometer, a small, fine, pith ball; a wire connects with a similar cylinder and electrometer in a distant apartment; and his wife, by remarking the corresponding motions of the ball, writes down the words they indicate; from which it appears that he has formed an alphabet of motions. As the length of the wire makes no difference in the effect, a correspondence might be carried on at any distance. Whatever the use may be, the invention is beautiful."

The possibility of applying electricity to telegraphic communication was conceived by several other persons, long before it was attempted upon a practical scale. The Rev. Mr. Gamble, in his description of his original shutter-telegraph, published towards the close of the last century, alludes to a project of electrical communication. Mr. Francis Ronalds, in a pamphlet on this subject, published in 1823, states that Cavallo proposed to convey intelligence by passing given numbers of sparks through an insulated wire; and that, in 1816, he himself made experiments upon this principle, which he deemed more promising than the application of galvanic or voltaic electricity, which had been projected by some Germans and Americans. He succeeded perfectly in transmitting signals through a length of eight miles of insulated wire; and he describes minutely the contrivances necessary for adapting the principle to telegraphic communication.

It is, however, to the joint labours of Messrs. W. F. Cooke and Professor Wheatstone, that electric telegraphs owe their practical application; and, in a statement of the facts respecting their relative positions in connection with the invention, drawn up at their request by Sir M. I. Brunel and Professor Daniell, it is observed that "Mr. Cooke is entitled to stand alone, as the gentleman to whom this country is indebted for having practically introduced and carried out the electric telegraph as a useful undertaking, promising to be a work of national importance; and Professor Wheatstone is acknowledged as the scientific man whose profound and successful researches had already prepared the public to receive it as a project capable of practical application."—(Penny Cyclopædia.)

LESS THAN NO TIME.

By the electric telegraph on the Great Western Railway has been accomplished the apparent paradox of sending a message in 1845, and receiving it in 1844! Thus, a few seconds after the clock had struck twelve, on the night of the 31st of December, the superintendent at Paddington signalled his brother officer at Slough, that he wished him a happy New Year. An answer was instantly returned, suggesting that the wish was premature, as the year had not yet arrived at Slough! The fact is—the difference of longitude makes the point of midnight at Slough a little *after* that at Paddington; so that a given instant, which was after midnight at one station, was before midnight at the other. Or, the wonder may be more readily understood, when it is recollected that the motion of electricity is far more rapid than the diurnal motion of the earth.

We hear of similar feats in the United States. Thus, a letter from Indiana says, "That wonderful invention, the magnetic telegraph, passes through our country from the eastern cities, communicating intelligence almost instantaneously. News has been transmitted from Philadelphia to Cincinnati, a distance of 750 miles, on one unbroken chain of wires. Of course, as Cincinnati is 13 degrees west of Philadelphia, or 40 minutes of time later, the news is that much a-head of the time."—(London Anecdotes.)

TELEGRAPHIC REPORTING IN AMERICA.

The *Pittsburgh Chronicle* gives the following striking instance of the use of the electric telegraph on the other side of the Atlantic, and of enterprise on the part of a publisher. A speech by Mr. Clay was much looked for. It was delivered in Lexington on a Saturday, and the proprietor of the *New York Herald* determined on beating his contemporaries. Express riders were ready, and in less than five hours his report of the speech (a full one) was in Cincinnati. Notifications had been sent along the line of telegraph to "look out;" and at four o'clock on Sunday morning, the publisher of the *Herald* received in New York a copy of the speech,—the distance being more than 1100 miles! This was done during a heavy rain, and while a thunder-shower was passing over a portion of both the eastern and western lines. At Cincinnati, where it was to be copied in passing, the telegraph suddenly ceased working, to the dismay of the superintendent. Being short of proper hands, he mounted a horse, and followed the line, through the pelting storm, until he found a break, caused by the falling of a tree, beyond Turtle Creek, a distance of twenty-one miles. He finished mending it at dark, and then returned to the city, and in the temporary absence of other competent operators, received the speech and sent it to New York, finishing it at four o'clock in the morning.

The first message of Governor Young to the New York Legislature was commenced reading in the House of Assembly at Albany, on Tuesday (Jan. 5, 1847), at 18 minutes before 12, New York time, and was transmitted to New York by the New York, Albany, and Buffalo Telegraph Company, and the entire document complete was placed in possession of the editors of that city at three o'clock p.m. The message contained 5000 words, or 25,000 letters, and was written from two instruments in the Albany office, by Messrs. Carter, Buel, and Johnson, and read in the New York office by the Messrs. Woods, at the rate of 83 letters per minute, or two and a-half hours for each instrument. Professor Morse's original estimate to Congress for the despatch with which communications could be sent by his telegraph, was thirty letters per minute. Here we see the number almost trebled in a long public document.

THE LIGHTNING STEED.

The following versified pedigree is from the *Boston Chronotype*:—

" That steed called 'Lightning,' (say the Fates,)
Is owned in the United States.
'Twas Franklin's hand that caught the horse ;
'Twas harnessed by Professor Morse!"

PARLIAMENTARY ELECTRIC TELEGRAPH.

Both Houses of Parliament have a telegraph of their own, communicating with the offices of clerks, cloisters, and committee-rooms. As a specimen of the information conveyed from the House, we have the following :—" Committee has permission to sit until five o'clock ;" and among the questions sent down from the committee are the following :—"What is before the House ?" "Who is speaking ?" " How long before the House divides ?" This will supersede the old form of ringing a bell, and the startling and stentorian announcements by the messengers to wearied wights in committee, of ".The Speaker's at prayers!" There will be no complaints for the future in the newspapers, by members indulging after dinner at Bellamy's, of being "barred out" of a division. A "call" of the House may be known in a twinkling of time throughout the country. His constituents may know in a moment when the Hon. Mr. —— is "up," when the "perpetual motion member" is *in pendulo.*

Accommodation has been afforded to an agent of the Electric Telegraph Company in the reporters' gallery; and his business will be that of communicating the results or the progress of debates and divisions up to the rising of the House.— (London Anecdotes.)

MARRIAGE BY TELEGRAPH.

The American journals report a story, which, if true, throws into the shade all the feats that have been performed by our British telegraph. It appears that a daughter of one of the wealthiest merchants in Boston had formed an attachment for a handsome young man, who was a clerk in her father's counting-house; and she determined to marry him, although her father had previously promised her in marriage to another suitor. The father having heard of the attachment; feigned ignorance of it, but determined to cause it to be broken off. For this purpose he directed the young man to proceed to England by steamer, upon business; and the lover accordingly arrived, *en route*, in New York. In the meantime, the young lady had gained some knowledge of her father's intentions, and sent a message to that effect to her lover in New York, by the following expedient: —She took her place in the telegraphic office in Boston, and he did the same, with a magistrate, in the office in New York; and the exchange of consent being given by the electric flash, they were thus married by telegraph! Shortly after, the lady's father insisted upon her marriage with the gentleman he had selected for her; and judge of his amazement when she told him she was already the wife of Mr. B., then on his way to England; adding an explanation of the novel way in which the ceremony was performed. The merchant threatened to protest against the validity of the marriage, but did not carry his threat into execution.

VELOCITY OF ELECTRICITY.

One of our most profound electricians is reported to have exclaimed, "Give me but an unlimited length of wire, with a small battery, and I will girdle the universe with a sentence in forty minutes." Yet this is no vain boast; for so rapid is the transition of the electric current along the lines of the telegraph wire, that, supposing it were possible to carry the wires eight times round the earth, it would but occupy *one second of time*.

The immense velocity of electricity makes it impossible to calculate it by direct observation; it would require to be many thousands of leagues long before the result could be expressed in the fractions of a second. Yet, Professor Wheatstone has devised some apparatus for this purpose, among which is a double metallic mirror, to which he has given a velocity of eight hundred revolutions in a second of time.

The Professor concludes, from his experiments with this apparatus, that the velocity of electricity through a copper wire, one-fifteenth of an inch thick, exceeds the velocity of light across the planetary spaces; that it is at least 288,000 miles per second! The Professor adds, that the light of electricity, in a state of great intensity, does not last the millionth part of a second; but that the eye is capable of distinctly perceiving objects which present themselves for this short space of time.

A TELEGRAPHIC BLUNDER.

During the revolutionary excitement in 1848, it was reported in the papers that the King of Prussia had abdicated. The mistake originated with the electric telegraph, which sent the following despatch: —" The—King—of—Prussia—has —gone—to—Pot—" In another minute, the communication was on its way to a newspaper office. Not long after, however, the dial was again agitated, and then " s—dam." Making it read thus—"The King of Prussia has gone to Potsdam."

STORM IN A TELEGRAPH OFFICE.

Recently, at Buffalo, United States, a driving snow-storm came on from the north-east, accompanied by vivid flashes of lightning and heavy peals of thunder. The atmosphere, and all objects upon which the eye rested, and especially the falling snow, put on a sallow, sickly hue; and this was rendered occasionally more singular by the repeated flashes of electricity, which worked wonders in the Telegraph-office. The battery-room was for some time lit up by one constant sheet of electric flame that played around its walls. It was a thrilling scene, and one calculated to fill the mind of the observer with serious apprehension: it proved, however, harmless in its consequences. A very strong current was attracted to the writing instrument of the Lockport line, by the large iron wire used. The power was so great, that it became necessary to detach the wire, in order to prevent the instrument from melting. One of the most intense flashes of electricity took effect upon one of the operators, by removing him, almost instantaneously, from his seat at the machine.

THE ELECTRIC SPARK.

Faraday was the first to elicit the electric spark from the magnet: he found that it is visible at the instants of breaking and of renewing the contact of the conducting wires, and only then:—

Around the Magnet Faraday
Is sure that Volta's lightnings play;
But *how* to draw them from the wire?
He took a lesson from the heart:
'Tis when we meet, 'tis when we part,
Breaks forth the electric fire.
Blackwood's Magazine.

It has been established, that Faraday obtained a spark from a temporary or electro-magnet, as far back as November, 1831.

SIR HARRY SMITH AND THE CAFFRES.

In the course of the pacification conference of Sir Harry Smith (governor of the Cape of Good Hope) with the Caffres, at King William's Town, a voltaic battery was fired on the opposite slope, about a quarter of a mile distant. Here a waggon had been placed at 300 yards' distance from the battery, communicating in the usual manner by means of wires. The object of His Excellency was to convey to the Caffre mind an idea of sudden and irresistible power. Accordingly, on a given signal from him—the waving of a small flag—the discharge instantly took place. The explosion shattered the carriage of the waggon, canting up the body of the vehicle, so that it remained fixed by one end on the ground, at an angle of forty-five degrees. The action was so sudden, as scarcely to afford time to his Excellency to direct the attention of the Caffres to the experiment; but, in those who were looking towards the spot, and saw the power exercised on a distant object, the surprise manifested was amusing. "There," exclaimed Sir Harry Smith, "is a lesson to you not to meddle with waggons; as you now see the power I possess, should you do so, to punish you."

FOURDRINIER'S PAPER-MAKING MACHINERY.

On April 25, 1839, some very interesting details of Fourdrinier's machinery for making paper of endless length, were elicited during a debate in the House of Commons, upon the presentation of a petition from these ingenious manufacturers. It appears that 1000 yards, or any given quantity of yards of paper, could be continuously made by it. Many years since, the invention was patented; but, owing to a mistake in the patent—the word "machine" being written instead of "machines"—the property was pirated, and that led to litigations, in which the patentees' funds were exhausted before they could establish their rights. They then became bankrupts, and thus all the fruits of their invention, on which they had spent £40,000, were entirely lost to them.

The evidence of Mr. Brunel, and of Mr. Lawson, the printer of the *Times*, proved the invention of the Fourdriniers to be one of the most splendid discoveries of the age. Mr. Lawson stated that the conductors of the metropolitan newspapers could never have presented to the world such an immense mass of news and advertisements as was now contained in them, had not this invention enabled them to make use of any size required. By the revolution of the great cylinder employed in the process, an extraordinary degree both of rapidity and convenience in the production is secured. One of its chief advantages is the prevention of all risk of combination among the workmen, the machine being so easily managed that the least skilful person can attend to it. It was added, that the invention had caused a remarkable increase in the revenue: in the year 1800, when this machine was not in existence, the amount of the paper duty was £195,641; in 1821, when the machinery was in full operation, the amount of duty was £579,867; in 1835, it was £833,822. No doubt, part of this increase must be set down to other causes; still, it was impossible, but for this discovery, that such a quantity of paper could have been made and consumed. The positive saving to the country effected by it has not been less than £8,000,000; the increase in the revenue not less than £500,000 a-year. At length, in May, 1840, the sum of £7000 was voted by Parliament to Messrs. Fourdrinier, as some compensation for their loss by the defective state of the patent law.

In 1839, there was made by this machinery at Colinton, a single sheet of paper weighing 533 lbs., and measuring upwards of a mile and a half in length, the breadth being only 50 inches. Were a ream of paper of similar sheets made, it would weigh 266,500 lbs. or upwards of 123 tons.—(London Anecdotes.)

ARCHIMEDES AND THE LEVER.

Archimedes said, "Give me a lever long enough, and a prop strong enough, and with my own weight I will move the world." "But," says Dr. Arnott, " he would have required to move with the velocity of a cannon-ball for millions of years, to alter the position of the earth a small part of an inch. This feat of Archimedes is, in mathematical truth, performed by every man who leaps from the ground; for he kicks the world away from him whenever he rises, and attracts it again when he falls."

THE DRUMMOND LIGHT.

The importance of simplicity in inventions for popular use, has been shown in the late Lieutenant Drummond's apparatus for illuminating lighthouses with his oxyhydrogen light; that is, a stream of oxygen and another of hydrogen, directed upon a ball of lime. Experimentally, the light has succeeded beyond the expectation of the inventor; but the machinery or apparatus remains to be simplified before it can be worked by the keepers of lighthouses. The light is seen at a distance of 60 miles.

MYTHOLOGY OF SCIENCE.

M. Arago, in his brilliant *eloge* on Fourier, observes:—"The ancients had a taste, or rather a passion, for the marvellous, which made them forget the sacred ties of gratitude. Look at them, for instance, collecting into one single group the high deeds of a great number of heroes, whose names they have not even deigned to preserve, and attributing them all to Hercules. The lapse of centuries has not made us wiser. The public in our time also delight in mingling fiction with history. In all careers, particularly in that of the sciences, there is a design to create Herculeses. According to the vulgar opinion, every astronomical discovery is attributable to Herschel. The theory of the motions of the planets is identified with the name of Laplace, and scarcely any credit is allowed to the important labours of D'Alembert, Clairaut, Euler, and Lagrange. Watt is the sole inventor of the steam-engine, whilst Chaptal has enriched the chemical arts with all those ingenious and productive processes which secure their prosperity." To countervail this error, Arago continues: "Let us hold up to legitimate admiration those chosen men whom nature has endowed with the valuable faculty of grouping together isolated facts, and deducing beautiful theories from them; but do not let us forget that the sickle of the reaper must cut down the stalks of corn, before any one can think of collecting them into sheaves."

A DESCENT IN A DIVING-BELL.

Sir George Head, in his humorous *Home Tour*, gives an amusing picture of a pair of operative divers whom he saw in the Hull docks. Sir George was passing as the workmen were raising the diving-bell, when he stepped into the lighter to observe the state of the labourers on their return from below. He had a remarkably good view of their features, at a time when they had no reason to expect any one was looking at them; for, as the bell was raised very slowly, he had an opportunity of seeing within it, by stooping, the moment its side was above the gunwale of the lighter. But, Sir George shall relate what he saw:—

"A pair of easy-going, careless fellows, each with a red night-cap on his head, sat opposite one another, by no means over-heated or exhausted, and apparently with no other want in the world than that of 'summut to drink;' they had been under water exactly two hours. I asked them what were their sensations on going down? They said that, before a man was used to it, it produced a feeling as if the ears were bursting; that, on the bell first dipping, they were in the habit of holding their noses; at the same time of breathing as gently as possible, and that thus they prevented any disagreeable effect: they added, the air below was hot, and made a man thirsty; —the latter observation, though in duty bound I received as a hint, I believe to be true; nevertheless, the service cannot be formidable, as the extra pay is only one shilling per day. Had there been anything extraordinary to see below, I should have asked permission to go down; but the water was by no means clear, and the muddy bottom of the docks was not a sufficient recompense for the disagreeable sensation. Two men descend at a time, and four pump the air into the bell through the leathern hose; the bell is nearly a square, or rather an oblong vessel of cast-iron, with ten bull's-eye lights at the top, which lights are fortified within by a lattice of strong iron wire, sufficient to resist an accidental blow of a crowbar, or other casualty. * * Notwithstanding the great improvements made in diving-bells since their invention, after all precautions, a man in a diving-bell is, certainly, in a state of awful dependence upon human aid: in case of the slightest accident to the air-pump, or even a single stitch of the leathern hose giving way, long before the ponderous vessel could be raised to the surface, life must be extinct."

"WET THE ROPES."

The property of cords contracting their length by moisture became generally known, it is said, on the raising of the Egyptian obelisk in the square facing St. Peter's, at Rome, by order of Pope Sixtus V. The great work was undertaken in the year 1586, and the day for raising the obelisk was marked with great solemnity. High mass was celebrated at St. Peter's, and the architect and workmen received the benediction of the Pope. The blast of a trumpet was the given signal, when engines were set in motion by an incredible number of horses; but not until after fifty-two unsuccessful attempts had been made was the huge block lifted from the earth. As the ropes which held it had somewhat stretched, the base of the obelisk could not reach the summit of the pedestal, when a man in the crowd cried out, "*Wet the ropes!*" This advice was followed, and the column, as of itself, gradually rose to the required height, and was placed upright on the pedestal prepared for it.

THE RAILWAY SYSTEM—COAL, STEAM, AND IRON.

Coal, steam, and iron, are the threefold power which has created the vast system of railways. It has, chiefly in England and Scotland, and betwixt the years 1843 and 1849, increased the number of miles of railway previously constructed from 1857 to 5000 miles; and the year 1848 conveyed from one part of the kingdom to another 57,965,000 passengers, and expended on these works the enormous sum of £200,000,000, double the amount being required in order to complete the existing and the contemplated lines. Miss Martineau, after travelling in the East, and seeing the Pyramids of Egypt, in the account of her journey, expressed regret that the art by which the stones of these immense structures were elevated is lost. An engineer, in reference to this regret, sent a letter to the *Times*, stating, in effect, that he, or any engineer of the day, would have no objection to undertake the erection of a pyramid equal to the largest and the loftiest in Egypt. To show that this is no idle boast, the following facts may be mentioned:—According to ancient authors, betwixt 100,000 and 300,000 men were engaged for twenty years in building the great Pyramid of Egypt, at an expenditure of labour which has been estimated as equal to lifting fifteen thousand seven hundred and thirty-three millions (15,733,000,000) of cubic feet of stone one foot high. From a computation by M. Dupin, it appears that the steam-engines of England would equal the whole product of this immense application of human labour, in lifting stones, within the short space of eighteen hours. In the construction of the *southern* division of the London and North Western Railway, the labour, as estimated in the same manner, is twenty-five thousand millions (25,000,000,000) of cubic feet of similar material lifted to the same height, being 9,267,000,000 (nine thousand two hundred and sixty-seven millions) *more* than was lifted for the Pyramids, and yet the English work was performed by about 20,000 men, in less than five years. According to another calculation, illustrating the enormous extent of these works, called into existence by the united influence of iron coal, and steam, in making the division of railway just referred to, and which is 112 miles in length, as much earth was removed as would form a footpath a foot high and a yard broad, round the whole circumference of the earth;—the cost of this division of the railway in penny pieces, being sufficient to form a copper kerb or edge to it.—When the train has been connected, consisting of passenger-carriages, luggage-vans, horse-boxes, carriage-trucks, and, as on the leading English lines, a travelling post-office—the locomotive engine is moved to the front. This is the steam-horse, which has drunk a thousand gallons of cold water to prepare him for his journey, and taken in provender to the extent of one ton of fuel. The engine-driver takes his place, and opens a valve, the steam enters and commences its work, the engine works, the train follows, and in a brief space, at the rate of forty, fifty, and even sixty miles an hour, it rushes through tunnels which have been cut for miles in the solid rock, along embankments which have been piled up in the valleys, over morasses whose profoundest depths have been fathomed and piled, through cuttings on the sides of mountains, along precipices with the ocean lashing their bases —across viaducts, over rivers and ravines, crossing arms of the sea by means of tubular bridges of iron. "While the train is almost on the wing," observes Sir F. B. Head, "beating the eagle in its flight, the passengers are reclining in their easy-chairs, thinking or sleeping, reading or writing, as if they were in their own happy homes—safer, indeed, than there, for thieves cannot rob them by day, nor burglars alarm them by night. The steam-horse starts neither at the roar of the thunderstorm, nor the flash of its fire. Draughts of a purer air expel the marsh poison from its seat before it has begun the work of death, and, surrounded by conductors, the delicate and timid traveller looks without dismay on the forked messengers of destruction, twisting the spire, or rending the oak, or raging above the fear-stricken dwellings of man."

The Atlantic is now crossed almost every week from January to December, and the passage seldom lasts beyond twelve days; insomuch that the merchants of Liverpool on the one side, and Boston and New York on the other, calculate to an hour on the arrival of the steamer, and are seldom disappointed.

LAVOISIER'S DISCOVERIES AND FATE.

Lavoisier proved that the fixed air (carbonic acid) of Black was a compound of carbon and oxygen; that atmospheric air consisted of oxygen and nitrogen; and that oxygen was the agent in combustion and respiration, as well as in the process of oxidizing metals, and in the formation of acids (the acids formed by hydrogen being then unknown to the science). Lavoisier thus generalized the discovery of Priestley, and superseded the phlogiston theory by that of oxygen. Lavoisier's theory of combustion, if we may be allowed the metaphor, kindled the torch which has lighted succeeding chemists along the path of discovery. Lavoisier enjoyed the privilege—rarely awarded to great discoverers in science—of seeing his views speedily adopted throughout Europe. Such, also, we are reminded, was the reward of Hervey, who, after suffering years of obloquy and persecution for promulgating the doctrine of the circulation of the blood, had the satisfaction of living to witness his principles taught in all the medical schools of the civilized world. But, less fortunate than Hervey, Lavoisier was persecuted by more unrelenting men, who struck him down in the heyday of his scientific reputation and usefulness. During the French Revolution, he was thrown into prison on a charge of adulterating tobacco, factitiously brought against him as a pretext for confiscating his property. He became a victim of the guillotine in 1794—" A melancholy proof," Mr. Whewell remarks, "that in periods of political ferocity, innocence and merit, private virtues and public services, amiable manners and the love of friends, literary fame and exalted genius, are all as nothing to protect their possessor from the last extremes of violence and wrong, inflicted under judicial forms."

GUTTA PERCHA.

The tree yielding this useful substance was first observed by Mr. Lobb, while engaged in a botanical mission in Singapore, in the Eastern Archipelago; but gutta percha was first brought into general notice in 1845, by Dr. Montgomery, whose attention was attracted to it by seeing it employed by the Malays to make handles for implements. He found that the material could be advantageously substituted for caoutchouc in the construction of the parts of surgical instruments hitherto made of that substance; for which discovery the London Society of Arts awarded him its gold medal. He ascertained from the natives that the tree yielding the gutta (Malayan for *gum*) attains a height of 60 or 70 feet, and a diameter of 3 or 4 feet, that its wood is valueless as timber, but that its fruit yields a concrete oil, which is used for food. The tree is found in Singapore, Borneo, and the adjacent islands. Dr. Montgomery was assured by Mr. Brook, the Rajah of Sarawak, that in the woods of Borneo it acquires a diameter of 6 feet. Several hundred tons of gutta percha are now annually exported from Singapore; but there is reason to apprehend, from the wasteful method in which the natives collect it, that this supply must speedily be diminished, if it do not altogether cease. The largest quantity of juice yielded by a single trunk is only 20 or 30 lbs.; and the improvident Malays will rather sacrifice a tree of a hundred years' growth, for the sake of obtaining all its juice at once, than submit to the process of tapping the trunk, and allowing the gum to exude in small quantities annually. The people fell the trees, strip off the bark, and collect the milky juice in a cavity formed by the hollow stem of the plantain leaf—when, being exposed to the air, it coagulates. Dr. Oxley, who writes a description of the tree in the *Journal of the Indian Archipelago*, printed at the Mission Press of Singapore, mentions that only a short time ago the tree was tolerably abundant in the island of Singapore, but that already all the large timber has been felled, and few, if any, other than small plants are now to be found. The range of its production, however, appears to be considerable, it being found all up the Malayan peninsula as far as Penang. Numerous patents have been taken out for applications of gutta percha to the arts and sciences. Like caoutchouc it is soluble in naphtha. Hot water (above 150°) has a remarkable action upon the substance; contrary to the usual effect of heat, the gum contracts and becomes plastic, and may then be made to assume any form, which will be permanent at an ordinary temperature. This property fits it for many important purposes to which caoutchouc cannot be adapted. In surgical practice it renders gutta percha of great value. Amongst the ornamental purposes to which it has been successfully applied are casts of medals, and other objects requiring a smooth surface and sharp impression. The Gutta Percha Company alone imported between 600 and 700 tons of the material, chiefly for commercial purposes, betwixt the years 1844 and 1848. From 60 to 80 tons are said to be imported monthly. The sonorous property of gutta percha is interesting. By speaking in a voice little above a whisper, it will be heard through a tube of the substance at the distance of three-quarters of a mile.

POETICAL PREDICTION OF THE CRYSTAL PALACE.

It is a curious fact that the Crystal Palace realized the conceptions of one of the earliest poetical dreams in the language; and one would almost believe that when Chaucer, four centuries and a half ago, delineated the following scene in the "House of Fame," his pen, which, as Spenser said of it, was dipped in the "pure well of English undefiled," drew its inspiration from the prophetic as well as the poetic faculty—"the vision and the faculty divine:"—

"I dreamt I was
Within a *temple made of glass,*
In which there were more images,
Of *gold* standing in sundry stages,
In more rich tabernacles,
And with *jewels* more pinnacles,
And more curious *portraitures,*
And quaint manner of figures
Of gold work than I saw ever.
* * * *
"Then saw I stand on either side
Straight down to the doors wide
*From the dais many a pillar
Of metal* that shone out full clear.
* * * *
"Then gan I look about and see
That there came ent'ring in the hall,
A right great company withal,
*And that of sundry regions
Of all kinds of conditions,*
That dwell in earth beneath the moon,
Poor and rich.
* * * *
"*Such a great congregation
Of folks as I saw roam about,*
Some within and some without,
Was never seen or shall be more!"

THE CRYSTAL PALACE.

The Crystal Palace and the Great Exhibition will render the year 1851 for ever memorable, and perpetuate the honoured name of his Royal Highness Prince Albert as the projector of the most extensive and varied collection of the products of nature, art, and manufacturing industry ever witnessed in the world. To Sir J. Paxton belongs the honour of designing the spacious structure of glass and iron; and to Messrs. Fox and Henderson that of its erection. The general plan was that of a parallelogram, 1848 feet long, and 408 feet wide. The total area roofed over was 772,784 square feet, equal to about 19 acres; 217,100 square feet of additional area was obtained by cross galleries. There were about 200 miles of sash bars and 896,000 square feet of glass required for the roof; 700 tons of wrought iron and 3800 tons of cast iron were used in the construction of the building. The Exhibition was opened by the Queen on the 1st of May, in presence of 25,000 spectators, whilst 650,000, it was estimated, crowded the surrounding parks. The total number of visits to the Exhibition was 6,039,195, the daily average being 42,831, and the greatest number in any one day, 109,915 persons. The receipts amounted to £506,100, and the expenditure to £292,794, leaving a surplus of £213,305 to be applied to the promotion of industrial art. The value of the articles exhibited was £2,000,000. The total number of exhibitors was 13,937; of whom 7381 belonged to Great Britain and her colonies, and 6556 to foreign countries.

THE THAMES TUNNEL.

The engineer of this great work, Mr., now Sir Mark Isambard Brunel, completed his design in 1823; and amongst those who then regarded it as practicable were the late Duke of Wellington and the late Dr. Wollaston. The works were commenced in 1825, and the tunnel itself in 1826; and by March, 1827, it had advanced about one-third of the whole length. All proceeded well till May 18, when the river burst into the tunnel with such velocity and volume, as to fill it in fifteen minutes; but, although the men were at 'work, no lives were lost. The hole, thirty-eight feet deep, was closed with bags of clay and hazel-rods, the water pumped out, and the works resumed in September. On Jan. 12, 1828, the river broke in a second time, and filled the tunnel in less than ten minutes; when the rush of water brought with it a strong current of air that put out the lights; six of the workmen were lost. For some distance, Mr. Brunel, junior, struggled in total darkness, and the rush of the water carried him up the shaft. The tunnel was again cleared, and the part completed found to be sound. Hundreds of plans were proposed for its completion; the funds of the company were too low to proceed, and above £5000 was raised by public subscription.

For seven years the work was suspended; but, by advances from Government, it was resumed in 1835. On April 23, 1837, there was a third irruption of the river; a fourth on Nov. 2, 1837, with the loss of one life; and, on March 6, 1838, the fifth and last irruption took place. Thus, of the Tunnel there were completed—

In 1836 .... 117 feet.
— 1837 .... 28 „
— 1838 .... 80 „
— 1839 .... 194 „
— 1840 .... 76 „

Leaving only 60 feet to complete.

Meanwhile, the tunnel works proved a very attractive exhibition. In 1838, they were visited by 23,000 persons, and, in 1839, by 34,000. By January 1841, the tunnel was completed from shore to shore—1140 feet, and Sir I. Brunel, on August 13, was the first to pass through. On March 25, 1843, the tunnel was opened to the public, with a demonstration of triumph.

The cost of the work has been nearly four times the sum at first contemplated; the actual expense being upwards of £600,000.

WEIGHING MACHINE AT THE BANK OF ENGLAND.

The most interesting place connected with the machinery of the Bank of England is the weighing-office, which was established a few years ago. In consequence of a proclamation concerning the gold circulation, it became very desirable to obtain the most minute accuracy, as coins of different weight were plentifully offered. Many complaints were made, that sovereigns which had been issued from one office were refused at another; and though these assertions were not, perhaps, always founded on truth, yet it is indisputable that the evil occasionally occurred. Every effort was made by the directors to remedy this, some millions of sovereigns being weighed separately, and the light coins divided from those which were full weight. Fortunately, the governor for the time being (Mr. W. Cotton), before whom the complaints principally came, was attached to scientific pursuits; and he at once turned his attention to discover the causes which operated to prevent the attainment of a just weight. In this he was successful, and the result of his inquiry was a machine, remarkable for an almost elegant simplicity. About 80 or 100 light and heavy sovereigns are placed indiscriminately in a round tube; as they descend on the machinery beneath, those which are light receive a slight touch, which moves them into their proper receptacle; while those which are the legitimate weight, pass into their appointed place. The light coins are then defaced by a sovereign-cutting machine, remarkable alike for its accuracy and rapidity. By this 200 may be defaced in one minute; and, by the weighing machinery, 35,000 may be weighed in one day.

An eminent member of the Royal

Society mentioned to the writer, that, amongst scientific men, it is a question whether the weighing-machine of Mr. Cotton is not the finest thing in mechanics; and that there is only one other invention— the envelope-machine of De la Rue —to be named with it.—(Francis's History of the Bank of England.)

POETICAL PREDICTION OF RAILWAYS AND STEAMBOATS.

In Dr. Darwin's *Botanic Garden*, first published in 1789, but written, it is well-known, at least twenty years before the date of its publication, occurs the following prediction respecting steam:—

" Soon shall thy arm, unconquer'd steam, afar
Drag the slow barge, or drive the rapid car;
Or, on wide-waving wings expanded bear
The flying chariot through the fields of air,
Fair crews triumphant leaning from above,
Shall wave their fluttering 'kerchiefs as they move;
Or warrior bands alarm the gaping crowd,
And armies shrink beneath the shadowy cloud:
So mighty Hercules o'er many a clime
Waved his huge mace in virtue's cause sublime;
Unmeasured strength with early art combined,
Awed, served, protected, and amazed mankind."

FRANKLIN'S DISCOVERIES.

Of all this great man's scientific excellencies, the most remarkable is the smallness, the simplicity, the apparent inadequacy of the means which he employed in his experimental researches. His discoveries were all made with hardly any apparatus at all; and if, at any time, he had been led to employ instruments of a somewhat less ordinary description, he never rested satisfied until he had, as it were, afterwards translated the process, by resolving the problem with such simple machinery, that you might say he had done it wholly unaided by apparatus. The experiments by which the identity of lightning and electricity was demonstrated, were made with a sheet of brown paper, a bit of twine or silk thread, and an iron key!—(Lord Brougham.)

SIR ISAAC NEWTON'S MAGNET.

The smallest natural magnets generally possess the greatest proportion of attractive power. Sir Isaac Newton wore in his ring a magnet which weighed only three grains; yet it was able to take up 746 grains, or nearly 250 times its own weight — whereas magnets weighing above two pounds seldom lift more than five or six times their own weight.

GUN-COTTON AND COLLODION.

Cotton, after contributing to the manufacturing prosperity of the nation, promised a few years ago to form a very important part of its munitions of war. Professor Schönbein, of Basle, discovered that by combining cotton with nitric acid, an explosive compound was formed, capable of being substituted for gunpowder. Its power in blasting and mining, and its projectile force in fire-arms, were satisfactorily tested; but gunpowder still maintains its supremacy. Gun-cotton is remarkable for the low temperature at which it explodes. Hence, when pure, it may be burnt on the palm of the hand, without inconvenience, on the application of a moderately-heated wire. Professor Schönbein attended the meeting of the British Association for the Advancement of Science, held at Southampton, in 1846, when the operation of this new power was explained and experimented with. Subsequently, the professor attended at Osborne House, to exhibit the properties of his gun-cotton to Prince Albert, when Schönbein offered to explode a portion on the hand of Colonel B——; who would, however, have nothing to do with the novel power. Prince Albert himself submitted to the test, and off went the cotton, without smoke, stain, or burning of the skin. Thus encouraged, the colonel took his turn; but whether the material was changed or not for the coarser preparation, it gave him such a singeing that he leaped up with a cry of pain. A hearty laugh was all the commiseration he received. After this, Professor Schönbein loaded a fowling-piece with cotton in the place of powder, and the prince fired both ball and shot from it with the usual effect. Dissolved in ether, gun-cotton forms the collodion now extensively employed in photography. Collodion is also used by surgeons, as affording a ready and efficacious plaster for cuts and flesh wounds.

LAW AND LAWYERS.

LUBRICATING BUSINESS.

One day, when some one objected to the practice of having dinners for parish or public purposes, "Sir," said Lord Stowell, "I approve of the dining system: it puts people in a good humour, and makes them agree when they otherwise might not: a dinner *lubricates* business."

RELIGION AND LAW.

When Sir E. Coke was made Solicitor-General, Whitgift, the Archbishop of Canterbury, sent him a Greek Testament, with a message, that "he had studied the common law long enough, and that he ought hereafter to study the law of God."

LORD STOWELL.

Sir William Scott (Lord Stowell) was the enemy of every change; and careless, and even distrustful of all improvement. As he could imagine nothing better than the existing state of any given thing, he could see only peril and hazard in the search for anything new; and with him it was quite enough to characterize a measure as "a mere novelty," to deter him at once from entertaining it—a phrase of which Mr. Speaker Abbott, with some humour, once took advantage to say, when asked by his friend what that mass of papers might be, pointing to the huge bundle of the Acts of a single session—"Mere novelties, Sir William—mere novelties!"—(Lord Brougham.)

Sir William Scott, however, possessed much pungent wit. A celebrated physician having said, somewhat more flippantly than beseemed the gravity of his cloth, "Oh, you know, Sir William, after forty a man is always either a fool or a physician!" "Mayn't he be both, Doctor?" was the arch rejoinder, —with a most arch leer and an insinuating voice, half drawled out.

LORD ELDON.

We quote the following from Mr. Horace Twiss' *Life of Lord-Chancellor Eldon*:—

"I have seen it remarked," says Lord Eldon, in his *Anecdote Book*, "that something which in early youth captivates attention, influences future life in all stages. When I left school, in 1766, to go to Oxford, I came up from Newcastle to London in a coach, then denominated, on account of its quick travelling, as travelling was then estimated, a fly; being, as well as I remember, nevertheless, three or four days and nights on the road. There was no such velocity as to endanger overturning, or other mischief. On the panels of the carriage were painted the words, '*Sat cito, si sat bene*,'—words which made a lasting impression on my mind, and have had their influence upon my conduct in all subsequent life. Their effect was heightened by circumstances during and immediately after the journey. Upon the journey, a Quaker, who was a fellow-traveller, stopped the coach at the inn at Tuxford, desired the chambermaid to come to the coach-door, and gave her a sixpence, telling her that he forgot to give it her when he slept there two years before. I was a very saucy boy; and said to him, 'Friend, have you seen the motto on this coach?' 'No.' 'Then look at it: for I think giving her only sixpence *now* is neither *sat cito* nor *sat bene*.' After I got to town, my brother, now Lord Stowell, met me at the White Horse, in Fetter Lane, Holborn, then the great Oxford house, as I was told. He took me to see the play at Drury Lane. Love played *Jobson* in the farce, and Miss Pope played *Nell*. When we came out of the house it rained hard. There were then few hackney-coaches, and we got both into one sedan-chair. Turning out of Fleet Street into Fetter Lane, there was a sort of contest between our chairmen and some persons who were coming up Fleet Street, whether they should first pass Fleet Street, or we in our chair first get out of Fleet Street into Fetter Lane. In the struggle, the sedan-chair was overset, with us in it. This, thought I, is more than *sat cito*, and certainly it is not *sat bene*. In short, in all that I have had to do in my future life, professional and judicial, I have always felt the effect of this early admonition, on the panels of the vehicle which conveyed me from school—'*Sat cito, si sat bene.*' It was the impression of this which made me that deliberative judge—as some have said, too deliberative—and reflection upon all that is past will not authorize me to deny that, whilst I have been thinking, *sat cito, si sat bene*, I may not have sufficiently recollected whether *sat bene, si sat cito* has had its due influence."

ROMILLY'S AFFECTION.

Sir Samuel Romilly, when a child, was intrusted to a female domestic, whom he thus tenderly refers to in his *Diary*:—" The servant whom I have mentioned was to me in the place of a mother. I loved her to adoration. I remember, when quite a child, kissing, unperceived by her, the clothes which she wore; and when she once entertained a design of quitting our family, and going to live with her own relations, receiving the news as that of the greatest misfortune that could befall me, and going up into my room in an agony of affliction, and imploring God, upon my knees, to avert so terrible a calamity."

JOHNSON'S BOSWELL.

Lord Eldon relates in his *Anecdote Book*:—" At an assizes at Lancaster, we found Dr. Johnson's friend, Jemmy Boswell, lying upon the pavement—*inebriated*. We subscribed at supper a guinea for him, and half-a-crown for his clerk, and sent him, when he waked next morning, a brief, with instructions to move, for what we denominated the writ of '*Quare adhæsit pavimento*,' with observations duly calculated to induce him to think that it required great learning to explain the necessity of granting it to the judge, before whom he was to move. Boswell sent all round the town to attorneys for books, that might enable him to distinguish himself; but in vain. He moved, however, for the writ, making the best use he could of the observations in the brief. The judge was perfectly astonished, and the audience amazed. The judge said, 'I never heard of such a writ; what can it be that adheres *pavimento?* Are any of you gentlemen at the bar able to explain this?' The Bar laughed. At last, one of them said, 'My Lord, Mr. Boswell last night *adhæsit pavimento.* There was no moving him for some time. At last, he was carried to bed, and he has been dreaming about himself and the pavement.'"

PARLIAMENTARY REPRIMAND.

In the reign of George II., one Crowle, a counsel of some eminence, made some observation before an election committee, which was considered to reflect on the House itself. He was accordingly summoned to appear at their bar; and, on his knees, he received a reprimand from the Speaker. As he rose from the floor, with the utmost *nonchalance,* he took out his handkerchief, and wiping his knees, coolly observed, that "it was the dirtiest house he had ever been in in his life."

EQUIVOCAL ILLUSTRATION.

Sir Fletcher Norton was noted for his want of courtesy. When pleading before Lord Mansfield on some question of manorial right, he chanced unfortunately to say:— "My Lord, I can illustrate the point in an instance in my own person: I myself have two little manors." The judge immediately interposed, with one of his blandest smiles, "We all know it, Sir Fletcher."

LORD ERSKINE'S POINTS.

A gentleman, who has examined several of Lord Erskine's briefs, states that the notes and interlineations were few, but that particular parts were doubled down, and dashed with peculiar emphasis; his plan being to throw all his strength upon the grand features of the case, instead of frittering it away upon details.

LORD KENYON'S LAPSUS.

Lord Kenyon, on the trial of a bookseller for publishing Paine's *Age of Reason,* in his charge to the jury, enumerated many celebrated men who had been sincere Christians; and, after having enforced the example of Locke and Newton, proceeded:—"Nor, gentlemen, is this belief confined to men of comparative seclusion, since men, the greatest and most distinguished, both as philosophers and as monarchs, have enforced this belief, and shown its influence by their conduct. Above all, gentlemen, need I name to you the Emperor Julian, who was so celebrated for the practice of every Christian virtue, that he was called Julian the *Apostle!*"

A MONOMANIAC.

It is very well known that, by the laws of England, the Lord-Chancellor is held to be the guardian of the persons and property of all such individuals as are said to be no longer of sound mind and good disposing memory—in fine, to have lost their senses. Lord-Chancellor Loughborough once ordered to be brought to him a man against whom his heirs wished to take out a statute of lunacy. He examined him very attentively, and put various questions to him, to all of which he made the most pertinent and apposite answers. "This man mad!" thought he; "verily, he is one of the ablest men I ever met with." Towards the end of his examination, however, a little scrap of paper, torn from a letter, was put into Lord Loughborough's hands, on which was written "Ezekiel." This was enough for such a shrewd and able man as his lordship. He forthwith took his cue. "What fine poetry," said the Chancellor, "is in Isaiah!" "Very fine," replied the man, "especially when read in the original Hebrew." "And how well Jeremiah wrote!" "Surely," said the man. "What a genius, too, was Ezekiel!" "Do you like him?" said the man; "I'll tell you a secret—*I am Ezekiel!*"

LORD BROUGHAM'S CHANCELLORSHIP.

Lord Brougham had a great horror of hearing the almost interminable speeches which some of the junior counsel were in the habit of making, after he conceived everything had been said which could be said on the real merits of the case before the court by the gentlemen who preceded them. His hints to them to be brief on such occasions were sometimes extremely happy. Once, after listening with the greatest attention to the speeches of two counsel on one side, from ten o'clock until half-past two, a third rose to address the court on the same side. His lordship was quite unprepared for this additional infliction, and exclaimed, "What! Mr. A——, are you really going to speak on the same side?"

"Yes, my lord, I mean to trespass on your lordship's attention for a short time."

"Then," said his lordship, looking the orator significantly in the face, and giving a sudden twitch of his nose—"then, Mr. A——, you had better cut your speech as short as possible, otherwise you must not be surprised if you see me dozing; for really this is more than human nature can endure."

The young barrister took the hint: he kept closely to the point at issue—a thing very rarely done by barristers—and condensed his arguments into a reasonable compass.

NATURAL PORTRAITS.

The *Entomological Magazine* (vol. i. p. 518) states, that "on the reverse of *Hipparchia Janira* (a butterfly), may be traced a very tolerably defined profile, and some specimens, no very bad likeness, of Lord Brougham. The *Caricature Plant* in Kew Gardens has been observed to represent on its fantastically variegated leaves the same remarkable profile; and a more permanent likeness than either is pointed out to visitors to the island of Arran, sculptured by nature on the rugged peaks of Goatfell.

LITERARY DIVERSION.

About the middle of the seventeenth century the scribes, or rather those whose ambition was not of the most soaring order, used to divert themselves, and rack their inventive powers, by torturing and twisting their verses into odd devices and shapes, expressive of the themes they discussed—as might be expected, to the serious detriment of their poetic merit. Many of these fantastic performances were of grotesque or even ludicrous description, such as fans, and toilet-glasses, and frocks, for love songs; wine-glasses, bottles, and flagons, for drinking songs: pulpits, altars, and tomb-stones, for religious verses and epitaphs; and even flying angels, Grecian temples, and Egyptian pyramids, for patriotic effusions.

Another species of literary diversion may be noticed in the curious combination of words, mostly in Latin, by some of the early writers, in which, however, their wit is less discernible than their patient ingenuity. One of these has calculated that the following verses might be changed in their order, and re-combined in thirty-nine million, nine hundred and sixteen thousand eight hundred different ways: and that to complete the writing out of this series of combinations, it would occupy a man ninety-one years and forty-nine days, if he wrote at the rate of twelve hundred verses daily. This is the wondrous distich:—

"Lex, grex, rex, spes, res, jus thus, sal, sol bona lux, laus!
Mars, mors, sors, fraus, fœx, styx, nox, crux, pus, mala cis, lis!"

This singular jumble in poetry has been thus rendered into English:—

"Law, flocks, king, hopes, riches, right incense, salt, sun good torch, praise to you.
Mars, death, destiny, fraud, impurity, Styx, night, the cross, bad humours, and evil power, may you be condemned."

Among the ingenious pastimes of poets, we must notice the following, which is unique in its way—each word reads the same backwards and forwards:—

"Odo tenet mulum,
Madidam mappam tenet anna."

This couplet cost the author, says an old book, a world of foolish labour.

The following Latin verse, which is composed with much ingenuity, affords two very opposite meanings by merely transposing the order of the words—

"Prospicimus modo, quod durabunt tempore longo,
Fœdera, nec patriæ pax cito diffugiet."

"Diffugiet cito pax patriæ, nec fœdera longo,
Tempore durabunt, quod modo prospicimus."

The following is another specimen of literary ingenuity. Two words of opposite meanings, spelled with exactly the same letters, form a Telestick; that is, the letters beginning the lines, when united, were to give one of the words, and the letters at the end were to produce the others—thus:—

"U-nite and untie are the same—so say yo-U
N-ot in wedlock, I ween has the unity bee-N
I-n the drama of marriage each wandering gou-T
T-o a new face would fly—all except you and I
E-ach seeking to alter the *spell* in their scen-E."

LITERARY PROPERTY AND REMUNERATION.

SALE OF LITERARY WORKS.

The ultimate sale of the copyright of *Paradise Lost* produced to Milton's widow eight pounds; and Dryden received from Tonson two pounds thirteen shillings and nine pence for every hundred lines of his poetry.

From an old account-book of Bernard Lintot, the bookseller, the following information respecting the prices paid heretofore for the copyright of plays is obtained. Tragedies were then the fashionable drama, and obtained the best price. Dr. Young received for his *Busiris* eighty-four pounds; Smith for his *Phædra and Hippolytus*, fifty pounds; Rowe for his *Jane Shore*, fifty pounds and fifteen shillings; and for *Lady Jane Gray*, seventy-five pounds and five shillings; and Cibber, for his *Nonjuror*, obtained one hundred and five pounds.

LALLA ROOKH.

The publisher of *Lalla Rookh* gave three thousand guineas for the copyright of that poem.

JACOB TONSON AND DRYDEN.

Jacob Tonson, the most eminent of his profession as a publisher, having refused to advance Dryden a sum of money for a work in which he was engaged, the enraged bard sent a message to him, and the following lines, adding, "Tell the dog that he who wrote these can write more :—

'With leering looks, bull-faced, and freckled skin,
With two left legs, and Judas-coloured hair,
And frowsy pores, that taint the ambient air.'"

The bookseller felt the force of the description, and to avoid the completion of the portrait, immediately sent the money.

CHEAPNESS OF LITERARY WORKS.

"As a curious literary fact," says Cottle, "I might mention that the sale of the first edition of the *Lyrical Ballads* was so slow, and the severity of most of the reviews so great, that their progress to oblivion, notwithstanding the merit which I was quite sure they possessed, seemed to be ordained to be as rapid as it was certain. I had given thirty guineas for the copyright; but the heavy sale induced me at length to part with them at a loss —the largest proportion of the impression of five hundred to Mr. Arch, a London bookseller.

"On my reaching London, having an account to settle with Messrs. Longman and Rees, the booksellers of Paternoster Row, I sold them all my copyrights, which were valued as one lot, by a third party. On my next seeing Mr. Longman, he told me that, in estimating the value of the copyrights, Fox's *Achmed* and Wordsworth's *Lyrical Ballads* were 'reckoned as *nothing*.' 'That being the case,' I replied, 'as both these authors are my personal friends, I should be obliged if you would return me again these two copyrights, that I may have the pleasure of presenting them to the respective writers.' Mr. Longman answered, with his accustomed liberality, ' You are welcome to them.' On my reaching Bristol, I gave Mr. Fox his receipt for twenty guineas, and on Coleridge's return from the north, I gave him Mr. Wordsworth's receipt for his thirty guineas; so that whatever advantage has arisen subsequently from the sale of this volume of the *Lyrical Ballads*, I am happy to say, has pertained exclusively to Mr. Wordsworth."

MAGAZINES.

Sir John Hawkins, in his *Memoirs of Johnson*, ascribes the decline of literature to the ascendency of frivolous Magazines, between the years 1740 and 1760. He says that they render smatterers conceited, and confer the superficial glitter of knowledge instead of its substance.

Sir Richard Phillips, upwards of forty years a publisher, gives the following evidence as to the sale of the Magazines in his time :—

" For my own part, I know that in 1790, and for many years previously, there were sold of the trifle called the *Town and Country Magazine*, full 15,000 copies per month; and, of another, the *Ladies' Magazine*, from 16,000 to 22,000. Such circumstances, were, therefore, calculated to draw forth the observations of Hawkins. The *Gentleman's Magazine*, in its days of popular extracts, never rose above 10,000 ; after it became more decidedly antiquarian, it fell in sale, and continued for many years at 3000. There was also a lighter work, the *European Magazine*, and one better selected, called the *Universal Magazine*, both of which sold also to the latter extent. These were the periodicals with which I had to contend when I began the *Monthly Magazine* in 1795; but, till 1824, when I sold that work, the average regular sale did not exceed 3500 or 3750.

THE FIRST MAGAZINE.

The *Gentleman's Magazine* unaccountably passes for the earliest periodical of that description; while, in fact, it was preceded nearly forty years by the *Gentleman's Journal* of Motteux, a work much more closely resembling our modern magazines, and from which Sylvanus Urban borrowed part of his title, and part of his motto; while on the first page of the first number of the *Gentleman's Magazine* itself, it is stated to contain "more than any book of the *kind* and price."—(Mr. Watts, of the British Museum.)

MARRIAGES OF MEN OF GENIUS.

Marriages of men of genius is one of the strangest themes in the history of literature. Goethe married to become respectable; Niebuhr to please a mistress; Churchill because he was miserable; Napoleon to get a command; Wilkes to oblige his friends; Wycherly to spite his relations. The author of *Salad for the Solitary*, furnishes the following piquant *morceaux*, touching the marriage of two French *litterateurs* of celebrity:—

"M. Balzac, the French novelist, exhibits another example of eccentricity in matrimonial affairs. According to a Parisian correspondent, the arrival of this celebrated author from Germany caused an immense sensation in certain circles, owing to the romantic circumstances connected with his marriage. When Balzac was at the zenith of his fame, he was travelling in Switzerland, and had arrived at the inn just at the very moment the Prince and Princess Hanski were leaving it. Balzac was ushered into the room they had just vacated, and was leaning from the window to observe their departure, when his attention was arrested by a soft voice at his elbow, asking for a book which had been left behind upon the window-seat. The lady was certainly fair, but appeared doubly so in the eyes of the poor author, when she intimated that the book she was in quest of was the pocket edition of his own works, adding that she never travelled without it, and that without it she could not exist! She drew the volume from beneath his elbow, and flew down stairs, obedient to the screaming summons of her husband—a pursy old gentleman, who was already seated in the carriage, railing in a loud voice against dilatory habits of women in general and his own spouse in particular; and the emblazoned vehicle drove off, leaving the novelist in a state of self-complacency the most enviable to be conceived. This was the only occasion upon which Balzac and the Princess Hanski had met, till his recent visit to Germany, when he presented himself as her accepted husband. During these long intervening fifteen years, however, a literary correspondence was steadily kept up between the parties, till at length instead of a letter containing literary strictures upon his writings, a missive of another kind—having a still more directly personal tendency, reached him from the fair hand of the princess. It contained the announcement of the demise of her husband the prince—that he had bequeathed to her his domains, and his great wealth—and consequently, that she felt bound to requite him in some measure for his liberality, and had determined upon giving him a successor—in the person of Balzac. It is needless to state that the delighted author waited not a second summons; they were forthwith united in wedlock, at her château on the Rhine, and a succession of splendid fêtes celebrated the auspicious event. The story of the marriage of Lamartine is also one of romantic interest. The lady, whose maiden name was Birch, was possessed of considerable property, and when past the bloom of youth, she became passionately enamoured of the poet, from the perusal of his 'Méditations;' for some time she nursed this sentiment in secret, and being apprised of the embarrassed state of his affairs, she wrote him, tendering him the bulk of her fortune. Touched with this remarkable proof of her generosity, and supposing it could only be caused by a preference for himself, he at once made an offer of his hand and heart. He judged rightly, and the poet was promptly accepted."

MECHANICAL TRIUMPHS.

Contributing, as they do, to our most immediate and pressing wants—appealing to the eye by their magnitude, and often by their grandeur, and associated in many cases with the warmer impulses of humanity and personal safety—the labours of the mechanist and engineer acquire a contemporary celebrity, which is not vouchsafed to the results of scientific research, or to the productions of literature and the fine arts. The gigantic steam-vessel, which expedites and facilitates the intercourse of nations—the canal, which unites two distant seas—the bridge and the aqueduct, which span an impassable valley—the harbour and the breakwater, which shelter our vessels of peace and of war—the railway, which hurries us along on the wings of mechanism, and the light beacon which throws its directing beams over the deep—address themselves to the secular interests of every individual, and obtain for the engineer who invented or who planned them a high and well-merited popular reputation.—(Macaulay.)

MEDICAL MEN.

HARVEY.

After Harvey had made the great discovery of the circulation of the blood, he durst not for many years even drop a hint upon the subject in his comparatively private lectures, and it was not until nearly thirty years had elapsed that he ventured to publish to the world, not in his own country, but at Frankfort, the results of his experiments. And then nothing could exceed the contempt and ridicule with which it was received. Had he lived in a country unblessed with the light of the Reformation, he would probably have shared the fate of Galileo. As it was, he was accused of propagating doctrines tending to subvert the authority of Holy Scripture; the epithet circulator, in its Latin invidious signification (quack), was applied to him; it was given out that he was "crack-brained," and his practice as a physician sensibly declined. In a quarter of a century more his system was received in all the universities of the world, and Harvey lived to enjoy the reputation he so justly merited.

ECONOMY OF TIME.

Dr. Bateman, the well-known physician, and author of a number of medical works, was a great economist of time. In the intervals of professional duty his pen was always in his hand, and he was accustomed to write with great fluency. In preparing his manuscript upon any particular subject—as, for instance, more especially his articles for the *Cyclopædia*—he was in the habit of noting down on a scrap of paper the heads into which he thought of dividing his subject, of then reading all the books upon it which he had occasion to consult, after which he arranged in his mind all he proposed to say, so that when he began to write he considered his labour done. He wrote, indeed, as fast as his pen could move, and with so little necessity of correction or interlineation, that his first copy always went to the printer. Neither was any part of this process hastily or inconsiderately performed. He said that to prepare for the single article on "Imagination," in the *Edinburgh Encyclopædia*, he read the greater part of one-and-twenty volumes.

DISCOVERY OF VACCINATION.

It was long after Dr. Jenner first conceived the idea of preventing small-pox by vaccination that he elaborated his great discovery, and still longer before he durst promulgate it to the world. In 1780, he divulged his views to a friend, expressing his confident conviction that it was destined to benefit the human race. It was not till after sixteen years of patient and searching investigation that the efficacy of the discovery was effectually tested on the human subject. The causes of failure, in the casual dissemination of the disease, were next ascertained, and his chief care was to avoid them in attempting to propagate it by artificial means. He has left us an interesting picture of his feelings during this eventful period. "While the vaccine discovery was progressive, the joy I felt at the prospect before me, of being the instrument destined to take away from the world one of its greatest calamities, blended with the fond hope of enjoying independence, and domestic peace and happiness, were often so excessive, that, in pursuing my favourite subject among the meadows, I have sometimes found myself in a kind of reverie. It is pleasant to me to recollect that those reflections always ended in devout acknowledgments to that Being from whom this and all other blessings flow."

At length, on the 14th of May, 1796, an opportunity occurred of making a decisive trial.—(On the annual occurrence of this day a festival is held at Berlin to commemorate the event.)—Matter was taken from the hand of Sarah Nelmes, who had been infected by her master's cows, and inserted by two superficial incisions into the arms of James Phipps, a healthy boy of about eight years of age. He went through the disease apparently in a very satisfactory manner, but the most anxious part of the trial still remained to be performed. Was he secure against the contagion of small-pox? This point was fully put to issue. Variolous matter immediately taken from a pustule was carefully inserted by several incisions, and the result is related by Jenner to his friend Gardner in the following language:—"But now listen to the most delightful part of my story. The boy has since been inoculated for the small-pox, which, as I ventured to predict, produced no effect. I shall now pursue my studies with redoubled ardour."

After zealously multiplying his experiments, Jenner published his first memoir in June, 1798. He had originally intended, it appears, to have announced them to the world, in the *Transactions of the Royal Society.* In Moore's "History of Vaccination," we find the true cause of their not appearing in that form. He had been seriously admonished, *not* to present his paper, lest it should *injure* the character he had acquired amongst scientific men by a paper he had already published in those "*Transactions*" on the "Cuckoo!" Before the publication of this work, Jenner went up to London for the purpose of exhibiting the cow-pox, and of demonstrating to his professional friends, the accuracy of his delineations and the truth of his assertions. All were received with the greatest distrust. During a residence of three months, he could not obtain permission to exhibit the vaccine disease upon one individual.

Mr. Cline was the only professional man who perceived the importance of Jenner's discovery, and predicted his success. He advised Jenner to come to London and settle as a practitioner; but nothing could induce him to leave Gloucestershire. The nobility of his nature is shown in the reply he made to the tempting prospect set before him by his adviser. "Shall I," he writes, "who, even in the morning of my days, sought the lowly and sequestered paths of life, the valley and not the mountain,—shall I, now my evening is fast approaching, hold myself up as an object for fortune and for fame? Admitting it is a certainty that I obtain both, what stock shall I add to my little fund of happiness? And as for fame what is it? A gilded bait for ever pierced with the arrows of malignancy."

But nothing could arrest the progress of Jenner's brilliant and beneficent discovery, which at last bore down incredulity, indifference, hostility, and ridicule. In 1799, thirty-three of the leading physicians, and forty eminent surgeons of London, signed an expression of their confidence in the efficacy of vaccination. The confidence of the public was speedily won for it by the remarkable diminution of mortality which followed its introduction. Jenner bore his success with the same equanimity which he evinced under the neglect and ridicule of the profession, and always manifested a forgiving spirit towards those who had been his calumniators. He died in 1823, full of years and honours.

VACCINATION.

The Empress Dowager Mary of Russia, and several foreign potentates, sent gratulatory addresses to Dr. Jenner on his discovery of vaccination, which has rapidly gained ground in every quarter of the globe. A few instances of this kind are worthy of being recorded.

When Dr. Wickham was made prisoner in France, Dr. Jenner was applied to as the fittest person for addressing to Bonaparte a petition soliciting that physician's liberation. This was at the time of Napoleon's greatest animosity to this country. It happened thus: the emperor was in his carriage, and the horses were being changed. The petition was then presented to him. He exclaimed, "Away! away!" The Empress Josephine, who accompanied him, said, "But, emperor, do you see who this comes from? Jenner!" He changed his tone of voice that instant, and said, "What that man asks is not to be refused;" and the petition was immediately granted. The emperor also liberated many others, even whole families, from time to time, at the request of Dr. Jenner. Indeed, he never refused any request made by Dr. Jenner, who, of course, observed proper delicacy in not applying too often.

LADY MONTAGU'S RESIDENCE IN TURKEY, AND INTRODUCTION OF INOCULATION INTO BRITAIN.

The heat of Constantinople, during the summer months, is excessive, and the European embassies usually retire to the shores of the Bosphorus, or the village of Belgrade, about fourteen miles distant. In these delicious shades, and most beautiful forest scenery, Lady Mary was happy to pass her days. No English traveller visits Belgrade without participating in her pleasure in her description, and inquiring after the site of her residence. At present no part of the house remains, for such is the fragility of Turkish structures, excepting their mosques, that they seldom last a century.

There was a custom prevalent among the villagers, and, indeed, universal in the Turkish dominions, which she examined with philosophical curiosity, and at length became perfectly satisfied with its efficacy. It was that of ingrafting, or, as it is now called, inoculating with variolous matter, in order to produce a milder disease, and to prevent the ravages made by the small-pox on the lives and beauty of European patients. The process was simple, and she did not hesitate to apply it to her son, at that time about three years old. This was in March, 1717.

National gratitude, if directed by justice, will not overlook, in favour of more recent discoveries, the original obligation to Lady Mary Wortley Montagu, for the introduction of the art of inoculation into this kingdom. Mr. Maitland, who had attended the embassy in a medical character, first endeavoured to establish the practice of it in London, and was encouraged by her patronage. In 1721, as its expediency had been much agitated among scientific men, an experiment, to be sanctioned by the College of Physicians, was allowed by Government. Five persons, under condemnation, willingly encountered the danger with the hopes of life. Upon four of them the eruption appeared on the seventh day; the fifth was a woman, on whom it never appeared, but she confessed that she had it when an infant. With so much ardour did Lady Mary enforce this salutary innovation among mothers of her own rank in life, that, as we find in her letters, much of her time was necessarily dedicated to various consultations, and in superintending the success of her plan.—(Memoirs by Dallaway.)

ABERNETHY AND JOHN PHILPOT CURRAN.

A curious scene once took place between Abernethy and the famous John Philpot Curran. Mr. Curran being personally unknown to Mr. Abernethy, had visited him repeatedly without having had an opportunity of explaining to the surgeon so fully as he thought necessary the nature of his malady. At last he determined on obtaining a hearing, and fixing his keen dark eye on the "doctor," he said, "Mr. Abernethy, I have been here on eight different days, and I have paid you eight different guineas; but you have never yet listened to the symptoms of my complaint. I am resolved, sir, not to leave this room till you satisfy me by doing so." Struck by his manner, Mr. Abernethy threw himself back in his chair, and assuming the posture of an indefatigable listener, replied in a tone of half humour, half sarcasm,—"O, very well, sir! I am ready to hear you out; go on: give me the whole, your birth, parentage, and education: I wait your pleasure; go on." Upon which, Curran, not a whit disconcerted, gravely began:—"My name is John Philpot Curran. My parents were poor, but, I believe, honest people, of the province of Munster, where also I was born, at Newmarket, in the county of Cork, in the year 1750. My father being employed to collect the rents of a Protestant gentleman of small fortune, in that neighbourhood, procured my admission into one of the Protestant free schools, where I obtained the first rudiments of my education. I was next enabled to enter Trinity College, Dublin, in the humble sphere of a sizer." And so he continued for several minutes, giving his astonished hearer a true but irresistibly laughable account of his "birth, parentage, and education," as desired, till he came to his illness and sufferings, the detail of which was not again interrupted. It is hardly necessary to add, that Mr. Abernethy's attention to his gifted patient was, from that time to the close of his life, assiduous and devoted.

ABERNETHY—A CLASS ILLUSTRATION.

Few old pupils (says M'Ilwaine, who was one of them) will forget the story of the major who had dislocated his jaw. This accident is a very simple one, and easily put right; but having once happened, is apt to recur on any unusual extension of the lower jaw. Abernethy used to represent this as a frequent occurrence with the hilarious major; but, as it generally happened at mess, the surgeon went round to him, and immediately put it in again. One day, however, the major was dining about fourteen miles from the regiment, and, in a hearty laugh, out went his jaw. They sent for the medical man, whom, said Abernethy, we must call the apothecary. Well, at first he thought the jaw was dislocated; but he began to pull and to show that he knew nothing about the proper mode of putting it right again. On this the major began to be very excited, and vociferated inarticulately in a strange manner; when, all at once, the doctor, as if he had just hit on the nature of the case, suggested that the major's complaint was in his brain, and that he could not be in his right mind. On hearing this, the major became furious, which was regarded as confirmatory of the doctor's opinion. They accordingly seized him, confined him in a strait-waistcoat, and put him to bed, and the doctor ordered that the barber should be sent for to shave the head, and a blister to be applied to the part affected. The major, fairly beaten, ceased making resistance, but made the best signs his situation and his imperfect articulation allowed for pen and paper. This being hailed as indicative of returning rationality, writing materials were set before him; and as soon as he was sufficiently freed from his bonds, he wrote—"For God's sake send for the surgeon of the regiment." This was accordingly done, and the jaw readily reduced, as it had been often before. "I hope," added Abernethy, "you will never forget how to reduce a dislocated jaw."

JENNER AND THE FOREIGN POTENTATES.

When the foreign potentates arrived in this country in 1814, they all expressed a wish to see Dr. Jenner; he was first introduced to the Grand Duchess of Oldenburgh, when the conversation turned upon philosophical subjects, and her imperial highness astonished the doctor by the extent of her information. Dr. Jenner requested her imperial highness, when she wrote to her august mother, to have the goodness to say that he had a grateful remembrance of the kind attention which she showed him. "*When I write?*" she replied, "I will write this very evening!"—At parting she said, "Dr. Jenner, you must see the emperor, my brother, who is expected here soon." Dr. Jenner bowed acquiescence and withdrew.

The emperor arrived, and the promised interview took place in the most gracious form. The Doctor was ushered into a room, which soon after his imperial majesty entered alone. He pronounced the words "Dr. Jenner!" (which was returned with a respectful bow), and then advanced and touched his right shoulder. Alexander shortly commenced a discourse upon the astonishing effects of vaccination in Russia; and Dr. Jenner had the pleasure of hearing him declare, that the vaccine had nearly subdued small-pox throughout that country. Dr. Jenner then told the emperor that he had the highest gratification at hearing such an important fact from his majesty himself. The Doctor next presented the monarch with a volume of his own works upon the subject; and added, "that in whatever country vaccination was conducted in a similar way to that which his majesty had commanded in the Russian empire, the small-pox must necessarily become extinct."

In a few days afterwards Count Orloff, with whom he had been long acquainted, from attendance on his countess, waited on Dr. Jenner, and asked him if a Russian order would be acceptable to him, should his majesty be graciously pleased to confer it. Dr. Jenner replied, that he thought this exclusively belonged to men of perfect independence. The count expressed his surprise at his not possessing a pecuniary independence. Dr. Jenner answered, that he possessed a village fortune, though not what came under the general acceptation of the term independence.

By appointment Dr. Jenner waited on the King of Prussia. The Dr. came rather late, and the king was in haste to go to church. His majesty, however, gave him a very polite reception, and apologized for being under the necessity of going to church; but made, as did the other sovereigns, a general acknowledgment of the obligations of the world to Dr. Jenner. His Prussian majesty was the first crowned head who submitted his own offspring to vaccination; and the Emperor of Austria followed his example. After the king was gone, the crown-prince, and many others of the illustrious foreigners, honoured Dr. Jenner with particular notice, and gave him a pressing invitation to Berlin.

Dr. Jenner's next presentation was to Blucher. He was very polite, and rather facetious. Before the general entered the room, a Turkish tobacco-pipe (a Turkey bowl with an alder stick) was brought in by a servant, upon a velvet cushion.

The next interview was with Platoff. To the astonishment of Dr. Jenner, who was accompanied by Dr. Hamel (a physician born on the banks of the Don, and acquainted with the Cossack language), the count proved to be quite a polished gentleman, had a knowledge of vaccination and practised it. He said, "Sir, you have extinguished the most pestilential disorder that ever appeared on the banks of the Don."

SIR RICHARD JEBB.

This eminent physician used to tell a story of himself, which made even rapacity comical. He was attending a nobleman, from whom he had a right to expect a fee of five guineas: he received only three. Suspecting some trick on the part of the steward, from whom he received it, he, at the next visit, contrived to drop three guineas. They were picked up, and again deposited in his hand; but he still continued to look on the carpet. His lordship asked if all the guineas were found. "There must be two still on the floor," replied Sir Richard, "for I have but three." The hint was taken as he meant.

SIR HANS SLOANE'S LIBERALITY.

Sir Hans Sloane was a governor in almost every hospital about London; to each he gave a hundred pounds in his life-time; and, at his death, a sum more considerable. He formed the plan of a dispensatory, where the poor might be furnished with proper medicines at prime cost; which, with the assistance of the College of Physicians, was afterwards carried into execution. He gave the company of apothecaries the entire freehold of their botanical garden at Chelsea; in the centre of which a marble statue of him is erected, admirably executed, by Rysback, and the likeness striking. He did all he could to forward the colony in Georgia, in 1732; of the Foundling Hospital, in 1739, and formed the plan for bringing up the children. He was the first in England who introduced, into general practice, the use of bark, not only in fevers, but in a variety of other cases; particularly in nervous disorders, in mortifications, and in violent hæmorrhages. His cabinet of curiosities, which he had taken so much pains to collect, he bequeathed to the public; on condition, that the sum of £20,000 should be paid to his family; which sum, though large, was not the original cost, and scarce more than the intrinsic value of the gold and silver medals, the ores and precious stones, that were found in it. Besides these, there was his library, consisting of more than 50,000 volumes, 347 of which were illustrated with cuts, finely engraven, and coloured from nature; 3566 manuscripts; and an infinite number of rare and curious books. The Parliament accepted his bequest; and that magnificent structure, called Montague House, in great Russell Street, Bloomsbury, was purchased for the reception of this collection, as well as for that of the Cottonian Library, and the Harlëian manuscripts; and thus, Sir Hans Sloane became the founder of the British Museum, one of the noblest collections in the world. But the wits, who never spare a character, however eminently great and useful, more than once took occasion to ridicule this good man for a taste, the utility of which they did not comprehend, but which was honoured with the unanimous approbation of the British legislature. Thus Young, in his *Love of Fame* :—

" But what address can be more sublime
Than Sloane—the foremost *toyman* of
his time ?
His nice ambition lies in curious fancies,
His daughter's portion a rich *shell* enhances,
And Ashmole's baby-house is, in his
view,
Britannia's golden mine—a rich Peru !
How his eyes languish ! how his
thoughts adore,
That painted coat which Joseph *never*
wore !
He shows, on holidays, a sacred pin,
That touch'd the ruff, that touch'd
Queen Bess's chin."
SAT. IV. 113–122.

MRS. SARAH HASTINGS AND MRS. FRENCH.

The memory of female doctors soon vanishes, and seldom reaches beyond their cotemporaries. They sink into the grave, together with their patients, and all remembrance of their deeds is lost.

A few doctresses, however, have by accident acquired a more permanent fame, by their names being mentioned in some standard work, which preserves their memory: this is the case with Mrs. Sarah Hastings and Mrs. French, of Leicester, who have had their names immortalized by their cures being recorded in the *Philosophical Transactions*.

OLD AGE OF BOERHAAVE.

The name of Boerhaave is justly regarded as one of the most illustrious in the calendar of modern medicine. After having vigorously struggled with poverty in his youth, his talents and his fame at length created a fortune for him; and, it is said, that he left two millions of florins to his only son. Did this wealth alter the man? Let us learn from his own mouth what he was in his sixty-seventh year; when, in a letter to his old scholar, J. B. Bassaud, then physician to the Emperor of Germany, he writes thus:—

"My health is very good. I sleep at my country-house. I go to town every morning by five o'clock; and I occupy myself there, from that time until six in the evening, in relieving the sick. I understand chemistry; I amuse myself in reading it; I revere, I love, I adore, the only God! When I return to the country, I visit my plants: I acknowledge and admire the presents with which the liberality of my friend Bassaud has enriched me. My garden seems to be proud of the variety and strength of its trees. I pass my life in contemplating my plants; I grow old in the desire of possessing new ones. Amiable and sweet folly! Thus riches only serve to irritate the thirst of possession, and the miser is miserable from the liberality of his benefactor. Forgive the madness of an old friend, who wishes to plant trees, the beauty and shade of which will be destined to give delight only to his nephews. It is thus that my life passes, without any other chagrin than my distance from you, and happy in every thing else."

What an amiable picture does this present of that great and good man! What activity, and what zeal for the relief of suffering humanity! The original letter is written in Latin, and it has been found difficult to catch the spirit of the original.

ANCIENT STATE OF SURGERY IN SCOTLAND.

When the surgeons of Edinburgh were, in 1505, incorporated, under the denominations of surgeons and barbers, it was required of them to be able to *read and write!* "to know anatomie, nature, and complexion of everie member of humanis bodie, and lykwayes to know all vaynes of the samyn, that he may make flewbothemie in dew time;" together with a perfect knowledge of shaving beards. These were all the qualifications that seemed necessary to the art of surgery, at the beginning of the sixteenth century. The practice of physic was, if possible, in a still more deplorable state.—(Campbell's Journey from Edinburgh to the Highlands.)

ZIMMERMAN.

This eminent physician went from Hanover to attend Frederick the Great in his last illness. One day the king said to him, "You have, I presume, sir, helped many a man into another world?" This was rather a bitter pill for the doctor; but the dose he gave the king in return, was a judicious mixture of truth and flattery:— "Not so many as your majesty, nor with so much honour to myself."

JOHN ABERNETHY—HIS WIT AND ECCENTRICITY.

A lady consulted him on a nervous disorder, and gave him a long, frivolous, and fantastic detail of her symptoms. He referred her, as was his wont, to his "book," but she persisted in endeavouring to extract further information from him. "May I eat oysters, Doctor? may I take supper?" "I'll tell you what, Madam," replied Mr. Abernethy impatiently, "you may eat anything but the poker and the bellows; for the one is too hard of digestion, and the other is full of wind." Mr. Abernethy was once prodigiously pleased with the course pursued by a lady who was aware of his aversion to idle loquacity and silly affectation. Entering his consulting-room, without uttering a word, she thrust towards him her finger which had sustained a severe injury. Mr. Abernethy looked first at her face, and then at her finger, which he dressed. The fair patient then silently withdrew. In a few days she called again, and presented the affected digit. "Better?" inquired the surgeon. "Better," replied the patient. The finger was again dressed, and the lady tacitly retired. After several similar calls, the lady at length held out her finger free from bandages, and healed. "Well?" asked Mr. Abernethy. "Well," responded the laconic lady. "Upon my word, Madam," exclaimed the delighted surgeon, "you are the most rational woman I ever met with!"

"Pray, Mr. Abernethy, what is a cure for gout?" inquired a luxurious and indolent citizen. "Live upon sixpence a-day—and earn it!" was the pithy answer.

JOHN ABERNETHY—HIS INTEGRITY AND HONOUR.

On his receiving the appointment of Professor of Anatomy and Surgery to the Royal College of Surgeons, a professional friend observed to him that they should now have something new. "What do you mean?" asked Mr. Abernethy. "Why," said the other, "of course you will finish up the lectures which you have been so long delivering at St. Bartholomew's Hospital, and let us have them in an improved form." "Do you take me for a fool or a knave?" rejoined Mr. Abernethy; "I have always given the students at the Hospital that to which they were entitled—the best produce of my mind. If I could have made my lectures to them better, I would instantly have made them so. I will give the College of Surgeons precisely the same lectures, down to the smallest details—nay, I will tell the old fellows how to make a poultice." Soon after, when he was lecturing to the students at St. Bartholomew's, and adverting to the College of Surgeons, he exclaimed, gleefully, "I told the big wigs how to make a poultice!" The great surgeon's description of poultice-making is said to have been extremely diverting.

JOHN ABERNETHY—HIS GENEROSITY.

In the year 1818, Lieutenant D—— fell from his horse in London, and sustained a fracture of the skull and arm. Mr. Abernethy was the nearest surgeon, and being sent for, continued his attendance daily, for months. When the patient became convalescent, he was enjoined by Abernethy to proceed to Margate and adopt shell-fish diet. The patient requested to know the extent of his pecuniary liability. "Who is that young woman?" inquired Abernethy, smilingly. "She is my wife." "What is your rank in the army?" "I am a half-pay Lieutenant." "Oh! very well, wait till you are a General; then come and see me, and we'll talk about it."

One of the students at the Hospital indicated to Mr. Abernethy his desire to be appointed his "dresser," the usual fee for which was sixty guineas for the year. Abernethy invited the youth to breakfast with him next morning, to make arrangements; and, in the meantime, on inquiry, found that the young man was attentive and clever, but in straitened circumstances. At the breakfast table, the student produced a small bag, containing the sixty guineas, and presented it to

Mr. Abernethy, who, in the kindest and most considerate manner, declined it, insisting upon his applying the money to the purchase of books and other means of improvement. That student is now a practitioner of considerable eminence in the metropolis.

ETHER AND CHLOROFORM, AS ANÆSTHETIC AGENTS.

The practice of the inhalation of sulphuric ether as an anæsthetic agent dates no further back than the year 1846. In describing its effects to the Philosophical Society of Glasgow, Dr. Andrew Buchanan, who had at first distrusted the astounding properties attributed to it, said, " I have carefully examined the subject by actual observation and experiment, and I have now to state, as the result, that I am fully satisfied that the statements originally made to me were in no way exaggerated; that the inhalation of ether really has the power of suspending, for a time, the sensibility of the nerves; and that, during the period of suspended sensibility, the most formidable surgical operations may be performed—amputation of the limbs—the dissecting out of tumors, and cutting for the stone — without any perception of pain by the person operated upon, and without reason to apprehend any bad consequences, either immediate or subsequent. I can honestly declare that I have seen all these, and many other operations performed; and that the patients, when put fully under the influence of the ether, gave no indications of feeling pain during these operations, and declared afterwards that they had felt none, which is the whole evidence that the case admits of. So great a triumph of the medical art I never expected to witness; but it should not excite feelings of exultation merely, but should be received with gratitude and with thankfulness, as a great boon which it has pleased the Giver of all good to bestow, in his compassion for the sufferings of mankind." (Proceedings of Philosophical Society of Glasgow, 1847.)

In the same year, Dr. Simpson of Edinburgh found that chloroform, when inhaled into the lungs, produced the same effect as ether, and could be more readily and easily administered. This body (which was only discovered in 1831) has now entirely superseded ether in surgical and midwifery practice. The same property has been observed (1853) to be possessed by a lycoperdon (or puff-ball), which has been employed to render bees insensible without destroying them.

DR. PARR AND DR. S. JOHNSON.

Dr. Robert Gooch published in *Blackwood's Magazine* a lively account of a visit to the venerable Dr. Parr at Warwick, in 1822. Speaking of the advantages and disadvantages of different professions, Parr naturally gave the preference to that of physic, as being equally favourable to a man's moral sentiments and intellectual faculties.—One of the party reminded him of his first interview with Dr. Johnson. "I remember it well," said Parr, "I gave him no quarter,—the subject of our dispute was the liberty of the press. Dr. Johnson was very great; whilst he was arguing, I observed that he stamped; upon this I stamped. Dr. Johnson said, 'Why do you stamp, Dr. Parr?' I replied, 'Sir, because you stamped, and I was resolved not to give you the advantage even of a stamp in the argument.'"

DR. JAMES HOPE AND THE STETHOSCOPE.

The late Dr. James Hope had long assigned to himself the execution of two works—*A Treatise on*

Diseases of the Heart, and on *Morbid Anatomy*, illustrated by plates; and, for the completion of them, he allotted seven years. The materials for the latter work were nearly prepared, and the only difficulty he had to encounter in its publication was the enormous expense of the engravings. But the subject of "Diseases of the Heart" was then not very well understood. He had bestowed much thought upon it, from the period of his medical studies at Edinburgh. It appeared essential that he should continue his studies at some large hospital, and he selected St. George's, London, as the one to which his ambition prompted him to hope he should one day be physician, which he afterwards became. Here he soon became conspicuous for his regular attendance and unvarying application. Never was he to be seen without his stethoscope, his book for taking notes of cases, and a small ink-bottle attached to his button. At that time there was much prejudice in England, and especially at St. George's, against "*auscultation*," (the use of the stethoscope,) in the examination of diseases of the chest. This Dr. Hope determined to remove, and he adopted the most judicious course, that, namely, of leaving facts to speak for themselves. He took the most minute notes of them all, wrote down the conclusions to which he was led in as great detail as possible, and, before proceeding to a post mortem examination, publicly placed his book on the table that it might be read by every one. He was invariably correct. Attention was soon drawn to him. His accuracy silenced every objection, and all intelligent and candid men became convinced of the utility of the stethoscope.

MISCELLANEOUS.

DR. JOHNSON, AND OSBORNE THE BOOKSELLER.

Tom Osborne, the bookseller, was one of "that mercantile, rugged race, to which the delicacy of the poet is sometimes exposed;" as the following anecdote will more fully evince: Johnson being engaged by him to translate a work of some consequence, he thought it a respect which he owed his own talents, as well as the credit of his employer, to be as circumspect in the performance of it as possible; in consequence of which, the work went on, according to Osborne's ideas, rather slowly; in consequence, he frequently spoke to Johnson of this circumstance, and, being a man of a coarse mind, sometimes, by his expressions, made him feel the situation of dependence. Johnson, however, seemed to take no notice of him, but went on according to the plan which he had prescribed for himself. Osborne, irritated by what he thought an unnecessary delay, went one day into the room where Johnson was sitting, and abused him in the most illiberal manner: amongst other things, he told Johnson he had been much mistaken in his man; that he was recommended to him as a good scholar, and a ready hand; but he doubted both; for "Tom Such-a-one would have turned out the work much sooner; and that being the case, the probability was, that by this *here* time the first edition would have moved off." Johnson heard him for some time unmoved; but, at last, losing all patience, he seized a huge folio, which he was at that time consulting, and, aiming it at the bookseller's head, succeeded so forcibly as to send him sprawling on the floor. Osborne alarmed the family with his cries; but Johnson, clapping his foot on his breast, would not let him stir till he had exposed him in that situation; and then left him, with this triumphant expression: "Lie there, thou son of dulness, ignorance, and obscurity!"

MANUSCRIPT OF ROBINSON CRUSOE.

Robinson Crusoe, in manuscript, ran through the whole trade; nor would any one print it, though the writer, Defoe, was in good repute as an author. One bookseller, at last, not remarkable for his discernment, but for his speculative turn, engaged in this publication. This bookseller got above a thousand guineas by it; and the booksellers are accumulating money every hour by editions of this work in all shapes. The second volume of this work, however, met with a small sale. The bookseller would have given two hundred pounds that it never had been printed; the first would have been so much more saleable without it.

HAYDON PAINTING CLARKSON THE PHILANTHROPIST.

Found the dear old man at tea with his niece and wife, looking much better than when in town. Playford is a fine old building: 1593 the last date, but must be much older, they say. It is surrounded by a moat with running water. Clarkson has a head like a patriarch, and in his prime must have been a noble figure. He was very happy to see me, but there is a nervous irritability which is peculiar. He lives too much with adorers, especially women. As he seemed impatient at my staying beyond a certain time, I went to bed, and wished him good night. I slept well, and the next morning walked in the garden and fields. He breakfasted on milk and bread (alone), and I breakfasted with Mrs. T. Clarkson, up stairs. I promised to sketch him at ten, and at ten I was ready . . . . When all was ready, the windows fitted, he said, "Call in the maids." In came six servant girls, and washerwomen (it being washing-day). "I am determined they shall see the first stroke." In they all crowded, timidly wondering. Clarkson said, "There now, that is the first stroke; come again in an hour, and you shall see the last!" We now began to talk. He said, "When Christophe's wife and daughters, all accomplished women, were brought or introduced by him to Wilberforce, and others in high life, there was a sort of shrink at admitting them into society." I told him I believed it, because when I resolved to place the African in front of the picture on the same level as the Europeans, there was the same delicacy; but I got him and put him in at once. Shame prevented remonstrance. . . . Why was I not so impressed as when I visited the Duke? Here was a man who in his Christian and peaceable object had shown equal perseverance, equal skill, equal courage, and yet I was not so affected. Clarkson has more weaknesses than the Duke. He is not so high bred. He makes a pride of his debilities. He boasts of his swollen legs and his pills as if they were so many claims to distinction. The Duke did not let you see him in his infirmities. He was deaf, but he would not let you see it if possible. He dined like others, ate like others, and did everything like others; and what he did not do like others, he did not do before others. Lord Grey and Clarkson have both that infirmity of asking questions about themselves, as if they had forgot the answers, that they may elicit again the answers for the pleasure of hearing the repetition. The Duke —never. He is too much a man. Himself seems the last thing he remembers, except when others presume on his modesty. He never obtruded Waterloo unless it was forced on him, or arose out of the conversation; nor did he shrink if the company seemed to press it. In fact, the Duke was a high bred man. The want of this is never compensated for—never.—(Haydon.)

MISAPPLICATION OF WORDS BY FOREIGNERS.

The misapplication of English words by foreigners is often very ludicrous. It is said that Dr. Chalmers once entertained a distinguished guest from Switzerland, whom he asked if he would be helped to kippered salmon. The foreign divine asked the meaning of the uncouth word kippered, and was told that it meant preserved. The poor man, in a public prayer soon after, offered a petition that the distinguished divine might long be "kippered to the Free Church of Scotland."

"COMING EVENTS CAST THEIR SHADOWS BEFORE."

In Beattie's *Life of Thomas Campbell*, the following anecdote is preserved respecting the well-known couplet in "Lochiel":—

"'Tis the sunset of life gives me mystical lore,
And coming events cast their shadows before."

The happy thought first presented itself to his mind during a visit at Minto. He had gone early to bed, and still meditating on the wizard's "warning," fell fast asleep. During the night he suddenly awoke, repeating:—

"Events to come cast their shadows before"

This was the very thought for which he had been hunting during the whole week! He rang the bell more than once with increased force. At last, surprised and annoyed by so unseasonable a peal, the servant appeared. The poet was sitting with one foot in the bed and the other on the floor, with an air of mixed impatience and inspiration.

"Sir, are you ill?" inquired the servant. "Ill! never better in my life. Leave me the candle, and oblige me with a cup of tea as soon as possible." He then started to his feet, seized the pen, and wrote down the "happy thought," but as he wrote, changed the words "events to come," into "coming events," as they now stand. Looking to his watch, he observed that it was two o'clock—the right hour for a poet's dream, and over his cup of tea, he completed the first sketch of "Lochiel's Warning."

SHAKSPEARE AND THE CLIMATE OF SCOTLAND.

A French writer mentions as a proof of Shakspeare's attention to particulars, his allusion to the climate of Scotland, in the words, " Hail, hail, all hail!" " *Grêle, grêle, toute grele!*"

ASININE BISHOPRIC.

It was customary in the time of Henry VIII., when speaking of St. Asaph's, to abbreviate it into St. As's. Standish, the bishop, having irritated Erasmus by an idle sarcasm, the latter retaliated by sometimes calling him *Episcopus a Sancto Asino*.

THE ROXBURGH CLUB.

Among other follies of the age of paper, which took place in England at the end of the reign of George III., a set of book-fanciers, who had more money than wit, formed themselves into a club, and appropriately designated themselves the *Bibliomaniacs*. Dr. Dibdin was their organ; and among the club were several noblemen, who, in other respects, were esteemed men of sense. Their rage was, not to estimate books according to their intrinsic worth, but for their rarity. Hence, any volume of the vilest trash, which was scarce, merely because it never had any sale, fetched fifty or a hundred pounds; but if it were but one of two or three known copies, no limits could be set to the price. Books altered in the title-page, or in a leaf, or any trivial circumstance which varied a few copies, were bought by these *soi-disant* maniacs, at one, two, or three hundred pounds, though the copies were not really worth more than threepence per pound. A trumpery edition of Boccaccio, said to be one of two known copies, was thus bought by a noble marquis for £1475, though in two or three years afterwards he resold it for £500. First editions of all authors, and editions by the first clumsy printers, were never sold for less than £50, £100, or £200.

To keep each other in countenance, these persons formed themselves into a club, and, after a duke, one of their fraternity, called themselves the *Roxburgh Club*. To gratify them, *facsimile* copies of clumsy editions of trumpery books were reprinted; and, in some cases, it became worth the while of more ingenious persons to play off forgeries upon them. This mania after a while abated; and, in future ages, it will be ranked with the tulip and the picture mania, during which, estates were given for single flowers and pictures.

A GOOD SERMON TO A SMALL AUDIENCE.

A story is told of Dr. Beecher, of Cincinnatti, that is worth recording, as illustrating the truth that we can never tell what may result from an apparently insignificant action. The Doctor once engaged to preach for a country minister, on exchange, and the Sabbath proved to be excessively stormy, cold, and uncomfortable. It was in mid-winter, and the snow was piled in heaps all along the roads so as to make the passage very difficult. Still the minister urged his horse through the drifts till he reached the church, put the animal into a shed, and went in. As yet there was no person in the house, and after looking about, the old gentleman, then young, took his seat in the pulpit. Soon the door opened, and a single individual walked up the aisle, looked about, and took a seat. The hour came for commencing service, but no more hearers. Whether to preach to such an audience or not was now the question; and it was one that Lyman Beecher was not long in deciding. He felt that he had a duty to perform, and he had no right to refuse to do it, because only one man could reap the benefit of it; and accordingly he went through all the services, praying, singing, preaching, and the benediction, with only one hearer. And when all was over, he hastened down from the desk to speak to his "congregation," but he had departed. A circumstance so rare was referred to occasionally, but twenty years after it was brought to the Doctor's mind quite strangely. Travelling somewhere in Ohio, the Doctor alighted from the stage one day, in a pleasant village, when a gentleman stepped up and spoke to him, familiarly calling him by name. "I do not remember you," said the Doctor. "I suppose not," said the stranger; "but we spent two hours together in a house alone once, in a storm." "I do not recal it, sir," added the old man; "pray, pray, when was it?" "Do you remember preaching twenty years ago, in such a place, to a single person?" "Yes, yes," said the Doctor, grasping his hand, "I do, indeed; and if you are the man, I have been wishing to see you ever since." "I am the man, sir; and that sermon saved my soul, made a minister of me, and yonder is my church. The converts of that sermon, sir, are all over Ohio."—(Hogg's Instructor).

CONVERSATION OF LITERARY MEN.

The most extraordinary conversations men whom I have known, were Sheridan, Sydney Smith, Canning, and Theodore Hook; but they were all dissimilar to each other, as if the realm of wit and humour were peopled by different races. Sheridan charmed, Canning fascinated, Sydney Smith entertained, and Theodore Hook amazed you.

SILENCE NOT ALWAYS THE INDICATION OF WISDOM.

Coleridge once dined in company with a person who listened to him, and said nothing for a long time; but he nodded his head, and Coleridge thought him intelligent. At length, towards the end of the dinner, some apple-dumplings were placed on the table, and the listener had no sooner seen them than he burst forth "Them's the jockeys for me!" Coleridge adds, "I wish Spurzheim could have examined the fellow's head."

JUDICIAL ANIMOSITY.

Mr. Curran distinguished himself not more as a barrister than as a member of Parliament; and in the latter character, it was his misfortune to provoke the enmity of a man whose thirst for revenge was only satiated by the utter ruin of his adversary. On the discussion of a bill of a penal nature, Mr. Curran inveighed in warm terms against the attorney-general, Mr. Fitzgibbon, for sleeping on the bench, when statutes of the most cruel kind were enacting; and he ironically lamented that the slumber of guilt should so nearly resemble the repose of innocence. A message from Mr. Fitzgibbon was the consequence of this sally; and the parties, having met, were left to fire when they chose. "I never," said Mr. Curran, relating the circumstances of the duel, "saw any one whose determination seemed more malignant than Fitzgibbon's: after I had fired, he took aim at me for at least half a minute; and on its proving ineffectual, I could not help exclaiming to him, 'It was not your fault, Mr. Attorney; you were deliberate enough.'" The attorney-general declared his honour satisfied; and here at least for the present, the dispute appeared to terminate. Not here, however, terminated Fitzgibbon's animosity. Soon after, he became Lord-Chancellor and a Peer in Ireland, and, in the former capacity, found an opportunity, by means of his judicial authority, ungenerously to crush the rising power of his late antagonist. Mr. Curran, who was at this time a leader, and one of the senior practitioners at the chancery bar, soon felt all the force of his rival's vengeance. The chancellor is said to have yielded a reluctant attention to every motion he made; he frequently stopped him in the midst of a speech; questioned his knowledge of law; recommended to him more attention to facts; in short, he succeeded not only in crippling all his professional efforts, but actually to leave him without a client. Mr. Curran, indeed, appeared as usual in the three other courts; but he had been already stripped of his most profitable practice; and as his expenses nearly kept pace with his gains, he was almost left a beggar; for all hopes of the wealth and honours of the long robe were now denied him. The memory of this persecution imbittered the last moments of Curran's existence; and he could never even allude to it without evincing a just and excusable indignation. In a letter which he addressed to a friend twenty years after, he says, "I make no compromise with power. I had the merit of provoking and despising the personal malice of every man in Ireland who was the known enemy of the country. Without the walls of the court of justice, my character was pursued with the most persevering slander; and within those walls, though I was too strong to be beaten down by any judicial malignity, it was not so with my clients; and my consequent losses in professional income have never been estimated at less, as you have often heard, than thirty thousand pounds." The incidents attendant upon this disagreement were at times ludicrous in the extreme. One day, when it was known that Curran was to make an elaborate argument in chancery, Lord Clare (the title of Fitzgibbon) brought a large Newfoundland dog upon the bench with him; and during the progress of the argument, he lent his ear much more to the dog than to the barrister. At last the Chancellor seemed to lose all regard to decency. He turned himself quite aside, in the most material part of the case, and began in full court to fondle the animal. Mr. Curran stopped short. "Go on, go on, Mr. Curran," said Lord Clare. "O," replied Mr. Curran, "I beg a thousand pardons, my lord; I really took it for granted that your lordship was employed in consultation."

LIBERTY A PLANT.

During the progress of a political meeting held in the town of Cambridge, it so happened that the late Dr. Mansel, then public orator of the University of Cambridge, but afterwards master of Trinity College and Bishop of Bristol, came to the place of meeting just as Musgrave, the well-known political tailor of his day, was in the midst of a most pathetic oration, and emphatically repeating "Liberty, liberty, gentlemen ——" he paused—" Liberty is a plant——" "So is a cabbage!" exclaimed the caustic Mansel, before Musgrave had time to complete his sentence, with so happy an allusion to the trade of the tailor, that he was silenced amid roars of laughter.

BACON.

Lord Bacon wrote in his will, "For my name and memory, I leave it to men's charitable speeches, and to foreign nations, and the next ages."

NOVELS AND NOVELISTS.

SCOTT'S HABITS OF COMPOSITION.

"*To J. G. Lockhart, Esq.*

"Edinburgh, 16th February, 1833.

"Sir,—Having been for a few days employed by Sir Walter Scott, when he was finishing his *Life of Bonaparte*, to copy papers connected with that work, and to write occasionally to his dictation, it may perhaps be in my power to mention some circumstances relative to Sir Walter's habits of composition, which could not fall under the observation of any one except a person in the same situation with myself, and which are therefore not unlikely to pass altogether without notice.

"When, at Sir Walter's request, I waited upon him to be informed of the business in which he needed my assistance, after stating it, he asked me if I was an early riser, and added that it would be no great hardship for me, being a young man, to attend him the next morning at six o'clock. I was punctual, and found Sir Walter already busy writing. He appointed my tasks, and again sat down at his own desk. We continued to write during the regular work hours till six o'clock in the evening, without interruption, except to take breakfast and dinner, which were served in the room beside us, so that no time was lost; we rose from our desks when everything was ready, and resumed our labours when the meals were over. I need not tell you, that during these intervals Sir Walter conversed with me as if I had been on a level of perfect equality with himself.

"I had no notion it was possible for any man to undergo the fatigue of composition for so long a time at once, and Sir Walter acknowledged he did not usually subject himself to so much exertion, though it seemed to be only the manual part of the operation that occasioned him any inconvenience. Once or twice he desired me to relieve him, and dictated while I wrote with as much rapidity as I was able. I have performed the same service to several other persons, most of whom walked up and down the apartment while excogitating what was to be committed to writing; they sometimes stopped too, and like those who fail in a leap and return upon their course to take the advantage of another race, endeavoured to hit upon something additional by perusing over my shoulder what was already set down —mending a phrase, perhaps, or recasting a sentence, till they should recover their wind. None of these aids were necessary to Sir Walter: his thoughts flowed easily and felicitously, without any difficulty to lay hold of them, or to find appropriate language; which was evident by the absence of all solicitude (*miseria cogitandi*) from his countenance. He sat in his chair, from which he rose now and then, took a volume from the bookcase, consulted it, and restored it to the shelf—all without intermission in the current of ideas, which continued to be delivered with no less readiness than if his mind had been wholly occupied with the words he was uttering. It soon became apparent to me, however, that he was carrying on two distinct trains of thought, one of which was already arranged, and in the act of being spoken, while at the same time he was in advance considering what was afterwards to be said. This I discovered by his sometimes introducing a word which was wholly out of place—*entertained* instead of *denied*, for example—but which I presently found to belong to the next sentence, perhaps four or five lines further on, which he had been preparing at the very moment that he gave me the words of the one that preceded it. Extemporaneous orators, of course, and no doubt many writers, think as rapidly as was done by Sir Walter; but the mind is wholly occupied with what the lips are uttering or the pen is tracing. I do not remember any other instance in which it could be said that two threads were kept hold of at once—connected with each other indeed, but grasped at different points. I was, as I have said, two or three days beside Sir Walter, and had repeated opportunities of observing the same thing.—I am, Sir, respectfully your obliged humble servant,

"ROBERT HOGG."

SIR WALTER SCOTT'S EARLY LIFE.

Walter Scott was twenty years of age when, in 1791, he was admitted to the Speculative Society of Edinburgh. He was chosen librarian, and shortly afterwards the secretary and treasurer. He kept the accounts and records very faithfully, and wrote essays and joined in debates on the commonplace questions usually proposed in such clubs. The following, from the *Life of Scott* by Lockhart, relates to this part of his life:—

"Lord Jeffrey remembers being struck, the first night he spent at the Speculative, with the singular appearance of the secretary, who sat gravely at the bottom of the table in a huge woollen night-cap; and, when the president took the chair, pleaded a bad toothache as his apology for coming into that worshipful assembly in such a 'portentous machine.' He read that night an essay on ballads, which so much interested the new member that he requested to be introduced to him. Mr. Jeffrey called on him next evening, and found him 'in a small den on the sunk floor of his father's house in George's Square, surrounded with 'dingy books,' from which they adjourned to a tavern and supped together. Such was the commencement of an acquaintance, which by degrees ripened into friendship, between the two most distinguished men of letters whom Edinburgh produced in their time. I may add here the description of that early den, with which I am favoured by a lady of Scott's family. 'Walter had soon begun to collect out-of-the-way things of all sorts. He had more books than shelves; a small painted cabinet, with Scotch and Roman coins in it, &c. A claymore and Lochaber axe, given him by old Ivernahyle, mounted guard on a little print of Prince Charlie; and 'Broughton's saucer' was hooked up against the wall below it.' Such was the germ of the magnificent library and museum of Abbotsford; and such were the 'new realms' in which he, on taking possession, had arranged his little paraphernalia about him, 'with all the feelings of novelty and liberty.' Since those days the habits of life in Edinburgh, as elsewhere, have undergone many changes; and the 'convenient parlour,' in which Scott first showed Jeffrey his collections of minstrelsy, is now, in all probability, thought hardly good enough for a menial's sleeping room."

HABITS OF SIR WALTER SCOTT.

There was no feature more conspicuous in the life of the great enchanter than the economical division of his time, and the entire occupancy of it to the best account. Mr. Lockhart furnishes this description, by James Skene, of Rubislow, who was very intimate with Scott.

He rose by five o'clock, lit his own fire, when the season required one, and shaved and dressed with great deliberation; for he was a very martinet as to all but the mere coxcombries of the toilet, not abhorring effeminate dandyism itself so cordially as the slightest approach to personal slovenliness, or even those "bed-gown and slipper tricks," as he called them, in which literary men are so apt to indulge. Arrayed in his shooting-jacket, or whatever dress he meant to use till dinner time, he was seated at his desk by six o'clock, all his papers arranged before him in the most accurate order, and his books of reference marshalled around him on the floor, while at least one favourite dog lay watching his eye just beyond the line of circumvallation. Thus, by the time the family assembled for breakfast, between nine and ten, he had done enough, in his own language, "*to break the neck of the day's work.*" After breakfast a couple of hours more were given to his solitary tasks, and by noon he was, as he used to say, his "own man." When the weather was bad, he would labour incessantly all the morning; but the general rule was to be out and on horseback by one o'clock at the latest; while, if any more distant excursion had been proposed over night, he was ready to start on it by ten; his occasional rainy days of unintermitted study forming, as he said, a fund in his favour, out of which he was entitled to draw for accommodation, whenever the sun shone with special brightness.

It was another rule, that every letter he received should be answered that same day. Nothing else could have enabled him to keep abreast with the flood of communication that in the sequel put his good nature to the severest test; but already the demands on him in this way also were numerous; and he included attention to them among the necessary business, which must be despatched before he had a right to close his writing-box. In turning over his enormous mass of correspondence, I have almost invariably found some indication that, when a letter had remained more than a day or two unanswered, it had been so because he found occasion for inquiry or deliberate consideration.

I ought not to omit that in those days Scott was far too zealous a dragoon not to take a principal share in the stable duty. Before beginning his desk-work in the morning, he uniformly visited his favourite steed, and neither *Captain* nor *Lieutenant*, nor the *Lieutenant's* successor, *Brown Adam*, so called after one of the heroes of the Minstrelsy, liked to be fed except by him. The latter charger was indeed altogether intractable in other hands, though in his the most submissive of faithful allies. The moment he was bridled and saddled, it was the custom to open the stable door, as a signal that his master expected him, when he immediately trotted to the side of the leaping-on-stone, of which Scott, from his lameness, found it convenient to make use, and stood there, silent and motionless as a 'rock, until he was fairly in his seat, after which he displayed his joy by neighing triumphantly through a brilliant succession of curvettings. *Brown Adam* never suffered himself to be backed but by his master. He broke, I believe, one groom's arm and another's leg, in the rash attempt to tamper with his dignity.

Camp was at this time the constant parlour dog. He was very handsome, very intelligent, and naturally very fierce, but gentle as a lamb among the children. As for the more locomotive *Douglas* and *Percy*, he kept one window of his study open, whatever might be the state of the weather, that they might leap out and in as the fancy moved them. He always talked to *Camp* as if he understood what was said, and the animal certainly did understand not a little of it; in particular, it seemed as if he perfectly comprehended, on all occasions, that his master considered him as a sensible and steady friend, and the greyhounds as volatile young creatures, whose freaks must be borne with.

SCOTT'S REVERSES.

Sir Walter Scott was engaged, at the time of his misfortunes, in writing the *Life of Bonaparte*, taking up his new novel of *Woodstock* at intervals by way of relief. These tasks he continued, with steady perseverance, in the midst of all his distresses. Even on the day which brought him assurance of the grand catastrophe, he resumed in the afternoon the task which had engaged him in the morning. There was more triumph over circumstances here than might be supposed, for he had lately begun to feel the first touches of the infirmities of age—age to which ease, not hard work, is naturally appropriate. His sleep was now less sound than it had been; his eyesight was failing; and, above all, he felt that backwardness of the intellectual power which is inseparable from years. The will, however, was green as ever, and under the prompting of an honourable spirit, it did its work nobly. Doggedly, doggedly did the energetic old man rouse himself from his melancholy couch, and set to his task at an hour when gaiety had little more than sought his. Firmly did he keep to his desk during long hours, till he could satisfy himself that he had done his utmost. The temptations of society, the more insinuating claims of an overworked system for rest, were alike resolutely rejected. The world must ever hear with wonder, that between the third day after his bankruptcy and the fifteenth day thereafter, he had written a volume of *Woodstock*, although several of these days had been spent in comparative vacancy, to allow the imagination time for brooding. He believed, that, for a bet, he could have written this volume *in ten days*. Just a fortnight after his final breach with fortune, he says in his journal, " I have now no pecuniary provisions to embarrass me, and I think, now the shock of the discovery is past and over, I am much better off on the whole. . . . I shall be free of a hundred petty public duties imposed on me as a man of consideration, of the expense of a great hospitality, and, what is better, of the waste of time connected with it. I have known in my day all kinds of society, and can pretty well estimate how much or how little one loses by retiring from all but that which is very intimate. . . . If I could see those about me as indifferent to the loss of rank as I am, I should be completely happy. As it is, time must salve that sore, and to time I trust it."

SIR WALTER SCOTT AND THE AMERICAN AUTHORESS.

"One morning," said Scott, "I opened a huge lump of a despatch, without looking to know how it was addressed, never doubting that it had travelled under some omnipotent frank, like the first lord of admiralty's, when, lo and behold, the contents proved to be a manuscript play, by a young lady of New York, who kindly requested me to read and correct it, equip it with prologue and epilogue, procure for it a favourable reception from the manager of Drury Lane, and make Murray or Constable bleed handsomely for the copyright; and, inspecting the cover, I found that I had been charged five pounds odd for the postage. This was bad enough; but there was no help, so I groaned and submitted. A fortnight or so after, another packet, of not less formidable bulk, arrived, and I was absent enough to break its seal too, without examination. Conceive my horror, when out jumped the same identical tragedy of the "Cherokee Lovers," with a second epistle from the authoress, stating that, as the winds had been boisterous, she feared the vessel intrusted with her former communication might have foundered, and therefore judged it prudent to forward a duplicate."

CHARLES DICKENS.

Having stated, in the original preface to *Nicholas Nickleby*, that the *Brothers Cheeryble* were portraits from the life, and that they yet exercised their unbounded benevolence in the town of which they are the pride and honour, Dickens thus laments over the applications to which his statement has given rise:—

"If I were to attempt to sum up the hundreds upon hundreds of letters from all sorts of people, in all sorts of latitudes and climates, to which this unlucky paragraph has since given rise, I should get into an arithmetical difficulty from which I could not easily extricate myself. Suffice it to say, that I believe the applications for loans, gifts, and offices of profit, that I have been requested to forward to the originals of the Brothers Cheeryble (with whom I never interchanged any communication in my life), would have exhausted the combined patronage of all the lord-chancellors since the accession of the house of Brunswick, and would have broken the rest of the Bank of England."

DICKENS AND SQUEERS.

Prefixed to Dickens's second edition of *Nicholas Nickleby*, we find the following allusion to Yorkshire schools:—

"I cannot call to mind, now, how I came to hear about Yorkshire schools, when I was not a very robust child, sitting in by-places, near Rochester Castle, with a head full of Partridge, Strap, Tom Pipes, and Sancho Panza; but I know that my first impressions of them were picked up at that time, and that they were somehow or other connected with a suppurated abscess that some boy had come home with, in consequence of his Yorkshire guide, philosopher, and friend, having ripped it open with an inky penknife. The impression made upon me, however made, never left me. I was always curious about them—fell, long afterwards, and at sundry times, into the way of hearing more about them—at last, having an audience, resolved to write about them. With that intent I went down into Yorkshire before I began this book, in very severe winter time, which is pretty faithfully described herein. As I wanted to see a schoolmaster or two, and was forewarned that those gentlemen might, in their modesty, be shy of receiving a visit from the author of the *Pickwick Papers*, I consulted with a professional friend here, who had a Yorkshire connection, and with whom I concerted a pious fraud. He gave me some letters of introduction, in the name, I think, of my travelling companion: they bore reference to a supposititious little boy who had been left with a widowed mother who didn't know what to do with him; the poor lady had thought, as a means of thawing the tardy compassion of her relations in his behalf, of sending him to a Yorkshire school. I was the poor lady's friend, travelling that way; and if the recipient of the letter could inform me of a school in his neighbourhood, the writer would be very much obliged. I went to several places in that part of the country where I understood these schools to be most plentifully sprinkled, and had no occasion to deliver a letter until I came to a certain town which shall be nameless. The person to whom it was addressed was not at home; but he came down at night, through the snow, to the inn where I was staying. It was after dinner, and he needed little persuasion to sit down by the fire in a warm corner, and take his share of the wine that was on the table. I am afraid he is dead now. I recollect he was a jovial, ruddy, broad-faced man; that we got acquainted directly; and that we talked on all kinds of subjects, except the school, which he showed a great anxiety to avoid. 'Was there any large school near?' I asked him, in reference to the letter. 'O, yes,' he said, 'there was a pratty big 'un.' 'Was it a good one?' I asked. 'Ey,' he said, 'it was as good as anoother; that was a' a matther of opinion;' and fell to looking at the fire, staring round the room, and whistling a little. On my reverting to some other topic that we had been discussing, he recovered immediately; but, though I tried him again and again, I never approached the question of the school, even if he were in the middle of a laugh, without observing that his countenance fell, and that he became uncomfortable. At last, when we had passed a couple of hours or so, very agreeably, he suddenly took up his hat, and, leaning over the table, and looking me full in the face, said, in a low voice, 'Weel, misther, we've been vary pleasant toogather, and ar'll spak' my moind tiv'ee. Dinnot let the weedur send her lattle boy to yan o' our schoolmeasthers, while there's a harse to hold in a' Lunnun, or a gootther to lie asleep in. Ar wouldn't mak' ill words amang my neeburs, and ar spak' tiv'ee quiet loike. But I'm doom'd if ar can gang to bed and not tellee, for weedur's sak', to keep the lattle boy from a' sike scoundrels while there's a harse to hold in a' Lunnun, or a gootther to lie asleep in.' Repeating these words with great heartiness, and with a solemnity on his jolly face that made it look twice as large as before, he shook hands and went away."

MAGNANIMITY OF CERVANTES.

Michael Cervantes Saavedra, the author of *Don Quixote*, gave a proof that his generosity was equal to his genius. He was, in the early part of his life, for some time a slave in Algiers, and there he concerted a plan to free himself and thirteen fellow-sufferers. One of them traitorously betrayed the design, and they were all conveyed to the Dey of Algiers; and he promised them their lives on condition they discovered the contriver of the plot. "I was that person," exclaimed the intrepid Cervantes; "save my companions, and let me perish." The Dey, struck with his noble confession, spared his life, allowed him to be ransomed, and permitted him to depart home.

This writer of an incomparable romance, replete with character, incident, pleasantry, and humour, without any alloy of vulgarity, obscenity, or irreligion, and which is held in admiration throughout the civilized world, starved in the midst of a high reputation, and died in penury.

As Philip III., King of Spain, was standing in a balcony of his palace at Madrid, and viewing the prospects of the surrounding country, he observed a student on the banks of the river Manzanares, reading a book, and from time to time breaking off, and beating his forehead with extraordinary tokens of pleasure and delight; upon which the king said to those about him, "That scholar is either mad, or he is reading *Don Quixote*."

This anecdote is worth a volume of panegyric.

STERNE'S HARD-HEARTEDNESS.

"What is called sentimental writing," says Horace Walpole, "though it be understood to appeal solely to the heart, may be the product of a bad one. One would imagine that Sterne had been a man of a very tender heart; yet I know, from indubitable authority, that his mother, who kept a school, having run in debt on account of an extravagant daughter, would have rotted in jail if the parents of the scholars had not raised a subscription for her. Her son had too much sentiment to have any feeling. A dead ass was more important to him than a living mother."

DANIEL DEFOE.

The name of the interesting writer of *Robinson Crusoe* was not originally *Defoe*, but *Foe*—the prefix being added by himself. He was born in London in 1663. His early education and habits were such as to promise almost any other results than works of fiction. And yet we find him, at twenty-one years of age, the author of a treatise against the Turks. He joined the insurrection of the Duke of Monmouth, but had the good fortune to escape to London unscathed, where he engaged, first as a horse-factor, and then as a brickmaker. Failing in business, however, he became insolvent, and compounded with his creditors as best he could. It is to his credit, however, that when his circumstances were afterwards improved, he paid the full amount of all his obligations. In 1697, he again became an author; and more than twenty years later—when about fifty years of age—his romance of *Robinson Crusoe* appeared. His subsequent productions were very numerous; and a few of them were works of merit.

GOËTHE'S NOVELS.

The regular novels of Goëthe are of a very questionable sort. The vivacity of his imagination and fineness of feeling, supply good individual pictures and acute remarks, but they cannot be praised either for incident or character. They are often stained, too, with the degradation to which he unfortunately reduces love, where liking and vice follow fast upon each other. *The Apprenticeship of William Meister*, for instance, is a very readable book, in so far as it contains a great deal of acute and eloquent criticism; but who would purchase the criticism, even of Goëthe, at the expense of the licentiousness of incident and pruriency of description with which the book teems?—(Russell's Germany.)

MISS BURNEY.

Miss Burney, afterwards Madame D'Arblay, wrote her celebrated novel of *Evelina* when only seventeen years of age, and published it without the knowledge of her father, who, having occasion to visit the metropolis, soon after it had issued from the press, purchased it as the work then most popular, and most likely to prove an acceptable treat to his family.

When Dr. Burney had concluded his business in town, he went to Chessington, the seat of Mr. Crisp, where his family were on a visit. He had scarcely dismounted and entered the parlour, when the customary question of "What news?" was rapidly addressed to him by the several personages of the little party. "Nothing," said the worthy doctor, "but a great deal of noise about a novel which I have brought you."

When the book was produced, and the title read, the surprised and conscious Miss Burney turned away her face to conceal the blushes and delighted confusion which otherwise would have betrayed her secret; but the bustle which usually attends the arrival of a friend in the country, where the monotonous but peaceful tenor of life is agreeably disturbed by such a change, prevented the curious and happy group from observing the agitation of their sister.

After dinner, Mr. Crisp proposed that the book should be read. This was done with all due rapidity; when the gratifying comments made during its progress, and the acclamations which attended its conclusion, ratified the approbation of the public. The amiable author, whose anxiety and pleasure could with difficulty be concealed, was at length overcome by the delicious feelings of her heart; she burst into tears, and throwing herself on her father's neck, avowed herself the author of *Evelina*.

The joy and surprise of her sisters, and still more of her father, cannot easily be expressed. Dr. Burney, conscious as he was of the talents of his daughter, never thought that such maturity of observation and judgment, such fertility of imagination, and chasteness of style, could have been displayed by a girl of seventeen—by one who appeared a mere infant in artlessness and inexperience, and whose deep seclusion from the world had excluded her from all visual knowledge of its ways.

Soon after 1774, she settled at Rome, and was admitted a member of the Academy of the Arcadi, under the name of Corilla Olympica, and for some time continued to charm the inhabitants of Rome by her talents in improvisation. At length, when Pius VI. became Pope, he determined that she should be solemnly crowned—an honour which had been granted to Petrarch only.

Twelve members of the Arcadian Academy were selected out of thirty, publicly to examine the new edition of the "Tenth Muse," which has so often been dedicated to ladies of poetical and literary talents. Three several days were allotted for this public exhibition of poetical powers, on the following subjects:—sacred history, revealed religion, moral philosophy, natural history, metaphysics, epic poetry, legislation, eloquence, mythology, fine arts, and pastoral poetry.

In the list of examiners appeared a prince, an archbishop, three monseigneurs, the Pope's physician, *abati, avocati*, all of high rank in literature and criticism. These severally gave her subjects, which, besides a readiness at versification in all the measures of Italian poetry, required science, reading, and knowledge of every kind.

In these severe trials, she acquitted herself to the satisfaction and astonishment of all the personages, clergy, literati, and foreigners then resident at Rome. Among the latter was the brother of George III., the Duke of Gloucester. Nearly fifty sonnets, by different poets, with odes, canzoni, terze rime, attave, canzonette, &c., produced on the subject of the event, are inserted at the end of a beautiful volume containing a description of the order and ceremonials of this splendid, honourable, and enthusiastic homage paid to poetry, classical taste, talents, literature, and the fine arts.

THE AUTHORSHIP OF WAVERLEY.

Mrs. Murray Keith, a venerable Scotch lady, from whom Sir Walter Scott derived many of the traditionary stories and anecdotes wrought up in his novels, taxed him one day with the authorship, which he, as usual, stoutly denied. "What!" exclaimed the old lady, "d'ye think I dinna ken my ain groats among other folk's kail?"

THE "VICAR OF WAKEFIELD."

This beautiful little work remained unnoticed, and was attacked by the reviews, until Lord Holland, who had been ill, sent to his bookseller for some amusing book. This was supplied, and he was so pleased that he spoke of it in the highest terms to a large company who dined with him a few days after. The consequence was, that the whole impression was sold off in a few days.

ORATORY AND ELOCUTION,
PULPIT, PARLIAMENTARY, AND JUDICIAL.

BISHOP ATTERBURY.

Dr. Doddridge, in his unpublished lectures on preaching, gives a short view of the characters and qualifications of the most celebrated divines of the last and present age, both conformists and non-conformists. Under the former head he thus describes Atterbury as a preacher:—"Atterbury. The glory of English orators! His language in its strictest purity and beauty: nothing dark, nothing redundant, nothing defective, nothing misplaced. Trivial thoughts avoided; uncommon ones introduced; set in a clear and strong light in a few words; a few admirable similies; graceful allusions to Scripture beyond any other writer. On the whole, he is a model for courtly preachers."

SHERIDAN.

Sheridan was one day much annoyed by a fellow-member of the House of Commons, who kept crying out every few minutes, "Hear! hear!" During the debate he took occasion to describe a political cotemporary who wished to play the rogue, but had only sense enough to act the fool. "Where," exclaimed he, with great emphasis, "where shall we find a more foolish knave or a more knavish fool than he?" "Hear! hear!" was shouted by the troublesome member. Sheridan turned round, and, thanking him for the prompt reply, sat down amid a general roar of laughter.

APPLAUSE IN THE GALLERY OF THE HOUSE OF COMMONS.

The late William Gardiner, of Leicester, related the following story of himself, in his work called *Music and Friends:*—

"I was presented with an order to the gallery of the House of Commons. That night there was a grand debate upon Mr. Grey's motion touching the seizure of Oczakow by the Empress of Russia, in which I heard all the principal speakers. Mr. Grey's style was that of sober argument; Sheridan's, playful; Burke's, imaginative and lofty; Pitt's (what little he said), supercilious and scornful; Fox's, powerful and eloquent. He was the last speaker, and I was so excited by his oratory, that, without reflecting where I was, I vehemently called out 'Bravo!' I was delighted to that degree that I made the house ring again. The speaker, Addington, immediately got up and said, that more unwarrantable conduct he had never witnessed than that of the person who had interrupted the proceedings. Strangers were upon sufferance in that house, and could not be permitted to applaud or disapprove anything that was passing. It was a high breach of privilege, and a sergeant-at-arms was ordered to bring the offender to the bar. A tall, handsome man, sitting alone in the side gallery, approached me, and said, with a countenance almost breaking into a laugh, 'How could you be so indiscreet, young man?' 'Sir,' I replied, 'I hope you will excuse me; I am but a countryman.' By this time the officer was making his way to take me up, when this person, waving his hand, caused him to desist. It was no other than the Prince of Wales, whom the importance of the debate had brought into the house, and who, most probably, saved me from Newgate. The gallery, however, in consequence of my indiscretion, was ordered to be cleared; and as I passed through the crowd, I had the execration of the whole company. Many years afterwards, when on a journey to the south of England, I arrived late in the evening at the Single Star, in Exeter, and was shown into the travellers' room, where a merry party were discussing the merits of the different speakers in the House of Commons. A gentleman told us that he was in the gallery one night, enjoying the debate, when he had the mortification to be turned out, in consequence of the folly of some fellow calling out 'Bravo!' I kept my countenance, and joined in the laugh, and did not reveal to the gentleman that I was the very person who had committed this outrage, till I met him the next morning at breakfast."

GRATTAN,—CONCENTRATED CONTEMPT.

Thomas Campbell repeated the following anecdote of Grattan, on the authority of Samuel Rogers:— Grattan was once violently attacked in the Irish House of Commons by an inveterate Orangeman, who made a miserable speech. In reply, Grattan said—"I shall make no other remark on the personalities of the honourable gentleman who spoke last, than—As he rose without a friend, so he has sat down without an enemy." Was ever contempt (adds Campbell) so concentrated in expression!

BURKE PUT TO FLIGHT.

Mr. Burke, on one occasion, had just risen in the House of Commons, with some papers in his hand, on the subject of which he intended to make a motion, when a rough-hewn member, who had no ear for the charms of eloquence, rudely started up, and said, "Mr. Speaker, I hope the honourable gentleman does not mean to read that large bundle of papers, and to bore us with a long speech into the bargain." Mr. B. was so swollen with rage, as to be incapable of utterance, and absolutely ran out of the house. On this occasion, George Selwyn remarked, that it was the only time he ever saw the fable realized—*a lion put to flight by the braying of an ass.*

FARADAY AS A LECTURER.

Von Raumer acutely observes:— "Mr. Faraday is not only a man of profound chemical and physical science (which all Europe knows), but a very remarkable lecturer. He speaks with ease and freedom, but not with a gossiping unequal tone, alternately inaudible and bawling, as some very learned professors do; he delivers himself with clearness, precision, and ability. Moreover, he speaks his language in a manner which confirmed me in a secret suspicion I had, that a great number of Englishmen speak it very badly. Why is it that French in the mouth of Mdlle. Mars, German in that of Tieck, and English in that of Faraday, seems a totally different language? Because they articulate what other people swallow or chew. It is a shame that the power and harmony of simple speech (I am not talking of eloquence, but of vowels and consonants), that the tones and inflexions which God has given to the human voice, should be so neglected and abused. And those who think they do them full justice —preachers—generally give us only the long straw of pretended connoisseurs, instead of the chopped straw of the dilettanti."

BROUGHAM AND LYNDHURST.

Brougham, speaking of the salary attached to a rumoured appointment to a new judgeship, said it was all moonshine. Lyndhurst, in his dry and waggish way, remarked, "May be so, my Lord Harry; but I have a strong notion that, moonshine though it be, you would like to see the first quarter of it."

LORD BROUGHAM.

It is related of Lord Brougham that on one occasion, after having practised all day as a barrister, he went to the House of Commons, where he was engaged in active debate through the night, till three o'clock in the morning: he then returned home; wrote an article for the *Edinburgh Review;* spent the next day in court, practising law, and the succeeding night in the House of Commons; returned to his lodgings at three o'clock in the morning, and "retired simply because he had nothing else to do."

It is known that Brougham was laboriously studying optics in the brief intervals of the Queen's trial, one of the most absorbing judicial proceedings of modern times, and in which he took a leading part as counsel.

LORD ERSKINE.

When Lord Erskine made his *début* at the bar, his agitation almost overcame him, and he was just going to sit down. "At that moment," said he, "I thought I felt my little children tugging at my gown, and the idea roused me to an exertion of which I did not think myself capable."

JEFFREY AND JOHN KEMBLE.

In February 1818, he did what he never did before or since. He stuck a speech. John Kemble had taken his leave of our stage, and before quitting Edinburgh, about sixty or seventy of his admirers gave him a dinner and a snuff-box. Jeffrey was put into the chair, and had to make the address previous to the presentation. He began very promisingly, but got confused, and amazed both himself and everybody else, by actually sitting down, and leaving the speech unfinished; and, until reminded of that part of his duty, not even thrusting the box into the hand of the intended receiver. He afterwards told me the reason of this. He had not premeditated the scene, and thought he had nothing to do, except, in the name of the company, to give the box. But as soon as he rose to do this, Kemble, who was beside him, rose also, and with the most formidable dignity. This forced Jeffrey to look up to his man; when he found himself annihilated by the tall tragic god; who sank him to the earth at every compliment, by obeisances of overwhelming grace and stateliness. If the chairman had anticipated his position, or re- covered from his first confusion, his mind and words could easily have subdued even Kemble.—(Life of Lord Jeffrey.)

CHARLES JAMES FOX.

"What a man," says Walpole, "Fox is! After his long and exhausting speech on Hastings's trial, he was seen handing ladies into their coaches, with all the gaiety and prattle of an idle gallant."

MELODRAMATIC TRICK.

Burke's was a complete failure, when he flung the dagger on the floor of the House of Commons, and produced nothing but a smothered laugh, and a joke from Sheridan:— "The gentleman has brought us the knife, but where is the fork?"

DR. CHALMERS IN LONDON.

When Dr. Chalmers first visited London, the hold that he took on the minds of men was unprecedented. It was a time of strong political feeling; but even that was unheeded, and all parties thronged to hear the Scottish preacher. The very best judges were not prepared for the display that they heard. Canning and Wilberforce went together, and got into a pew near the door. The elder in attendance stood alone by the pew. Chalmers began in his usual unpromising way, by stating a few nearly self-evident propositions, neither in the choicest language, nor in the most impressive voice. "If this be all," said Canning to his companion, "it will never do." Chalmers went on—the shuffling of the conversation gradually subsided. He got into the mass of his subject; his weakness became strength, his hesitation was turned into energy, and, bringing the whole volume of his mind to bear upon it, he poured forth a torrent of the most close and conclusive argument, brilliant with all the exuberance of an imagination which ranged over all nature for illustrations, and yet managed and applied each of them with the same unerring dexterity, as if that single one had been the study of a whole life. "The tartan beats us," said Mr. Canning; "we have no preaching like that in England." "Canning," says Sir James Mackintosh, "told me that he was entirely converted to admiration of Chalmers." Wilberforce noted in his diary, that Canning was affected to tears.

PITT, FOX, AND SHERIDAN.

Pitt and Fox were listened to with profound respect, and in silence broken only by occasional cheers; but from the moment of Sheridan's rising, there was an expectation of pleasure, which, to his last days, was seldom disappointed. A low murmur of eagerness ran round the house; every word was watched for, and his pleasantry set the whole assemblage in a roar. Sheridan was aware of this, and has been heard to say, that if a jester would never be an orator, yet no speaker could expect to be popular in a *full house*, without a jest; and that he always made the experiment, good or bad; as a laugh gave him the country gentlemen to a man.

PREACHERS AND ACTORS.

"Pray, Mr. Betterton," asked the good Archbishop Sancroft, of the celebrated actor, "can you inform me what is the reason you actors on the stage, speaking of things imaginary, affect your audience as if they were real, while we in the church speak of things real, which our congregations receive only as if they were imaginary?" "Why, really, my Lord," answered Betterton, "I don't know, unless we actors speak of things imaginary as if they were real, while you in the pulpit speak of things real as if they were imaginary."

CANNING AND GRATTAN.

Canning said of Grattan's eloquence, that, for the last two years, his public exhibitions were a complete failure, and that you saw all the mechanism of his oratory without its life. It was like lifting the flap of a barrel-organ, and seeing the wheels; you saw the skeleton of his sentences without the flesh on them; and were induced to think that what you had considered flashes, were merely primings kept ready for the occasion.—(Moore.)

READING.

The late Isaac Hawkins Brown declared, that he never felt the charms of Milton until he heard his exordium read by Sheridan.

Virgil pronounced his own verses with such an enticing sweetness and enchanting grace, that Julius Montanus, a poet who had often heard him, used to say that he could steal Virgil's verses, if he could steal his voice, expression, and gesture; for the same verses, that sounded so rapturously when he read them, were not always excellent in the mouth of another.

DOING JUSTICE TO THE CONSONANTS.

Mr. Jones, in his life of Bishop Horne, speaking of Dr. Hinchcliffe, Bishop of Peterborough, says, that in the pulpit he spoke with the accent of a man of sense, such as he really was in a superior degree; but it was remarkable, and, to those who did not know the cause, mysterious, that there was not a corner of the church in which he could not be heard distinctly. The reason which Mr. Jones assigned was, that he made it an invariable rule *to do justice to every consonant, knowing that the vowels would speak for themselves.* And thus he became the surest and clearest of speakers; his elocution was perfect, and never disappointed his audience.

THE PULPIT.

A celebrated divine, who was remarkable in the first period of his ministry for a boisterous mode of preaching, suddenly changed his whole manner in the pulpit, and adopted a mild and dispassioned mode of delivery. One of his brethren, observing it, inquired of him what had induced him to make the change. He answered, "When I was young, I thought it was the *thunder* that killed the people; but when I grew wiser, I discovered that it was the *lightning;* so I determined in future to thunder less, and lighten more."

EFFECT OF MANNER.

"The Duke of Argyle," says Lord Chesterfield, "though the weakest reasoner, was the most pleasing speaker I ever heard in my life. He charmed, he warmed, he forcibly ravished the audience; not by his matter, certainly, but by his manner of delivering it. A most genteel figure, a noble air, an harmonious voice, an elegance of style, and a strength of emphasis, conspired to make him the most affecting, persuasive, and applauded speaker I ever heard. I was captivated like others; but when I came home, and coolly considered what he had said, stripped of all those ornaments in which he had dressed it, I often found the matter flimsy, the arguments weak, and I was convinced of the power of those adventitious concurring circumstances, which it is ignorance of mankind to call trifling."

WHITEFIELD.

Garrick said he would give a hundred guineas if he could say "Oh!" as Whitefield did.

EDMUND BURKE.

The agitation produced by Burke's speech at the trial of Warren Hastings was such that the whole audience appeared to have felt one convulsive emotion; and when it was over, it was some time before Mr. Fox could obtain a hearing. Amidst the assemblage of concurring praises, which this speech excited, none was more remarkable than the tribute of Mr. Hastings himself. "For half an hour," said that gentleman, "I looked up at the orator in a reverie of wonder; and during that space I actually felt myself the most culpable man on earth." Had the sentiment concluded here, our readers would not believe that it was in the language or manner of Mr. Hastings. "But," continued he, "I recurred to my own bosom, and there found a consciousness which consoled me under all I heard, and all I suffered." A friend of Hastings' thus satirized Burke on the occasion:—

" Oft have I wondered that on Irish
  ground
No *venomous* reptile ever yet was
  found;
The secret stands revealed in nature's
  work—
She saved her venom TO CREATE A
  BURKE!"

SHERIDAN'S POTIONS.

In the year 1805, on the day when the very animated debate took place upon the celebrated Tenth Report of the Commissioners of Naval Inquiry, the attention of a gentleman, who happened to enter a coffee-house near the House of Commons, was instantly fixed by another gentleman, whom he observed at one of the tables, with tea, and pen, ink, and paper before him. For some time the latter sat alternately drinking tea and taking down memoranda, and then called to the waiter to bring him some brandy; when to the observer's great surprise, a half-pint tumbler-full was brought. The gentleman placed it by him, continuing a while alternately to write and drink tea;

when, at length, collecting his papers together, he put them in his pocket, and swallowing the half pint of brandy as if it had been water, went out of the coffee-house. The stranger was so much struck by all he had observed, particularly at the facility with which such a quantity of spirits was taken, that he could not forbear to ask the waiter who that gentleman was? The man replied, "Pshaw! don't you know him? Why, that's Sheridan; he's going now to the House of Commons." It will be remembered that in the course of this debate Mr. Sheridan made one of the finest speeches ever delivered by him, alike remarkable for keenness of argument and brilliancy of wit, and this under the influence of a potion that would wholly have deprived most men of their faculties.

The following anecdote of Sheridan was related by one of the oldest surviving friends and followers of Fox. This gentleman and Sheridan had dined together at Bellamy's. Sheridan, having taken his allowance, said as usual, "Now I shall go down and see what's doing in the house;" which in reality meant, and was always so interpreted by whoever dined in his company, "I have drank enough; my share of the business is done; now do yours; call for the bill, and pay it." The bill having been settled by Sheridan's friend, the latter, hearing that Sheridan was "up," felt curious to know what he could possibly be at, knowing the state in which he had just departed. Accordingly, he entered the house, and, to his no small astonishment, found Sheridan in a fit of most fervent oratory, thundering forth the following well-known passage: "Give them a corrupt House of Lords; give them a venal House of Commons; give them a tyrannical prince; give them a truckling court; and let me have but an unfettered press, and I will defy them to encroach a hair's-breadth upon the liberties of England!"

PHILOLOGY AND LINGUISTS.

SIR WILLIAM JONES.

That wonderful scholar, Sir William Jones, who, in addition to great acquirements in various other departments of knowledge, had made himself acquainted with no fewer than twenty-eight different languages, was studying the grammars of several of the Oriental dialects up till within a week of his lamented death. At an earlier period of his life, when he was in his thirty-third year, he had resolved, as appears from a scheme of study found among his papers, "to learn no more rudiments of any kind, but to perfect himself in, first, twelve languages, as the means of acquiring accurate knowledge of history, arts, and sciences." These were the Greek, Latin, Italian, French, Spanish, Portuguese, Hebrew, Arabic, Persian, Turkish, German, and English. When he was afterwards induced, however, from the situation he held in India, to devote himself more especially to Oriental learning, he extended his researches a great way even beyond these ample limits. In addition to the tongues already enumerated, he made himself not only completely master of Sanscrit, as well as less completely of Hindostanee and Bengalee, but to a considerable extent, also, of the other Indian dialects, called the Thibetian, the Pali, the Phaluvi, and the Deri; to which are to be added, among the languages which he describes himself to have studied least perfectly, the Chinese, Russian, Runic, Syriac, Ethiopic, Coptic, Dutch, Swedish, and Welsh.

MITHRIDATES AND CLEOPATRA.

Mithridates, King of Pontus, knew twenty-two languages, and spoke them correctly.

And Plutarch says that Cleopatra knew almost all the languages spoken by the people of the Levant.

MADAME ANNA BISHOP.

When Madame Anna Bishop was giving concerts in Guanajuato, Mexico, in the winter of 1849, her placards announced that she would sing in *ten* languages, viz., Spanish, Italian, French, German, Russian, Tartar, English, Irish, Scotch, and Ethiopian!

THE TRAVELLING LIBRARY.

Professor Porson, the celebrated Grecian, was once travelling in a stage-coach, where a young Oxonian, fresh from college, was amusing the ladies with a variety of talk, and, amongst other things, with a quotation, as he said, from Sophocles. A Greek quotation, and in a coach too, roused the slumbering professor from a kind of dog-sleep, in a snug corner of the vehicle. Shaking his ears and rubbing his eyes, " I think, young gentleman," said he, " you favoured us just now with a quotation from Sophocles; I do not happen to recollect it there." "O, sir," replied the tyro, "the quotation is word for word as I have repeated it, and from Sophocles, too; but I suspect, sir, it is some time since you were at college." The professor, applying his hand to his great-coat pocket, and taking out a small pocket edition of Sophocles, quietly asked him if he would be kind enough to show him the passage in question in that little book. After rummaging the pages for some time, he replied, "Upon second thoughts, I now recollect that the passage is in Euripides." " Then, perhaps, sir," said the professor, putting his hand again into his pocket, and handing him a similar edition of Euripides, "you will be so good as to find it for me in that little book." The young Oxonian again returned to his task, but with no better success, muttering, however, to himself, a vow never again to quote Greek in a stage-coach. The tittering of the ladies informed him plainly that he had got into a hobble. At last, "Why, sir," said he, "how dull I am! I recollect now; yes, now I perfectly remember that the passage is in Æschylus." The inexorable professor returned to his inexhaustible pocket, and was in the act of handing him an Æschylus, when our astonished freshman vociferated, "Coachman! holloa, coachman! let me out; I say instantly let me out! There's a fellow here has the whole Bodleian library in his pocket."

THE RETORT NOT COURTEOUS.

"Dr. Porson," said a gentleman to the great "Grecian," with whom he had been disputing—"Dr. Porson, my opinion of you is most contemptible." "Sir," returned the doctor, "I never knew an opinion of yours that was not contemptible."

DR. JOHNSON.

Dr. Johnson had a veneration for the voice of mankind beyond what most people will own; and, as he liberally confessed that all his own disappointments proceeded from himself, he hated to hear others complain of general injustice. "I remember," says Mrs. Piozzi, "when lamentation was made of the neglect showed to a great philologist, as some one ventured to call him, ' He is a scholar, undoubtedly, sir,' replied Dr. Johnson ; 'but remember that he would run from the world, and that it is not the world's business to run after him. I hate a fellow whom pride, or cowardice, or laziness drives into a corner, and does nothing, when he is there, but sit and *growl;* let him come out as I do, and *bark.*'"

CLASSICAL GLORY.

Dr. George, the celebrated Grecian, upon hearing the praises of the great King of Prussia, entertained considerable doubt whether the king, with all his victories, knew how to conjugate a Greek verb in $\mu\iota$.

CAN SHE SPIN ?

A young girl was presented to James I. as an English prodigy, because she was deeply learned. The person who introduced her boasted of her proficiency in ancient languages. "I can assure your majesty," said he, "that she can both speak and write Latin, Greek, and Hebrew." "These are rare attainments for a damsel," said James; "but, pray tell me, can she spin?"

DRS. PORSON AND GILLIES.

Dr. Gillies, the historian of Greece, and Dr. Porson, used now and then to meet. The consequence was certain to be a literary contest. Porson was much the deeper scholar of the two. Dr. Gillies was one day speaking to him of the Greek tragedies, and of Pindar's odes. "We *know nothing,*" said Dr. Gillies, emphatically, "of the Greek metres." Porson answered, "If, doctor, you will put your observation in the *singular* number, I believe it will be very accurate."

ELIHU BURRITT, THE LEARNED BLACKSMITH.

A letter written by Elihu Burritt, the learned blacksmith, contains some interesting incidents of his career.

Mr. Burritt mentions that, being one of a large family, and his parents poor, he apprenticed himself, when very young, to a blacksmith, but that he had always had such a taste for reading, that he carried it with him to his trade. He commenced the study of Latin when his indentures were not half expired, and completed reading Virgil in the evenings of one winter. He next studied Greek, and carried the Greek Grammar about in his hat, studying it for a few moments while heating some large iron. In the evenings, he sat down to Homer's *Iliad,* and read twenty books of it during the second winter. He next turned to the modern tongues, and went to Newhaven, where he recited to native teachers in French, Spanish, German, and Italian, and at the end of two years he returned to his forge, taking with him such books as he could procure. He next commenced Hebrew, and soon mastered it with ease, reading two chapters in the Bible before breakfast; this, with an hour at noon, being all the time he could spare from work. Being unable to procure such books as he desired, he determined to hire himself to some ship bound to Europe, thinking he would there meet with books at the different ports he touched at. He travelled more than a hundred miles on foot to Boston with this view, but was not able to find what he sought; and at that period he heard of the American Antiquarian Society at Worcester. Thither he bent his steps, and arrived in the city in utter indigence. Here he found a collection of ancient, modern, and Oriental books, such as he never imagined to be collected in one place. He was there kindly allowed to read what books he liked, and reaped great benefit from this permission.

He used to spend three hours daily in the hall, and made such use of these privileges, as to be able to read upwards of *fifty* languages with greater or less facility.

FRANKLIN.

Franklin commenced the study of the languages at twenty-seven years of age. We quote his account of the manner in which he pursued this branch of his studies:—

"I had begun," says he, "in 1733 to study languages. I soon made myself so much a master of the French as to be able to read the books in that language with ease. I then undertook the Italian. An acquaintance, who was also learning it, used often to tempt me to play chess with him. Finding this took up too much of the time I had to spare for study, I at length refused to play any more, unless on this condition—that the victor in every game should have a right to impose a task, either of parts of the grammar to be got by heart, or in translations, &c., which task the vanquished was to perform upon honour before our next meeting. As we played pretty equally, we thus beat one another into that language. I afterwards, with a little painstaking, acquired as much of the Spanish as to read their books also. I have already mentioned that I had had only one year's instruction in a Latin school, and that when very young, after which I neglected that language entirely. But when I had attained an acquaintance with the French, Italian, and Spanish, I was surprised to find, on looking over a Latin Testament, that I understood more of that language than I had imagined, which encouraged me to apply myself to the study of it again; and I met with more success, as those preceding languages had greatly smoothed my way."

A FEMALE LINGUIST.

Maria Cajetana Agnesi, an Italian lady of great learning, was born at Milan, March 16, 1718. Her inclinations, from her earliest youth, led her to the study of science, and at an age when young persons of her sex attend only to frivolous pursuits, she made such astonishing progress in mathematics, that when, in 1750, her father, professor in the University of Bologna, was unable to continue his lectures, from infirm health, she obtained permission from the Pope, Benedict XIV., to fill his chair. Before this, at the early age of nineteen, she had supported one hundred and ninety-one theses, which were published in 1738, under the title of *Propositiones Philosophicæ*. She was mistress of Latin, Greek, Hebrew, French, German, and Spanish. At length she gave up her studies, and went into the monastery of the Blue Nuns, at Milan, where she died, January 9, 1799. In 1740, she published a discourse, tending to prove "that the study of the liberal arts is not incompatible with the understandings of woman." This was written when she was very young; she wrote upon mathematics of a high order —fluxions and analytics. The commentators of Newton were acquainted with her mathematical works while they were in manuscript. In 1801, these works were published in two volumes, at the expense of Mr. Baron Maseres, to do honour to her memory, and to prove that women have minds capable of comprehending the most abstruse studies. Her eulogy was pronounced by Frisi, and translated into French by Boulard.

PIRACY IN THE PULPIT.

DR. SOUTH.

Webster, in his "great india-rubber speech" at Trenton, related the following anecdote: "May it please your honours—I remember having heard an anecdote of a celebrated divine, Dr. South, a man of great learning and virtue. He relieved himself of his clerical duties one summer by travelling *incog*. He went into a country church in the north of England one Sabbath morning, and heard the rector read a sermon. In coming from the church, the rector suspected him to be a brother of the ministry, and spoke to him. He received the rector's courtesies, and thanked him for the very edifying sermon he had preached, suggesting that it must have been the result of a good deal of labour. 'Oh, no,' said the rector, 'we turn off these things rapidly. On Friday afternoon and Saturday morning I produced this discourse.' 'Is that possible, sir,' said Dr. South, 'it took me three weeks to write that very sermon.' 'Your name is not Dr. South?' said the rector. 'It is, sir,' said Dr. South. 'Then,' said the rector, 'I have only to say that I am not ashamed to preach Dr. South's sermons anywhere.'"

PLEASURES AND TOILS OF LITERATURE.

Literature has its solitary pleasures, and they are many; it has also its social pleasures, and they are more. The Persian poet, Sadi, teaches a moral in one of his apologues. Two friends passed a summer day in a garden of roses; one satisfied himself with admiring their colours and inhaling their fragrance; the other filled his bosom with the leaves, and enjoyed at home, during several days, with his family, the deliciousness of the perfume. The first was the solitary, the second the social student. He wanders among many gardens of thought, but always brings back some flower in his hand. Who can estimate the advantages that may result from this toil, and this application of it!

The domestic history of the amiable Cowper, notwithstanding his abiding melancholy, presents us with some placid and even glowing pictures—when contemplated seated on his sofa, rehearsing each newly constructed passage to his faithful Mary Unwin.

In their method of economizing time, we find a certain uniformity in the practice of authors and students, of gathering up their spare minutes. Some writers yielding to their pleasing toils over the midnight lamp; others, again, devoting the early dawn of day to the sweet and silent communings of their muse. Says an anonymous writer: "The morning has been specially consecrated to study by the example of the Christian scholar. Hackett calls it, very prettily, and in the spirit of Cowley or Carew, 'the mother of honey dews and pearls which drop upon the paper from the student's pen.' The learned and excellent Bishop Jewell affords a very delightful specimen of the day of an English scholar, who not only lived among his books but among men. He commonly rose at four o'clock, had private prayers at five, and attended the public service of the church in the cathedral at six. The remainder of the morning was given to study. One of his biographers has drawn a very interesting sketch of Jewell during the day.

"At meals, a chapter being first read, he recreated himself with scholastic wars between young scholars whom he entertained at his table. After meals, his doors and ears were open to all suits and causes; at these times, for the most part, he despatched all those businesses which either his place, or others' importunity forced upon him, making gain of the residue of this time for study. About the hour of nine at night he called his servants to an account of how they had spent

I

the day, and admonished them accordingly. From this examination to his study, (how long it is uncertain, oftentimes after midnight) and so to bed; wherein, after some part of an author read to him by the gentlemen of his bed-chamber, commending himself to the protection of his Saviour, he took his rest."

So it was with Fielding, Goldsmith, Steele, and many others, honourable in literature; so also with Handel, Mozart, and Weber, in music; and it is one of the kindly recompenses of nature, by which she contrives to adjust, so equitably, the good and evil in this life. We owe that magnificent oratorio, the "Messiah," and others of his masterly productions to the author's most adverse circumstances; and it is doubted whether men of genius generally would have achieved half as much as they have, had their circumstances in life been more propitious. Sir Walter Scott wrote his *Waverley*, however, for love — not of pelf, but his pen. Not so his subsequent romances. Beaumont was of opinion that a man of genius could no more help putting his thoughts on paper than a traveller in a burning desert can help drinking when he sees water.

POETICAL HEROINES.

BYRON'S "MAID OF ATHENS."

"Maid of Athens, ere we part,
Give, O give me back my heart."

The *Maid of Athens*, in the very teeth of poetry, has become Mrs. Black, of Egina! The beautiful Teresa Makri, of whom Byron asked back his heart, of whom Moore and Hobhouse, and the poet himself, have written so much and so passionately, has forgotten the sweet burden of the sweetest of love-songs, and taken the unromantic name, and followed the unromantic fortunes, of a Scotchman! The commodore proposed that we should call upon her on our way to the temple of Jupiter, this morning. We pulled up to the town in the barge, and landed on the handsome pier built by Dr. Howe (who expended thus, most judiciously, a part of the provisions sent from our country in his charge), and, finding a Greek in the crowd who understood a little Italian, we were soon on our way to Mrs. Black's. Our guide was a fine, grave-looking man of forty, with a small cockade on his red cap, which indicated that he was some way in the service of the government. He laid his hand on his heart when I asked him if he had known any Americans in Egina. "They built this," said he, pointing to the pier, the handsome granite posts of which we were passing at the moment. "They gave us bread, and meat, and clothing, when we should otherwise have perished." It was said with a look and tone that thrilled me. I felt as if the whole debt of sympathy which Greece owes our country were repaid by this one energetic expression of gratitude. We stopped opposite a small gate, and the Greek went in without cards. It was a small stone house of a story and a half, with a ricketty flight of wooden steps at the side, and not a blade of grass or sign of a flower in court or window. If there had been but a geranium in the porch, or a rose-tree by the gate, for description's sake. Mr. Black was *out*—Mrs. Black was *in*. We walked up the creaking steps, with a Scotch terrier barking and snapping at our heels, and were met at the door by, really, a very pretty woman. She smiled as I apologized for our intrusion, and a sadder or a sweeter smile I never saw. She said her welcome in a few simple words of Italian, and I thought there were few sweeter voices in the world. I asked her if she had not learned English yet. She coloured, and said, "No, signore!" and the deep spot in her cheek faded gradually down in tints a painter would remember. Her husband, she said, had wished to learn her language, and would never let her speak English. I began to feel a prejudice against him. Presently a boy of perhaps three years came into the room—an ugly, white-headed, Scotch-looking little ruffian, thin-lipped and freckled, and my aversion for Mr. Black became quite decided. "Did you not regret leaving Athens?" I asked. "Very much, signore," she answered with half a sigh; "but my husband dislikes Athens." Horrid Mr. Black! thought I. I wished to ask her of Lord Byron, but I had heard that the poet's admiration had occasioned the usual scandal attendant on every kind of pre-eminence, and her modest and timid manners, while they assured me of her purity of heart, made me afraid to venture where there was even a possibility of wounding her. She sat in a drooping attitude on the coarsely-covered divan, which occupied three sides of the little room, and it was difficult to believe that any eye but her husband's had ever looked upon her, or that the "wells of her heart" had ever been drawn upon for anything deeper than the simple duties of a wife and mother. She offered us some sweetmeats, the usual Greek compliment to visitors, as we rose to go, and, laying her hand upon her heart, in the beautiful custom of the country, requested me to express her thanks to the commodore for the honour he had done her in calling, and to wish him and his family every happiness. A servant-girl, very shabbily dressed, stood at the side door, and we offered her some money, which she might have taken unnoticed. She drew herself up very coldly, and refused it, as if she thought we had quite mistaken her. In a country where gifts of the kind are so universal, it spoke well for the pride of the family, at least. I turned after we had taken leave, and made an apology to speak to her again; for in the interest of the general impression she had made upon me I had forgotten to notice her dress, and I was not sure that I could remember a single feature of her face. We had called unexpectedly, of course, and her dress was very plain. A red cloth cap, bound about the temples with a coloured shawl, whose folds were mingled with large braids of dark-brown hair, and decked with a tassel of blue silk, which fell to her left shoulder, formed her head-dress. In other respects she was dressed like a European. She is a little above the middle height, slight and well formed, and walks weakly, like most Greek women, as if her feet were too small for her weight. Her skin is dark and clear, and she has a colour in her cheek and lips that looks to me consumptive. Her teeth are white and regular, her face oval, and her forehead and nose form the straight line of the Grecian model—one of the few instances I have ever seen of it. Her eyes are large, and of a soft, liquid hazel, and this is her chief beauty. There is that "looking out of the soul through them," which Byron always described as constituting the loveliness that most moved him. I made up my mind, as we walked away, that she would be a lovely woman anywhere. Her horrid name, and the unprepossessing circumstances in which we found her, had uncharmed, I thought, all poetical delusion that would naturally surround her as the "Maid of Athens." We met her as simple Mrs. Black, whose Scotch husband's terrier had worried us at the door, and we left her, feeling that the poetry which she had called forth from the heart of Byron was her due by every law of loveliness.—(N. P. Willis's Cruise in the Mediterranean.)

BURNS' "CHLORIS."

"Lassie wi' the lint-white locks,
Bonnie lassie, artless lassie."

Mr. Lorimer's eldest daughter Jean was at this time a very young lady, but possessed of uncommon personal charms. Her form was symmetry itself, and, notwithstanding hair of flaxen lightness, the beauty of her face was universally admired. A Mr. Gillespie, a brother-officer of Burns, settled at Dumfries, was already enslaved by Miss Lorimer; and to his suit the poet lent all his influence. But it was in vain. Miss Lorimer became the wife of another, under somewhat extraordinary circumstances. A young gentleman named Whelpdale, connected with the county of Cumberland, and who had already signalized himself by profuse habits, settled at Barnhill, near Moffat, as a farmer. He was acquainted with a respectable farmer named Johnston, at Drumcrieff, near Craigieburn, where Miss Lorimer visited. He thus became acquainted with the young beauty. He paid his addresses to her, and it is supposed that she was not adverse to his suit. One night, in March 1793, when the poor girl was still some months less than eighteen years of age, and of course possessed of little prudence or knowledge of the world, he took her aside, and informed her that he could no longer live except as her husband; he therefore entreated her to elope with him that very night to Gretna Green, in order that they might be married, and threatened to do himself some extreme mischief if she should refuse. A hard-wrung consent to this most imprudent step fixed her fate to sorrow through life. The pair had not been united for many months, when Mr. Whelpdale was obliged by his debts to remove hastily from Barnhill, leaving his young wife no resource but that of returning to her parents at Kemmishall. She saw her husband no more for twenty-three years. * *

The subsequent history of the lady is pitiful. Some years after this outpouring of poesy in her praise, her father was unfortunate in business, and ceased to be the wealthy man he once was. The tuneful tongue which had sung her praise was laid in silence in Dumfries church-yard. She continued to derive no income from her husband, and scarcely even to know in what part of the world he lived. She was now, therefore, compelled to accept of a situation as plain governess in a gentleman's family; and in such situations she passed some years of her life. In 1816, returning from a visit to her brother in Sunderland, she inquired at Brampton for her husband, and learned that she had only missed seeing him by a few hours, as he had that day been in the village. He was now squandering some fourth or fifth fortune, which had been left to him by a relation. Not long after, learning that he was imprisoned for debt at Carlisle, she went to see him. Having announced to him her wish for an interview, she went to the place where he was confined, and was desired to walk in. His lodging was pointed out to her on the opposite side of a quadrangle, round which there was a covered walk, as in the ambulatories of the ancient religious houses. As she walked along one side of this court, she passed a man whose back was towards her—a bulky-looking person, slightly paralytic, and who shuffled in walking as if from lameness. As she approached the door, she heard this man pronounce her name. "Jean," he said, and then immediately added, as under a more formal feeling, "Mrs. Whelpdale!" It was her husband—the gay youth of 1793 being now transformed into a broken-down middle-aged man, whom she had passed without even suspecting who he was. The wife had to ask the figure if he was her husband, and the figure answered that he was. To such a scene many a romantic marriage leads! There was kindness, nevertheless, between the long-separated pair. Jean spent a month in Carlisle, calling upon her husband every day, and then returned to Scotland. Some months afterwards, when he had been liberated, she paid him another visit; but his utter inability to make a prudent use of any money intrusted to him, rendered it quite impossible that they should ever renew their conjugal life. After this she never saw him again. It is understood that this poor, unprotected woman at length was led into an error which cost her the respect of society. She spent some time in a kind of vagrant life, verging on mendicancy, and never rising above the condition of a domestic servant. She never ceased to be elegant in her form and comely of face; nor did she ever cease to recollect that she had been the subject of some dozen compositions by one of the greatest modern masters of the lyre.—(Chambers's Life of Burns.)

POETRY AND POETS.

LORD BYRON AND MR. CURRAN.

When Lord Byron rose into fame, Curran constantly objected to his talking of himself, as the great drawback on his poetry. "Any subject," said he, "but that eternal one of self. I am weary of knowing once a month the state of any man's hopes or fears, rights or wrongs. I should as soon read a register of the weather, the barometer up so many inches to-day and down so many inches to-morrow. I feel scepticism all over me at the sight of agonies on paper, things that come as regular and as notorious as the full of the moon. The truth is, his lordship *weeps for the press,* and *wipes his eyes with the public.*"

POETS AT BREAKFAST.

The following specimen of the table-talk of poets is taken from "Moore's Diary." The entry is dated October 27, 1820:—

"Wordsworth came at half-past eight, and stopped to breakfast. Talked a good deal. Spoke of Byron's plagiarisms from him; the whole third canto of *Childe Harold* founded on his style and sentiments. The feeling of natural objects which is there expressed, not caught by B. from nature herself, but from him (Wordsworth), and spoiled in the transmission. *Tintern Abbey,* the source of it all; from which same poem, too, the celebrated passage about Solitude, in the first canto of *Childe Harold* is (he said) taken, with this difference, that what is naturally expressed by him, has been worked by Byron into a laboured and antithetical sort of declamation. Spoke of the Scottish Novels. Is sure they are Scott's. The only doubt he ever had on the question did not arise from thinking them too good to be Scott's, but, on the contrary, from the infinite number of clumsy things in them; commonplace contrivances, worthy only of the Minerva press, and such bad vulgar English as no gentleman of education ought to have written. When I mentioned the abundance of them, as being rather too great for one man to produce, he said, that great fertility was the characteristic of all novelists and storytellers. Richardson could have gone on for ever; his *Sir Charles Grandison* was originally in thirty volumes. Instanced Charlotte Smith, Madame Cottin, &c., &c. Scott, since he was a child, accustomed to legends, and to the exercise of the story-telling faculty, sees nothing to stop him as long as he can hold a pen. Spoke of the very little knowledge of real poetry that existed now; so few men had time to study. For instance, Mr. Canning; one could hardly select a cleverer man; and yet, what did Mr. Canning know of poetry? What time had he, in the busy political life that he led, to study Dante, Homer, &c., as they ought to be studied, in order to arrive at the true principles of taste in works of genius? Mr. Fox, indeed, towards the latter part of his life, made leisure for himself, and took to improving his mind; and, accordingly, all his later public displays bore a greater stamp of wisdom and good taste than his early ones. Mr. Burke alone was an exception in this description of public men; by far the greatest man of his age; not only abounding in knowledge himself, but feeding, in various directions, his most able contemporaries; assisting Adam Smith in his *Political Economy* and Reynolds in his *Lectures on Painting*. Fox, too, who acknowledged that all he had ever learned from books was nothing to what he had derived from Burke."

EDGAR ALLEN POE.

The conversation of Edgar Allen Poe, the gifted American poet, was at times, says R. W. Griswold, almost supermortal in its eloquence. His voice was modulated with astonishing skill, and his large and variably expressive eyes looked repose or shot fiery tumult into theirs who listened, while his own face glowed or was changeless in pallor as his imagination quickened his blood or drew it back frozen to his heart. His imagery was from the worlds which no mortal can see but with the vision of genius. Suddenly starting from a proposition exactly and sharply defined in terms of utmost simplicity and clearness, he rejected the forms of customary logic, and, by a crystalline process of accretion, built up his ocular demonstrations in forms of gloomiest and ghastliest grandeur, or in those of the most airy and delicious beauty—so minutely and distinctly, yet so rapidly, that the attention which was yielded to him was chained till it stood among his wonderful creations, till he himself dissolved the spell, and brought his hearers back to common and base existence by vulgar fancies or exhibitions of the ignoblest passion.

CHARLES LAMB.

It is told of Charles Lamb, that one afternoon returning from a dinner-party, having taken a seat in a crowded omnibus, a stout gentleman subsequently looked in, and politely asked, "All full inside?" "I don't know how it may be with the *other* passengers," answered Lamb, "but that last piece of oyster-pie did the business for *me*."

Coleridge, during one of his interminable table-talks, said to Lamb, "Charley, did you ever hear me preach?" "I never heard you do anything else," was the prompt and witty reply of Elia, which has become a favourite byword at the present day.

The regular routine of clerkly business ill suited the literary tastes and the wayward though innocent habits of our essayist. Once at the India House, one in authority said to him—:"I have remarked, Mr. Lamb, that you come very *late* in the morning." "Yes, sir," replied the wit, "but I go away *early* in the afternoon." The oddness of the excuse silenced the reprover, who turned away with a smile.

A retired cheesemonger, who hated any allusion to the business that had enriched him, once remarked to Charles Lamb, in the course of a discussion on the poor-law, "You must bear in mind, sir, that I have got rid of all that stuff which you poets call the 'milk of human kindness.'" Lamb looked at him steadily, and gave his acquiescence in these words: "Yes, sir, I am aware of it; you turned it all into cheese several years ago."

CHARLES LAMB AND THE POETASTER.

Lamb was once invited by an old friend to meet an author, who had just published a volume of poems. When he arrived, being somewhat early, he was asked by his host to look over the volume of the expected visitor. A few minutes convinced Elia that it possessed very little merit, being a feeble echo of different authors.

This opinion of the poetaster was fully confirmed by the appearance of the gentleman himself, whose self-conceit, and confidence in his own book, were so manifest as to awaken in Lamb that spirit of mischievous waggery so characteristic of the humorist. Lamb's rapid and tenacious memory enabled him during the dinner to quote fluently several passages from the pretender's volume. These he gave with this introduction—"This reminds me of some verses I wrote when I was very young." He then, to the astonishment of the gentleman in question, quoted something from the volume.

Lamb tried this a second time: the gentleman looked still more surprised, and seemed evidently bursting with suppressed indignation. At last, as a climax to the fun, Lamb coolly quoted the well-known opening lines of *Paradise Lost* as written by himself.

This was too much for the versemonger. He immediately rose to his legs, and with an impressive solemnity of manner thus addressed the claimant to so many poetical honours: "Sir, I have tamely submitted all this evening to hear you claim the merit that may belong to any little poems of my own; this I have borne in silence; but, sir, I never will sit quietly by and see the immortal Milton robbed of *Paradise Lost*."

DIPPING CHARLES LAMB.

"Coleridge," says De Quincey, "told me of a ludicrous embarrassment which Lamb's stammering caused him at Hastings. Lamb had been medically advised to a course of sea-bathing; and accordingly, at the door of his bathing-machine, whilst he stood shivering with cold, two stout fellows laid hold of him, one at each shoulder, like heraldic supporters; they waited for the word of command from their principal, who began the following oration to them: "Hear me, men! Take notice of this; I am to be dipped——"

What more he would have said is unknown to land or sea bathing machines; for, having reached the word *dipped*, he commenced such a rolling fire of di—di—di—di, that when at length he descended *à plomb* upon the full word *dipped*, the two men, rather tired of the long suspense, became satisfied that they had reached what lawyers call the "operative" clause of the sentence, and both exclaiming at once, "O, yes, sir, we're quite aware of *that*," down they plunged him into the sea.

On emerging, Lamb sobbed so much from the cold, that he found no voice suitable to his indignation; from necessity he seemed tranquil; and again addressing the men, who stood respectfully listening, he began thus: "Men, is it possible to obtain your attention?" "O, surely, sir, by all means." "Then listen: once more I tell you I am to be di—di—di—," and then, with a burst of indignation, " dipped, I tell you ——" "O, decidedly, sir." And down the stammerer went for the second time.

Petrified with cold and wrath, once more Lamb made a feeble attempt at explanation. "Grant me pa—pa—patience; is it mum—um—murder you me—me—mean? Again and a—ga—ga—gain, I tell you, I'm to be di—di—di—dipped ——" now speaking furiously with the voice of an injured man. "O, yes, sir," the men replied, "we know that—we fully understand it; and, for the third time, down went Lamb into the sea.

"O limbs of Satan!" he said, on coming up for the third time, "it's now too late. I tell you that I am —no, that I *was* to be di—di—di—dipped only *once*."

POPE'S ACCURACY.

"At fifteen years of age," says Pope, "I got acquainted with Mr. Walsh. He encouraged me much and used to tell me that there was one way left of excelling; for though we had several great poets, we never had any one great poet that was correct. He ended his remarks by desiring me to make accuracy my study and aim."

This, perhaps, first led Pope to turn his lines over and over again so often. This habit he continued to the last, and he did it with a surprising facility.

CAMPBELL AND WILSON.

"Campbell," says Dr. Beattie, "went to Paisley races, got prodigiously interested in the first race, and betted on the success of one horse, to the amount of fifty pounds, with Professor Wilson. At the end of the race he thought he had lost the bet, and said to Wilson, 'I owe you fifty pounds; but really, when I reflect that you are a professor of moral philosophy, and that betting is a sort of gambling only fit for blacklegs, I cannot bring my conscience to pay the bet.'

"'O,' said Wilson, 'I very much approve of your principles, and mean to act upon them. In point of fact, *Yellow Cap*, on whom you betted, has won the race; and, but for conscience, I ought to pay you the fifty pounds; but you will excuse me.'"

CHATTERTON'S MISERY.

A prodigy of genius, the unfortunate Chatterton, was amusing himself one day, in company with a friend, reading the epitaphs in Pancras Church-yard. He was so deep sunk in thought as he walked on, that, not perceiving a grave that was just dug, he tumbled into it.

His friend, observing his situation, ran to his assistance, and, as he helped him out, told him, in a jocular manner, he was happy in assisting at the resurrection of genius. Poor Chatterton smiled, and, taking his companion by the arm, replied, "My dear friend, I feel the sting of a speedy dissolution. I have been at war with the grave for some time, and find it is not so easy to vanquish it as I imagined. We can find an asylum to hide from every creditor but that."

His friend endeavoured to divert

his thoughts from the gloomy reflection: but what will not melancholy and adversity combined subjugate? In three days after, the neglected and disconsolate youth put an end to his miseries by poison.

JAMES MONTGOMERY.

A writer in the *Boston Atlas* gives the following account of an interview with Montgomery, the Cowper of his age:—

"I found Montgomery, in conversation, delightful. There was nothing of the 'I am a poet' about him; but he entered freely and familiarly into conversation, and expressed his opinions on the literature of the day with as much diffidence as if he had himself only worshipped the Muse 'afar off.' . .

"In the course of the evening, the conversation turned on Robert Montgomery's poetry, which was then making some noise. James, for some time, took no part in what was going on, but was an attentive listener. At last it seemed as if flesh and blood could bear it no longer, for he commented on the meanness of Satan Bob in assuming his name, for the purpose of cheating the public into the purchase of his wares. 'It has been a serious business to me,' said the true Montgomery, 'for I am constantly receiving letters, evidently intended for another person, in which I am either mercilessly abused for what I never wrote, or bespattered with compliments of the most nauseating character. Many, to this day, do not distinguish between me and Robert Montgomery; and so I am, in a great measure, robbed of what little hard-earned fame I possess.'

"The poet, evidently, was much mortified by Robert's assumption of his name, and did not endeavour to disguise his contempt for the literary pirate, who sailed under false colours. His intimate friends say that this is the only subject which ruffles the habitual serenity of his mind; and well it may, for it must be no trifling annoyance to see that fame, which was acquired by years of toil and patient endurance, perilled in the minds of many by the productions of such a popinjay as the author of *Oxford* and *Woman.*"

JOANNA BAILLIE.

"I believe," says Miss Sedgwick, "of all my pleasures here, dear J. will most envy me that of seeing Joanna Baillie, and of seeing her repeatedly at her home—the best point of view for all best women. She lives on Hampstead Hill, a few miles from town, in a modest house, with Miss Agnes Baillie, her only sister, a kindly and agreeable person.

"Miss Baillie—I write this for J., for women always like to know how one another look and dress—Miss Baillie has a well-preserved appearance: her face has nothing of the vexed or sorrowful expression that is often so deeply stamped by a long experience of life. It indicates a strong mind, great sensibility, and the benevolence that, I believe, always proceeds from it if the mental constitution be a sound one, as it eminently is in Miss Baillie's case.

"She has a pleasing figure, what we call lady-like, that is, delicate, erect, and graceful; not the large-boned, muscular frame of most English women. She wears her own gray hair—a general fashion, by the way, here, which I wish we elderly ladies of America may have the courage and the taste to imitate; and she wears the prettiest of brown silk gowns and bonnets, fitting the *beau-idéal* of an old lady—an ideal she might inspire, if it has no pre-existence.

"You would, of course, expect her to be free from pedantry and all modes of affectation; but I think you would be surprised to find yourself forgetting, in a domestic and confiding feeling, that you were talking with the woman whose name is best established among the female writers of her country; in short, forgetting everything but that you were in the society of a most charming private gentlewoman. She might—would that all female writers could—take for her device a flower that closes itself against the noontide sun, and unfolds in the evening shadows."

COWPER'S LETTERS.

William Cowper is pre-eminently the Christian poet of our age and nation, and, high as is the rank assigned to his verse by the unanimous consent of the whole literary world, it is not higher than that to which his prose is entitled. Robert Hall, himself a master of English, said—"I have always considered the letters of Mr. Cowper as the finest specimens of the epistolary style in our language." Southey, who was also distinguished as a prose-writer, pays a similar tribute to Cowper's letters. Such, indeed, is the universal judgment passed upon the unstudied grace and inimitable ease of those compositions with which the poet charmed his friends and occupied the leisure of his secluded life, when not engaged in the work of his high poetical vocation.

COWPER'S SCHOOLBOY TORMENTOR.

At school, first in his native village, and subsequently at Westminster, Cowper suffered much from the cruelty of boys older and stronger than himself, who took a malicious delight in tyrannizing over him; and such was the effect of the savage treatment upon his gentle spirit, that, speaking of a lad of about fifteen years of age, who acted towards him with peculiar barbarity, "I well remember," he says, "being afraid to lift my eye upon him higher than his knees, and that I knew him better by his shoe-buckles than by any other part of his dress. May the Lord pardon him, and may we meet in glory!"

FELICIA HEMANS.

A traveller who called on Mrs. Hemans, at Wavertree, in 183–, gives us some pleasing recollections. "After some conversation in the parlour," he says, "Mrs. H. proposed a visit to her study.

"'Come,' said she, 'I will show you my poetic mint;' and she led the way to a room over the one in which we were sitting. It was a very small place, but neat almost to a fault. There were no author litterings. Everything was in order. An open letter lay on the table. She pointed to it, and said, laughingly—

"'An application for my autograph, and the postage unpaid. You cannot imagine how I am annoyed with albums and such matters. A person who ought to have known better sent me an album lately, and begged a piece from me, if it were only long enough to fill up a page of sky-blue tinted paper, which he had selected for me to write upon.'

"In incidentally referring to her compositions, she said, 'They often remain chiming in my mind for days, before I commit them to paper; and sometimes I quite forget many, which I compose as I lie awake in bed. Composition is less a labour with me than the act of writing down what has impressed me, excepting in the case of blank verse, which always involves something like labour. My thoughts have been so used to go in the harness of rhyme, that when they are suffered to run without it, they are often diffused, or I lose sight, in the ardour of composition, of the leading idea altogether.'

"Mrs. Hemans' voice was peculiarly musical, and I would have given anything to have heard her recite some of her own poetry; but I did not dare to hazard such a request; and feeling that I had intruded quite long enough on her time, I intimated my intention of taking my departure, when she begged me to partake of some refreshment.

"I must not omit to mention, for the especial benefit of my fair readers, that Mrs. Hemans' dress was simple enough. She wore a white gown (I am really not learned nough in such matters to say whether it was of cotton or muslin), over which was thrown a black lace shawl; on her head was a cap of very open network, without flowers or ornament of any kind."

An American visitor gives the following description of Mrs. Hemans:—

"I cannot well conceive of a more exquisitely beautiful creature than Mrs. Hemans was. None of the portraits or busts I have ever seen of her do her justice, nor is it possible for words to convey to the reader any idea of the matchless yet serene beauty of her expression. Her glossy waving hair was parted on her forehead, and terminated, on the sides, in rich and luxuriant auburn curls; there was a dove-like look in her eyes, and yet there was a chastened sadness in their expression. Her complexion was remarkably clear, and her high forehead looked as pure and spotless as Parian marble. A calm repose, not unmingled with melancholy, was the characteristic expression of the face; but when she smiled, all traces of sorrow were lost, and she seemed to be but 'a little lower than the angels' —fitting shrine for so pure a mind. Let me not be deemed a flatterer or an enthusiast, in thus describing her, for I am only one of many who have been almost as much captivated by her personal beauty as charmed by the sweetness and holiness of her productions. If ever poesies were the reflex of the beauties, personal and mental, of their writers, they were indeed so in the case of Mrs. Hemans.

"We talked, of course, a great deal about poetry and poets, and she asked me if I had seen Wordsworth.

"On my replying that I had not, she said, 'You will be almost as much delighted with the man as with his works. He is delightful. I once saw him at St. Asaph, and he spent half a day with me reciting his own poetry.'

"We talked of L. E. L. Mrs. Hemans said she had received several letters from her, containing pressing invitations to visit London. 'A place I never was in, and never wish to be,' she observed. 'My heart beats too loudly, even in this quiet place, and there I think it would burst. The great Babel was not made for such as I.'"

GRAHAME'S "SABBATH."

When James Grahame composed the poem of *The Sabbath*, he sent it to the press unknown to his wife. When it was issued, he brought her a copy, and requested her to read it. As his name was not prefixed to the work, she did not dream that he had anything to do with it. As she went on reading, the sensitive author walked up and down the room. At length she broke out in praise of the poem, and turning to him, said, "Ah, James, if you could but produce a poem like this!" Judge, then, of her delighted surprise when she found he was the author. The effect upon her, it is said, was almost overwhelming.

COLERIDGE AS A SOLDIER.

"Mr. Coleridge," says Cottle, "told us of one of his Cambridge eccentricities, which highly amused us. He said that he had paid his addresses to a Mary Evans, who, rejecting his offer, he took it so much in dudgeon, that he withdrew from the university to London, when, in a reckless state of mind, he enlisted in the 15th regiment of Elliot's Light Dragoons. No objection having been taken to his height or age, he was asked his name. He had previously determined to give one that was thoroughly Kamschatkian, but having noticed that morning, over a door in Lincoln's Inn Fields, or the Temple, the name of 'Cumberbatch' (not Cumberback), he thought this word sufficiently outlandish, and replied 'Silas Tomken Cumberbatch;'* and such was the entry in the regimental book.

"Here, in his new capacity, laborious duties devolved on Mr. C. He endeavoured to think on Cæsar, and Epaminondas, and Leonidas, with other ancient heroes, and composed himself to his fate; remembering, in every series, there must be a commencement. But still he found confronting him no imaginary inconveniences. Perhaps he who had most cause for dissatisfaction was the drill sergeant, who thought his professional character endangered; for, after using his utmost efforts to bring his raw recruit into something like training, he expressed the most serious fears, from his unconquerable awkwardness, that he should never be able to make *a soldier of him.*

"Mr. C., it seemed, could not even rub down his own horse, which, however, it should be known, was rather a restive one, who, like Cowper's hare, 'would bite if it could,' and, in addition, kick not a little. We could not suppose that these predispositions in the martial steed were at all aggravated by the unskilful jockeyship to which he was subjected; but the sensitive quadruped did rebel a little in the stable, and wince a little in the field.

"Perhaps the poor animal was something in the state of the horse that carried Mr. Wordsworth's Idiot Boy, who, in his sage contemplations, 'wondered what he had got upon his back.'

"This rubbing down of his horse was a constant source of annoyance to Mr. C., who thought the most rational way was—to let the horse rub himself down, shaking himself clean, and so to shine in all his native beauty; but on this subject there were two opinions, and his that was to decide carried most weight. If it had not been for the foolish and fastidious taste of the ultra precise sergeant, this whole mass of trouble might be avoided; but seeing the thing must be done, or punishment, he set about the Herculean task with the firmness of a Wallenstein. But lo! the paroxysm was brief, as the necessity that called it forth.

"Mr. C. overcame this immense difficulty by bribing a young man of the regiment to perform the achievement for him, and that on very easy terms, namely, by writing him some love stanzas to send his sweetheart.

"Mr. Coleridge, in the midst of all his deficiencies, it appeared, was liked by the men, although he was the butt of the whole company; being esteemed by them as next of kin to a natural, though of a peculiar kind—a talking natural. This fancy of theirs was stoutly resisted by the love-sick swain; but the regimental logic prevailed; for, whatever they could do with masterly

---

* These three initials would be the proper S. T. C. affixed to his garments.

dexterity, he could not do at all; *ergo*, must he not be a natural?

"There was no man in the regiment who met with so many falls from his horse as Silas Tomken Cumberbatch. He often calculated, with so little precision, his due equilibrium, that, in mounting on one side—perhaps the wrong stirrup—the probability was, especially if his horse moved a little, that he lost his balance, and if he did not roll back on this side, came down ponderously on the other. Then the laugh spread amongst the men —'Silas is off again.' Mr. C. had often heard of campaigns, but he never before had so correct an idea of hard service.

"Some mitigation was now in store for Mr. C., arising out of a whimsical circumstance. He had been placed, as a sentinel, at the door of a ball-room, or some public place of resort, when two of his officers, passing in, stopped for a moment near Mr. C., talking about Euripides, two lines from whom one of them repeated.

"At the sound of Greek, the sentinel instinctively turned his ear, when he said, with all deference, touching his lofty cap, 'I hope your honour will excuse me, but the lines you have repeated are not quite accurately cited. These are the lines,' when he gave them in their more correct form. 'Besides,' said Mr. C., 'instead of being in Euripides, the lines will be found in the second antistrophe of the Œdipus of Sophocles.' 'Why, man, who are you?' said the officer; 'old Faustus ground young again?' 'I am your honour's humble sentinel,' said Mr. C., again touching his cap.

"The officers hastened into the room, and inquired of one and another about that 'odd fish' at the door, when one of the mess—it is believed the surgeon—told them that he had his eye upon him, but he could neither tell where he came from, nor any thing about his family of the Cumberbatches; 'but,' continued he, 'instead of his being an 'odd fish,' I suspect he must be a 'stray bird' from the Oxford or Cambridge aviary.' They learned also the laughable fact, that he was bruised all over by frequent falls from his horse. 'Ah!' said one of the officers, 'we have had, at different times, two or three of these 'university birds' in our regiment.'

"This suspicion was confirmed by one of the officers, Mr. Nathaniel Ogle, who observed that he had noticed a line of Latin chalked under one of the men's saddles, and was told, on inquiring whose saddle it was, that it was 'Cumberbatch's.'

"The officers now kindly took pity on the 'poor scholar,' and had Mr. C. removed to the medical department, where he was appointed assistant in the regimental hospital. This change was a vast improvement in Mr. C.'s condition; and happy was the day also, on which it took place, for the sake of the sick patients; for Silas Tomken Cumberbatch's amusing stories, they said, did them more good than all the doctor's physic.

"If he began talking to one or two of his comrades—for they were all on a perfect equality, except those who went through their exercises the best, and stretched their necks a little above the 'awkward squad,' in which ignoble class Mr. C. was placed as pre-eminent member, almost by acclamation—if he began to speak, notwithstanding, to one or two, others drew near, increasing momently, till by and by the sick beds were deserted, and Mr. C. formed the centre of a large circle.

"In one of these interesting conversations, when Mr. C. was sitting at the foot of the bed, surrounded by his gaping comrades, who were always solicitons of, and never wearied with, his stories, the door suddenly burst open, and in came two or three gentlemen (his friends), looking some time, in vain, amid the uniform dresses, for their man. At length they pitched on Mr. C., and, taking him by the arm, led him, in silence, out of the room—a picture, indeed, for a Wilkie. As the supposed *deserter* passed the threshold, one of the astonished auditors uttered, with a sigh, 'Poor Silas! I wish they may let him off with a cool five hundred!' Mr. C.'s ransom was soon joyfully adjusted by his friends, and now the wide world once more lay before him."

WORDSWORTH.

The *Lyrical Ballads* were mostly written at Allfoxden, near the Bristol Channel, in one of the deepest solitudes in England, amid woods, glens, streams, and hills. Here Wordsworth had retired with his sister; and Coleridge was only five miles distant, at Stowey.

Cottle relates some amusing anecdotes of the ignorance of the country people in regard to them, and to poets and lovers of the picturesque generally. Southey, Coleridge and his wife, Lamb, and the two Wedgewoods visited Wordsworth in his retirement, and the whole company used to wander about the woods, and by the sea, to the great wonder of all the honest people they met. As they were often out at night, it was supposed they led a dissolute life; and it is said that there are respectable people in Bristol who believe now that Mrs. Coleridge and Miss Wordsworth were disreputable women, from a remembrance of the scandalous tattle circulating then.

Cottle asserts that Wordsworth was driven from the place by the suspicions which his habits provoked, being refused a continuance of his lease of the Allfoxden house by the ignoramus who had the letting of it, on the ground that he was a criminal in the disguise of an idler.

One of the villagers said "that he had seen him wander about at night, *and look rather strangely at the moon ;* and then he roamed over the hills like a partridge." Another testified, "he had heard him mutter, as he walked, in some outlandish brogue that nobody could understand." This last, we suppose, is the rustic version of the poet's own statement,—

"He murmurs near the running brooks,
A music sweeter than their own.".

Others, however, took a different view of his habits, as little flattering to his morals as the other view to his sense. One wiseacre remarked confidently, "I know what he is. We have all met him tramping away towards the sea. Would any man in his senses take all that trouble to look at a parcel of water? I think he carries on a snug business in the smuggling line, and, in these journeys, is on the look-out for some *wet* cargo."

Another carrying out this bright idea, added, "I know he has got a private still in his cellar; for I once passed his house at a little better than a hundred yards' distance, and I could smell the spirits as plain as an ashen fagot at Christmas." But the charge which probably had the most weight in those times was the last. "I know," said one, "that he is surely a desperate French Jacobin; for he is so silent and dark that no one ever heard him say one word about politics."

While the ludicrous tattle to which we have referred was sounding all around him, he was meditating *Peter Bell* and the *Lyrical Ballads* in the depths of the Allfoxden woods, and consecrating the rustics who were scandalizing him. The great Poet of the Poor, who has made the peasant a grander object of contemplation than the peer, and who saw through vulgar externals and humble occupations to the inmost soul of the man, had sufficient provocations to be the satirist of those he idealized.

COWPER'S HABITS OF COMPOSITION.

We learn from Southey, who had seen his MS. letters, that they "were written as easily as they appear to have been; they would not otherwise (he observes) have been inimitable; they are written in a clear, beautiful, running hand, and it is rarely that an erasure occurs in them, or the slightest alteration of a phrase." Cowper himself describes the painstaking attention he bestowed upon his poetical composition:—"Whatever faults I may be chargeable with as a poet, I cannot accuse myself of negligence. I never suffer a line to pass till I have made it as good as I can."

FATE OF A LYRICAL WRITER.

As I sit in my garret here (in Washington) watching the course of great men, and the destiny of party, I meet often with strange contradictions in this eventful life. The most remarkable was that of J. Howard Payne, author of *Sweet Home*. I knew him personally. He occupied the rooms under me for some time, and his conversation was so captivating that I often spent whole days in his apartment. He was an applicant for office at the time—consul at Tunis—from which he had been removed. What a sad thing it was to see the poet subjected to all the humiliation of office-seeking. Of an evening we would walk along the streets. Once in a while we would see some family circle so happy, and forming so beautiful a group, that we would both stop, and then pass silently on. On such occasions he would give me a history of his wanderings, his trials, and all the cares incident to his sensitive nature and poverty.

"How often," said he once. "I have been in the heart of Paris, Berlin, and London, or some other city, and heard persons singing, or the hand-organ playing, *Sweet Home*, without a shilling to buy the next meal or a place to lay my head. The world has literally sung my song until every heart is familiar with its melody. Yet I have been a wanderer from my boyhood. My country has turned me ruthlessly from my office; and in my old age I have to submit to humiliation for bread." Thus he would complain of his hapless lot. His only wish was to die in a foreign land, to be buried by strangers, and sleep in obscurity. I met him one day looking unusually sad, "Have you got your consulate?" said I. "Yes, and leave in a week for Tunis; I shall never return." Poor Payne! his wish was realized—he died at Tunis.

POETICAL POPULARITY.

One of Campbell's most popular lyrics was the *Wounded Hussar*. In 1802 it was a street ballad, a fact which was very annoying to the sensitive poet, who was quizzed on this proof of his success by his waggish companions. In after years Campbell regarded his street popularity in a different light. "Coming home one evening to my house in Park Square (narrates Dr. Beattie), where as usual he had dropped in to spend a quiet hour, I told him that I had been agreeably detained listening to some street music near Portman Square." "Vocal or instrumental?" he inquired. "Vocal; the song was an old favourite, remarkably good, and of at least forty years' standing." "Ha!" said he, "I congratulate the author, whoever he is." "And so do I—it was your own song, the *Soldier's Dream;* and when I came away the crowd was still increasing." "Well," he added, musing, "this is something like popularity!"

He then, as an instance of real popularity, mentioned that, happening to enter a blacksmith's forge on some trifling errand many years ago, he saw a small volume lying on the bench, but so begrimmed and tattered, that its title-page was almost illegible. It was Goldsmith's *Deserted Village and other Poems*; every page of which bore testimony to the rough hands—guided by feeling hearts—that had so often turned over its leaves. "This," he added, "was one of the most convincing instances of an author's popularity I ever met with."

BOWLES.

The canon's absence of mind was very great, and when his coachman drove him into Bath, he had to practise all kinds of cautions to keep him to time and place. The act of composition was a slow and laborious operation with Mr. Bowles. He altered and re-wrote his MS., until, sometimes, hardly anything remained of the original, excepting the general conception. When we add that his handwriting was one of the worst that ever man wrote —insomuch that frequently he could not read that which he had written the day before—we need not say that his printers had very tough work in getting his works into type. At the time when we printed for Mr. Bowles, we had one compositor who had a sort of knack in making out the poet's hieroglyphics, and he was once actually sent for by Mr. Bowles into Wiltshire to copy some MS. written a year or two before, which the poet had himself vainly endeavoured to decipher.—(Newspaper.)

COWPER'S "TASK."

Cowper, like many other men of eminence, was often indebted to others for the subjects on which he wrote. Lady Austen was very fond of blank verse, and urged her friend to try his powers in that species of composition. At length he promised to do so if she would furnish him with a subject. She replied, "O you can never be in want of a subject: you can write upon any: write upon this sofa." The poet obeyed her command, and produced the *Task*.

This poem, which thus arose from the lively repartee of familiar conversation, presents a variety including almost every subject and every style, without the violation of order and harmony, while it breathes a spirit of the purest and most exalted morality.

Thomas Campbell finely remarks, that "his whimsical outset in a work, where he promises so little and performs so much, may be advantageously contrasted with those magnificent commencements of poems which pledge both the reader and the writer, in good earnest, to a task. Cowper's poem, on the contrary, is like a river, which rises from a playful little fountain, and which gathers beauty and magnitude as it proceeds."

"PARADISE LOST."

When this great production appeared, in 1667, the celebrated Waller wrote of it—"The old, blind schoolmaster, John Milton, hath published a tedious poem on the fall of man; if its length be not considered a merit, it has no other."

Thomas Ellwood, an intelligent and learned Quaker, who was honoured by the intimate friendship of Milton, used to read to him various authors in the learned languages, and thus contributed as well to his own improvement as to solace the dark hours of the poet when he had lost his sight.

"The curious ear of John Milton," said Ellwood, in his own *Life*, "could discover, by the tone of my voice, when I did not clearly understand what I read, and open the difficult passages."

Milton lent Ellwood the manuscript of *Paradise Lost* to read. When he returned it, Milton asked him how he liked it. "I like it much," said the judicious Quaker: "thou hast written well, and said much of *Paradise Lost;* but what hast thou to say of *Paradise Found?*" Milton made no answer, but sat musing for some time.

When business afterwards drew Ellwood to London, he called on Milton, who showed him the poem of *Paradise Regained;* and in a pleasant tone said to his friend, "This is owing to you; for you put it into my head by the question you asked me at Charlfont, which before I had not thought of."

JONATHAN SWIFT.

In one of his letters, Pope gives the following illustration of Dean Swift's eccentricity:—

"Dean Swift has an odd, blunt way, that is mistaken by strangers for ill nature: it is so odd that there is no describing it but by facts. I'll tell you that one first comes into my head.

"One evening, Gay and I went to see him: you know how intimately we were all acquainted. On our coming in, 'Heyday, gentlemen,' says the doctor, 'what's the meaning of this visit? How came you to leave all the great lords that you are so fond of, to come hither to see a poor dean?' 'Because we would rather see you than any of them.' 'Ay, anyone that did not know you so well as I do might believe you. But since you have come I must get some supper for you I suppose.' 'No, doctor, we have supped already.' 'Supped already? That's impossible: why, it is not eight o'clock yet. That's very strange: but if you had not supped, I must have got something for you. Let me see; what should I have had? A couple of lobsters? Ay that would have done very well—two shillings; tarts, a shilling.'

"'But you will drink a glass of wine with me, though you supped so much before your usual time only to spare my pocket.' 'No, we had rather talk with you than drink with you.' 'But if you had supped with me, as in all reason you ought to have done, you must then have drank with me. A bottle of wine, two shillings. Two and two are four, and one is five; just two and sixpence a piece. There, Pope, there's half a crown for you; and there's another for you, sir; for I won't save anything by you, I am determined.'

"This was all said and done with his usual seriousness on such occasions; and in spite of everything we could say to the contrary, he actually obliged us to take the money."

DRYDEN.

This poet, when a boy at Westminster school, was put with others to write a copy of verses on the miracle of the conversion of water into wine. Being a great truant, he had not time to compose his verses; and, when brought up, he had only made one line of Latin, and two of English:—

" *Videt et erubit lympha pudica Deum!*"
" The modest water, awed by power divine,
Beheld its God, and blushed itself to wine;"—

which so pleased the master, that, instead of being angry, he said it was a presage of future greatness, and gave the youth a crown on this occasion.

SIR WALTER SCOTT.

When Sir Walter Scott was a schoolboy, between ten and eleven years of age, his mother one morning saw him standing still in the street, and looking at the sky, in the midst of a tremendous thunder-storm. She called to him repeatedly, but he did not seem to hear: at length he returned into the house, and told his mother that if she would give him a pencil, he would tell her why he looked at the sky. She acceded to his request, and in a few minutes he laid on her lap the following lines:—

"Loud o'er my head what awful thunders roll!
What vivid lightnings flash from pole to pole!
It is thy voice, O God, that bids them fly;
Thy voice directs them through the vaulted sky;
Then let the good thy mighty power revere;
Let hardened sinners thy just judgments fear."

BURNS.

Burns, in his autobiography, informs us that a life of Hannibal, which he read when a boy, raised the first stirrings of his enthusiasm; and he adds, with his own fervid expression, that "the *Life of Sir William Wallace* poured a tide of Scottish prejudices into his veins, which would boil along them till the floodgates of life were shut in eternal rest." He adds, speaking of his retired life in early youth, "This kind of life, the cheerless gloom of a hermit, and the toil of a galley slave, brought me to my sixteenth year, *when love made me a poet.*"

BYRON.

Moore relates, in his *Life of Lord Byron*, that on a certain occasion, he found him occupied with the *History of Agathon*, a romance, by Wieland; and, from some remarks made at the time, he seemed to be of opinion that Byron was reading the work in question as a means of furnishing suggestions to, and of quickening his own imaginative powers. He then adds, "I am inclined to think it was his practice, when engaged in the composition of any work, to excite his vein by the perusal of others on the same subject or plan, from which the slightest hint caught by imagination, as he read, was sufficient to kindle there such a train of thought as but for that spark had never been awakened."

GOETHE.

The singular facility with which Goethe's poems were produced, resembling improvisation or inspiration rather than composition, has contributed in some cases, no doubt, to enhance their peculiar charm. "I had come," says he, "to regard the poetic talent dwelling in me entirely as nature; the rather that I was directed to look upon external nature as its proper subject. The exercise of this poetic gift might be stimulated and determined by occasion, but it flowed forth most joyfully, most richly, when it came involuntarily, or even against my will.

"I was so accustomed to say over a song to myself without being able to collect it again, that I sometimes rushed to the desk, and, without taking time to adjust a sheet that was lying crosswise, wrote the poem diagonally from beginning to end, without stirring from the spot. For the same reason I preferred to use a pencil, which gives the characters more willingly; for it had sometimes happened that the scratching and spattering of the pen would wake me from my somnambulistic poetizing, distract my attention, and stifle some small product in the birth. For such poetry I had a special reverence. My relation to it was something like a hen to the chickens, which, being fully hatched, she sees chirping about her. My former desire to communicate these things only by reading them aloud renewed itself again. To barter them for money seemed to me detestable."

CRABBE.

When the poet Crabbe once presented one of his poems to the late Lord-Chancellor Thurlow, his lordship said, "I have no time to read verses; my avocations do not permit it." Crabbe instantly retorted, "There was a time when the encouragement of literature was considered to be a duty appertaining to the illustrious situation which your lordship holds." Thurlow frankly acknowledged his error, and nobly returned it. He observed, "I ought to have noticed your poem, and I heartily forgive your rebuke." In proof of his sincerity he presented him with one hundred pounds, and subsequently gave him preferment in the church.

COWPER'S AMUSEMENTS.

"Amusements (he writes to Wm. Unwin) are necessary in a retirement like mine, especially in such a sable state of mind as I labour under. The necessity of amusement makes me a carpenter, a bird-cage maker, a gardener, and has lately taught me to draw, and to draw too with such surprising proficiency in the art, considering my total ignorance of it two months ago, that, when I show your mother my productions, she is all admiration and applause." To Mr. Newton he writes:—"I draw mountains, valleys, woods, and streams, and ducks, and dab-chicks. I admire them myself, and Mrs. Unwin admires them, and her praise and my praise put together are fame enough for me." The pleasure he derives from his pursuits he thus describes:—"I never received a *little* pleasure from anything in my life; if I am delighted, it is in the extreme. The unhappy consequence of this temperament is, that my attachment to any occupation seldom outlives the novelty of it. That nerve of my imagination, that feels the touch of any particular amusement, twangs under the energy of the pressure with so much vehemence, that it soon becomes sensible of weariness and fatigue." Adverting in another letter to his amusements, he says:—"Poetry above all things is useful to me in this respect. While I am held in pursuit of pretty images, or a pretty way of expressing them, I forget everything that is irksome." The remark may remind us of one of his verses:—

"There is a pleasure in poetic pains,
 Which only poets know."

QUEEN VICTORIA AND THOMAS CAMPBELL.

The following story narrates the most graceful compliment and delicate return ever made by royalty:—

"I was at her Majesty's coronation, in Westminster Abbey," said Campbell, "and she conducted herself so well, during the long and fatiguing ceremony, that I shed tears many times. On returning home, I resolved, out of pure esteem and veneration, to send her a copy of all my works.

"Accordingly, I had them bound up, and went personally with them to Sir Henry Wheatly, who, when he understood my errand, told me that her Majesty made it a rule to decline presents of this kind, as it placed her under obligations which were unpleasant to her. 'Say to her Majesty, Sir Henry,' I replied, 'that there is not a single thing the Queen can touch with her sceptre in any of her dominions which I covet; and I therefore entreat you, in your office, to present them with my devotion as a subject.' But the next day they were returned.

"I hesitated," continued Campbell, "to open the parcel; but, on doing so, I found, to my inexpressible joy, a note inclosed, desiring my autograph on them. Having complied with the wish, I again transmitted the books to her Majesty; and, in the course of a day or two, received in return this elegant engraving, with her Majesty's autograph, as you see below." He then directed particular attention to the royal signature, which was in her Majesty's usual bold and beautiful handwriting.

CANNING.

When Canning was challenged to find a rhyme for Julianna, he immediately wrote—

" Walking in the shady grove
With my Julianna,
For lozenges I gave my love
Ip-e-cac-u-an-ha."

There might be now as much fact as there was then fiction in the verses. Ipecacuanha lozenges are now sold by the apothecaries.

MISS LANDON—L.E.L.

We quote the following from William Howitt:—

"On the other hand, in mixed companies, witty and conversant as she was, you had a feeling that she was playing an assumed part. Her manner and conversation were not only the very reverse of the tone and sentiment of her poems, but she seemed to say things for the sake of astonishing you with the very contrast. You felt not only no confidence in the truth of what she was asserting, but a strong assurance that it was said merely for the sake of saying what her hearers would least expect to hear her say.

"I recollect once meeting her in company, at a time when there was a strong report that she was actually though secretly married. Mrs. Hofland, on her entering the room, went up to her in her plain, straightforward way, and said, 'Ah! my dear, what must I call you?— Miss Landon, or whom?'

"After a well-feigned surprise at the question, Miss Landon began to talk in a tone of merry ridicule at this report, and ended by declaring that as to love or marriage, they were things that she never thought of. 'What, then, have you been doing with yourself this last month?'

"'O, I have been puzzling my brain to invent a new sleeve; pray, how do you like it?' showing her arm.

"'You never think of such a thing as love!' exclaimed a sentimental young man; 'you, who have written so many volumes of poetry upon it!'

"'O that's all professional, you know,' exclaimed she, with an air of merry scorn.

"'Professional!' exclaimed a grave Quaker who stood near; 'why dost thou make a difference between what is professional and what is real? Dost thou write one thing and think another? Does not that look very much like hypocrisy?'

"To this the astonished poetess made no reply, but by a look of genuine amazement. It was a mode of putting the matter to which she had evidently never been accustomed. And, in fact, there can be no question that much of her writing was professional. She had to win a golden harvest for the comfort of others as dear to her as herself; and she felt, like all authors who have to cater for the public, that she must provide, not so much what she would of her free-will choice, but what they expected from her."

MRS. SOUTHEY.

And who was Mrs. Southey?— who but she who was so long known, and so great a favourite, as Caroline Bowles; transformed by the gallantry of the laureate, and the grace of the parson, into her matrimonial appellation. Southey, so long ago as the 21st of February, 1829, prefaced his most amatory poem of *All for Love* with a tender address, that is now, perhaps, worth reprinting:—

"TO CAROLINE BOWLES.

"Could I look forward to a distant day,
With hope of building some elaborate lay,
Then would I wait till worthier strains of mine
Might have inscribed thy name, O Caroline!
For I would, while my voice is heard on earth,
Bear witness to thy genius and thy worth.
But we have been both taught to feel with fear
How frail the tenure of existence here;
What unforeseen calamities prevent,
Alas! how oft, the best resolved intent;
And, therefore, this poor volume I address
To thee, dear friend, and sister poetess!
"ROBERT SOUTHEY.
"Keswick, Feb. 21, 1829."

The laureate had his wish; for in duty he was bound to say, that worthier strains than his bore inscribed the name of Caroline connected with his own; and, moreover, she was something more than a dear friend and sister poetess.

"The laureate," observes a writer in *Fraser's Magazine*, "is a fortunate man · his queen supplies him with *butts* (alluding to the laureateship), and his lady with *Bowls:* then may his cup of good fortune be overflowing."

MOORE, BOWLES, AND CRABBE.

Thomas Moore writes in his diary as follows, showing his excessive love of praise:—

"January 21, 1825.—The grand opening to-day of the Literary Institution at Bath. Attended the inaugural lecture by Sir G. Gibbs, at two. Walked about a little afterwards, and to the dinner at six—Lord Lansdowne in the chair. Two bishops present; and about 108 persons altogether. Bowles and Crabbe of the number. Lord L. alluded to us in his first speech, as among the literary ornaments, if not of Bath itself, of its precincts; and in describing our respective characteristics, said, beginning with me, 'the one, a specimen of the most glowing, animated, and impassioned style,' &c.; this word 'impassioned' spoken out strongly in the very ear of the Bishop of Bath and Wells, who sat next him. On the healths of the three poets being given, though much called for, I did not rise, but motioned to Crabbe, who got up and said a few words. When it came to my turn to rise, such a burst of enthusiasm received me as I could not but feel proud of. Spoke for some time, and with much success. Concluded by some tributes to Crabbe and Bowles, and said of the latter, that 'his poetry was the first fountain at which I had drunk the pure freshness of the English language, and learned (however little I might have profited by my learning) of what variety of sweetness the music of English verse is capable. From admiration of the poet, I had been at length promoted into friendship with the man, and I felt it particularly incumbent upon me,' from some late allusions, to say, that I had found the life and the poetry of my friend to be but echoes to each other; the same sweetness and good feeling pervades and modulates both. Those who call my friend a wasp, would not, if they knew him better, make such a mistake in natural history. They would find that he is a *bee*, of the species called the *apes neatina*, and that, however he may have a sting ready on the defensive, when attacked, his native element is that garden of social life which he adorns, and the proper business and delight of his life are sunshine and flowers.' In talking of the 'springs of health with which nature had gifted the fair city of Bath,' and of her physicians, I said, 'it was not necessary to go back to the relationship between Apollo and Esculapius to, show the close consanguinity that exists between literature and the healing art; between that art which purifies and strengthens the body, and those pursuits that refine and invigorate the intellect. Long,' I added, ' may they both continue to bless you with their beneficent effects! Long may health and the Muses walk your beautiful hills together, and mutually mingle their respective influences, till your springs themselves shall grow springs of inspiration, and it may be said,

' Flavus Apollo
Pocula Castaliâ plena ministrat aquâ.''

Quite overwhelmed with praises, I left the room. Elwyn and I, accompanied by Bayly, and a sensible Irishman, E. introduced me to (Ellis); went to the play together. Home to Elwyn's house, where I slept.

"Jan. 22, 1825.—Bowles highly gratified with what I said of him. Asked by every one to give a correct copy of it for the newspapers, but shall not, for it would break the charm which all lies in manner, the occasion, &c., &c. Duncan of Oxford said to me, 'I have had that sweet oratory ringing in my ears all night.'"

"April 11 to May 11.—For this whole month have been too closely occupied with my Sheridan task to write a word here, and must, therefore, only recollect what I can. Received a letter from some Mrs. F. (whom I never heard of before) in which she says, ' Your talents and excellence have long been the idols of my heart. With thee were the dreams of my earliest love,' &c. The object of the letter is to invite me to a dinner she is about to give to 'a few select friends in memory of Lord Byron!' Her husband, she adds, is a 'gentleman and a scholar;' I wish him joy of her."

WORDSWORTH AND SIR H. DAVY.

We talked of Wordsworth's exceedingly high opinion of himself; and she mentioned that one day, in a large party, Wordsworth, without any thing having been previously said that could lead to the subject, called out suddenly from the top of the table to the bottom, in his most epic tone, "Davy!" and, on Davy's putting forth his head in awful expectation of what was coming, said, "Do you know the reason why I published the *White Doe* in quarto?" "No, what was it?" "To show the world my own opinion of it."—(Moore.)

H. K. WHITE'S LOVE OF FAME.

That youthful poet and eminent scholar, Henry Kirke White, toiled hard for fame. His ambition was, that his name might not be forgotten; that among the aspirants to literary distinction he might be recognized, and his genius acknowledged. It was the fear of falling short of this that made him mournfully inquire,

" Fifty years hence, and who will hear of Henry ?"

Under this impulse he sacrificed health, and even life. He trimmed the midnight lamp with a tremulous hand, and scanned the classic page with an eye almost drowsy in death.

" He nursed the pinion that impelled the steel."

Having received, according to his aims, the highest honours of the university, he exclaimed, respecting these laurels, which he had so hardly won, and which, as the sequel proved, he was so soon to relinquish,

" What are ye now,
But thorns about my bleeding brow ?"

In sacrificing health to fame, however, Henry Kirke White saw his error in time to reach that higher, purer motive, which combines with feelings of regret and sorrow, the hopes and aspirations of the Christian.

WORDSWORTH, COLERIDGE, AND COTTLE.

Coleridge had met with Wordsworth's *Descriptive Sketches* in 1794, and discerned amid the faults of an immature understanding the promise of an original poetic genius. He, on his part, needed no other voucher for the possession of the richest intellectual gifts than what proceeded from his own most eloquent tongue. His mind, as yet undimmed by the fumes of opium, was now in its fullest and freshest bloom. Transcendental metaphysics had not monopolized his thoughts. His sympathies had a wider range than afterwards, and, if his discourse sometimes lost itself in clouds, they were clouds which glowed with gorgeous hues. All who saw him in his early prime are agreed that his finest works convey a feeble notion of the profusion of ideas, the brilliancy of imagery, the subtlety of speculation, the sweep of knowledge, which then distinguished his inexhaustible colloquial displays. Each poet had traversed regions of thought to which the other was comparatively a stranger: Wordsworth full of original contemplations upon nature — Coleridge more conversant with systems of philosophy, and all the varieties of general literature. Coleridge was astonished to find a man who, out of the common appearances of the world, could evolve new and unexpected feelings—Wordsworth was dazzled with the splendour of apparently boundless intellectual hoards. There sprang up between them on the instant the strongest sentiments of admiration and affection. "I feel myself," writes Coleridge, "a little man by his side." Of Miss Wordsworth he speaks with equal enthusiasm. "His exquisite sister is a woman indeed!—in mind, I mean, and heart; for her person is such that, if you expected to see a pretty woman, you would think her rather ordinary—if you expected to see an ordinary woman, you would think her pretty! Her manners are simple, ardent, impressive. In every motion her most innocent soul outbeams so brightly that who saw would say—

'Guilt was a thing impossible in her.'

Her information varies; her eye watchful in minutest observation of nature, and her taste a perfect electrometer—it bends, protrudes, and draws in at subtlest beauties and most recondite faults." What Wordsworth thought of his guest may be summed up in his well-known saying, that other men of the age had done wonderful things, but Coleridge was the only wonderful man he had ever known.

Here is an anecdote of these two poets and their publisher Cottle:—

"The publisher has preserved no memorials of his professional visit; but some particulars he has recorded of a former jaunt afford an amusing glimpse of the simplicity of living, and ignorance of common things, which then distinguished the gifted pair. Cottle drove Wordsworth from Bristol to Allfoxden in a gig, calling at Stowey by the way to summon Coleridge and Miss Wordsworth, who followed swiftly on foot. The Allfoxden pantry was empty—so they carried with them bread and cheese, and a bottle of brandy. A beggar stole the cheese, which set Coleridge expatiating on the superior virtues of brandy. It was he that, with thirsty impatience, took out the horse; but as he let down the shafts, the theme of his eloquence rolled from the seat, and was dashed to pieces on the ground. Coleridge, abashed, gave the horse up to Cottle, who tried to pull off the collar. It proved too much for the worthy citizen's strength, and he called to Wordsworth to assist. Wordsworth retired baffled, and was relieved by the ever-handy Coleridge. There seemed more likelihood of their pulling off the animal's head than his collar, and they marvelled by what magic it had ever been got on. 'La, master,' said the servant-girl who was passing by, 'you don't go the right way to work;' and turning round the collar, she slipped it off in an instant, to the utter confusion of the three luminaries. How Silas Cumberbatch could have gone through his cavalry training, and W. W. have spent nine-tenths of his life in the country, and neither of them have witnessed the harnessing or unharnessing of a horse, must remain a problem for our betters."

BOYSE.

Samuel Boyse, author of *The Deity*, a poem, was a fag author, and, at one time, employed by Mr. Ogle to translate some of Chaucer's tales into modern English, which he did with great spirit, at the rate of threepence a line for his trouble. Poor Boyse wore a blanket, because he was destitute of breeches; and was, at last, found famished to death, with a pen in his hand.

JOHN DRYDEN.

It was after preparing a second edition of *Virgil*, that the great Dryden, who had lived, and was to die, in harness, found himself still obliged to seek for daily bread. Scarcely relieved from one heavy task, he was compelled to hasten to another; and his efforts were now stimulated by a domestic feeling—the expected return of his son in ill health from Rome.

In a letter to his bookseller he pathetically writes, "If it please God that *I must die of over-study*, I cannot spend my life better than in preserving his."

It was on this occasion, on the verge of his seventieth year, as he describes himself in the dedication of his *Virgil*, that, "worn out with study, and oppressed with fortune," he contracted to supply the bookseller with ten thousand verses at sixpence a line.

RABELAIS' OPINION OF THE WORLD.

Rabelais had written some sensible pieces, which the world did not regard at all. "I will write something," says he, "that they shall take notice of." And so he sat down to writing nonsense.

GEORGE BUCHANAN.

This illustrious scholar, compelled to fly from his own country by the animosity of a priestly cabal, whose vices he had made the theme of his satire, sought refuge and protection under Henry VIII. of England. His appeal to that monarch was couched in terms of great pathos and elegance. "Look not," said the poet, "with an unrelenting countenance upon the humble advance of a man whose soul is devoted to your service; one who, a beggar, a vagrant, and an exile, has endured every species of misfortune which a perfidious world can inflict. A savage host of inveterate enemies pursued him, and the palace of his sovereign resounds with their menaces. *Over mountains covered in snow, and valleys flooded with rain, I come a fugitive to the Athenian altar of mercy, and, exhausted by calamities, cast myself at your feet.*"

Alas! London was not the Athens the fugitive sought, nor Henry the Pericles whose generosity was to succour him. But who can wonder that, after sacrificing to the axe that beauty on which he once reposed with delight, neither the misfortune of greatness, nor the eloquence of genius, should have been able to make the least impression on the heart of the savage Henry?

PEEL AND BYRON.

Sir Robert Peel was a contemporary of Byron, and a scholar at the same university. It is related that when a great fellow of a boy-tyrant, who claimed little Peel as a *fag*, was giving him a castigation, Byron happened to come by. While the stripes were succeeding each other, and poor Peel was writhing under them, Byron saw and felt for the misery of his friend; and although he was not strong enough to fight the tyrant with any hope of success, and it was dangerous even to approach him, he advanced to the scene of action, and with a blush of rage, tears in his eyes, and in a voice trembling with terror and indignation, asked very humbly if he would be pleased to tell him "how many stripes he meant to inflict."

"Why," replied the executioner, "you little rascal, what is that to you?"

"Because, if you please," said Byron, "*I would take half.*"

That Byron was thus originally of a noble nature, is proved beyond all contradiction by this little anecdote.

CAMPBELL.

"It is well known," says Frazer, "that Campbell's own favourite poem was his *Gertrude*. I once heard him say, 'I never like to see my name before the *Pleasures of Hope;* why, I cannot tell you, unless it was that, when young, I was always greeted among my friends as 'Mr. Campbell, author of the *Pleasures of Hope.*' 'Good morning to you, Mr. Campbell, author of the *Pleasures of Hope.*' When I got married, I was married as the author of the *Pleasures of Hope;* and when I became a father, my son was the son of the author of the *Pleasures of Hope.*' A kind of grim smile, ill subdued, we are afraid, stole over our features, when, standing beside the poet's grave, we read the inscription on his coffin :—

"'Thomas Campbell, LL.D., author of the *Pleasures of Hope*, died, June 15, 1844, aged 67.'

"The poet's dislike occurred to our memory—there was no getting the better of the thought."

CHURCHILL'S "ROSCIAD."

When Churchill finished his *Rosciad*, he waited on an eminent bookseller with the copy; but he had suffered so severely by the publication of poetry, that he was determined to have nothing more to do with any of the rhyming sons of Apollo, unless he was indemnified from sustaining any loss. This condition Churchill could not comply with. The bookseller, however, recommended a worthy young man to him, who had just ventured his little fortune in the uncertain sea of ink, and who would probably run the risk of publication.

Churchill waited on him, and found everything to his wish. The poem was printed, advertised, and at the end of five days ten copies were sold. Churchill was thunderstruck, and the bookseller was little less chagrined. At the end of four days more he found that six more copies were sold. The poet was almost frantic, and hurried away to a friend to acquaint him with his hard fate.

His friend, who was intimate with Garrick, posted to him the next morning, and informed him what a beautiful picture of his astonishing abilities had just appeared in the *Rosciad*. Garrick swallowed the gilded pill, instantly sent for the poem, read it, and sounded its praises wherever he went. The next evening the publisher had not a single copy left, and in a few weeks so many editions went off, that Churchill found himself richer than any poet whose estate lay at that time on Parnassus.

BLACKLOCK AND DAVID HUME.

Blacklock, the poet, certainly much better known for his blindness than for his genius, happened to call upon Hume, the historian, one day, and began a long dissertation on his misery, bewailing his loss of sight, his large family of children, and his utter incapacity to provide for them, or even to supply them, at that moment, with the necessaries of life.

Hume himself was, at that period, so little a favourite of fortune, from the smallness of his paternal estate, and the scantiness of his collegiate stipend, being then a member of the university, that he had solicited, and just then received, through the strenuous interest of a friend, a university appointment worth about forty pounds per annum.

The heart of the philosopher, however, was softened by the complaint of his friend; and being destitute of the pecuniary means of immediate assistance, he ran to his desk, took out the newly-received grant, and presented it to the unhappy poet, with a promise, which he faithfully performed, of using his best interest to have the name of Hume changed for that of Blacklock. In this generous attempt he was finally successful, and, by his noble philanthropy, had the pleasure of saving his friend and family from starvation.

VOLTAIRE AND POPE.

Voltaire, when in London, was very intimate with Pope: he was familiar at his table, and introduced to the circle of his acquaintance. But gratitude, and a respect to the laws of hospitality, seemed not to govern the conduct of Voltaire.

One day, when he knew Pope was from home, he called on his ancient mother, who lived with him, and told her that he should be very sorry to do anything to displease her, but really it was very hard living in London; that he had a poem, a severe lampoon upon her, which he was going to publish, but which he would recommend her to give him a sum of money to suppress.

The fear of the poor old woman at length prevailed over her indignation, and she bribed him not to publish, which he agreed to, on one condition—that she would never mention the subject. She promised, and she kept her word. Having so well succeeded once, he made a second attempt on the yielding prey. The indignation of the injured lady was at its height, when Pope entered the room, and, perceiving her agitation, insisted on knowing the cause. She informed him, in half-stifled accents.

Voltaire had neither time to run off nor to make up an excuse, when the enraged poet, who was never deficient in filial respect, flew with resentment on the unfeeling Frenchman, striking him vehemently. Voltaire, in the attempt to retreat precipitately, fell over a chair.

CAMOENS.

When Camoens published his poem of the *Lusiad*, King Sebastian was so pleased with it that he gave the author a pension of four thousand reals, on condition that he should reside at court; but this salary was withdrawn by Cardinal Henry, who succeeded to the throne of Portugal, which Sebastian had lost at the battle of Alcazar. The bard of the Tagus was utterly neglected by Henry, under whose inglorious reign it was that he perished in poverty.

Camoens had a black servant who was grown old with him, and who had long experienced his master's humanity. This grateful Indian, who was a native of Java, is said by some writers to have saved the life of his master in that unhappy shipwreck by which he lost all his property, except his poems, which he preserved. When Camoens became so reduced as no longer to maintain his servant, this faithful creature begged in the streets of Lisbon for the only man in Portugal on whom God had bestowed those talents which have a tendency to erect the spirit of a sinking age.

BOILEAU AND RACINE.

Boileau and Racine derived little or no profit from the booksellers. Boileau particularly, though fond of money, was so delicate on this point, that he gave all his works away. It was this that made him so bold in railing at those authors *qui mettent leur Apollon aux gages d'un libraire*, and he declared that he had inserted only these verses,—

"*Je sois qu'un noble esprit peut sans honte et sans crime
Tirer de son travail un tribut légitime*,"

to console Racine, who had received some profits from the printing of his tragedies. These profits, were, however, inconsiderable: the truth is, the king remunerated the poets.

Racine's first royal mark of favour was an order signed by Colbert for six hundred livres, *to give him the means of continuing his studies for the belles-lettres.* He received, by an account found among his papers, above forty thousand livres from the *cassette* of the king, by the hand of the first *valet-de-chambre*. Besides these gifts, Racine had a pension of four thousand livres, as historiogra-pher, and another pension as a man of letters.

BUTLER'S PRIDE.

It is said that Butler, the celebrated author of *Hudibras*, was equally remarkable for poverty and pride. A friend of his one evening invited him to supper, and contrived to place in his pocket a purse containing one hundred guineas. This was found by the poet the following morning, and, feeling uneasy, he ascertained by whom it was given, and then returned it, expressing his warm displeasure at the insult which had been thus offered him.

DR. WATTS AND MRS. ROWE.

Dr. Watts, whose passion for the justly celebrated Mrs. Rowe, then Miss Singer, is well known, having called one winter morning upon that lady, and perceiving that the fire and the conversation were getting dull, took up the poker, and putting it in the fire said, "Allow me, madam, to raise a flame."

LITERARY CAUTIOUSNESS.

Pope published nothing until it had been a year or two before him, and even then the printer's proofs were very full of alterations; and, on one occasion, Dodsley, his publisher, thought it better to have the whole recomposed than make the necessary corrections.

Goldsmith considered four lines a-day good work, and was seven years in beating out the pure gold of the *Deserted Village.*

SHOOTING A BOOKSELLER.

Campbell produced the *Pleasures of Hope* at Edinburgh, being then but twenty-one years of age. This fine performance at once gave him fame, and for twenty years afterward brought to the publishers between two and three hundred pounds annually. They had originally given him ten pounds for the poem. Afterwards he received some further remuneration, and was allowed the profit accruing from a quarto edition of his works.

"Many a true word is spoken in jest," the proverb teaches; and an anecdote told of Campbell may be thought to indicate a feeling within not very favourable to those who had given his poem to the world. Being in a festive party at a period when the actions of Bonaparte were most severely condemned, on being called upon for a toast, Campbell gave, 'The health of Napoleon.' This caused great surprise to all the company, and an explanation was called for.

"The only reason I have for proposing to honour Bonaparte," said he, "is, that he had the *virtue to shoot a bookseller.*" Palm, a bookseller, had recently been executed in Germany, by order of the French chief.

MILTON'S SONNETS.

A lady having expressed her wonder to Dr. Johnson, that "Milton, who had written so sublime a poem as the *Paradise Lost*, should have been so inferior to himself in the composition of the Sonnets," he replied, "Is it a matter of surprise, madam, that the hand which was able to scoop a colossus, of the most *perfect symmetry*, from a *rock*, should fail in an attempt to form the head of Venus out of a cherry-stone?"

POPE'S ENEMIES.

According to the scandalous chronicle of the day, Pope, shortly after the publication of the *Dunciad*, had a tall Irishman to attend him. Colonel Duckett threatened to cane him for a licentious stroke aimed at him, which Pope recanted. Thomas Bentley, nephew to the doctor, for the treatment his uncle had received, sent Pope a challenge. The modern like the ancient Horace was of a nature liable to panic at such critical moments. Pope consulted some military friends who declared that his *person* ought to protect him from any such redundance of valour as was thus formally required; however, one of them accepted the challenge for him, and gave Bentley the option of fighting or apologizing, who, on this occasion, proved what is usual—that the easiest of the two is the quickest performed.

REWARDS.

Goldsmith was astonished when the bookseller gave him five shillings a couplet for his delightful poem of the *Deserted Village*, when each line was fairly worth as many pounds; but an instance of liberality has occurred in Russia, which really deserves recording. Alexander Paselikin, a young poet, has recently produced a work, which does not contain above six hundred lines, and for which he has received three thousand rubles, nearly one pound sterling per line.

POPE'S EARLY POPULARITY.

"A remarkable fact," says Professor Wilson, "is the early acknowledgment of Pope by his contemporaries. At sixteen he is a poet for the world by his *Pastorals*, and at that age he has a literary adviser in Walsh, and a literary patron in Trumbull. He does not seem to court. He is courted. He is the intimate friend, we do not know how soon, of scholars and polite writers, of men and women high in birth, in education, in station. Scarce twenty, by his *Essay on Criticism*, he assumes a chair in the school of the Muses. At five-and-twenty, he is an acknowledged dictator of polite letters.

"So early, rapid, untroubled an ascension to fame it would require some research to find a parallel to. Our literature has it not. And this acknowledgment, gratulation, triumph, which friends and circles, and the confined literary world of that day in this country, could furnish, a whole age, and a whole country, and a whole world, the extended republic of letters, confirm.

"At the age of thirty-seven, Pope declares that henceforward he will write *from*, as well as *to*, his own mind. The *Essay on Man* follows. It expresses that graver study of the universal subject, MAN, which appeared to Pope, now self-known, to be, for the time of poetical literature to which he came, the most practicable—for his own ability the aptest; and it embodies that part of anthropology which doubtless was the most congenial to his own inclination—the philosophical contemplation of man's nature, estate, destiny.

"The success of this enterprise was astonishing. Be the philosophy what and whose it may, the poem revived to the latest age of poetry the phenomenon of the first, when precept and maxim were modulated into verse, that they might write themselves in every brain, and live upon every tongue."

HENRY W. LONGFELLOW.

We know of nothing which, in few words, gives more information concerning this distinguished American poet than the following anecdote.

"About the year, 1837, Longfellow," says a Dublin paper, "being engaged in making the tour of Europe, selected Heidelberg for a permanent winter residence. There his wife was attacked with an illness which ultimately proved fatal.

"It so happened, however, that some time afterward there came to the same romantic place a young lady of considerable personal attractions. The poet's heart was touched — he became attached to her; but the beauty of sixteen did not sympathize with the poet of six-and-thirty, and Longfellow returned to America, having lost his heart as well as his wife.

"The young lady, also an American, returned home shortly afterwards. Their residences, it turned out, were contiguous, and the poet availed himself of the opportunity of prosecuting his addresses, which he did for a considerable time with no better success than at first. Thus foiled, he set himself resolutely down, and instead, like Petrarch, of laying siege to the heart of his mistress through the medium of sonnets, he resolved to write a whole book ; a book which would achieve the double object of gaining her affections, and of establishing his own fame. *Hyperion* was the result.

"His labour and his constancy were not thrown away: they met their due reward. The lady gave him her hand as well as her heart; and they now reside together at Cambridge, in the same house which Washington made his headquarters when he was first appointed to the command of the American armies. These interesting facts were communicated to us by a very intelligent American gentleman, whom we had the pleasure of meeting in the same place which was the scene of the poet's early disappointment and sorrow."

ADDISON AND THE POETASTER.

Addison, the sublime moralist, elegant critic, and humorous describer of men and manners, whose works furnish instruction to youth, amusement to age, and delight to all who peruse them, was remarkable for his taciturnity. Conscious of his talents as a writer, he acknowledged his deficiency in conversation. "I can draw," said he, "a bill for a thousand pounds, although I have not a guinea in my pocket."

A poetaster brought Addison one of his compositions, and begged his opinion of it. It was a copy of very indifferent verses, and they appeared the worse because he had prefixed to them several lines from Homer, and thus exposed them to a very disadvantageous contrast. Addison, with great warmth, struck out the lines from Homer; and when the surprised poetaster asked the reason, "Do you not recollect," said Addison, "the Roman emperor, whose statues appeared to him very ridiculous when they were placed near those of the gods?"

MILTON AND JAMES II.

James II., when Duke of York, made a visit to Milton, out of curiosity. In the course of their conversation, the duke said to the poet, that he thought his blindness was a judgment of heaven on him, because he had written against Charles I., his (the duke's) father, when the immortal poet replied, "If your highness thinks that misfortunes are indexes of the wrath of heaven, what must you think of your father's tragical end? I have only lost my *eyes*—he lost his *head*."

POE THE AMERICAN POET.

Edgar A. Poe, whose genius even those who most dislike his wild extravagances and psychological transcendentalism will at once acknowledge, thus vents his bitterest sarcasm upon the *North American Review*:—

"I cannot say that I ever fairly comprehended the force of the term 'insult,' until I was given to understand, one day, by a member of the *North American Review* clique, that this journal was 'not only willing, but anxious, to render me that justice which had been already rendered me by the *Revue Française*, and the *Revue des Deux Mondes*,' but was 'restrained from so doing' by my 'invincible spirit of antagonism.' I wish the *North American Review* to express *no* opinion of me whatever—for I have none of it. In the meantime, as I see no motto on its title-page, let me recommend it one from Sterne's Letter from France. Here it is: 'As we rode along the valley, we saw a herd of asses on the top of one of the mountains—how they viewed and *reviewed* us.'"

A ROBBER'S REMORSE.

Somebody once robbed the poet Montgomery of an inkstand, presented to him by the ladies of Sheffield. The public execration was so loud, that the thief restored the booty with the following note:—

"Birmingham, March, 1812.

"Honoured Sir: When we robbed your house we did not know that you wrote such beautiful verses as you do. I remember my mother told some of them to me when I was a boy. I found what house we robbed by the writing on the inkstand. Honoured sir, I send it back. It was my share of the booty, and I hope you and God will forgive me."

GOLDSMITH'S "DESERTED VILLAGE."

"The *Deserted Village*," says Mr. Best, an Irish clergyman, "relates to the scenes in which Goldsmith was an actor. Auburn is a poetical name for the village of Lissoy, in the county of Westmeath, barony of Kilkenny West. The name of the schoolmaster was Paddy Burns. I remember him well. He was, indeed, a man severe to view. A woman called Walsey Cruse kept the alehouse.

'Imagination fondly stoops to trace
 The parlour splendours of that festive place.'

I have been often in the house. The hawthorn bush was remarkably large, and stood opposite the alehouse.

"I was once riding with Brady, titular Bishop of Ardagh, when he observed to me, 'Ma foy! Best, this huge overgrown bush is mightily in the way; I will order it to be cut down.' 'What, sir!' said I, 'cut down Goldsmith's hawthorn bush, that supplies so beautiful an image in the *Deserted Village?*' 'Ma foy!' exclaimed the bishop, 'is that the hawthorn bush? Then ever let it be sacred from the edge of the axe, and evil to him that would cut from it a branch.'"

TIT FOR TAT.

Campbell, the poet, and Turner, the artist, were dining together with a large party, a few years ago. The poet was called upon for a toast, and, by way of a joke upon the great professor of the sister art, gave, "The Painters and Glaziers." After the laughter had subsided, the artist was of course summoned to propose a toast also. He rose, and, with admirable tact and ready wit, discharged the debt of his craft to the author of the *Pleasures of Hope*, by giving the "Paper-stainers."

COLERIDGE'S YOUTH.

"From eight to fourteen I was a playless dreamer," he observes, "a *helluo librorum*, my appetite for which was indulged by a singular incident: a stranger, who was struck by my conversation, made me free of a circulating library in King Street, Cheapside."

"This incident," says Gilman, "was indeed singular. Going down the Strand in one of his day-dreams, fancying himself swimming the Hellespont, thrusting his hands before him as in the act of swimming, one hand came in contact with a gentleman's pocket. The gentleman seized his hand: turning round, he looked at him with some anger, exclaiming, 'What, so young, and so wicked!' at the same time accusing him of an attempt to pick his pocket.

"The frightened boy sobbed out his denial of the intention, and explained to him how he thought himself Leander trying to swim the Hellespont.

"The gentleman was so struck and delighted with the novelty of the thing, and with the simplicity and intelligence of the boy, that he subscribed, as before stated, to the library; in consequence of which, Coleridge was further enabled to indulge his love of reading. It is stated that at this school he laid the foundation of those bodily sufferings, which made his life one of sickness and torture, and occasioned his melancholy resort to opium. He greatly injured his health, it is said, and reduced his strength, by his bathing excursions; but is it not quite as likely that the deficiency of food, and those holidays when he was turned out to starvation, had quite as much to do with it?"

COLERIDGE'S OPIUM-EATING.

One of the most melancholy facts in the history of Coleridge is his indulgence in the use of opium. It had been continued for a long time, and had begun to weaken and obscure his vigorous and brilliant intellect before his friend Cottle became aware that he used it.

In 1814, Cottle wrote to him a very faithful letter, full of dissuasives against the habit; and in Coleridge's reply occur the following affecting paragraphs:—

"For ten years the anguish of my spirit has been indescribable, the sense of my danger staring, but the consciousness of my guilt worse —far worse than all. I have prayed, with drops of agony on my brow; trembling, not only before the justice of my Maker, but, even before the mercy of my Redeemer. 'I gave thee so many talents; what hast thou done with them?'

"Secondly, overwhelmed as I am with a sense of my direful infirmity, I have never attempted to disguise or conceal the cause. On the contrary, not only to friends have I stated the whole case with tears, and the very bitterness of shame, but in two instances I have warned young men, mere acquaintances, who had spoken of taking laudanum, of the direful consequences, by an awful exposition of its tremendous effects on myself.

"Thirdly, though before God I cannot lift up my eyelids, and only do not despair of his mercy, because to despair would be adding crime to crime, yet to my fellow-men I may say, that I was seduced into the accursed habit ignorantly. I had been almost bedridden for many months, with swellings in my knees. In a medical journal, I unhappily met with an account of a cure performed in a similar case, or what appeared to me so, by rubbing in laudanum, at the same time taking a given dose internally. It acted like a charm—like a miracle! I recovered the use of my limbs, of my appetite, of my spirits, and this continued for near a fortnight. At length the unusual stimulus subsided, the complaint returned, the supposed remedy was recurred to; but I cannot go through the dreary history.

"Suffice it to say, that effects were produced which acted on me by terror and cowardice; of pain and sudden death, not—so help me God—by any temptation of pleasure, or expectation or desire of exciting pleasurable sensations. On the very contrary, Mrs. Morgan and her sister will bear witness so far as to say that the longer I abstained, the higher my spirits, the keener my enjoyments, till the moment, the direful moment arrived, when my pulse began to fluctuate, my heart to palpitate, and such falling down as it were, of my whole frame, such intolerable restlessness, and incipient bewilderment, that in the last of my several attempts to abandon the dire poison, I exclaimed in agony, which I now repeat in seriousness and solemnity, 'I am too poor to hazard this.' Had I but a few hundred pounds,—but two hundred pounds,—half to send Mrs. Coleridge, and half to place myself in a private mad-house, where I could procure nothing but what a physician thought proper, and where a medical attendant could be constantly with me for two or three months (in less than that time life or death would be determined), then there might be hope. Now there is none! You bid me rouse myself: go bid a man, paralytic in both arms, to rub them briskly together, and that will cure him. 'Alas!' he would reply, 'that I cannot move my arms is my complaint and my misery.'"

Writing to another friend, a short time after, he says, "Conceive a poor miserable wretch, who for many years has been attempting to beat off pain by a constant recurrence to the vice that reproduces it. Conceive a spirit in hell, employed in tracing out for others the road to that heaven from which his crimes exclude him. In short, conceive whatever is most wretched, helpless, and hopeless, and you will form as tolerable a notion of my state as it is possible for a good man to have. I used to think the text in St. James, that 'he who offends in one point offends in all,' very harsh;' but I now feel the awful, the tremendous truth of it. In the one crime of opium, what crime have I not made myself guilty of! Ingratitude to my Maker, and to my benefactors injustice, *and unnatural cruelty to my poor children*, self-contempt for my repeated promise, breach, nay, too often, actual falsehood."

It is interesting to know that

Coleridge afterwards broke away from this dreadful habit, and that his life was lengthened out some twenty years longer.

BARON HALLER.

Poets change their opinions of their own productions wonderfully at different periods of life. Baron Haller was in his youth warmly attached to poetic composition. His house was on fire, and to rescue his poems, he rushed through the flames. He was so fortunate as to escape with his beloved manuscripts in his hands. Ten years afterwards, he condemned to the flames those very poems which he had ventured his life to preserve.

POPULARITY OF POETS.

When Lord Byron was presented with an American edition of *Childe Harold*, he exclaimed, "This, now, is something like immortality."

We are reminded of his remark by meeting in the Mexican correspondence of the *Boston Atlas* with this statement: "At Puebla I found in a convent a volume of *Lalla Rookh*, and another of the *Lady of the Lake*. On the battle-field of Contreras I picked up a volume of Burns' poems."

VALUE OF A MANUSCRIPT.

The original manuscript of Gray's *Elegy* was lately sold by auction in London. There was really quite "a scene" in the auction-room. Imagine a stranger entering in the midst of a sale of some rusty-looking old books. The auctioneer produces *two small half sheets of paper*, written over, torn, and mutilated. He calls it a "most interesting article," and apologizes for its condition. Pickering bids ten pounds! Rodd, Foss, Thorpe, Bohn, Holloway, and some few amateurs, quietly remark, twelve, fifteen, twenty, twenty-five, thirty, and so on, till there is a pause at *sixty-three pounds!* The hammer strikes. "Hold!" says Mr. Foss. "It is mine," says the amateur. "No, I bid sixty-five in time." "Then I give seventy." "Seventy-five," says Mr. Foss; and fives are repeated again until the two bits of paper are knocked down, amidst a general cheer, to Payne and Foss, for *one hundred pounds sterling!* On these bits of paper are written the first draught of the *Elegy in a Country Churchyard*, by Thomas Gray, including five verses which were omitted in publication, and with the poet's interlinear corrections and alterations—certainly an "interesting article:" several persons supposed it would call for a ten pound note, perhaps even twenty. A single volume with "W. Shakspere," in the fly-leaf, produced, sixty years ago, a hundred guineas; but, probably, with that exception, no mere autograph, and no single sheet of paper, ever before produced the sum of *five hundred dollars!*

COLERIDGE'S ABSENCE OF MIND.

Mr. Coleridge had solicited permission of Mr. Southey to deliver his fourth lecture on the Rise, Progress, and Decline of the Roman Empire, as a subject to which he had devoted especial attention. The request was immediately granted, and at the end of the third lecture it was formally announced to the audience that the next lecture would be delivered by Mr. Samuel Taylor Coleridge, of Jesus College, Cambridge.

At the usual hour the room was thronged. The moment of commencement arrived. No lecturer appeared. Patience was preserved for a quarter of an hour or more; but still no lecturer. At length it was communicated to the impatient assemblage, that a circumstance exceedingly to be regretted would prevent Mr. Coleridge from giving his lecture that evening, as intended.

Some few present learnt the truth, but the major part of the company retired not very well pleased, and under the impression that Mr. Coleridge had either broken his leg, or that some severe family affliction had occurred.

Mr. Coleridge's rather habitual absence of mind, with the little importance he generally attached to engagements, renders it likely that at this very time he might have been found at T——, College Street, composedly smoking his pipe, and lost in profound musings on his divine Susquehanna.

An eminent medical man in Bristol, who greatly admired Mr. Coleridge's conversation and genius, on one occasion invited Mr. C. to dine with him on a given day. The invitation was accepted, and this gentleman, willing to gratify his friends with an introduction to Mr. Coleridge, invited a large assembly for the express purpose of meeting him, and made a splendid entertainment, anticipating the delight which would be universally felt from Mr. Coleridge's far-famed eloquence.

It unfortunately happened that Mr. Coleridge had forgotten all about it; and the gentleman, with his guests, after waiting till the hot became cold, under his mortification consoled himself by the resolve never again to subject himself to the like disaster. No explanation or apology from Mr. Coleridge's friends could soothe the choler of this disciple of Galen.

A dozen subscribers to his lectures fell off from this slip of his memory.

WORDSWORTH'S WANT OF SMELL.

Wordsworth had no sense of smell. Once, and once only in his life, the dormant power awakened. It was by a bed of stocks in full bloom, at a house which he inhabited in Dorsetshire, and he said it was like a vision of paradise to him; but it lasted only a few moments, and the faculty continued torpid from that time.

THEODORE E. HOOK.

I remember, one day at Sydenham, Mr. Theodore Hook coming in unexpectedly to dinner, and amusing us very much with his talent at extempore verse. He was then a youth, tall, dark, and of a good person, with small eyes, and features more round than weak; a face that had character and humour, but no refinement. His extempore verses were really surprising.

It is easy enough to extemporize in Italian. One only wonders how, in a language in which every thing conspires to render verse-making easy, and it is difficult to avoid rhyming, this talent should be so much cried up. But in English it is another matter. I have known but one other person besides Hook who could extemporize in English; and he wanted the confidence to do it in public. Of course, I speak of rhyming. Extempore blank verse, with a little practice, would be found as easy in English, as rhyming is in Italian.

In Hook the faculty was very unequivocal. He could not have been aware of the character of all the visitors, still less of the subject of conversation when he came in, and he talked his full share till called upon. Yet he ran his jokes and his verses upon us all in the easiest manner, saying something characteristic of every' body, or avoiding it with a pun; and he introduced so agreeably a piece of village scandal, upon which the party had been rallying Campbell, that the poet, though not unjealous of his dignity, was, perhaps, the most pleased of us all.

Theodore afterwards sat down to the pianoforte, and enlarging upon this subject made an extempore parody of a modern opera, introducing sailors and their claptraps, rustics, &c., and making the poet and his supposed flame the hero and heroine.

He parodied music as well as words, giving us the most received cadences and flourishes, and calling to mind—not without some hazard to his filial duties—the commonplaces of the pastoral songs and duets of the last half century; so that if Mr. Dignum, the Damon of Vauxhall, had been present, he would have doubted whether to take it as an affront or a compliment.

Campbell certainly took the theme of the parody as a compliment; for having drunk a little more wine than usual that evening, and happening to wear a wig on account of having lost his hair by a fever, he suddenly took off the wig, and dashed it at the head of the performer, exclaiming, "You dog! I'll throw my laurels at you."

SWIFT AND MR. SERGEANT BETTESWORTH.

The following lines on Sergeant Bettesworth, which Swift inserted in one of his poems, gave rise to a violent resentment on the part of the barrister:—

" So at the bar the booby Bettesworth,
Though half-a-crown o'erpays his sweat's worth,
Who knows in law nor text nor margent,
Calls Singleton *his brother sergeant.*"

The poem was sent to Bettesworth at a time when he was surrounded with his friends in a convivial party. He read it aloud till he had finished the lines relative to himself. He then flung it down with great violence—trembled and turned pale—and after some pause, his rage for a while depriving him of utterance, he took out his penknife, and opening it vehemently, swore, "With this very penknife I will cut off his ears."

He then went to the dean's house, and, not finding him at home, followed him to the house of a friend, where being shown into a back room, he desired the doctor might be sent for; and on Swift entering the room, and asking what were his commands, "Sir," said he, "I am Sergeant Bettesworth."

"Of what regiment, pray, sir?" said Swift.

"O, Mr. Dean, we know your powers of raillery—you know me well enough; I am one of his majesty's sergeants-at-law, and I am come to demand if you are the author of this poem, [producing it,] and these villanous lines on me."

"Sir," said Swift, "when I was a young man, I had the honour of being intimate with some great legal characters, particularly Lord Somers, who, knowing my propensity to satire, advised me, when I lampooned a *knave* or *fool*, never to own it. Conformably to that advice, I tell you I am not the author."

ROBERT POLLOK.

Robert Pollok, author of the *Course of Time*, while a student of theology, once delivered a trial discourse before the Secession Divinity Hall, Glasgow, the subject of which was Sin. His manner of treating it, in the opinion of his fellow-students, was rather turgid; and at those passages which they considered to be particularly outrageous, they did not scruple to give audible symptoms of the amusement they derived from Mr. Pollok's highflown phrases. At last one flight was so extravagant that the professor himself was fairly obliged to give way—and smiled.

At this moment the young preacher was just upon the point of a climax expressing the dreadful evils which sin had brought into the world, and he closed it with the following remark: "And had it not been for sin, the smile of folly had never been seen upon the brows of wisdom."

This anecdote is related upon the authority of a person who was present; but it may be remarked that, perhaps, if Mr. Pollok's discourse had been listened to with that decorum which the gravity of the occasion demanded, it might not, to an unprejudiced auditor, have seemed deserving of the unfavourable reception it met with. But when the speaker became sensible that his compeers were making merry at his expense, it must have produced in his manner a degree of confusion, or perhaps of vehemence, by which language and ideas, in themselves not inappropriate, might be rendered ridiculous. It is also to be kept in view that Pollok was not popular among his fellow-students: so that they may be supposed to have been on the watch for an opportunity to testify their jealousy of him.

DEATH OF CAMPBELL, THE POET.

On the 16th he was able to converse more freely; but his strength had become more reduced, and being assisted to change his posture, he fell back insensible. Conversation was carried on in the room in whispers; and Campbell uttered a few sentences, so unconnected, that his friends were doubtful whether he was conscious or not of what was going on in his presence, and had recourse to an artifice to learn.

One of them spoke of the poem of *Hohenlinden*, and pretending to forget the author's name, said he had heard it was by Mr. Robinson. Campbell saw the trick, was amused, and said playfully, but in a calm and distinct tone, "No; it was one Tom Campbell."

The poet had, as far as a poet can, become for years indifferent to posthumous fame. In 1838, five years before this time, he had been speaking to some friends in Edinburgh on the subject. "When I think of the existence which shall commence when the stone is laid over my head, how can literary fame appear to me, to any one, but as nothing? I believe, when I am gone, justice will be done to me in this way—that I was a pure writer. It is an inexpressible comfort, at my time of life, to be able to look back and feel that I have not written one line against religion or virtue."

COLERIDGE.

Mr. Coleridge was a remarkably awkward horseman, so much so as generally to attract notice.

On a certain occasion he was riding along the turnpike road, in the county of Durham, when a wag, approaching him, noticed his peculiarity, and, quite mistaking his man, thought the rider a fine subject for a little sport; when, as he drew near, he thus accosted Mr. C.: "I say, young man, did you meet a *tailor* on the road?" "Yes," replied Mr. C., who was never at a loss for a rejoinder, "I did; and he told me if I went a little farther I should meet a *goose!*" The assailant was struck dumb, while the traveller jogged on.

IZAAK WALTON.

Dr. Hawes bequeathed a great portion of his library to the dean and chapter of Salisbury; and his executor and friend presented the celebrated prayer-book, which was Walton's, to Mr. Pickering, the publisher. The watch which belonged to Walton's connection, the excellent Bishop Ken, has been presented to his amiable biographer, the Rev. W. Lisle Bowles.

Walton died at the house of his son-in-law, Dr. Hawkins, at Winchester. He was buried in Winchester Cathedral, in the south aisle, called Prior Silkstead's Chapel. A large black marble slab is placed over his remains; and to use the poetical language of Mr. Bowles, "the morning sunshine falls directly on it, reminding the contemplative man of the mornings when he was, for so many years, up and abroad with his angle, on the banks of the neighbouring stream."

CURIOUS TITLE.

The title which George Gascoigne, who had great merit in his day, has given to his collection, may be considered a specimen of the titles of his times. They were printed in 1576. He calls it "A Hundred Sundrie Flowres bounde vp in one small Poesie: gathered partly by translation in the fyne and outlandish gardens of Euripides, Ovid, Petrarke, Ariosto, and others; and partly by invention out of our own fruitefull orchardes in Englande; yielding sundrie sweet savours of tragicall, comicall, and morall discourses, both pleasaunt and profitable to the well-smelling noses of learned readers."

THE FIRST POET LAUREATE.

The first mention of the king's poet, under the appellation of laureate, was John Kay, who was appointed poet laureate to Edward IV. It is extraordinary that he should have left no pieces of poetry to prove his pretensions in some degree to this office, with which he is said to have been invested by the king, at his return from Italy.

The only composition he has left to posterity is a prose English translation of a Latin history of the siege of Rhodes. In the dedication, addressed to King Edward, —or rather in the title,—he styles himself "hys humble poete laureate." Although this our laureate furnishes us with no materials as a poet, yet his office, which here occurs for the first time under this denomination, must not pass unnoticed in the annals of literature.

SAMUEL ROGERS.

A writer in an American periodical, in 1845, gives the following description of a visit to Samuel Rogers:—

"Samuel Rogers is an exception to the almost general rule, that authors are poor. And who has not, at some time or other, heard of the author of *Pleasures of Memory?* He is not gifted, as Byron was, with beauty of person; so far from it, he is the very opposite of 'good looking,' as it is termed; but he is rich—a very Crœsus. A London banker, he can draw checks alike on the Bank of England and on the treasury of the Muses; and, what is better, find each duly honoured. He has an exquisite taste, and possesses abundantly the means of gratifying it. Art lays her tributes at his feet, and Genius is at his beck and call. For him Science labours, and at his bidding Music pours forth its melodious offerings. He possesses the magic talisman MONEY—which, like the slave of the lamp, in the Arabian tale, fulfils all his requirements, and surrounds him with all that heart can wish. Verily, if wealth, taste, and refinement can confer happiness on mortals, Samuel Rogers must be a satisfied man.

"About six years ago, while on a visit to some friends in London, I spent a day with Coleridge, who then resided with Mr. Gilman, at Highgate. While there, the poet received a note from Mr. Rogers, inviting him to breakfast, in St. James's Place on the following morning. Coleridge, knowing that it would gratify me to accompany him, very kindly asked me to do so, saying that he could take the liberty of introducing a friend, and I agreed to go.

"On the following morning, for a wonder, Mr. Coleridge called for me at the time he had appointed, and we proceeded together in a hack carriage to St. James's Place. Mr. Rogers himself received us, and as none of the other invited guests had arrived, I had a favourable opportunity of observing the venerable poet.

"I had anticipated seeing what is termed a *plain* face, but I had not pictured to myself one so unpoetical as Rogers'. Byron's lines on it, ill-natured and uncalled for as they were, were at least *pictorially* true to nature. There was recently published in the *Pictorial Times*, or *London Illustrated News*, I forget which, a sketch of him, taken at the National Gallery, in the act of examining a painting.

"That likeness is correct in every respect. The sunken eye, shrivelled nose, toothless jaws, and retracted lips are to the life. But though time has been busy with the poet's mortal part, he has not interfered with the jewel it contains. That remains undimmed, and although it emits fewer rays than of yore, its capability of doing so is not destroyed.

"The poet is of middle stature, and unbowed by age. Indeed, in his motions he is, to use a common but expressive figure, 'as brisk as a boy.' Nothing on earth is more delightful, I think, than a cheerful, intelligent old man. And such is Samuel Rogers. He, indeed, possesses all 'the pleasures of memory,' and has had the rare good fortune to live and experience what he sang about years and years ago.

"His conversation was lively and piquant, but did not exhibit any of those sallies of wit which are so often attributed to him in the newspapers, under the head of 'Sam Rogers' last,' &c. To Coleridge's observations he was profoundly attentive; but the great conversationalist was not in a very talking humour, and I was rather glad of it, as it gave me a better opportunity of using my eyes than I should have had, had his words fallen on my charmed ear.

"Mr. Rogers received me very kindly, without an introduction; for Coleridge, with his usual absence of mind, or rather utter disregard of all the minor courtesies and usages of society, neglected to present me to Mr. Rogers, until the latter looked very hard at me, and I reminded Coleridge that he had a companion.

"What a magnificent room was that library of Rogers'! There were paintings from the hands of the best ancient and modern masters, in gorgeous frames; portfolios of the choicest and rarest prints; water-colour drawings, by every artist of celebrity of past and present times; rare specimens of *vertu*, which would have thrown the proprietor of Strawberry Hill into a very flutter of excitement; busts, some brown with age, and others in all the brilliant modern whiteness of Carrara marble; costly gems and princely intaglios; books curious in their old literal board covers, with ancient silver clasps and venerable letters; manuscripts so precious from time, and in consequence of the labour which had been bestowed on them by gray monks, in solemn old cells, ages since, that they were shrined in crystal cases.

"There was a large piece of amber, in which was a fly inclosed, perfect and unmutilated, leaving us to wonder how it got there, and achieved its transparent immortality. Sidney Smith, once taking it up, said, 'Perhaps it buzzed in Adam's ear.' And there were vases of exquisite form and workmanship—relics from Pompeii and from far away Ind; and all so tastefully disposed that no *museum* effect was produced, nor did any one object.

obtrude itself so as to detract from the apparent value of the impression produced by another.

"On a pedestal was a bust of Pope, modelled, at least so far as a part of the drapery was concerned, by the artist (Roubilliac, I believe) in the presence of Mr. Rogers. But there were two objects in the room which, more than any others, engrossed my attention—the one represented the enormous wealth of its possessor, and the other indicated his keen appreciation of the value of mind.

"These articles were simply two small pieces of paper, in gold frames. One of them was a Bank of England note for one million pounds sterling, and the other the original receipt of John Milton for five pounds (the sum he received for the copyright of *Paradise Lost*, from Simmonds, the bookseller). The bank-note was one of the only four which were ever struck from a plate, which was afterwards destroyed. The Rothschilds have one impression; the late Mr. Coutts had another; the Bank of England the third; and, as I have said, Mr. Rogers decorates his parlour with the remaining one.

"There it hangs, within any one's reach; a fortune for many, but valueless to all excepting its owner. No one would think of stealing it, for it would be only as so much waste paper. It never could be negotiated without detection, and, were it destroyed by fire, from its peculiar character, no loss would ensue to Mr. Rogers. At his word, however, it might be transformed into a golden shower. He, alone, is the magician who can render it all-powerful for good or evil."

CHARLES LAMB AND THE COMPTROLLER OF STAMPS.

On December 28th the immortal dinner came off in my painting-room, with Jerusalem towering up behind us as a background. Wordsworth was in fine cue, and we had a glorious set-to on Homer, Shakspeare, Milton, and Virgil. Lamb got exceedingly merry and exquisitely witty, and his fun in the midst of Wordsworth's solemn intonations of oratory was like the sarcasm and wit of the fool in the intervals of Lear's passion. Lamb soon got delightfully merry. He made a speech and voted me absent, and made them drink my health. "Now," said Lamb, "you old lake poet, you rascally poet, why do you call Voltaire dull?" We all defended Wordsworth, and affirmed there was a state of mind when Voltaire would be dull. "Well," said Lamb, "here's Voltaire, the Messiah of the French nation, and a very proper one too." He then, in a strain of humour beyond description, abused me for putting Newton's head into my picture. "A fellow," said he, "who believed nothing unless it was as clear as the three sides of a triangle." And then he and Keats agreed he had destroyed all the poetry of the rainbow, by reducing it to the prismatic colours. It was impossible to resist him, and we all drank, "Newton's health, and confusion to mathematics." It was delightful to see the good-humour of Wordsworth in giving in to all our frolics without affectation, and laughing as heartily as the best of us. By this time other friends joined, amongst them poor Ritchie, who was going to penetrate by Fezzan to Timbuctoo. I introduced him as "A gentleman going to Africa." Lamb seemed to take no notice; but all of a sudden, he roared out, "Which is the gentleman we are going to lose?" We then drank the victim's health, in which Ritchie joined. In the morning of this delightful day a gentleman, a perfect stranger, had called on me. He said he knew my friends, had an enthusiasm for Wordsworth, and begged I would procure him the happiness of an introduction. He told me he was a comptroller of stamps, and often had correspondence with the poet. I thought it a liberty; but still, as he seemed a gentleman, I told him he might come. When we retired to tea we found the comptroller. In introducing him to Wordsworth I forgot to say who he was. After a little time the comptroller looked down, looked up, and said to Wordsworth, "Don't you think, sir, Milton was a great genius?" Keats looked at me, Wordsworth looked at the comptroller. Lamb, who was dozing by the fire, turned round and said, "Pray, sir, did you say Milton was a great genius?" "No, sir, I asked Mr. Wordsworth if he were not." "O!" said Lamb, "then you are a silly fellow." "Charles, my dear Charles," said Wordsworth; but Lamb, perfectly innocent of the confusion he had created, was off again by the fire. After an awful pause the comptroller said, "Don't you think Newton a great genius?" I could not stand it any longer. Keats put his head into my books. Ritchie squeezed in a laugh. Wordsworth, seemed asking himself, "Who is this?" Lamb got up, and taking a candle, said, "Sir, will you allow me to look at your phrenological development?" He then turned his back on the poor man, and at every question of the comptroller he chaunted:

"Diddle diddle dumpling, my son John
Went to his bed with his breeches on."

The man in office, finding Wordsworth did not know who he was, said in a spasmodic and half-chuckling anticipation of assured victory, "I have had the honour of some correspondence with you, Mr. Wordsworth." "With me, sir?" said Wordsworth; "not that I remember." "Don't you, sir? I am a comptroller of stamps." There was a dead silence; the comptroller evidently thinking that was enough. While we were waiting for Wordsworth's reply, Lamb sung out:

"Hey diddle diddle,
The cat and the fiddle."

"My dear Charles," said Wordsworth:

"Diddle diddle dumpling, my son John," chaunted Lamb; and then, rising, exclaimed, "Do let me have another look at that gentleman's organs!" Keats and I hurried Lamb into the painting-room, shut the door, and gave way to inextinguishable laughter. Monkhouse followed, and tried to get Lamb away. We went back, but the comptroller was irreconcileable. We soothed and smiled, and asked him to supper. He stayed, though his dignity was sorely affected. However, being a good-natured man, we parted all in good humour, and no ill effects followed. All the while, until Monkhouse succeeded, we could hear Lamb struggling in the painting-room, and calling at intervals, "Who is that fellow? Allow me to see his organs once more."—(Life of Benjamin R. Haydon.)

LEIGH HUNT'S DESCRIPTION OF CAMPBELL.

"They who knew Mr. Campbell," says Leigh Hunt, "only as the author of *Gertrude of Wyoming*, and the *Pleasures of Hope*, would not have suspected him to be a merry companion, overflowing with humour and anecdote, and anything but fastidious.

"The Scotch poets have always something in reserve. It is the only point in which the major part of them resemble their countrymen. He was one of the few men whom I could at any time have walked half-a-dozen miles through the snow to spend an evening with.

"No man felt more kindly towards his fellow-creatures, or took less credit for it. When he indulged in doubt and sarcasm, and spoke contemptuously of things in general, he did it, partly, no doubt, out of actual dissatisfaction, but more perhaps, than he suspected out of a fear of being thought weak and sensitive; which is a blind that the best men very commonly practise.

"When I first saw this eminent person, he gave me the idea of a French Virgil. I found him as handsome as the Abbé Delille is said to have been ugly. But he seemed to me to embody a Frenchman's ideal notion of the Latin poet; something a little more cut and dry than I had looked for; compact and elegant, critical and acute, with a consciousness of authorship upon him; a taste over-anxious not to commit itself, and refining and diminishing nature as in a drawing-room mirror.

"This fancy was strengthened, in the course of conversation, by his expatiating on the greatness of Racine. I think he had a volume of the French poet in his hand.

"His skull was sharply cut and fine, with a full share, according to the phrenologists, both of the reflective and amative organs; and his poetry will bear them out. His face and person were rather on a small scale; his features regular; his eye lively and penetrating; and when he spoke, dimples played about his mouth; which, nevertheless, had something restrained and close in it. Some gentle Puritan seemed to have crossed the breed, and to have left a stamp on his face, such as we often see in the female Scotch face, rather than the male."

"GERTRUDE OF WYOMING."

Some fourteen or fifteen years after the publication of *Gertrude*, Campbell found himself engaged in a correspondence with the son of Brandt, the Indian chief, who was represented by the poet as the leader of a savage party, whose ferocity gave to war more than its own horrors. Campbell had abused him, almost in the language of an American newspaper:—

"The mammoth comes, the foe, the monster Brandt,
With all his howling, desolating band."

It was rather a serious moment when a gentleman with an English name called on Campbell, demanding, on the part of the son of Brandt, some explanation of this language, as applied to his father. A long letter from Campbell is printed in Stone's *Life of Brandt*, addressed to the Mohawk chief, Ahyonwalgs, commonly called John Brandt, Esq., of the Grand River, Upper Canada, in which he states the various authorities which had misled him into the belief of the truth of the incidents on which his notion of Brandt's character was founded, and which, it seems, misrepresented it altogether.

It was, no doubt, a strange scene, and the poet could with some truth say, and with some pride, too, that when he wrote his poem, it was unlikely that he should ever have contemplated the case of the son or daughter of an Indian chief being affected by its contents. He promises in future editions to correct the involuntary error, and he does so by saying, in a note, that the Brandt of the poem is a pure and declared character of fiction.

This does not satisfy Mr. Stone's sense of justice, who would have the tomahawk applied to the offending rhyme, and who thinks anything less than this is a repetition of the offence.

POETIC INSPIRATION.

We hear much about "poetic inspiration," and the "poet's eye in a fine frenzy rolling;" but Sir

Joshua Reynolds gives an anecdote of Goldsmith, while engaged upon his poem, calculated to cure our notions about the ardour of composition.

Calling upon the poet one day, he opened the door without ceremony, and found him in the double occupation of turning a couplet and teaching a pet dog to sit upon his haunches. At one time he would glance his eye at his desk, and at another shake his finger at the dog to make him retain his position. The last lines on the page were still wet; they form a part of the description of Italy:—

"By sports like these are all their cares beguiled;
The sports of children satisfy the child."

Goldsmith, with his usual good humour, joined in the laugh caused by his whimsical employment, and acknowledged that his boyish sport with the dog suggested the stanza.

LEIGH HUNT'S DESCRIPTION OF THOMAS MOORE.

"Moore's forehead," says Leigh Hunt, "was bony and full of character, with 'bumps' of wit, large and radiant enough to transport a phrenologist. In this particular he strongly resembled Sterne. His eyes were as dark and fine as you would wish to see under a set of vine-leaves; his mouth generous and good-humoured, with dimples; and his manner as bright as his talk, full of the wish to please and be pleased. He sang and played with great taste on the pianoforte, as might be supposed from his musical compositions. His voice, which was a little hoarse in speaking,—at least I used to think so,—softened into a breath, like that of the flute, when singing.

"In speaking he was emphatic in rolling the letter *r*, perhaps out of a despair of being able to get rid of the national peculiarity. The structure of his versification, when I knew him, was more artificial than it was afterwards; and in his serious compositions it suited him better. He had hardly faith enough to give way to his impulses in writing, except when they were festive and witty; and artificial thoughts demand a similar embodiment. Both patriotism and personal experience, however, occasionally inspired him with lyric pathos; and in his naturally musical perception of the right principles of versification, he contemplated the fine, easy playing, muscular style of Dryden, with a sort of perilous pleasure. I remember his quoting with delight a couplet of Dryden's which came with a peculiar grace out of his mouth:—

'Let honour and preferment go for gold;
But glorious beauty isn't to be sold.'

"Besides the pleasure I took in Moore's society as a man of wit, I had a great esteem for him as a man of candour and independence. His letters were full of all that was pleasant in him. As I was a critic at that time, and in the habit of giving my opinion of his works in the *Examiner*, he would write me his *opinion* of the *opinion*, with a mixture of good humour, admission, and deprecation, so truly delightful, and a sincerity of criticism on my own writings so extraordinary for so courteous a man, though with abundance of balm and eulogy, that never any subtlety of compliment could surpass it."

MISS JEWSBURY'S DESCRIPTION OF MRS. HEMANS.

In the following passage from Miss Jewsbury's *Three Histories*, she avowedly describes Mrs. Hemans:—

"Egeria was totally different from any other woman I had ever seen, either in Italy or in England. She did not dazzle; she subdued me. Other women might be more commanding, more versatile, more acute, but I never saw any one so exquisitely feminine. . . . . . Her birth, her education, but, above all, the genius with which she was gifted, combined to inspire a passion for the ethereal, the tender, the imaginative, the heroic, in one word the beautiful. It was in her faculty divine, and yet of daily life; it touched all things, but, like a sun-beam, touched them with a golden finger.

"Any thing abstract or scientific was unintelligible or distasteful to her. Her knowledge was extensive and various; but, true to the first principle of her nature, it was poetry that she sought in history, scenery, character, and religious belief— poetry that guided all her studies, governed all her thoughts, coloured all her imaginative conversation. Her nature was at once simple and profound; there was no room in her mind for philosophy, nor in her heart for ambition. The one was filled by imagination, the other engrossed by tenderness.

"She had a passive temper, but decided tastes; any one might influence, but very few impressed her. Her strength and her weakness lay alike in her affections: these would sometimes make her weep, at others imbue her with courage; so that she was, alternately, 'a falcon-hearted dove,' and a 'reed broken with the wind.' Her voice was a sweet, sad melody, and her spirits reminded me of an old poet's description of the orange-tree, with its

'Golden lamps, hid in a night of green,'

or of those Spanish gardens where the pomegranate blossoms beside the cypress. Her gladness was like a burst of sunlight; and if in her sadness she resembled night, it was night wearing her stars. I might describe and describe forever, but I should never succeed in portraying Egeria. She was a Muse, a Grace, a variable child, a dependent woman, the Italy of human beings."

COWLEY AND HIS MISFORTUNES.

Cowley, in an ode, had commemorated the genius of Brutus, with all the enthusiasm of a votary of liberty. After the king's return, when Cowley solicited some reward for his sufferings and services in the royal cause, the chancellor is said to have turned on him with a severe countenance, saying, "Mr. Cowley, your pardon is your reward."

It seems that the ode was then considered to be of a dangerous tendency among half the nation; Brutus would be the model of enthusiasts, who were sullenly bending their necks under the yoke of royalty. Charles II. feared the attempt of desperate men; and he might have forgiven Rochester a loose pasquinade, but not Cowley a solemn invocation.

This fact, then, is said to have been the true cause of the despondency so prevalent in the latter poetry of "the melancholy Cowley." And hence the indiscretion of the Muse, in a single flight, condemned her to a painful, rather than a voluntary, solitude, and made the poet complain of "barren praise" and "neglected verse."

No wonder, therefore, that he thus expresses himself in the preface to his *Cutter of Coleman Street:*—

"We are, therefore, wonderfully wise men, and have a fine business of it; we, who spend our time in poetry. I do sometimes laugh, and am often angry with myself, when I think on it; and if I had a son inclined to the same folly by nature, I believe I should bind him from it by the strictest conjurations of a parental blessing. For what can be more ridiculous than to labour to give men delight, whilst they labour, on their part, most earnestly, to take offence?"

And thus he closes the preface,

in all the solemn expression of injured feelings: "This I do affirm, that *from all which I have written, I never received the least benefit or the least advantage, but, on the contrary, have felt sometimes the effects of malice and misfortune.*"

ADDISON'S COMPANIONS.

Addison's chief companions, before he married Lady Warwick, in 1716, were Steele, Budgell, Philips, Carey, Davenant, and Colonel Brett. He used to breakfast with one or other of them, at his lodgings in St. James's Place; dine at taverns with them; then to Button's; and then to some tavern again for supper in the evening: and this was then the usual round of his life.

PERCIVAL THE AMERICAN POET.

Dr. Percival is one of the most eccentric men in the world, and one of the most learned. He lived a long time in a garret—literally a garret, after the manner of the old poets—at New Haven, and had very few companions, save his books, cabinets, and herbarium. He reads with fluency ten languages, and is so familiar with the Latin, Greek, French, Spanish, German, and Italian, that he can take a work never before seen by him, in any of those languages, and read it in English with as much correctness and ease as he would one of his own poems.

For several years, he was engaged in making a geological survey of Connecticut; and his report was laid before the legislature of that state, when a proposal to give the copyright to the author, after a certain number of copies should be printed for the use of the state, was discussed. On this occasion, one of the members said, that "in his examination of our geology, Dr. Percival had been upon one side at least of every square mile in the state, except where river or lake had interrupted his progress. He had walked over every hill, plain, and morass in Connecticut, with his basket on his arm and his bag on his back; stopping at the farm-houses at night, and resuming his examination at early light."

He was engaged in this work for five years, and his salary never exceeded three hundred dollars per annum. The legislature of course adopted the proposal of giving to him the copyright. He is one of the poorest, as well as one of the most meritorious, of our authors.— (Arvine.)

NIGHT THOUGHTS.

Dr. Young was fond of coffee in an afternoon; till, finding it prejudicial to his nerves, he intimated his intention of abstaining from it. His grandson, who was then a little boy, inquired into the particular motive that led him to this resolution. "My reason is," answered the doctor, "because it keeps me awake at night. I can't sleep for it." "Then I beg you, sir, not to leave off your coffee; otherwise you will give us no more *Night Thoughts.*"

TASSO.

Tasso's contradictory critics perplexed him with the most intricate literary discussions, and probably occasioned a mental alienation. We find, in one of his letters, that he repents the composition of his great poem; for although his own taste approved of the marvellous, which still forms the nobler part of its creation, yet he confesses that his critics have decided that the history of his hero, Godfrey, required another species of conduct. "Hence," cries the unhappy bard, "doubts vex me; but for the past, and what is done, I know of no remedy;" and he longs to precipitate the publication, that "he may be delivered from misery and agony." He solemnly swears that "did not the circumstances of my situation compel me, I would not print it, even, perhaps, during my life, I so much doubt of its success."

Such was that painful state of fear and doubt experienced by the author of the *Jerusalem Delivered*, when he gave it to the world—a state of suspense, among the children of imagination, of which none are more liable to participate in than the too sensitive artist.

THOMSON AND QUIN.

Thomson, the poet, when he first came to London, was in very narrow circumstances, and was many times put to his shifts even for a dinner. Upon the publication of his *Seasons*, one of his creditors arrested him, thinking that a proper opportunity to get his money.

The report of this misfortune reached the ears of Quin, who had read the *Seasons*, but never seen their author; and he was told that Thomson was in a sponging-house in Holborn. Thither Quin went, and being admitted into his chamber, "Sir," said he, "you don't know me, but my name is Quin." Thomson said, that though he could not boast of the honour of a personal acquaintance, he was no stranger either to his name or his merit, and invited him to sit down. Quin then told him he was come to sup with him, and that he had already ordered the cook to provide supper, which he hoped he would excuse.

When supper was over, and the glass had gone briskly about, Mr. Quin told him it was "now time to enter upon business." Thomson declared he was ready to serve him as far as his capacity would reach, in anything he should command (thinking he was come about some affair relating to the drama). "Sir," says Quin, "you mistake me. I am in your debt. I owe you a hundred pounds, and I am come to pay you."

Thomson, with a disconsolate air, replied, that, as he was a gentleman whom he had never offended, he wondered he should seek an opportunity to trifle with his misfortunes. "No," said Quin, raising his voice, "I say I owe you a hundred pounds, and there it is;" and, suiting the action to the word, immediately laid a bank-note of that value before him.

Thomson, astonished, begged he would explain himself. "Why," says Quin, "I will tell you. Soon after I had read your *Seasons*, I took it into my head, that, as I had something to leave behind me when I died, I would make my will. Among the rest of my legatees, I set down the author of the *Seasons* for a hundred pounds; and, this day hearing that you were in this house, I thought I might as well have the pleasure of paying the money myself, as order my executors to pay it, when perhaps you might have less need of it; and this, Mr. Thomson, is my business."

RIVAL REMEMBRANCE.

Mr. Gifford to Mr. Hazlitt.
"What we read from your pen we remember no more."

Mr. Hazlitt to Mr. Gifford.
"What we read from your pen we remember before."

FIRST POETIC EFFUSION ON AMERICAN SOIL.

The *Bangor Whig*, in 1850, gave the following statement, as derived from the archives of the ancient Historical Society in Boston:—

"The first poetic effusion ever produced on American soil originated in a circumstance which was handsomely explained by one of the full bloods of the Jibawa, or, as we call them, Chippewas. All those who have witnessed the performances of the Indians of the far west, recently in our city, must recollect the cradle, and the mode in which the Indians bring up their children.

"Soon after our forefathers landed at Plymouth, some of the young people went out into a field where Indian women were picking strawberries, and observed several cradles hung upon the boughs of trees, with the infants fastened into them — a novel and curious sight to any European. A gentle breeze sprang up, which waved the cradle to and fro. A young man, one of the party, peeled off a piece of birch bark, and upon the spot wrote the following lines, which have been repeated thousands of times, by thousands of American mothers, very few of whom ever knew or cared for its origin :—

'Lullaby baby, upon the tree top ;
 When the wind blows the cradle will rock ;
 When the bough breaks the cradle will fall ;
 And down comes lullaby, baby, and all.'"

LORD BYRON'S MOTHER.

Lord Byron was afflicted with a club foot, and when young he submitted to some very painful operations to have the deformity removed, but with no success. His mother was a proud, passionate, and wicked woman, in whom even the yearnings of natural affection seemed stifled. Let us see the influence his mother exerted on this brilliant and powerful mind.

The readers of *Byron's Life* must have shuddered to hear him speak of his mother. Moore, the biographer of Byron, speaks three times of this fact, and the passages are so remarkable that we will transcribe them literally. The first is brief, but significant:—

"On the subject of his deformed foot," says Moore, in his *Byron* (vol. i. p. 21), "Byron described the feeling of horror and humiliation that came over him when his mother, in one of her fits of passion, called him a '*lame brat!*'"

The second passage is scarcely less significant:—

"But in the case of Lord Byron, disappointment met him at the very threshold of life. His mother, to whom his affections first naturally and with order turned, either repelled them rudely, or capriciously trifled with them. In speaking of his early days to a friend at Genoa, a short time before his departure for Greece, he traced his first feelings of pain and humiliation to the coldness with which his mother had received his caresses in infancy, and the frequent taunts on his personal deformity with which she wounded him."

This passage, found on the 146th page, is only excelled in dreadfulness by the following, on the 198th page :—

"He had spoken of his mother to Lord Sligo, and with a feeling that seemed little short of aversion. 'Some time or other,' said Byron, 'I will tell you why I thus feel towards her.' A few days after, when they were bathing together in the Gulf of Lepanto, he referred to his promise, and pointing to his naked leg, exclaimed, 'Look there! it is to her false delicacy at my birth I owe that deformity; and yet, as long as I can remember, she has never ceased to taunt and reproach me with it. Even a few days before we parted for the last time, on my leaving England, she, in one of her fits of passion, uttered an imprecation on me, praying that I might prove as ill-formed in mind as I am in body!' His look and manner, in relating the frightful circumstance, can only be conceived by those who have seen him in a similar state of excitement."

What an imprecation from the lips of a woman, and that woman a mother—"Praying that I might prove as ill-formed in mind as I am in body!"

HANNAH MORE AND ANN YEARSLEY.

"I was well acquainted with Ann Yearsley," says Cottle, "and my friendship for Hannah More did not blind my eyes to the merits of her opponent. Candour exacts the acknowledgment that the Bristol milkwoman was a very extraordinary individual. Her natural abilities were eminent, united with which she possessed an unusually sound masculine understanding, and altogether evinced, even in her countenance, the unequivocal marks of genius.

"It has been customary to charge her with ingratitude (at which all are ready to take fire), but without sufficient cause, as the slight services I rendered her were repaid with a superabundant expression of thankfulness. What then must have been the feelings of her heart towards Mrs. Hannah More, to whom her obligations were so surpassing?

"The merits of the question involved in the dissension between Ann Yearsley and Mrs. Hannah More lie in a small compass, and they deserve to be faithfully stated. The public are interested in the refutation of charges of ingratitude, which, if substantiated, would tend to repress assistance towards the humbler children of genius. The baneful effects arising from a charge of ingratitude in Ann Yearsley towards her benefactress might be the proximate means of dooming to penury and death some unborn Chatterton, or of eclipsing the sun of a future Burns.

"Hannah More discovered that the woman who supplied her family daily with milk was a respectable poetess. She collected her productions, and published them for her benefit, with a recommendatory address. The poems, as they deserved, became popular, doubtless, in a great degree, through the generous and influential support of Mrs. H. More; and the profits of the sale amounted to some hundreds of pounds.

"The money thus obtained the milkwoman wished to receive herself, for the promotion of herself in life, and the assistance of her two promising sons, who inherited much of their mother's talent. Hannah More, on the contrary, in conjunction with Mrs. Montague, thought it most advisable to place the money in the funds, in the joint names of herself and Mrs. Montague, as trustees for Ann Yearsley, so that she might receive a small permanent support through life.

"The great error on the part of the milkwoman was in not prevailing on some friend thus to interfere, and calmly to state her case; instead of which, in a disastrous moment, she undertook to plead her own cause, and, without the slightest intention of giving offence, called on her patroness. Ann Yearsley's suit, no doubt, was urged with a zeal approaching to impetuosity, and not expressed in that measured language which propriety might have dictated, and any deficiency in which could not fail to offend her polished and powerful patroness.

"Ann Yearsley obtained her object, but she lost her friend. Her name, from that moment, was branded with ingratitude; and severe indeed was the penalty entailed on her by this act of indiscretion. Her good name, with the rapidity of the eagle's pinion, was forfeited. Her talents, in a large circle, at once became questionable, or vanished away. Her assumed criminality also was magnified into audacity, in daring to question the honour or oppose the wishes of two such women as Mrs. Hannah More and Mrs. Montague. And thus, through this disastrous turn of affairs, a dark veil was suddenly thrown over prospects so late the most unsullied and exhilarating; and the favourite of fortune sank to rise no more.

"Gloom and perplexities in quick succession oppressed the Bristol milkwoman, and her fall became more rapid than her ascent. The eldest of her sons, William Cromartie Yearsley, who had bidden fair to be the prop of her age, and whom she had apprenticed to an eminent engraver, with a premium of one hundred guineas, prematurely died; and his surviving brother soon followed him to the grave. Ann Yearsley, now a childless and desolate widow, retired, heart-broken, from the world, on the produce of her library, and died many years after, in a state of almost total seclusion, at Melksham. An inhabitant of the town lately informed me that she was never seen, except when she took her solitary walk in the dusk of the evening. She lies buried in Clifton Church-yard."

WRITING FOR THE PRESENT—THOMAS CARLYLE.

The editor of the *London Monthly Magazine* relates an anecdote characteristic of Carlyle, and from which others may take a useful hint. "We recollect," says the editor, "walking with Mr. Thomas Carlyle down Regent Street, when he remarked, that we poets had all of us mistaken the argument that we should treat.

"The past," he said, "is too cool for this age of progress. Look at this throng of carriages, this multitude of men and horses, of women and children. Every one of these had a reason for going this way, rather than that. If we could penetrate their minds, and ascertain their motives, an epic poem would present itself, exhibiting the business of life as it is, with all its passions and interests, hopes and fears. A poem, whether in verse or prose, conceived in this spirit, and impartially written, would be the epic of the age." And in this spirit it was that he conceived the plan of his own *French Revolution*, a History.

POPE'S "ESSAY ON MAN."

"In a rough attack upon Warburton," says D'Israeli, "respecting Pope's privately printing fifteen hundred copies of the *Patriot King* of Bolingbroke, which I conceive to have been written by Mallet, I find a particular account of the manner in which the *Essay on Man* was written, over which Johnson seems to throw great doubts.

"The writer of this angry epistle, in addressing Warburton, says, 'If you were as intimate with Pope as you pretend, you must know the truth of a fact which several others, as well as I, who never had the honour of a personal acquaintance with Lord Bolingbroke or Mr. Pope, have heard. The fact was related to me by a certain senior fellow of one of our universities, who was very intimate with Mr. Pope.

"'He started some objections one day, at Mr. Pope's house, to the doctrine contained in the ethic Epistles; upon which Mr. Pope told him that he would soon convince him of the truth of it, by laying the argument at large before him; for which purpose he gave him *a large prose manuscript* to peruse, telling him, at the same time, the author's name. From this perusal, whatever other conviction the doctor might receive, he collected at least this—that Mr. Pope had from his friend not only the *doctrine*, but even the *finest and strongest ornaments of his ethics.*

"'Now, if this fact be true,—as I question not but you know it to be so,—I believe no man of candour will attribute such merit to Mr. Pope as you would insinuate, for acknowledging the wisdom and the friendship of the man who was his instructor in philosophy, nor, consequently, that this acknowledgment, and the *dedication of his own system, put into a poetical dress by Mr. Pope*, laid his lordship under the necessity of never resenting any injury done to him afterwards. Mr. Pope said no more than the literal truth in calling Lord Bolingbroke his *guide, philosopher, and friend.*"

The existence of this very manuscript volume was authenticated by Lord Bathurst, in a conversation with Dr. Blair and others, where he said "he had read the manuscript in Lord Bolingbroke's hand-writing, and was at a loss whether most to admire the elegance of Lord Bolingbroke's prose, or the beauty of Mr. Pope's verse."—(See the letter of Dr. Blair in Boswell's Life of Johnson.)

DUNGEON COMPOSITIONS.

It was behind the bars of a gloomy window in the Tower, where "every hour appeared to be a hundred winters,"- that Chaucer, recently from exile, and sore from persecution, was reminded of a work popular in those days, and which had been composed in a dungeon,—the *Consolations of Philosophy*, by Boethius —and which he himself had formerly translated. He composed his *Testament of Love*, substituting for the severity of an abstract being the more genial inspiration of love itself. But the fiction was a reality, and the griefs were deeper than the fancies.

In this chronicle of the heart the poet moans over "the delicious hours he was wont to enjoy," of his "richesse," and now of his destitution—the vain regret of his abused confidence—the treachery of all that "summer brood" who never approach the lost friend in "the winter hour" of an iron solitude. The poet energetically describes his condition : there he sat, "witless, thoughtful; and sightless, looking." This work the poet has composed in prose; but in the leisure of a prison the diction became more poetical in thoughts and in words than the language at that time had yet attained to, and for those who read the black letter, it still retains its impressive eloquence.

ORIGIN OF "JOAN OF ARC."

Mr. Southey, the poet laureate, gives the following as the origin of the publication of his poem of *Joan of Arc:*—

"Towards the close of the year 1794, the poem was announced to be published by subscription, in a quarto volume, at one pound one shilling. Soon afterwards, I became acquainted with my fellow-townsman, Joseph Cottle, who had just commenced business as a printer and bookseller in the city of Bristol. One evening I read to him part of the poem, without any thought of making a proposal concerning it, or expectation of receiving one. He offered me fifty guineas for the copyright, and fifty copies for my subscribers, which was more than the list amounted to; and the offer was accepted as readily as it was proposed.

"It rarely happens that a young author meets with a bookseller as inexperienced and as ardent as himself; and it would be still more extraordinary if such mutual indiscretion did not bring with it cause for regret to both. But this transaction was the commencement of an intimacy which has continued, without the slightest displeasure, to this day.

"At that time few books were printed in the country; and it was seldom indeed that a quarto volume issued from a provincial press. A fount of new types was ordered for what was intended to be the handsomest book that Bristol had ever yet sent forth; and when the paper

M

arrived, and the printer was ready to commence his operations, nothing had been done towards preparing the poem for the press, except that a few verbal alterations had been made. I was not, however, without misgivings; and when the first proof-sheet was brought me, the more glaring faults of the composition stared me in the face.

"But the sight of a well-printed page, which was to be set off with all the advantages that fine-wove paper and hot-pressing could impart, put me in spirits, and I went to work with good will. About half the first book was left in its original state; and the rest of the poem was recast and recomposed while the printing went on.

"This occupied six months. I corrected the concluding sheet of the poem, left the preface in the publisher's hands, and departed for Lisbon, by way of Corunna and Madrid."

GOD SAVE THE KING.

It is said that the English national hymn, so called, "God save the King," is of French origin, both the words and the music. In the *Memoirs of the Marquise de Crequy*, published in 1844, and containing her souvenirs from 1710 to 1800, the original words are given in French, as sung in French before Louis XIV., when he entered the Chapel of St. Cyr. The words are as follows:—

> "*Grand Dieu, Sauvez le Roi!*
> *Grand Dieu, Venez le Roi!*
> *Vive le Roi!*
> *Qui toujours Glorieux*
> *Louis Victorieux!*
>
> *Voyez vos ennemis*
> *Toujours soumis!*
> *Grand Dieu, Sauvez le Roi!*
> *Grand Dieu, Venez le Roi!*
> *Vive le Roi!*"

The words are said to have been written by Madame de Brinon, and the music by the famous Sully. It is also said that Handel, during a visit to Paris, got possession of the music, and on his return dedicated it to King George I. It must be rather galling for a loyal Englishman, while bursting his lungs in roaring "God save the Queen," and knocking the hats over the eyes of the refractory individuals who refuse to join him in his folly, to remember that he is glorifying his "Mrs. Cobourg" in a French song to French music.—(American Anecdotes.)

COWPER'S "JOHN GILPIN."

It happened one afternoon, in those years when Cowper's accomplished friend Lady Austen made a part of his little evening circle, that she observed him sinking into increased dejection. It was her custom, on these occasions, to try all the resources of her sprightly powers for his immediate relief. She told him the story of John Gilpin (which had been treasured in her memory from her childhood), to dissipate the gloom of the passing hour. Its effects on the fancy of Cowper had the air of enchantment.

He informed her, the next morning, that convulsions of laughter, brought on by his recollection of her story, had kept him waking during the greatest part of the night, and that he had turned it into a ballad. So arose the pleasant poem of *John Gilpin*.

HENRY KIRKE WHITE.

This youthful bard, whose premature death was so sincerely regretted by every admirer of genius, manifested an ardent love of reading in his infancy; it was a passion to which everything else gave way.

"I could fancy," says his oldest sister, "I see him in his little chair, with a large book upon his knee, and my mother calling 'Henry, my love, come to dinner;' which was repeated so often without being regarded, that she was obliged to change the tone of her voice before she could rouse him.

"When he was about seven, he would creep unperceived into the kitchen, to teach the servant to read and write; and he continued this for some time before it was discovered that he had been thus laudably employed.

"He wrote a tale of a Swiss emigrant, which was probably his first composition, and gave it to this servant, being ashamed to show it to his mother." "The consciousness of genius," says Mr. Southey, "is always at first accompanied with this diffidence; it is a sacred, solitary feeling. No forward child, however extraordinary the promise of his childhood, ever produced anything truly great."

When Henry was about eleven years old, he one day wrote a separate theme for every boy in his class, which consisted of about twelve or fourteen. The master said he had never known them write so well upon any subject before, and could not refrain from expressing his astonishment at the excellence of Henry's own. At the age of thirteen he wrote a poem, "On being confined to School one pleasant Morning in Spring," from which the following is an extract:—

"How gladly would my soul forego
All that arithmeticians know,
Or stiff grammarians quaintly teach,
Or all that industry can reach,
To taste each morn of all the joys
That with the laughing sun arise,
And unconstrained to rove along
The bushy brakes and glens among,
And woo the Muse's gentle power,
In unfrequented rural bower!
But ah! such heaven-approaching joys
Will never greet my longing eyes;
Still will they cheat in vision fine,
Yet never but in fancy shine."

The parents of Henry were anxious to put him to some trade; and when he was in his fourteenth year he was placed at a stocking-loom, with the view, at some future period, of getting a situation in a hosier's warehouse; but the youth did not conceive that nature intended to doom him to spend seven years of his life in folding up stockings, and he remonstrated with his friends against the employment.

Young White was soon removed from the stocking-loom to the office of a solicitor, which was a less obnoxious employment. He became a member of a literary society in Nottingham, and delivered an extempore lecture on genius; in which he displayed so much talent that he received the unanimous thanks of the society, and they elected this young Roscius of oratory their professor of literature. At the age of fifteen he gained a silver medal for a translation from Horace; and the following year a pair of globes, for an imaginary tour from London to Edinburgh. He determined upon trying for this prize one evening when at tea with his family; and at supper he read to them his performance.

In his seventeenth year he published a small volume of poems, which possessed considerable merit. Soon after, he was sent to Cambridge, and entered at St. John's College, where he made the most rapid progress. But the intensity of his studies ruined his constitution, and he fell a victim to his ardent thirst for knowledge. He died about two years after, aged twenty-one, leaving behind him several poems and letters, which gave earnest of the high rank he would have attained in the republic of letters had his life been spared.

HABITS OF MILTON.

He arose at four in the morning; had some one to read the Bible to him for about half an hour; contemplated till seven; read and wrote until dinner; walked, or swung, and played music three or four hours; entertained visitors until eight; took a light supper; smoked his pipe; drank a glass of water, and went to bed. He never drank strong liquors, and seldom drank anything at all between his meals.

GOLDSMITH'S HABITS.

In the house he usually wore his shirt-collar open, in the manner represented in the portrait by Sir Joshua. Occasionally he read much at night when in bed; at other times, when not disposed to read, and yet unable to sleep, which was not an unusual occurrence, the candle was kept burning, his mode of extinguishing which, when out of immediate reach, was characteristic of his fits of indolence or carelessness: he flung his slipper at it, which in the morning was in consequence usually found near the overturned candlestick, daubed with grease.

THE AMERICAN GOETHE.

When the young gentleman who styles himself the American Goethe was asked why he did not write something equal to Goethe's, he testily answered, "Because I haven't a *mind* to."

DEATH AND FUNERAL OF SHELLEY.

It is well known that Shelley was wrecked and drowned in a storm, with his friend, Captain Williams, on their way from Leghorn to Leria.

"The remains of Shelley and Mr. Williams," says Leigh Hunt, "were burnt, after the good ancient fashion, and gathered into coffers. Those of Mr. Williams were subsequently taken to England. Shelley's were interred at Rome, in the Protestant burial-ground, the place which he had so touchingly described in recording its reception of Keats.

"The ceremony of the burning was alike beautiful and distressing. Trelawney, who had been the chief person concerned in ascertaining the fate of his friends, completed his kindness by taking the most active part on this last mournful occasion. He and his friend, Captain Shenley, were first upon the ground, attended by proper assistants. Lord Byron and myself arrived shortly afterwards. His lordship got out of his carriage, but wandered away from the spectacle, and did not see it. I remained inside the carriage, now looking on, now drawing back, with feelings that were not to be witnessed.

"None of the mourners, however, refused themselves the little comfort of supposing that lovers of books and antiquity, like Shelley and his companion—Shelley in particular, with his Greek enthusiasm—would not have been sorry to foresee this part of their fate. The mortal part of him, too, was saved from corruption—not the least extraordinary part of his history.

"Among the materials for burning were many of the more graceful and more classical articles, such as could readily be procured—frankincense, wine, &c. To these was added Keats' volume, found in his vest pocket.

"The beauty of the flame arising from the funeral pile was extraordinary. The weather was beautifully fine. The Mediterranean, now soft and lucid, kissed the shore as if to make peace with it. The yellow sand and blue sky were intensely contrasted with one another; marble mountains touched the air with coolness; and the flame of the fire bore away towards heaven in vigorous amplitude, waiving and quivering with a brightness of inconceivable beauty. It seemed as though it contained the glassy essence of vitality. You might have expected a seraphic countenance to look out of it, turning once more, before it departed, to thank the friends that had done their duty.

"Shelley, when he died, was in

his thirtieth year. His figure was tall and slight, and his constitution consumptive. He was subject to violent spasmodic pains, which would sometimes force him to lie on the ground till they were over; but he had always a kind word to give to those about him, when his pangs allowed him to speak. In this organization, as well as in some other respects, he resembled the German poet Schiller. Though well turned, his shoulders were bent a little, owing to premature thought and trouble. The same causes had touched his hair with gray; and though his habits of temperance and exercise gave him a remarkable degree of strength, it is not supposed he could have lived many years."

ORIGIN OF THE "MARSEILLAISE."

M. de Lamartine, in his *Histoire des Girondins*, published in Paris, gives the following account of the origin of the French national air, the *Marseillaise*.

"In the garrison of Strasburg was quartered a young artillery officer, named Rouget de Lisle, a native of Louis de Salnier, in the Jura. He had a great taste for music and poetry, and often entertained his comrades during their long and tedious hours in the garrison. Sought after for his musical and poetical talent, he was a frequent and familiar guest at the house of one Dietrich, an Alsatian patriot, mayor of Strasburg.

"The winter of 1792 was a period of great scarcity at Strasburg. The house of Dietrich was poor, his table was frugal, but a seat was always open to Rouget de Lisle.

"One day there was nothing but bread and some slices of smoked ham on the table. Dietrich, regarding the young officer, said to him, with sad serenity, 'Abundance fails at our boards; but what matters that, if enthusiasm fails not at our civic *fêtes*, nor courage in the hearts of our soldiers? I have still a last bottle of wine in my cellar. Bring it,' said he to one of his daughters, 'and let us drink France and Liberty! Strasburg should have its patriotic solemnity. De Lisle must draw from these last drops one of those hymns which raise the soul of the people.'

"The wine was brought and drank, after which the officer departed. The night was cold. De Lisle was thoughtful. His heart was moved, his head heated. He returned staggering to his solitary room, and slowly sought inspiration sometimes in the fervour of his citizen soul, and anon on the keys of his instrument, composing now the air before the words, and then the words before the air. He sung all, and wrote nothing, and at last, exhausted, fell asleep with his head resting on his instrument, and awoke not till daybreak.

"The music of the night returned to his mind like the impression of a dream. He wrote it, and ran to Dietrich, whom he found in the garden digging winter lettuces. The wife and daughters of the old man were not up. Dietrich awoke them, and called in some friends, all as passionate as himself for music, and able to execute the composition of De Lisle. At the first stanza cheeks grew pale; at the second, tears flowed; and at last the delirium of enthusiasm burst forth. The wife of Dietrich, his daughters, himself, and the young officer, threw themselves, crying, into each other's arms.

"The hymn of the country was found. Executed some days afterwards in Strasburg, the new song flew from city to city, and was played by all the popular orchestras. Marseilles adopted it to be sung at the commencement of the sittings of the clubs, and the Marseillaise spread it through France, singing it along the public roads. From this came the name of *Marseillaise!*"

THOMSON'S "WINTER."

Many writers of popular name have been indebted to casual circumstances for their elevated distinction. When Thomson produced his "Winter," the best of his *Seasons*, the poem lay like waste-paper in the shop of the bookseller, and to the great mortification of the author. At last Mr. Mitchell, a gentleman of taste and rank, having read the piece with pleasure, took it in his pocket, read passages from it in all companies where he visited, and in a few days the whole impression being disposed of, the poet was enabled to complete his design.

CAMPBELL'S "HOHENLINDEN."

The following is an extract from a letter written by Thomas Campbell to a relative in America, and affords us the first impressions of the battle of Hohenlinden.

"Never shall time efface from my memory the recollections of that hour of astonishment and suspended breath, when I stood with the good monks of St. Jacob, to overlook a charge of Klenau's cavalry upon the French under Grennier, encamped below us. We saw the fire given and returned, and heard distinctly the sound of the French *pas de charge*, collecting the lines to attack in close column. After three hours' awaiting the issue of a severe action, a park of artillery was opened just beneath the walls of the monastery, and several waggoners, who were stationed to convey the wounded in spring-waggons, were killed in our sight. My love of novelty now gave way to personal fear; and I took a carriage, in company with an Austrian surgeon, back to Landshut."

"I remember," he adds, on his return to England, "how little I valued the art of painting, before I got into the heart of such impressive scenes; but in Germany I would have given anything to have possessed an art capable of conveying ideas inaccessible to speech and writing. Some particular scenes were rather overcharged with that degree of the terrific which oversteps the sublime; and I own my flesh yet creeps at the recollection of spring-waggons and hospitals; but the sight of Ingolstadt in ruins, or Hohenlinden covered with fire, seven miles in circumference, were spectacles never to be forgotten."

THE THREE VERSES OF EURIPIDES.

Euripides once said that three of his verses had cost him the labour of three days. "I could have written a hundred in that time," said another poet of ordinary abilities. "I believe it," replied Euripides; "but they would have lived only three days."

AN OVER-POETIC POET.

Dr. Glover was on a visit at Stowe, when he wrote his celebrated ballad of *Admiral Hosier's Ghost*, perhaps the most spirited of all his productions. The idea occurred to him during the night; he rose early, and went into the garden to compose.

In the heat of his composition, he walked into the tulip-bed; unfortunately, he had a stick in his hand, and with a true poetical fervour, he hewed down the tulips in every direction. Lady Temple was particularly fond of tulips, and some of the company, who had seen the doctor slashing around him, and suspected how his mind was occupied, asked him, at breakfast, how he could think of thus wantonly destroying her ladyship's favourite flowers.

The poet, perfectly unconscious of the havoc he had made, pleaded not guilty. There were witnesses enough to convict him. He acknowledged that he had been composing in the garden, and made his peace by repeating the ballad.

JAMES MONTGOMERY, THE POET.

Professor Durbin, an American tourist, in his letters from England, writes, "The day I left Sheffield, at five o'clock, P.M., for Manchester, Dr. Newton, and Mr. Jones, his host, were so good as to afford several of us the great pleasure of spending an hour or two in the company of Mr. Montgomery, the poet. It was at the dinner-table at Mr. Jones'.

"Conference business required that the company should sit down to dinner early, and it chanced to be before Mr. Montgomery arrived. As soon as he was seen through the window approaching the door, Mr. Jones rose and went out to meet him, and led him into the room. All rose, and stood while he passed round the table, shaking each one by the hand, and then took his seat with Mr. Newton, between him and myself.

"The conversation was interrupted but a moment; and the intelligence, vivacity, and piety of the poet instantly diffused a glow and elevation of thought and feeling which true consecrated genius only can inspire. The topics were various — grave, gay, amusing, sometimes witty, but always marked with great propriety, and often with deep piety.

"He is now quite advanced in years, and nervous, his health not being good; yet in company he is very cheerful. He is exceedingly easy and agreeable in manner, and his whole bearing very gentlemanly.

"No man in any community was ever more respected; and he enters into all the great benevolent movements in his vicinity, and generally presides, at least once a-year, at one of the principal missionary meetings of the Wesleyans in Sheffield. He is a truly religious man; the son of a Moravian missionary, who died in the West Indies.

"Some time ago there was a proposition to re-establish the mission on the same island; and, out of respect to Mr. Montgomery, all classes contributed, and the funds were immediately raised. He has a small income from his works, and a small pension from the government; and thus passes his days in sweet retirement, coming forth only to countenance the cause of religion and benevolence, or to shine upon his friends. I was obliged to take my leave of him and the entire company around him ere the dinner-party broke up."

SWIFT'S MENTAL MALADY.

Sometimes, during his mental affliction, he continued walking about the house for many consecutive hours; sometimes he remained in a kind of torpor. At times, he would seem to struggle to bring into distinct consciousness and shape into expression, the intellect that lay smothering under gloomy obstruction in him. A pier-glass falling by accident, nearly fell on him. He said he wished it had! He once repeated, slowly, several times, "I am what I am." The last thing he wrote was an epigram on the building of a magazine for arms and stores, which was pointed out to him as he went abroad during his mental disease:—

"Behold a proof of Irish sense;
Here Irish wit is seen;
When nothing's left that's worth defence,
They build a magazine!"

SWIFT'S RUDENESS.

An anecdote which, though only told by Mrs. Pilkington, is well attested, bears, that the last time he was in London he went to dine with the Earl of Burlington, who was but newly married. The Earl, it is supposed, being willing to have a little diversion, did not introduce him to his lady, nor mention his name. After dinner, said the Dean, "Lady Burlington, I hear you can sing; sing me a song." The lady looked on this unceremonious manner of asking a favour with distaste, and positively refused. He said, "She should sing, or he would make her. Why, madam, I suppose you take me for one of your poor English hedge-parsons; sing when I bid you." As the Earl did nothing but laugh at this freedom, the lady was so vexed that she burst into tears, and retired. His first compliment to her when he saw her again was, "Pray, madam, are you as proud and ill-natured now as when I saw you last?" To which she answered, with great good-humour, "No, Mr. Dean, I'll sing for you if you please." From which time he conceived a great esteem for her.—(Scott's Life of Swift.)

SWIFT'S RELIGION.

I know of few things more conclusive as to the sincerity of Swift's religion than his advice to poor John Gay to turn clergyman, and look out for a seat on the bench. Gay, the author of the *Beggar's Opera*—Gay, the wildest of the wits about town—it was this man that Jonathan Swift advised to take orders—to invest in a cassock and bands—just as he advised him to husband his shillings and put his thousand pounds out at interest. The Queen, and the bishops, and the world, were right in mistrusting the religion of that man.—(Thackeray.)

SWIFT'S CONVERSATION.

The style of his conversation was very much of a piece with that of his writings, concise, and clear, and strong. Being one day at a Sheriff's feast, who among other toasts called out to him, "Mr. Dean, the trade of Ireland!" He answered quick, "Sir, I drink no memories!"

Happening to be in company with a petulant young man who prided himself on saying pert things . . . and who cried out—"You must know, Mr. Dean, that I set up for a wit!" "Do you so," says the Dean, "take my advice, and sit down again!"

At another time, being in company, when a lady whisking her long train [long trains were then in fashion] swept down a fine fiddle, and broke it; Swift cried out—

"Mantua væ miseræ nimium vicina Cremonæ!"
—(Dr. Delany.)

ADDISON'S DIFFIDENCE.

Mr. Addison wrote very fluently; but he was sometimes very slow and scrupulous in correcting. He would show his verses to several friends; and would alter almost everything that any of them hinted at as wrong. He seemed to be too diffident of himself; and too much concerned about his character as a poet; or (as he worded it) too solicitous for that kind of praise, which, God knows, is but a very little matter after all!—(Pope.)

ADDISON'S GRAVITY AND TACITURNITY.

Addison was perfect good company with intimates, and had something more charming in his conversation than I ever knew in any other man; but with any mixture of strangers, and sometimes only with one, he seemed to preserve his dignity much, with a stiff sort of silence.—(Pope.)

The remark of Mandeville, who, when he had passed an evening in his company, declared that he was "a parson in a tyewig," can detract little from his character. He was always reserved to strangers, and was not incited to uncommon freedom by a character like that of Mandeville.—(Johnson.)

Old Jacob Tonson did not like Mr. Addison: he had a quarrel with him, and, after his quitting the secretaryship, used frequently to say of him—"One day or other you'll see that man a bishop—I'm sure he looks that way; and, indeed, I ever thought him a priest in his heart."—(Pope.)

It was my fate to be much with the wits; my father was acquainted with all of them. *Addison was the best company in the world.* I never knew anybody that had so much wit as Congreve.—(Lady Wortley Montagu.)

PRIOR.—SINGING AND DANCING DIPLOMATISTS.

Matthew Prior was made Secretary of Embassy at the Hague! I believe it is dancing, rather than singing, which distinguishes the young English diplomatists of the present day; and have seen them in various parts perform that part of their duty very finely. In Prior's time it appears a different accomplishment led to preferment. Could you write a copy of *Alcaics?* that was the question. Could you turn out a neat epigram or two? Could you compose *The Town and Country Mouse?* It is manifest that, by the possession of this faculty, the most difficult treaties, the laws of foreign nations, and the interests of our own, are easily understood. Prior rose in the diplomatic service, and said good things that proved his sense and his spirit. When the apartments at Versailles were shown to him, with the victories of Louis XIV. painted on the walls, and Prior was asked whether the palace of the king of England had any such decorations, "The monuments of my master's actions," Mat said, of William, whom he cordially revered, "are to be seen everywhere, except in his own house." Bravo, Mat! Prior rose to be full ambassador at Paris, where he somehow was cheated out of his ambassadorial plate; and in a heroic poem, addressed by him to her late lamented majesty Queen Anne, Mat makes some magnificent allusions to these dishes and spoons, of which Fate had deprived him. All that he wants, he says, is her Majesty's picture; without that he can't be happy:—

"Thee, gracious Anne, the present I adore;
Thee, Queen of Peace, if Time and Fate have power
Higher to raise the glories of thy reign,
In words sublimer and a nobler strain.
May future bards the mighty theme rehearse.
Here, Stator Jove, and Phœbus, king of Verse,
The votive tablet I suspend."

With that word the poem stops abruptly. The votive tablet is suspended for ever, like Mahomet's coffin. News came that the Queen was dead. Stator Jove, and Phœbus, king of verse, were left there, hovering to this day over the votive tablet. The picture was never got any more than the spoons and dishes—the inspiration ceased—the verses were not wanted—the ambassador was not wanted. Poor Mat was recalled from his embassy, suffered disgrace along with his patrons, lived under a sort of cloud ever after, and disappeared in Essex. When deprived of all his pensions and emoluments, the hearty and generous Oxford pensioned him. They played for gallant stakes—the bold men of those days—and lived and gave splendidly.—(Thackeray's English Humourists.)

GAY'S WEALTH AND IMPROVIDENCE.

Gay, says Pope, was quite a natural man — wholly without art or design, and spoke just what he thought, and as he thought it. He dangled for twenty years about a court, and at last was offered to be made usher to the young princess. Secretary Craggs made Gay a present of stock in the South Sea year; and he was once worth £20,000, but lost it all again. He got about £500 by the first *Beggar's Opera*, and £1100 or £1200 by the second. He was negligent, and a bad manager. Latterly, the Duke of Queensberry took his money into his keeping, and let him only have what was necessary out of it, and, as he lived with them, he could not have occasion for much. He died worth upwards of £3000.—(Pope.)

GAY'S PORTRAIT.

In the portraits of the literary worthies of the early part of the last century, Gay's face is the pleasantest perhaps of all. It appears adorned with neither periwig nor night-cap (the full dress and *negligée* of learning, without which the painters of those days scarcely ever pourtrayed wits), and he laughs at you over his shoulder with an honest boyish glee — an artless sweet humour. It was so kind, so gentle, so jocular, so delightfully brisk at times, so dismally woe-begone at others, such a natural good creature, that the giants loved him. —(Thackeray.)

GAY'S APPETITE AT TABLE.

Thackeray says that the Duke and Duchess of Queensberry over-fed the poetical Gay, who "was lapped in cotton, and had his plate of chicken, and his saucer of cream, and frisked, and barked, and wheezed, and grew fat, and so ended." Congreve testified that Gay was a great eater. "As the French philosopher used to prove his existence by *cogito, ergo sum*, the greatest proof of Gay's existence is *edit, ergo est*."

CRITICISM ON GRAY'S "ELEGY."

This work was published anonymously, and was designed to form a continuation of Dr. Johnson's *Criticism on the Poems of Gray*. It was written by Professor Young, of Glasgow, who has imitated, with singular felicity, the style and construction of the fabric of which it was to form a part. Dr. Johnson says, "Of the imitation of my style in a criticism on Gray's *Churchyard*, I forgot to make mention. The author is, I believe, utterly unknown, for Mr. Stevens cannot hunt him out. I know little of it; for though it was sent me I never cut the leaves open. I had a letter with it representing it to me as my own work. In such an account to the public there may be humour, but to me it was neither serious nor comical. I suspect the writer to be wrong-headed. As to the noise which it makes I have never heard it, and am inclined to believe that few attacks, either of ridicule or invective, make much noise, but by the help of those that they provoke."—(Dr. Johnson to Mrs. Thrale.)

EXTEMPORE POETS OF ITALY.

The *improvvisatori*, or extempore poets in Italy, are actually what they are called. They do it with great emulation and warmth, generally in octaves, in which the answerer is obliged to form his octave to the concluding line of the challenger, so that all the octaves after the first must be extempore, unless they act in concert together. "The first time I heard them," says Spence, "I thought it impossible for them to go on so readily as they did, without having arranged things beforehand.

"It was at Florence, at our resident's, Mr. Colman. When Mr. C. asked me what I thought of it, I told him that I could not conceive how they could go on so readily and so evenly, without some collusion between them. He said that it amazed everybody at first; that he had no doubt of its being all fair, and desired me, to be satisfied of it, to give them some subject myself, as much out of the way as I could think of. As he insisted upon my doing so, I offered a subject which must be new to them, and on which they could not well be prepared. It was but a day or two before that a band of musicians and actors set out from Florence, to introduce operas for the first time in the Empress of Russia's court. This advance of music, and that sort of dramatic poetry which the Italians at present look upon as the most capital parts of what they call *virtu*, so much farther north than ever they had been under the auspices of the then great duke, was the subject I offered for them. They shook their heads a little, and said it was a very difficult one. However, in two or three minutes' time, one of them began with his octave upon it; another answered him immediately, and they went on for five or six stanzas, alternately, without any pause, except that very short one which is allowed them by the giving off of the tune on the guitar, at the end of each stanza. They always improvise to music — at least all that I ever heard — and the tune is somewhat slow; but when they are thoroughly warmed, they will sometimes call out for quicker time. If two of these guitar-players meet in the summer nights in the very streets of Florence, they will challenge one another, and improvise sometimes as rapidly as those in set companies. Their most common subject is the commendation of their several mistresses, or two shepherds contending for the same, or a debate which is the best poet. They often put one in mind of Virgil's third, fifth, and seventh eclogues, or what he calls the contention of his shepherds, in alternate verse; and, by the way, Virgil's shepherds seem sometimes to be tied down by the thought in the preceding stanza, as these extempore poets are by the preceding rhyme."

PONDEROUS ERUDITION.

Dr. Walter Anderson, who was afflicted with an incurable *cacoethes scribendi*, was for half a century minister of Chirnside. Complaining to David Hume that the successful authors had pre-occupied all the popular subjects, the historian jocularly suggested the *Life of Croesus*, king of Lydia, as a suitable subject for a book. Anderson seized the idea, and wrote the life, containing also " Observations on the ancient notion of Destiny, or Dreams, on the origin and credit of the Oracles," &c. The work received a serio-burlesque notice in the second number of the first *Edinburgh Review*, conducted by Hume, Smith, Carlyle, and others. Undeterred by the failure of his first attempt, he produced in succession five quarto volumes of history, which nobody read or bought. As he published at his own risk, it is related that the cost of print and paper was defrayed by the sale, one by one, as each successive ponderous 4to appeared, of some houses which he possessed in the town of Dunse, till all had become the property of another.

PRINTING AND PRINTERS.

THE ART OF PRINTING.

When, where, and by whom printing was invented are equally unknown; and it may, perhaps, be matter of surprise to many that the art of printing, which throws so much light upon almost every other subject, should throw little upon its own origin. The most we know is, that it was discovered either in Germany or Holland, about 1440 —only about four hundred years ago; that the first types were made of wood, not metal; and that some of the earliest printed works were passed off as manuscripts.

The two principal cities which lay claim to the invention are Haerlem and Mentz; and either from one or the other, or perhaps from both, it was conveyed to the different cities and countries of Europe.

The introduction of printing into England is undoubtedly to be ascribed to William Caxton, a modest, worthy, and industrious man, who went to Germany entirely to learn the art; and having practised it himself at Cologne, in 1471, brought it to England two years afterwards. He was not only a printer, but an author; and the book which he translated, called the *Game at Chess*, and which appeared in 1474, is considered as the first production of the English press.

The seal-engravers were, however, the first printers; and the art of printing with blocks was merely an extension of the art, from impressions on wax to impressions on paper or vellum.

Though a variety of opinions exist as to the individual by whom the art of printing was first discovered, yet all authorities concur in admitting Peter Schœffer to be the person who invented cast-metal types; having learned the art of cutting the letters from the Guttembergs: he is also supposed to have been the first who engraved on copper-plates.

The following testimony has been preserved in the family, by Jo. Fred. Faustus, of Ascheffenburg:—

"Peter Schœffer, of Gernsheim, perceiving his master Faust's design, and being himself desirous ardently to improve the art, found out —by the good providence of God—the method of cutting (*incidendi*) the characters in a matrix, that the letters might easily be singly cast, instead of being cut. He privately cut matrices for the whole alphabet. Faust was so pleased with the contrivance, that he promised Peter to give him his only daughter, Christiana, in marriage—a promise which he soon after performed."

PUNCTUATION.

The dash, or perpendicular line, thus, |, was the only punctuation the first printers used. It was, however, discovered, that "the craft of poynting well used makes the sentence very light." The more elegant comma supplanted the long, uncouth |; the colon was a refinement, "showing that there is more to come." But the semicolon was a Latin delicacy which the obtuse English typographer resisted. So late as 1580 and 1590, treatises on orthography do not recognize any such innovator; the Bible of 1592, though printed with appropriate accuracy, is without a semicolon; but in 1633, its full rights are established by Charles Butler's *English Grammar*. From this chronology of the four points of punctuation, it is evident that Shakspeare could never have used the semicolon; a circumstance which the profound George

Chalmers mourns over, opining that semicolons would often have saved the poet from his commentators.

PRINTING AND BURNING OF TINDAL'S NEW TESTAMENT.

Tonstall, Bishop of London, in the reign of Henry VIII., and whose extreme moderation, of which he was accused at the time, preferred burning books to burning authors, which was then getting into practice, to testify his abhorrence of Tindal's principles, who had printed a translation of the New Testament, a sealed book for the multitude, thought of purchasing all the copies of Tindal's translation, and annihilating them in one common flame. This occurred to him when passing through Antwerp, in 1529, then a place of residence for the Tindalists. He employed an English merchant there for this business, who happened to be a secret follower of Tindal, and acquainted him with the bishop's intention. Tindal was extremely glad to hear of the project, for he was desirous of printing a more correct edition of his version, but the first impression still hung on his hands, and he was too poor to make a new one. He furnished the English merchant with all his unsold copies, which the bishop as eagerly bought, and had them all publicly burned in Cheapside; which the people not only declared was "a burning of the Word of God," but it so inflamed the desire of *reading that volume,* that the second edition was sought after at any price; and when one of the Tindalists, who was sent here to sell them, was promised by the Lord-Chancellor, in a private examination, that he should not suffer if he would reveal who encouraged and supported his party at Antwerp, the Tindalist immediately accepted the offer, and assured the Lord-Chancellor that the greatest encouragement they had was from Tonstall, Bishop of London, who had bought up half the impression, and enabled them to produce a second!

ENGLISH BIBLES.

The number of typographical inaccuracies which abound in the Bibles printed by the king's printers is remarkable. Dr. Lee states, " I do not know any book in which it is so difficult to find a very correct edition as the English Bible.". What is in England called the *Standard* Bible, is that printed at Oxford, in 1769, which was superintended by Dr. Blayney; yet it has been ascertained that there are at least one hundred and sixteen errors in it.

These errors were discovered in printing an edition in London, in 1806, which has been considered as very correct; yet Dr. Lee says that that edition contains a greater number of mistakes. The Rev. T. Curtis corroborates Dr. Lee's testimony. He states his general impression to be, that the text of the common English Bible is incorrect, and he gives a great variety of instances.

Dr. A. Clarke, in his preface to the Bible, states that he has corrected many thousand errors in the Italics, which, in general, are said to be in a very incorrect state. Between the Oxford edition of 1830 and the Cambridge edition, there are eight hundred variations in the Psalms alone.

The Rev. T. H. Horne, in his *Introduction to the Study of the Scriptures,* makes the following observation: "Booksellers' edition, 1806. In the course of printing, by Woodfall, this edition from the Cambridge copy, a great number of very gross errors were discovered in the latter, and the errors of the common Oxford edition were not so few as twelve hundred."

Mr. Offor, a retired bookseller, and who made a collection of upwards of four hundred Bibles of different editions, states that he was not aware of any edition he had examined which was without errors; but Pasham's Bible, in 1776, and another printed at Edinburgh, in 1811, were the most accurate and the most beautiful he had found.

Now, it will be observed, that the former was printed by a private individual, the monopoly being evaded by putting at the bottom of the pages very short notes, which were cut off in the binding.

The same witness afterwards remarks, that "there never was an elegant edition of the Bible printed at the king's printers'; the elegant editions have been those of Baskerville, Macklin, Heptinstall, Ritchie, and Bowyer, and the whole of these were printed with colourable notes." He also stated, that the effect of the patents was to limit the circulation of the Scriptures; and that, if the patents were intended to protect the purity of the text, and improve the printing, they had certainly been productive of a very different result.

THE FIRST PRINTED BOOK, OR THE DEVIL AND DOCTOR FAUSTUS.

The first printed book on record is the *Book of Psalms*, by one Faust, of Mentz, and his son-in-law, Schœffer. It appeared in 1457, less than four hundred years ago. Several works were printed many years before, by Guttemberg; but as the inventors wished to keep the secret to themselves, they sold their first printed works as manuscripts.

This gave rise to an adventure that brought calamity on Faust. Having in 1450, begun an edition of the Bible, and finished it in 1460, he carried several printed copies of it to Paris, and offered them for sale as manuscripts. This made him at once an object of suspicion.

It was in those days when Satan was thought to be ready at every man's elbow, to offer his magic if called upon, and as the French could not conceive how so many books should perfectly agree in every letter and point, they ascribed it to infernal agency, and poor Faust had the misfortune to be thrown into prison.

Here it was, that, in order to prove he had no aid from the devil, as well as to gain his liberty, he was obliged to reveal the secret, and show to the proper officers how the work was done.

Perhaps it was upon this adventure that somebody built up the story of the league of the devil and Dr. Faustus, as well as wrote those ludicrous dialogues, which, in some of the puppet-shows, Faust, under the name of Dr. Faustus, is made to hold with the devil.

FIRST ENGLISH PRINTING-PRESS.

The first printing-press in England was set up in the almonry of Westminster, where Caxton, probably encouraged by the learned Thomas Milling, then abbot, produced the moral treatise entitled the *Game and Playe of the Chesse*, the first book printed in that country. The ancient printing-house contains nothing of the interior appearance peculiar to its original arrangement, having been for a long time let in tenements, and divided according to the convenience of the generation of lodgers that have inhabited it.

ATTEMPT TO PRINT A PERFECT BOOK.

"Whether such a miracle as an immaculate edition of a classical author does exist," says one, "I have never learnt; but an attempt has been made to obtain this glorious singularity, and was as nearly realized as is perhaps possible—the magnificent edition of *Os Lusiadas* of Camoens by Don Joze Souza, in 1817. This amateur spared no prodigality of cost and labour, and flattered himself that, by the assistance of Didot, not a single typographical error should be found in that splendid volume.

"But an error was afterwards discovered in some of the copies, occasioned by one of the letters in the word *Lusitano* having got misplaced during the working of one of the sheets. It must be confessed that this was an accident or misfortune, rather than an erratum!"

The celebrated Foulises, of Glasgow, attempted to publish a work which should be a perfect specimen of typographical accuracy. Every precaution was taken to secure the desired result. Six experienced proof-readers were employed, who devoted hours to the reading of each page; and after it was thought to be perfect, it was posted up in the hall of the university, with a notification that a reward of fifty pounds would be paid to any person who could discover an error. Each page was suffered to remain two weeks in the place where it had been posted, before the work was printed, and the printers thought that they had attained the object for which they had been striving. When the work was issued, it was discovered that several errors had been committed, one of which was in the first line of the first page. The Foulis' editions of classical works are still much prized by scholars and collectors.

BURNS IN A PRINTING-OFFICE.

The following anecdote is related by Robert Chambers:—

"Meanwhile the preparation of the new edition was going rapidly on in the printing-office of William Smellie—a man who, like Creech, mingled literary labours with those attending one of the trades of literature.

"There was a vast fund of knowledge, shrewdness, and talent under the rude exterior of Smellie. In his office, at the foot of Anchor Close, he had done typographic duty for Gilbert Stuart, Robert Fergusson, Dr. Robertson, Hugo Arnot, Adam Smith, and many others of the recent and living literati of Scotland, all of whom had been his personal friends.

"His son, Alexander, who lately died at an advanced age, perfectly remembered the visits of the Ayrshire Ploughman to the composing-room, along which he would walk about three or four times, cracking a whip which he carried, to the no small surprise of the men. He paid no attention to his own copy under their hands, but looked at any other which he saw lying on the cases.

"One day he asked a man how many languages he was acquainted with. 'Indeed, sir,' replied the man, 'I've enough ado wi' my ain.' Burns remarked that behind there was one of his companions setting up a Gaelic Bible, and another composing from a Hebrew Grammar. 'These two,' said the compositor, 'are the greatest dolts in the house.' Burns seemed amused by the remark, and said he would take a note of it.

"Mr. Alexander Smellie also communicated the following anecdote: There was a particular stool in the office, which Burns uniformly occupied while correcting his proof-sheets; as he would not sit on any other, it always bore the name of Burns' stool. It is still (1844) in the office, and in the same situation where it was when Burns sat on it.

"At this time, Sir John Dalrymple was printing, in Mr. Smellie's office, an *Essay on the Properties of Coal Tar*. One day it happened that Sir John occupied the stool, when Burns came into the correcting-room, looking for his favourite seat. It was known that what Burns wanted was his stool; but before saying anything to Sir John on the subject, Burns was requested to walk into the composing-room.

"The opportunity was taken in his absence to request of Sir John to indulge the bard with his favourite seat, but without mentioning his name. Sir John said, 'I will not give up my seat to yon impudent, staring fellow.' Upon which it was replied, 'Do you not know that that staring fellow, as you call him, is Burns, the poet?' Sir John instantly left the stool, exclaiming, 'Good gracious! Give him all the seats in your house!' Burns was then called in, took possession of his stool, and commenced the reading of his proofs."

ERRORS OF THE PRESS.

The original memoirs of Cowper, the poet, were apparently printed from an obscurely written manuscript. Of this there is a whimsical proof, where the *Persian Letters* of Montesquieu are spoken of, and the compositor, unable to decipher the author's name, has converted it into *Mules Quince!*

A newspaper heads an advertisement, "*Infernal* Remedy." This may be quite true, but we imagine that "*internal* remedy" was intended. Mistakes, even of single letters, are sad things.

An important house in New York had occasion to advertise for sale a quantity of brass hoppers, such as are used in coffee-mills. But instead of brass hoppers, the newspaper read *grasshoppers*. In a short time the merchant's counting-room was thronged with inquirers respecting the new article of merchandise.

The editor of the *Evangelical Observer*, in reference to an individual, took occasion to write that he was *rectus in ecclesia*, that is, *in good standing in the church*. The type-setter, to whom this was a dead language, in the editor's absence, converted it into *rectus in culina*, which, although pretty good Latin, alters, in some degree, the sense, as it accorded to the reverend gentleman spoken of only a *good standing in the kitchen.*

By a ridiculous error of the press, the *Eclectic Review* was advertised as the *Epileptic Review*, and, on inquiry being made for it at a bookseller's shop, the bibliopole replied: "He knew of no periodical called the *Epileptic Review*, though there might be such a publication coming out by fits and starts."

JEALOUSY OF BOOKSELLERS AND PRINTERS.

Day, the printer, in Elizabeth's time, envied by the rest of his fraternity, who did what they could to hinder the sale of his books, had books upon his hands, in the year 1572, to the value of £3000 or £4000—a great sum in those days. But living under Aldersgate, an obscure corner of the city, he wanted a good vent for them. His friends, who were among the learned, procured aid from the dean and chapter of St. Paul's Church-yard, so that he had a neat, handsome shop framed. It was little and low, and flat-roofed, and leaded like a terrace, railed and posted, fit for men to stand upon in any triumph or show, but could not in any wise either hurt or deface the same. This cost him £40 or £50.

But his brethren, the booksellers, envied him, and, by their interest, got the mayor and aldermen to forbid him setting it up. Archbishop Parker interfered, and obtained the queen's permission on his behalf, and he at length succeeded.

STATIONERS' COMPANY.

The Stationers' Company existed as a fraternity long previous to the invention of printing. Some of its members, indeed, have acquired immortality by being among the first to introduce this new power into the world. Wynkyn de Worde, and Pynson, and "learned John Day," were all of the Stationers' Company.

INTENTIONAL ERRATA.

Besides the ordinary mistakes which take place in printing, there are others which are sometimes purposely committed, in order to have an opportunity of introducing into the Errata, what could not have been permitted in the body of the work. In those countries, for instance, where the Inquisition exists, and particularly in Rome, the use of the word *Fatum*, or *Fata*, in any printed work is forbidden. An author who wished to make use of the latter, adopted this scheme:— He printed the word throughout his book, *Facta;* and then, in the Errata, he placed a notice, For Facta, read Fata. A similar expedient was resorted to by Scarron. He had composed some verses, to which he had prefixed a dedication in these words:—"A Guillemette, chienne de ma soeur." Some time after, having quarrelled with his sister, just as he was preparing for the press a collection of his poems, he maliciously printed among the Errata of the book, For "Chienne de ma soeur," read "Ma chienne de soeur."

PUBLISHERS.

THE HARPERS OF NEW YORK.

In 1826, James and John Harper worked as journeymen in a printing-office in New York. They were distinguished, like Franklin, for industry, temperance, and economy. The well-known editor of the *Albany Evening Journal* worked as a journeyman printer at that time in the same establishment. "James," says he, "was our partner at the press. We were at work as soon as the day dawned; and though, on a pleasant summer afternoon, *we* used to sigh occasionally for a walk upon the Battery before sundown, *he* never would allow the 'balls to be capped' until he had broken the back of the thirteenth 'token.'"

What is the sequel? The journeyman printer of 1826 has become the head of one of the first—if not the first—publishing houses in the world; a man of ample fortune, and enjoying the confidence of his fellow-citizens in an eminent degree. It was in 1844 that, in the city in which he was first known as a journeyman printer, his name was made the rallying cry of a new political party, whose irresistible enthusiasm and overwhelming numbers speedily elevated him to the chief magistracy of the great metropolis of the western world.—(Arvine.)

WILLIAM HUTTON, THE BOOKSELLER.

William Hutton, well known in the literary world as a bookseller, struggled in early life with innumerable difficulties. His own account of his first adventure as a bookseller is a good specimen of that spirit of indomitable perseverance which is ever the forerunner of success. He determined to set up in that character in the town of Southwell, about fourteen miles from Nottingham. Here he accordingly opened a shop, with, as he expresses it, about twenty shillings' worth of trash for all his stock.

"I was," says he, "my own joiner, put up my shelves and furniture, and in one day became the most eminent bookseller in the place." Being employed, however, during the other days of the week, in working at Nottingham as a bookbinder, he could only give his attendance at

N

Southwell on Saturdays, that being besides, quite enough for the literary wants of the place. "Throughout a very rainy summer, I set out," says he, "at five every Saturday morning, carried a burden of from three pounds' weight to thirty, opened shop at ten, starved in it all day upon bread, cheese, and a half pint of ale, took from one to six shillings, shut up at four, and, by trudging through the solitary night and the deep roads five hours more, I arrived at Nottingham at nine, where I always found a mess of milk porridge by the fire, prepared by my valuable sister." This humble attempt, however, was the beginning of his prosperity. Next year he was offered about two hundred pounds' weight of old books, on his note-of-hand, for twenty-seven shillings, by a Dissenting minister, to whom he was known; and upon this he immediately determined to break up his establishment at Southwell, and to transfer himself to Birmingham. He did so, and succeeded so well, that by never suffering his expenses to exceed five shillings a-week, he found that by the end of the first year he had saved about twenty pounds. This, of course, enabled him to extend his business, which he soon made a very valuable one. Birmingham was to Hutton what Philadelphia was to Franklin. The first time he had ever seen it was when he entered it after running away from his uncle's, a wearied and a homeless wanderer, with scarcely a penny in his pocket, and not a hope in the world to trust to. Yet in this place he was destined to acquire, some years after, an ample fortune, and to take his place among the most honoured of its citizens.

PUNS AND ANAGRAMS.

A MONUMENTAL CONCEIT.

The following epitaph is on an old monument in St. Ann and St. Agnes Church:—

Qu an tris di c vul stra
os guis ti ro um nere vit
H san Chris mi c mu la

In this distich, the last syllable in each word in the upper line is the same as that of each corresponding word in the last line, and is to be found in the centre. It reads thus:—

" *Quos anguis tristi diro cum vulnere stravit,*
Hos sanguis Christi miro cum munere lavit."

TRANSLATION.

"Those who have felt the serpent's venomed wound,
In Christ's miraculous blood have healing found."

ELEANOR DAVIES.

Perhaps the happiest of anagrams was that produced on a singular person and occasion. Lady Eleanor Davies, the wife of the celebrated Sir John Davies, the poet, was a very extraordinary character. She was the Cassandra of her age; and several of her predictions warranted her to conceive she was a prophetess. As her prophecies, in the troubled times of Charles I., were usually against the government, she was at length brought by them into the Court of High Commission.

The prophetess was not a little mad, and fancied the spirit of Daniel was in her, from an anagram she had formed of her name:—

Eleanor Davies,
Reveal, O Daniel!

The anagram had too much by an L, and too little by an S; yet

Daniel and *reveal* were in it, and that was sufficient to satisfy her inspirations. The court attempted to dispossess the spirit from the lady, while the bishops were in vain reasoning the point with her out of the Scriptures, to no purpose, she poising text against text. One of the deans of the arches, says Heylin, shot her through and through with an arrow borrowed from her own quiver; he took a pen, and at last hit upon this excellent anagram:—

Dame Eleanor Davies,
Never so mad a ladie!

The happy fancy put the solemn court into laughter, and Cassandra into the utmost dejection of spirit. Foiled by her own weapons, her spirit suddenly forsook her; and either she never afterwards ventured on prophesying, or the anagram perpetually reminded her hearers of her state—and we hear no more of this prophetess!

WILLIAM OLDYS.

The following anagram on the well-known bibliographer, William Oldys, may claim a place among the first productions of this class. It was written by Oldys himself, and found by his executors in one of his manuscripts:—

" W. O.
In word and WILL I AM a friend to you,
And one friend OLD IS worth a hundred now."

BURNEY'S ANAGRAM ON NELSON— "PENDU A RIOM."

None of the anagrams of the sixteenth and seventeenth centuries exceed in felicity Dr. Burney's on Lord Nelson: " Horatio Nelson, Honor est a Nilo."

Of all the extravagances occasioned by the anagrammatic fever, when at its height, none probably equals what is recorded of an eccentric Frenchman in the seventeenth century, André Pujom. He read, in his own name, the anagram "Pendu à Riom" (the seat of criminal justice in the province of Auvergne), felt impelled to fulfil his destiny, committed a capital offence in Auvergne, and was actually hung in the place to which the omen pointed.

ON NAPOLEON.

The following anagram on the original name of Napoleon I., the most renowned conqueror of the age in which he lived, may claim a place among the first productions of this class, and fully shows, in the transposition, the character of that extraordinary man, and points out that unfortunate occurrence of his life which ultimately proved his ruin. Thus: "Napoleon Bonaparte" contains—"No, appear not on Elba."

TU DOCES.

A singular pun is produced in the following words, which were inscribed on a tea-chest: " *Tu doces*, which is the second person singular of the verb *doceo*, to teach, and, when literally translated, becomes *Thou Tea-Chest*."

PUNNING IN FRENCH.

Mr. Moore records in his diary of table-talk, as a specimen of French punning, that the following was among the Potierana lately published:—"Il a l' esprit *seize*," *i.e.*, *treize et trois* (très etroit). Mercer (says he) told me of a punster, who had so much the character of never opening his mouth without a pun, that one day, upon his merely asking some one at dinner for a little spinage, the person stared, looked puzzled, and said, "*Je vous demande pardon, monsieur, mais, pour cette fois, je ne comprend pas.*" The quickness of the French at punning arises (Mr. Moore adds), very much from their being such bad spellers.

Not having the fear of orthography before their eyes, they have at least one restraint less upon their fancy in this sort of exercise.

PUNNING IN LATIN.

Thomas Moore notes in his diary, that dining at Bowles's, his host mentioned that at some celebration at Reading school, when the patrons or governors of it (beer and brandy merchants), were to be welcomed with a Latin address, the boy appointed to the task, thus bespoke them, "*Salvete, hospites sele*beeri*mi*," and then turning to the others, "Salvete, hospites *cele*brandi."

Among our collection of ingenious literary productions, Dean Swift's celebrated Latin puns deserve a place; they will live with the language, for they have never been excelled. This species of composition consists of Latin words, and allowing for false spelling, and the running the words into each other, contain good sense in English as well as Latin. For example:—

"Apud in is almi de si re,
Mimis tres I ne ver re qui re,
Alo veri findit a gestis,
Ilis miseri ne ver at restis."

"A pudding is all my desire,
My mistress I never require,
A lover I find it a jest is,
His misery never at rest is."

"Mollis abuti,
Has an acuti,
No lasso finis,
Omni de armistress.
Cantu disco ver,
Meas alo ver?"

"Moll is a beauty,
Has an acute eye,
No lass so fine is,
O my dear mistress,
Can't you discover
Me as a lover?"

READING.

ALFRED THE GREAT LEARNING TO READ.

Alfred the Great ascended the throne in 872. Born when his country was involved in the most profound darkness and deplorable condition, and when learning was considered rather as a reproach than an honour to a prince, he was not taught to know one letter from another till he was above twelve years of age, when a book was put into his hand, by accident more than by previous design. Judith, his step-mother, was sitting one day, surrounded by her family, with a book of Saxon poetry in her hands. With a happy judgment, she proposed it as a gift to him who would first learn to read it. The elder princes thought the reward inadequate to the task, and retired from the field of emulation. But the mind of Alfred, captivated by the prospect of information, and pleased with the neatness of the writing and the beauty of the illuminations, inquired if she actually intended to give it to the person who would soonest learn to read it. His mother repeating the promise, with a smile of joy at the question, he took the book, found out an instructor, and learned to read it, recited it to her, and received it for his reward. It is said that he imbibed such a passion for reading that he never stirred abroad without a book in his bosom. He founded and endowed schools (among others Oxford), and brought teachers of learning from all parts of the world, purchased books, ordered the Bible to be translated into the Anglo-Saxon, undertaking the version of the Psalms himself, but did not live to complete it; and, in short, encouraged education and learning equally by precept and example.

SOUTH SEA ISLANDER'S NOTION OF WRITING.

The Rev. J. Williams, in his *Narrative of Missionary Enterprise*, gives the following interesting anecdote:—

"In the erection of this chapel (at Rarotonga), a striking instance occurred of the feelings of an untaught people, when observing, for the first time, the effects of written communications. As I had come to work one morning without my square, I took up a chip, and, with a piece of charcoal, wrote upon it a request that Mrs. Williams would send me that article. I called a chief, who was superintending his portion of the work, and said to him:—

"'Friend, take this, go to our house, and give it to Mrs. Williams.'

"He was a singular-looking man, remarkably quick in his movements, and had been a great warrior; but in one of the numerous battles he had fought he had lost an eye, and, giving me an inexpressible look with the other, he said:—

"'Take that! She will call me a fool, and scold me, if I carry a chip to her.'

"'No,' I replied, 'she will not; take it, and go immediately, for I am in haste.'

"Perceiving me to be in earnest, he took it and asked—

"'What must I say?'

"I replied—

"'You have nothing to say; the chip will say all I wish.'

"With a look of astonishment and contempt, he held up the piece of wood, and said—

"'How can this speak? Has it a mouth?'

"I desired him to take it immediately, and not spend so much time in talking about it. On arriving at the house, he gave it to Mrs. Williams, who read it, threw it away, and went to the tool-chest, whither the chief, resolving to see the result of this mysterious proceeding, followed her closely. On receiving the square from her, he said—

"'Stay, daughter: how do you know that this is what Mr. Williams wants?'

"'Why,' she replied, 'did you not give me a chip just now?'

"'Yes,' said the astonished warrior, 'but I did not hear it say anything.'

"'If you did not, I did,' was the reply, 'for it made known to me what he wanted; and all you have to do is to return as fast as possible.'

"With this the chief leaped out of the house, and catching up the mysterious piece of wood, he ran through the settlement with the chip in one hand and the square in the other, holding them up as high as his arm would reach, and shouting as he went—

"'See the wisdom of these English people: they can make chips talk! they can make chips talk!'

"On giving me the square, he wished to know how it was possible thus to converse with persons at a distance. I gave him all the information in my power; but it was a circumstance involved in so much mystery, that he actually tied a string to the chip, hung it around his neck, and wore it for some time. During several following days, we frequently saw him surrounded by a crowd, who were listening with intense interest while he narrated the wonders which the chip had performed."

FREDERICK THE GREAT AND HIS LIBRARIES.

The principal amusement of Frederick's leisure hours, at all periods of his life, was his library. The plan for his reading in general, which he adopted in his youth, and to which he constantly adhered, was this:—He divided all books that he chose to read into two classes—those for study, and those for amusement. The second class, by far the more numerous of the two, comprehended all the works which he wished to know something of, and which he merely skimmed, or read once through. The first consisted of those which he meant to study, to read over again, or to consult as long as he lived; these he took up continually, one after another, in the order which he had ranged them, unless upon occasions when he only wanted to verify, to quote, or to imitate some passage. He had five libraries absolutely alike, and composed of the same books—at Potsdam, at old Sans Souci, at Berlin, at Charlottenburg, and at Breslau. When he removed from one of these residences to another, he had only to note how far he had got in a book, and on his arrival, he could proceed as though he were on the same spot. Hence he always bought five copies of every book that he wished to have. To the five libraries above-mentioned were afterwards added another in the new palace of Sans Souci, and a travelling library for the review time. The books belonging to all these libraries were uniformly bound in red morocco, with gilt leaves. Each book had its particular place, and on the cover was a letter, denoting the library to which it belonged.

METHODICAL READING.

Gibbon, the celebrated author of the *Decline and Fall of the Roman Empire*, has furnished a new idea in the art of reading. "We ought," says he, "not to attend to the order of our book, so much as of our thoughts. The perusal of a particular work gives birth, perhaps, to ideas unconnected with the subject it treats; I pursue these ideas and quit my proposed plan of reading." Thus in the midst of Homer he read Longinus; a chapter of Longinus led to an epistle of Pliny; and having finished Longinus, he followed the train of his ideas of the sublime and beautiful in the inquiry of Burke, and concluded with comparing the ancient with the modern Longinus. Of all our popular writers, the most experienced reader was Gibbon, and he offers important advice to an author engaged on a particular subject: "I suspended my perusal of any new book on the subject till I had reviewed all that I knew, or believed, or had thought on it, that I might be qualified to discern how much the authors added to my original stock."

KNOWING AND JUDGING.

Pope says that from fourteen to twenty, he read only for amusement; from twenty to twenty-seven, for improvement and instruction; that in the first part of his time he desired only to know, and in the second he endeavoured to judge.

A MOTHER'S ADVICE.

Sir William Jones, when a mere child, was very inquisitive. His mother was a woman of great intelligence, and he would apply to her for the information which he desired; but her constant reply was, "Read, and you will know." This gave him a passion for books, which was one of the principal means of making him what he was.

THOMAS HOOD THE HUMOURIST ON THE BENEFITS OF READING.

The secretaries of the Manchester Athenæum bazaar committee addressed to Thomas Hood a request that he would allow his name to be placed on the list of patrons of an approaching bazaar. To this request the secretaries received the following characteristic reply:—

"ST. JOHN's WOOD, July 18, 1843. (From my bed,) 17, Elm-tree Road.

"Gentlemen,—If my humble name can be of the least use for your purpose, it is heartily at your service, with my best wishes for the prosperity of the Manchester Athenæum, and my warmest approval of the objects of that institution.

"I have elsewhere recorded my own deep obligations to literature, —that a natural turn for reading and intellectual pursuits probably preserved me from the moral shipwreck, so apt to befall those who are deprived in early life of the paternal pilotage. At the very least, my books kept me aloof from the ring, the dog-pit, the tavern, and the saloon, with their degrading orgies. For the closet associate of Pope and Addison—the mind accustomed to the noble, though silent, discourse of Shakspeare and Milton—will hardly seek, or put up with, low company and slang. The reading animal will not be content with the brutish wallowings that satisfy the unlearned pigs of the world.

"Later experience enables me to depose to the comfort and blessing that literature can prove in seasons of sickness and sorrow—how powerfully intellectual pursuits can help in keeping the head from crazing, and the heart from breaking,—nay, not to be too grave, how generous mental food can even atone for a meagre diet—rich fare on the paper for short commons on the cloth.

"Poisoned by the malaria of the Dutch marshes, my stomach, for many months, resolutely set itself against fish, flesh, or fowl; my appetite had no more edge than the German knife placed before me. But, luckily, the mental palate and digestion were still sensible and vigorous; and whilst I passed untasted every dish at the Rhenish *table d'hôte*, I could yet enjoy my *Peregrine Pickle*, and the feast after the manner of the ancients. There was no yearning towards calf's head *à la tortue*, or sheep's heart; but I could still relish Head *à la Brunnen*, and the *Heart of Mid-Lothian*.

"Still more recently, it was my misfortune, with a tolerable appetite, to be condemned to lenten fare, like Sancho Panza, by my physician— to a diet, in fact, lower than any prescribed by the poor-law commissioners; all animal food, from a bullock to a rabbit, being strictly interdicted; as well as all fluids stronger than that which lays dust, washes pinafores, and waters polyanthus. But 'the feast of reason and the flow of soul' were still mine. Denied beef, I had *Bul*wer and *Cow*per,—forbidden mutton, there was *Lamb*,—and in lieu of pork, the great *Bacon* or *Hogg*.

"Then, as to beverage, it was hard, doubtless, for a Christian to set his face like a Turk against the juice of the grape. But, eschewing wine, I had still my *Butler;* and in the absence of liquor, all the *choice spirits* from Tom Browne to Tom Moore.

"Thus, though confined, physically, to the drink that drowns kittens, I quaffed mentally, not merely the best of our own home-made, but the rich, racy, sparkling growths of France and Italy, of Germany and Spain—the champagne of Molière, and the Monte Pulciano of Boccaccio, the hock of Schiller, and the sherry of Cervantes. Depressed bodily by the fluid that damps every thing, I got intellectually elevated with Milton, a little merry with Swift, or rather jolly with Rabelais, whose Pantagruel, by the way, is quite equal to the best gruel with rum in it.

"So far can literature palliate or compensate for gastronomical privations. But there are other evils, great and small, in this world, which try the stomach less than the head, the heart, and the temper—bowls that will not roll right—well-laid schemes that will 'gaug aglee'—and ill winds that blow with the pertinacity of the monsoon. Of these, Providence has allotted me a full share; but still, paradoxical as it may sound, my *burden* has been greatly lightened by *a load of books*. The manner of this will be best understood from a feline illustration. Everybody has heard of the two Kilkenny cats, who devoured each other; but it is not so generally known that they left behind them an orphan kitten, which, true to the breed, began to eat itself up, till it was diverted from the operation by a mouse. Now, the human mind, under vexation, is like that kitten, for it is apt to *prey upon itself*, unless drawn off by a new object; and none better for the purpose than a book; for example, one of Defoe's; for who, in reading his thrilling *History of the Great Plague*, would not be reconciled to a few little ones?

"Many, many a dreary, weary hour have I got over—many a gloomy misgiving postponed—many a mental or bodily annoyance forgotten, by help of the tragedies and comedies of our dramatists and novelists! Many a trouble has been soothed by the still small voice of the moral philosopher—many a dragon-like care charmed to sleep by the sweet song of the poet; for all which I cry incessantly, not aloud, but in my heart, Thanks and honour to the glorious masters of the pen, and the great inventors of the press!

"Such has been my own experience of the blessing and comfort of literature and intellectual pursuits; and of the same mind, doubtless, was Sir Humphry Davy, who went for 'consolations in *Travel*,' not to the inn or the posting house, but to his library and his books. I am, gentlemen, yours, very truly,

"THOS. HOOD."

REPORTING AND REPORTERS.

WILBERFORCE AND MORGAN O'SULLIVAN.

A certain popular debate, which was about English labourers, being one evening unusually dull, Jack Finnarty, who had but a short time before been imported from Tipperary, said to the only other reporter in the gallery at the time, that he felt very drowsy, and that he would be after taking a little bit of a nap, if he would tell him when he awoke anything which might take place. The other agreed, and Jack, in a moment, was fast locked in the arms of Morpheus. An hour elapsed, and after half a dozen yawns, Jack opened his eyes.

"Has anything happened?" was his first question to his friend.

"To be sure there has," said the other, whose name was Morgan O'Sullivan.

"Has there, by the powers?" exclaimed Jack, pricking up his ears in the plenitude of his anxiety to learn what it was.

"Yes, Jack, and very important, too."

"And why don't you be after telling it me at once? What was it about?"

"About the virtue of the Irish potato, Jack."

"Was it the Irish potato, you said, Morgan?"

"The Irish potato, and a most eloquent speech it was."

"Thunder and lightning, then, and why don't you tell it me?"

"I'll read it from my note-book, Jack, and you'll take it down as I go on," said Morgan.

"Och, it's myself, sure, that's ready at any time to write what any mimber says about our praties. Are you ready to begin?"

"Quite ready," answered Morgan.

"Now, then," said Jack, with an energy which strangely contrasted with the previous languor of his manner,—"now, then, Morgan, my boy."

Morgan, affecting to read from his note-book, commenced thus: "The honourable mimber said, that if—"

"Och, be aisy a little bit," interrupted Jack; "*who* was the honourable mimber?"

Morgan, hesitating for a moment—"Was it his name you asked? Sure it was Mr. Wilberforce."

"Mr. Wilberforce! Och, very well then."

Morgan resumed. "Mr. Wilberforce said, that it always appeared to him beyond all question that the great cause why the Irish labourers were, as a body, so much stronger, and capable of enduring so much greater fatigue than the English, was the surpassing virtues of their potato. And he—"

"Morgan, my dear fellow," shouted Jack, at the mention of the Irish potato, his countenance lighting up with ecstasy as he spoke,—"Morgan, my dear fellow, this is so important that we must give it in the first person."

"Do you think so?" said Morgan.

"Throth, and I do," answered Jack.

"Very well," said the other.

Morgan then resumed: "And I have no doubt, continued Mr. Wilberforce, that had it been my lot to be born and reared in—"

"Did the mimber say *reared?*" interrupted Jack exultingly, evidently associating the word with the growth of potatoes in his "own blessed country."

"He said 'reared,'" observed the other, who then resumed: "Had it been my lot to be born and reared in Ireland, where my food would have principally consisted of the potato—that most nutritious and salubrious root,—instead of being the poor, infirm, shrivelled, and stunted creature you, sir, and honourable gentlemen, now behold me, I would have been a tall, stout, athletic man, and able to carry an enormous weight."

Here Jack Finnarty observed, looking his friend eagerly in the face, "Faith, Morgan, and that's what I call thrue eloquence! Go on."

"I hold that root to be invaluable; and the man who first cultivated it in Ireland I regard as a benefactor of the first magnitude to his species. And my decided opinion is, that never, till we grow potatoes in England, in sufficient quantities to feed all our labourers, will those labourers be so able-bodied a class as the Irish. (Hear, hear! from both sides of the house.")

"Well, by St. Patrick, but that bates everything," observed Jack, on finishing his notes. "That's rare philosophy. And the other mimbers cried 'Hear, hear,' did they?"

"The other members cried 'Hear, hear,'" answered Morgan.

In a quarter of an hour afterwards the house rose. Morgan went away direct to the office of the paper for which he was employed; while Jack, in perfect ecstasies at the eulogium which had been pronounced on the virtue of the potatoes of "ould Ireland," ran in breathless haste to a public-house, where the reporters who should have been on duty for the other morning papers were assembled. He read over his notes to them, which they copied *verbatim;* and not being at the time in the best possible condition for judging of the probability of Mr. Wilberforce delivering such a speech, they repaired to their respective offices, and actually gave a copy of it into the hands of the printer. Next morning it appeared in all the papers, except the one with which Morgan O'Sullivan was connected. The sensation and surprise it created in town exceeded everything. Had it only appeared in one or two of the papers, persons of ordinary intelligence must at once have concluded that there was some mistake about the matter. But its appearing in all the journals except one forced, as it were, people to the conclusion that it must have been actually spoken. The inference was plain. Everybody, while regretting that the necessity should exist, saw that no other course was left but to put Mr. Wilberforce at once into a strait jacket, and provide him with a keeper. In the evening, the house met as usual, and Mr. Wilberforce, on the speaker taking the chair, rose and begged the indulgence of the house for one moment to a matter which concerned it, as well as himself, personally. "Every honourable member," he observed, "has doubtless read the speech which I am represented as having made on the previous night. With the permission of the house, I will read it. (Here the honourable member read the speech amidst deafening roars of laughter.) I can assure honourable members that no one could have read this speech with more surprise than I myself did this morning, when I found the paper on my breakfast table. For myself, personally, I care but little about it, though, if I were capable of uttering such nonsense as is here put into my mouth, it is high time that, instead of being a member of this house, I were an inmate of some lunatic asylum. It is for the dignity of this house that I feel concerned; for if honourable members were capable of listening to such nonsense, supposing me capable of giving expression to it, it were much more appropriate to call this a theatre for the performance of farces, than a place for the legislative deliberations of the representatives of the nation."

It was proposed by some members to call the printers of the different papers in which the speech appeared to the bar of the house, for a breach of privilege; but the matter was eventually allowed to drop.

THE HUMOROUS REPORTER MARK SUPPLE.

Mark took his wine frequently at Bellamy's, and then went up into the gallery, and reported like a gentleman and a man of genius. The members hardly knew their own speeches again; but they admired his free and bold manner of dressing them up. None of them ever went to the printing-office of the *Morning Chronicle*, to complain that the tall Irishman had given a lame sneaking version of their sentiments. They pocketed the affront of their metamorphosis, and *fathered* speeches they had never made. His way was the hyperbole; a strong spice of Orientalism, with a dash of the *bogtrotter*. His manner seemed to please, and he presumed upon it. One evening, as he sat at his post in the gallery, waiting the issue of things, and a hint to hang his own tropes and figures upon, a dead silence happened to prevail in the house. It was when Mr. Addington was speaker. The bold leader of the *press-gang* was never bent upon serious business much, and at this time he was particularly full of meat and wine.

Delighted, therefore, with the pause, but thinking that something might as well be going forward, he called out lustily, "A song from Mr. Speaker." Imagine Addington's long, prim, upright figure, his consternation, and utter want of preparation for, or of a clew to repel, such an interruption of the rules and orders of Parliament. The house was in a roar. Pitt, it is said, could hardly keep his seat for laughing. When the bustle and the confusion were abated, the sergeant-at-arms went into the gallery to take the audacious culprit into custody, and indignantly desired to know who it was; but nobody would tell. Mark sat like a tower on the hindermost bench of the gallery, imperturbable in his own gravity, and safe in the faith of the brotherhood of reporters, who alone were in the secret. At length, as the mace-bearer was making fruitless inquiries, and getting impatient, Supple pointed to a fat Quaker, who sat in the middle of the crowd, and nodded assent that he was the man. The Quaker was, to his great surprise, taken into immediate custody; but after a short altercation and some further explanation, he was released, and the hero of our story put in his place for an hour or two, but let off on an assurance of his contrition, and of showing less wit and more discretion in future.

JOHN PROBY.

John Proby had never been out of London, never in a boat, never on the back of a horse. To the end of bagwigs he wore a bag; he was the last man that walked with a cane as long as himself, ultimately exchanged for an umbrella, which he was never seen without in wet weather or dry; yet he usually reported the whole debates in the Peers from memory, without a note, for the *Morning Chronicle*, and wrote two or three novels, depicting the social manners of the times. He was a strange feeder, and ruined himself in eating pastry at the confectioners' shops (for one of whose scores Taylor and I bailed him); he was always in a perspiration, whence George christened him "King Porus;" and he was always so punctual to a minute that when he arrived in sight of the office window, the hurry used to be, "There's Proby—it is half-past two," and yet he never set his watch. If ever it came to right time I cannot tell; but if you asked him what o'clock it was, he would look at it, and calculate something in this sort—"I am twenty-six minutes past seven—four, twenty-one from twelve forty,—it is just three minutes past three!" Poor, strange, and simple, yet curiously-informed Proby, his last domicile was the Lambeth parish workhouse, out of which he would come in his coarse gray garb, and call upon his friends as freely and unceremoniously as before, to the surprise of servants, who entertain "an 'orrid" jealousy of paupers, and who could not comprehend why a person so clad was shown in. The last letter I had from him spoke exultingly of his having been chosen to teach the young children in the house their A B C, which conferred some extra accommodations upon him. Among my other coadjutors were Mr. Robinson, educated for the Kirk, and a quiet man; and Mr. Cooper, the author of a volume of poetry, which procured him the countenance of the beautiful Duchess of Devonshire; and Mark Supple, an Irish eccentric of the first water.—(Jerdan's Autobiography.)

THE FIRST PARLIAMENTARY REPORTS.

The first attempt at a monthly publication of the parliamentary debates was made in the *Gentleman's Magazine*, for August, 1735; and the practice was continued in succeeding numbers. The reports were of the most timid and cautious description, the names of the speakers being given only by the first and last letters, and, in many cases, no speaker's name is mentioned; all that appears is a summary of the argument and discussion. They got bolder by degrees, and at last published the names at full length. This audacity, coupled with the fact that some of the members appeared in a light not very satisfactory to themselves, either from their own defects, or the incorrect version of their oratory, caused the attention of the Commons to be drawn to the subject. It was brought under notice, April 13, 1738, by the speaker, who was followed by Yonge, Windham, and Sir Thomas Winnington. The last concluded a very angry speech with these words: "Why, sir, you will have the speeches of this house every day printed, even during your session; and we shall be looked upon as the most contemptible assembly on the face of the earth." The result was a thundering resolution, unanimously agreed to, declaring it "a high indignity to, and a notorious breach of, the privileges of the house to publish the debates, either while Parliament is sitting or during the recess," and threatening to proceed against offenders "with the utmost severity." Accounts of parliamentary business were now obtained with greater risk, and various contrivances were employed to disguise a version of them. The *Gentleman's Magazine* published them under the title of the "Debates of the Senate of Lilliput," and the *London Magazine* under that of a "Journal of the Proceedings and Debates in the Political Club;" giving Roman names to the speakers, while each publication printed an explanatory key at the end of the year. The two gentlemen principally occupied in this mystification were William Gurthrie and Thomas Gordon, both Scotchmen. About this time, Dr. Johnson arrived in London, and was immediately engaged by the editor of the *Gentleman's Magazine* (Cave), in the composition of the parliamentary debates. Gurthrie, who had a good memory, brought home as much as he could recollect from the house, mending his draught by whatever other assistance he could command; after which, the matter thus collected underwent the finishing touches of Johnson. At times, according to Boswell, Johnson had no other aid than the names of the speakers, and the side they took, being left to his own resources for the argument and language. A speech—the celebrated speech, commencing, "The atrocious crime of being a young man," which he put into the mouth of Pitt, when that distinguished orator replied to the taunts of Walpole—Johnson afterwards declared, in the company of Francis, Wedderburn, Foote, and Murphy, that he "wrote in a garret in Exeter Street." His reports, however, are considered by the editor of Hansard's *Parliamentary History*, the most authentic extant, faithfully embodying the argument, if not the style, of the speakers. It was once observed to him, that he dealt out reason and eloquence with an equal hand to both parties. "That is not quite true," said Johnson; "I saved appearances pretty well; but I took care that the Whig dogs should not have the best of it." The reports increased immensely the sale of the magazines; they enabled Cave to set up an equipage, on the door-panel of which, instead of a crest, he had painted a representation of his office at St. John's Gate, Clerkenwell, where Johnson sometimes ate his dinner, concealed behind a screen, not having suitable clothes to appear before the more modish visitors of his employer; some of them, perhaps, members of the house, who dropped in to see or correct the maiden proofs of their oratory in the senate.

LORD LOUGHBOROUGH.

Mr. Wedderburn, afterwards Lord Loughborough, was once asked whether he really delivered in the House of Commons, a speech which the newspapers ascribed to him. "Why, to be sure," said he, "there are many things in that speech which I did say, and there are more which I wish I had said."

REPORTING FROM MEMORY.

Mr. William Woodfall, the son of the celebrated printer of the *Public Advertiser*, in which the Letters of Junius first appeared, undertook, without any assistance, the arduous task of reporting the debates of both houses of Parliament, day by day, in his father's paper, and afterwards in other daily journals. This gentleman possessed a most extraordinary memory, as well as wonderful powers of literary labour. It is asserted that he has been known to sit through a long debate of the House of Commons, not making a single note of the proceedings, and afterwards to write out a full and faithful account of what had taken place, extending to sixteen columns, without allowing himself an interval of rest. The remarkable exertions of this most famous reporter gave the newspaper for which he wrote a celebrity which compelled other newspapers to aim at the same fulness and freshness in their parliamentary reports. What Woodfall accomplished by excessive bodily and mental exertion, his contemporaries succeeded in bringing to a higher degree of perfection by the division of labour; and thus, in time, each morning newspaper had secured the assistance of an efficient body of reporters, each of whom might in turn take notes of a debate, and commit a portion of it to the press several hours before the whole debate was concluded.

ROYAL SOCIETY OF LONDON.

ITS MACE.

The mace of the Royal Society, made of silver, weighing 149 oz. avoirdupois, was presented by the King, along with its second charter, in 1663. Of late years it acquired from another source a *prestige* which has been dissipated in a manner not unlike that of the "pretorium" in the *Antiquary*. It was long the popular belief, Sir D. Brewster mentions, in the *N. Brit. Review*, that this was the mace ordered by Cromwell out of the House of Commons, and numberless visitors came to the apartments of the Royal Society to see the famous "bauble." It was even figured in the Abbotsford edition of *Woodstock* as being the mace which belonged to the Long Parliament. Mr. Weld, in his *History of the Royal Society*, has dispelled this pleasing illusion, he having not only traced the history of the "bauble" mace, but discovered the warrant for preparing the new one as a gift to the Society. "We cannot forbear observing," he says, "that though the mace may not be as curious as before to the antiquary, divested as it now is of its fictitious historical interest, yet it is much more to be respected ; for surely a mace designated a 'bauble,' and spurned from the House of Commons, by a republican, will scarcely be an appropriate gift to the Royal Society." Still, it would be a cherished national relic of the time of Old Knoll, who rises in popular estimation as the character of Charles II. sinks.

SCIENCE AND SUPERSTITION.

This great scientific body was established in 1660, deriving its origin from previous societies of learned men, who met together for the discussion of subjects of science and art. The meetings were sometimes held at Dr. Goddard's lodgings in Wood Street, where he kept an operator for grinding lenses; sometimes at the Bull Head Tavern in Cheapside; and sometimes at Gresham College. Amongst the celebrated names connected with the proceedings of the infant association, are those of Boyle, Evelyn, Cowley the poet, and Wren the architect. One result of its labours was remarkable. During the civil war, no fewer than eighty persons were executed in Suffolk for witchcraft; and, in 1649, fourteen men and women were burned for witchcraft in a little village near Berwick, where the entire population consisted only of fourteen families. It is stated by Hutchinson that there were but two witches executed in England after the Royal Society published their *Transactions*, and Sir Walter Scott has given it as his opinion, that the establishment of the Royal Society tended greatly to destroy the belief in witchcraft and superstition generally. The discontinuance of "touching" for scrofula, or "king's evil," by the royal hand, was due to the same wholesome influence, although this superstition held out the longest. Dr. Samuel Johnson was "touched" by Queen Anne so late as 1712.

TRANSFUSION OF BLOOD.

In the year 1667, the Royal Society successfully performed the experiment of transfusing the blood of a sheep into a man in perfect health. The subject of the experiment was Arthur Coga, who, as Pepys says, was a kind of minister, and, being in want of money, hired himself for a guinea. Drs. Lower and King performed the experiment, injecting twelve oz. of sheep's blood, without producing any inconvenience. The patient drank a glass or two of Canary, took a pipe of tobacco, and went home with a stronger and fuller pulse than before. The experiment was in a day or two afterwards repeated on Coga, when fourteen oz. of sheep's blood was substituted for eight oz. of his own. Pepys went to see him, and heard him give an account in Latin of the operation and its effects.

SAVANS OF FRANCE.

The following reminiscences of Cuvier, Humboldt, Gay-Lussac, Berthollet, and La Place are from memoranda by Sir Humphry Davy:—

"Cuvier had even in his address and manner the character of a superior man;—much general power and eloquence in conversation, and a great variety of information on scientific as well as popular subjects. I should say of him, that he is the most distinguished man of *talents* I have known; but I doubt if he is entitled to the appellation of a man of genius."

"De Humboldt was one of the most agreeable men I have ever known; social, modest, full of intelligence, with facilities of every kind: almost *too fluent* in conversation. His travels display his spirit of enterprise. His works are monuments of the variety of his knowledge and resources."

"Gay-Lussac was quick, lively, ingenious, and profound, with great activity of mind, and great facility of manipulation. I should place him at the head of the living chemists of France."

"Berthollet was a most amiable man; when the friend of Napoleon even, always good, conciliatory, and modest, frank and candid. He had no airs, and many graces. In every way below La Place in intellectual powers, he appeared superior to him in moral qualities. Berthollet had no appearance of a man of genius; but one could not look on La Place's physiognomy without being convinced that he was a very extraordinary man."

"La Place, when a minister of Napoleon, was rather formal and grand in manner, with an air of protection rather than of courtesy. He spoke like a man not merely feeling his own power, but wishing that others should be immediately conscious of it. I have heard, from good authority, that he was exceedingly proud of his orders, and that he had the star of the order of Reunion affixed to his dressing-gown. This was in 1813. In 1820, when I saw him again, his master had fallen. His manners were altered. He was become mild and gentlemanlike; and had a softer tone of voice, and more grace in the forms of salutation. I remember the first day I saw him, which was, I believe, in November, 1813. On my speaking to him of the atomic theory in chemistry, and expressing my belief that the science would ultimately be referred to mathematical laws, similar to those which he had so profoundly and successfully established with respect to the mechanical properties of matter, he treated my idea in a tone bordering on contempt, as if angry that any results in chemistry could, even in their future possibilities, be compared with his own labours. When I dined with him, in 1820, he discussed the same opinion with acumen and candour, and allowed all the merit of John Dalton. It is true our positions had changed. *He* was now amongst the old aristocracy of France, and was no longer the intellectual head of the new aristocracy; and, from a young and humble aspirant to chemical glory, I was about to be called, by the voice of my colleagues, to a chair which had been honoured by the last days of Newton."

SCIENCE—ITS TRIUMPHS.

It has lengthened life; it has mitigated pain; it has extinguished diseases; it has increased the fertility of the soil; it has given new securities to the mariner; it has furnished new arms to the warrior; it has spanned great rivers and estuaries with bridges of form unknown to our fathers; it has guided the thunderbolt innocuously from heaven to earth; it has lighted up the night with the splendour of the day; it has extended the range of the human vision; it has multiplied the power of the human muscles; it has accelerated motion; it has annihilated distance; it has facilitated intercourse, correspondence, all friendly offices, all despatch of business; it has enabled man to descend to the depths of the sea, to soar into the air, to penetrate securely into the noxious recesses of the earth, to traverse the land in cars which whirl along without horses, and the ocean in ships which run ten knots an hour against the wind. These are but a part of its fruits, and of its first fruits. For it is a philosophy which never rests, which has never attained, which is never perfect. Its law is progress. A point which yesterday was invisible is its goal to-day, and will be its starting-post to-morrow.—(Macaulay.)

SCIENTIFIC ADVENTURE.

ASCENT OF THE JUNGFRAU.

In 1841, Professor Forbes, along with M. Agassiz, and others, made a successful ascent of the great Swiss mountain, the Jungfrau, whose summit is 13,720 feet above the level of the sea.

Of six travellers and seven guides who formed the party, four of each reached the top—viz., of the former, MM. Forbes, Agassiz, Desor, and Duchatelies; of the latter, Jacob Leutvold (who ascended the Finster Aarhorn), Johan Jannon, Melchior, Baucholzer, and Andreas Aplanalp. They left the Grimsel on the morning of the 27th of August, 1841, ascended the whole height of the Ober-Aar Glacier, and descended the greater part of that of Viesch. Crossing a col to the right, they slept at the chalet of Aletsch, near the lake of that name. This was twelve hours' hard walking, the descent of the glaciers being difficult and fatiguing. Next day, the party started at six A.M., having been unable sooner to procure a ladder, to cross the crevasses; they then traversed the upper part of the glacier of Aletsch in its whole extent for four hours and a half, until the ascent of the Jungfrau began.

The party crossed with great caution extensive and steep fields of fresh snow, concealing crevasses, till they came to one which opened vertically, and behind which rose an excessively steep wall of hardened snow. Having crossed the crevasses with the ladder, they ascended the snow without much danger, owing to its consistency. After some similar walking they gained the col which separates the Aletsch Glacier from the Rothal, on the side of Lauterbrunnen, by which the ascent has usually been attempted. Thus, the travellers, although now at a height of between 12,000 and 13,000 feet, had by far the hardest and most perilous part of the ascent to accomplish. The whole upper part of the mountain presented a steep, inclined surface of what at first seemed snow, but which soon appeared to be hard ice. This slope was not less than 800 or 900 feet in perpendicular height, and its surface (which Professor Forbes measured several times with a clinometer), in many places rose at 45 degrees, and in few much less; and all Alpine travellers know well what an inclined surface of 45 degrees is to walk up. Of course, every step taken was cut with the hatchet, whilst the slope terminated below, on both sides in precipices some thousand feet high. After very severe exertion, they reached the top of this great mountain at four P.M. The summit was so small that but one person could stand upon it at once, and that not until the snow had been flattened. The party returned as they came up, step by step, and backwards, and arrived at the chalet of Aletsch, and by beautiful moonlight, at half-past eleven at night.

PROFESSOR FORBES IN THE ALPS.

Strange incidents befell Professor Forbes and his companions, in their travels through the Alps of Savoy. On one occasion, they got so near a thunder-cloud, as to be highly electrified by induction, with all the angular stones round them hissing like points near a powerful electrical machine; on another, whilst crossing one of the loftiest passes, the Col de Collon, they discovered a dark object lying on the snow, which proved to be the body of a man, with the clothes hard-frozen and uninjured. "The effect on us all," says the Professor, "was electric; and had not the sun shone forth in its full glory, and the very wilderness of eternal snow seemed gladdened under the serenity of such a summer's day, as is rare at these heights, we should certainly have felt a deeper thrill, arising from the sense of personal danger. As it was, when we had recovered our first surprise, and interchanged our expression of sympathy for the poor traveller, and gazed with awe on the disfigured relics of one who had so lately been in the same plight with ourselves, we turned and surveyed, with a stronger sense of sublimity than before, the desolation by which we were surrounded; and became still more sensible of our isolation from human dwellings, human help, and human sympathy, our loneliness with nature, and as it were, the more immediate presence of God."

SCIENTIFIC MEN.

NAPOLEON'S SAVANS IN EGYPT.

During the Egyptian campaign, no sooner were the Mameluke horse descried than the word was given—"Form square; artillery to the angles; *asses* and *savans* to the centre;" a command which afforded no small merriment to the soldiers, and made them call the asses *demi-savans*.—(Alison.)

HUMBOLDT AND THE FRENCH SAVANS IN EGYPT.

In the diary of Thomas Moore appears the following notice of the great work which was the joint production of the *savans* who accompanied Napoleon to Egypt:—
"Aug., 1820.—Went to call on Madame de Souza, for the purpose of being taken by her to the Institute. Was received there with much kindness by M. Fourrier, one of the Egyptian *savans*, and author of the 'Memoire' prefixed to the great work on Egypt. He said that he merely held the pen, for that every word in it was *disputé* among the whole number of those on the expedition, and that it was the result of their collected knowledge on the subject. When I mentioned to Madame de Souza what he said about the concoction of the memoir, she told me it was all done too in the presence of the Emperor!" Afterwards meeting with Baron Humboldt, that distinguished philosopher "spoke contemptuously of the great government work as a confused heap of common-places; Fourrier's a pompous preface with nothing in it. Said the Egyptians were blackish, with good aquiline noses; the Sphynx a negro face. Asked him if he thought Cleopatra was 'blackish?' 'Yes, certainly.'"

DR. WHEWELL AND THE COLLEGE "DONS."

Dr. Whewell's accession to the Mastership of Trinity might well have been an era in the history of that "royal and religious foundation." The new head was a gentleman of most commanding personal appearance, and the very sound of his powerful voice betokened no ordinary man. He was a remarkably good rider even in a country of horsemen, and the anecdote was often told, and not altogether repudiated by him, how, in his younger days, about the time of his ordination, a pugilist, in whose company he accidentally found himself while travelling, audibly lamented that such lusty thews and sinews should be thrown away on a parson. With these physical advantages was combined a knowledge almost literally universal. Some people are said to know a little of everything; he might be truly said to know a great deal of everything. Second Wrangler of his year, Professor of Mineralogy, and afterwards of Moral Philosophy, author of a *Bridgewater Treatise*, and writer on a diversity of subjects, scientific and ethical, he kept up his classics to an extent unusual for a scientific man, and did not neglect the lighter walks of literature. His name is on the list of the Cambridge prize poets, and is also known in connection with several translations from the German. In conversation it was scarcely possible to start a subject without finding him at home in it. A story is current about him, not absolutely authenticated, but certainly of the *se non vero ben trovato* sort; that some of the Dons who were tired of hearing him explain everything, and enlighten everybody in Combination-room, laid a trap to catch him in this wise. They determined to get themselves up thoroughly in some out-of-the-way topic, and introduce it, as if by accident, on the first convenient occasion. Accordingly they pitched upon something connected with China, either (for there are two versions of the story) Chinese musical instruments or the Chinese game of chess. Various odd books, and particularly a certain volume of a certain cyclopædia, were dragged out of their dusty repose and carefully perused. Next Sunday, when the College dignitaries and some stranger guests were marshalled over their port and biscuit, the conspirators thoroughly primed, and with their parts artistically distributed, watched their time and adroitly introduced the prepared topic. One after the other they let drop most naturally a quantity of strange erudition, marvellously astounding, no doubt to the small-college Dons present, and apparently puzzling to the object of attack, for he actually remained silent for a full quarter of an hour, till, just as the parties were congratulating themselves on their success, he turned to the principal speaker, and remarked, "O, I see you've been reading the article I wrote for such a cyclopædia in such a year!" They gave it up after that.—(Bristed's Five Years in an English University.)

YOUTHFUL PURSUITS OF GALILEO.

The early years of Galileo were spent in the construction of instruments and pieces of machinery, which were calculated chiefly to amuse himself and his schoolfellows. Sir David Brewster, in mentioning this fact, remarks that in this respect the early life of the future astronomer, resembled that of almost all great experimental philosophers.

GALILEO'S ADJURATION.

In the year 1615, Galileo was called to account by the Inquisition at Rome for maintaining the motion of the earth and the stability of the sun, and teaching and promulgating this doctrine. He was enjoined by Cardinal Bellarmine to renounce this opinion as heretical, and it was decreed that if he refused he should be cast into prison. The astronomer appeared before the cardinal, and declared that he abandoned the doctrine of the earth's motion, and would cease to propagate it. Under the pontificate of Urban VIII., however, he began anew to teach the doctrine of the earth's motion. This pope had once been his friend, but now became his accuser; and in 1633, Galileo was again summoned before the Inquisition, and put upon his trial for holding and teaching the heretical opinion. He again abjured the doctrine, kneeling before the assembled cardinals, and clothed in sackcloth of a penitent criminal. Laying his hands upon the gospels, he invoked the Divine aid in abjuring and detesting, and vowing never again to teach, the doctrine of the earth's motion, and of the sun's stability. When he rose from his knees, he stamped on the ground and said in a whisper to a friend, "*E pur si muove.*" "It does move, though." Having signed his recantation, he was, in conformity to his sentence, confined in the prison of the Inquisition.

SCIENTIFIC AND LITERARY PURSUITS OF AGE.

HUMBOLDT.

"In my eightieth year" (writes Baron Humboldt, in the *Aspects of Nature*, 1849), "I am still enabled to enjoy the satisfaction of completing a third edition of my work, remoulding it entirely to meet the requirements of the present time." The Nestor of science is now (1854) engaged in completing his *Cosmos*.

ARNAULD AND SPELMAN.

The great Arnauld retained the vigour of his genius, and the command of his pen, to his last day. He translated Josephus when eighty years old, and at the age of eighty-two was still the great Arnauld.

Sir Henry Spelman neglected the sciences in his youth, but cultivated them at fifty years of age, and produced good fruit. His early years were chiefly passed in farming, which greatly diverted him from his studies: but a remarkable disappointment respecting a contested estate disgusted him with these rustic occupations. Resolved to attach himself to regular studies and literary society, he sold his farms, and became the most learned antiquary and lawyer.

JOHNSON, CHAUCER, CELLINI, AND FRANKLIN.

Dr. Johnson applied himself to the Dutch language but a few years before his death. In one morning of advanced life, he amused himself by committing to memory 800 lines of Virgil. At the age of seventy-three, when staggering under an immediate attack of paralysis — sufficiently severe to render him speechless—he composed a Latin prayer, in order to test the loss or retention of his mental faculties.

Chaucer's *Canterbury Tales* were the composition of his latest years. They were begun in his fifty-fourth year, and finished in his sixty-first.

The most delightful of autobiographers, for artists, is that of Benvenuto Cellini—a work of great originality, which was not begun till "the clock of his age had struck fifty-eight."

Franklin's philosophical pursuits began when he had nearly reached his fiftieth year.

DRYDEN, ANGELO, WREN, FRANKLIN, AND ACCORSO.

Dryden's complete works form the largest body of poetry from the pen of one writer in the English language; yet he gave no public testimony of poetical abilities till his twenty-seventh year. In his sixty-eighth year he proposed to translate the whole *Iliad;* and the most pleasing productions were written in his old age.

Michael Angelo preserved his

creative genius even to extreme old age: there is a device said to be invented by him of an old man represented in a *go-cart*, with an hour-glass upon it; the inscription *Ancora impara!*—YET I AM LEARNING!

Sir Christopher Wren retired from public life at eighty-six; and after that he spent five years in literary, astronomical, and religious engagements.

Dr. Franklin exhibited a striking instance of the influence of reading, writing, and conversation, in prolonging a sound and active state of all the faculties of the mind. In his eighty-fourth year he discovered no one mark in any of them of the weakness of decay usually observed in the minds of persons at that advanced period of life.

Accorso, a great lawyer, being asked why he began the study of the law so late, answered, that indeed he began it late, but should therefore master it the sooner.

NECKER AND LE VEGER.

Necker offers a beautiful instance of the influence of late studies in life; for he tells us, that "the era of threescore and ten is an agreeable age for writing: your mind has not lost its vigour, and envy leaves you in peace."

The opening of one of La Mothe le Veger's Treatises is striking: " I should but ill return the favours God has granted me in the eightieth year of my age, should I allow myself to give way to that shameless want of occupation which I have condemned all my life:" and the old man proceeds with his "observations on the composition and reading of books."

WALTON AND REID.

Izaak Walton still glowed while writing some of the most interesting biographies in his eighty-fifth year, and in his ninetieth enriched the poetical world with the first publication of a romantic tale by Chalkhill, "the friend of Spenser."

The revelations of modern chemistry kindled the curiosity of Dr. Reid to his latest days.

ADAM SMITH.

Professor Dugald Stewart says, that Adam Smith observed to him that "of all the amusements of old age, the most grateful and soothing is a renewal of acquaintance with the favourite studies and favourite authors of youth—a remark which in his own case seemed to be more particularly exemplified while he was reperusing, with the enthusiasm of a student, the tragic poets of ancient Greece. I heard him repeat the observation more than once while Sophocles and Euripides lay open on his table."

TABLE-TALK AND VARIETIES.

SPEAKING A FOREIGN LANGUAGE.

Miss Selina Bunbury, the writer of a *Tour in Norway and Sweden*, relates some amusing blunders committed in the course of her attempts to secure the services of a travelling companion who could drive her into the country. After sundry failures, a Scandinavian professor succeeded in finding a collector of fairy legends who was desirous of making a tour in quest of the lore of faëryland, and consented to take the whip and reins in Miss Bunbury's carriole:—

"The Professor had told me (she writes) that the fairy-legend hunter spoke English; a delightful knowledge this was to me, for I am by no means strong in northern tongues. Thus, in the hope of using and hearing my own, I was quite at ease, when the next day they both made their appearance. The Professor presented me formally. Herr Fairy-hunter made a great many bows; and as so many bows involve a good many curtsies, I inclined nearly as often. Then, with a last reverence he spoke, in English, and said, very slowly,— 'I complain of you much, that you are so disagreeable; but now I make an extra.' I made my last reverence in reply. Such a speech, by way of a complimentary one, was rather startling, and not a little alarming. I looked nervously at the Professor, who, with profound gravity, interpreted his friend's meaning thus,—'He pities you for being so disagreeably circumstanced; but he is making an abridgment of his book, and, therefore, cannot now make his tour.' I bowed with a sense of relief, and the fairy-hunter and myself exchanged some sentences which I do not record, as I believe the fairies alone would be able to understand the language. 'I have got another plan for you,' said the Professor; 'yes, this is the very thing. A teacher of music here wishes to take his wife and child into the country, and one of our opera-voices, who also speaks Italian—which you do likewise—will go with them. They will all join you; but as they must leave their affairs here, they expect you will pay all the travelling expenses. They will bring their own provisions, because there are none to be got on the road. That is fair.'—'Very fair, indeed,' I answered, 'the very thing.'—'I complain of you much!' murmured the fairy-hunter, looking at me compassionately.—'You must, then, take a carriage,' said the Professor.—'It will be quite filled,' I replied. 'Four persons, with horse-cloaks, pipes, tobacco-pouches, provisions, and luggage!'—'And the child,' added the Professor.—'Ah! I suppose I must take it on my knee.'—'You are very disagreeable,' said the fairy-hunter, with a look of commiseration at me: but I thought, secretly, that others were still more disagreeable. 'But Mr Murray's *Hand-book* says it is dangerous to take a heavy carriage over the hills of Norway, and certainly a roll down among such *et ceteras* would not be pleasant,' I added. Herr Fairy-hunter moved uneasily on his chair, worked his hands together, shook his head disprovingly, and said, 'You must be complained of.'" Miss Bunbury at last succeeded in finding a guide and companion.

SCIENCE AND COMMERCE.

The commercial world owes to two retired philosophers, in the solitude of their study, Locke and Smith, those principles which dignify trade into a liberal pursuit, and connect it with the happiness of a people.

DEDICATIONS.

The virtuous Duke of Montausier, governor of the Dauphin of France in the reign of Louis XIV., would never suffer his pupil to read the dedications that were addressed to him. One day, however, he discovered him reading one of these epistles in private; but, instead of taking it from him, he obliged him to read it aloud, and, stopping him at the end of every phrase, said, "Do you not see, sir, that they are laughing at you with impunity? Can you sincerely believe yourself possessed of all the good qualities ascribed to you? Can you read, without indignation, such gross flattery, which they would not presume to offer without having the lowest opinion of your understanding?"

At a time when the ministers of state were frequently changed in

France, a certain author dedicated his piece to the Brazen Horse, on the Pont-Neuf; "for I am persuaded," said he, "that my patron *will long remain in place.*"

LITERARY DINNERS.

"I knew a person," says Menage, "who occasionally gave entertainments to authors. His fancy was to place them at table, each according to the size and thickness of the volumes they had published, commencing with the folio authors, and proceeding through the quarto and octavo, down to the duodecimo, each according to his rank."

SIDNEY SMITH.

Smith observing Lord Brougham's one-horse carriage, he remarked to a friend, alluding to the B surrounded by a coronet on the panel, "There goes a carriage with a B outside and a *wasp* within."

MADAME NECKER'S TABLE-TALK.

During one day, at Madame Necker's, the Chevalier de Chastellux happened to arrive first of the company, and so early that the mistress of the house was not in the drawing-room. In walking about, he saw on the ground, under Madame Necker's chair, a little book, which he picked up; it was a white paper book, of which several pages were in the handwriting of Madame Necker. It was the *preparation* for the very dinner to which he was invited. Madame Necker had written it the evening before, and it contained all she was to say to the most remarkable persons at table. After reading the little book, M. de Chastellux hastened to replace it under the chair. A moment afterwards, a valet-de-chambre entered to say, that Madame Necker had forgotten her pocket-book in the drawing-room. It was found and carried to Madame Necker. The dinner was delightful to M. de Chastellux, who saw that Madame Necker said word for word what she had written in her pocket-book.

SIDNEY SMITH AND LANDSEER.

A friend once sent Smith a note, requesting him to sit for his portrait to Landseer, the great animal-painter. Sidney wrote back, "Is thy servant a *dog* that he should do this thing?"

LOCKE AND SCOTT—ON ACQUIRING KNOWLEDGE.

Mr. Locke was asked how he had contrived to accumulate a mine of knowledge so rich, yet so extensive and deep. He replied, that he attributed what little he knew to the not having been ashamed to ask for information, and to the rule he had laid down of conversing with all descriptions of men, on those topics chiefly that formed their own peculiar professions or pursuits.

Sir Walter Scott gives us to understand, that he never met with any man, let his calling be what it might, even the most stupid fellow that ever rubbed down a horse, from whom he could not, by a few moments' conversation, learn something which he did not before know, and which was valuable to him. This will account for the fact that he seemed to have an intuitive knowledge of everything.

AMERICAN PRONUNCIATION.

Noah Webster, in the preface to his own *Dictionary of the English Language*, thoroughly disparages Dr. Johnson's, and most Americans are of Webster's opinion. When Stuart, their distinguished painter, was introduced to the leviathan of our literature, Johnson, surprised at his speaking such good English, asked him where he learnt it; and Stuart's cool reply was, "Not in your dictionary!" In addition to the use of words which are only to be found in their own vocabulary, they have notions of pronunciation that are peculiarly their private property. It is not the fashion with us, as we have already observed, to call "beauty" *booty*, nor "duty" *dooty*, nor "due" *doo*; neither would the adoption of *tew* for "too," nor of *noos* for "news," nor of en-*gine* for "éngine," nor of genu-*ine* for "génuine," of *deefe* for "deaf," of *en-quirry* for "enquiry," and countless similar expressions, slip very glibly off our tongues; but if you only ask an American why he so pronounces them, he will tell you that he believes it to be the right way; and if you remind him that there are no such words as he occasionally uses, in the English language, his answer will be, "There mayn't be in *yours*, but there are in *ours!*"—(Alfred Bunn's Old England and New England.)

GOLDSMITH AT GREEN ARBOR COURT.

The lover of literature will walk up the Break-neck Stairs, between Seacoal Lane and the Old Bailey, with great pleasure, when he reflects that it will lead to Green Arbor Court, where Goldsmith wrote his *Vicar of Wakefield* and his *Traveller*.

A friend of the doctor, paying him a visit in this place in March, 1759, found him in a lodging so poor and miserable that, he says, he should not have thought it proper to have mentioned the circumstance did he not consider it as the highest proof of the splendour of Goldsmith's genius and talents, that, by the bare exertion of their powers, under every disadvantage of person and fortune, he could gradually emerge from such obscurity to the enjoyment of all the comforts and even the luxuries of life, and admission into the best societies of London.

The doctor was writing his *Inquiry into the present State of Polite Learning* in a wretched, dirty room, in which there was but one chair; and when he, from civility, offered it to his visitant, he was obliged to seat himself in the window. Such was the humble abode of one of the first of English writers; and such was the place where two of the finest productions of English literature were written.

ADAM SMITH.

This distinguished philosopher was remarkable for absence of mind. As an anecdote of this peculiarity, it is related of him, that having one Sunday morning walked into his garden at Kirkaldy, dressed in little more than his night-gown, he gradually fell into a reverie, from which he did not awaken till he found himself in the streets of Dunfermline, a town at least twelve miles off. He had in reality trudged along the king's highway all that distance in the pursuit of a certain train of ideas, and he was only eventually stopped in his progress by the bells of Dunfermline, which happened at the time to be ringing the people to church. His appearance in a crowded church, on a Scotch Sunday morning, in his night-gown, is left to the imagination of the reader.

BISHOP NEWTON AND HAWKESWORTH.

So sensible was even the calm Bishop Newton to critical attacks, that Whiston tells us he lost his favour, which he had enjoyed for twenty years, by contradicting Newton in his old age; for no man was of "a more fearful temper." Whiston declares that he would not have thought proper to have published his work against Newton's *Chronology* in his lifetime, "because I knew his temper so well, that I should have expected it would have killed him; as Dr. Bentley, Bishop Stillingfleet's chaplain, told me that he believed Mr. Locke's thorough confutation of the bishop's metaphysics about the Trinity hastened his end." Dr. Hawkesworth *died of criticism.* Singing birds cannot live in a storm.

A POEM ON TOBACCO.

The authors of the time of Elizabeth and James I. often put quaint and ridiculous titles to their books. Amongst others we may mention Joshua Sylvester, a Puritanical poet, who wrote a poem against tobacco, which bears this title: Tobacco battered, and the Pipes shattered about their Ears that idly idolize so loathsome a Vanity, by a Volley of holy Shot thundered from Mount Helicon.

CAVENDISH'S DISREGARD OF MONEY.

To the anecdotes given in a previous part of this volume, illustrative of the eccentricities of this great chemist, may here be added the following, characteristic of his disregard of money:—

"The bankers (says Mr. Pepys) where he kept his accounts, in looking over their affairs, found he had a considerable sum in their hands, some say nearly eighty thousand pounds, and one of them said, that he did not think it right that it should lie so without investment. He was therefore commissioned to wait upon Mr. Cavendish, who at that time resided at Clapham. Upon his arrival at the house he desired to speak to Mr. Cavendish.

"The servant said, 'What is your business with him?'

"He did not choose to tell the servant.

"The servant then said, 'You must wait till my master rings his bell, and then I will let him know.'

"In about a quarter of an hour the bell rang, and the banker had the curiosity to listen to the conversation which took place.

"'Sir, there is a person below, who wants to speak to you.'

"'Who is he? Who is he? What does he want with me?'

"'He says he is your banker, and must speak to you.'

"Mr. Cavendish, in great agitation, desires he may be sent up, and, before he entered the room, cries, 'What do you come here for? What do you want with me?'

"'Sir, I thought it proper to wait upon you, as we have a very large balance in hand of yours, and wish for your orders respecting it.'

"'If it is any trouble to you, I will take it out of your hands. Do not come here to plague me.'

"'Not the least trouble to us, sir, not the least; but we thought you might like some of it to be invested.'

"'Well! well! What do you want to do?'

"'Perhaps you would like to have forty thousand pounds invested.'

"'Do so! Do so, and don't come here and trouble me, or I will remove it.'"

BURKE.

It was a fine compliment which Johnson, when debilitated by sickness, paid to Burke—the only man who was a match for that conversational tyrant: "That fellow calls forth all my powers. Were I to see Burke now it would kill me." "Can he *wind into a subject, like a serpent*, as Burke does?" was the shrewd question put to Boswell by Goldsmith.

DOCTOR JOHNSON IN CONVERSATION.

Tyers says of Johnson, though his time seemed to be bespoke, and quite engrossed, his house was always open to all his acquaintance, new and old. His amanuensis has given up his pen, the printer's devil has waited on the stairs for a proof-sheet, and the press has often stood still, while his visitors were delighted and instructed. No subject ever came amiss to him. He could transfer his thoughts from one thing to another with the most accommodating facility. He had the art, for which Locke was famous, of leading people to talk of their favourite subjects, and on what they knew best. By this he acquired a great deal of information. What he once learned he rarely forgot. They gave him their best conversation, and he generally made them pleased with themselves for endeavouring to please him.

Poet Smart used to relate, "that his first conversation with Johnson was of such variety and length, that it began with poetry and ended in fluxions." He always talked as if he was talking upon oath. He was the wisest person, and had the most knowledge in ready cash, that I ever had the honour to be acquainted with. Johnson's advice was consulted on all occasions. He was known to be a good casuist, and therefore had many cases submitted for his judgment. His conversation, in the judgment of several, was thought to be equal to his correct writings. Perhaps the tongue will throw out more animated expressions than the pen. He said the most common things in the newest manner. He always commanded attention and regard.

DOCTOR BIRCH.

Of Dr. Birch, Johnson was used to speak in this manner: "Tom is a lively rogue; he remembers a great deal, and can tell many pleasant stories; but a pen is to Tom a torpedo; the touch of it benumbs his hand and his brain. Tom can talk; but he is no writer."

COLERIDGE'S TALK.

Dr. Dibdin has given an animated description of Coleridge's lecturing and conversation, which concurs with the universal opinion.

"I once came from Kensington, in a snow-storm, to hear Mr. Coleridge lecture on Shakspeare. I might have sat as wisely, and more comfortably, by my own fireside, for no Coleridge appeared. I shall never forget the effect his conversation made upon me at the first meeting at a dinner-party. It struck me not only as something quite out of the ordinary course of things, but as an intellectual exhibition altogether matchless. The viands were unusually costly, and the banquet was at once rich and varied; but there seemed to be no dish like Coleridge's conversation to feed upon; and no information so instructive as his own. The orator rolled himself up, as it were, in his chair, and gave the most unrestrained indulgence to his speech; and how fraught with acuteness and originality was that speech, and in what copious and eloquent periods did it flow! The auditors seemed rapt in wonder and delight, as one conversation, more profound or clothed in more forcible language than another, fell from his tongue. He spoke for nearly two hours with unhesitating and uninterrupted fluency. As I returned homewards to Kensington, I thought a second Johnson had visited the earth, to make wise the sons of men, and regretted that I could not exercise the powers of a second Boswell, to record the wisdom and the eloquence that fell from the orator's lips.

"The manner of Coleridge was emphatic rather than dogmatic, and thus he was generally and satisfactorily listened to. It might be said of Coleridge, as Cowper has so happily said of Sir Philip Sidney, that he was the 'warbler of poetic prose.' There was always this characteristic feature in his multifarious conversation—it was always delicate, reverent, and courteous. The chastest ear could drink in no startling sound; the most serious believer never had his bosom ruffled by one sceptical or reckless assertion.

Coleridge was eminently simple in his manner. Thinking and speaking were his delight; and he would sometimes seem, during the most fervid moments of discourse, to be abstracted from all, and everything around and about him, and to be basking in the sunny warmth of his own radiant imagination."

THE TERM "WE."

The plural style of speaking ("we") among kings was begun by King John of England, A.D. 1119. Before that time sovereigns used the singular person in their edicts. The German and the French sovereigns followed the example of King John in 1200. When editors began to say "we" is not known.

KNOCKING OUT AN I.

Mr. Curran, the late celebrated Irish advocate, was walking one day with a friend, who was extremely punctilious in his conversation. Hearing a person near him say curosity, for curiosity, he exclaimed, "How that man murders the English language!" "Not so bad," replied Curran, "he has only *knocked an i out!*"

PROFITS OF RECENT AUTHORSHIP.

The late Mr. Tegg, the publisher in Cheapside, gave the following list of remunerative payments to distinguished authors in his time; and he is believed to have taken considerable pains to verify the items:—Fragments of History, by Charles Fox, sold by Lord Holland, for 5000 guineas. Fragments of History, by Sir James Mackintosh, £500. Lingard's History of England, £4683. Sir Walter Scott's Bonaparte was sold, with the printed books, for £18,000; the net receipts of copyright on the first two editions only must have been £10,000. Life of Wilberforce, by his sons, 4000 guineas. Life of Byron, by Moore, £4000. Life of Sheridan, by Moore, £2000. Life of Hannah More, £2000. Life of Cowper, by Southey, £1000. Life and Times of George IV., by Lady C. Bury, £1000. Byron's Works, £20,000. Lord of the Isles, half share, £1500. Lalla Rookh, by Moore, £3000. Rejected Addresses, by Smith, £1000. Crabbe's Works, republication of, by Mr. Murray, £3000. Wordsworth's Works, republication of, by Mr. Moxon, £1050. Bulwer's Rienzi, £1600. Marryat's Novels, £500 to £1500 each. Trollope's Factory Boy, £1800. Hannah More derived £30,000 per annum for her copyrights, during the latter years of her life. Rundell's Domestic Cookery, £2000. Nicholas Nickleby, £3000. Eustace's Classical Tour, £2100. Sir Robert Inglis obtained for the beautiful and interesting widow of Bishop Heber, by the sale of his Journal, £5000.

JAMES BOSWELL.

The moment Johnson's voice burst forth, the attention which it excited in Mr. Boswell amounted almost to pain. His eyes goggled with eagerness; he leaned his ear almost on the shoulder of the doctor, and his mouth dropped open to catch every syllable that might be uttered; nay, he seemed not only to dread losing a word, but to be anxious not to miss a breathing, as if hoping from it latently, or mystically, some information.

On one occasion, the doctor detected Boswell, or Bozzy, as he called him, eavesdropping behind his chair, as he was conversing with Miss Burney at Mr. Thrale's table. "What are you doing there, sir?" cried he, turning round angrily, and clapping his hand upon his knee. "Go to the table, sir!"

Boswell obeyed with an air of affright and submission, which raised a smile on every face. Scarce had he taken his seat, however, at a distance, than, impatient to get again at the side of Johnson, he rose, and was running off in quest of something to show him, when the doctor roared after him authoritatively, "What are you thinking of, sir? Why do you get up before the cloth is removed? Come back to your place, sir;" and the obsequious spaniel did as he was commanded. "Running about in the middle of meals!" muttered the doctor, pursing his mouth at the same time to restrain his rising risibility.

Boswell got another rebuff from Johnson, which would have demolished any other man. He had been teasing him with many direct questions, such as, "What did you do, sir?" "What did you say, sir?" until the great philologist became perfectly enraged. "I will not be put to the *question!*" roared he. "Don't you consider, sir, that these are not the manners of a gentleman? I will not be baited with *what* and *why*. What is this? What is that? Why is a cow's tail long? Why is a fox's tail bushy?" "Why, sir," replied Pilgarlic, "you are so good that I venture to trouble you." "Sir," replied Johnson, "my being so *good* is no reason why you should be so *ill.*" "You have but two topics, sir," exclaimed he, on another occasion, "yourself and me, and I am sick of both."

DR. CHALMERS' LITERARY HABITS.

In October, 1841, Dr. Chalmers commenced two series of biblical compositions, which he continued with unbroken regularity till the day of his decease, May 31, 1847. Go where he might, however he might be engaged, each week-day had its few verses read, thought over, written upon—forming what he denominated *Horæ Biblicæ Quotidianæ:* each Sabbath-day had its two chapters, one in the Old and the other in the New Testament, with the two trains of meditative devotion recorded to which the reading of them respectively gave birth—forming what he denominated *Horæ Biblicæ Sabbaticæ*. When absent from home, or when the manuscript books in which they were ordinarily inserted were not beside him, he wrote in short-hand, carefully entering what was thus written in the larger volumes afterwards. Not a trace of haste nor of the extreme pressure from without, to which he was so often subjected, is exhibited in the hand-writing of these volumes. There are but few words omitted—scarcely any erased. This singular correctness was a general characteristic of his compositions. His lectures on the Epistle to the Romans were written *currente calamo,* in Glasgow, during the most hurried and overburdened period of his life. And when, many years afterwards, they were given out to be copied for the press, scarcely a blot, or an erasure, or a correction, was to be found in them, and they were printed off exactly as they had originally been written.

In preparing the *Horæ Biblicæ Quotidianæ,* Chalmers had by his side, for use and reference, the *Concordance,* the *Pictorial Bible,* Poole's *Synopsis,* Henry's *Commentary,* and Robinson's *Researches in Palestine.* These constituted what he called his "Biblical Library." "There," said he to a friend, pointing, as he spoke, to the above-named volumes, as they lay together on his library-table, with a volume of the *Quotidianæ,* in which he had just been writing, lying open beside them,—"There are the books I use —all that is Biblical is there. I have to do with nothing besides in my Biblical study." To the consultation of these few volumes he throughout restricted himself.—(Memoir by Dr. Hanna.)

JUDGE BURNET.

Judge Burnet, son of the famous Bishop of Salisbury, when young, is said to have been of a wild and dissipated turn. Being one day found by his father in a very serious humour, "What is the matter with you, Tom?" said the bishop: "what are you ruminating on?" "A greater work than your lordship's *History of the Reformation*," answered the son. "Ay! what is that?" asked the father. "The reformation of myself, my lord," replied the son.

FALSTAFF'S BUCKRAM-MEN.

Sir John Falstaff was a benefactor to Magdalen College. He bequeathed estates to that society, part of which were appropriated to buy liveries for some of the senior demies. But this benefaction, in time, yielding no more than a penny a week to those who received the liveries, they were called by way of contempt, *Falstaff's Buckram-men.*

The proper name of this knight was Fastolff. He was a celebrated general and nobleman in France during our conquests in that kingdom, and intimate with the founder of Magdalen College. It is thought that the name which Shakspeare gave to his humorous knight was merely accidental; and that he did not intend the least allusion to this great warrior, under the name of Sir John Falstaff. It is evident, indeed, that although their names are somewhat similar, their characters are very different.—(Warton.)

CARDINAL WOLSEY.

"King Henry," says Fuller, "took just offence that the cardinal set his own arms above the king's, on the gate-house, at the entrance into the colledg (at Oxford). This was no verbal but a real *Ego et Rex meus,* excusable by no plea in manners or grammar, except only by that (which is rather fault than figure) a harsh downright *Hysterosis;* but to humble the cardinal's pride, some afterwards set up on a window a painted mastiff dog, gnawing the spate-bone of a shoulder of mutton, to minde the cardinal of his extraction, being the son of a butcher, it being utterly improbable (as some have fancied) that that picture was placed there by the cardinal's own appointment, to be to him a monitour of humility."

SUGAR PLUMS.

We meet with extravagances in the world, which we must endure, and, indeed adopt, while they last. Their absurdity does not completely appear till after they are over. During the reign of Henry III. there was a time when it was thought impossible to exist without sugar plums. Every one carried his box of sugar plums in his pocket, as he now does his snuff-box. It is related in the history of the Duke de Guise, that when he was killed at Blois, he had his comfit-box in his hand.

MRS. HANNAH MORE—TRUE AND FALSE SYMPATHY.

The author of this anecdote (Mrs. Hannah More), many years ago, made one in a party of friends. An unexpected guest, who was rather late, at length came in; she was in great agitation, having been detained on the road by a dreadful fire in the neighbourhood. The poor family, who were gone to bed, had been with difficulty awakened; the mother had escaped by throwing herself from a two pair of stairs window into the street: she then recollected that, in her extreme terror, she had left her child in bed. To the astonishment of all present, she instantly rushed back through the flames, and, to the general joy, soon appeared with the child in her arms. While she was expressing her gratitude, the light of the lamps fell on its face, and she perceived, to her inexpressible horror, that she had saved the child of another woman—that her own had perished! It may be imagined what were the feelings of the company. A subscription was immediately begun. Almost every one had liberally contributed, when a nobleman, who could have bought the whole party, turning to Mrs. Hannah More, said, "Madam, I will give you—" every expecting eye was turned to the peer, knowing him to be unused to the giving mood: the person addressed joyfully held out her hand, but drew it back on his coolly saying, "I will give you this afflicting incident for the subject of your next tragedy."

PERFUMED GLOVES.

In the *computus* of the bursars of Trinity College, for the year 1631, the following article occurs: "*Solut. pro fumigandis chirothecis.*" Gloves make a constant and considerable article of expense in the earlier accompt-books of the college here mentioned; and without doubt in those of many other societies. They were annually given (a custom still subsisting) to the college-tenants, and often presented to guests of distinction. But it appears (at least, from accompts of the said college in preceding years), that the practice of perfuming gloves for this purpose was fallen into disuse soon after the reign of Charles the First.—(Warton.)

Stowe's continuator, Edmund Howes, informs us, that *sweet* or *perfumed* gloves, were first brought into England by the Earl of Oxford, who came from Italy in the 14th or 15th year of Queen Elizabeth, during whose reign, and long afterwards, they were very fashionable.

They are frequently mentioned by Shakspeare. Autolycus in *The Winter's Tale*, has among his wares, "*Gloves as sweet as damask roses.*"

FIELDING'S "AMELIA."

Andrew Millar, the bookseller, gave Fielding a thousand pounds for his *Amelia;* but showing the MS. to Sir Andrew Mitchell, afterwards ambassador to Prussia, he was told that it was much inferior to *Tom Jones*, and advised to get rid of it as soon as he could. Millar soon thought of a stratagem by which he could at least push it off to the trade, if he could not make it popular. At a sale made to the booksellers previous to the publication, Millar offered his friends all his other publications on the usual terms of discount; but when he came to *Amelia*, he laid it aside as a work in such demand, that he could not afford to deliver it to the trade in the usual manner. The *ruse* succeeded; the impression, though very large, was anxiously bought up, and the bookseller relieved from every apprehension as to the popularity of Fielding's *Amelia*.

GRUB STREET.

"Grub Street," says Pennant, "has long been proverbial for the residence 'of authors of the less fortunate tribe, and the trite and illiberal jest of the more favoured.'" This character it seems to have obtained so far back as during the protectorate of Cromwell, when a great number of seditious pamphlets and papers, tending to exasperate the people against the existing government, were published. The authors of these writings were generally men of very indigent circumstances, who were compelled to live in a cheap or obscure part of the town. Grub Street then abounded with mean and old houses, which were let out in lodgings, at low rents, to persons of this description, whose occupation was publishing anonymously, what were then deemed libellous or treasonable works.

But it was here that honest John Foxe compiled the greatest portion of his *Martyrology;* and it is generally believed that John Speed wrote his *Chronicle,* and Daniel Defoe several of his publications, in the much-abused Grub Street.

SCHILLER'S NOBILITY.

Schiller, the German poet, had a patent of nobility conferred upon him by the Emperor of Germany, which he never used. Turning over a heap of papers one day, in the presence of a friend, he came to his patent, and showed it carelessly to his friend, with this observation, "*I suppose you did not know I was a noble;*" and then buried it again in the mass of miscellaneous papers in which it had long lain undisturbed. Schiller's friend might have answered, after this action, "If I did not before know you were noble, I know it now."

ADDISON.

The following curious particulars relating to this celebrated man deserve to be revived, and will be interesting to his admirers.

Budgell gives this account of a conversation between Lord Halifax and Addison, at which he himself was present: it happened a little before they went to wait on George the First at Greenwich, at his first landing after his accession to the throne. Lord Halifax told them that he expected the white staff, and intended to recommend Mr. Addison to the king for one of the secretaries of state. "Mr. Addison, I believe," says Budgell, "very sincerely told his lordship that he did not aim at so high a post, and desired him *to remember that he was not a speaker in the house.* Lord Halifax briskly replied, 'Come, prithee, Addison, no unseasonable modesty. I made thee secretary to the regency with this very view. Thou hast the best right, of any man in England, to be secretary of state; nay, it will be a sort of displacing thee not to make thee so. If thou couldst but get over that *silly sheepishness* of thine, that makes thee sit in the house and hear a fellow prate, for half an hour together, who has not a tenth part of thy good sense, I should be glad to see it; but since I believe that is impossible, we must contrive as well as we can. Thy pen has already been an honour to thy country, and will be a credit to thy king.'"

The well-known modesty of Addison is confirmed by this conversation; but Lord Halifax was too partial to his friend, when he supposed him endowed with the talents of a statesman.

CHEMICAL EXPERIMENTING.

M. Roulle, an eminent French chemist, was not the most cautious of operators. One day, while performing some experiments, he observed to his auditors, "Gentlemen, you see this cauldron upon this brazier; well, if I were to cease stirring a single moment, an explosion would ensue, which would blow us all into the air." The company had scarcely time to reflect on this comfortable piece of intelligence, before he did forget to stir, and his prediction was accomplished. The explosion took place with a horrible crash; and all the windows of the laboratory were smashed to pieces. Fortunately, no one received any serious injury, the greatest violence of the explosion having been in the direction of the chimney. The demonstrator escaped without further harm than the loss of his wig.

A professor of a northern university, who was as remarkable for his felicity in experimenting as Roulle could be for his failures, was once repeating an experiment with some combustible substances, when the mixture exploded, and the phial which he held in his hand blew into a hundred pieces. "Gentlemen," said the doctor to his pupils, with the most unaffected gravity, "I have made this experiment often with the very same phial, and never knew it break in my hands before!" The simplicity of this rather superfluous assurance produced a general laugh, in which the learned professor, instantly discerning the cause of it, joined most heartily.

PETER THE GREAT A SURGEON.

The czar, excited by natural curiosity, and his love for the sciences, took great pleasure in seeing dissections and chirurgical operations. It was Peter who first made these known in Russia, and he was so fond of them, that he gave orders to be informed whenever anything of the kind was going on in the hospitals, and he seldom failed to be present. He frequently lent his assistance, and had acquired sufficient skill to dissect according to the rules of art, to bleed, draw teeth, and perform other operations, as well as one of the faculty. It was an employment to which he was very partial, and besides his case of mathematical instruments which he always carried with him, he had a pouch well stocked with chirurgical instruments.

The czar once exercised his dexterity as a dentist in a very laughable manner on the wife of one of his *valets-de-chambre*, who wished to be revenged upon her for some supposed injuries. Perceiving the husband, whose name was Balboiarof, sitting in the ante-chamber with a sad and pensive countenance, the czar inquired the cause of his sorrow? "Nothing, sire," answered Balboiarof, "except that my wife refused to have a tooth drawn which gives her the most agonizing pain." "Let me speak to her," replied the czar, "and I warrant I'll cure her."

He was immediately conducted by the husband to the apartments of the supposed sick person, and made her sit down that he might examine her mouth, although she protested she had not the toothache. "Ah, this is the mischief," said her husband; "she always pretends not to suffer when we wish to give her ease, and renews her lamentations as soon as the surgeon is gone." "Well, well," said the czar, "she shall not suffer long. Do you hold her head and arms." Then taking out the instrument, he, in spite of her cries, extracted the tooth which he supposed to be the cause of her complaint, with admirable address.

Hearing, a few days after, that this was a trick of the husband to torture his wife, Peter chastised him severely with his own hands.

HUNTER AND CULLEN.

The celebrated Dr. William Hunter and Dr. Cullen, formed a copartnership of as singular and laudable a kind as is to be found in the annals of science. Being natives of the same part of the country, and neither of them in affluent circumstances, these two young men, stimulated by the impulse of genius, to prosecute their medical studies with ardour, but thwarted by the narrowness of their fortunes, entered into partnership as surgeons and apothecaries in the country. The chief object of their contract being to furnish each of the parties with the means of prosecuting their medical studies, which they could not separately so well enjoy, it was stipulated that one of them, alternately, should be allowed to study in what college he pleased during the winter, while the other should carry on the business in the country for their common advantage. In consequence of this agreement, Cullen was first allowed to study at the University of Edinburgh for one winter; but when it came to Hunter's turn next winter, he preferring London to Edinburgh, went thither. There his singular neatness in dissecting, and uncommon dexterity in making anatomical preparations, his assiduity in study, and amiable manners, soon recommended him to the notice of Dr. Douglas, who then read lectures upon anatomy in London. Hunter was engaged as an assistant, and afterwards filled the chair itself with honour.

The scientific partnership was by this means prematurely dissolved; but Cullen was not a man of that disposition to let any engagement with him prove a bar to his partner's advancement in life. The articles of the treaty were freely given up, and Cullen and Hunter ever after kept up a very cordial and friendly correspondence; though it is believed, they never, from that time, had a personal interview.

BOSWELL'S BEAR-LEADING.

It was on a visit to the parliament house that Mr. Henry Erskine (brother of Lord Buchan and Lord Erskine), after being presented to Dr. Johnson by Mr. Boswell, and having made his bow, slipped a shilling into Boswell's hand, whispering that it was for the sight of his *bear*.—(Sir Walter Scott.)

THE COMMON LOT OF THE ALCHYMISTS.

Fuller relates, that "one Thomas Charnoc, in pursuit of the philosopher's stone, which so many do *touch*, few *catch*, and none *keep*, met a very sad disaster. Once, when he was on the point of *completing* the grand operation, his work unhappily fell into the fire." "This," says Mr. D'Israeli, "is a misfortune which I observe has happened to all alchymists."

LORD BYRON'S "CORSAIR."

The Earl of Dudley, in his *Letters* (1818), says:—"To me Byron's *Corsair* appears the best of all his works. Rapidity of execution is no sort of apology for doing a thing ill, but when it is done well, the wonder is so much the greater. I am told he wrote this poem at ten sittings—certainly it did not take him more than three weeks."

LORD ELIBANK AND DR. JOHNSON.

Lord Elibank made a happy retort on Dr. Johnson's definition of oats, as the food of horses in England, and men in Scotland. "Yes," said he, "and where else will you see *such horses*, and *such men?*"—(Sir Walter Scott.)

A SNAIL DINNER.

The chemical philosophers, Dr. Black and Dr. Hutton, were particular friends, though there was something extremely opposite in their external appearance and manner. Dr. Black spoke with the English pronunciation, and with punctilious accuracy of expression, both in point of matter and manner. The geologist, Dr. Hutton, was the very reverse of this: his conversation was conducted in broad phrases, expressed with a broad Scotch accent, which often heightened the humour of what he said. It chanced that the two Doctors had held some discourse together upon the folly of abstaining from feeding on the testaceous creatures of the land, while those of the sea were considered as delicacies. Wherefore not eat snails? they are known to be nutritious and wholesome, and even sanative in some cases. The epicures of old praised them among the richest delicacies, and the Italians still esteem them. In short, it was determined that a gastronomic experiment should be made at the expense of the snails. The snails were procured, dieted for a time, and then stewed for the benefit of the two philosophers, who had either invited no guests to their banquet, or found none who relished in prospect the *pièce de resistance*. A huge dish of snails was placed before them: still, philosophers are but men, after all; and the stomachs of both doctors began to revolt against the experiment. Nevertheless, if they looked with disgust on the snails, they retained their awe for each other, so that each, conceiving the symptoms of internal revolt peculiar to himself, began, with infinite exertion, to swallow, in very small quantities, the mess which he internally loathed.

Dr. Black, at length, showed the white feather, but in a very delicate manner, as if to sound the opinion of his messmate. "Doctor," he said, in his precise and quiet manner— "Doctor—do you not think that they taste a little—a very little, green?" "Horribly green! horribly green! indeed—tak' them awa',—tak' them awa'!" vociferated Dr. Hutton, starting up from table, and giving full vent to his feelings of abhorrence. So ended all hopes of introducing snails into the modern *cuisine;* and thus philosophy can no more cure a nausea than honour can set a broken limb.—(Sir Walter Scott.)

DULL AUTHORS.

Marchand, commonly called Marchand du Maine, brother of Prosper Marchand of Amsterdam, said that he had been a whole winter by the side of the Duchess du Maine's bed, reading the first ten pages of a book. The moment he began to read she fell asleep, which he not immediately perceiving, proceeded; but the next day she always made him begin again. We are not told the name of this composing book. Its qualities, however, are by no means rare.

LETTER-WRITING.

"Sprightliness and wit," says a learned author, "are graceful in letters, just as they are in conversation; when they flow easily, and without being studied; when employed so as to season, not to cloy. One who, either in conversation or in letters, affects to shine and sparkle always, will not please long. The style of letters should not be too highly polished. All nicety about words betrays study, and hence, musical periods, and appearance of number and harmony in arrangement, should be carefully avoided in letters."

COWPER AND HIS CRITIC.

Cowper had sent a small poem to the publishers, when some friendly critic took the liberty to alter a line in the poem, to *make it smoother*, supposing, of course, he had made the line much better, *because it was smoother*, and that Cowper would be grateful for such a favour; but Cowper did not think "oily smoothness" the only merit of poetry, and so was quite indignant at the liberty taken with his poem.

"I did not write the line," says he, "that has been tampered with, hastily or without due attention to the construction of it; and what appeared to me its only merit is, in its present state, entirely annihilated.

"I know that the ears of modern verse-makers are delicate to an excess, and their readers are troubled with the same squeamishness as themselves; so that if a line does not run as smooth as quicksilver, they are offended. A critic of the present day serves a poem as a cook serves a dead turkey, when she fastens the legs of it to a post, and draws out all its sinews. For this we may thank Pope; but give me a manly, rough line, with a deal of meaning in it, rather than a whole poem of music periods, that have nothing but their oily smoothness to recommend them.

"In a much longer poem which I have just finished, there are many lines which an ear so nice as the gentleman's who made the above-mentioned alteration would undoubtedly condemn; and yet (if I may be allowed the expression) they cannot be made smoother without being made the worse for it. There is a roughness on a plum which nobody that understands fruit would rub off, though the plum would be much more polished without it. But lest I tire you, I will only add, that I wish you to guard me for the future from all such meddling, assuring you that I always write as smoothly as I can, but that I never did, never will, sacrifice the spirit or sense of a passage to the sound of it."

BUNYAN AND THE BOOK OF MARTYRS.

There is no book, except the Bible, which Bunyan is known to have perused so intently as the *Acts and Monuments* of John Foxe, the martyrologist, one of the best of men; a work more hastily than judiciously compiled, but invaluable for that greater and far more important portion which has obtained for it its popular name of the *Book of Martyrs*. Bunyan's own copy of this work is in existence, and valued, of course, as such a relic of such a man ought to be. It was purchased, in the year 1780, by Mr. Wantner, of the Minories; from him it descended to his daughter, Mrs. Parnell, of Botolph Lane; and it was afterwards purchased by subscription for the Bedfordshire General Library.

This edition of the *Acts and Monuments* is of the date 1641, three volumes folio, the last of those in the black letter, and probably the latest when it came into Bunyan's hands. In each volume he has written his name beneath the title-page, in a large and stout print-hand. Under some of the woodcuts he has inserted a few rhymes, which are undoubtedly his own composition; and which, though much in the manner of the verses that were printed under the illustrations of his own *Pilgrim's Progress*, are very much worse than even the worst of these. Indeed, it would not be possible to find specimens of more miserable doggerel.

Here is one of the Tinker's tetrastichs, penned in the margin, beside the account of Gardiner's death:—

"The blood, the blood that he did shed
Is falling one his one head;
And dreadfull it is for to see
The beginers of his misere."

One of the signatures bears the date of 1662; but the verses must undoubtedly have been some years earlier, before the publication of his first tract. These curious inscriptions must have been Bunyan's first attempts in verse. He had, no doubt, found difficulty enough in tinkering them to make him proud of his work when it was done, otherwise he would not have written them in a book which was the most valuable of all his goods and chattels. In later days, he seems to have taken this book for his art of poetry. His verses are something below the pitch of Sternhold and Hopkins. But if he learnt there to make bad verses, he entered fully into the spirit of its better parts, and received that spirit into as resolute a heart as ever beat in a martyr's bosom.—(Southey.)

EDWARD IRVING.

Mr. P. invited a party to supper. Some of his guests had three miles to walk home after the meal. But *before* its commencement, Mr. P. requested Irving, who was one of the party, to read the Bible and expound. He began and continued a discourse which manifested not even a tendency towards termination until midnight. The supper was, of course, either burnt up or grown cold. When the clock struck twelve, Mr. P. tremblingly and gently suggested to him that it might be desirable to draw to a close. "Who art *thou*," he replied with prophetic energy, "who darest to interrupt the man of God in the midst of his administrations?" He pursued his commentary for some time longer, then closed the book, and waving his long arm over the head of his host, uttered an audible and deliberate prayer that his offence might be forgiven.

WRITING HISTORY.

When Leti, the historian, was one day attending the levee of Charles the Second, he said to him, "Leti, I hear that you are writing the *History of the Court of England*." "Sir, I have been for some time preparing materials for such a history." "Take care that your work give no offence," said the prince. Leti replied, "Sir, I will do what I can; but if a man were as wise as Solomon, he would scarcely be able to avoid giving offence." "Why, then," rejoined the king, "be as wise as Solomon; write proverbs, not histories."

SIR JAMES MACKINTOSH'S HUMOUR.

Sir James Mackintosh had a great deal of humour; and, among many other examples of it, he kept a dinner-party at his own house for two or three hours in a roar of laughter, playing upon the simplicity of a Scotch cousin, who had mistaken the Rev. Sidney Smith for his gallant synonym, the hero of Acre.

HISTORICAL OMISSIONS.

In Goldsmith's *History of England* no mention is made of the great plague or the great fire of London.

BERZELIUS THE CHEMIST.

This devoted chemist continued to labour in the cause of science when the lower part of his body was paralyzed, and he was dying by inches. His death took place in 1848, in the 69th year of his age.

CRITICIZED POET.

An indifferent poet, who had been severely handled by the critics, yet continued to go on publishing his crudities, said one day to an acquaintance, that he had found out a way to be revenged of his reviewers, and that was by laughing at them. "Do you so?" said the other; "then let me tell you, you lead the merriest life of any man in Christendom."

CHRISTIANITY.

Sir Humphry Davy observes—"Of all the religions which have operated upon the human mind, Christianity alone has the consistent character of perfect truth; all its parts are arranged with the most beautiful symmetry; and its grand effects have been constantly connected with virtuous gratification, with moral and intellectual improvement, with the present and future happiness."

COLERIDGE'S "WATCHMAN."

Coleridge, among his many speculations, started a periodical, in prose and verse, entitled *The Watchman*, with the motto, "that all might know the truth, and that the truth might make us free." He watched in vain! Coleridge's incurable want of order and punctuality, and his philosophical theories, tired out and disgusted his readers, and the work was discontinued after the ninth number. Of the unsaleable nature of this publication, he related an amusing illustration. Happening one morning to rise at an earlier hour than usual, he observed his servant-girl putting an extravagant quantity of paper into the grate, in order to light the fire, when he mildly checked her for her wastefulness: "La! sir," replied Nanny; "why, it's only *Watchmen*."

FUSELI ON SMALL TALK.

Fuseli had a great dislike to common-place observations. After sitting perfectly silent for a long time in his own room, during " the bald, disjointed chat" of some idle callers-in, who were gabbling with one another about the weather, and other topics of as interesting a nature, he suddenly exclaimed, "We had pork for dinner to-day!" "Dear Mr. Fuseli, what an odd remark!" "Why, it is as good as anything you have been saying for the last hour."

SIR W. SCOTT—SIR H. DAVY—SPECKBACKER THE TYROLESE PATRIOT.

Speaking of Sir H. Davy, Sir Walter Scott, in his kind manner, mentioned to Mrs. Davy, wife of Dr. Davy, his brother's biographer, the following circumstance respecting Sir Humphry:—

"There was one very good thing about him, he never forgot a friend; and I'll tell you a thing he did to me that makes me particularly say so. When he was travelling in the Tyrol, the old patriot leader, Speckbacker, was very ill, suffering from rheumatism, or something of that sort: and when he heard there was a great philosopher in the neighbourhood, he thought of course he must be a doctor, and sent to beg some advice about his complaint. Sir Humphry did not profess to know much of medicine, but he gave him something, which luckily relieved his pain; and then the gratitude of the old chief made him feel quite unhappy because he refused to take any fee. So Sir Humphry said, 'Well, that you may not feel unhappy about not making me any return for my advice, I'll ask if you have any old pistol, or rusty bit of a sword, that was used in your Tyrolese war of defence, for I have a friend that would be delighted to have any such article; and you may depend on its being hung up in his hall, and the story of it told for many a year to come.' Speckbacker struck his hands together, much pleased with the request, and said, 'Oh, I have the very thing! you shall have the gun that I used myself when I shot thirty Bavarians in one day.' The illustrious gun was given accordingly to Sir Humphry, who brought it with him on his next visit, to Scotland, and deposited it with me, at Abbotsford, himself."

GRAY AND THE DUCHESS OF NORTHUMBERLAND.

Gray, the elegant author of the *Elegy in a Country Churchyard*, being in London, before his promotion to the chair of modern history in the University of Cambridge, and when his circumstances were so cramped that he could indulge himself in very few gratifications, went with a friend to a private sale of books, in which the lots were very large. Amongst the rest there was a very elegant bookcase, filled with a select collection of the French classics, handsomely bound, the price 100 guineas. Gray had a great longing for this lot, but could not afford to buy it. The conversation between him and his friend was overheard by the Duchess of Northumberland, who, knowing the other gentleman, took an opportunity to ask who his friend was. She was told it was the celebrated Gray. Upon their retiring, she bought the book-case and its contents, and sent it to Gray's lodgings, with a note, importing that she was ashamed of sending so small an acknowledgment for the infinite pleasure she had received in reading the *Elegy in a Country Churchyard* — of all others her favourite poem.

JAMES SMITH.

The following playful colloquy in verse took place at a dinner-table between Sir George Rose and James Smith, one of the authors of the *Rejected Addresses*, in allusion to Craven Street, Strand, where he resided:—

"J. S —' At the top of my street the
attorneys abound,
And down at the bottom the barges
are found:
Fly, Honesty, fly to some safer retreat,
For there's craft in the river, and
craft in the street.'"

"Sir G. R.—' Why should Honesty fly
to some safer retreat,
From attorneys and barges, od rot
'em ?
For the lawyers are *just* at the top of
the street,
And the barges are *just* at the bottom.'"

BISHOP HOUGH.

Doctor Hough, bishop of Worcester, who was as remarkable for the evenness of his temper as for many other qualities, having a good deal of company at his house, a gentleman present desired his lordship to show him a curious weather-glass, which the bishop had lately purchased, and which cost him above thirty guineas. The servant was accordingly desired to bring it, who, in delivering it to the gentleman, accidentally let it fall, and broke it to pieces. The company were all a little deranged by the accident.

"Be under no concern, my dear sir," says the bishop, smiling, "I think it is rather a lucky omen; we have hitherto had a dry season; and I hope we shall have some rain, for I protest I do not remember ever to have seen the glass so low."

STERNE REBUKED.

Sterne being in company with three or four clergymen, was relating a circumstance which happened to him at York.

After preaching at the cathedral, an old woman, whom he observed sitting on the pulpit stairs, stopped him as he came down, and begged to know where she should have the honour of hearing him preach the next Sunday. Mr. Sterne having mentioned the place where he was to exhibit, found her situated in the same manner on that day; when she put the same question to him as before.

The following Sunday he was to preach four miles out of York, which he told her; and to his great surprise, found her there too; and, that the same question was put to him as he descended from the pulpit. On which, adds he, I took for my text these words, expecting to find my old woman as before:—" I will grant the request of this poor widow; lest by her often coming, she weary me." One of the company immediately replied, "Why, Sterne, you omitted the most applicable part of the passage, which is, 'Though I neither fear God nor regard man.'" This unexpected retort silenced the wit for the whole evening.

INVITATION TO DINNER BY MOORE.

The following was one of the latest productions of the poet Moore, addressed to the Marquis of Lansdowne. It is full of those felicitous turns of expression in which the English Anacreon excels. It breathes the very spirit of classic festivity:—

"Some think we bards have nothing real—
  That poets live among the stars, so
Their very dinners are ideal,—
  (And heaven knows, too oft they are so:)
For instance, that we have, instead
  Of vulgar chops and stews, and hashes,
First course,—a phœnix at the head,
  Done in its own celestial ashes:
At foot, a cygnet, which kept singing
  All the time its neck was wringing.
Side dishes, thus,—Minerva's owl,
  Or any such like learned fowl.
Doves, such as heaven's poulterer gets
  When Cupid shoots his mother's pets.
Larks stew'd in morning's roseate breath,
Or roasted by a sunbeam's splendour;
And nightingales, be-rhymed to death—
  Like young pigs whipp'd to make them tender.
Such fare may suit those bards who're able
To banquet at Duke Humphrey's table;
But as for me, who've long been taught
  To eat and drink like other people,
And can put up with mutton, bought
  Where Bromham rears its ancient steeple;
If Lansdowne will consent to share
My humble feast, though rude the fare,
Yet, seasoned by that salt he brings
From Attica's salinest springs,
'Twill turn to dainties; while the cup,
Beneath his influence brightening up,
Like that of Baucis, touched by Jove,
  Will sparkle fit for gods above!"

LOCKE.

John Locke, having been introduced by Lord Shaftesbury to the Duke of Buckingham and Lord Halifax; these three noblemen, instead of conversing with the philosopher, as might naturally have been expected, on literary subjects, in a very short time sat down to cards. Mr. Locke, after looking on for some time, pulled out his pocket-book, and began to write with great attention. One of the company observing this, took the liberty of asking him what he was writing.

"My lord," says Locke, "I am endeavouring, as far as possible, to profit by my present situation; for having waited with impatience for the honour of being in company with the greatest geniuses of the age, I thought I could do nothing better than to write down your conversation; and, indeed, I have set down the substance of what you have said for this hour or two."

This well-timed ridicule had its desired effect; and these noblemen, fully sensible of its force, immediately quitted their play, and entered into a conversation more rational, and better suited to the dignity of their characters.

STAMMERING WIT.

Stammering (says Coleridge), is sometimes the cause of a pun. Some one was mentioning in Lamb's presence the cold-heartedness of the Duke of Cumberland, in restraining the duchess from rushing up to the embrace of her son, whom she had not seen for a considerable time, and insisting on her receiving him in state. "How horribly *cold* it was," said the narrator. "Yes," said Lamb, in his stuttering way; "but you know he is the Duke of *Cu-cum-ber-land.*"

MEDICINAL ANECDOTE.

A gentleman of narrow circumstances, whose health was on the decline, finding that an ingenious physician occasionally dropped into a coffee-house that he frequented, not very remote from Lincoln's-Inn, always placed himself *vis-à-vis* the doctor, in the same box, and made many indirect efforts to withdraw the doctor's attention from the newspaper to examine the index of his constitution. He at last ventured a bold push at once, in the following terms:—" Doctor," said he, " I have for a long time been very far from being well, and as I belong to an office, where I am obliged to attend every day, the complaints I have prove very troublesome to me, and I should be glad to remove them." The doctor laid down his paper, and regarded his patient with a steady eye, while he proceeded: "I have but little appetite, and digest what I eat very poorly; I have a strange swimming in my head," &c. In short, after giving the doctor a full quarter of an hour's detail of all his symptoms, he concluded the state of his case with a direct question: "Pray, doctor, what shall I take?" The doctor, in the act of resuming his newspaper, gave him the following laconic prescription : "Take, why, take advice!"

LORD BOLINGBROKE.

The famous Lord Bolingbroke being at Aix-la-Chapelle, during the treaty of peace at that place (at which time his attainder was not taken off), was asked by an impertinent Frenchman, Whether he came there in any public character? "No, sir," replied his lordship; "I come like a French minister, with no character at all."

BURN'S "JUSTICE."

Everybody has heard of the book entitled, Burn's *Justice of the Peace.* The author of that book, Mr. Burn, was a curate in one of the northern counties of England. When he had completed it, he set out for London to dispose of it in the best way he could. When he arrived there, being an entire stranger in town, he applied to the landlord of the inn where he stopped, a decent-looking, obliging sort of a man, to see if he could recommend him to any bookseller, who might be likely to purchase his manuscript. The landlord readily introduced him to a bookseller of his acquaintance, who upon having the matter explained to him, begged to look at the manuscript. The papers were put into his hands, which he returned in a few days, telling the disappointed author, that he could not venture to give more than twenty pounds for the book. This offer Burn could not think of accepting. He returned very melancholy to his lodging, sincerely repenting that he had ever put pen to paper on that subject.

By this time, Mr. Andrew Millar was well established in business, and his name had been several times mentioned with some degree of respect to Mr. Burn; so that he resolved to wait upon him, without any person to introduce him. He went, communicated his business in a few words, was politely received, and informed, that if he would trust the manuscript with him for a few days, he should be able to give him an answer; and in the meantime, as he was from home, he asked the author to dine with him each day, till they should conclude about the business. Mr. Millar, who did not depend upon his own judgment in cases of this sort, sent the manuscript to a young lawyer, with whom he usually advised in regard to law-books. The gentleman after reading the performance, returned it to Mr. Millar, and informed him, that if he could purchase the copyright for 200 pounds, he would certainly have a great bargain; for the book was extremely well written, and much wanted, so that the sale of it must be very considerable.

Mr. Millar having received this information, met the author the next day as usual, and then asked what price he demanded for his work? The author, dispirited with the former offer, said he was at a loss what to ask; for he had been already offered so small a price, that rather than accept of anything like it, he would throw the papers into the fire. What was this offer? said Mr. Millar. Only twenty pounds, said Mr. Burn, with great ingenuousness. But, said Mr. Millar, would you think 200 guineas too little? Too little! says Burn in surprise; No. Well then, said Mr. Millar, the book shall be mine, and you shall have the money when you please. The bargain was instantly struck, and a bottle of old port was drank to the good luck of it. Mr. Millar found no reason to repent of his frankness, for the book sold amazingly well; nor had the author any reason to be dissatisfied with his bargain, for Mr. Millar, with a spirit of candour and liberality that does not always belong to men of his profession, frankly sent 100 guineas to the author for every edition of the book that was printed in his life-time; and these were many: insomuch, that by the sale of this book alone, he cleared no less than £11,000.

CATO.

Cato being asked how it happened, that he had no statues erected to him, whilst Rome was crowded with those of so many others: "I would rather," answered he, "people should inquire why I have them not, than complain that I have."

EXCERPTS FROM DIARY OF THOMAS MOORE.

"Aug. 20, 1818.—Some tolerable stories told: mistakes in acts of Parliament — 'the new jail to be built from the materials of the old one, and the prisoners to remain in the latter till the former was ready' — a sentence of transportation of seven years, 'half to go to the king, and the other half to the informer;' it had been, of course, formerly a pecuniary punishment, and, upon its being altered, they overlooked the addition."

"Aug. 21, 1818.— Dined with Dr. Parr: himself, his wife, and a friend he called 'Jack,' a clergyman of £1000 a-year, who lives in his neighbourhood, very much devoted to him, and ready at a call to come and write letters for him, &c. &c.; his own hand being quite illegible (see what he says of it in preface to Fox's *Characters*). He was very cordial and animated; hob-nobbed with me across the table continually; told me he had written whole sheets of Greek verses against Big Ben (the Regent); showed them to me: the name he designated him by, I saw, was Φυσκων, inflated or puffy. Told me they were full of wit, which I took his word for, as they seemed rather puzzling Greek. Talked a good deal of Halhed, Sheridan's friend, and mentioned a curious interview which took place between them about the time of Hastings' business, by his (Parr's) intervention, in consequence of an attack made by Major Scott upon Fox in the house, charging him with having set on foot a negotiation with Mr. Hastings some years before. Fox, who knew nothing of the matter, had nothing to say in reply. Scott was present at this interview procured by Parr, and it appeared that the negotiation had been set on foot without the knowledge of Fox, and that Sheridan was the chief agent in it. An explanation was accordingly made next night in the house by Scott. Parr's account of the abuse he poured out upon Scott at that interview—'Hot scalding abuse; it was downright lava, sir.' Spoke of the poem of *Fracastorius* as very nearly equal to Virgil."

"Aug. 22, 1818.—A gentleman told a punning epigram of Jekyl's upon an old lady being brought forward as a witness to prove a tender made:—

Garrow, forbear! that tough old jade
Can never prove a tender maid."

"Aug. 29, 1818.—A good story in Mrs. Crouch's *Memoirs of Stephen Kemble*, who, sleeping at an inn in a country town, was waked about daybreak by a strange figure, a dwarf, standing by his bed in extraordinary attire. Kemble raised himself up in the bed, and questioned the figure, which said, 'I am a dwarf, as you perceive; I am come to exhibit at the fair to-morrow, and I have mistaken the bed-chamber: I suppose you are a giant come for the same purpose.'"

"Sept. 1, 1818.—Interrupted by Bowles, who never comes amiss; the mixture of talent and simplicity in him delightful. His parsonage-house at Bremhill is beautifully situated; but he has a good deal frittered away its beauty with grottoes, hermitages, and Shenstonian inscriptions: when company is coming he cries, 'Here John, run with the crucifix and missal to the hermitage, and set the fountain going.' His sheep-bells are tuned in thirds and fifths; but he is an excellent fellow notwithstanding; and, if the waters of his inspiration be not those of Helicon, they are at least very *sweet* waters, and to my taste pleasanter than some that are more strongly impregnated."

ROLINUS' SERMONS.

The story which is so pleasantly told by *Rabelais*, chap. vii. of Book III., and the answer of Pantagruel to Panurge, when he consults him on his intended marriage, are copied from a sermon of John Rolinus, doctor of Paris, and monk of Cluny, on widowhood. The passage appears to me singular enough to deserve translation. He tells us, that a certain widow having gone to ask the advice of her curé, whether she ought to marry again, told him she was without support, and that her servant, for whom she had taken a fancy, was industrious, and well acquainted with her husband's trade. The curé's answer was, that she ought to marry him. "And yet," said the widow, "I am afraid to do it; for when we marry, we run some risk of finding a master in our servants." "Well, then," said the curé, "don't take him." "But what shall I do?" said the widow. "I cannot support the labour of my husband's business without assistance." "Marry him, then," said the curé. "Very well," said the widow; "but if he turns out a worthless fellow, he may get hold of my property and spend it." "Then you need not take him," replied the curé. In this way the curé always coincided with the last opinion expressed by the widow; but seeing, at last, that her mind was really made up, and that she would marry the servant, he told her to take the advice of the bells of the church, and that they would counsel her best what to do. The bells rang, and the widow distinctly heard them say, "*Prends ton valet: Prends ton valet.*"* She accordingly returned and married him immediately. Some time afterwards, he drubbed her heartily, and she found, that, instead of being mistress, she had really become the servant. She returned to the curé, and cursed the moment when she had been credulous enough to act upon his advice. "Good woman," said the curé, "I am afraid you have not rightly understood what the bells said to you." He rang them again; and then the poor widow heard clearly,— "*Ne le prends pas: Ne le prends pas*" (Don't take him: Don't

* Take your servant: Take your servant.—This incident will probably remind our readers of Whittington.

take him); for the drubbing and bad treatment she had received had opened her eyes.—(Menage.)

NATIONAL CHARACTERISTICS.

Charles V. used to say, that the Portuguese appeared to be fools, and were so; that the Spaniards appeared wise, and were not so; that the Italians seemed to be wise, and were so; and that the French seemed fools, and were not so: That the Germans spoke like carters, the English like blockheads, the French like masters, and the Spaniards like kings. The Sicilians used to call him, Scipio Africanus; the Italians, David; the French, Hercules; the Turks, Julius Cæsar; the Africans, Hannibal; the Germans, Charlemagne; and the Spaniards, Alexander the Great.

SCARRON.

M. Scarron was one day attacked so violently by hiccup, that his friends were apprehensive for his life. When the violence of the attack was a little abated, "If I survive," said he, turning to his friends, "if I survive, I shall write a tremendous satire against the hiccup." His friends certainly expected some very different resolution.

M. D'USEZ—COMPLAISANCE.

M. d'Usez was gentleman of honour to the French queen. This princess one day asked him what o'clock it was. He replied, "Madam, any hour your majesty pleases."

THE JESUIT IN A STORM.

A Jesuit who had been particularly recommended to the captain of a vessel, was sailing from France to America. The captain, who saw that a storm was approaching, said to him, "Father, you are not accustomed to the rolling of a vessel, you had better get down as fast as possible into the hold. As long as you hear the sailors swearing and blaspheming, you may be assured that there are good hopes: but if you should hear them embracing and reconciling themselves to each other, you may make up your accounts with heaven." As the storm increased, the Jesuit, from time to time, despatched his companion to the hatchway to see how matters went upon deck. "Alas! father," said he, returning, "all is lost, the sailors are swearing like demoniacs; their very blasphemies are enough to sink the vessel." "Oh! heaven be praised," said the Jesuit, "then all's right."

CLASSICAL APPLICATION.

A person meeting another riding, with his wife behind him, applied to him Horace's line—" Post equitem sedet atra cura" (gloomy care sits behind the rider).

ORACLES.

A person who had some dangerous enemies, whom he believed capable of attempting anything, consulted the Oracle to know whether he should leave the country. The answer he obtained was, "*Domine, stes securus;*" a reply which led him to believe he might safely remain at home. Some days afterwards, his enemies set fire to his house, and it was with difficulty that he escaped with his life. Then recollecting the answer of the Oracle, he perceived, when too late, that the word was not *Domine,* but *Domi ne stes securus.*—(Menage.)

MARY DE MEDICIS.

Fabro Chigi, who was afterwards Pope, under the title of Alexander VII., while nuncio in France, was present at the death of Mary de Medicis. He asked her if she pardoned all her enemies, and particularly Cardinal Richelieu. She said she did from her heart. "Madame," said he, "as a mark of reconciliation, will you send him the

LOUIS XIV. AND SPINOLA.

Louis XIV., grave and dignified as he was, could not restrain the joy he felt on the birth of the Duke of Burgundy, on the 6th of August, 1682. He refused the attendance of his guards, and every one was allowed to address him. As all were admitted to the honour of kissing his hand, the Marquis Spinola, in the ardour of his zeal, bit his finger in doing so, and that so sharply, that the king was forced to call out. "I beg your majesty's pardon," said the marquis; "if I had not bit your finger, you would not have distinguished me from the crowd."

LONG SPEECHES AND GRAY HAIRS.

Louis XII. one day looking at himself in his mirror, was astonished to see a number of gray hairs on his head. "Ah!" said he, "these must be owing to the long speeches I have listened to; and it is those of M. le —— in particular, that have ruined my hair."

MARCO DE LODI.

Marco de Lodi having presented a sonnet of his own composition to Clement VII., the Pope found one of the lines in the first quatrain deficient in a syllable. "Do not let that disturb your Holiness," said the poet; "in the next you will probably find a syllable too much, which will balance the defect."

RACAN.

Racan was a man of talent, and frequently said good things; but his voice was weak, and he spoke rather indistinctly. One day in a numerous company, when he was present, the conversation turned on some subject which gave an opportunity of introducing an agreeable story. When he had finished, seeing that the company, who probably had not heard it, did not laugh, he turned to Menage, who was sitting near him, and said, "I see plainly that these gentlemen have not understood me—translate me, if you please, into the vulgar tongue."

JOHNSONIANA.

The following are extracts from Boswell's *Life*:—

When the dictionary was upon the eve of publication, Lord Chesterfield, who, it is said, had flattered himself with expectations that Johnson would dedicate the work to him, attempted, in a courtly manner, to soothe and insinuate himself with the sage, conscious, as it should seem, of the cold indifference with which he had treated its learned author; and further attempted to conciliate him, by writing two papers in *The World*, in recommendation of the work: and it must be confessed, that they contain some studied compliments, so finely turned, that, if there had been no previous offence, it is probable Johnson would have been highly delighted. Praise, in general, was pleasing to him; but, by praise from a man of rank and elegant accomplishments, he was peculiarly gratified.

This courtly device failed of its effect. Johnson, who thought that "all was false and hollow," despised the honeyed words, and was even indignant that Lord Chesterfield should, for a moment, imagine that he could be the dupe of such an artifice. His expression to Boswell concerning Lord Chesterfield, upon this occasion, was, "Sir, after making great professions, he had, for many years taken no notice of me; but when my dictionary was coming out, he fell a-scribbling in *The World* about it. Upon which I wrote him a letter, expressed in civil terms, but such as might show him that I did not mind what he said or wrote, and that I had done with him."

Dr. Johnson appeared to have had a remarkable delicacy with respect to the circulation of this letter; for Dr. Douglas, Bishop of Salisbury, informed Boswell, that, having many years ago pressed him to be allowed to read it to the second Lord Hardwicke, who was very desirous to hear it (promising at the same time that no copy of it should be taken), Johnson seemed much pleased that it had attracted the attention of a nobleman of such a respectable character; but, after pausing some time, declined to comply with the request, saying, with a smile, "No, sir, I have hurt the dog too much already;" or words to this purpose.

Dr. Adams expostulated with Johnson, and suggested that his not being admitted when he called on him, to which Johnson had alluded in his letter, was probably not to be imputed to Lord Chesterfield; for his Lordship had declared to Dodsley, that "he would have turned off the best servant he ever had, if he had known that he denied him to a man who would have been always more than welcome." And in confirmation of this, he insisted on Lord Chesterfield's general affability and easiness of access, especially to literary men. Johnson: "Sir, that is not Lord Chesterfield; he is the proudest man this day existing." Adams: "No, there is one person, at least, as proud; I think, by your own account, you are the prouder man of the two." Johnson: "But mine was *defensive* pride." This, as Dr. Adams well observed, was one of those happy turns for which he was so remarkably ready.

Johnson having now explicitly avowed his opinion of Lord Chesterfield, did not refrain from expressing himself concerning that nobleman with pointed freedom. "This man," said he, "I thought had been a lord among wits, but I find he is only a wit among lords!" And when his letters to his natural son were published, he observed, "They teach the morals of a whore, and the manners of a dancing-master."

In 1776, Boswell showed him, as a curiosity which he had discovered, his *Translation of Lobo's Account of Abyssinia* which Sir John Pringle had lent, it being then little known as one of his works. He said, "Take no notice of it," or, "don't talk of it." He seemed to think it beneath him, though done at six-and-twenty. Boswell said to him, "Your style, sir, is much improved since you translated this." He answered, with a sort of triumphant smile, "Sir, I hope it is."

Mr., afterwards Dr., Burney, during a visit to the capital, had an interview with him in Gough Square, where he dined and drank tea with him, and was introduced to the acquaintance of Mrs. Williams. After dinner, Dr. Johnson proposed to Mr. Burney to go up with him into his garret, which being accepted, he there found five or six Greek folios, a deal writing-desk, and a chair and a half. Johnson, giving to his guest the entire seat, tottered himself on one with only three legs and one arm. Here he gave Mr. Burney Mrs. Williams' history, and showed him some volumes of his Shakspeare already printed, to prove that he was in earnest. Upon Mr. Burney opening the first volume, at the *Merchant of Venice*, he observed to him, that he seemed to be more severe on Warburton than Theobald. Johnson: "O, poor Tib! he was ready knocked down to my hands; Warburton stands between me and him." Burney: "But, sir, you'll have Warburton upon your bones, won't you?" Johnson: "No, sir, he'll not come out; he'll only growl in his den." Burney: "But you think, sir, that

Warburton is a superior critic to Theobald?" Johnson: "O, sir, he'd make two-and-fifty Theobalds cut into slices. The worst of Warburton is, that he has a rage for saying something, when there's nothing to be said." Burney: "Have you seen the letters which Warburton has written in answer to a pamphlet addressed *To the Most Impudent Man alive?*" Johnson: "No, sir." Burney: "It is supposed to be written by Mallet." The controversy at this time raged between the friends of Pope and Bolingbroke; and Warburton and Mallet were the leaders of the several parties. Mr. Burney asked him then if he had seen Warburton's book against Bolingbroke's philosophy? Johnson: "No, sir, I have never read Bolingbroke's impiety, and therefore am not interested about its confutation."

Sir Thomas Robinson sitting with Johnson, said, that the King of Prussia valued himself upon three things:—upon being a hero, a musician, and an author. Johnson: "Pretty well, sir, for one man. As to his being an author, I have not looked at his poetry; but his prose is poor stuff: he writes just as you may suppose Voltaire's footboy to do, who had been his amanuensis. He has such parts as the valet might have, and about as much of the colouring of the style as might be got by transcribing his works." When Boswell was at Ferney, he repeated this to Voltaire, in order to reconcile him somewhat to Johnson, whom he, in affecting the English mode of expression, had previously characterized as "a superstitious dog;" but after hearing such a criticism on Frederick the Great, with whom he was then on bad terms, he exclaimed, "An honest fellow!"

Upon this contemptuous animadversion on the King of Prussia, Boswell observed to Johnson, "It would seem then, sir, that much less parts are necessary to make a king than to make an author; for the king of Prussia is confessedly the greatest king now in Europe, yet you think he makes a very poor figure as an author."

Of Burke he said, "It was commonly observed, he spoke too often in Parliament; but nobody could say he did not speak well, though too frequently, and too familiarly."

Talking of Tacitus, Boswell hazarded an opinion, that with all his merit for penetration, shrewdness of judgment, and terseness of expression, he was too compact, too much broken into hints, as it were, and therefore too difficult to be understood. Dr. Johnson sanctioned this opinion. "Tacitus, sir, seems to me rather to have made notes for a historical work, than to have written a history."

He said, "Burnet's *History of his own Times* is very entertaining: the style, indeed, is mere chit-chat. I do not believe that Burnet intentionally lied; but he was so much prejudiced, that he took no pains to find out the truth. He was like a man who resolves to regulate his time by a certain watch, but will not inquire whether the watch is right or not."

Goldsmith being mentioned—Johnson: "It is amazing how little Goldsmith knows: he seldom comes where he is not more ignorant than any one else." Sir Joshua Reynolds: "Yet there is no man whose company is more liked." Johnson: "To be sure, sir, when people find a man of the most distinguished abilities as a writer, their inferior while he is with them, it must be highly gratifying to them. What Goldsmith comically says of himself, is very true—he always gets the better when he argues alone; meaning, that he is master of a subject in his study, and can write well upon it; but when he comes into company, he grows confused, and unable to talk. Take him as a poet, his *Traveller* is a very fine performance; ay, and so is his *Deserted Village*, were it not sometimes too much the echo of his *Traveller*. Whether, indeed, we take him as a poet, as a comic writer, or as an historian, he stands in the first class." Boswell: "An historian! my dear sir, you will not surely rank his compilation of the *Roman History* with the works of other historians of this age?" Johnson: "Why, who are before him?" Boswell: "Hume, Robertson, Lord Lyttelton." Johnson: (His antipathy to the Scotch beginning to rise.) "I have not read Hume; but doubtless, Goldsmith's *History* is better than the *verbiage* of Robertson, or the foppery of Dalrymple." Boswell: "Will you not admit the superiority of Robertson, in whose history we find such penetration—such painting?" Johnson: "Sir, you must consider how that penetration and that painting are employed; it is not history, it is imagination. He who describes what he never saw, draws from fancy. Robertson paints minds, as Sir Joshua paints faces in a history piece; he imagines an heroic countenance. You must look upon Robertson's work as romance, and try it by that standard: history it is not."

Johnson praised John Bunyan highly. "His *Pilgrim's Progress* has great merit both for invention, imagination, and the conduct of the story; and it has had the best evidence of its merit, the general and continued approbation of mankind: few books, I believe, have had a more extensive sale. It is remarkable, that it begins very much like the poem of Dante; yet there was no translation of Dante when Bunyan wrote. There is reason to think that he had read Spenser."

He talked of Izaak Walton's *Lives*, which was one of his most favourite books. *Dr. Donne's Life*, he said, was the most perfect of them. He observed, that "it was wonderful that Walton, who was in a very low situation in life, should have been familiarly received by so many great men, and that at a time when the ranks of society were kept more separate than they are now."

Johnson praised the *Spectator*, particularly the character of Sir Roger de Coverley. He said, "Sir Roger did not die a violent death, as has generally been fancied: he was not killed; he died only because others were to die, and because his death afforded an opportunity to Addison of some very fine writing. We have the example of Cervantes making Don Quixote die. I never could see why Sir Roger is represented as a little cracked. It appears to me, that the story of the widow was intended to have something superinduced upon it; but the superstructure did not come."

Burton's *Anatomy of Melancholy*, he said, was the only book that ever took him out of bed two hours sooner than he wished to rise.

Goldsmith, to divert the tedious minutes, while waiting for one of the guests at a dinner-party, strutted about, bragging of his dress, and appeared seriously vain of it (for his mind was wonderfully prone to such expressions): "Come, come," said Garrick, "talk no more of that: you are, perhaps, the worst —eh, eh!" Goldsmith was eagerly attempting to interrupt him, when Garrick went on laughing ironically, "Nay, you will always *look* like a gentleman; but I am talking of being well or *ill dressed*."—"Well, let me tell you," said Goldsmith, "when my tailor brought home my blossom-coloured coat, he said, 'Sir, I have a favour to beg of you:— when anybody asks you who made your clothes, be pleased to mention

John Filby, at the Harrow, in Water Lane.'" Johnson: "Why, sir, that was because he knew the strange colour would attract crowds to gaze at it, and thus they might hear of him, and see how well he could make a coat even of so absurd a colour."

Johnson: "I remember once being with Goldsmith in Westminster Abbey. While we surveyed the Poets' Corner, I said to him, from Ovid,

Forsitan et nostrum nomen miscebitur istis.

When we got to Temple-bar, he stopped me, pointed to the heads upon it, and slily whispered me,

Forsitan et nostrum nomen miscebitur istis."

"At the Literary Club," says Boswell, "before Johnson came in, we talked of his *Journey to the Western Islands*, and of his coming away 'willing to believe the second sight,' which seemed to excite some ridicule. I was then so impressed with the truth of many of the stories which I had been told, that I avowed my conviction, saying, 'He is only *willing* to believe—I *do* believe; the evidence is enough for me, though not for his great mind. What will not fill a quart bottle will fill a pint bottle; I am filled with belief.'—'Are you?' said Colman; 'then cork it up.'"

Being by no means pleased with their inn at Bristol, Boswell said, "Let us see now how we should describe it." Johnson was ready with his raillery. "Describe it, sir? Why, it was so bad, that Boswell wished to be in Scotland!"

CLASSIFICATION OF NOVELS.

Novels may be arranged according to the botanical system of Linnæus.

Monandria Monogynia is the usual class, most novels having one hero and one heroine. *Sir Charles Grandison* belongs to the Monandria Digynia. Those in which the families of the two lovers are at variance may be called Diœcious. The Cryptogamia are very numerous, so are the Polygamia. Where the lady is in doubt which of her lovers to choose, the tale is to be classed under the Icosandria. Where the party hesitates between love and duty, or avarice and ambition, Didynamia. Many are poisonous, few of any use, and far the greater number are annuals.

ROMAN CALENDAR.

Most of those who are acquainted with the Roman manner of computation by Kalends, Ides, and Nones, are ignorant of the reason, which is this: The ancient Romans at first regulated their months according to the course of the moon, and having observed that it presented three remarkable varieties every month,—the first when it is concealed in conjunction with the sun; the second, when it begins to be seen at setting; the third, when opposite to the sun, it is seen fully illuminated by his rays,—they called the first day of the month the *Kalends*, from the Latin word *Celare*, because for this day the planet was concealed; or, according to Juba, from the Greek word *Kalein*, because they then assembled the people to announce that the *Nones*, that is, the fair or market, would take place on the fifth day after. The day when the moon, beginning to re-appear, was in its first quarter, they called the *Nones*, from the Greek *Neos*, and the day when it appeared full, the *Ides*, from the word *Eidos, face*, because it was then in its beauty, and showed its entire face. From the *Ides*, till the end of the month, they reckoned 14, 13, 12, &c., before the *Kalends* of the following month; and from the first day of that month till the *Nones*, the 2d, 3d, 4th, &c., after the Kalends.

AN EXTEMPORE DISCOURSE.

A young preacher of a prepossessing appearance, and an agreeable voice and manner, having mounted the pulpit, was suddenly seized with loss of memory, and completely forgot his sermon. To have come down again would have been disgraceful. If he tried to preach, he had nothing to say. What was to be done in this extremity? He resolved to stand firm and to make the most of his voice and gestures, without using any but imperfect or unconnected expressions, such as, in fact, but, if, and again, to conclude, and so on. Never did a preacher appear to possess such fire. He bellowed, he uttered pathetic exclamations, he clapped his hands, he stamped with his feet. Everything shook about him, the very vault of the church echoed with his vehemence. The audience remained in profound silence; every one put forward his head, and redoubled his attention, to understand what was perfectly unintelligible. Those who were near the pulpit said, we are too near, we can hear nothing. Those who were farther off, regretted the distance at which they sat, thinking they were losing the finest things in the world. In short, the preacher kept his audience on the stretch for three quarters of an hour; and retired with the applause of the whole audience, each of whom determined next time to choose his seat better, in order not to lose the fruits of such a discourse.—(Melange d'Hist. et de Lit.)

HOW TO TURN THE BRAIN.

Nothing is so likely to turn the brain as intense application directed to one of six things—the quadrature of the circle; the multiplication of the cube; the perpetual motion; the philosopher's stone; judicial astrology; and magic. In youth, we may exercise our imagination upon them, in order to convince ourselves of their impossibility; but it argues a want of judgment to occupy ourselves with such inquiries at a more advanced age. "Nevertheless," says Fontenelle, "the search has its advantages, for we find many things on the way that we never looked for."

JULIUS SCALIGER.

Julius Scaliger used to say, that he was ignorant of three things; of the cause of the interval which takes place between the paroxysms of fever; how an idea, once forgotten, may be recalled to the memory; and the cause of the flux and reflux of the sea. Alas! of how many things was he ignorant of which he says nothing.

SOCIETY OF PORT-ROYAL.

The society of Port-Royal des Champs was so called from a valley near Chartreuse, about six leagues from Paris. In 1637, the celebrated advocate, Le Maitre, abandoned the bar, and resigned his office of Councillor of State, which his extraordinary merit had procured him at the age of twenty-eight. His brother, de Sericourt, who had followed the profession of arms, quitted it at the same time. Both resolved henceforth to dedicate themselves to God, and retired to a small mansion near Port-Royal de Paris. Their brothers De Sacy, De St. Elmi, and De Valmont joined them. After the arrest of the Abbe de St. Cyrian, which took place in 1638, Francis de Sondy, Archbishop of Paris, intimated to them by order of the court, that they must leave their house. They did so the next day, and went to reside at Port-Royal des Champs, where they had not remained more than two months, when they were again dislodged by order of the court. Thirteen months afterwards, however, they were allowed to return. Several persons of distinguished merit joined these hermits, and from these the Society, which afterwards received the title of Port-Royal, was formed. Among its members were the celebrated Arnauld, M. de Suylin, M. de Sacy, Arnaud d'Andilly, de Luzancy, De Pomponne, De Beauropaire, Ste Marthe, Nicole, and Lancelot, who afterwards turned Benedictine.

The Society had no rules, no vows, no constitution, no cells, nor anything of the kind. They employed themselves assiduously in prayer and study, and in the instruction of youth in the sciences and the practice of virtue. Racine was educated there, and requested to be buried in the cemetery of Port-Royal, at the feet of his old master M. Hamon.—(Matanasiana.)

GREGORY VII.

We find, in Machiavel and Cardan, that Pope Gregory VII. caused most of the valuable works of the ancients to be burned. It was this Pope who burned the works of the learned Varro, to prevent St. Augustin from being accused of plagiarism, the saint having stolen from him the greater part of his *Treatise de Civitate Dei.*

AN ARACHNOID GARMENT.

Chapelain, the author of the *Pucelle*, was called by the academicians the Knight of the Order of the Spider, because he wore a coat so patched and pieced, that the stitches exhibited no bad resemblance of the fibres produced by that insect. Being one day present at a large party given by the great Condé, a spider of uncommon size fell from the ceiling upon the floor. The company thought it could not have come from the roof, and all the ladies at once agreed that it must have proceeded from Chapelain's wig; the wig so celebrated by the well-known parody. He was so avaricious, that though he had an income of 13,000 livres, and more than 240,000 in ready money, he used to wipe his hands on a handful of rushes, in order to save towels. His avarice was the cause of his death; he preferred crossing the street, while inundated with water, to paying a liard for the use of a plank which was laid across. He caught a cold and oppression of breathing, of which he died.—(Charpentier.)

TALMUD.

The *Talmud* has been composed by certain Jewish doctors of the kingdom of Pontus, who had been summoned for that purpose by their own nation, in order that they might have something to oppose to the Christians. These doctors were descendants of the ten tribes of Israel, who were carried into captivity from Samaria by King Psalmanazar, the father of Sennacherib, in the time of Hosea. The "Talmud" was valued at 100 livres during the time of Joseph Scaliger. This book is a mixture of Syriac, Hebrew, and the Vulgar Hebrew, which was the language of the school of the Rabbis, and which differs as much from the other as the Latin of Bartolus from that of Cicero.

GASSENDI, SIR MATTHEW HALE, AND OTHERS.

Gassendi was accustomed to read, throughout the greater part of the night, by the lamp in the parish church, his parents being too poor to supply him with candles.

Sir Matthew Hale relates, with regard to himself, that he laboured for sixteen hours in the day during the first two years that he spent in the Inns of Court.

William Prynne was exceedingly diligent; he read or wrote about sixteen hours in the day. To prevent loss of time, he caused his food to be laid on a table in his study; and when he was hungry, he made a scanty meal.

Descartes frequently studied fifteen hours in the day.

M. de Buffon studied twelve or fourteen hours.

Joseph Scaliger was so exceedingly fond of intellectual engagements, that he would sometimes remain in his study for two or three days without food.

John Knox evinced a high opinion of the value of learning, when he said to Queen Mary of Scotland, in his blunt phraseology, "I am here now; yet I cannot tell what other men shall judge of me, that, at this time of day, I am absent from my book, and waiting at court."

Carneades was so enamoured with the pursuits of knowledge, that he scarcely allowed himself time to pare his nails or comb his hair.

Budæus and Turnebus spent their wedding-days in the study.

THE DUTCH.

The Dutch may be compared to their own turf, which kindles and burns slowly, but which, when once kindled, retains its fire to the last.

ENGLISH AND GERMAN.

An English lady resident at Coblentz, one day wishing to order of her German servant (who did not understand English) a boiled fowl for dinner, Grettel was summoned, and the experiment began. It was one of the lady's fancies, that the less her words resembled her native tongue, the more they must be like German. So her first attempt was to tell the maid that she wanted a *cheeking*, or *keeking*. The maid opened her eyes and mouth, and shook her head. "It's to cook," said the mistress, "to cook, to put in an iron thing, in a pit—pat—pot." "Ish understand risht," said the maid, in her Coblentz *patois*. "It's a thing to eat," said her mistress, "for dinner—for deener—with sauce, soace—sowose. What on earth am I to do?" exclaimed the lady in despair, but still making another attempt. "It's a little creature—a bird—a bard—a beard—a hen—a hone—a fowl—a fool; it's all covered with feathers—fathers—feeders!" "Ha, ha!" cried the delighted German, at last getting hold of a catchword, "Ja, ja! fedders—ja woh!" and away went Grettel, and in half an hour returned triumphantly, with a bundle of stationers' quills.

An Englishman talking with a German friend, a man of a remarkably philosophical cast of mind, and fond of clothing his sentiments in the graces of classical allusion, the discourse happened to turn upon the mortifications to which those subject themselves who seek after the vanities of this world. Our friend was for a stoical independence, and had Diogenes in his eye. "For mine self," he exclaimed, with rising enthusiasm, "I should be quite contentment for to live all my days in a dub, eating nothing else but unicorns!" (acorns.)

MENAGE.

The Queen of Sweden (Christina) said of him, after he published his work on the *Origin of the French Language*, "Menage is undoubtedly a very learned and excellent person, but he is very unaccommodating; he will never allow a word to pass without its passport: he must always know whence it comes, and where it is going."

WHAT SHOULD BE DONE AT ONCE.

Shutting one's self up in a convent, marrying, and throwing one's self over a precipice, are three things which must be done without thinking too much about them.

KING EDWARD VI.

Though considerable talents and attainments have not always been associated with eminent stations, a goodly number of the great are to be found in the list of those who have been richly endowed by their Creator, and have diligently improved his gifts. The young King Edward VI. stands among the most prominent of these examples.

This amiable prince was born in 1537, at Hampton Court. His mother was Jane Seymour, the third wife of Henry VIII. At the early age of six years, he was committed to the care of Sir Anthony Cook, and other learned preceptors, who were intent on his improvement in spiritual knowledge, as well as in science and learning. The manner in which these gentlemen performed their duties, and in which the prince improved, may be ascertained from an account written by William Thomas, a learned man, who was afterwards clerk of the council. He says—

"If ye knew the towardness of that young prince, your hearts would melt to hear him named, and your stomach abhor the malice of them that would him ill. The beautifulest creature that liveth under the sun, the wittiest, the most amiable, and the gentlest thing of all the world. Such a capacity in learning the things taught him by his schoolmaster, that it is a wonder to hearsay. And, finally, he hath such a grace of posture, and gesture in gravity, when he comes into a presence, that it should seem he were already a father, and yet passes he not the age of ten years. A thing, undoubtedly, much rather to be seen than believed."

In his ninth year he wrote letters in Latin and French; and in the British Museum are themes and orations in Latin, which he then composed. Curio, the Italian reformer, told his tutors, "that by their united prayers, counsels, and industry, they had formed a king of the highest, even divine hopes."

His ardent attachment and reverence to the Holy Scriptures are well known; and Foxe tells us that "he was not wanting in diligence to receive whatever his instructors would teach him. So that, in the midst of all his play and recreation, he would always keep the hours appointed to study, using the same with much attention, till time called him again from his book to pastime.

"In this, his study and keeping of his hours, he so profited, that Cranmer, beholding his towardness, his readiness in both tongues, in translating from Greek to Latin, from Latin to Greek again, in declaiming with his schoolfellows, without help of his teachers, and that extempore, wept for joy, declaring to Dr. Cox, his schoolmaster, that he would never have thought it to have been in the prince, except he had seen it himself."

He became acquainted with seven languages, and well understood logic and theology.

PRECOCITY OF GUIZOT.

Guizot, the distinguished French statesman and historian, gave early promise of his great talents. He is called by a French writer "a child who had no childhood." When only seven years of age, young Guizot was placed at the gymnasium of Geneva, and devoted his whole soul to study. His first and only playthings were books; and at the end of four years the scholar was able to read, in their respective languages, the works of Thucydides and Demosthenes, of Cicero and Tacitus, of Dante and Alfieri, of Schiller and Goethe, of Gibbon and Shakspeare. His last two years at college were especially consecrated to historical and philosophical studies. Philosophy, in particular, had powerful attractions for the young man. His mind, endowed by nature with a remarkable degree of logical strength, was just the one to unfold and ripen in the little Genevan republic, which has presented something of the learned and inflexible physiognomy of its patron John Calvin.

ROBERT HALL.

Rev. Robert Hall, when a boy about six years of age, was sent to a boarding-school, where he spent the week, coming home on Saturday and returning on Monday. When he went away on Monday morning he would take with him two or three books from his father's library, to read at the intervals between school-hours. The books he selected were not those of mere amusement, but such as required deep and serious thought. Before he was nine years old, he had read over and over again, with the deepest interest, Edwards *on the Affections* Edwards *on the Will*, and Butler's *Analogy*.

THE DOCTORS MATHER, OF BOSTON.

Dr. Cotton Mather, who died in Boston, in 1728, was a man of unequalled industry, vast learning, and most disinterested benevolence. No person in America had at that time so large a library, or had read so many books, or had retained so much of what they had read. It was his custom to read fifteen chapters in the Bible every day. He wrote over his study-door, in capital letters, "BE SHORT." In one year he kept sixty fasts and twenty vigils, and published fourteen books. His publications amounted in all to 382, some of them being of huge dimensions. His *Magnalia* was the largest; it consisted of seven folio volumes. His *Essays to do Good* are read with pleasure and profit even now. He lived to the age of sixty-five years.

His father, Dr. Increase Mather, was also a man of great industry and erudition for the age in which he lived, and but little behind the son in point of mental activity and usefulness. He is said to have spent sixteen hours a-day in his study; and his sermons and other publications were very numerous. In a volume entitled, *Remarkables of the Life of Dr. Increase Mather,* is a catalogue of no less than eighty-five of his publications, not including many learned and useful prefaces written for other books. He died in his eighty-fifth year, having been a preacher sixty-six years.

QUEEN ELIZABETH'S MANUSCRIPTS.

In 1825, the son of Mr. Lemon, the keeper of the state-papers, discovered, on examining some of the papers of the reign of Elizabeth, a paper in the handwriting of the queen, and marked "The Third Booke." Conceiving this to belong to something of importance, he placed it carefully aside, and, by a diligent search, at length obtained the papers of four other books, which proved to be an entire translation of Boëthius *de Consolatione Philosophiæ*. In Walpole's *Royal and Noble Authors*, it is mentioned that Queen Elizabeth had translated this work; but no vestige of it was known to exist. Nearly the whole of the work is in her majesty's own handwriting; but there are parts evidently written by her private secretary, and by the secretary of state at the time. All the difficult passages and all the poetical portions are in the queen's own hand, and it is not a little curious, that in the translation of the latter she had imitated all the variety of metre which is found in the work. It is therefore a literal, rather than a poetical translation. There are letters also discovered which identify this translation to have been made by the queen, and it is to be hoped that the public will yet be gratified with the publication of this literary curiosity. From a document accompanying this translation, it appears that her majesty composed the work at Windsor, during five weeks of the winter season; and from a courtly computation made by the queen's secretary, we collect the information, that less than twenty-four hours of labour were actually bestowed upon this manuscript of many pages.

SHELLEY'S LIBRARY.

Shelley's library was a very limited one. He used to say that a good library consisted not of many books, but a few chosen ones; and being asked what he considered such, he said, "I'll give you my list—catalogue it can't be called: the Greek Plays, Plato, Lord Bacon's Works, Shakspeare, the Old Dramatists, Milton, Goethe, Schiller, Dante, Petrarch and Boccaccio, Machiavelli and Guicciardini,—not forgetting Calderon; and last, yet first, the Bible." It is not meant that this was all his collection. He had read few English works of the day; scarcely a novel except Walter Scott's, for whose genius he had sovereign respect; Anastasius, by which he thought Lord Byron profited in his *Don Juan*; and the *Promissi Sposi*. In speaking of *Hope* and *Manzoni*, he said, "that one good novel was enough for any man to write, and he thought both judicious in not risking their fame by a second attempt."

THE SCHOOLMASTER ABROAD.

A modern writer, in a sketch of Lord Brougham, gives the origin of this popular phrase:—

" No orator of our times is more successful in embalming phrases full of meaning, in the popular memory. The well-known talismanic sentiment, 'The schoolmaster is abroad,' is an instance. In a speech on the elevation of Wellington, a mere 'military chieftain,' to the premiership, after the death of Canning, Brougham said, 'Field-marshal the Duke of Wellington may take the army—he may take the navy—he may take the great seal—he may take the mitre. I make him a present of them all. Let him come on with his whole force, sword in hand, against the constitution, and the English people will not only beat him back, but laugh at his assaults. In other times the country may have heard with dismay that 'the soldier was abroad.' It will not be so now. Let the soldier be abroad if he will; he can do nothing in this age. There is another personage abroad—a personage less imposing —in the eyes of some, perhaps, insignificant. *The schoolmaster is abroad;* and I trust to him, armed with his primer, against the soldier in full military array.'"

POSTSCRIPTS TO LADIES' LETTERS.

George Selwyn once affirmed in company, that no woman ever wrote a letter without a postscript. "My next letter shall refute you," said Lady G. Selwyn soon after received a letter from her ladyship, when, after her signature, stood " P. S. Who is right now, you or I ?"

WILKINS AND THE DUCHESS'S VOYAGE TO THE MOON.

Dr. John Wilkins, a man of uncommon parts and abilities, in the reign of Charles II., has been laughed at, together with his chimeras; but even these proclaim themselves the chimeras of a man of genius.

Such was his attempt to show the possibility of a voyage to the moon. In a conversation with the Duchess of Newcastle, her grace asked him, "Doctor, where am I to find a place for baiting at, in the way up to that planet?" "Madam," said he, "of all the people in the world, I never expected that question from you, who have built so many castles in the air, that you might lie every night at one of your own."

LE CLERC.

Some person observed to this acute and profound scholar, "I think '*De mortuis nil nisi bonum*' is a good saying." "'*De mortuis nil nisi verum.*'" said Le Clerc, "is a better." "Why so?" "Because truth can do no harm to the dead, and may do great good to the living."

BURKE AND LONSDALE'S NINEPINS.

The Earl of Lonsdale was so extensive a proprietor, and patron of boroughs, that he returned nine members every Parliament, who were facetiously called Lord Lonsdale's ninepins. One of the members thus designated, having made a very extravagant speech in the House of Commons, was answered by Mr. Burke, in a vein of the happiest sarcasm, which elicited from the house loud and continued cheers. Mr. Fox entering the house just as Mr. Burke was sitting down, inquired of Sheridan what the house was cheering. "O, nothing of consequence," replied Sheridan, "only Burke has knocked down one of Lord Lonsdale's ninepins."

LORD DERBY.

Lord Stanley (now Lord Derby), once alluded to Lord Brougham as "the noble lord who had just taken his seat;" but chancing to look round, and seeing the ex-chancellor jumping about like a cricket, begged pardon, and said he meant his noble friend who "never took his seat."

OLD LONDON RECOLLECTIONS—HOGARTH'S "APPRENTICES."

For the following genial and lively sketch, we are indebted to Mr. Thackeray's *Lectures on the English Humourists*. Its relish will be heightened to such readers as enjoyed the privilege of hearing the author deliver the lecture of which it forms a part.

"Fair-haired Frank Goodchild smiles at his work, whilst naughty Tom Idle snores over his loom. Frank reads the edifying ballads of Whittington and the London 'Prentice. Whilst that reprobate Tom Idle prefers *Moll Flanders*, and drinks hugely of beer, Frank goes to church of a Sunday, and warbles hymns from the gallery; while Tom lies on a tomb-stone outside playing at halfpenny-under-the-hat, with street blackguards, and deservedly caned by the beadle. Frank is made overseer of the business, whilst Tom is sent to sea. Frank is taken into partnership, and marries his master's daughter, sends out broken victuals to the poor, and listens in his night-cap and gown with the lovely Mrs. Goodchild by his side, to the nuptial music of the city bands and the marrow-bones and cleavers; whilst idle Tom, returned from sea, shudders in a garret lest the officers are coming to take him for picking pockets. The Worshipful Francis Goodchild, Esq., becomes Sheriff of London, and partakes of the most splendid dinners which money can purchase or alderman devour; whilst poor Tom is taken up in a night cellar, with that one-eyed and disreputable accomplice who first taught him to play chuck-farthing on a Sunday. What happens next? Tom is brought up before the justice of his country, in the person of Mr. Alderman Goodchild, who weeps as he recognizes his old brother 'prentice, as Tom's one-eyed friend peaches on him, as the clerk makes out the poor rogue's ticket for Newgate. Then the end comes. Tom goes to Tyburn in a cart with a coffin in it; whilst the Right Honourable Francis Goodchild, Lord Mayor of London, proceeds to his Mansion House, in his gilt coach, with four footmen and a sword-bearer, whilst the companies of London march in the august procession, whilst the train-bands of the city fire their pieces and get drunk in his honour; and oh, crowning delight and glory of all, whilst his majesty the king looks out from his royal balcony, with his ribbon on his breast, and his queen and his star by his side, at the corner house of St. Paul's Church-yard, where the toy-shop is now.

"How the times have changed! The new Post-office now not disadvantageously occupies that spot where the scaffolding is on the picture, where the tipsy trainband-man is lurching against the post, with his wig over one eye, and the 'prentice-boy is trying to kiss the pretty girl in the gallery. Past away 'prentice-boy and pretty girl! Past away tipsy trainband-man with wig and bandolier! On the spot where Tom Idle (for whom I have an unaffected pity) made his exit from this wicked world, and where you see the hangman smoking his pipe, as he reclines on the gibbet, and views the hills of Harrow or Hampstead beyond—a splendid marble arch, a vast and modern city—clean, airy, painted drab, populous with nursery-maids and children, the abodes of wealth and comfort—the elegant, the prosperous, the polite Tyburnia rises, the most respectable district in the habitable globe!

"In that last plate of the *London Apprentices*, in which the apotheosis of the Right Honourable Francis Goodchild is drawn, a ragged fellow is represented in the corner of the simple, kindly piece, offering for sale a broadside, purporting to contain an account of the appearance of the ghost of Tom Idle, executed at Tyburn. Could Tom's ghost have made its appearance in 1847, and not in 1747, what changes would have been remarked by that astonished escaped criminal! Over that road which the hangman used to travel constantly, and the Oxford stage twice a-week, go ten thousand carriages every day; over yonder road, by which Dick Turpin fled to Windsor, and Squire Western journeyed into town, when he came to take up his quarters at the Hercules Pillars on the outskirts of London, what a rush of civilization and order flows now! What armies of gentlemen with umbrellas march to banks, and chambers, and counting-houses! What regiments of nursery-maids and pretty infantry: what peaceful processions of policemen, what light broughams and what gay carriages, what swarms of busy apprentices and artificers, riding on omnibus-roofs, pass daily and hourly! Tom Idle's times are quite changed; many of the institutions gone into disuse which were admired in his day. There's more pity and kindness, and a better chance for poor Tom's successors now than at that simpler period, when Fielding hanged him, and Hogarth drew him."

STERNE'S MAUDLIN SENSIBILITY.

"Sterne (says Mr. Thackeray) used to blubber perpetually in his study, and finding his tears infectious, and that they brought him a great popularity, he exercised the lucrative gift of weeping, he utilized it, and cried on every occasion. I own that I don't value or respect much the cheap dribble of those fountains. He fatigues me with his perpetual disquiet, and his uneasy appeals to my risible or sentimental faculties. He is always looking in my face, watching his effect, uncertain whether I think him an impostor or not; posture-making, coaxing, and imploring me. 'See what sensibility I have—own now that I'm very clever—do cry now, you can't resist this.' The humour of Swift and Rabelais, whom he pretended to succeed, poured from them as naturally as song does from a bird; they lose no manly dignity with it, but laugh their hearty great laugh out of their broad chests as nature bade them. But this man —who can make you laugh, who can make you cry, too—never lets his reader alone, or will permit his audience repose; when you are quiet, he fancies he must rouse you, and turns over head and heels, or sidles up, and whispers a nasty story. The man is a great jester, not a great humourist. He goes to work systematically and of cold blood; paints his face, puts on his ruff and motley clothes, and lays down his carpet and tumbles on it."

GOLDSMITH'S PLAYFULNESS.

The younger Colman relates the following anecdote of Goldsmith's playfulness with children:—

"I was only five years old," he says, "when Goldsmith took me on his knee one evening whilst he was drinking coffee with my father, and began to play with me, which amiable act I returned, with the ingratitude of a peevish brat, by giving him a very smart slap on the face; it must have been a tingler, for it left the marks of my spiteful paw on his cheek. This infantile outrage was followed by summary justice, and I was locked up by my indignant father in an adjoining room to undergo solitary imprisonment in the dark. Here I began to howl and scream most abominably, which was no bad step towards my liberation, since those who were not inclined to pity me might be likely to set me free for the purpose of abating a nuisance.

"At length a generous friend appeared to extricate me from jeopardy, and that generous friend was no other than the man I had so wantonly molested by assault and battery — it was the tender-hearted Doctor himself, with a lighted candle in his hand, and a smile upon his countenance, which was still partially red from the effects of my petulance. I skulked and sobbed as he fondled and soothed, till I began to brighten. Goldsmith seized the propitious moment of returning good-humour, when he put down the candle, and began to conjure. He placed three hats, which happened to be in the room, and a shilling under each. The shillings he told me were England, France, and Spain. 'Hey presto cockalorum!' cried the Doctor, and lo, on uncovering the shillings, which had been dispersed each beneath a separate hat, they were all found congregated under one. I was no politician at five years old, and therefore might not have wondered at the sudden revolution which brought England, France, and Spain all under one crown: but, as also I was no conjuror, it amazed me beyond measure. . . . From that time, whenever the Doctor came to visit my father, 'I plucked his gown to share the good man's smile:' a game at romps constantly ensued, and we were always cordial friends and merry playfellows. Our unequal companionship varied somewhat as to sports as I grew older; but it did not last long; my senior playmate died in his forty-fifth year, when I had attained my eleventh. . . . In all the numerous accounts of his virtues and foibles, his genius and absurdities, his knowledge of nature and ignorance of the world, his 'compassion for another's woe' was always predominant; and my trivial story of his humouring a froward child weighs but as a feather in the recorded scale of his benevolence."

STERNE'S DEATH.

There is one passage in Sterne which the circumstances of his death render pathetic. A believer in the doctrine of presentiment would think it a prop to his theory. It is as striking as Swift's digression on madness, in the *Tale of a Tub*. "Was I in a condition to stipulate with death, I should certainly declare against submitting to it before my friends; and, therefore, I never seriously think upon the mode and manner of this great catastrophe, which generally takes up and torments my thoughts as much as the catastrophe itself; but I constantly draw the curtain across it with this wish, that the Disposer of all things may so order it, that it happen not to me in my own house—but rather in some decent inn. At home—I know it—the concern of my friends, and the last services of wiping my brows and smoothing my pillow, will so crucify my soul, that I shall die of a distemper which my physician is not aware of; but in an inn, the few cold offices I wanted would be purchased with a few guineas, and paid me with an undisturbed but punctual attention." It is known that Sterne died in hired lodgings, and I have been told that his attendants robbed him even of his gold sleeve-buttons while he was expiring.—(Ferriar's Illust.)

DAVID HUME.

Lord Charlemont relates the following anecdote of Hume, illustrating his generous appreciation of the talent of his opponents:—One day that he visited me in London, he came into my room laughing, and apparently well pleased. "What has put you into this good humour, Hume?" said I. "Why, man," replied he, "I have just now had the best thing said to me I ever heard. I was complaining in a company, where I spent the morning, that I was very ill-treated by the world, and that the censures put upon me were hard and unreasonable; that I had written many volumes, throughout the whole of which there were but a few pages that contained any reprehensible matter, and yet, that for those few pages I was abused and torn to pieces. 'You put me in mind,' said an honest fellow in the company, 'of an acquaintance of mine, a notary-public, who, having been condemned to be hanged for forgery, lamented the hardships of his case; that, after having written many thousand inoffensive sheets, he should be hanged for one line.'"

DOUBLING DOWN A PAGE, AND TURNING OVER A NEW LEAF.

It being reported that Lady Caroline Lamb had, in a moment of passion, knocked down one of her pages with a stool, the poet Moore, to whom this was told by Lord Strangford, observed, "O! nothing is more natural for a literary lady than to double down a page." "I would rather," replied his lordship, "advise Lady Caroline to turn over a new leaf."

DECIMALS.

It is at first sight surprising, that in the progression of numbers, and in calculation, the number of ten, and the decimal progression, should have been preferred to all others. The cause of this preference is, that it corresponds with the number of our fingers; in which all men are accustomed to reckon from their infancy. They count, in the first place, the number of their fingers. When the units exceed the number of their fingers, they pass to a second ten. If the number of tens increases, they count these also on their fingers; and when the number of tens exceeds the number of their fingers, they recommence on their fingers a new sort of calculation; that is to say, of tens of tens, or hundreds; and afterwards, of thousands, and so on. Thus, it is the number of the fingers with which nature has furnished man, as an instrument always ready to assist him in his calculations, which has led to the adoption of this number—a number, in other respects less useful, and less fitted for the purpose, than the number of twelve, which is more susceptible of division; for 10 is divisible only by 2 and by 5, while 12 is divisible by 2, by 3, by 4, and by 6.

The Roman ciphers afford a proof of the origin which I have just stated. They express units by the I's, which represent the fingers. Five is represented by a V, which represents the first and last fingers of the hand. Ten is represented by an X, being two V's united at their bases, and expressing the contents of both hands. Fifty is marked by an L, the half of the letter E, which is the same as C, and represents a hundred. Five hundred by a D, the half of the letter O, which is the same as M, and represents a thousand.—(Huet.)

BOXHORN.

A gentleman who had studied under Boxhorn, in Holland, told me that that professor had the most extraordinary passion for smoking and reading. In order to enjoy both at once, he had a hole made in the middle of the brim of his hat, through which he used to stick his lighted pipe when he intended to read or to compose. When it was empty, he refilled it, stuck it into the hole, and smoked away without requiring to put his hand to it; and this was his occupation almost every hour of the day.

A FAIR EXCHANGE.

Brebeuf, when young, had no taste for any author but Horace. One of his friends, named Gautier, on the contrary, liked nothing but Lucan. This preference was the cause of frequent disputes. To put an end to these, at last they agreed that each should read the poem which his companion preferred, examine it, and estimate its merits impartially. This was done, and the consequence was, that Gautier, having read Horace, was so delighted with him, that he scarcely ever left him; while Brebeuf, enchanted with Lucan, gave himself so wholly up to the study of his manner, that he carried it to a greater extent than Lucan himself, as is evident from the translation of that poem which he has left us in French verse.

ARCHBISHOP LEIGHTON.

Used often to say that, if he were to choose a place to die in, it should be an inn, it looking like a pilgrim's going home, to whom this world was all as an inn, and who was weary of the noise and confusion in it. He added that the officious tenderness and care of friends was an entanglement to a dying man; and that the unconcerned attendance of those that could be procured in such a place would give less disturbance.—(Burnet's History of his Times.)

VOLTAIRE AND HIS CUP.

Voltaire, when he was in Paris in 1778, lived in the house of the Marquis de Villette. One day tho Marquis had invited a large party to dinner. Coming to table, Voltaire did not find in its place before him his own particular cup, which he had marked with his catchet. "Where is my cup?" he inquired, his eye sparkling, of a tall, simple domestic, whose special duty it was to wait upon him. The poor fellow, quite at a loss, stammered out some words. "Enemy of your master!" exclaimed the old man in a fury, "go, seek for my cup; I must have my cup, or *I shall not dine to-day.*" The cup could not be found; and, leaving the table in his passion, he walked off to his apartment and shut himself up. The guests were confounded and disappointed by the scene. At length it was agreed that Mr. Villevielle, to whom he was much attached, should go to him and try to soothe him. He knocked gently at the door. "Who is there?" "It is I, Villevielle." "Ah," opening the door, "it is you, my dear Marquis. What is the purpose of this visit?" "I am here in name of all our friends, who are grieved at your absence, to request you will come down, and to express the regret of M. de Villette, who has dismissed the simpleton who was the cause of your anger." "They invite me to come down?" "Yes, they implore you." "My friend, I dare not." "And why so?" "They must laugh at me below." "Can you admit such a thought? have we not all our notions in such matters? has not every one his own glass, his own knife, his own pen?" "I see very well you are anxious to excuse me. Let us rather allow frankly that every one has his weaknesses; I blush at mine. Do you go down first, and I shall follow." Voltaire re-appeared a few minutes after, and seated himself at table with the awkward timidity of a child who has been detected in something foolish, and fears to be scolded.

POETRY AND PRACTICE.

1. It is a fine thing for children to learn to make verse; but when they come to be men, they must speak like other men, or else they will be laughed at. It is ridiculous to speak, or write, or preach in verse. As it is good to learn to dance; a man may learn his leg, learn to go handsomely; but it is ridiculous for him to dance when he should go.

2. It is ridiculous for a lord to print verses: it is well enough to make them to please himself, but to make them public is foolish. If a man, in a private chamber, twirls his band-strings, or plays with a rush to please himself, it is well enough; but if he should go into Fleet Street, and sit upon a stall, and twirl a band-string, or play with a rush, then all the boys in the street would laugh at him.

3. Verse proves nothing but the quantity of syllables; they are not meant for logic.—(Selden).

AKENSIDE AND ROLT.

Akenside's *Pleasures of Imagination* attracted much notice on the first appearance, from the elegance of its language, and the warm colouring of the descriptions. But the Platonic fanaticism of the foundation injured the general beauty of the edifice. Plato is indeed the philosopher of imagination; but is not this saying that he is no philosopher at all? I have been told that Rolt, who afterwards wrote many books, was in Dublin when that poem appeared, and actually passed a whole year there, very comfortably, by passing for the author.—(Walpole.)

SIR THOMAS MORE.

The greatest of men are sometimes seized with strange fancies at the very moment when one would suppose they had ceased to be occupied with the things of this world. Sir Thomas More, at his execution, having laid his head upon the block, and perceiving that his beard was extended in such a manner that it would be cut through by the stroke of the executioner, asked him to adjust it properly upon the block; and when the executioner told him he need not trouble himself about his beard, when his head was about to be cut off, "It is of little consequence to me," said Sir Thomas, "but it is a matter of some importance to you, that you should understand your profession, and not cut through my beard, when you had orders only to cut off my head."

ANAGRAMS.

The best anagram I have met with, is one which was shown me by the Duchess de la Tremouille. She was the sister of the Duke de Bouillon and of Marshal Turrenne, and her name was Marie de la Tour; in Spanish, Maria de la Torre, which a Spanish anagrammatist found to be exactly *Amor de la Tierra*.—(Chevreau.)

DR. CHALMERS—BUTLER'S "ANALOGY."

In the memoir of Dr. Chalmers, inserted in the *Transactions of the Royal Society of Edinburgh*, it is said that, on one occasion, when some person present was animadverting upon the wealth of the Church of England, and gave as an example of its over-abundance the revenues of the see of Durham, the Doctor exclaimed, with characteristic eagerness:—

"Sir, if all that has been received for the bishopric of Durham, since the foundation of the see, were set down as payment for Butler's *Analogy*, I should esteem it as a cheap purchase."

P. CORNEILLE.

Pierre Corneille, who has given such splendour of expression to the thoughts and sentiments of his heroes, had nothing in his external appearance that gave any indication of his talent, and his conversation was so tiresome, as to weary every one who listened to it. A great princess, who had felt much curiosity to see him, used to say, after the visit was over, that Corneille ought never to be heard but at the Hotel de Bourgogne.* Nature, which had been so liberal to him in extraordinary gifts, had denied him more common accomplishments. When his friends used to remind him of these defects, he would smile gently, and say, "I am not the less Pierre Corneille."

SCEPTICISM.

The sceptics, who doubt of everything, and whom Tertullian calls professors of ignorance, do affirm something, when they say we can affirm nothing, and admit that something is certain, when they maintain that nothing can be certainly known.—(Chevreau.)

CARMELINE THE DENTIST.

Carmeline, the famous tooth-drawer, and maker of artificial teeth, had his portrait painted and placed in his chamber window, with a motto taken from Virgil's line on the *Golden Bough*, in the sixth book of the *Æneid*.

"Uno avulso, non deficit alter." †

The application was extremely happy.

HELEN.

Every one speaks of the beautiful Helen, but few are aware that she had five husbands, Theseus, Menelaus, Paris, Deiphobus, and Achilles; that she was hanged in the Isle of Rhodes by the servants of Polixo; and that, in the war of which she was the cause, 886,000 Greeks and 670,000 Trojans lost their lives.

A QUID PRO QUO.

Masson, Regent of Trinity College, had asked one of his friends to lend him a book, which he

* The theatre.
† When one is drawn out, another is never wanting.

wished to consult, and received for answer,—" That he never allowed his books to go out of his room, but that, if he chose to come there, he was welcome to read as long as he pleased." Some days afterwards this pedant applied to Masson for the loan of his bellows, who replied, —" That he never allowed his bellows to go out of his room, but that, if he chose to come there, he was welcome to blow as long as he pleased."

BURTON, AUTHOR OF THE "ANATOMY OF MELANCHOLY."

In 1599, he was elected student of Christ Church, and "for form sake," says Wood, "though he wanted not a tutor, he was put under the tuition of Dr. John Bancroft, after Bishop of Oxon. In 1614, he was admitted to the reading of the sentences, and on the 29th of Nov., 1616, he had the vicaridge of St. Thomas parish, in the west suburb of Oxon, conferred on him by the dean and canons of Christ Church (to the parishioners whereof he always gave the sacrament in wafers), which, with the rectory of Segrave, in Leicestershire, given to him some years after by George Lord Berkeley, he kept with much ado to his dying day. He was an exact mathematician, a curious calculator of nativities, a general read scholar, a through-paced philologist, and one that understood the surveying of lands well. As he was by many accounted a severe student, a devourer of authors, a melancholy and humorous person ; so by others, who knew him well, a person of great honesty, plain-dealing, and charity. I have heard some of the antients of Ch. Ch. often say that his company was very merry, facete, and juvenile, and no man in his time did surpass him for his ready and dextrous interlarding his common discourses among them with verses from the poets, or sentences from classical authors, which being then all the fashion in the university, made his company more acceptable." He died in 1639.—*Oxoniana.*

DR. BAINBRIDGE.

Dr. Walter Pope, in his life of Seth Ward, Bishop of Salisbury, speaking of the Doctor, says, "This was the same Dr. Bainbridge who was afterwards Savilian professor of astronomy at Oxford, a learned and good mathematician ; yet there goes a story of him which was in many scholars' mouths, when I was first admitted there, that he put upon the school-gate an *affiche*, or written paper, as the custom is, giving notice at what time, and upon what subject, the professor will read, which ended in these words, *lecturus de polis et axis*, under which was written by an unknown hand as follows :—

Doctor Bainbridge
Came from Cambridge,
To read *de polis et axis :*
Let him go back again,
Like a dunce as he came,
And learn a new syntaxis."

He died in the year 1643.

CHILLINGWORTH.

"Mr. Chillingworth," says Bishop Hare, "is certainly a good reasoner, and may be read with much advantage : but I fear the reading of him by young divines hath had one great inconvenience. They see little show of reading in him, and from thence are induced to think, there is no necessity of learning, to make a good divine ; nay, that if he had been more a scholar, he had been a worse reasoner ; and therefore not to study the ancient writers of the church, is one step to the being Chillingworths themselves : I fear, I say, the reading Mr. Chillingworth in their first years has had this influence, to make them think, that good parts and good sense would do without learning, and that learning is rather a prejudice than an improvement of them. But 'tis a great mistake to judge of a man's learning by the show that is made of it. Mr. Chillingworth had studied hard, and digested well what he had read; and so must they who hope to write as well, and be as much esteemed."

DR. ALDRICH.

The learning of Dr. Aldrich, and his skill in polite literature, were evinced by his numerous publications, particularly of many of the Greek classics, one of which he generally published every year as a gift to the students of his house. He also wrote a system of logic for the use of a pupil of his, and printed it; but he possessed so great a skill in architecture and music, that his excellence in either would alone have made him famous to posterity. The three sides of the quadrangle of Christ Church, called Peck-water Square, were designed by him, as was also the elegant chapel of Trinity College, and the church of All Saints, in the High Street, to the erection whereof Dr. Radcliffe, at his solicitation, was a liberal contributor.

Amidst a variety of honourable pursuits, and the cares which the government of his college subjected him to, Dr. Aldrich found leisure to study and cultivate music, particularly that branch of it which related both to his profession and his office. To this end he made a noble collection of church-music, consisting of the works of Palestrina, Carissimi, Victoria, and other Italian composers for the church, and by adapting with great skill and judgment English words to many of their motets, enriched the stores of our church, and in some degree made their works our own.

In the *Pleasant Musical Companion*, printed in 1726, are two catches of Dr. Aldrich, the one, "Hark the bonny Christ-Church Bells," the other entitled "A smoking catch, to be sung by four men smoking their pipes, not more difficult to sing than diverting to hear."

Dr. Aldrich's exclusive love of smoking was an entertaining topic of discourse in the university, concerning which the following story, among others, passed current:—A young student of the college once finding some difficulty to bring a young gentleman—his chum—into the belief of it, laid him a wager that the dean was smoking at that instant, viz., about ten o'clock in the morning. Away, therefore, went the student to the deanery, where, being admitted to the dean in his study, he related the occasion of his visit. To which the dean replied, in perfect good humour, "You see you have lost your wager, for I'm not smoking, but filling my pipe." The catch above mentioned was made to be sung by the dean, Mr. Sampson Estwick, then of Christ Church, and afterwards of St. Paul's, and two other smoking friends. Mr. Estwick is plainly pointed out by the words, "I prithee Sam, fill."—(Oxoniana.)

SIR WILLIAM DAWES, ARCHBISHOP OF YORK.

Sir William was the youngest son of Sir John Dawes, Bart. In 1687, he was sent to St. John's College, from Merchant Tailor's school, but his father's title and estate descending to him, upon the death of his two elder brothers, about two years after, he left Oxford, and entered himself a nobleman in Catharine Hall, Cambridge. "His discourses," says the writer of his life, "were plain and familiar, and such as were best adapted to a country audience, yet under his management and manner of expression, they far surpassed the most elaborate compositions of other men. For such was the comeliness of his person, the melody of his voice, the decency of his action, and the majesty of his whole appearance, that he might well be pronounced the most complete pulpit orator of his age." He was the author of several works, and died in 1724.

The following story is told as a proof of the Archbishop's good nature and fondness of a pun. His clergy dining with him, for the first time after he had lost his lady, he told them, he feared they did not find things in so good order as they used to be in the time of poor Mary; and, looking extremely sorrowful, added with a deep sigh, "She was, indeed, *Mare Pacificum!*" —A curate, who pretty well knew what she had been, called out, "Ay, my Lord, but she was *Mare Mortuum* first." Sir William gave him a living of £200 per annum within two months afterwards.

LATINIZED NAMES.

The custom of persons Latinizing their names was formerly very common. Of Oxford men, who frequently wrote their names in Latin, the following occur to my recollection:—Andrew Borde, *Andreas Perforatus;* Nightingale, *Philomelus;* Bridgewater, *Aquepontanus;* Gayton, *De Speciosâ Villâ;* Turberville, *De Turbidâ Villâ;* Flood, *De Fluctibus;* Holyoke, *De Sacrâ Quercu;* Payne Fisher, *Paganus Piscator;* and John Aubrey, *Joannes Albericus.*—(Oxoniana.)

COLLINS, THE POET.

Collins was sent very young to Winchester College, where he was soon distinguished for his early proficiency, and his turn for elegant composition. In the year 1740, he came off first on the roll for New College, but there being no vacancy in that society, he entered a commoner of Queen's. On the expiration of the year, no vacancy having happened during that time at New College, he left Queen's on being elected a Demy of Magdalen. He was soon tired of a college life, resigned his demyship, and went to London, where he commenced a man of the town, and was romantic enough to suppose that his superior abilities would draw the attention of the great world, by means of whom he was to make his fortune. In this pleasurable way of life he soon wasted his little property, but was relieved by a considerable legacy left him by a maternal uncle, a colonel in the army. He soon afterwards fell into a most deplorable state of mind.

Without books, or steadiness and resolution to consult them if he had been possessed of any, he was always planning schemes for elaborate publications, which were carried no further than drawing up proposals for subscriptions, some of which were published; and in particular one for "A History of the Darker Ages."

He was passionately fond of music; good-natured and affable; warm in his friendships, visionary in his pursuits, and temperate in his diet. He was of moderate stature, of a light and clear complexion, with gray eyes, so very weak at times as hardly to bear a candle in the room, and to give him apprehensions of blindness.

The following story is told of him while he was resident at Magdalen College:—It happened one afternoon, at a tea-visit, that several intelligent friends were assembled at his rooms to enjoy each other's conversation, when in comes a certain member of the university, as remarkable at that time for his brutal disposition as for his good scholarship; who, though he met with a circle of the most peaceable people in the world, was determined to quarrel; and, though no man said a word, raised his foot, and kicked the tea-table and all its contents, to the other side of the room. Our poet, though of a warm temper, was so confounded at the unexpected downfall, and so astonished at the unmerited insult, that he took no notice of the aggressor at that time, but getting up from his chair calmly began to pick up the slices of bread and butter, and the fragments of his china, repeating very mildly,

" Invenias etiam disjecti membra poetæ."

—(Oxoniana.)

SIDNEY SMITH.

A gentleman, residing in Bristol, in 1838, who signs himself R——, was invited by Southey to accompany him and his son on a visit to Sidney Smith at Combe Fleury. He says,—

"We arrived at the village about noon, and, having alighted at the little inn, we all four proceeded towards the vicarage where Mr. Smith resided, a country lad officiating as our guide through the somewhat intricate lanes. We had proceeded about three-quarters of a mile, when the clodhopper, mounting a gate, pointed with his huge hand to a portly gentleman in a black dress and top-boots, who was leisurely riding along on a rough-looking cob, and opening his eyes and capacious mouth to the fullest extent of which each was capable, exclaimed, 'There be Passon Smith yander.' And, surely enough, the 'passon' it was, and towards him we made our way.

"He did not recognize Southey, but looking hard at him and us, was about to pass on, when the laureate went towards him and accosted him by name. Almost instant recognition took place, and the personal friends, although violent political enemies, cordially greeted each other. Smith alighted from his horse, and directing our guide to take it to the stable, turned with us towards the house, asking a hundred questions, and ever and anon expressing his delight at the unexpected visit.

"The vicarage was anything but pleasantly situated, and, in itself, more resembled a farm-house than a village pastor's 'modest mansion.' Everything about it was in sad disorder, and plainly enough evidenced that no woman's hand presided over the arrangement of the establishment. We got to the front door through a littered-up courtyard, and, after passing through a stone-paved hall, were conducted into the library, a large room, full of old-fashioned furniture, where books, parliamentary reports, pamphlets, and letters, lay all about, in most admired confusion.

"'This is my workshop,' he observed to Southey; 'as black as any smithy in Christendom.'

"And the neat and precise laureate seemed to think so, for he looked cautiously about for a clean chair, folded up his coat-tails, and was preparing to sit down, when Smith, with a sly gravity, wiped with his handkerchief (none of the cleanest) the dust from an old folio edition of the works of one of the fathers of the church, and requested his friend to sit on it.

"Southey shrunk from the profanation, and, respectfully removing the work, preferred the dusty chair. I do not think he much relished the joke, although he said nothing. I could not help thinking that he was mentally comparing, or rather contrasting, the appearance of Smith's library with that of his own exquisitely neat one at Keswick. Alas! ere long he would wander into that learned retreat, there gaze for hours, with an idiotic smile, on a favourite black letter volume, and then submit himself, like a child, to the guiding hand of an attendant, and be led out; for, in the days of his insanity, it was a strange fact, that although fond of finding his way into his beloved library, he never could discover the way *out* of it.

"The conversation was pretty general, and chiefly related to the old friends of either party. Mr. Smith spoke of Coleridge in the highest terms, but severely deprecated his indolence. Referring to Charles Lamb's intemperate habits, he remarked, 'He draws so much beer that no wonder he buffoons people—he must have a *butt* to put it in.'

"At this time, the question of the authorship of that strange, but clever and learned book, the *Doctor*, was a doubtful one, and much mooted in literary circles. Many suspected, and indeed named, Southey as the writer; but he never either admitted or denied the fact of his being so. The conversation turned on the subject, and Smith, with a roguish twinkle in his eye, told Southey that he knew who was the author. Southey calmly inquired the name, and the ex-reverend gentleman remarked, 'I remember, some years since, enjoying a conversation with one Robert Southey, in which he used the exact words which I find here,' and he read from a page of the *Doctor* a passage, and then said, 'Now, Mr. Laureate, it needs no conjuror to convince any one of common sense that the writer of the passage I have read, and the utterer of those very words to me seven years since, are one and the same person.' Southey bit his lip, but said nothing. After his death, Mrs. Southey divulged the secret, which her husband kept till his death. I question whether she would have made known the fact of the authorship, had not some shabby fellows, by judicious nods and well-timed faint denials, gained the credit of being connected with the work.

"We sat down to a plain country dinner, after which

'The glasses sparkled on the board.'

"Like Friar Tuck, the canon of St. Paul's enjoyed creature comforts, and many were the flashes of wit which set us in a roar. Southey was very abstemious, and refused wine, alleging his recent seizure as an excuse. Smith rattled away like a great boy, and, with the sole exception of Theodore Hook, I never heard any one so brilliant in conversation. No subject came amiss to him, and he seemed at home in every one. Of humbugs, both political and personal, he had the most utter detestation, and freely expressed his opinions. I shall not soon forget the ridicule which he that day heaped on the head of Robert Montgomery, who had then just published his poem, *Satan*.

"As to personal appearance, Sidney Smith was about the average height, or a trifle above it, inclined to corpulency, and of a fresh red-and-white complexion. The expression of his features was pleasing, and his snowy hair gave him an air of venerability. Good humour was the prevailing characteristic; but when he talked with severity, his aspect became changed, and few could have beheld unmoved his withering glance."

THOMAS HOOD.

Mr. Hood was born under Gresham's Grasshopper, in the city of London, in the year 1790, the son of Hood, of the firm of Vernor & Hood, in the Poultry, the publishers of Bloomfield and Kirke White, and the booksellers to whom we are indebted for the *Beauties of England and Wales*. One of his biographers has told us that he completed his education at a *finishing* school at Camberwell, upon which Tom has some twenty good jokes in his *Literary Reminiscences.* From Camberwell he went to Dundee, and soon after he was apprenticed to his uncle, Mr. Robert Sands, to learn the art and mystery of engraving. Here he soon found out the drift of his own genius; he left the burin for the pen, composed a few light pieces of poetry, got into notice, and, after Scott's death in 1821, became a sort of sub-editor of the *London Magazine.* It was at this time that he acquired the friendship of Lamb, Hazlitt, Cary, Allan Cunningham, Clare, and others, so delightfully pictured by Mr. Hood himself in his two short *Literary Reminiscences.* A volume of *Odes and Addresses to Great People* gave him a rank and a reputation in literature for something done in a better kind of Colman vein. It was some time, however, before the real author was known; and Coleridge, after two perusals, wrote and taxed Lamb with the authorship of the work. This was high praise, and, as the young lady said of Dr. Johnson, from one who could not lie, and could not be mistaken.

A Plea for the Midsummer Fairies was followed by a volume of *Whims and Oddities,* inscribed to Sir Walter Scott; then came the *Comic Annual,* with its six or seven years of clever and lively existence ; then *Tylney Hall,* a story in three volumes, with one super-excellent character in it, called Unlucky Joe; then *Up the Rhine,* the result of a residence on the banks of that *hurrying* river; then *Hood's Own,* a volume of cullings from his comic lucubrations, with what he calls a new infusion of blood for general circulation. Here he gave us his two short *Literary Reminiscences* already alluded to. On Hook's death, Hood became editor of the *New Monthly Magazine,* and, upon some disagreement with Mr. Colburn, editor of a magazine of his own, bearing his own name.

Hood was a little below the middle size, with a grave face, which habitually wore an air of melancholy. He was mistaken more than once in Germany, he tells us, for a regimental chaplain. His mouth, he informs us, was a little *wry,* as if it had always laughed on the wrong side. But Hood's was no *willow-pattern* face. He was silent in mixed company; a kind of Puritan in look, till an opportunity for a joke appeared, which he rose at like a trout—not, however, to be caught, but to catch others ; his countenance brightened up with the rising wit; you saw a play around his mouth ; his eyes sparkled, and all the genius of the man stood full in the face before you.

CHARACTERISTICS OF BYRON'S WRITINGS.

Never had any writer so vast a command of the whole eloquence of scorn, misanthropy, and despair. That Marah was never dry. No art could sweeten, no draughts could exhaust its perennial waters of bitterness. Never was there such variety in monotony as that of Byron. From maniac laughter to piercing lamentation, there was not a single note of human anguish of which he was not master. He always described himself as a man of the same kind with his favourite creations, as a man whose heart had been withered, whose capacity for happiness was gone and could not be restored, but whose invincible spirit dared the worst that could befall him here or hereafter.

How much of this morbid feeling sprang from an original disease of the mind, how much from real misfortune, how much from the nervousness of dissipation, how much was fanciful, how much was merely affected, it is impossible for us, and would probably have been impossible for the most intimate friends of Lord Byron, to decide. Whether there ever existed, or can ever exist, a person answering to the description which he gave of himself may be doubted; but that he was not such a person is beyond all doubt. It is ridiculous to imagine that a man whose mind was really imbued with scorn of his fellow-creatures, would have published three or four books every year in order to tell them so; or that a man who could say with truth that he neither sought sympathy nor needed it, would have admitted all Europe to hear his farewell to his wife, and his blessings on his child. In the second canto of *Childe Harold*, he tells us that he is insensible to fame and obloquy:—

"Ill may such contest now the spirit move,
Which heeds not keen reproof nor partial praise."

Yet we know, on the best evidence, that, a day or two before he published these lines, he was greatly, indeed childishly, elated by the compliments paid to his maiden speech in the House of Lords.

What our grandchildren may think of the character of Lord Byron, as exhibited in his poetry, we will not pretend to guess. It is certain, that the interest which he excited during his life is without a parallel in literary history. The feelings with which young readers of poetry regarded him can be conceived only by those who have experienced it. To people who are unacquainted with real calamity, "nothing is so dainty sweet as lovely melancholy." This faint image of sorrow has in all ages been considered by young gentlemen as an agreeable excitement. Old gentlemen and middle-aged gentlemen have so many real causes of sadness, that they are rarely inclined "to be as sad as night only for wantonness." Indeed, they want the power almost as much as the inclination.

Among that large class of young persons whose reading is almost entirely confined to works of imagination, the popularity of Lord Byron was unbounded. They bought pictures of him: they treasured up the smallest relics of him; they learned his poems by heart, and did their best to write like him, and to look like him. Many of them practised at the glass in the hope of catching the curl of the upper lip, and the scowl of the brow, which appear in some of his portraits. A few discarded their neckcloths in imitation of their great leader. For some years the Minerva press sent forth no novel without a mysterious, unhappy, Lara-like peer. The number of hopeful undergraduates and medical students who became things of dark imaginings, on whom the freshness of the heart ceased to fall like dew, whose passions had consumed themselves to dust, and to whom the relief of tears was denied, passes all calculation. This was not the worst. There was created in the minds of many of these enthusiasts a pernicious and absurd association between intellectual power and moral depravity.

This affectation has passed away; and a few more years will destroy whatever yet remains of that magical potency which once belonged to the name of Byron.—(Macaulay.)

CHARACTERS IN WRITING.

The characters of writing have followed the genius of the barbarous ages; they are well or ill formed, in proportion as the sciences have flourished more or less. Antiquaries remark, that the medals struck during the consulship of Fabius Pictor, about 250 years before Augustus, have the letters better formed than those of an older date. Those of the time of Augustus, and of the following age, show characters of perfect beauty. Those of Diocletian, and Maximian are worse formed than those of the Antonines; and again, those of the Justins and Justinians degenerate into a Gothic taste. But it is not to medals only that these remarks are applicable; we see the same inferiority of written characters generally following in the train of barbarism and ignorance. During the first race of our kings, we find no writing which is not a mixture of Roman and other characters. Under the empire of Charlemagne and of Louis le Débonnaire, the characters returned almost to the same point of perfection which characterized them in the time of Augustus, but in the following age there was a relapse to the former barbarism; so that for four or five centuries we find only the Gothic characters in manuscripts; for it is not worth while making an exception for some short periods, which were somewhat more polished, and when there was less inelegance in the formation of the letters.—(Melange, d'Histoire et de Litterature.)

HOW TO CIRCULATE A SATIRE.

Mignot, the famous pastry-cook, having learned that he had been ill-treated by Despreaux, in his third satire, brought an action against him; but finding that he was merely laughed at, he determined to be more effectually revenged. As he was celebrated for the excellence of his biscuits, and all Paris used to send for them to his shop, he caused to be printed, at his own expense, a great many copies of the Abbé Cotin's satire against Despreaux, and wrapped them round the biscuits he sold, in order to give them circulation; thus associating his own talents with those of the Abbé. His indignation, however, abated, when he found that Boileau's satire, far from being injurious to him, had completely brought him into fashion.

DEODATI AND DUMOULIN.

Deodati, professor at Geneva, was one day asked what he thought of the preaching of Dumoulin; to which he answered sneeringly, "Clear waters are never deep." Shortly afterwards, Deodati himself delivered a sermon, and Dumoulin was asked his opinion. Dumoulin, who had learned the remark of the critic, parodied the expression, and answered, "Deep waters are never clear."

ERASMUS' "COLLOQUIES."

Simon Colinet, a bookseller in Paris, in printing the *Colloquies* of Erasmus, threw off an impression of 80,000 copies. This number appears surprising; but we must recollect, that books were then more rare than they are now, and were consequently sought after with more avidity. The bookseller, also, had the address to circulate a report, that the *Colloquies* had been prohibited, in order to increase the demand—a device which was successful.

DON CARLOS.

Don Carlos, son of Philip II. of Spain, had composed a book on the subject of his father's travels, with the title, *The Great and Wondrous Travels of King Philip*. As these travels consisted merely of excursions from Madrid to the Escurial, and from the Escurial to Madrid, Philip caused Don Carlos to be tried by the Inquisition. The cause of this unfortunate prince's death is not exactly known. Some say that his father put him to death through jealousy; others, that it was done in order to be revenged for his railleries and insults; and others, in order to free the kingdom from a troublesome prince. Neither is the manner of his death known—whether he died by bleeding, like Seneca, or was suffocated between two mattresses, or strangled by the executioner. After his death, a collection of his extravagances was made in Spanish. He possessed talents, but so unregulated by judgment, that it cannot be denied that he was in a great measure the author of his fate.

The little romance of *Don Carlos*, by the Abbé St. Real, is extremely well written, and paints exactly the character of this young prince; but the truth of history is violated, as is generally the case in such works.

ORIGINES.

Paulus Jovius is the first who has introduced mottoes: Dorat the first who brought anagrams into fashion. Rabelais is the first who has written satires in French prose: Etienne Jodelle the first who introduced tragedies into France. The Cardinal of Ferrara, archbishop of Lyons, is the first person who had a tragi-comedy performed on the stage by Italian comedians. The first sonnet which appeared in French, is attributed to Jodelle.

INTELLECTUAL GLADIATORSHIP.

The celebrated Father Simon, of the Oratoire, had long delayed taking on himself the order of priesthood, on account of his great and profound study; but in consequence of a peremptory order from his superior, he was at last obliged to leave his house at July, and to set out for Meaux, to receive his ordination. He arrived, with two of his companions, after the usual hour of examination. M. de Ligny, who was then bishop of the diocese, seeing these fathers arrive at this uncommon hour, thought they must be some ignorant fellows, who had come with the view of annoying him; and under this impression, he recommended to the examiner, whom he had kept to dine with him, not to spare them. The signal being given, the examiner, turning to M. de Simon, said to him, in a grave tone, "I shall not ask you if you understand Latin : I know it is taught in your college with reputation. Horace, however, has his difficulties. Will you explain to me the first satire ?" presenting to him the book. M. Simon having acquitted himself well, the examiner went on—" And philosophy — I suppose you are pretty fairly stocked with ?" M. Simon, who was in the practice of teaching it, answered modestly, that he studied it every day. The examiner having stated a captious argument, M. Simon escaped adroitly by a distinguo. "I see," said the examiner, "you know something of philosophy — and theology no doubt ? a priest of the Oratoire without theology, would be as bad as a Cordelier without Latin." With this, the examiner attacked M. Simon on the controversial questions of the time; but finding him orthodox on them, he abandoned them for more solid discussion. "We see enough," said he, "of theologians and philosophers in the ecclesiastical state, but we have but few who devote themselves to the study of the Oriental languages, and read the Scriptures in the original. Ah ! how delightful," said he, turning to the bishop, " to read these sacred volumes as they were written ! what charms does the Hebrew possess for men of learning !" The prelate casting down his eyes, answered, that he had *heard* as much from Messieurs de Muys and de Flavigny, both very learned Hebraists. The examiner, turning to M. Simon, asked him if he had any taste for this beautiful language? M. Simon observed, that he was acquainted with its elements, and had always had a peculiar pleasure in the study of the Scriptures in the original. "How delighted I am to hear it!" said the examiner; "and how seldom do we meet with minds so well-directed as yours! Tell me, however, what is the Hebrew name for Genesis?" "*Beresith*," replied M. Simon. The field being thus opened, the combat began; both parties became animated; they declaimed, they argued, they cited polyglots, and rabbis ancient and modern. The examiner, confounded at such a display of erudition, made but a feeble resistance. M. Simon pressed him, pushed him on all sides, and gave him no quarter. The examiner stumbled at last, and was fairly beaten down, and trampled under foot by his tremendous antagonist. The bishop, who laughed from his very heart, was delighted to witness and prolong the battle; but seeing that dinner was getting cold, and taking pity, too, on the discomfited examiner, he gave his benediction to M. Simon, assuring him that, next day, he and his brethren should be admitted to holy orders without farther examination. The prelate went to dinner, the examiner to dry the perspiration produced by the debate, and M. Simon to his lodging, along with his companions, laughing in his sleeve at the result of the examination.—(Melange, d'Histoire et de Litterature.)

DESCARTES.

Descartes, when in Holland, had, with a great deal of industry, constructed an automaton girl, (which gave rise to the report that he had a daughter named Franchine), in order to prove demonstratively that brutes have no souls, and are merely well-constructed machines, which are put in motion by the impression of external substances that strike against them, and communicate to them a portion of their motion. Having put this machine on board a vessel, the captain had the curiosity to open the chest in which it was packed, and, surprised at the appearance of the automaton, which moved like an animated being, he got frightened, and threw it into the sea, thinking it was the devil.

DEDICATIONS.

Authors are frequently but very ill repaid by those to whom they dedicate their books. The only reward which Theodore Gaza received from Sixtus IV. for his dedication of the *Treatise of Aristotle on the Nature of Animals*, was the price of the binding of his book, which the Pope generously repaid to him. Tasso was not more successful with his dedications. Ariosto, in presenting his poems to the Cardinal d'Este, was saluted with a sarcasm, which will be remembered as long as his works. The historian Dupliex, a very fertile author, presenting one of his books to the Duke d'Epernin, that nobleman, turning abruptly towards the Pope's nuncio, who was present, remarked, "This is one of your breeding authors; he is delivered of a book every month."

BIBLIOMANIA.

The bibliomania has been on the increase among men of letters for a century past: and some wishing to form vast libraries, have searched not only the whole of Europe, but also the East, to discover ancient books and rare manuscripts; which has been the source of many impostures and ridiculous mistakes. Towards the close of last century, some cheats or ignorant persons sent over from India to Paris a number of Arabian manuscripts, in excellent condition, and written in a very beautiful character. They were received with profound respect by those who knew nothing of the matter; but as soon as those acquainted with the language cast their eyes upon them, they discovered that these rare volumes were common registers and account-books of Arabian merchants! *Risum teneatis amici.*

SWIFT'S POWER OF INVECTIVE.

Jeffrey, in his review of the works of Swift, more especially the *Tale of a Tub, Gulliver,* and the *Polite Conversation,* characterizes them as follows:—"Their distinguishing feature, however, is the force and vehemence of the invective in which they abound; the copiousness, the steadiness, the perseverance, and the dexterity with which abuse and ridicule are showered upon the adversary. This, we think, was, beyond all doubt, Swift's great talent, and the weapon by which he made himself formidable. He was, without exception, the greatest and most efficient *libeller* that ever exercised the trade; and possessed, in an eminent degree, all the qualifications which it requires:—a clear head—a cold heart—a vindictive temper—no admiration of noble qualities—no sympathy with suffering—not much conscience—not much consistency—a ready wit—a sarcastic humour—a thorough knowledge of the baser parts of human nature—and a complete familiarity with everything that is low, homely, and familiar in language. These were his gifts; and he soon felt for what ends they were given. Almost all his works are libels; generally upon individuals, sometimes upon sects and parties, sometimes upon human nature. Whatever be his end, however, personal abuse, direct, vehement, unsparing invective, is his means. It is his sword and his shield, his panoply, and his chariot of war. In all his writings, accordingly, there is nothing to raise or exalt our notions of human nature—but everything to vilify and degrade. We may learn from them, perhaps, to dread the consequences of base actions, but never to love the feelings that lead to generous ones. There is no spirit, indeed, of love or of honour in any part of them; but an unvaried and harassing display of insolence and animosity in the writer, and villany and folly in those of whom he is writing. Though a great polemic, he makes no use of general principles, nor ever enlarges his views to a wide or comprehensive conclusion. Everything is particular with him, and, for the most part, strictly personal. To make amends, however, we do not think him quite without a competitor in personalities. With a quick and sagacious spirit, and a bold and popular manner, he joins an exact knowledge of all the strong and the weak parts of every cause he has to manage; and, without the least restraint from delicacy, either of taste or of feeling, he seems always to think the most effectual blows the most advisable, and no advantage unlawful that is likely to be successful for the moment. Disregarding all the laws of polished hostility, he uses, at one and the same moment, his sword and his poisoned dagger—his hands, and his teeth, and his envenomed breath—and does not even scruple, upon occasion, to imitate his own yahoos, by discharging on his unhappy victims a shower of filth, from which neither courage nor dexterity can afford any protection.—Against such an antagonist, it was, of course, at no time very easy to make head; and accordingly his invective seems, for the most part, to have been as much dreaded, and as tremendous as the personal ridicule of Voltaire. Both were inexhaustible, well-directed, and unsparing; but even when Voltaire drew blood, he did not mangle the victim, and was only mischievous when Swift was brutal. Any one who will compare the epigrams on M. Franc de Pompignan with those on Tighe or Bettesworth, will easily understand the distinction."

SWIFT'S PERSONAL CHARACTER.

Of Swift's personal character, his ingenious biographer has given almost as partial a representation, as of his political conduct—a great part of it indeed has been anticipated, in tracing the principles of that conduct—the same arrogance and disdain of mankind, leading to profligate ambition and scurrility in public life, and to domineering and selfish habits in private. His character seems to have been radically overbearing and tyrannical; for though, like other tyrants, he could stoop low enough where his interests required it, it was his delight to exact an implicit compliance with his humours and fancies, and to impose upon all around him the task of observing and accommodating themselves to his habits, without the slightest regard to their convenience or comfort. Wherever he came, the ordinary forms of society were to give way to his pleasure; and everything, even to the domestic arrangements of a family, to be suspended for his caprice. If he was to be introduced to a person of rank, he insisted that the first advances and the first visit should be made to him. If he went to see a friend in the country, he would order an old tree to be cut down, if it obstructed the view from his window—and was never at his ease unless he was allowed to give nicknames to the lady of the house, and make lampoons upon her acquaintance. On going for the first time into any family, he frequently prescribed beforehand the hours for their meals, sleep, and exercise: and insisted rigorously upon the literal fulfilment of the capitulation. From his intimates he uniformly exacted the most implicit submission to all his whims and absurdities; and carried his prerogative so far, that he sometimes used to chase the Grattans and other accommodating friends, through the apartments of the deanery, and up and down stairs, driving them like horses, with a large whip, till he thought he had enough of exercise. All his jests have the same character of insolence and coarseness. When he first came to his curate's house, he announced himself as "his master;" took possession of the fireside, and ordered his wife to take charge of his shirts and stockings. When a young clergyman was introduced to him, he offered him the dregs of a bottle of wine, and said, he always kept a poor parson about him to drink up his dregs. Even in hiring servants, he always chose to insult them, by inquiring into their qualifications for some filthy and degrading office. And though it may be true, that his after-conduct was not exactly of a piece with those preliminaries, it is obvious, that as no man of proper feelings could submit to such impertinence, so no man could have a right to indulge in it. Even considered merely as a manner assumed to try the character of those with whom he lived, it was a test which no one but a tyrant could imagine himself entitled to apply; and Swift's practical conclusion from it was just the reverse of what might be expected. He attached himself to those only who were mean enough to bear this usage, and broke with all who resented it. While he had something to gain or to hope from the world, he seems to have been occasionally less imperious; but, after he retired to Ireland, he gave way without restraint to the native arrogance of his character; and, accordingly, confined himself almost entirely to the society of a few easy-tempered persons, who had no talents or pretensions to come in competition with his; and who, for the honour of his acquaintance, were willing to submit to the dominion he usurped. A singular contrast to the rudeness and arrogance of this behaviour to his friends and dependents, is afforded by the instances of extravagant adulation and base humility, which occur in his addresses to those upon whom his fortune depended.—(Jeffrey.)

PORSON.

Professor Porson being once at a dinner-party where the conversation turned upon Captain Cook and his celebrated voyages round the world, an ignorant person, in order to contribute his mite towards the social intercourse, asked him, "Pray, was Cook killed on his first voyage?" "I believe he was," answered Porson, "though he did not mind it much, but immediately entered on a second."

Porson said of a prospect shown to him, that it put him in mind of a fellowship—a long, dreary walk, with a church at the end of it.

POPULAR TEACHING.

Bulwer, in his *England and the English*, hits off the literary charlatans most aptly:—

"At present a popular instructor is very much like a certain master in Italian, who has thriven prodigiously upon a new experiment on his pupils.

"J—— was a clever fellow, and full of knowledge which nobody wanted to know. After seeing him in rags for some years, I met him the other day most sprucely attired, and with the complacent and sanguine air of a prosperous gentleman.

"'I am glad to see, my dear sir,' said I, 'that the world wags well with you.'

"'It does.'

"'Doubtless your books sell famously.'

"'Bah, no bookseller will buy them. No, sir, I have hit on a better *metier* than that of writing books. I am giving lessons in Italian.'

"'Italian! why, I thought when I last saw you, that you told me Italian was the very language you knew nothing about.'

"'Nor did I, sir; but as soon as I had procured scholars, I began to teach myself. I bought a dictionary. I learnt that lesson in the morning which I taught my pupils at noon. I found I was more familiar and explanatory, thus *fresh from knowing little*, than if I had been confused and over-deep by knowing much. I am a most popular teacher, sir; and my whole art consists in being just one lesson in advance of my scholars.'

PROFESSOR WHITE.

White was a very extraordinary man, of great profundity as an Asiatic linguist. He was first discovered by the late Dean Tucker, working as an apprentice to a poor weaver, in a village either in Gloucestershire or Somersetshire. At this village, on a certain day, was to be a dinner-party. The dean, strolling about before dinner, chanced to go into a poor weaver's shop. He took up a dirty, tattered Greek Testament. "How comes this here? who reads this book?" "Sir, my lad is always poring over such books." On speaking to the lad, he found him well versed in Greek and Latin. By appointment he waited upon the dean in the afternoon, who introduced him to the company. A collection was made for him. Tucker undertook the care of him, put him to school at Gloucester, and from thence sent him to Oxford. Here he gradually rose in academical success—fellow of Wadham, professor of Arabic, canon of Christ Church, and Hebrew professor.

HUMOROUS SAYING OF CHARLES V.

Charles V., who spoke fluently several European languages, used to say, that we should speak Spanish with the gods, Italian with our female friends, French with our male friends, German with soldiers, English with geese, Hungarian with horses, and Bohemian with the devil.

THE VINEGAR BIBLE.

There is an edition of the Bible known by the name of the *Vinegar Bible*, from the *erratum* in the title to the twentieth chapter of St. Luke, in which "Parable of the *Vineyard*" is printed "Parable of the *Vinegar*." It was printed in 1717, at the Clarendon press.

A DICTIONARY LIBRARY.

The apt reply of a distinguished American scholar to a benefactor of the institution of learning with which he was connected, when an increase of the library was the subject of discussion, deserves perpetual remembrance.

"We need more books," said the professor.

"More books!" said the merchant; "why, have you read through all you have already?"

"No; I never expect to read them all."

"Why, then, do you want more?"

"Pray, sir, did you ever read your dictionary through?"

"Certainly not."

"Well, a library is my dictionary."

SCHOLASTIC CONTROVERSY.

Henry, in his *History of England*, states that the following parts of learning were cultivated, in some degree, in Britain, during the period from 1066 to 1216: grammar, rhetoric, logic, metaphysics, physics, ethics, scholastic divinity, the canon law, arithmetic, geometry, astronomy, astrology, and medicine. He also gives the following, to show the trifling questions that were agitated by the logicians of that period:—

"When a hog is carried to market, with a rope tied about its neck, which is held at the other end by a man, whether the hog is carried to market by the rope or the man?"

"Literary wars," says Bayle, "are sometimes as lasting as they are terrible." A disputation between two great scholars was so interminably violent, that it lasted thirty years! He humorously compares it to the German war, which lasted as long.

ROME.

Some one telling the famous Jerome Bignon, that Rome was the seat of faith; "That is true," said he; "but then faith is like some people, who are never to be found at home."

FRANCIS I.

Francis I. was one day playing at tennis, when a monk, who was playing on his side, by a successful stroke, insured the victory to the king's party. "Well done," said the king; "a brave stroke for a monk!" "Sire," replied the monk, "your majesty can make it the blow of an abbé when you please." Some days afterwards the abbacy of Bourmayen became vacant, and the king presented the situation to him.

LOSS OF TIME.

A female devotee, who confessed the great attachment she had to play, was reminded by her confessor of the sad loss of time which it occasioned. "Ah, true," said she, "there is a deal of time lost in shuffling the cards."

POPE INNOCENT XI.

Pope Innocent XI. was the son of a banker. He was elected on St. Matthew's day, and in the evening a pasquinade appeared on the statue:—"They found a man sitting at the receipt of custom."

QUANTITY AND QUALITY.

A marquis said to a financier, "I would have you to know that I am a man of quality." "And I," replied the financier, "am a man of quantity."

BOSSUET.

M. Bossuet, Bishop of Meaux, at eight years of age, preached with grace; he delivered a sermon at that age at the Hotel de Rambouillet. It was nearly midnight when he closed, and Voiture, who was present, remarked as he rose to go, "I have never heard a sermon so early—or so late."

CANDOUR.

The first president of the parliament of Paris, asked M. Montauban, one day as he rose to speak, whether he would be long. "Very," replied the advocate coolly. "At least," replied the magistrate, "you are candid."

SANTEUIL.

Santeuil was crossing the court of the College of Cardinal le Morne, when he met a scholar who was walking up and down, composing his theme which he held in his hand. Santeuil, guessing what he was employed about, pulled the paper out of his hand with a tremendous expression of countenance, translated it instantly into elegant Latin, and returned it to him, saying, "If your regent asks you who composed this theme, tell him it was the devil." He then hurried off, making his cloak fly about him, and raising a cloud of dust all about. The terrified student retreated instantly into college, and repeated to the regent the history of the apparition of the devil. The Jesuit, who saw that the theme was composed in the most elegant Latin, and that the student told the story with perfect sincerity and good faith, was puzzled what to think of the matter. Soon after, Santeuil was present at a public discussion which took place in the hall of the Jesuits. The scholar recognized his old acquaintance, and immediately called out in an agony of fear, "The devil! the devil!" Santeuil, perceiving that he was detected, related the story, to the infinite amusement of the audience, who found this explanation much more interesting than the former subject of discussion.

BREVITY.

Henry IV. liked a brief reply. He once met an ecclesiastic, to whom he said, "Whence do you come? Where are you going? What do you want?" The ecclesiastic replied instantly, "From Bourges—to Paris—a benefice." "You shall have it," replied the monarch.

THE SUN.

Some astronomers, who had been making observations, thought they perceived several spots in the sun. Voitiere happened shortly afterwards to be in a company, where he was asked if there were any news. "None," said he; "but that I hear very bad reports of the sun."

SHAKSPEARE.

"Foreigners cannot enjoy our Shakspeare," said Sherlock to Voltaire. "That is true," replied he; "they are acquainted with his plays only through translations, which retain slight faults, while the great beauties are lost: a blind man cannot be persuaded of the beauty of the rose, when his fingers are pricked by the thorns."

THE PREACHER.

A Gascon preacher stopped short in the pulpit; it was in vain that he scratched his head; nothing would come out. "My friends," said he, as he walked quietly down the pulpit stairs, "my friends, I pity you, for you have lost a fine discourse."

VOLTAIRE AND MONTESQUIEU.

Voltaire having given a representation of his *Orphan of China*, at the Delices near Geneva, before it appeared in Paris, the President Montesquieu, who was present, fell fast asleep. Voltaire threw his hat at his head, saying, "He thinks he is in court."—"No, no," said Montesquieu, awaking, "in church."

VOLTAIRE'S "MARIANNE."

Voltaire's *Marianne* was at first only once acted. It is said, that the public being divided as to the merit of the work, the question was oddly settled. The farce, which happened to be played that evening, was entitled, *The Mourning:*—" For the deceased play, I suppose," said a critic in the pit; and this decided the fate of the piece.

VOLTAIRE'S EAGLE.

The greatest geniuses have always their weaknesses to connect them with the ordinary race of mankind. Voltaire was not exempt from this tribute which nature seems to exact from great men, as an expiation for their superiority. The following anecdote is in point:—"Voltaire took great delight in a young eagle which he kept chained in the court of his chateau at Ferney. One day the eagle fell to fighting with two cocks, and was severely wounded. Voltaire, disconsolate, sent an express to Geneva, with directions to bring a man who passed there as a pretty expert *animal doctor*. In his impatience, he did nothing but move between the cage of the eagle and the window of his apartment, from which he had a view of the great road. At length his courier appeared, and along with him, the Esculapius so much wished for; Voltaire raised a cry of joy; flew to meet him, gave him a most distinguished reception, and lavished on him prayers and promises to interest him for his sick favourite. The man, astonished at a reception to which he was little accustomed, examined the wounds of the eagle. Voltaire, full of anxiety, sought to read in his eyes his hopes and fears. The doctor declared, with the air of a professor, that he would not venture to pronounce on the case until after the first dressing was removed; but promised to repeat his visit on the morrow, and departed, handsomely paid. On the morrow Voltaire was on thorns, and at last the decision was, that the physician could not answer for the life of the eagle; a new source of disquietude. Voltaire's first question every morning to one of his servants, named Madeline, whose business it was to wake him, was, "How is my eagle?" "Very poorly, sir,—very poorly." One day at length Madeline answered, laughing: "Ah, sir, your eagle is no longer sick." "It is cured then! What happiness!" "No; it is dead!" "Dead! my eagle dead! and this you tell me laughing?" "Why, sir, it was so lean, it is all the better dead." "How, lean!" exclaimed Voltaire in a rage; "an excellent reason, truly! I suppose you must kill me also because I am lean. You baggage! to laugh at the death of my poor eagle, because it was lean! because you are in good condition yourself, you think it is only people of your stamp that should have a right to live? Out of my sight! begone!" Madame Denis, hearing the noise, ran to her uncle, and asked what had discomposed him. Voltaire told her the particulars, continuing to repeat: "Lean! lean! So then I must be killed too ——." At length he insisted that Madeline should be dismissed. His niece feigned compliance, and ordered the poor girl to keep herself out of sight in the chateau. And it was only after two months that Voltaire asked about her. "She is very unfortunate," said Madame Denis, "she has not succeeded in getting a place at Geneva; which happens from its being known that she was turned off from the chateau." "It is all her own fault. Why laugh at the death of my eagle because it was lean? However, she must not be allowed to starve; let her come back, but let her beware of presenting herself before me, do you hear?" Madame Denis promised she should not, and upon this Madeline came forth from her concealment, but carefully kept out of the way of her master. One day, however, Voltaire rising from table, found her standing opposite to him; Madeline coloured, and, with downcast eyes, wished to stammer out some excuses: "Not a word more of it," said he; "but mind you at least, that it is not necessary to kill everything which happens to be lean."

JOHNSON AND THE POETESS.

"When last in Lichfield," says Anna Seward, "Johnson told me that a lady in London once sent him a poem which she had written, and afterwards desired to know his opinion of it. 'Madam, I have not cut the leaves. I did not even peep between them.' He met her again in company, and she again asked him after the 'trash.' He made no reply, and began talking to another person. The next time they met, she asked him if he had yet read her poem. He answered, 'No, madam, nor never intend to!' Shocked at the unfeeling rudeness he thus recorded of himself, I replied, that I was surprised any person should obtrude their writings upon his attention; adding, that if I could write as well as Milton or Gray, I should think the best fate to be desired for my compositions was exemption from his notice. I expected a sharp sarcasm in return, but he only rolled his large head in silence.

"Johnson told me once, he 'would hang a dog that read the Lycidas of Milton twice.' 'What, then,' replied I, 'must become of me, who can say it by heart, and who often repeat it to myself with a delight which grows by what it feeds upon?' 'Die!' returned the growler, 'in a surfeit of bad taste.' Thus it was that the wit and aweless impoliteness of the stupendous creature bore down by storm every barrier which reason attempted to rear against his injustice."

CRITICISM OF A HATTER'S SIGN.

A journeyman hatter, a companion of Dr. Franklin, on commencing business for himself, was anxious to get a handsome signboard, with a proper inscription. This he composed himself, as follows:—"John Thompson, *hatter, makes and sells hats for ready money,*" with the figure of a hat subjoined. But he thought he would submit it to his friends for their amendments. The first he showed it to thought the word *hatter* tautologous, because followed by the words "makes hats," which showed he was a hatter. It was struck out. The next observed, that the word "makes" might as well be omitted, because his customers would not care who made the hats; if good, and to their mind, they would buy, by whomsoever made. He struck that out also. A third said, he thought the words "for ready money" were useless; as it was not the custom of the place to sell on credit, every one who purchased expected to pay. These, too, were parted with, and the inscription then stood, "John Thompson sells hats." "*Sells* hats!" says his next friend; "why, who expects you to give them away? What, then, is the use of the word?" It was struck out, and *hats* was all that remained attached to the name of John Thompson. Even this inscription, brief as it was, was reduced ultimately to "John Thompson," with the figure of a hat subjoined.

RICHARD I.

Foulques de Neully, a celebrated preacher of his day, addressing himself in a prophetic style to Richard I., King of England, told him he had three daughters to marry, and that, if he did not dispose of them soon, God would punish him severely. "You are a false prophet," said the king; "I have no daughter." "Pardon me, sir," replied the priest, "your majesty has three, ambition, avarice, and luxury; get rid of them as fast as possible, else assuredly some great misfortune will be the consequence." "If it must be so then," said the king, with a sneer, "I give my ambition to the templars, my avarice to the monks, and my luxury to the prelates."

IMPROMPTUS.

It is a difficult matter to make a good impromptu. I believe, for my own part, that none are good but those that are made at leisure. —(Menage.)

VOLTAIRE'S GENIUS.

It was observed by Madame Necker, that Voltaire had extracted from his genius everything of which it was susceptible; that in his case it was like a sponge, which he had drained of its contents to the last drop.

VOLTAIRE AND THE ENGLISHMAN.

An Englishman who stopped at Ferney, in his way to Italy, offered to Voltaire to bring him from Rome whatever he desired. "Good," said the philosopher, "bring me the ears of the grand Inquisitor." The Englishman, in the course of a familiar conversation with Clement XIV., related to him this piece of pleasantry. "Tell Voltaire from me," answered the pope, laughing, "that our Inquisitor is no longer possessed of ears."

IMMORTALITY.

Bautru, in presenting a poet to M. d'Hemery, addressed him, "Sir, I present to you a person who will give you immortality; but you must give him something to live upon in the meantime."

THE LATEST INFORMATION.

M. de E—— was relating a story. M. de B—— said to him, "That cannot be, for I have a letter of the 31st, which says the contrary." "Ah," replied the narrator, "but mine is of the 32d!"

CASAUBON.

Casaubon being present during the discussion of a thesis in the Sorbonne, listened to a very long and stubborn dispute, which was carried on in a style so barbarous and unintelligible to him, that he could not help remarking, as he left the hall, "I never listened to so much Latin before without understanding it!"

BACON'S INCONSISTENCIES.

The difference between the soaring angel and the creeping snake was but a type of the difference between Bacon the philosopher and Bacon the attorney-general, Bacon seeking for truth, and Bacon seeking for the seals. Those who survey only one half of his character may speak of him with unmixed admiration, or with unmixed contempt. But those only judge of him correctly who take in at one view Bacon in speculation and Bacon in action. They will have no difficulty in comprehending how one and the same man should have been far before his age and far behind it, in one line the boldest and most useful of innovators, in another line the most obstinate champion of the foulest abuses. In his library, all his rare powers were under the guidance of an honest ambition, of an enlarged philanthropy, of a sincere love of truth. There, no temptation drew him away from the right course. Thomas Aquinas could pay no fees. Duns Scotus could confer no peerages. The master of the sentences had no rich reversions in his gift. Far different was the situation of the great philosopher when he came forth from his study and his laboratory to mingle with the crowd which filled the galleries of Whitehall. In all that crowd there was no man equally qualified to render great and lasting services to mankind. But in all that crowd there was not a heart more set on things which no man ought to suffer to be necessary to his happiness, on things which can often be obtained only by the sacrifice of integrity and honour. To be the leader of the human race in the career of improvement, to found on the ruins of ancient intellectual dynasties a more prosperous and a more enduring empire, to be revered by the latest generations as the most illustrious among the benefactors of mankind, all this was within his reach. But all this availed him nothing while some quibbling special pleader was promoted before him to the bench, while some heavy country gentleman took precedence of him by virtue of a purchased coronet, while some pander, happy in a fair wife, could obtain a more cordial salute from Buckingham, while some buffoon, versed in all the latest scandal of the court, could draw a louder laugh from James.—(Macaulay.)

THE RETORT COURTEOUS.

M. le Comte de —— was, like many others who take the name of Count, without the property. In a company where I was present, he once endeavoured to turn into ridicule an abbé, who, according to custom, had assumed the name, without possessing a benefice. "It is strange," said he, "that we should have known each other so long, and yet that I don't know whereabouts your abbey lies." "What!" said the abbé, "don't you know? It is within *your* county."—(Menage.)

THE FIRST SMOKER.

Tobacco was first brought into repute in England by Sir Walter Raleigh. By the caution he took in smoking it privately, he did not intend it should be copied. But sitting one day, in deep meditation, with a pipe in his mouth, he inadvertently called to his man to bring him a tankard of small-beer. The fellow, coming into the room, threw all the liquor into his master's face, and running down stairs, bawled out, "Fire! Help! Sir Walter has studied till his head is on fire, and the smoke bursts out at his mouth and nose!"

M. DE BAUTRU.

M. de Bautru had been often pressed by the Queen to show her his wife. At last she told him plainly, that she was determined to be presented to her. Bautru, who had resisted as long as he possibly could, promised to bring her with him after dinner; "but, please your Majesty," added he, "she is terribly deaf." "O, no matter," said the Queen, "I will talk loud." He immediately went home to prepare his wife for the interview, and warned her to speak as loud as possible, as the Queen would be unable otherwise to understand her. He brought her to the Louvre in the evening, and the Queen immediately opened the conference by bawling as loudly as possible, while Madame de Bautru answered her in the same tone. The King, who had been apprised of the whole by Bautru, laughed with all his heart at the scene. At last the Queen, who perceived it, said to Madame de Bautru, "Is it not the case that Bautru has made you believe that I am deaf?" Madame de Bautru admitted that it was so. "Ah, the villain!" continued the Queen, "he told me the same of you."—(Menage.)

AMERICAN COPYRIGHTS.

American publishers usually pay authors 10 per cent. on the retail price of their works. But authors of extraordinary popularity in some instances have received from 20 to 40 per cent.

Stephens, author of *Travels in the Holy Land*, &c., had received from his publishers, the Harpers, as early as 1848, more than fifteen thousand dollars; and Prescott, for his *Life of Ferdinand and Isabella*, and his *Conquest of Mexico*, had received some twenty or twenty-five thousand dollars from the same firm.

THE "COTTER'S SATURDAY NIGHT."

The early patroness of Burns, Mrs. Dunlop, of Dunlop, had an old housekeeper, a sort of privileged person, who had certain aristocratical notions of the family dignity, that made her utterly astonished at the attentions that were paid by her mistress to a man in such low worldly estate as the rustic poet. In order to overcome her prejudice and surprise, her mistress persuaded her to peruse a MS. copy of the *Cotter's Saturday Night*, which the poet had just then written. When Mrs. Dunlop inquired her opinion of the poem, she replied, with a quaint indifference, "Aweel, madam, that's vera weel." "Is that all you have to say in its favour?" asked the mistress. "'Deed, madam," she returned, "the like o' you quality may see a vast in't; but I was aye used to the like o' all that the poet has written about in my ain father's house, and atweel I dinna ken how he could hae described it ony other gate." When Burns heard of the old woman's criticism, he remarked that it was one of the highest compliments he had ever received.

INVITATIONS.

You are not invited to an entertainment, it is because you have not bought the invitation, which he who makes it sells to those who flatter him, and are obsequious to him. Instead of a good supper, then, I have nothing. Yes; you have the pleasure of knowing you have not commended the man you disliked, nor endured his insolent behaviour.—(Epictetus.)

EVIL SPEAKING.

If anybody tells you such an one has spoken ill of you, do not refute them in that particular; but answer, had he known all my vices he had not spoken only of that one.—(Ibid.)

CARDINAL RICHELIEU.

Amidst the important occupations of the Cardinal Richelieu, he generally found time to unbend a little from the fatigue attendant on the ministry. He was fond of violent exercises, particularly after meals, but did not like to be surprised in these moments of amusement and pleasure. M. de Boisrobert, who was constantly with him, told me that one day M. de Grammont, who, at the Palais Royal, was considered as one of the family (having espoused one of the Cardinal's nieces), and who, of course, possessed the liberty of free entry at all times, broke in upon the Cardinal after dinner, while amusing himself with leaping in the great gallery. M. de Grammont, like an able courtier, told the Cardinal he could leap much better than he, and immediately began leaping five or six times. The Cardinal, who was as accomplished a courtier as himself, perfectly understood his meaning, and afterwards distinguished him more than ever by his favour.

SYMPTOMS OF GREATNESS.

I flatter myself (says Beattie) I shall soon get rid of this infirmity [a distressing giddiness from which he was slowly recovering]; nay, that I shall ere long be in the way of becoming a great man. For, have I not headache, like Pope? vertigo, like Swift? gray hairs, like Homer? Do I not wear large shoes (for fear of corns), like Virgil? and sometimes complain of sore eyes (though not of lippitude), like Horace? Am I not at this present writing invested with a garment not less ragged than that of Socrates? Like Joseph, the patriarch, I am a mighty dreamer of dreams; like Nimrod, the hunter, I am an eminent builder of castles (in the air). I procrastinate like Julius Cæsar; and very lately, in imitation of Don Quixote, I rode a horse, lean, old, and lazy, like Rosinante. Sometimes, like Cicero, I write bad verses; and sometimes bad prose, like Virgil. This last instance I have on the authority of Seneca. I am of small stature, like Alexander the Great; I am somewhat inclinable to fatness, like Dr. Arbuthnot and Aristotle; and I drink brandy and water, like Mr. Boyd. I might compare myself in relation to many other infirmities, to many other great men; but if fortune is not influenced in my favour by the particulars already enumerated, I shall despair of ever recommending myself to her good graces.—(Dr Beattie to Hon. C. Boyd.)

THE FAIR SEX, BY THE FAIREST OF THE SEX.

I have never had any great esteem for the generality of the fair sex; and my only consolation for being of that gender has been, the assurance it gave me of never being married to any one among them; but, I own, at present, I am so much out of humour with the actions of Lady H——, that I never was so heartily ashamed of my petticoats before. You know, I suppose, that by this discreet match she renounces the care of her children; and I am laughed at by all my acquaintance for my faith in her honour and understanding. My only refuge is the sincere hope that she is out of her senses, and taking herself for Queen of Sheba, and Mr. M—— for King Solomon. I do not think it quite so ridiculous; but the men, you may well imagine, are not so charitable, and they agree in the kind reflection, that nothing hinders women from playing the fool but not having it in their power. The many instances that are to be found to support this opinion, ought to make the few reasonable more valued—but where are the reasonable ladies?—(Lady M. W. Montagu.)

AN AUTHOR SOLICITING PATRONAGE.

The distresses of authors, sometimes, on receiving patronage, are as great as that which renders patronage necessary. On this subject, a story is told of the eccentric Wynne.

A short time previous to his publishing his *History of Ireland*, he expressed a desire to dedicate it to the Duke of Northumberland, who was just returned from being lord-lieutenant of that country. For this purpose he waited on Dr. Percy, and met with a very polite reception. The Duke was made acquainted with his wishes, and Dr. Percy went as the messenger of good tidings to the author. But there was more to be done than a formal introduction: the poor writer intimated this to the good doctor; who, in the most delicate terms, begged his acceptance of an almost new suit of black, which, with a very little alteration, might be made to fit. This, the doctor urged, would be best, as there was not time to provide a new suit, and other things necessary for his *debut*, as the Duke had appointed Monday in the next week to give the historian an audience. Mr. Wynne approved of the plan in all respects, and in the meantime had prepared himself with a set speech, and a manuscript of the dedication. But, to digress a little, it must be understood that Dr. Percy was considerably in stature above Mr. Wynne, and his coat sufficiently large to wrap round the latter, and conceal him. The morning came for the author's public entry at Northumberland House; but, alas! one grand mistake had been made: in the hurry of business, no application had been made to the tailor for the necessary alteration of his clothes: however, great minds are not cast down by ordinary occurrences. Mr. Wynne dressed himself in Dr. Percy's friendly suit, together with a borrowed sword, and a hat under his arm of great antiquity; then taking leave of his trembling wife, he set out for the great house. True to the moment he arrived. Dr. Percy attended, and the Duke was ready to receive our poet, whose figure at this time presented the appearance of a suit of sables hung on a hedge-stake, or one of those bodiless forms we see swinging on a dyer's pole. On his introduction, Mr. Wynne began his formal address; and the noble Duke was so tickled at the singularity of the poet's appearance that, in spite of his gravity, he burst the bonds of good manners; and at length, agitated by an endeavour to restrain risibility, he leaped from his chair, forced a purse of thirty guineas into Mr. Wynne's hand, and hurrying out of the room, told the poet he was welcome to make what use he pleased of his name and patronage.

IGNORANCE.

Sir John Germain was so ignorant, that being told that Sir Matthew Decker wrote St. Matthew's Gospel, he firmly believed it. I doubted this tale very much, says Walpole, till I asked a lady of quality, his descendant, about it, who told me it was most true. She added, that Sir John Germain was in consequence so much persuaded of Sir Matthew's piety, that, by his will, he left two hundred pounds to Sir Matthew, to be by him distributed among the Dutch paupers in London.

SIR JOHN HARRINGTON'S EXTRAVAGANCE.

Sir John Harrington, the celebrated epigrammatist in the reign of Queen Elizabeth, was a man of great wit, but thoughtless in his conduct, and extremely careless in the management of his affairs; so that, in consequence of his extravagance, he was obliged to part with several of his estates. Among the rest, he sold a very fine one, called Nyland, in Somersetshire, concerning which Dr. Fuller, in his account of Harrington, relates a whimsical anecdote.

Sir John while riding over this manor, accompanied by an old and trusty servant, suddenly turned round, and with his usual pleasantry said,

> John, John, this Nyland.
> Alas! once was my land.

To whom John, as merrily and truly replied,

> If you had had more wit, sir,
> It might have been yours yet, sir.

THE BRISTOL MILKWOMAN'S POETRY.

The anecdote of Mason is well known, when solicited to subscribe five guineas in support of Ann Yearsley, the Bristol milkwoman and poetess. He observed to his friend, who was rather hyperbolical in his praises—"Here are five pounds for her book, and five shillings for her heaven-born genius." Perhaps this was illiberal; but the force of its reasoning may be applied and rendered even *poetically* just by analogy.

CONVERSATION.

Gibbon, one of the most fastidious of men, and disposed by neither party nor personal recollections to be enamoured of Fox, describes his conversation as admirable. They met at Lausanne, spent a day without other company, "and talked the whole day." The test was sufficiently long under any circumstances, but Gibbon declares that Fox never flagged; his animation and variety of topic were inexhaustible.

Dr. Bentley was loquacious. Dr. Stillingfleet, Bishop of Worcester, to whom this talented man was chaplain, said that if Bentley had been a little more diffident, he would have been the most extraordinary man in Europe.

Grotius was very talkative, but he was thoughtful, and richly stored with learning.

Of Goldsmith, it was said, "He wrote like an angel, and talked like poor Poll."

James Smith says, "I don't fancy painters. General Phipps used to have them much at his table. He once asked me if I liked to meet them. I answered, 'No; I know nothing in their way, and they know nothing out of it.'"

MADAME DE BOURDONNE.

Madame de Bourdonne, Canoness of Remiremont, had been present at a discourse full of fire and eloquence, but deficient in solidity and arrangement. One of her friends, who felt an interest in the preacher, asked her, as she came out of church, how she liked it? "Is it not full of *spirit?*" said she. "So full," replied Madame de Bourdonne, "that I could not perceive any *body*."

THE ARCHBISHOP OF LYONS.

The Archbishop of Lyons had his hands completely distorted and disfigured by the gout. He was once engaged in play at cards, and had gained a thousand pistoles. "I should not mind it," said the losing party, "if my money had not got into the ugliest hand in the kingdom." "That is false," said the Archbishop; "I know one that is still uglier." "I'll wager thirty pistoles you don't," said the other. The Archbishop immediately drew off the glove which covered his left hand, and the gamester acknowledged he had lost his wager.

ART CRITICISM.

Ambrose Philips, the poet, was very solemn and pompous in conversation. At a coffee-house he was discoursing upon pictures, and pitying the painters who in their historical pieces always draw the same sort of sky. "They should travel," said he, "and then they would see that there is a different sky in every country, in England, France, Holland, Italy, and so forth." "Your remark is just," said a grave gentleman who sat just by: "I have been a traveller myself, and can testify that what you observe is true; but the greatest variety of skies that ever I found was in Poland." "In Poland, sir?" said Philips. "Yes, in Poland; for there is Sobiesky, and Sarbiensky, and Jablonsky, and Podebrasky, and many more skies, sir."

LAUDAMY AND CALAMY.

The following is related by Mr. Gillies, in his *Reminiscences of Sir Walter Scott:*—"It happened, at a small country town, that Scott suddenly required medical advice for one of his servants, and, on inquiring if there was any doctor at the place, was told that there were two —one long established, and the other a new-comer. The latter gentleman, being luckily found at home, soon made his appearance —a grave, sagacious-looking personage, attired in black, with a shovel hat, in whom, to his utter astonishment, Sir Walter recognized a Scotch blacksmith, who had formerly practised, with tolerable success, as a veterinary operator in the neighbourhood of Ashestiel. 'How, in all the world!' exclaimed he, 'can it be possible that this is John Lundie?'—'In troth is it, your honour—just a' that's for him.'—'Well, but let us hear: you were a *horse*-doctor before; now, it seems, you are a *man*-doctor; how do you get on?'—'Ou, just extraordinar weel; for your honour maun ken my practice is vera sure and orthodox. I depend entirely upon twa *simples*.'—'And what may their names be? Perhaps, it is a secret?—'I'll tell your honour,' in a low tone; 'my twa simples are just *laudamy* and *calamy!*'—'Simples with a vengeance!' replied Scott. 'But John, do you never happen to *kill* any of your patients?'—'Kill? Ou ay, may be sae! Whiles they die and whiles no;—but it's the will o' Providence. Ony how, your honour, it wad be lang before it makes up for Flodden!'"

CENTENNIAL CELEBRATION AT GÖTTINGEN.

The Society of Philologists, formed in Germany a few years ago, originated thus:—In 1837, the University of Göttingen held its centennial celebration. The festival of a university, which could look back upon so proud a century as that which marked the history of this celebrated seat of learning, naturally attracted an unusual assemblage of scholars. Distinguished philologists of all parties met together, forgetting their animosities, and embracing each other as fellow-labourers in the same great enterprise, though contemplating it from different points of view.

So touching was the scene, and so delightful the magnanimous feelings with which those who participated in it greeted each other, that Thiersch, the pillar of Greek learning in Bavaria—a man of the noblest enthusiasm, as well as of great eloquence—gave utterance to his struggling emotions, and ventured, in his remarks, to propose the formation of a society which should secure the annual recurrence of such occasions. A special meeting was called to consider the subject, at which Humboldt presided. The proposal was received with acclamation, and the first meeting was appointed to be held in Nuremberg, in 1838, at which Thiersch was to preside. In 1839, the society met at Manheim.

Frederic Jacobs, whose age and partial deafness prevented him from attending the first meeting, where his name had been mentioned with particular marks of respect, had also decided not to attend the second. But Rost of Gotha resorted to a stratagem, which was successful in procuring the attendance of Jacobs. At the age of seventy-five, he undertook his four days' journey, travelling forty miles a day, and calling, as he went, on his literary friends at Frankfort, Darmstadt, and Heidelberg. When this amiable old man and popular writer—the favourite of all parties—arrived, he could not decline addressing the assembled classical teachers of his country, mostly of the younger generation. He spoke in an affecting strain of eloquence, which was received with unusual applause. After the meeting, the principal members of the society appointed Hermann of Marburg to draw up a special communication in Latin, addressed to Jacobs, testifying, in the warmest terms, their respect for him as one of the most accomplished of classical scholars, and their personal regards for him as a man and as a friend. This circumstance called him out, in another public speech, on a subsequent day, so that the occasion was a kind of jubilee to that noble representative of the past generation.

JAMES HOGG AND SIR WALTER SCOTT.

Speaking of Scott's acquaintance with the Ettrick Shepherd, Mr. Lockhart relates the following anecdotes of the latter:—Shortly after their first meeting, Hogg, coming into Edinburgh with a flock of sheep, was seized with a sudden ambition of seeing himself in type, and he wrote out that same night *Willie and Katie*, and a few other ballads, already famous in the Forest, which some obscure bookseller gratified him by printing accordingly; but they appear to have attracted no notice beyond their original sphere. Hogg then made an excursion into the Highlands, in quest of employment as overseer of some extensive sheep-farm; but, though Scott had furnished him with strong recommendations to various friends, he returned without success. He printed an account of his travels, however, in a set of letters in the *Scots Magazine*, which, though exceedingly rugged and uncouth, had abundant traces of the native shrewdness and genuine poetical feeling of this remarkable man. These also failed to excite attention; but, undeterred by such disappointments, the Shepherd no sooner read the third volume of the *Minstrelsy*, than he made up his mind that the Editor's *Imitations of the Ancients* were by no means what they should have been. "Immediately," he says, in one of his many memoirs of himself, "I chose a number of traditional facts, and set about imitating the manner of the ancients myself." These imitations he transmitted to Scott, who warmly praised the many striking beauties scattered over their rough surface. The next time that Hogg's business carried him to Edinburgh, he waited upon Scott, who invited him to dinner in Castle Street, in company with William Laidlaw, who happened also to be in town, and some other admirers of the rustic genius. When Hogg entered the drawing-room, Mrs. Scott, being at the time in a delicate state of health, was reclining on a sofa. The Shepherd, after being presented, and making his best bow, forthwith took possession of another sofa placed opposite to hers, and stretched himself thereupon at all his length; for, as he said afterwards, 'I thought I could never do wrong to copy the lady of the house.' As his dress at this period was precisely that in which any ordinary herdsman attends cattle to the market, and as his hands, moreover, bore most legible marks of a recent sheep-smearing, the lady of the house did not observe with perfect equanimity the novel usage to which her chintz was exposed. The Shepherd, however, remarked nothing of all this—dined heartily and drank freely, and, by jest, anecdote, and song, afforded plentiful merriment to the more civilized part of the company. As the liquor operated, his familiarity increased and strengthened; from "Mr. Scott," he advanced to "Sherra," and thence to "Scott," "Walter," and "Wattie," until at supper, he fairly convulsed the whole party by addressing Mrs. Scott as "Charlotte."

PEVERIL OF THE PEAK, AND PETER OF THE PAUNCH.

One morning (says Mr. Lockhart, in his *Life of Scott*) soon after Peveril came out, one of our most famous wags (now famous for better things), namely, Mr. Patrick Robertson, commonly called by the endearing Scottish *diminutive* "Peter," observed that tall conical white head advancing above the crowd towards the fireplace, where the usual roar of fun was going on among the briefless, and said, "Hush, boys, here comes old Peveril—I see *the Peak*." A laugh ensued, and the Great Unknown, as he withdrew from the circle after a few minutes' gossip, insisted that I should tell him what our joke upon his advent had been. When enlightened, being by that time half-way across the "babbling hall," towards his own *Division*, he looked round with a sly grin, and said, between his teeth, "Ay, ay, my man, as weel Peveril o' the Peak ony day, as Peter o' the Painch" (paunch)—which, being transmitted to the brethren of *the stove school*, of course delighted all of them, except their portly Coryphœus. But *Peter's* application stuck; to his dying day, Scott was in the Outer House *Peveril of the Peak*, or *Old Peveril*—and, by and by, like a good cavalier, he took to the designation kindly. He was well aware that his own family and younger friends constantly talked of him under this *sobriquet*. Many a little note have I had from him (and so probably has *Peter* also), reproving, or perhaps encouraging, Tory mischief, and signed, "Thine, PEVERIL."

WORDSWORTH'S FAREWELL VISIT TO SCOTT.

A few days before Scott's departure for Italy in search of health, in 1831, Mr. Wordsworth and his daughter arrived from Westmoreland to take farewell of him. This was a very fortunate circumstance; nothing could have gratified Sir Walter more, or sustained him better, if he needed any support from without. On the 22d—all his arrangements being completed, and Laidlaw having received a paper of instructions, the last article of which repeats the caution to be "very careful of the dogs"—these two great poets—who had through life loved each other well, and, in spite of very different theories as to art, appreciated each other's genius more justly than inferior spirits ever did either of them—spent the morning together in a visit to Newark; hence the last of the three poems by which Wordsworth has connected his name to all time with the most romantic of Scottish streams. But I need not transcribe a piece so well known as the *Yarrow Revisited*.

Sitting that evening in the library, Sir Walter said a good deal about the singularity that Fielding and Smollett had both been driven abroad by declining health, and never returned—which circumstance, though his language was rather cheerful at this time, he had often before alluded to in a darker fashion; and Mr. Wordsworth expressed his regret that neither of those great masters of romance appeared to have been surrounded with any due marks of respect in the close of life. I happened to observe that Cervantes, on his last journey to Madrid, met with an incident which seemed to have given him no common satisfaction. Sir Walter did not remember the passage, and desired me to find it out in the *Life* by Pellicer, which was at hand, and translate it. I did so, and he listened with lively though pensive interest. Our friend Allan, the historical painter, had also come out that day from Edinburgh, and he lately told me, that he remembers nothing he ever saw with so much sad pleasure as the attitudes and aspect of Scott and Wordsworth as the story went on. Mr. Wordsworth was at that time, I should notice—though indeed his noble stanzas tell it—in but a feeble state of general health. He was, moreover, suffering so much from some malady in his eyes, that he wore a deep green shade over them. Thus he sat between Sir Walter and his daughter: *absit omen*—but it was no wonder that Allan thought as much of Milton as of Cervantes. The anecdote of the young student's raptures on discovering that he had been riding all day with the author of *Don Quixote*, is introduced in the preface to *Count Robert*, and *Castle Dangerous*, which (for I may not return to the subject) came out at the close of November in four volumes, as the Fourth Series of *Tales of My Landlord*.—(Lockhart.)

A ROYAL PROBLEM IN SCIENCE.

When King Charles II. dined with the members on the occasion of constituting them a Royal Society, towards the close of the evening he expressed his satisfaction at being the first English monarch who had laid a foundation for a society which proposed that their whole studies should be directed to the investigation of the arcana of nature, and added, with that peculiar gravity of countenance he usually wore on such occasions, that among such learned men he now hoped for a solution to a question which had long puzzled him. The case he thus stated:— Suppose two pails of water were fixed in two different scales that were equally poised, and which weighed equally alike, and two live bream, or small fish, were put into either of these pails; he wanted to know the reason why that pail, with such addition, should not weigh more than the other pail which was against it. Every one was ready to set at quiet the royal curiosity; but it appeared that every one was giving a different opinion. One at length offered so ridiculous a solution, that another of the members could not refrain from a loud laugh; when the king, turning to him, insisted that he should give his sentiments as well as the rest. This he did without hesitation; and told his majesty, in plain terms, that he denied the fact; on which the king, in high mirth, exclaimed: "Odds fish, brother, you are in the right!" The jest was not ill designed. The story is often useful to cool the enthusiasm of the scientific visionary, who is apt to account for what never existed.

"EDINBURGH REVIEW."

Sir Walter Scott ascribes the great success of this periodical to two circumstances:—that it was above the influence of the puffing booksellers, and that the recompense per sheet was not only liberal in itself, but was actually forced on all contributors, however high their rank and fortune, by the editor, whose saying was, that Czar Peter, when working in the trenches, received pay as a common soldier. This general rule removed all scruples of delicacy, and fixed the services of men of talent and enterprise, who were glad of a handsome apology to work for fifteen or twenty guineas, though they would not willingly have been considered as hackney writers.

VULGAR PRONUNCIATION.

One of the peculiarities of vulgar English pronunciation is to put the letter *r* at the end of words ending with a vowel. Some of the inhabitants of London, if they had to speak the following sentence, "A fellow broke the window, and hit Isabella on the elbow, as she was playing a sonata on the piano," would give it in the following manner :—"A fellor broke the windor, and hit Isabellar on the elbor, as she was playing a sonatar on the pianar." Others adopt the contrary plan, and leave out the *r* as often as they can. There are magistrates of high pretensions to education, who would say, "The conduct of the prisna' and his general characta' render it propa' that he should no longa' be a memba' of this community." Equally glaring is the taking away of *h* from places where it is required, and giving it where its absence is desirable. The termination of words ending in *ing* with a *k*, as *somethink*, is not less incorrect or less disagreeable. It is worth while occasionally to point out these errors, as many must be disposed to correct them, on being made aware of their existence.

SERVANTS.

In France, servants always walk before their masters. It is otherwise in Italy. Masters walk before their servants in summer, on account of the dust, and in winter behind them, on account of the badness of the roads.

BOOK-STALL READERS.

There is a class of street-readers whom I can never contemplate without affection—the poor gentry who, not having wherewithal to buy or hire a book, filch a little learning at the open stalls; the owner, with his hard eye, casting envious looks at them all the while, and thinking when they will have done. Venturing tenderly, page after page, expecting every moment when he shall interpose his interdict, and yet unable to deny themselves the gratification, they "snatch a fearful joy."

BURKE AND THE RIOT ACT.

During one of the debates on the affairs of America, Hartley, the member for Hull, after having driven four-fifths of a very full house from the benches by an unusually dull speech, at length requested that the Riot Act might be read, for the purpose of elucidating one of his propositions. Burke, who was impatient to address the house himself, immediately started up and exclaimed, "The Riot Act, my dearest friend: why, in the name of everything that's sacred, have the Riot Act read? The mob, you see, is already dispersed." Peals of laughter followed the utterance of this comic appeal, which Lord North frequently declared to be one of the happiest instances of wit he ever heard.

THE CALCULATING MACHINE.

Mr Babbage, the inventor of this machine, has (in his *Bridgewater Treatise*) referred to its present state. He mentions that, as early as 1821, he undertook to superintend for the Government the construction of an engine for calculating and printing mathematical and astronomical tables. Early in 1833 a small portion of the machine was put together, and it performed its work with all the precision which had been anticipated. At that period circumstances caused a suspension of its progress, and the Government, on whose decision the continuance or discontinuance of the work depends, have not yet communicated to Mr. Babbage their wishes on the question. Since the commencement of the original machine, Mr. Babbage has projected another and far more powerful engine; the former could employ about 120 figures in its calculations, the latter is intended to compute with about 4000.

LORD CHATHAM.

It is said of the eloquence of the Earl of Chatham, that "his voice, even when it sank to a whisper, was heard to the remotest benches; when he strained it to its full strength, the sound rose like the swell of an organ of a great cathedral, shook the house with its peal, and was heard through lobbies and down staircases to the Court of Requests and the precincts of Westminster Hall."

DR. PITCAIRNE AND ACADEMIC DEGREES.

Dr. Alexander Pitcairne, who died in 1713, and who was long remembered most distinctly in Scotland for his strong Jacobitism, his keen wit, and his eminence as a physician, studied his profession in Holland, where he was for some time the preceptor of Boerhaave. His political principles causing him to be no friend to the republican Dutch, he amused himself with satirizing them in verse. Dull, however, as the Dutch are generally esteemed, they had once paid him very smartly in his own coin. Pitcairne, it seems, took great offence at the facility with which the University of Leyden, like some of those in this country at a more recent period, conferred degrees upon those applying for them. To ridicule them, he sent for a diploma for his footman, which was granted. He next sent for another for his horse. This, however, was too gross an affront for even Dutchmen to swallow. In a spirit of resentment an answer was returned, to the effect, that "search having been made in the books of the University, they could not find one instance of the degree of doctor having been ever conferred upon a horse, although, in the instance of one Dr. Pitcairne, it appeared that the degree had once been conferred on an ass."

DRS. BARTON AND NASH.

Dr. Barton was in company with Dr. Nash, just as he was going to publish his work on the antiquities of Worcestershire. "I fear," said Dr. Barton, "there will be a great many inaccuracies in your books when they come out." "How are errors to be avoided?" said Dr. Nash. "Very easily," said Dr. Barton. "Are you not a justice of peace?" "I am," said Dr. Nash. "Why, then," replied the old warden, "you have nothing to do but to send your books to the *house of correction*."

COBBETT'S EARLY RECOLLECTIONS.

Perhaps, in Cobbett's voluminous writings, there is nothing so fine as the following picture of his boyish scenes and recollections. It has been well compared to the most simple and touching passages in Richardson's *Pamela*:—

"After living within a hundred yards of Westminster Hall, and the Abbey Church, and the bridge, and looking from my own window into St. James's Park, all other buildings and spots appeared mean and insignificant. I went to-day to see the house I formerly occupied. How small! It is always thus: the words large and small are carried about with us in our minds, and we forget real dimensions. The idea, such as it was received, remains during our absence from the object. When I returned to England in 1800, after an absence from the country parts of it for sixteen years, the trees, the hedges, even the parks and woods, seemed so small! It made me laugh to hear little gutters, that I could jump over, called rivers. The Thames was but 'a creek.' But when, in about a month after my arrival in London, I went to Farnham, the place of my birth, what was my surprise! Everything was become so pitifully small! I had to cross in my post-chaise the long and dreary heath of Bagshot; then, at the end of it, to mount a hill called Hungry Hill; and from that hill I knew that I should look down into the beautiful and fertile vale of Farnham. My heart fluttered with impatience, mixed with a sort of fear, to see all the scenes of my childhood; for I had learned, before, the death of my father and mother. There is a hill not far from the town, called Crooksbury Hill, which rises up out of a flat in the form of a cone, and is planted with Scotch fir-trees. Here I used to take the eggs and young ones of crows and magpies. This hill was a famous object in the neighbourhood. It served as the superlative degree of height. 'As high as Crooksbury Hill,' meant with us the utmost degree of height. Therefore the first object my eyes sought was this hill. I could not believe my eyes! Literally speaking, I for a moment thought the famous hill removed, and a little heap put in its stead; for I had seen in New Brunswick, a single rock, or hill of solid rock, ten times as big, and four or five times as high! The postboy, going down hill, and not a bad road, whisked me in a few minutes to the Bush Inn, from the garden of which I could see the prodigious sand hill where I had begun my gardening works. What a nothing! But now came rushing into my mind, all at once, my pretty little garden, my little blue smock-frock, my little nailed shoes, my pretty pigeons that I used to feed out of my hands, the last kind words and tears of my gentle, and tender-hearted, and affectionate mother. I hastened back into the room. If I had looked a moment longer, I should have dropped. When I came to reflect, what a change! What scenes I had gone through! How altered my state! I had dined the day before at a secretary of state's, in company with Mr. Pitt, and had been waited upon by men in gaudy liveries. I had had nobody to assist me in the world; no teachers of any sort; nobody to shelter me from the consequence of bad, and nobody to counsel me to good, behaviour. I felt proud. The distinctions of rank, birth, and wealth, all became nothing in my eyes; and from that moment (less than a month after my arrival in England) I resolved never to bend before them."

Cobbett was, for a short time, a labourer in the kitchen-grounds of the Royal Gardens at Kew. King George the Third often visited the gardens to inquire after the fruit and esculents; and one day he saw Cobbett here, then a lad, who, with a few halfpence in his pocket, and Swift's *Tale of a Tub* in his hand, had been so captivated by the wonders of the Royal Gardens, that he applied there for employment. The king, on perceiving the clownish boy, with his stockings tied about his legs by scarlet garters, inquired about him, and specially desired that he might be continued in his service.

PERCY BYSSHE SHELLEY.

Shelley had a pleasure in making paper boats, and floating them on the water. The *New Monthly* has the following curious anecdote on this subject:—So long as his paper lasted he remained rivetted to the spot, fascinated by this peculiar amusement; all waste-paper was rapidly consumed, then the covers of letters, next letters of little value; the most precious contributions of the most esteemed correspondents, although eyed wistfully many times, and often returned to the pocket, were sure to be sent at last in pursuit of the former squadrons. Of the portable volumes which were the companions of his rambles, and he seldom went out without a book, the fly-leaves were commonly wanting—he had applied them as our ancestor Noah applied gopher-wood; but learning was so sacred in his eyes, that he never trespassed further upon the integrity of the copy; the work itself was always respected. It has been said that he once found himself on the north bank of the Serpentine river without the materials for indulging those inclinations which the sight of water invariably inspired, for he had exhausted his supplies on the round pond in Kensington Gardens. Not a single scrap of paper could be found, save only a bank post bill for fifty pounds; he hesitated long, but yielded at last; he twisted it into a boat with the extreme refinement of his skill, and committed it with the utmost dexterity to fortune—watching its progress, if possible, with a still more intense anxiety than usual. Fortune often favours those who frankly and fully trust her; the north-east wind gently wafted the costly skiff to the south bank, where during the latter part of the voyage the venturous owner had waited its arrival with patient solicitude.

SIR WALTER SCOTT'S BREAKFASTS.

Sir Walter Scott's chief meal was breakfast. No fox-hunter ever prepared himself for the field by more substantial appliances. His table was always provided, in addition to the usually plentiful delicacies of a Scotch breakfast, with some solid article, on which he did most lusty execution; a round of beef, a pasty such as made Gil Blas' eyes water, or, most welcome of all, a cold sheep's head. A huge brown loaf flanked his elbow, and it was placed upon a broad wooden trencher, that he might cut and come again with the bolder knife. Often did the *clerk's coach* — commonly called among themselves the "Lively," which trundled round every morning to pick up the brotherhood, and then deposited them at the proper minute in the Parliament-close—often did this lumbering hackney arrive at his door before he had fully appeased what Homer calls the "sacred rage of hunger," and vociferous was the merriment of the learned scribes when the surprised poet swung forth to join them, with an extemporized sandwich, that looked like a ploughman's luncheon, in his hand. But this robust supply would have served him, in fact, for the day. He never tasted anything more before dinner, and at dinner he ate almost as sparingly as Squire Tovell's niece in Crabbe's tale.— (Lockhart.)

WILL'S COFFEE-HOUSE, TOM'S, AND BUTTON'S.

Three of the most celebrated resorts of the literati of the last century were the following:—Will's Coffee-house, No. 23, on the north side of Great Russell Street, Covent Garden, at the end of Bow Street. This was the favourite resort of Dryden, who had here his own chair, in winter, by the fireside, in summer in the balcony; the company met on the first floor, and there smoked; and the young beaux and wits were sometimes honoured with a pinch out of Dryden's snuff-box. Will's was the resort of men of genius till 1710. It was subsequently occupied by a perfumer.

Tom's, No. 17, Great Russell Street, had nearly 700 subscribers, at a guinea a head, from 1764 to 1768, and had its card, conversation, and coffee-rooms, where assembled Dr. Johnson, Garrick, Murphy, Goldsmith, Sir Joshua Reynolds, Foote, and other men of talent. The tables and books of the club are preserved in the house, the first floor of which is occupied by Mr. Webster, the medallist.

Button's, "over against" Tom's, was the receiving-house for contributions to the *Guardian*, in a lion-head box, the aperture for which remains (1849) in the wall to mark the place. Button had been servant to Lady Warwick, whom Addison married, and the house was frequented by Pope, Steele, Swift, Arbuthnot, and Addison. The lion's head for a letter-box, "the best head in England," was set up in imitation of the celebrated lion at Venice. It was removed from Button's to the Shakspeare's Head, under the arcade in Covent Garden, and in 1751 was placed in the Bedford, next door. This lion's head is now treasured as a relic by the Bedford family.

LITERATURE AS A PROFESSION.

Sir Walter Scott, in conversing with a young man who was about to embark upon the perilous voyage of letters, in search of fortune and fame, made to him this pithy remark — it contains a volume :— "Literature, my young friend, is a good staff, but a bad crutch."

"PAMELA."

I recollect an anecdote (said Sir John Herschel, in the opening address to the subscribers to the Windsor and Eton public library, when the learned knight was president), told me by a late highly respected inhabitant of Windsor, as a fact which he could personally testify, having occurred in a village where he resided several years, and where he actually was at the time it took place. The blacksmith of the village had got hold of Richardson's novel of *Pamela, or Virtue Rewarded*, and used to read it aloud in the long summer evenings, seated on his anvil, and never failed to have a large and attentive audience. It is a pretty long-winded book; but their patience was fully a match for the author's prolixity, and they fairly listened to it all. At length when the happy turn of fortune arrived which brings the hero and heroine together, and describes them as living long and happily, according to the most approved rules, the congregation were so delighted as to raise a great shout, and procuring the church keys, actually set the parish bells a-ringing.

A WHIMSICAL LORD OF QUEEN ANNE'S TIME.

Lord Wharncliffe, in his new and extended edition of the works of Lady Mary Wortley Montagu, gives the following amusing anecdotes of a noble lord of the early part of the last century:—Mary Howe, daughter of Lord Viscount Howe, married to Thomas, eighth Earl of Pembroke, 1725— the Lord Pembroke, who collected the statues and models at Wilton, and whose knowledge of classical antiquity might therefore make his praise flattering to Lady Mary Wortley, had been a principal member of the Whig administrations under King William and Queen Anne, and the last person who held the office of Lord High Admiral; but now being old and a great humourist, distinguished himself by odd whims and peculiarities; one of which was a fixed resolution not to believe that anything he disliked, ever did or could happen. One must explain this by instances. He chose that his eldest son should always live in the house with him while unmarried. The son, who was more than of age, and had a will of his own, often chose to live elsewhere. But let him be ever so distant, or stay away ever so long, his father still insisted on supposing him present; every day bidding the butler tell Lord Herbert dinner was ready: and the butler every day as gravely bringing word, that "his lordship dined abroad." Marrying for the third time at seventy-five, he maintained strict dominion over a wife whom other people thought safely arrived at years of discretion, and quite fit to take care of herself. She had leave to visit in an evening, but must never on any account stay out a minute later than ten o'clock, his supper-hour. One night, however, she staid till past twelve. He declined supping, telling the servant it could not be ten o'clock, as their lady was not come home; when at last she came, in a terrible fright, and began making a thousand apologies. "My dear," said he very coolly, "you are under a mistake, it is but just ten; your watch, I see, goes too fast, and so does mine: we must have the man to-morrow to set them to rights; meanwhile let us go to supper." His example on another occasion might be worth following. Of all the Mede and Persian laws established in his house, the most peremptory was, that any servant who once got drunk should be instantly discharged; no pardon granted, no excuse listened to. Yet an old footman, who had lived with him many years, would sometimes indulge in a pot of ale extraordinary, trusting to the wilful blindness which he saw assumed when convenient. One fatal day, even this could not avail. As my Lord crossed the hall, John appeared in full view; not rather tipsy, or a little disguised, but dead drunk, and unable to stand. Lord Pembroke went up to him. "My poor fellow, what ails you? you seem dreadfully ill; let me feel your pulse. God bless us, he is in a raging fever; get him to bed directly, and send for the apothecary." The apothecary came, not to be consulted—for his Lordship was physician-general in his own family—but to obey orders; to bleed the patient copiously, clap a huge blister on his back, and give him a powerful dose of physic. After a few days of this treatment, when the fellow emerged weak and wan as the severest illness could have left him, "Hah, honest John," cried his master, "I am truly glad to see thee alive; you have had a wonderful escape though, and ought to be thankful; very thankful, indeed. Why, man, if I had not passed by at the time and spied the condition you were in, you would have been dead before now. But, John, John," lifting up his finger, "NO MORE OF THESE FEVERS!"

PORSON'S MEMORY.

"I had invited Porson," says an English author, "to meet a party of friends in Sloane Street, where I lived; but the professor had mistaken the day, and made his appearance in full costume the preceding one. We had already dined, and were at our cheese. When he discovered his error, he made his usual exclamation of a *whooe!* as long as my arm, and, turning to me, with great gravity, said, 'I advise you in future, sir, when you ask your friends to dinner, to ask your wife to write your cards. Sir, your penmanship is abominable; it would disgrace a cobbler. I swear that your day is written Thursday, not Friday,' at the same time pulling the invitation out of his pocket. A jury was summoned, and it was decided *nem. con.*, 'that for once the professor was in the wrong,' which he instantly admitted. 'Your blunder,' I replied, 'my friend, will cost me a beef-steak and a bottle of your favourite Trinity ale, so that you will be the gainer.'

"He sat on, 'as was his custom in the afternoon,' till past midnight, emptying every flask and decanter that came to his way. As I knew there was no end to his bacchanalia when fairly seated with plenty of drink and a listener, I retired, leaving him to finish the remains of some half-dozen of bottles; for it was immaterial to the professor the quality of the stuff, provided he had quantity.

"On my descending, the following morning, to breakfast, I was surprised to find my friend lounging on a sofa, and perusing with great attention a curious volume of Italian tales, which I had picked up in my travels. I learned that, having found the liquor so choice, and the *Novelle Antiche* so interesting, he had trimmed his lamp and remained on the premises. 'I think,' said he, 'that with the aid of a razor, and a light-coloured neckcloth, and a brush, I shall be smart enough for your fine party.'

"A pretty large company assembled in the evening, and Porson treated them with a translation (without book) of the curious tale which had excited his notice. So extraordinary was his memory, that although there were above forty names introduced into the story, he had only forgotten one. This annoyed him so much, that he started from the table, and after pacing about the room for ten minutes, he stopped short, exclaiming, 'Eureka! The count's name is Don Francesco Averani.' The party sat till three o'clock in the morning, but Porson would not stir, and it was with no small difficulty that my brother could prevail on him to take his departure at five; having favoured me with his company exactly thirty-six hours. During this time, I calculated he finished a bottle of alcohol, two of Trinity ale, six of claret, besides the lighter sort of wines, of which I could take no account; he also emptied a half-pound canister of snuff, and, during the first night, smoked a bundle of cigars.

"Professor Porson, most unhappily, gave way to his inclination to drinking, and died of apoplexy at the age of forty-nine years. At a *post-mortem* examination, it was ascertained that his skull was one of the thickest that had ever been observed. And this, too, notwithstanding the fact that he was one of the most remarkable scholars of the age in which he lived."

THE SON OF BUFFON.

The son of Buffon one day surprised his father by the sight of a column, which he had raised to the memory of his father's eloquent genius. "It will do you honour," observed the Gallic sage. And when that son, in the revolution, was led to the guillotine, he ascended in silence, so impressed with his father's fame, that he only told the people, "I am the son of Buffon."

PORSON AT SCHOOL.

Professor Porson, when a boy at Eton school, discovered the most astonishing powers of memory. In going up to a lesson one day, he was accosted by a boy in the same form—"Porson, what have you got there?" "*Horace.*" "Let me look at it." Porson handed the book to the boy, who, pretending to return it, dexterously substituted another in its place, with which Porson proceeded. Being called on by the master, he read and construed Carm. 1, x. very regularly. Observing the class to laugh, the master said, "Porson, you seem to me to be reading on one side of the page, while I am looking at the other; pray whose edition have you?" Porson hesitated. "Let me see it," rejoined the master; who, to his great surprise, found it to be an English *Ovid*. Porson was ordered to go on; which he did easily, correctly, and promptly, to the end of the ode.

PUNCTUATION.

When Lord Timothy Dexter, of Newburyport, wrote his famous book, entitled *A Pikel for the Knowing Ones*, there happened to be many heresies, schisms, and false doctrines abroad in the land regarding punctuation, and as many diverse systems appeared, for the location of commas, semicolons, periods, dashes, &c., as there were works published. To obviate this difficulty, and to give every one an opportunity of suiting himself, his lordship left out all marks of punctuation from the body of his work, and at the ending of the book had printed four or five pages of nothing but stops and pauses, with which he said the reader could pepper his dish as he chose.

PASCAL.

It is reported of that prodigy of parts, Monsieur Pascal, that, till the decay of his health had impaired his memory, he forgot nothing of what he had done, read, or thought during any part of his rational age.

SIDNEY SMITH.

Sidney Smith had an extraordinary memory, always ready. He could repeat pages of poetry, English, Latin, and French; when, where, or how he learned them no one of his family pretended to know; but they were always ready and appropriate in company, when conversation turned that way. He was equally ready in enlivening a party of young ladies, by every variety of charades and conundrums, generally made on the spur of the moment, by cutting paper into curious figures, and by a display of clever tricks; for all which his demand in payment was a kiss from each. His company was much sought after. He was always lively and agreeable, and his conversation full of variety and interesting anecdotes.

SIR JAMES MACKINTOSH AND MADAME DE STAEL.

Sir J. Mackintosh, who spoke of Madame de Stael as the most celebrated woman of this, or, perhaps, any age, said: "She treats me as the person whom she most delights to honour. I am generally ordered with her to dinner as one orders beans and bacon. She is one of the few persons who surpass expectation; she has every sort of talent, and would be universally popular if, in society, she were to confine herself to her inferior talents — pleasantry, anecdote, and literature — which are so much more suited to conversation than her eloquence and genius."

HUMANITY OF MR. DAY.

While Mr. Day, the eccentric author of *Sandford and Merton*, was visiting his friend, Sir William Jones, at his chambers, the latter, in removing some books, perceived a spider fall from them; on which he cried hastily — "Kill that spider, Day; kill that spider!" "No," said Mr. Day, with that coolness for which he was conspicuous, "I will not kill that spider, Jones; I do not know that I have a right to kill that spider! Suppose when you are going in the coach to Westminster Hall, a superior being who, perhaps, may have as much power over you as you have over this insect, should say to his companion, 'Kill that lawyer! kill that lawyer!' how should you like that, Jones?—and I am sure, to most people, a lawyer is a more noxious animal than a spider."

CORRUPTIONS OF WORDS.

Many of our most popular vulgarisms have their origin in some whimsical perversion of language or of fact. St. Martin is one of the worthies of the Romish calendar, and a form of prayer commences with the words, "*O, mihi, beate Martine*," which was corrupted to "My eye and Betty Martin."

"The Goat and Compasses," with appropriate emblazonment, was a favourite name for the old English hostelries. The name is a corruption of the ancient legend, "God encompasseth us."

DR. JOHNSON'S STYLE.

Macaulay, in his *Review of Boswell's Johnson*, says he wrote in a style in which no one ever made love, quarrelled, drove bargains, or even thinks. When he wrote for publication, "he did his sentences into Johnsonese."

Goldsmith remarked to him, "If you were to write a fable about little fishes, doctor, *you* would make the little fishes to talk like whales."

LITERARY ACQUIREMENTS IN THE ARMY.

Lieut.-Gen. Sir George Murray served in the expedition to Egypt, and when before Alexandria, the troops having suffered severely from want of water, his literary acquirements were of the greatest service, instructing him that Cæsar's army had suffered from the same cause, and in very nearly the same place. Referring to his *Cæsar*, which he always carried in his travelling portable library, he found his recollection right, and that water had been obtained by the Romans from digging wells to a certain depth in the sands. The trial was immediately made, and the result was a most copious supply of that necessary article, which enabled the British troops to hold their ground, and ultimately to triumph.

PASCAL'S "LETTERS."

When Pascal became warm in his celebrated controversy, he applied himself with incredible labour to the composition of his *Provincial Letters*. He was frequently occupied twenty days on a single letter. He recommenced some above seven or eight times, and by this means obtained that perfection which has made his work, as Voltaire says, one of the best books ever published in France.

ORIGIN OF THE WORD "TEETOTAL."

The word *teetotal* originated with a Lancashire working-man, who, being unused to public speaking, and wishing to pronounce the word "total" in connection with "abstinence from intoxicating liquors," hesitated, and pronounced the first letter by itself, and the word after it, making altogether *t-total*. This fact it is well to be acquainted with, because it sufficiently refutes the vulgar notion that *tee* has reference to *tea*.

PHYSIOGNOMY.

Lavater, in his *Physiognomy*, says that Lord Anson, from his countenance, must have been a very wise man. He was one of the most stupid men I ever knew.—(Walpole.)

LORD WILLIAM POULET.

Lord William Poulet, though often chairman of committees of the House of Commons, was a great dunce, and could scarce read. Having to read a bill for naturalizing Jemima, Duchess of Kent, he called her Jeremiah, Duchess of Kent.

Having heard south walls commended for ripening fruit, he showed all the four sides of his garden for south walls.

A gentleman writing to desire a fine horse he had, offered him any *equivalent*. Lord William replied, that the horse was at his service, but he did not know what to do with an *elephant*.

A pamphlet, called *The Snake in the Grass*, being reported (probably in joke) to be written by this Lord William Poulet, a gentleman, abused in it, sent him a challenge. Lord William professed his innocence, and that he was not the author; but the gentleman would not be satisfied without a denial under his hand. Lord William took a pen, and began, "This is to scratify, that the buk called the Snak—" "O, my Lord," said the person, "I am satisfied; your Lordship has already convinced me you did not write the book."

EXCUSE FOR A LONG LETTER.

In a postscript to one of the *Provincial Letters*, Pascal excuses himself for the letter being so long, on the plea that he had not had time to make it shorter.

WIT AND WISDOM.

Philip, King of Macedon, having invited Dionysius the younger to dine with him at Corinth, attempted to deride the father of his royal guest, because he had blended the characters of prince and poet, and had employed his leisure in writing odes and tragedies. "How could the king find leisure," said Philip, "to write such trifles?" "In those hours," answered Dionysius, "which you and I spend in drunkenness and debauchery."

STUPID STORIES.

A stupid story, or idea, will sometimes make one laugh more than wit. I was once removing from Berkeley Square to Strawberry-hill, and had sent off all my books when a message unexpectedly arrived, which fixed me in town for that afternoon. What to do? I desired my man to rummage for a book, and he brought me an old Grub Street thing from the garret. The author, in sheer ignorance, not humour, discoursing of the difficulty of some pursuit, said, that even if a man had as many lives as a cat, nay, as many lives as one Plutarch is said to have had, he could not accomplish it. This odd *quid pro quo* surprised me into vehement laughter.—(Walpole.)

SYMPTOMS OF INSANITY.

My poor nephew, Lord ——, was deranged. The first symptom that appeared was, his sending a chaldron of coals as a present to the Prince of Wales, on learning that he was loaded with debts. He delighted in what he called *book-hunting*. This notable diversion consisted in taking a volume of a book, and hiding it in some secret part of the library, among volumes of similar binding and size. When he had forgot where the game lay, he hunted till he found it.—(Walpole.)

PENNANT'S TOUR IN CHESTER.

Mr. Pennant is a most ingenious and pleasing writer. His *Tours* display a great variety of knowledge, expressed in an engaging way. In private life, I am told, he has some peculiarities, and even eccentricities. Among the latter may be classed his singular antipathy to a wig—which, however, he can suppress, till reason yields a little to wine. But when this is the case, off goes the wig next to him, and into the fire.

Dining once at Chester with an officer who wore a wig, Mr. Pennant became half-seas over; and another friend that was in company carefully placed himself between Pennant and wig, to prevent mischief. After much patience, and many a wistful look, Pennant started up, seized the wig, and threw it into the fire. It was in flames in a moment, and so was the officer, who ran to his sword. Down stairs runs Pennant, and the officer after him, through all the streets of Chester. But Pennant escaped, from superior local knowledge. A wag called this "Pennant's Tour in Chester."—(Walpole.)

ENGLISH LANGUAGE.

Some years ago a gentleman, after carefully examining the folio edition of Johnson's *Dictionary*, formed the following table of English words derived from other languages:—

Latin,	6732
French,	4812
Saxon,	1665
Greek,	1148
Dutch,	691
Italian,	211
German,	106
Welsh,	95
Danish,	75
Spanish,	56
Icelandic,	50
Swedish,	34
Gothic,	31
Hebrew,	16
Teutonic,	15
Arabic,	13
Irish,	6
Runic,	4
Flemish,	4
Erse,	4
Syriac,	3
Scottish,	3
Irish and Erse,	2
Turkish,	2
Irish and Scottish,	1
Portuguese,	1
Persian,	1
Frisi,	1
Persic,	1
Uncertain,	1
Total,	15,784

TWO MINISTERS.

Mr. Pitt's plan, when he had the gout, was to have no fire in his room, but to load himself with bed-clothes. At his house at Hayes he slept in a long room, at one end of which was his bed, and his lady's at the other. His way was, when he thought the Duke of Newcastle had fallen into any mistake, to send for him, and read him a lecture. The Duke was sent for once, and came, when Mr. Pitt was confined to bed by the gout. There was, as usual, no fire in the room; the day was very chilly, and the Duke, as usual, afraid of catching cold. The Duke first sat down on Mrs. Pitt's bed, as the warmest place; then drew up his legs into it, as he got colder. The lecture unluckily continuing a considerable time, the Duke at length fairly lodged himself under Mrs. Pitt's bed-clothes. A person, from whom I had the story, suddenly going in, saw the two ministers in bed, at the two ends of the room; while Pitt's long nose, and black beard unshaved for some days, added to the grotesque of the scene.—(Walpole.)

BOOKSELLERS.

The manœuvres of bookselling are now equal in number to the stratagems of war. Publishers open and shut the sluices of reputation as their various interests lead them; and it is become more and more difficult to judge of the merit or fame of recent publications.—(Walpole.)

WORTHLESS WRITING.

Gilbert Wakefield tells us that he wrote his own memoirs (a large octavo) in six or eight days. It cost him nothing, and, what is very natural, is worth nothing. One might yawn scores of such books into existence; but who could be the wiser or the better?

DR. JOHNSON.

I cannot imagine that Dr Johnson's reputation will be very lasting. His *Dictionary* is a surprising work for one man; but sufficient examples in foreign countries show that the task is too much for one man, and that a society should alone pretend to publish a standard dictionary. In Johnson's *Dictionary*, I can hardly find anything I look for. It is full of words nowhere else to be found, and wants numerous words occurring in good authors. In writing it is useful; as, if one be doubtful in the choice of a word, it displays the authorities for its usage.

His essays I detest. They are full of what I call *triptology*, or repeating the same thing thrice over, so that three papers to the same effect might be made out of any one paper in the *Rambler*. He must have had a bad heart—his story of the sacrilege in his *Voyage to the Western Islands of Scotland* is a lamentable instance.—(Walpole.)

FRENCH NATIONALITY.

The Abbé Raynal came, with some Frenchmen of rank, to see me at Strawberry-hill. They were standing at a window, looking at the prospect to the Thames, which they found flat, and one of them said in French, not thinking that I and Mr. Churchill overheard them, "Everything in England only serves to recommend France to us the more." Mr. Churchill instantly stepped up and said, "Gentlemen, when the Cherokees were in this country they could eat nothing but train-oil."—(Walpole.)

THE VICTORIA REGIA AND THE CRYSTAL PALACE.

On new-year's day, 1837, a traveller, proceeding in a native boat up the river Berbice, in Demerara, discovered on the margin of a lake into which the river expanded, a Titanic waterplant, unlike any other he had before seen, though an accomplished botanist, and familiar with the flora of South America.

"I felt as a botanist," said Sir Richard Schomburg, "and felt myself rewarded. All calamities were forgotten. A gigantic leaf, from five to six feet in diameter, salver-shaped, with a broad rim of a light green above, and a vivid crimson below, rested on the water. Quite in character with the wonderful leaf was the luxuriant flower, consisting of an immense number of petals, passing in alternate tints from pure white to rose and pink," (and in some instances fifteen inches across.) "The smooth water was covered with blossoms; and, as I rowed from one to the other, I always observed something new to admire."

Sir Robert dug up whole plants, and sent first them, and afterwards seeds, to England, where the magnificent lily was named Victoria Regia. After some unsuccessful attempts, the task of forcing it to blossom in an artificial climate was confided to Mr. (now Sir Joseph) Paxton, the celebrated horticulturist of the Duke of Devonshire's celebrated Chatsworth.

When the Victoria Regia was to be flowered, Mr. Paxton determined to imitate nature so closely as to make the innocent offspring of the great mother lily fancy itself back again in the broad waters, and under the burning heats of British Guiana. He deceived the roots by imbedding them in a hillock of burnt loam and peat; he deluded the great circular leaves by letting them float in a tank, to which he communicated, by means of a little wheel, the gentle ripple of their own tranquil river; and he coaxed the flower into bloom by manufacturing a Berbician climate in a tiny South America, under a spacious and splendid *glass* house, invented by himself, and beautifully adapted for the purpose.

This at length suggested the giant palace in Hyde Park; and so it proved that the parent of the most extensive building in Europe was the largest known floral structure in the world.

The Victoria Regia was planted in Mr. Paxton's greenhouse, Aug. 10, 1849. So well had everything been prepared, and so vigorously did it flourish, that, on the 9th of November, a flower was produced of large circumference.

Success, however, brought a fresh embarrassment; the great plant outgrew the dimensions of its home in little more than a month. A new house, of proper dimensions for the plant when it should arrive at maturity, must be constructed at once. Mr. Paxton went to work, and combining all his improvements in constructing greenhouses with special inventions for maturing the Victoria Regia, he soon produced the desideratum in the shape of a novel and elegant conservatory, sixty feet long by forty broad. While Mr. Paxton was busy with this model garden-house, a hot war was raging in London against having the building for the World's Fair erected in Hyde Park, having that great popular resort invaded by armies of excavators, bricklayers, blacksmiths, and timber-fellers, and against having the fashionable roads broken up by the carting of more brick and mortar than were contained in the pyramids of Gizeh. The necessary spoliation of a large number of ornamental trees in the Park, and the impossibility of such a mass of brick and mortar properly drying before the time for opening the Fair, were urged in the public journals against the locality and the plan of the building, as chosen by the committee.

These things meeting the eye of Mr. Paxton as he read the *Times*, the thought struck him that such objections might be mostly obviated, provided the building for the exhibition should be constructed on the plan of his conservatory for the Victoria Regia. All that seemed to him to be wanting was a great number of his lily-houses, made on a larger scale, and joined compactly together.

The proposed edifice could thus be constructed in the great workshops of Birmingham, at Dudley, and at Thames Bank, brought home to Hyde Park ready made, and put up like a bedstead, with none of the popular annoyances urged against the committee's plan. As to the trees, he would remove them, and bring them back again in due time, without injury, or he would clap the trees, all standing, under his great glass-case.

Mr. Paxton drew up his plans and specifications. They were presented for inspection to Mr. Stephenson, the engineer, one of the royal commissioners appointed for the management of the Fair. Mr. Stephenson was delighted with them, and laid them before the royal commission. Sir Robert Peel and Prince Albert strongly favoured Mr. Paxton's scheme; but on its reference to the building committee, it was promptly rejected like many others, the committee having devised a plan of its own.

Nothing daunted, Paxton appealed to the British public; and this he did by the aid of the woodcuts and pages of the *London Illustrated News*. Everybody but the committee was at once convinced of the practicability, simplicity, and beauty of Paxton's scheme. The people and the Prince were heartily with him. Thus encouraged, the indomitable architect and his friends determined to make another effort with the building committee.

It happened that the committee had invited candidates for raising their edifice, to suggest any improvements in it that might occur to them. This opened a crevice for the tender of Paxton's plan as an "improvement" on that of the com mittee. The result was, that the glazed palace was at length chosen unanimously, not only by the building committee, but by the royal commission also. Sir Joseph Paxton has acknowledged, not only that the Victoria Lily first started the idea of a palace of glass, but that the wonderful venation in the under surface of its leaves suggested the mechanical arrangement of its iron girders.

TOWNLEY'S ANTIQUARIAN ENTHUSIASM.

The following anecdote is related in Nichols' *Illustrations of Literature*, upon the authority of Mr. Dallaway. Upon receipt of a letter from Mr. Jenkins, the then English banker at Rome, promising him the first choice of some discovered statues, Mr. Townley "instantly set off for Italy, without companion or baggage, and, taking the common post conveyance, arrived *incognito* at Rome on the precise day when a very rich *cava* was to be explored. He stood near, as an uninterested spectator, till he perceived the discovery of an exquisite statue, little injured, and which decided his choice. Observing that his agent was urgent in concealing it, he withdrew to await the event. Upon his calling at Mr. Jenkins' house in the Corso, who was not a little surprised by his sudden appearance, the statue in question was studiously concealed, while the other pieces were shared between them with apparent liberality. Mr. Townley remonstrated, and was dismissed with an assurance that, after due restoration, it should follow him to England. In about a year after, Mr. Townley had the mortification to learn that the identical young Hercules had been sold to Lord Lansdowne at an extreme, yet scarcely an equivalent price." This transaction must have occurred some time before 1790. It was in that year that the Hercules was sold by Mr. Jenkins to Lord Lansdowne. A different story is, however, told of this Hercules in the account of it in the first Dilettante volume. Mr. Townley is there stated to have had the choice of the two statues at the time they were discovered; to have fixed from description, but afterwards to have repented of his choice.

THE FRENCH ACADEMY.

It was from a private meeting that the "French Academy" derived its origin; and the true beginners of that celebrated institution assuredly had no foresight of the object to which their conferences tended. Several literary friends in Paris, finding the extent of the city occasioned much loss of time in their visits, agreed to meet on a fixed day every week, and chose Conrat's residence as central. They met for the purposes of general conversation, or to walk together, or, what was not least social, to partake in some refreshing *collation.* All being literary men, those who were authors submitted their new works to this friendly society, who, without jealousy or malice, freely communicated their strictures; the works were improved, the authors were delighted, and the critics were honest. Such was the happy life of the members of this private society during three or four years. Pelisson, the earliest historian of the French Academy, has delightfully described it: "It was such that now, when they speak of these first days of the Academy, they call it the golden age, during which, with all the innocence and freedom of that fortunate period, without pomp and noise, and without any other laws than those of friendship, they enjoyed together all which a society of minds and a rational life can yield of whatever softens and charms."

They were happy, and they resolved to be silent; nor was this bond and compact of friendship violated till one of them, Malleville, secretary of Marshal Bassompierre, being anxious that his friend Faret, who had just printed his *L'Honnete Homme*, which he had drawn from the famous Il Cortigiano of Castiglione, should profit by all their opinions, procured his admission to one of their conferences. Faret presented them with his book, heard a great deal concerning the nature of his work, was charmed by their literary communications, and returned home ready to burst with the secret. Could the society hope that others would be more faithful than they had been to themselves? Faret happened to be one of those light-hearted men who are communicative in the degree in which they are grateful, and he whispered the secret to Des Marets and to Boisrobert. The first, as soon as he heard of such a literary senate, used every effort to appear before them and read the first volume of his *Ariane*. Boisrobert, a man of distinction, and a common friend to them all, could not be refused an admission; he admired the frankness of their mutual criticisms. The society, besides, was a new object; and his daily business was to furnish an amusing story to his patron Richelieu. The cardinal-minister was very literary, and apt to be so hipped in his hours of retirement, that the physician declared, that "all his drugs were of no avail, unless his patient mixed with them a drachm of Boisrobert." In one of those fortunate moments when the cardinal was "in the vein," Boisrobert painted, with the warmest hues, this region of literary felicity, of a small, happy society formed of critics and authors. The minister, who was ever considering things in that particular aspect which might tend to his own glory, instantly asked Boisrobert whether this private meeting would not like to be constituted a public body, and establish itself by letters patent, offering them his protection. The flatterer of the minister was overjoyed, and executed the important mission; but not one of the members shared in the rapture, while some regretted an honour which would only disturb the sweetness and familiarity of their intercourse. Malleville, whose master was a prisoner in the Bastile, and Serisay, the *intendant* of the Duke of Rochefoucauld, who was in disgrace at court, loudly protested, in the style of an opposition party, against the protection of the minister; but Chapelain, who was known to have no party interests, argued so clearly, that he left them to infer that Richelieu's *offer* was a *command;* that the cardinal was a minister who willed not things by halves; and was one of those very great men who avenge any contempt shown to them, even on such little men as themselves. In a word, the dogs bowed their necks to the golden collar. However, the appearance, if not the reality, of freedom was left to them; and the minister allowed them to frame their own constitution, and elect their own magistrates and citizens in this infant and illustrious republic of literature. The history of the further establishment of the French Academy is elegantly narrated by Pelisson. The usual difficulty occurred of fixing on a title; and they appear to have changed it so often, that the academy was at first addressed by more than one title:— Academie *des beaux Esprits;* Academie *de l'Eloquence;* Academie *Eminente*, in allusion to the quality of the cardinal, its protector. Desirous of avoiding the extravagant and mystifying titles of the Italian academies, they fixed on the most unaffected, *L'Academie Française;* but though the national genius may disguise itself for a moment, it cannot be entirely got rid of, and they assumed a vaunting device of a laurel wreath, including their epigraph, "*a l'Immortalite.*"

MODERN SNAIL-EATING.

The practice of *eating*, if not of talking to, snails seems not to be so unknown in this country as some of your readers might imagine. I was just now interrogating a village child in reference to the addresses to snails, quoted under the head of *Folk Lore*, vol. iii., pp. 132 and 179, when she acquainted me with the not very appetising fact, that she and her brothers and sisters had been in the constant habit of indulging this horrible *Limacotrophy.* " We hooks them out of the wall," she says, " with a stick in winter time, and not in summer time (so it seems they have their seasons), and we roasts them, and when they've done spitting they be a-done; and we takes them out with a fork, and eats them. Sometimes we has a jug heaped up, pretty near my pinafore full. I loves them dearly." Surely this little bit of practical cottage economy is worth recording.—Your correspondent, C. W. B., does not seem to be aware that " a ragout of borror (snails)" is a regular dish with English gipsies. Vide Borrow's *Zincali*, part 1. c. v. He has clearly not read Mr. Borrow's remarks on the subject:—" Know, then, O Gentile, whether thou be from the land of Gorgois (England), or the Busue (Spain), that the very gipsies, who consider a ragout of snails a delicious dish, will not touch an eel, because it bears a resemblance to a snake; and that those who will feast on a roasted hedgehog, could be induced by no means to taste a squirrel!" Having tasted of roasted hotchiwitchu (hedgehog) myself among the " gentle Rommanys," I can bear witness to its delicate fatness; and, though a ragout of snails was never offered for my acceptance, I do not think that those who consider (as most " Gorgois" do) stewed eels a delicacy ought to be too severe on "Limacotrophists!"—(Notes and Queries.)

CONCHOLOGY AND COLLECTORS.

Conchology, as seen in museums and cabinets, is but a collection of husks and rinds of things that are dead and gone. We treasure the envelope, having lost the letter; the book is destroyed, and we preserve the binding. Not one person in a hundred who decorates his apartment with shells can tell whether the living creatures they once contained had eyes or no eyes, were fixed to the rock or drifted with the sea-weed, were purely herbivorous, or, by an insinuating but unamiable process, dieted on the vitals of other molluscs their neighbours.—(Quarterly Review.)

THE LUNATIC AND THE SPORTSMAN.

In an article on "The World 'at Large'"—the purport of which is to show that men who are reputedly sane often act very insanely—a writer in *Chambers's Journal* reproduces this good old story:—"A gentleman of fortune visited a lunatic asylum, where the treatment consisted chiefly of forcing the patients to stand in tubs of cold water, those slightly affected up to the knees; others, whose cases were graver, up to the middle; while persons very seriously ill were immersed up to the neck. The visitor entered into conversation with one of the patients, who appeared to have some curiosity to know how the stranger passed his time out of doors. "I have horses and greyhounds for coursing," said the latter in reply to the other's question. "Ah! these are very expensive." "Yes; they cost me a great deal of money in the year, but they are the best of their kind." "Have you anything more?" "Yes; I have a pack of hounds for hunting the fox." "And they cost a great deal too?" "A very great deal." "And I have birds for hawking." "I see; birds for hunting birds. And these swell up the expense, I daresay?" "You may say that, for they are not common in this country. And then I sometimes go out along with my gun, accompanied by a setter and a retriever." "And these are expensive too?" "Of course. After all, it is not the animals of themselves that run away with the money: there must be men; you know, to feed and look after them, houses to lodge them in—in short the whole sporting establishment." "I see, I see. You have horses, hounds, setters, retrievers, hawks, men—and all for the capture of foxes and birds. What an enormous revenue they must cost you! Now, what I want to know is this, what return do they pay?—what does your year's sporting produce?" "Why, we kill a fox now and then—only they are getting rather scarce hereabouts—and we seldom bag less than fifty brace of birds each season." "Hark!" said the lunatic, looking anxiously round him. "My friend"—in an earnest whisper—"there is the gate behind you; take my advice, and be off out of this place while you are safe. Don't let the doctor get his eyes upon you. He ducks *us* to some purpose; but as sure as you are a living man, he will half-drown *you!*"

PLAYFULNESS OF ANIMALS.

Small birds chase each other about in play, but perhaps the conduct of the crane and the trumpeter (*Psophia crepitans*) is the most extraordinary. The latter stands on one leg, hops about in the most eccentric manner, and throws somersets. The Americans call it the mad bird, on account of these singularities. The crane expands its wings, runs round in circles, leaps, and throwing little stones and pieces of wood in the air, endeavours to catch them again, or pretends to avoid them, as if afraid. Waterbirds, such as ducks and geese, dive after each other, and cleave the surface of the water with outstretched neck and flapping wings, throwing an abundant spray around. Deer often engage in a sham battle or a trial of strength, by twisting their horns together and pushing for the mastery. All animals that pretend violence in their play stop short of exercising it; the dog takes the greatest precaution not to injure by his bite; and the ourang-outang, in wrestling with his keeper, attempts to throw him, and makes feints of biting him. Some animals carry out in their play the semblance of catching their prey; young cats, for instance, leap after every small and moving object, even to the leaves strewed by the autumn wind; they crouch and steal forward ready for the spring; the body quivering and the tail vibrating with emotion, they bound on the moving leaf, and again watch, and again spring forward at another. Rengger saw young jaguars and cuguars playing with round substances like kittens. Young lambs collect together on the little hillocks and eminences in their pastures, racing and sporting with each other in the most interesting manner. Birds of the pie kind are the analogues of monkeys, full of mischief, play, and mimicry. There is a story told of a tame magpie, which was seen busily employed in a garden gathering pebbles, and with much solemnity and a studied air dropping them in a hole about eighteen inches deep made to receive a post. After dropping each stone, it cried "currack!" triumphantly, and set off for another. On examining the spot, a poor toad was found in this hole, which the magpie was stoning for his amusement.—(Thompson's Passions of Animals.)

BURNET.

Bishop Burnet's absence of mind is well known. Dining with the Duchess of Marlborough, after her husband's disgrace, he compared this great general to Belisarius. "But," said the Duchess, eagerly, "how came it that such a man was so miserable, and universally deserted?" "O, madam," exclaimed the *distrait* prelate, "he had such a brimstone of a wife!"

CASTLE OF OTRANTO.

Lady Craven has just brought me from Italy a most acceptable present, a drawing of the castle of Otranto. Here it is. It is odd that that back-window corresponds with the description in my romance. When I wrote it, I did not even know that there was a castle at Otranto. I wanted a name of some place in the south of Italy, and Otranto struck me in the map.

I wrote the *Castle of Otranto* in eight days, or rather eight nights; for my general hours of composition are from ten o'clock at night till two in the morning, when I am sure not to be disturbed by visitants. While I am writing I take several cups of coffee.—(Walpole.)

PROVING AN ALIBI.

A clergyman at Cambridge preached a sermon which one of his auditors commended. "Yes," said the gentleman to whom it was mentioned, "it was a good sermon, but he stole it." This was told to the preacher. He resented it, and called on the gentleman to retract what he had said. "I am not," replied the aggressor, "very apt to retract my words, but in this instance I will. I said you had stolen the sermon. I find I was wrong, for on returning home, and referring to the book whence I thought it was taken, I found it there."

FRENCH AND ENGLISH.

A Frenchman, wishing to speak of the cream of the English poets, forgot the word, and said, "de *butter* of poets." A wag said that he had fairly churned up the English language.

We often laugh at our neighbours' mistakes; they might have smiled at our own, had they overheard a passenger in one of our steam-packets, who wished to inform a French lady on board that her "berth was ready," make the communication as follows:—"Madame, *votre* NAISSANCE *est arrangée*."

THE ENGLISH WIFE ON SATURDAY EVENING.

And to see in every humble home the preparation for to-morrow! What a mopping and scrubbing! What a magnificent polishing of candlesticks and saucepan-lids; the latter to be arranged in effective devices on the kitchen walls! What a dusting, and rubbing, and bees'-waxing of incongruous furniture—beaufets and bedsteads, chairs with cane seats, rush seats, horse-hair seats, and no seats at all; and all to be arrayed against the walls with a mathematical precision which only a rash man would dare disturb. Above all, to what brilliance are stove, and fender, and the poker wrought! It is here the good thoughtful English wife lingers longest. "The fire-place" is her shrine and altar; she returns to it, brush in hand, again and again; she brings forth all sorts of ornamental nicknackeries, shells, flowers, real and artificial, and all sorts of decorative crockery, to embellish it; and when it is done, and she is convinced of that fact by repeated observation at a distance, the rest of her household work is as nothing. This finished, all the little boots and shoes come in for their share of polish, the bare brown places cunningly disguised beneath extra blacking; and these being disposed under a table in the order of their size, in readiness for the morrow, their infant wearers are next soaked, soaped, and scrubbed desperately, indued in clean night-gown and close-fitting cap, fresh from the fire, and hot enough to make the little eyes water, and off they go to bed, all but one wise old woman of say twelve years, already choke-full of domestic economy, and the importance of "the farthing out." In quiet the poor mother now sits down to a lifetime of patching, darning, and translation of cloaks into frocks, and frocks into pinafores, or anything else that may most be required, lost, the while, in subtle calculations bearing upon the possibility of purchasing some article of apparel or household use, the necessity of which is no longer to be overlooked, until her husband comes home; and then she takes her careful face and market basket among the crowd we have already seen, the husband, meanwhile, concentrating all his attention upon the fire and frying-pan in sleepy expectation of sausages. — (Tait's Magazine.)

LITERARY LABOUR.

I do not believe that anything worth reading or hearing can be produced without labour; and the labour of writing weighs upon the nerves and exhausts the spirits more perhaps than any other. Let any man sit down to prepare an address for some public occasion, and he will have an idea of this labour. Doubtless it becomes easier by habit, but the effect of routine, and the perpetual recurrence of the demand, once, if not twice, in every week, creates a difficulty on the other side. My own habit has been, never to sit down to consider what I shall write, as many do. I find that my mind, such as it is, acts most freely away from the study and in the presence of nature. I therefore construct in my own mind an exact image of everything which I intend to write; and this, when completed, can either be spoken or written as the case requires. My sermons are thus written in my mind during the walks in the fields, the cemetery, or the garden, and when matured are committed to paper in very little time. This has given the impression that I write easily and rapidly, when, in truth, I have no advantage in this respect, except, perhaps, that of a better system, which, after the experience of years, I would recommend to every writer, whatever his profession may be.—(Peabody).

ORIGIN OF THE WORD DOLLAR.

The derivation suggested for this in Todd's edition of Johnson, is confirmed by the particular explanation of later lexicographers. In 1516, a silver mine was discovered at Joachim's Thal (St. Joachim's Dale) in Bohemia, and the proprietors in the following year issued a great number of silver pieces, of about the value of the Spanish psoduro, which bore the name of Joachim's thaler, subsequently abbreviated into dollar. Thus the dollar, like the guinea, commemorates the place from which it was originally coined.

LESSON FOR YOUNG MEN.

One day when Patrick Henry, the American statesman, was sitting in his office, a tall, thin, plainly dressed young man, who had descended the Cahawba alone in a small boat, came in and inquired for a school. The statesman saw that there was something in him, and after eyeing him for a moment replied, "I don't know of any school you can get here, but remain, my young friend. You form your own character, and mould your own destiny." These words of wisdom sunk down into the young man's heart. Musing upon them, he returned to his little boat, shot out again into the stream, found a school somewhere below, and that young man was John Price, who afterwards became one of the most distinguished preachers and theological professors in Virginia. His perseverance and self-reliance made him a great man.—(American Paper.)

FOOT-PRINTS OF ANIMALS ON ANCIENT ROCKS.

Sir Charles Lyell delivered a lecture "On impressions of Rain-drops in Ancient and Modern Strata." In illustration of the foot-tracks of quadrupeds, such as the musk-rat, the minx, the dog, and others, so common on the recent red sand of Kentville, on the borders of the Bay of Fundy in Nova Scotia, Sir C. Lyell exhibited a copy of a brick, one foot square, from Babylon, now in the British Museum, on which the track of a small animal of the ichneumon tribe, apparently the Asiatic mongoose, is distinctly seen. This brick has been sun-dried (not baked in a kiln), and must have been traversed by the creature when the clay mixed with straw was still very soft. Sir C. Lyell verified the character of the track by getting a living ichneumon in the Zoological Gardens to walk over a cake of soft mud, which he afterwards sun-dried. In the middle of the brick is an inscription, in the Babylonian cuneiform character, which, according to Colonel Rawlinson's interpretation, signifies that Nabokodnossor, King of Babylon, built certain cities, &c. This king is the same as the Nebuchadnezzar of Scripture, so that the brick is twenty-four centuries old.

SINGULAR DIET.

The celebrated modern sceptic, Benedict Spinoza, was accustomed to spend from twopence-halfpenny to threepence a-day upon his nourishment. But he was beaten hollow by Buttner, a German naturalist and philologist of the eighteenth century; such was the zeal of this individual in the pursuit of his favourite studies, that, in order to buy books, he restricted himself to what was barely sufficient to sustain life—he only ate one meal a-day, which cost him exactly three-half-pence. It is very generally known that the eminent French astronomer Lalande either really possessed, or else affected, an excessive fondness for spiders and caterpillars as articles of diet, and would eat them with apparent relish. He always carried a supply of these insects about with him in a *bonbonnière*.—(Critic.)

DAY IN THE CRYSTAL PALACE.

There was music echoing through the transparent fabric. Fragrant flowers and graceful shrubs flashing and sparkling in the subdued sunlight; in living sculpture were suddenly seen the grand, the grotesque, the terrible, the beautiful objects of every form and colour imaginable, far as the eye could reach, were dazzlingly intermingled, and there were present sixty thousand sons and daughters of Adam, passing and repassing ceaselessly, bewildered, charmingly; gliding amidst bannered nations, through country after country renowned in ancient name and great in modern: civilized and savage. From the far east and west, misty in distance, faintly echoed martial music, or the solemn anthem! The soul was approached through its highest senses, flooded with excitement, all its faculties were appealed to at once, and it sank for a while exhausted, overwhelmed. — (Warren's "Lily and the Bee.")

KING JAMES I. IN LANCASHIRE.

On the way from Preston his attention was attracted by a huge boulder stone which lay in the roadside, and was still in existence not a century ago. "O my saul (cried he), that meikle stane would build a braw chapping block for my Lord Provost. Stop; there be letters thereon; unto what purport?" Several voices recited the inscription:—

"Turne me o'er and I'll tell thee plaine."

"Then, turn it ower," said the monarch; and a long and laborious toil brought to light the following satisfactory intelligence:—

"Hot porritch makes hard cake soft,
So turne me o'er again."

"My saul (said the king), ye shall gang roun to your place again; these country gouks mauna ken the riddle without the labour."—(Notes and Queries.)

RELICS.

In the grounds of Abbington Abbey, Northamptonshire, stands Garrick's mulberry-tree, with this inscription upon copper attached to one of its limbs: "This tree was planted by David Garrick, Esq., at the request of Anne Thursby, as a growing testimony of their friendship, 1778."

Henry Kirke White's favourite tree, whereon he had cut "H. K. W. 1805," stood on the sands at Whitton, in Northumberland, till it was cut down by the woodman's axe; but in veneration for the poet's memory, the portion bearing his initials was carefully preserved in an elegant gilt frame.

An English traveller, desirous of possessing a memorial of Madame de Sèvigné, purchased, for the sum of 18,000 francs, the staircase of her chateau at Provence.

Sir Isaac Newton's solar dial, which was cut in stone, and attached to the manor-house at Woolstrop, Lincolnshire, is now placed in the Royal Society's collection.

Some years ago, a curious arm-chair, which had belonged to Gay, the poet, was sold at public auction at Barnstable, his native place. It contained a drawer underneath the seat, at the extremity of which was a smaller drawer, connected with a rod in front, by which it was drawn out.

Benjamin Franklin's "fine crab-tree walking-stick, with a gold head curiously wrought in the form of a cap of liberty," is bequeathed in a codicil to his will, "to the friend of mankind, General Washington;" adding, that "if it were a sceptre, he has merited it, and would become it."

Thrope's *Catalogue of Autographs* (1843) includes a letter from a Miss Smith, of Arundale, forwarding to the Earl of Buchan "a chip, taken from the coffin of the poet Burns, when his body was removed from his first grave to the mausoleum erected to his memory in St. Michael's church-yard, Dumfries."

LIBRARY OF THE BRITISH MUSEUM.

The library of the British Museum ranks third amongst the national collections in Europe, and is inferior to none in the curiosities and rarities of literature. The following notes of a visit to the library may not be unacceptable. The number of volumes it contains is 450,000; and one of the librarians assured us that they occupy *fifteen miles of book-shelves!* The position of the British Museum Library among the principal libraries of

Europe is seen in the following comparative statement:—

	Vols.
Paris (1), National Library,	824,000
Munich, Royal Library,	600,000
London, British Museum Library,	450,000
Petersburg, Imperial Library,	446,000
Copenhagen, Royal Library,	412,000
Berlin, Royal Library,	410,000
Vienna, Imperial Library,	313,000
Dresden, Royal Library,	300,000
Madrid, National Library,	200,000
Wolfenbüttel, Ducal Library,	200,000
Stuttgard, Royal Library,	187,000
Paris (2), Arzenal Library,	180,000
Milan, Brera Library,	170,000
Paris (3), St. Génévieve Library,	150,000
Darmstadt, Grand Ducal Library,	150,000
Florence, Magliabecchian Library,	150,000
Naples, Royal Library,	150,000
Brussels, Royal Library,	133,500
Rome (1), Casanate Library,	120,000
Hague, Royal Library,	100,000
Paris (4), Mazarino Library,	100,000
Rome (2), Vatican Library,	100,000
Parma, Ducal Library,	100,000

To the books of Sir Hans Sloane, forming the nucleus of the library, George II. added in 1757, the books collected by the Kings of England from the time of Henry VII., and which included amongst others the library of Archbishop Cranmer. The King annexed to this gift the right, which the Royal Library had acquired in Queen Anne's reign, to a copy of every new book entered at Stationers' Hall. In 1823, the magnificent library of George III. was presented to the Museum by George IV., on condition that it should for ever be kept separate from the rest of the collection. This library, which was commenced when the establishments of the Jesuits were broken up and their books dispersed, was enriched from these sources with some of the rarest works of antiquity. It also contains choice early editions of the classics, reports of learned bodies, productions of the Caxton press, the histories of the European states, in their respective languages, and a celebrated geographical and topographical collection, itself a great curiosity. The mere catalogue of the contents of this inedited Royal Atlas fills two octavo volumes. For state reasons, it was customary in former times—and the rule is not yet, we believe, altogether relaxed—to withhold this collection from the public eye, and especially from the examination of foreigners. In addition to the general topographical description of the country by counties, it contains sketches of every place of strength in the kingdom, showing how they could be put in a posture of defence, and rendered available either against "malice domestic" or "foreign levy." The curator favoured us with a sight of the illustrations of two Scottish counties; they happened to be those of Lanark and Dumbarton, and resembled large scrap-books, containing maps, old pictures of towns and villages, landscapes, sketches of old castles and peel-houses, views of mansion-houses and demesnes, plans of Dumbarton Castle, statistical notes, entries, and odds and ends connected with the district. These multifarious materials are arranged with clearness and neatness, so as to be of ready reference. The labour of their compilation must have been prodigious. The entire of the King's library is in beautiful order.

In one apartment we were allowed to examine Henry the Eighth's Bible, beautifully printed on vellum, in three volumes, with illuminated initial letters, and gorgeously bound. It bears this inscription:— "This Booke is presented unto your most excellent highness by youre loving, faithfull, and obedient subject and daylye oratour, Anthonie Master of London, haberdasher. The Byble in Englyshe. 1541." It is something to know that bluff King Hal possessed a Bible. It does not, to be sure, bear marks of having been much used by its royal owner. At all events, it was not from this source he derived the materials of his *Defence of the Seven Sacraments*, for which Pope Leo the Tenth conferred upon him the title of "Defender of the Faith," ever since borne by the British sovereigns. Nor could it be from his father that the youthful and pious Edward VI. acquired that reverence for the Scriptures, which led him to reprove a companion for laying upon the floor a Bible—who can say but it was this identical copy?—that by standing on it he might reach a shelf in an apartment where they were amusing themselves.

Here also are the Elector of Saxony's copy of Martin Luther's translation of the Bible, with illuminations; Martin Luther's own copy of the Bible, 1542; Myles Coverdale's Bible, 1530, the first printed in England; Charlemagne's Bible, &c.

In glancing cursorily over a collection of letters and other manuscripts of celebrated individuals, the following were noticed:—The handwritings of Shakspeare, Newton, Voltaire, Tasso, Lady Jane Grey, Edward the Sixth, Queen Elizabeth, Oliver Cromwell, and Melancthon, —the latter broad, massive, angular, and strongly resembling Dr. Chalmers'; Lady Jane Grey's prayerbook; Pope's Homer, with the elaborate erasures, interlineations, and re-castings, of which examples are given in Johnson's *Life* of the poet, by way of illustrating the intellectual process by which that great work was performed, and the gradations by which it advanced to correctness. This original copy of the *Iliad*, it is stated by Johnson, was "obtained by Bolingbroke as a curiosity, descended from him to Mallet, and is now, by the solicitation of the late Dr. Maty, deposited in the Museum." A variety of Oriental manuscripts are included in this miscellaneous department, amongst which are copies of the Koran.

But the interest felt by the visitor here is centred chiefly on two documents which belong to history. The first is superscribed—"Bull of Pope Innocent III., whereby he receives in fee the Kingdom of England, given to the Roman Church by virtue of a Charter confirmed by the Golden Seal of King John, and takes it into his apostolical protection. Given at St. Peter's, 11 Kalends of May, A.D. 1214, and of the Pontificate of Pope Innocent the 17th year." The surrender of his dominions to the Papal authority by this weak and worthless monarch, is one of the dark spots of our history. King John quarrelled with Pope Innocent III. about the appointment of an Archbishop of Canterbury. The Pope quashed a double election by the monks, and appointed by his own authority Stephen Langton, to whom we owe the first division of the Bible into chapters and verses. The King espoused the cause of a favourite bishop. The grand instrument of the power and policy of the Romish Church in those days was the sentence of interdict. The Pope launched this sentence against England. The King made ineffectual attempts to resist and roll it back. But the priesthood stood by the Pope, and the people by the priests. The churches were closed; the bells were silent which summoned the people to prayers; the dead were buried in unconsecrated places, thrown into ditches or huddled away in common fields; marriages were celebrated in church-yards, that the most gladsome occurrences of life might be shaded by the all-pervading gloom; the statues and pictures of the saints were invested in sable, or laid prostrate on the ground; no religious ordinance was dispensed, save baptism to those who had come into the world, and extreme unction to those going out of it. The rupture continued for several years; but the King remained obstinate, and retaliated by confiscating the estates of the clergy. The Pope again applied the screw. He declared that John had forfeited his crown, released his subjects from their allegiance, proclaimed a crusade against England, and commissioned the French King to execute it. Craven and treacherous, as he was truculent and tyrannical, John surrendered to the Pontiff, acknowledged his appointment to the primacy of the English Church, consented to do homage to the Pope — which, presently, with bended knees and folded hands, he accorded to the Pope's legate, who, with insolent triumph, trampled under foot the first instalment of the abject sovereign's tribute-money; and finally the degraded monarch drew up the charter cited in the bull now before us, in which he formally resigned England and Ireland to God, to St. Peter and St. Paul, and to Pope Innocent and his successors in the apostolical chair, agreeing to hold his dominions as feudatory of the Romish Church, by paying a thousand marks yearly.

The other historical deed is Magna Charta. A year had scarcely elapsed after his reconciliation with the Pope, when King John became involved in the contest with the Barons of England, which resulted in establishing the foundations of our national liberty. The King had rendered himself obnoxious to all ranks, by the oppressive and arbitrary character of his government. His rapacious exactions, his licentious habits, and the surrender of the independence of the kingdom to the Pope, had sunk their monarch so low in the eyes of his subjects, that everything seemed favourable for their striking a blow, not merely at the arbitrary prerogative of the reigning sovereign, but for the recovery of the ancient Saxon privileges of which they had been deprived by their Norman conquerors. In this cause the clergy joined the nobles, and even the power of the Pope failed to repress their ardour or daunt their resolution. They persevered and triumphed. On the plains of Runnymede, in the year 1215, was extorted from the tyrant John the *Magna Charta Communium Libertatum,* the Great Charter of the Common Liberties. By this deed the clergy and nobility secured various provisions advantageous to their respective orders. But its effect upon the common people, then in a state of villainage, or vassalage to the landed proprietors, although less direct and apparent, was destined to be greatly more important and permanent. The rise of towns and the origin of burghal privileges, conduced more to the extinction of villainage than any other cause; and without intending it, the barons and clergy gave an irresistible impulse to the progress of freedom amongst the lower classes, by introducing into the Charter a clause consolidating and protecting the liberties and privileges of towns. But the article by which the foundations of our free constitution were laid broad and deep was that which proclaimed that "No freeman shall be apprehended or imprisoned, or disseised (that is, deprived of anything he possesses), or outlawed, or banished, or any way destroyed, nor will we go upon him, nor will we send upon him (pronounce sentence against him, or allow any of the judges to do so), except by the legal judgment of his peers, or by the law of the land. (*Nulli vendemus, nulli negabimus, aut differemus rectum aut judicium.*) To none will we sell, to none will we deny, to none will we delay right or justice." From this epoch the distinction between the Norman and the Saxon race began to melt away, and it is here, as Mr. Macaulay has observed, that the history of the English nation commences. Hitherto the history of successive reigns had been a record of wrongs inflicted and sustained by different tribes. "When John became king," remarks the historian just named, "the distinction between Saxons and Normans was strongly marked, but before the end of the reign of his grandson it had almost disappeared. In the time of Richard the First, the ordinary imprecation of a Norman gentleman was, 'May I become an Englishman!' His ordinary form of indignant denial was, 'Do you take me for an Englishman?' The descendant of such a gentleman, a hundred years later, was proud of the English name."

In the memorable interview between the King and the barons, the latter appear to have submitted their demands drawn up in the form of preliminary articles of agreement, to which John affixed his seal. The articles were then embodied in the Charter, copies of which were sent, after being signed, to each county or each diocese in England; but of these only three are now known to exist. One is preserved in the library of the cathedral at Salisbury, and two are deposited in the British Museum. One of the latter is said to have been rescued from the scissors of a tailor, who was proceeding to cut the parchment into measures. They bear the marks of fire, having been slightly injured when part of the Cottonian library, before it was deposited in the Museum, was burnt, in 1731. In one copy, the waxen seal affixed by the King has been partially melted; in the other, it is destroyed.

Amongst the ancient charters in this part of the collection is the Bull of Pope Leo X., conferring on Henry VIII. the title of "Defender of the Faith." This document was also injured by the fire which partly destroyed the Cottonian collection. A set of the Great Seals of the British sovereigns is preserved here. One of the oldest English charters is the title to Battle Abbey, in Sussex, granted by William the Conqueror. This once famous ecclesiastical foundation owed its origin to the battle of Hastings, which decided the Norman conquest, in 1066. The Abbey was commenced by the Conqueror the year after.

The library contains a collection of English newspapers, stretching back to the first periodical publication, which is a pamphlet, dated 1588, and called the *English Mercurie*. The first newspaper, properly so called, did not appear till many years after. The oldest newspaper we noticed in the collection was dated 1616, and was occupied with "News out of Holland." Till long after this period occasional pamphlets and tracts served the purpose of the newspaper, which did not assume anything like its present character till after the Revolution of 1688. Mr. Macaulay describes the earlier efforts at newspaper literature in his *History of England*. He mentions that in 1685 nothing like the London daily paper of our time existed, or could exist, for want of capital, skill, and freedom. The political conflicts which preceded the Revolution gave rise to a number of publications, which are thus described:—
"None exceeded in size a single small leaf. The quantity of matter which one of them contained in a year was not more than is often found in two numbers of the *Times*." Then came the *London Gazette*. "The contents generally were a royal proclamation, two or three Tory addresses, notices of two or three promotions, an account of a skirmish between the Imperial troops and the Janissaries on the

Danube, a description of a highwayman, an announcement of a grand cockfight between two persons of honour, and an advertisement offering a reward for a stray dog. The whole made up two pages of moderate size. Whatever was communicated respecting matters of the highest moment, was communicated in the most meagre and formal style. The most important parliamentary debates, the most important state trials recorded in our history, were passed over in profound silence. In the capital the coffee-houses supplied in some measure the place of a journal. Thither the Londoners flocked, as the Athenians of old flocked to the market-place, to hear whether there was any news. There men might learn how brutally a Whig had been treated the day before in Westminster Hall, or what horrible accounts the letters from Edinburgh gave of the torturing of Covenanters." In 1690 there were nine London newspapers published weekly. In Queen Anne's reign, in 1709, they had increased to eighteen, including one daily paper. In the reign of George I. there were three daily, six weekly, and ten three times a-week. The collection of newspapers in the Museum was commenced by Sir Hans Sloane. The Burney Collection was added to these in 1818, at the cost of £1000. This department of the library is now supplied by the Commissioners of Stamps, who forward to the Museum the copies deposited in their office by the publishers.

There are two extensive collections of music in the library, one of which belonged to Dr. Charles Burney, the composer, and father of Madame D'Arblay, the novelist; and the other to Sir John Hawkins. The Rev. Dr. Burney, son of the composer, and a ripe scholar, left a library which was purchased for the British Museum at the expense of £14,000. Sir Joseph Banks' library of natural history, Garrick's dramatic collection, Musgrave's extensive biographical collection, four collections of French political tracts, belonging to the period of the first Revolution, and a similar collection of political pamphlets published in England during the civil wars of Charles the First's time, are amongst the notable features of the library.

Amongst the manuscripts, not the least curious we saw, was the *Basilicon Doron of King James the First*, in his own hand-writing—a treatise on the art of government, addressed by the King to his promising son Prince Henry, who died young, and showing (what was by no means peculiar to "the wisest fool in Christendom") how much easier it is to speculate plausibly, than to rule well. There are many manuscripts here which had found their way into the ancient royal library of England, at the period of the breaking up of the monastic institutions of this country, and some of these documents retain upon their blank leaves the maledictions denounced upon those who should alienate them from the places where they were deposited. One of the most ancient manuscripts is the "*Codex Alexandrinus*," written in uncial characters on vellum, in four quarto volumes, and supposed to be the oldest existing Greek manuscript of the Bible in existence, dating betwixt the fourth and sixth centuries. It was a gift to Charles the First from the Patriarch of Constantinople. There are several early copies of the Latin gospels, one written about the year 800, splendidly illuminated, and believed to have once belonged to the Venerable Bede. A collection of MSS. formed by the first Marquis of Lansdowne, cost the British Parliament £4925; they are chiefly historical, but include a rare version of the Bible in French, upon vellum, of Charles V.'s time. Amongst the classical manuscripts is one of the earliest extant of Homer's *Odyssey*, and another of the *Iliad*, the latter having cost 600 guineas. There is an extensive collection of ancient Irish manuscripts, including *The Brehon Laws*, by which Ireland was governed before the Anglo-Norman invasion. A selection from the manuscript collections of the late Richard Heber was purchased at £2000. There are in the Museum numerous Egyptian and Greek papyri, or writings on the material formed from the cellular tissue of the papyrus plant, which was used for this purpose before the invention of modern paper. From the ruins of Herculaneum there have been dug up no fewer than 1800 papyri, which have been deposited in the museum at Naples. The manuscript department of the library is rapidly increasing. Independently of those MSS. classed under the names of their collectors, there have been added 17,416, of which 2416 have been obtained since the year 1844. These are in Hebrew, Syriac, Greek, Armenian, Persian, Venetian, Portuguese, Chinese, Mexican, Russian, German, Italian, Welsh, French, Flemish, and early English. The illuminated manuscripts are objects of much interest. They are generally curious examples of conventual art in the middle ages, and some of them are eminently beautiful.

THE FOSSIL HUMAN SKELETON OF GUADELOUPE IN THE BRITISH MUSEUM.

The fossil human skeleton of Guadeloupe, which was brought to this country by Admiral Sir Alexander Cochrane, and presented to the Museum by the Lords of the Admiralty, is one of the most attractive objects in that unrivalled collection. It was found imbedded in a mass of limestone in the island of Guadeloupe; and as this was the first instance in which human bones had ever been discovered in the solid rock, not a few inconsiderate reasoners leaped to the conclusion that here at last was evidence irrefragable of a greatly higher antiquity for the human race than is assigned to it by the most ancient writings in the world; the pretensions of which writings to a Divine authority were believed by this class of thinkers to succumb to the same conclusive testimony. But when the fossil and the rock in which it was entombed came to be examined, the idea of its geological antiquity was declared to be utterly untenable, and the hopes which infidelity had begun to found upon it were most effectually dissipated. There are not now two opinions amongst geologists as to the age of the skeleton, or the nature of the rock in which it was preserved. The bones themselves are not mineralized or petrified, but retain, according to the analysis of Sir Humphry Davy, the usual constituents of fresh bone, namely, animal matter and phosphate of lime, and in fact they were of a somewhat soft consistency when first exposed to the air. These facts were alone sufficient to have upset the wild notions which took possession of the minds of sceptics in religion and sciolists in science, when the Guadeloupe skeleton was discovered. But its presumed high antiquity was still further disproved by the condition of the rock, which is a bed of limestone forming a sloping bank betwixt the island cliffs and the sea, and lying within high-water mark; consisting of consolidated sand, with fragments of shells and madrepores or corals, of species inhabiting the present seas; and stone arrow-heads, carved stone and wooden ornaments, and remains of pottery, have also been found imbedded in it. The rock is in the vicinity of the volcano called the Souffriere. It is not surprising, therefore, that in an island liable to volcanic convulsions, earthquakes, hurricanes, and inundations both of water and of sand, human bodies should occasionally have been overwhelmed in the drifting sand, which has ultimately become indurated. Similar aggregations of sand, gravel, and other detritus, consolidated by means of deposits of iron or lime from their solutions in water, are familiar to all observers. Such deposits on a large scale are in progress on the shores of the Mediterranean, on the coast of Sicily, and of the West Indies, the Bermudas, and other islands, and in which the remains of plants and animals, and articles of human fabric, are becoming incrusted and intombed. In the museum of the American Philosophical Society at Philadelphia, Sir Chas. Lyell was shown a slab of limestone from Santas in Brazil, procured by Capt. Elliot of the United States navy, which contains a human skull and other bones, with fragments of shells, some of them partially retaining their colour. Sir Charles observed that the calcareous rock resembles that of Guadeloupe, but is less solid; and he mentions that he was informed that several hundreds of human skeletons had been dug out of the same deposit about the year 1827. He supposes that the soil now indurated may have at one time been an Indian burial-ground, which had become submerged in the sea, as he observed serpulæ upon the rock, and had again been elevated above the water. Even in the lakes of Forfarshire there is a deposit of fresh-water limestone in progress, containing recent shells and aquatic plants.

The unrivalled researches of M. Cuvier in comparative anatomy enabled that profound philosopher to declare his conviction, before the skeleton of Guadeloupe had been described, that no human remains had ever been discovered in a fossil state. To this subject he devotes a chapter in his *Theory of the Earth*. The reader may remember the gypsum quarries about Paris, whence Cuvier derived so many of the osteological relics, which at the bidding of his reconstructive genius, bone uniting to bone, sprung into primitive forms, unknown to the present world, and which had been buried for ages at unfathomable depths under the earth. The inductive process by which these results—this "resurrection in miniature," as he described it—was attained, is without a parallel in the history of science. The labourers in these quarries, the unconscious instruments of his brilliant discoveries, were under the firm persuasion that a great proportion of the bones which they brought to his museum were those of the human skeleton. But he informs us that "having seen and carefully examined many thousands of these bones, I may safely affirm that not a single fragment of them has ever belonged to our species." Again, in reference to the supposed human remains which Spallanzani brought to Pavia from the island of Cerigo, M. Cuvier affirms "that there is not a single fragment among them that ever formed part of a human skeleton." And the general conclusion of this sagacious naturalist has been confirmed by all subsequent observations:—"The establishment of mankind in those countries in which the fossil bones of land-animals have been found, that is to say, in the greatest part of Europe, Asia, and America, must necessarily have been posterior not only to the revolutions which covered up these bones, but also to those other revolutions by which the strata containing the bones have been laid bare. Hence it clearly appears," he adds, "that no argument for the antiquity of the human race in those countries, can be founded either upon these fossil bones, or upon the more or less considerable collections of rocks or earthy materials by which they are covered."

The occurrence of human skeletons at Guadeloupe was first announced by General Ernouf in 1805. The skeleton in the Museum was described in the *Philosophical Transactions*, in 1814, by Mr. Charles Konig, the same gentleman, we presume, who, till lately, superintended the Natural History department of the Museum. The paper is accompanied by an accurate representation of the skeleton, a fair transcript of which is given in Mantell's *Wonders of Geology*. The skeleton wants the skull, and it is a curious fact, mentioned by Sir Charles Lyell, in his *Travels in North America*, in 1842, that in the Museum at Charleston, South Carolina, he was shown a fossil human skull from Guadeloupe, imbedded in solid limestone, "which they say belongs to the same skeleton of a female as that now preserved in the British Museum, where the skull is wanting." Dr. Moultrie, of the Medical College of that State, has described the bones, together with the entire skeleton disentombed from the limestone deposit at Guadeloupe, and is of opinion — taking for granted the relation of the skull at Charleston to the headless trunk in London — that the latter is not the skeleton of a Carib, as has been generally supposed, but that of one of the Peruvians, or of a tribe possessing a similar craniological development.

The slab of limestone in which the skeleton is imbedded is 4 feet 2 inches long by 2 feet in breadth; it has been considerably reduced since it was deposited in the Museum, having originally measured nearly double the size, and weighed about two tons. As described by Mr. Konig, the whole had very much the appearance of a huge nodule disengaged from a surrounding mass; and the situation of the skeleton must have been so superficial, that its presence in the rock on the coast had probably been indicated by the projection of part of one of the arms. The rock has a reddish hue, caused by the detritus of a madrepore of that colour. Several shells were also found in the rock, along with the fragment of a tusk, a piece of basaltic stone, and a small quantity of powdery matter of the nature of charcoal. In reducing the slab to convenient dimensions, its resistance to the tool showed it to be harder than statuary marble. Dr. Thomson found phosphate of lime in the stone, derived, doubtless, from the bones of the skeleton. The vertebræ of the neck have been lost along with the head, and the bones of the thorax are considerably dislocated and shattered. The vertebræ of the spinal column are all present, although they are individually not well defined. The bones of one of the legs are in a good state of preservation; those of the other are less entire. Both the arms are broken, and their parts displaced. But notwithstanding these and other defects, the outline of the skeleton is sufficiently complete to indicate to the least practised eye, that when these imprisoned bones were united by ligaments, and clothed with muscles and sinews, and the system was permeated by blood-vessels, and instinct with nervous sensibility, the life which animated the whole was human — the spirit which inhabited the mortal frame, was immortal — and survives! Mr. Hugh Miller, in his too brief sketch of the British Museum, finely apostrophises this "prisoner of the marble, haply once an Indian wife and mother:"— "Mysterious framework of bone, locked up in the solid marble, unwonted prisoner of the rock!—an irresistible voice shall yet call thee from out the stony matrix. The other organisms, thy partners in the show, are incarcerated in the lime for ever—thou but for a term!"

THE NINEVEH SCULPTURES IN THE BRITISH MUSEUM.

Antiquarian and archæological research is treading hard after the investigations of geology itself. For the purpose of establishing the succession and superposition of rocks, as first elaborated in our own island, geologists have extended their explorations from the back woods of America on the west, to the confines of Asia on the east—demonstrating the vast and prolonged preparations made by Creative Wisdom and Benevolence to fit the surface of the globe for becoming the habitation of rational and immortal beings;—and what an august light does science thus shed on the power and progress of creative agency! Where geology terminates the record of creation, archæology begins to illustrate the history of God's Providence in his dealings with the early races of man—"the gray fathers of the world." Carrying us back to the earliest era of post-diluvian history, and setting us down in the country which was the cradle of the human race, it disentombs from the oblivion of ages confirmations the most unequivocal of the statements of the Sacred Writings, historical and prophetic, respecting the first dwellers on the plains of the Tigris and the Euphrates. It places before our eyes the monuments on which the Assyrian kings recorded their victories—deciphers inscriptions, and interprets bass-reliefs, sculptured in the infancy of art, twenty centuries before the Christian era; and describes Assyrian arts and manners which long afterwards effloresced into the myths and symbols of the Greeks. Nineveh, the metropolis of the Assyrians, had been levelled with the ground before the period of authentic profane history began; even its site was involved in doubt when Xenophon and his army encamped upon its ruins, (for the Mespila of the *Anabasis* is understood to have been the ancient Nineveh,) during the celebrated retreat of the Ten Thousand. According to the chronology adopted by Mr. Layard, whose authority we shall follow, and of whose singularly interesting work we shall freely avail ourselves in the notice of his discoveries, it was in the year 606 B.C. that Nineveh was captured by Cyaxares, king of Persia and Media, a date which agrees with the period assigned both by the Sacred Scriptures and by Herodotus to the conquest and destruction of "that great city." Of the history of Nineveh few particulars that can be relied on have descended to us in profane history. The extraordinary feats related of Ninus and Semiramis, the two founders of the Assyrian empire—the vast armies of men at their command, their immense treasures, their stupendous buildings and hanging gardens, are evidently in a large degree fabulous. It is from the incidental allusions to Nineveh in the Bible that we derive our chief knowledge of the actual condition of the Assyrian capital; and the corroborative light reflected upon the statements of the Bible by the discoveries of Mr. Layard, is probably the most important and valuable contribution of modern times to the external evidences of the Divine origin of our holy religion.

There is monumental evidence that of the various buildings which he excavated, that of the palace of Nimroud was older by several centuries than the edifices of Khorsabad and Kouyunjik, which he also uncovered, and which he proves by the same undoubted evidence to have been built by a later dynasty of kings. The palace of Nimroud represents the original site of Nineveh. To this, the first palace, the son of its founder added a second; subsequent additions are recorded in the inscriptions; and the place at last attained the dimensions ascribed to it by Jonah and Diodorus. "If (says Mr. Layard) we take the four great mounds of Nimroud, Kouyunjik, Khorsabad, and Karamles, as the angle of a square, it will be found that its four sides corresponded pretty accurately with the 480 stadia, or 60 miles of the geographer, which makes the three days' journey of the prophet." Within this space there are many mounds, ruins of edifices, vestiges of streets and gardens; and the face of the country is strewed with fragments of pottery and bricks. As to the number of inhabitants, mentioned in the book of Jonah to be above 120,000, a number apparently incommensurate with a city of such magnitude, Mr. Layard remarks that cities in the East are not like those in Europe; for a place like London or Paris would not contain above a third of the number of their inhabitants. The women have separate apartments from the men; there is a separate house for each family; and gardens and arable land are inclosed by the city walls. Hence it is mentioned in Jonah that there was "much cattle" within the walls, and of course there was pasture for them. Damascus, Ispahan, and other Eastern cities are thus built at the present day. The existing ruins, our author adds, "show that Nineveh acquired its greatest extent in the time of the kings of the second dynasty, that is, of the kings mentioned in Scripture; it was then that Jonah visited it, and that reports of its magnificence were carried to the west, and gave rise to the traditions from which the Greek authors mainly derived the information which has been handed down to us."

At different periods between the years 1812 and 1820, the late Mr. Rich, the East India Company's resident at Bagdad, partially examined some of the mounds on the site of Nineveh, and to his investigations we owe the little knowledge we possessed of these ruins up till the present time. Mr. Layard commenced his explorations in 1845— his education, his indomitable energy, his knowledge of eastern manners and languages, acquired during prolonged journeyings in Asia Minor and Syria, and his strong antiquarian tastes, all qualifying him for the task he had undertaken.

In one respect the monuments of Assyria appear in striking contrast to those of Egypt. On the banks of the Nile rise the stupendous structures of the Pyramids, the only edifices built by the hand of man which appear likely to last as long as time lasts. The vast plains of the Tigris and the Euphrates only exhibit at distant intervals green and shapeless mounds, the ruins of ancient towns and villages. Mr. Layard counted, from the walls of an upland fort, "above a hundred mounds throwing their dark and lengthening shadows across the plain;— these were the remains of Assyrian civilization and prosperity." The difference between the monumental remains of the Egyptians and the Assyrians, shows how much a nation's architectural taste may be modified by the geological features of a country. The Egyptians embodied their conceptions in granite and marble. The Assyrians had not the means of building in either, else, our author is of opinion, they would have rivalled or excelled the Pyramids. They lived upon an alluvial soil, sufficiently tenacious to be formed into bricks, with the addition of a little chopped straw, and which, being dried in the sun, furnished the building materials for their houses and palaces. But a more compact and durable material was required for their sculptures and written characters, and such a substance was found in the coarse alabaster or gypsum occurring abundantly in the plains of Mesopotamia, and which was cut into slabs and used for the ornamental parts of the public buildings. It is of this material that the monuments brought to this country by Mr. Layard chiefly consist. The are generally slabs of from nine to twelve feet in height, and of a dark yellowish colour, resembling limestone. Some of the monuments are indeed limestone (carbonate of lime), the rock named gypsum or alabaster being sulphate of lime. The alabaster slabs, which were covered with carved figures or inscriptions, occupied the place of panels in the walls of the palaces. The walls themselves, constructed of sun-dried brick, were from five to fifteen feet in thickness. The slabs stood upright against the walls, and were carved after being placed in their position, as is shown by continuous series of figures and inscriptions. The door-ways were formed of human-headed lions and bulls, from ten to sixteen feet in height, the wall being carried some feet above them. In excavating the ruins, it was observed that the upper wall was built of baked bricks richly coloured, or of sun-dried bricks covered by a thin coat of plaster, on which were painted various ornaments. These colours had lost little of their original freshness and brilliancy. It is interesting to notice that it is to these upper walls that the complete covering of the building, and the consequent preservation of the sculptures, is attributed by the excavator, who observes that when the edifices had been deserted, they fell in, and the unbaked bricks, having again softened and assumed their original earthy consistency, incased the whole ruin. The structure of the edifices has been so satisfactorily examined, that no part of them has been left to conjecture except the roof, which is naturally supposed to have been formed of beams supported by the walls. The apartments were long and narrow, one at Nimroud being 160 feet in length by 35 in breadth; and it appears that they must have been lighted from above. We conclude by quoting Mr. Layard's description (or restoration) of an Assyrian palace, premising that these buildings were of a monumental character, in which the chronicles of the empire were inscribed, the achievements of heroes were commemorated, and the power and majesty of the nation's deities were celebrated. The author supposes a stranger ushered for the first time into the palace of the Assyrian kings:—

"He entered through a portal guarded by colossal lions or bulls, of white alabaster. In the first hall he found himself surrounded by sculptured records of the empire. Battles, sieges, triumphs, exploits of the chase, ceremonies of religion, were portrayed on its walls, sculptured in alabaster, and painted in gorgeous colours. Under each picture were engraved in characters filled up with bright copper, inscriptions describing the scenes represented. Above the sculptures were painted other events — the king, attended by his eunuchs and warriors, receiving his presents, entering into alliance with other monarchs, or performing some sacred duty. These representations were inclosed in coloured borders of elaborate and elegant design. The emblematic tree, with winged bulls, and monstrous animals, was conspicuous amongst the ornaments. At the upper end of the hall was the colossal figure of the king in adoration before the supreme deity, or receiving from his eunuch the holy cup. He was attended by warriors bearing his arms, and by the priests or presiding divinities. His robes and those of his followers were adorned with groups of figures, animals and flowers, all painted with brilliant colours. The stranger trode upon alabaster slabs, each bearing an inscription recording the titles, genealogy, and achievements of the great king. Several door-ways formed by gigantic winged lions or bulls, or by figures of guardian deities, led into other apartments, which again opened into more distant halls. In each were new sculptures. On the walls of some were processions of colossal figures, armed men and eunuchs following the king, warriors laden with spoil, leading prisoners, or bearing presents and offerings to the gods. On the walls of others were portrayed winged priests or presiding divinities, standing before the sacred trees. The ceiling was divided into square compartments, painted with flowers or figures of animals. Some were inlaid with ivory, each compartment being surrounded by elegant borders and mouldings. The rarest woods, in which the cedar was conspicuous, were used for the woodwork."

For the practice of ceiling, or panelling, or wainscoting with cedar wood, reference is made by the author to Zephaniah ii. 14, Jeremiah xxii. 14; 1 Kings vi. 15; vii. 3.

FANS.

Thomas Coryat's story about the use of forks in Italy, and his introduction of those cleanly and convenient implements into England, whereby, and "for no other cause," he obtained the nickname of *Furcifer*, is very generally known. The following description of fans by the same odd, fantastic traveller, which goes to prove that paper fans were not used in England at the time of his tour (1608), and that we borrowed them as well as forks from the Italians, has been less noticed.

"Here I will mention a thing, that although perhaps it will seeme but frivolous to divers readers that have already travelled in Italy, yet because unto many that neither have beene there, nor ever intend to go thither while they live, it will be a meere novelty, I will not let it passe unmentioned. The first Italian fannes that I saw in Italy did I observe in this space betwixt Pizighiton and Cremona; but afterwards I observed them common in most places of Italy where I travelled. These fannes *both men and women* of the country doe carry, to coole themselves withall in the time of heat, by the often fanning of their faces. Most of them are very elegant and pretty things. For whereas the fanne consisteth of a painted piece of paper and a little wooden handle; the paper, which is fastened into the top, is on both sides most curiously adorned with excellent pictures, having some witty Italian verses or fine emblems written under them; or of some notable Italian city, with a briefe description thereof added thereunto. These fannes are of a meane price, for a man may buy one of the fairest of them for so much money as countervaileth our English groate"—(Coryat's Crudities.)

THE DUCKING-STOOL.

Boswell relates that Dr. Johnson, in a conversation with Mrs. Knowles, the celebrated Quaker lady, said, "Madam, we have different modes of restraining evil—stocks for the men, a DUCKING-STOOL for WOMEN, and a pound for beasts."

In early times it was called the cucking-stool. Brand describes it as an engine invented for the punishment of scolds and unquiet women, by ducking them in the water, after having placed them in a stool or chair fixed at the end of a long pole, by which they were immerged in some muddy or stinking pond.

Blount thought this last name a corruption of ducking-stool; and another antiquary guessed that choking-stool was its etymology.— (See Brand's *Popular Antiquities*, vol. ii. p. 442.) But in a manuscript of the "Promptorium Parvulorum," "*csyn*, or CUKKYN, is interpreted by *stercoris;* and the etymology is corroborated by a no less ancient record than the Domesday Survey, where, at Chester, any man or woman who brewed bad ale, according to the custom of the city, had their choice either to pay a fine of four shillings, or be placed in the cathedra *stercoris.*"

Blount says this chair was in use in the Saxon times. In the Saxon dictionaries its name is Scealking-stool.

In Queen Elizabeth's time the ducking-stool was a universal punishment for scolds.

Cole, the antiquary, in his *Extracts from Proceedings in the Vice-chancellor's Court at Cambridge*, in that reign, quotes the following entries:—

"Jane Johnson, adjudged to the ducking-stool for scoulding, and commuted her penance.

"Katherine Sanders, accused by the churchwardens of St. Andrewe's for a common scold and slanderer of her neighbours, adjudged to the ducking-stool."

Every great town, at that time, appears to have had at least one of these penitential chairs in ordinary use, provided at the expense of the corporation.

Lysons, in his *Environs of London*, vol. i. p. 233, gives a bill of expenses for the making of one in 1572, from the churchwardens' and chamberlain's accompts at Kingston-upon-Thames. It is there called the cucking-stool.

1572.			
The making of the cucking-stool	£0	8	0
Iron-work for the same	0	3	0
Timber for the same	0	7	6
Three brasses for the same, and three wheels	0	4	10
	£1	3	4

In Harwood's *History of Lichfield* p. 383, in 1578, we find a charge "for making a cuck-stool, with appurtenances, 8*s.*" One was erected at Shrewsbury, by order of the corporation, in 1669.—See the history of that town, quarto, 1779, p. 172.

Misson, in his *Travels in England*, makes particular mention of the cucking-stool. He says, "This way of punishing scolding women is pleasant enough. They fasten an arm-chair to the end of two beams twelve or fifteen feet long, and parallel to each other; so that these two pieces of wood with their two ends embrace the chair, which hangs between them upon a sort of axle; by which means it plays freely, and always remains in the natural horizontal position in which a chair should be that a person may sit conveniently in it, whether you raise it or let it down. They set up a post upon the bank of a pond or river, and over this post they lay, almost in equilibrio, the two pieces of wood, at one end of which the chair hangs just over the water; they place the woman in this chair, and so plunge her into the water as often as the sentence directs, in order to cool her immoderate heat."

Cole, the antiquary already mentioned, in one of his manuscript volumes in the British Museum, says, "In my time, when I was a boy and lived with my grandmother in the great corner-house at the bridge-foot, next to Magdalen College, Cambridge, and re-built since by my uncle, Joseph Cock, I remember to have seen a woman ducked for scolding. The chair hung by a pulley fastened to a beam about the middle of the bridge, in which the woman was confined, and let down under the water three times, and then taken out. The bridge was then of timber, before the present stone bridge of one arch was builded. The ducking-stool was constantly hanging in its place, and on the back panel of it was engraved devils laying hold of scolds, &c. Some time after, a new chair was erected in the place of the old one, having the same devices carved on it, and well painted and ornamented. When the new bridge of stone was erected in 1754, this was taken away; and I lately saw the carved and gilt back of it nailed up by the shop of one Mr. Jackson, a whitesmith in the Butcher Row, behind the town-hall, who offered it to me, but I did not know what to do with it. In October, 1776, I saw in the old town-hall a third ducking-stool, of plain oak, with an iron bar before it to confine the person in the seat; but I made no inquiries about it. I mention these things, as the practice seems now to be totally laid aside." Mr. Cole died in the year 1782.

The custom of the ducking-stool was not confined to England. In the *Regiam Majestatem* of Sir John Skene it occurs as an ancient punishment in Scotland, under "Burrow Lawes," chap. 69, noticing Browsters, that is, "*Wemen quha brewes aill to be sauld*," it is said, "gif she makes gude Ail, that is sufficient; bot gif she makes evill Ail, contrair to the use and consuetude of the Burgh, and is convict thereof, she sall pay ane unlaw of aucht shillinges, or sall suffer the justice of the Burgh, that is, she sall be *put upon the* COCK-STULE, and the Ail sall be distributed to the pure folke."

Gay mentions the ducking-stool, in his Pastorals, as a punishment in use in his time:

"I'll speed me to the pond, where
    the high stool
On the long plank hangs o'er the
    muddy pool.
That stool, the dread of every scold-
    ing quean."

(The Shepherd's Week. Pastoral iii.)

BOTANICAL SATIRE.

Some of the systematic names of plants are very pretty little lampoons. Thus Sauvages having given the name *Buffonia*, in honour of Buffon, Linnæus added the epithet *tenuifolia*, which suits the slender leaves of the plant, and the slender pretensions of Buffon to the character of a botanist.

Another plant he named *Browallia*, after Browal, a scholar of his; and as Browal was of humble fortune, he called one of its species *Browallia depressa;* but when Browal rose in the world, and forgot his old friends, Linnæus gave another species the name of *Browallia elata*.

Thus, too, the *Petiveria alliacea*, while it commemorates the botanical zeal of Petiver, who a century ago was apothecary to the Charterhouse, at the same time points out by its acridity the defect of his temper.

Sometimes, again, the name of the plant, though equally epigrammatic, is kinder than in the instances just mentioned. Thus Linnæus gave the name of *Bauhinia* to a plant which has its leaves in pairs in honour of two brother-botanists, John and Gaspard Bauhins; and bestowed the name of *Banisteria* on a climbing-plant, in memory of M. Banister, who lost his life by falling from a rock while herborizing.

In the name *Salix Babylonica*, there is an elegant allusion to a well-known passage in the Psalms.

PULPIT CLIMAXES.

The late Rev. Robert Hall was remarkably happy and apt at hitting off in conversation, by a few bold strokes, dashed occasionally with sarcasm, the peculiarities of his acquaintance, whether they happened to lie in their style, their manners, or their character. We have not seen the following instance in print. It was told us by the gentleman to whom it was addressed. When talking of the Rev. —— of ——, one of the most popular preachers of the day among the Dissenters, in some of whose sermons there is a contrast between the plainness with which they begin, and the flights of metaphor in which they end, our friend asked Mr Hall how he liked this style of eloquence? He replied, "Not at all, sir; not at all. Why, sir, every sentence is a climax, every paragraph is a climax, every head is a climax, and the whole sermon is a climax. And then, at the end of every head and division of his sermon he shouts out, though scarcely audible at first, in a shrill voice that makes one's ears tingle, some text of Scripture in the shape of an exclamation. Why, sir, he puts me in mind of a little sweep boy, running up a succession of parallel chimneys, and at the top of each crying—sweep! sweep!"

PUNNING TEXT.

James the First of England, and Sixth of Scotland, was, as every one knows, deficient in vigour and steadiness. Having heard of a famous preacher who was very witty in his sermons, and peculiarly so in his choice of texts, he ordered this clergyman to preach before him. With all suitable gravity, the learned divine gave out his text in the following words:— "James, first and sixth, in the latter part of the verse, ' He that wavereth is like a wave of the sea, driven by the winds and tossed.'" "Ods chickens! he's at me already," exclaimed the king.

THE BUSY BEE IN THE CRYSTAL PALACE.

The primary object of the Great Exhibition was to collect from all nations the products of human industry. It was of course not only consistent with this end, but necessary to its attainment, to bring together specimens of the mineral, vegetable, and animal kingdom, constituting the materials upon which man exercises his industry and ingenuity. The processes of nature had therefore no place in the plan and purpose of this temple of science and art. It is human thought alone that operates upon the products of nature exhibited in the Crystal Palace, moulding and transforming them for the purposes of use and ornament. The few specimens of vegetable growth formed no exception to the rule excluding the works of nature from the processes and products of art, since the three elm-trees in the transept were left there less in virtue of the permission of the royal commissioners, than by the will of the people of London, who prohibited their being hewn down; while the tropical plants in the transept, and the Wardian cases in the eastern gallery—the meritorious but unrequited invention of our estimable friend at Clapham Rise, for the transportation of living plants from foreign lands,—were introduced chiefly as ornamental accessories, to refresh the eye fatigued by the artificial splendours of the Exhibition. The Irish Flax Society had indeed been allowed to add to its products exhibited in the gallery a living specimen of the common flax plant (*Linum usitatissimum*), which was the only instance in the Exhibition, so far as we could discover, in which a vegetable product was illustrated by a living plant. One exception there was also in favour of the animal kingdom, and one more appropriate could not have been chosen, to connect the processes of human skill and industry with the operations of instinct and the provident economy of nature. We refer to the bees in the north transept gallery, where, amongst different kinds of hives, there was a crystal palace in miniature, in which these interesting little insects were seen busily plying their respective avocations. The hives were variously constructed. There were cottage hive working bell glasses; the ladies' observatory hive, made of glass covered with straw; a collateral hive to obtain the honey without destroying the bees; besides other curious contrivances for apiarians. The Town Mansion Hive was inhabited by four swarms of July, 1850, from four distinct families, or stocks of bees, all living and working in perfect harmony. Till they were brought to the Great Exhibition, they had been kept in a secluded place on the border of a heath. The entrance to the hive was connected with an opening in the glass of the Crystal Palace, and the bees were seen constantly returning to the hive laden with their treasured sweets, or taking their departure for the fields and flower-gardens in the neighbourhood. For six months, they accommodated themselves to their very peculiar circumstances; and their curious operations, as seen distinctly through the glass covering, were not the least pleasing and instructive portion of the exhibition of the world's industry. You looked down into their miniature city, with its streets composed of houses built of a material which the skill of the chemist cannot produce, and on a plan of structural symmetry and geometrical exactness which it would puzzle the mathematician to imitate. In the formation of their cells, the bees solve the problem of accommodating the largest possible number in the least possible space, and with the smallest possible expenditure of material. Here, as in the great metropolis itself, were streets of plebeian houses, each of them consisting of a six-sided cell, the form best adapted for a cylindrical-bodied animal. These were inhabited by the workers. Houses of more spacious and palatial dimensions were tenanted by the males. There were store-houses, deeper and more capacious than the dwelling-houses, for the reception of the honey and pollen. And there was a Buckingham Palace for the Queen Bee. The workers of the hive illustrated the advantages of the division of labour, being classed into the nurse bees, whose function is to construct and unite the cells, collect the honey, and feed the larvæ; and the wax-makers, or labourers, who carry the stone and mortar, and lay the foundation upon which the nurse bees, or builders, raise their superstructure. When you looked out in the bright sunshine, you might see that the arrivals and departures were incessant. Where did the bees fly in quest of honey, and how did they find their way back again? How few of the strangers who went to London, like the bees, from secluded places on the borders of heaths, from quiet English villages, or distant manufacturing towns, could have gone as far from the Crystal Palace, and returned without losing their way? But where the stranger in London had only two eyes, the bee was possessed of myriads; and in addition to its compound eyes fitted for horizontal sight, it was supplied with a sort of secondary eyes, or stemmata, for vertical vision. And thus clear and comprehensive of sight, it winged its way to the wild-flowers in the Parks, and the cultivated flowers in Kensington Gardens and Hammersmith—to the banks of the Thames—"where Thames first rural grows"—perhaps to imperial Kew —perhaps to the forest glades of beautiful Richmond—

"To lofty Harrow now, and now to where
 Majestic Windsor lifts his princely brow;
 . . . . To royal Hampton's pile,
 To Clermont's terraced height, and Esher's groves.
 By the soft windings of the silent Mole."

The same wonderful instinct that guides the little busy bee in its wanderings amongst the fields and gardens, and brings it back again with unfailing certainty to the hive, laden with honey extracted from the nectaries of flowers, and pollen from their anthers, directs it also in selecting the plants suitable for its purpose, and in rejecting those which are pernicious or unproductive; and this discrimination the bee could exercise ages before the mind of man had elaborated the science which classifies plants according to their structure, and infers their qualities from their classification. In like manner, when the inhabitants of our island lived in huts of wattle and mud, painted their persons, and roamed about in the rude freedom of savage life, the bee constructed its cells on the same architectural and geometrical principles as it does at the present day, having neither fallen below nor improved upon the attainments of that sagacious instinct with which the God of nature has so wisely and beneficently endowed it. Instinct, perfect and persistent, constructs the curious prisms of the bee-hive, and governs the social economy of its industrious and orderly community. It was well to give a place to these social workers in the temple consecrated to the triumphs of reason and the trophies of art. In this the scene of his proudest achievements, man might learn a lesson, fitted at once to humble and exalt him, from "the little busy bee." "One thing," says Kirby, "is clear to demonstration, that by these creatures and their instincts, the power, wisdom, and goodness of the Great Father of the universe are loudly proclaimed; the atheist and infidel confuted, the believer confirmed in his faith and trust in Providence, which he thus beholds watching with incessant care over the welfare of the meanest of his creatures; and from which he may conclude that he, the prince of the creation, will never be overlooked or forsaken; and from these what lessons may be learned of patriotism and self-devotion to the public good—of loyalty—of prudence, temperance, diligence, and self-denial!"

THE WIG RIOT.

In the year 1764, owing to changes in the fashion, people gave over the use of that very artificial appendage—the wig, and wore their own hair, when they had any. In consequence of this, the wig-makers, who had become very numerous in London, were suddenly thrown out of work, and reduced to great distress. For some time both town and country rang with their calamities, and their complaints that men should wear their own hair instead of perukes; and at last it struck them that some legislative enactment ought to be procured in order to oblige gentlefolks to wear wigs, for the benefit of the suffering wig-trade. Accordingly they drew up a petition for relief, which, on the 11th of February, 1765, they carried to St. James's to present to his Majesty George the Third. As they went processionally through the town, it was observed that most of these wig-makers, who wanted to force other people to wear them, wore no wigs themselves; and this striking the London mob as something monstrously unfair and inconsistent, they seized the petitioners, and cut off all their hair *par force*.

Horace Walpole, who alludes to this ludicrous petition, says, "Should one wonder if carpenters were to remonstrate, that since the peace their trade decays, and that there is no demand for wooden legs?"—(*Letters to the Earl of Hertford*.)

PARLIAMENTARY REPARTEE.

Atterbury, the celebrated Bishop of Rochester, happened to say in the House of Lords, while speaking on a certain bill then under discussion, that "he had prophesied last winter this bill would be attempted in the present session; and he was sorry to find he had proved a true prophet." My Lord Coningsby, who spoke after the bishop, and always spoke in a passion, desired the House to remark, that one of the right reverend had set himself forth as a prophet; but, for his part, he did not know what prophet to liken him to, unless to that furious prophet Balaam, who was reproved by his own ass." Atterbury in reply, with great wit and calmness, exposed this rude attack, concluding thus:—"Since the noble lord has discovered in our manners such a similitude, I am well content to be compared to the prophet Balaam; but, my lords, I am at a loss how to make out the other part of the parallel; I am sure that I have been reproved by nobody but his lordship."—(*Political and Literary Anecdotes of his own Times*, by Doctor William King, Principal of St. Mary, Oxon.)

TRANSLATABLE PUNS.

Addison has given an excellent test by which we may know whether a piece of real wit has been achieved, or merely a pun perpetrated. We are to endeavour to translate the doubtful production into another language: and if it passes through this ordeal unharmed, it is true wit; if not, it is a pun. Like most tests, however, this fails occasionally; for there are some few puns that, in spite of the prohibitory law, can smuggle themselves into the regions of true wit—just as foreigners, who have perfectly learned the language of a country, can enter as natives, and set alien acts at defiance.

We will give two or three examples of these slippery fellows, who, to use a modern phrase, have succeeded in driving a coach-and-six through Addison's Act.

The lectures of a Greek philosopher were attended by a young girl of exquisite beauty. One day, a grain of sand happened to get into her eye, and, being unable to extricate it herself, she requested his assistance. As he was observed to perform this little operation with a zeal which, perhaps, a less sparkling eye might not have commanded, somebody called out to him, Μη την κορην διαφθειρης, *i.e.*, Do not spoil the pupil.

Cicero said of a man who had

ploughed up the ground in which his father was buried, *Hoc est verè colere monumentum patris*—This is really cultivating one's father's memory.

A punster, being requested to give a specimen of his art, asked for a subject. "The king." "The king is not a subject," he replied. This holds good in French likewise—(*Le roi n'est pas un sujet.*)

The last two cases belong to a class which is, perhaps, more extensive than is commonly supposed; where the two senses of the word are allied by an easy metaphor, and may consequently be found in more than one language. We will give another of the same kind.

Erskine was reproached with his propensity of punning, and was told that puns were the lowest kind of wit. "True," said he, "and therefore they are the foundation of all wit."

Madame de Lamotte was condemned to be marked with a hot iron on both shoulders, as well as to perpetual imprisonment, for her frauds in the affair of Marie Antoinette's diamond necklace. At the end of ten months, however, she made her escape from *l'hôpital*, where she was confined, by the aid of a *sœur*, who said, when quitting her, "Adieu, madame, prenez-garde de vous faire re-marquer." (Farewell, madam; take care not to be *re-marked*.)

A French editor, when quoting this, observes, "Nous ajouterons qu'il faut bien avoir la fureur de dire de tristes bons-mots pour en faire sur un pareil sujet."

At a time when public affairs were in a very unsettled state, M. de G——, who squinted terribly, asked Talleyrand how things were going on.

"Mais, comme vous voyez, monsieur." (Why, as you see, sir.)

Another pun, attributed to the same great master, is not only translatable, but is much better in English than in French. During the reign of Bonaparte, when an arrogant soldiery affected to despise all civilians, Talleyrand asked a certain general what was meant by calling people *pequins*. "Nous appelons pequin tout ce qui n'est pas militaire,' said the general. (We call everybody who is not a soldier, a *pequin*—a miserable creature.) "Eh! oui," replied Talleyrand, "comme nous autres nous appelons militaires tous ceux qui ne sont pas civiles." (Oh! yes; as we call military all those who are not civil.)

DOCTOR DALE.

"This makes me think on that famous civilian, Doctor Dale, who, being employed in Flanders by Q. Elizabeth, sent in a packet to the secretary of state two letters, one to the *queen*, the other to his *wife;* but that which was meant for the *queen* was superscribed, *To his dear wife;* and that for his wife, *To her most excellent majesty:* so that the *queen* having opened his letter, she found it beginning with *Sweetheart*, and afterwards with *My Dear*, and *Dear Love*, with such expressions; acquainting her with the state of his body, and that he began to want money. You may easily guess what motions of mirth this mistake raised; but the doctor by this *oversight* (or *cunningness* rather) got a supply of money. *   * And since I am fallen upon Doctor Dale, who was a witty kind of drole, I will tell you, instead of news (for there is little *good* stirring now), another facetious tale of his; and familiar tales may become *familiar letters* well enough. When Q. Elizabeth did first propose to him that foreign employment to *Flanders*, among other encouragements she told him that he should have twenty shillings *per diem* for his expenses: "Then, madam," *said he*, "I will spend nineteen shillings a-day." "What will you do with the odd shilling?" *the queen replied.* "I will reserve that for my *Kate,* and for *Tom* and *Dick;*" meaning his wife and children. This induced the queen to enlarge his allowance. —(Epistolæ Hoelinæ.)

SOUNDS INAUDIBLE BY CERTAIN EARS.

Dr. Wollaston says that in the natural and healthy state of the human ear, there seems to be no limit to the power of discerning low sounds, whereas acute ones are often inaudible by persons not otherwise deaf. His attention was called to this circumstance by finding a person insensible to the sound of a small organ-pipe, which was far within the limits of his own hearing. This person's hearing terminated at a note four octaves above the middle E of the pianoforte. Others again cannot hear the chirping of the grasshopper, the cricket, the sparrow, and the bat; the latter being about five octaves above the middle E of the piano. The limit of Wollaston's own hearing was about six octaves above the middle E. The range of human hearing includes more than nine octaves, the whole of which are distinct to most ears, though the vibrations of a note at the higher extreme are six hundred or seven hundred times more frequent than those which constitute the gravest audible sound; and as vibrations incomparably more frequent may exist, we may imagine, says Wollaston, that animals like the grylli, whose powers appear to commence nearly where ours terminate, may hear still sharper sounds which we do not know to exist; and that there may be insects hearing nothing in common with us, but endued with a power of exciting, and a sense that perceives, the same vibrations which constitute our ordinary sounds, but so remote that the animal who perceives them may be said to possess another sense, agreeing with our own solely in the medium by which it is excited, and possibly wholly unaffected by those slower vibrations of which we are sensible.

[If there be no limit to the power of discerning low sounds, the "gravest audible sound" is a nonentity, and we ought to read "the gravest known sound."]

THE WISE KING AND HIS COURT FOOL.

In his account of the court of King James the First, Sir Anthony Weldon describes the peculiar function of Archie Armstrong, the royal jester, as follows:—"For now began to appeare a glimering of a new favourite, one Mr. George Villiers, a younger son (by a second venter) of an ancient knight in Leicestershireas I take it; his father of an ancient family, his mother but of a meane, and a waiting gentlewoman, whom the old man fell in love with and married, by whom he had three sons, all raised to the nobility by meanes of their brother favourite. This gentleman was come also but newly from travell, and at that time did beleeve it a great fortune to marry a daughter of Sir Roger Astons, and in truth it was the highest of his ambition, and for that only end was an hanger-on upon the court; the gentlewoman loved him so well, as could all his friends have made her (for her great fortune) but an hundred markes' joynture, she had married him presently, in dispight of all her friends; and no question would have had him without any joynture at all.

"But, as the Fates would have it, before the closing up of this match, the king cast a glancing eye towards him, which was easily perceived by such as observed their prince's humour; and then the match was laid aside, some assuring him a great fortune was comming towards him. Then one gave him his place of cup-bearer, that he might be in the king's eye; another sent to his mercer and taylor to put good cloathes on him; a third, to his sempster for curious linnen; and all as prefacive insinuations to obtaine office upon his future rise: then others tooke upon them to be his bravoes, to undertake his quarrels upon affronts put on him by Somerset's faction: so all hands helped to the piecing up this new favourite.

"Then begun the King to eat abroad, who formerly used to eat in his bed-chamber, or if by chance supped in his bed-chamber, after supper would come forth to see pastimes and foolcries; in which Sir Ed. Zouch, Sir George Goring, and Sir John Finit were the chiefe and master fools; and surely this fooling got them more than any others' wisdome farre above them in desert. Zouch his part was to sing lewd songs, and tell lewd tales; Finit's, to compose these songs. Then was a set of fidlers brought to court on purpose for this fooling; and Goring was master of the game for fooleries, sometimes presenting David Droman, and Archee Armstrong the King's foole, on the back of the other fools, to tilt one at another till they fell together by the eares; sometimes the property was presented by them in antick dances. But Sir John Millicent (who was never known before) was commended for notable fooling, and so was he indeed the best extemporary foole of them all: with this jollity was this favourite ushered in."—(Court of King James, by Sir A. W. 12mo. London, 1651, p. 82.)

Archie became the victim of the ruthless bigot, Laud. When news arrived from Scotland of the bad reception which the King's proclamation respecting the Book of Common Prayer had met with there, Archibald, the King's fool, happening to meet the Archbishop of Canterbury, who was going to the council-table, said to his grace, "Wha's feule now? doth not your grace hear the news from Striveling about the Liturgy?" But the poor jester soon learned that Laud was not a person whom even his jester's coat and privileged folly permitted him to tamper with. The primate of all England immediately laid his complaint before the council. How far it was attended to, the following order of council, issued the very same day on which the offence was committed, will show. "At Whitehall, the 11th of March, 1637.—It is this day ordered by his Majesty, with the advice of the board, Archibald Armstrong, the King's fool, for certain scandalous words of a high nature spoken by him against the Lord Archbishop of Canterbury his grace, and proved to be uttered by him by two witnesses, shall have his coat pulled over his head, and be discharged of the King's service and banished the court; for which the lord chamberlain of the King's household is prayed and required to give order to be executed." And immediately the same was put in execution!* In a pamphlet printed in 1641, entitled *Archy's Dream*,† the following reason is given for Archy's banishment from court. A certain nobleman asking him what he would do with his handsome daughters, he replied he knew very well what to do with them, but he had sons whom he knew not well what to do with; he would gladly make scholars of them, but that he

* Rushworth, part ii. vol. i., pp. 470, 471. Welwood's Memoirs, p. 278.

† "Archy's Dream, sometime Jester to his Majestie; but exiled the court by Canterburio's malice: with a relation for whom an oddo chair stood void in ——. London, 1641."

x

feared the archbishop would cut off their ears.

STATUES TO GREAT MEN.

I may be askt by the studious, the contemplative, the pacifick, whether I would assign a higher station to any publick man than to a Milton and a Newton. My answer is plainly and loudly, *Yes.* But the higher station should be in streets, in squares, in houses of parliament; such are their places: our vestibules and our libraries are best adorned by poets, philosophers, and philanthropists. There is a feeling which street-walking and publick-meeting men improperly call *loyalty;* a feeling intemperate and intolerant, smelling of dinner and wine and toasts, which swell their stomachs and their voices at the sound of certain names reverberated by the newspaper press. As little do they know about the proprietary of these names as potwallopers know about the candidates at a borough election, and are just as vociferous and violent. A few days ago I received a most courteous invitation to be named on a committee for erecting a statue to Jenner. It was impossible for me to decline it; and equally was it impossible to abstain from the observations which I am now about to state. I recommended that the statue should be placed before a public hospital, expressing my sense of impropriety in confounding so great a benefactor of mankind, in any street or square or avenue, with the Dismemberer of America and his worthless sons. Nor would I willingly see him among the worn-out steam-engines of parliamentary debates. The noblest parliamentary men who had nothing to distribute, not being ministers, are without statues. The illustrious Burke, the wisest, excepting Bacon, who at any time sat within the people's house; Romilly, the sincerest patriot of his day; Huskisson, the most intelligent in commercial affairs; have none. Peel is become popular, not by his incomparable merits, but by his untimely death. Shall we never see the day when Oliver and William mount the chargers of Charles and George; and when a royal swindler is superseded by the purest and most exalted of our heroes, Blake?—(Walter Savage Landor.)

CLASSICAL SPOTS IN LONDON.

In Cannon Street we had the good fortune to stumble accidentally on the oldest existing memorial of ancient London, and which, probably, as the Londoners are said to know less of their own city than visitors, few of the multitudes passing it daily and hourly ever observe. It is the famous London Stone, which has been carefully preserved from age to age. It is found mentioned by this name in a record so early as the time of Ethelstan, king of the West Saxons. What was its original use does not appear. It is generally conjectured to have been erected by the Romans, and is believed to have marked the centre of the city burnt by Boadicea, and, like the *miliarium aureum,* the golden pillar in the Forum at Rome, to have been the point where all the ways met, and relatively to which their distances were measured by the Romans. At an early period the street where it is situated formed the centre of the ancient city, and appears to have been the place where proclamations were made to the citizens. Thus it is related in the English Chronicles that "When Jack Cade, the Kentish rebel, anno 1450, in Henry VI.'s time, who feigned himself the Lord Mortimer, came through Southwark into London, he marched to London Stone, amidst a great confluence of people, and the lord mayor among the rest;—he struck his sword upon it, and said, 'Now is Mortimer lord of this city;' and there making a formal but lying declaration to the mayor, departed back again to Southwark." This incident is introduced by Shakspeare in the second part of King Henry VI., one of the scenes of that drama being laid in Cannon Street, where Cade is represented as striking his staff on London Stone, and saying, "Now is Mortimer lord of this city. And here, sitting upon London Stone, I charge and command, that of the city's cost, the conduit run nothing but claret wine this first year of our reign." This venerable relic of antiquity is now built into the wall of St. Swithin's Church, where it is protected by iron bars; and as it existed before London was built or inhabited by the Anglo-Saxons, it may be destined to survive amongst the monuments of its fallen greatness, and attract the pensive regards of the wandering tourist from New Zealand, who in some distant epoch, according to Mr. Macaulay, is to take his station on the remaining arch of London Bridge, and contemplate the ruins of the modern Babylon.

Here, also, where the leading thoroughfares of William Street, Cannon Street, and East Cheap converge upon London Bridge, stood the famous Boar's-head Tavern, immortalized by Shakspeare, which Goldsmith made the subject of one of his pleasant essays, and Washington Irving in our own day delighted to visit for the sake of its ancient recollections, but which was removed a few years ago to make room for a statue of William IV. The most conspicuous object of all is the London Monument on Fish Street Hill, built in 1671-77 to commemorate the great fire, which commenced in this quarter in September, 1666, and covered 436 acres of the city with ruins, extending from the Tower to the Temple Church. The monument is a column of fluted Doric, 202 feet high, and was designed by Sir Christopher Wren. Cibber, father of the comedian, sculptured for the pedestal a representation in bas-relief of the destruction of the city; and the column is surmounted by a blazing urn which has recently been re-gilt. This noble pillar unfortunately stands in a low position, otherwise it would have been amongst the most conspicuous architectural ornaments of the city. It originally bore an inscription ascribing the fire in London to the malice of the Papists. It was to this accusation that Pope alluded in the well-known couplet—

" Where London's column pointing to
    the skies,
  Like a tall bully, lifts the head and
    lies."

The inscription was expunged in the time of James II., restored in the reign of William III., and finally obliterated in 1830, in accordance with a resolution of the Court of Common Council. The following were the terms of this notable inscription:—"This pillar was set up in perpetual remembrance of that most dreadful burning of this Protestant City, begun and carried on by the treachery and malice of the Popish faction, in the beginning of September, in the year of our Lord, 1666, in order to the carrying on their horrid plot for extirpating the Protestant religion and old English liberty, and the introducing Popery and slavery." A man named Hubert made a judicial confession that he set the first house on fire at the instigation of the Papists, and was executed for the crime. He was believed, by those who discredited the origin assigned by him to the conflagration, to be bereft of his senses. On the house in Pudding Lane, erected over the spot where the fire began, was placed by authority the following inscription, which was also removed in consequence of the inhabitants being incommoded by the multitudes who were thus induced to visit the place: "Here by the permission of Heaven, Hell broke loose upon this Protestant city, from the malicious hands of barbarous Papists, by the hand of their agent Hubert; who confessed, and, on the ruins of this place, declared this fact for which he was hanged, viz., that here began the dreadful fire, which is described and perpetuated, on and by the neighbouring pillar, erected anno," &c.

ELECTIONEERING EPIGRAM.

Thomas Moore has recorded in his diary, that Lord John Russell repeated to him the following epigram of Lord Holland's, on one of the two candidates for Bedfordshire saying in his address, that "the memory of his struggle would exist to the end of time":—

" When this earth to the work of destruction shall bend,
And the seasons be ceasing to roll,
How surprised will old Time be to see, at his end,
The state of the Bedfordshire poll!"

GALVANIZING AN INDIAN

On the afternoon of a very sultry day in June I had got a table out in the verandah of my bungalow, and was amusing myself with a galvanic apparatus, giving such of my servants as had the courage a taste of what they called *wulatee boinjee* (English lightning), when a long, gaunt figure, with his hair hanging down in disordered masses over his face, was observed to cross the lawn. On arriving within a few paces of where I stood he drew himself up in an imposing attitude, one of his arms akimbo, while the other held out towards me what appeared to be a pair of tongs, with a brass dish at the extremity of it. "Who are you?" I called out. "Fuqueer," was the guttural response. "What do you want?" "Bheek" (alms). "Bheek!" I exclaimed, "surely you are joking; a great stout fellow like you can't be wanting bheek?" The fuqueer paid not the slightest attention, but continued holding out his tongs with the dish at the end of it. "You had better be off," I said; "I never give bheek to people who are able to work." "We do Khooda's work," replied the fuqueer with a swagger. "Oh! you do; then," I answered, "you had better ask Khooda for bheek." So saying, I turned to the table, and began arranging the apparatus for making some experiments. Happening to look up about five minutes after I observed that the fuqueer was standing upon one leg, and struggling to assume as much majesty as was consistent with his equilibrium. The tongs and dish were still extended, while his left hand sustained his right foot across his abdomen. I turned to the table and tried to go on with my work; but I blundered awfully, broke a glass jar, cut my fingers, and made a mess on the table. I had a consciousness of the fuqueer's staring at me with his extended dish, and could not get the fellow out of my head. I looked up at him again. There he was as grand as ever, on his one leg, and with his eyes rivetted on mine. He continued this performance for nearly an hour, yet there did not seem to be the faintest indication of his unfolding himself; rather a picturesque ornament to the lawn if he should take it into his head, as these fellows sometimes do, to remain in the same position for a twelvemonth. "If," I said, "you stand there much longer, I'll give you such a taste of boinjee (lightning) as will soon make you glad to go." The only answer to this threat was a smile of derision that sent his moustache bristling against his nose. "Lightning!" he sneered; "your lightning can't touch a fuqueer; the gods take care of him." Without more ado I charged the battery and connected it with a coil machine, which, as those who have tried it are aware, is capable of racking the nerves in such a way as few people care to try, and which none are capable of voluntarily enduring beyond a few seconds. The fuqueer seemed rather amused at the queer-looking implements on the table, but otherwise maintained a look of lofty stoicism; nor did he seem in any way alarmed when I approached with the conductors. Some of my servants who had already experienced the process now came clustering about with looks of ill-suppressed merriment to witness the fuqueer's ordeal. I fastened one wire to his still extended tongs, and the other to the foot on the ground. As the coil machine was not yet in action, beyond disconcerting him a little, the attachment of the wires did not otherwise affect him. But when I pushed the magnet into the coil, and gave him the full strength of the battery, he howled like a demon; the tongs, to which his hand was now fastened by a force against his will, quivered in his unwilling grasp as if it were burning the flesh from his bones. He threw himself on the ground, yelling and gnashing his teeth, the tongs clanging an irregular accompaniment. Never was human pride so abruptly cast down. He was rolling about in such a frantic way that I began to fear he would do himself mischief; and, thinking he had now had as much as was good for him, I stopped the machine and released him.—(Household Words.)

· CRANMER AND HENRY VIII.

The following is Dr. Merle D'Aubigne's sketch of Cranmer at the time of his first introduction to the notice of Henry VIII. during the negotiations for that monarch's divorce:—

"Cranmer was descended from an ancient family, which came into England, as is generally believed, with the Conqueror. He was born at Aslacton, in Nottinghamshire, on the 2nd July 1489, six years after Luther. His early education had been very much neglected; his tutor, an ignorant and severe priest, had taught him little else than patiently to endure severe chastisement—a knowledge destined to be very useful to him in after-life. His father was an honest country gentleman, who cared for little besides hunting, racing, and military sports. At this school the son learnt to ride, to handle the bow and the sword, to fish, and to hawk; and he never entirely neglected these exercises, which he thought essential to his health. Thomas Cranmer was fond of walking, of the charms of nature, and of solitary meditations; and a hill, near his father's mansion, used often to be shown where he was wont to sit, gazing on the fertile country at his feet, fixing his eyes on the distant spires, listening with melancholy pleasure to the chime of the bells, and indulging in sweet contemplations. About 1504, he was sent to Cambridge, where barbarism still prevailed, says an historian. His plain, noble, and modest air conciliated the affections of many, and, in 1510, he was elected fellow of Jesus College. Possessing a tender heart, he became attached, at the age of twenty-three, to a young person of good birth (says Fox), or of inferior rank, as other writers assert. Cranmer was unwilling to imitate the disorderly lives of his fellow-students, and although marriage would necessarily close the career of honours, he married the young lady, resigned his fellowship (in conformity with the regulations), and took a modest lodging at the Dolphin. He then began to study earnestly the most remarkable writings of the times; polishing, it has been said, his old asperity on the productions of Erasmus, of Lefevre, of Etaples, and other great authors; every day his crude understanding received new brilliancy. He then began to teach in Buckingham (afterwards Magdalene) College, and thus provided for his wants. His lessons excited the admiration of enlightened men, and the anger of obscure ones, who disdainfully called him (because of the inn at which he lodged) *the hostler*. 'This name became him well,' said Fuller, 'for in his lessons he roughly rubbed the back of the friars, and famously curried the hides of the lazy priests.' His wife dying a year after his marriage, Cranmer was re-elected fellow of his old college, and the first writing of Luther's having appeared, he said: 'I must know on which side the truth lies. There is only one infallible source, the Scriptures; in them I will seek for God's truth.' And for three years he constantly studied the holy books, without commentary, without human theology, and hence he gained the name of the *Scripturist*. At last his eyes were opened; he saw the mysterious bond which unites all biblical revelations, and understood the completeness of God's design. Then, without forsaking the Scriptures, he studied all kinds of authors. He was a slow reader, but a close observer; he never opened a book without having a pen in his hand. He did not take up with any particular party or age; but possessing a free and philosophic mind, he weighed all opinions in the balance of his judgment, taking the Bible for his standard. Honours soon came upon him: he was made successively doctor of divinity, professor, university preacher, and examiner. * * Fox and Gardiner having renewed acquaintance with their old friend at Waltham Abbey, they sat down to table, and both the almoner and the secretary asked the doctor what he thought of the divorce. It was the usual topic of conversation, and not long before, Cranmer had been named member of a commission appointed to give their opinion on this affair. 'You are not in the right path,' said Cranmer to his friends; 'you should not cling to the decisions of the church. There is a surer and a shorter way, which alone can give peace to the king's conscience.'— 'What is that?' they both asked. —'The true question is this,' replied Cranmer: '*What says the Word of God?* If God has declared a marriage of this nature *bad*, the pope cannot make it *good*. Discontinue these interminable Roman negotiations. When God has spoken man must obey.'—'But how shall we know what God has said?' —'Consult the universities; they will discern it more surely than Rome.' * * The day after this conversation, Fox and Gardiner arrived at Greenwich, and the king summoned them into his presence the same evening. 'Well, gentlemen,' he said to them, 'our holidays are over; what shall we do now? If we still have recourse to Rome, God knows when we shall see the end of this matter.'—'It will not be necessary to take so long a journey,' said Fox; 'we know a shorter and surer way.'—'What is it?' asked the king eagerly.—'Doctor Cranmer, whom we met yesterday at Waltham, thinks that the Bible should be the sole judge in your cause.' Gardiner, vexed, at his colleague's frankness, desired to claim all the honour of this luminous idea for himself; but Henry did not listen to him. 'Where is Doctor Cranmer?' said he, much affected. 'Send, and fetch him immediately. Mother of God! (this was his customary oath) this man has the right sow by the ear. If this had only been suggested to me two years ago, what expense and trouble I should have been spared!' Cranmer had gone into Nottinghamshire; a messenger followed and brought him back. 'Why have you entangled me in this affair?' he said to Fox and Gardiner. 'Pray make my excuses to the king.' Gardiner, who wished for nothing better, promised to do all he could; but it was of no use. 'I will have no excuses,' said Henry. The wily courtier was obliged to make up his mind to introduce the ingenuous and upright man, to whom that station, which he himself had so coveted, was one day to belong. Cranmer and Gardiner went down to Greenwich, both alike dissatisfied. Cranmer was then forty years of age, with pleasing features, and mild and winning eyes, in which the candour of his soul seemed to be reflected. Sensible to the pains as well as to the pleasures of the heart, he was designed to be more exposed than other men to anxieties and falls; a peaceful life in some remote parsonage would have been more to his taste than the court of Henry VIII. Blessed with a generous mind, unhappily he did not possess the firmness necessary in a public man; a little stone sufficed to make him stumble. His excellent understanding showed him the better way; but his great timidity made him fear the more dangerous. He was rather too fond of relying upon the power of men, and made them unhappy concessions with too great facility. If the king had questioned him, he would never have dared advise so bold a course as that he had pointed out; the advice had slipped from him at table during the intimacy of familiar conversation. Yet he was sincere, and after doing everything to escape from the consequences of his frankness, he was ready to maintain the opinion he had given. Henry, perceiving Cranmer's timidity, graciously approached him. 'What is your name?' said the king, endeavouring to put him at his ease. 'Did you not meet my secretary and my almoner at Waltham?' And then he added: 'Did you not speak to them of my great affair?'—repeating the words ascribed to Cranmer. The latter could not retreat: 'Sir, it is true, I did say so.'—'I see,' replied the king with animation, 'that you have found the breach through which we must storm the fortress. Now, sir doctor, I beg you, and as you are my subject I command you, to lay aside every other occupation, and to bring my cause to a conclusion in conformity with the ideas you have put forth. All that I desire to know is, whether my marriage is contrary to the law of God or not. Employ all your skill in investigating the subject, and thus bring comfort to my conscience as well as to the queen's.' Cranmer was confounded; he recoiled from the idea of an affair on which depended, it might be, the destinies of the nation, and sighed after the lonely fields of Aslacton. But grasped by the vigorous hand of Henry, he was compelled to advance."

GOOD COMPANY

The Rev. Mr. Moffatt, the missionary in South Africa, relates the following incident, which it is to be feared will rebuke multitudes in more highly-favoured circumstances:—"Once there was a young man of talent and genuine piety, and from whom I expected valuable assistance; but the Lord took him to Himself. For a twelvemonth before his death he was speechless. During the greater part of that time he sat gazing on the New Testament, nodding to an attending relative when he wished the leaves turned over. On one occasion I entered and found him alone. On my saying to him, 'All alone, Andria?' he gave a negative shake of his head, and, with eyes full of animation, directed me to the Bible before him. It was as much as saying that he could not be alóne when he was in possession of that precious book."

RAPID DECAY OF NINEVEH.

The decay of Nineveh must have been very rapid, since, in the time of the young Cyrus, Xenophon seems to have passed close by its side, yet not even the name of the once mighty city appears to have survived its downfall. He only mentions a ruined town called Mespila, which probably the Medes had erected in the neighbourhood. Yet, according to Tacitus, Ninus or Nineveh was a city worthy of being captured even in the days of Claudius.—(Notes from Nineveh.)

SPANIARDS UNINTELLIGIBLE IN SPANISH TOWN.

At the stables I found two Spanish gentlemen, who had come with us in the steamer from Sta. Martha, in rather a "fix," for although in Spanish Town, they could not find any one who could speak that language; and when I came into the stable-yard I found the owner of the place and two or three hostlers going through all manner of indescribable pantomime; but of course the English people had no more idea of what the strangers wanted than the man in the moon. After enjoying the joke for some time, I came out of my hiding-place, and was immediately collared on both sides by the poor Spaniards, who were in a terrible state of perspiration, from their exertions both bodily and mental. It seems they wanted to go to and return from Old Harbour, but they had forgotten the name of the place, and had been for I do not know how long, roaring at the stable-owner, "*Vieja Puerta*" (Old Port). They might as well have cried "Oysters," or anything else, for no pantomime could transmogrify those words into Old Harbour in the mind of the Frenchmen. However, I soon sent them on their way rejoicing.—(A Ramble from Sydney to Southampton.)

THE PEDAGOGUE AND THE PIG-IRON.

The boys had no helps to information, bad or good, except what the master afforded them respecting manufactures; a branch of knowledge to which, as I before observed, he had a great tendency, and which was the only point on which he was enthusiastic and gratuitous. I do not blame him for what he taught us of this kind: there was a use in it beyond what he was aware of; but it was the only one on which he volunteered any assistance. In this he took evident delight. I remember, in explaining pigs of iron or lead to us, he made a point of crossing one of his legs with the other, and cherishing it up and down with great satisfaction, saying, "A pig, children, is about the thickness of my leg." Upon which, with a slavish pretence of novelty, we all looked at it, as if he had not told us so a hundred times. In everything else we had to hunt out our own knowledge.—(Autobiography of Leigh Hunt.)

CLAIRVOYANCE.

The laws of suggestion, and the occasional coincidences of a dream with facts, explain all the real phenomena connected with what is called *clairvoyance*, bearing any relation to a supernatural knowledge of events. There is nothing incredible in the statement of somnambulists predicting the hour of their sleeping or walking, nor in the dying foretelling the precise time of their decease. These are simply cases in which the mind, under the influence of a strong impression, and acting upon a feeble physical organization, has the power of fulfilling its own prophecy. It is otherwise with the prophecies relating to persons or events over which the somnambulist could have no control, which for the most part turn out unhappy guesses. Take, for example, the prophecies, of which there were several, from mesmeric patients in the clairvoyant state, that Sir John Franklin would return home about the middle of September, last year. Had the event been realized, the coincidence would not have been extraordinary, as September was the most likely season for him to be expected, and many persons were then looking for him; but its non-fulfilment, and the vagueness of the description of the circumstances of the position of Sir John Franklin and his companions, clearly proved that the clairvoyantes had not a single idea on the subject which had not been put into their heads by the conjectural paragraphs of newspapers, or by questions so framed as to suggest the answer expected. Indeed, *clairvoyance*, instead of being clear-sightedness, is about the obscurest kind of vision, and almost useless, that a human being can possess; for there is no well-authenticated case of a person discovering by it a single fact which it was of the slightest importance for him to know. A clairvoyante will describe a gentleman's country-seat, carriage-drive, lawn, trees, flowers, conservatory; but we never heard of a person who could find the road to it from such a description. A clairvoyante will talk generally of the seat of a disease, but never so as to guide an anatomist to the precise nerve, muscle, ligament, or bone affected. A clairvoyante will make revelations, but, like those of the American seer, revelations of old discoveries, or of old speculations, or of discoveries which cannot be tested. A clairvoyante will profess to read a book through a deal board, or a printed motto inclosed in a nut shell, but cannot make out the figures of a bank-note for £100, folded in a letter, even when the note is offered (which has been done), to any one who could declare the number without breaking the seal.—(*Westminster Review*.)

SKETCHES IN THE GREAT EXHIBITION.

A unit unperceived, I sink into the living stream again. Rich, poor, gentle, simple, wise, foolish, young, old, learned, ignorant, thoughtful, thoughtless, haughty, humble, frivolous, profound, every grade of intellect, every shade of character! Here is a voluble smatterer, suddenly discomfited by the chance question of a curious child; and rather than own ignorance, will tell him falsely. There a bustling piece of earth, earthy; testing everything by money value. Here comes one, serenely unconscious that he is a fool. There is one suddenly startled by a suspicion that he knows scarcely anything. Here is one listening with seeming lively interest, and assenting gesture, to a scientific explanation of which he comprehends nothing; but appearance must be kept up. There is one falsely thinking himself the observed of all observers; trying to look unconscious and distinguished. Here is one that will not see a timid, poor relation, or an humble friend, as fashionable folk are near. Yonder is a statesman, gliding about alone, watchful, thoughtful, cautious; pondering national character, habits, capabilities, localities, wants, superfluities, rival systems of policy, their fruits and workings, imagining new combinations, speculating on remote conseqnences. Here is one, little thinking that he will fall suddenly dead to-morrow; having much on hand, both of business and pleasure. Here sits a laughing child upon a gleaming cannon. Yonder is a blind man, sightless amidst surrounding pleasures; but there is one telling him tenderly that he stands beside the statue of Milton. There, in the glistening centre of the transept, stands an aged exile; venerable, widowed, once a queen; looking at the tranquil image of Victoria, meditating with a sigh on the happy security of her throne. Everywhere, gliding about, are forms of exquisite beauty, most delicate loveliness.—(Warren's Lily and the Bee.)

THE O'CARROLL.

My father now amused himself in writing cards to his intended guests, including the English officer who had been mentioned by Jack Walsh. A card was despatched to him in the customary style of our Milesian invitations, which, for the benefit of my readers on the eastern side of the Irish Sea, I transcribe—" The O'Carroll and Madame O'Carroll present their compliments to Major and Mrs. Bullman, and request the honour of their company to dinner at five o'clock on Thursday next. Castle Carroll, Monday." It so fell out that Bullman, who, being a stranger, was perfectly unacquainted with the style assumed by the representatives of ancient Celtic families, was extremely perplexed by my father's hereditary designation. Prior to answering the card, he chanced to meet Bodkin, whom he slightly knew, and to whom he immediately applied for information. "This is the oddest thing, Mr. Bodkin!" said the major; "I have got an invitation from a gentleman who does not call himself *Mister*, but prefixes *The* to his name; and his lady is *Madame*. Can you explain it at all?" "O, dear, yes," replied Bodkin, "it is the universal custom in this part of the world; and if you wish to pay a particular compliment, the rule is, that you must adopt precisely the same style yourself in your reply." "Certainly, whatever is right," said the unsuspecting major; "I wish to conform to the etiquette of the country in everything." Acting under the treacherous instructions of Bodkin, the major wrote the following answer: " The Bullman and Madame Bullman present their compliments to Mr. and Mrs. O'Carroll, and will have the honour of accepting their invitation to dinner on Thursday next." Words are indeed faint to describe my father's rage on receiving this answer. He stamped, stormed, and swore the English rascal should pay for his audacious insult. "How dares he ridicule my hereditary title with his rascally Bullman parody? The fellow shall fight me in the hall, since my evil fate confines me to the house."—(The Gentleman in Debt.)

OVERTASKING THE MIND.

Dr. Wigan remarks in his work on the mind, that he could not read the correspondence between William Pitt and his father, without a feeling allied to terror. Never did man go so near to destroy the intellect of his son by over-excitement, as the arrogant, unreasonable, imperious, and much over-rated man, the great Earl of Chatham, as he is called. " Courage, my son," said he in one of his letters, when the poor lad was complaining of the enormous variety of topics urged on his attention: "Courage, my boy, remember there is only the Cyclopædia to learn." William Pitt was near falling a sacrifice to his father's ambition. Great as were his talents, I do not doubt that they would have been much greater had they been more slowly cultivated; and he might then have attained the ordinary term of human life, instead of his brain wearing out his body at so early an age. To see him, as I have done, come into Bellamy's (a place for refreshments), after the excitement of debate, in a state of collapse that with his uncouth countenance gave the air of insanity, swallow a steak without mastication, and drink a bottle of port wine almost at a draught, and then be barely wound up to the level of ordinary impulse—repeat this process twice, or, I believe even three times during the night, was a fearful example of over-cultivation of the brain ere it had reached its full development. So much had its excitability been exhausted by premature and excessive moral stimuli, that when his ambition was sated, it was incapable of ever keeping itself in action without the physical stimulants I have spoken of. Men called the sad exhibition the triumph of mind over matter: I call it the contest of brain and body, where victory is attained at the sacrifice of life.

A SCARRED SCHOLAR.

At Swahn Khan's approach, a wild creature, all rags and gestures, rushed out, and embraced his knees, with many welcomes in Pushtoo, which he instantly turned into bad Persian when informed who I was. This prepared me for the announcement which followed, that he was the "Akhoond," or scholar of the place; but, as he had run out without his turban, I could not help smiling to see the scholar's skull scored all over with sabre cuts. He invited us all to stop and dine, and smoke a chillum; but as I insisted on proceeding, he made a last request, that "if ever I reduced the valley of Bunnoo, I would recover for him a certain long musket, which a Murwutee had taken as spoil, after killing the Akhoond's father in a raid, and then sold to a Bunnoochee, named Shah Abbas, for sixteen rupees, though (and this he whispered into my ear) it's worth forty!" I may as well mention here that I did not forget the Akhoond's request; but long afterwards, when all opposition had ceased in Bunnoo, discovered Shah Abbas, redeemed the paternal firelock which was, indeed, a long one, and had it duly conveyed to the delighted scholar of Kummur.—(Edwardes' Year on the Punjab Frontier).

THE PORTLAND VASE IN THE BRITISH MUSEUM.

In a small ante-room is exhibited the celebrated Portland or Barberini Vase, considered one of the principal ornaments of the Museum, and which has acquired fresh interest of late by the misfortune which threatened to deprive the world of this unique specimen of ancient art. It is a production of Grecian genius, and till a few years ago was as perfect as when it passed from the hands of its fabricator. In an unlucky hour, a madman, an artist, we believe, found his way into the Museum, and smashed the peerless vase to pieces. A skilful hand has with patient care, and no small degree of success, replaced and cemented the fragments, and restored the exquisite form and proportions of the vase; but its homogeneity of surface it is beyond the power of art to recover. The Portland vase was discovered about the middle of the 16th century, inclosed in a sarcophagus within the monument of the Emperor Alexander Severus, at a short distance from

Rome. The vase remained for about two centuries in the possession of the Barberini family, in the same city, and at last fell into the hands of Sir William Hamilton, from whom it was purchased by the Duke of Portland about the end of last century, for one thousand guineas, and who ultimately deposited it in the Museum. A mould of this noble work of art was taken at Rome before it came into the possession of Sir William Hamilton; and from this mould an English modeller took sixty casts in plaster of Paris, and then destroyed the mould. Wedgewood, the celebrated potter, also obtained a mould of the vase, from which he produced thirty copies, and after selling these at twenty-five guineas each, destroyed the cast, in order to prevent the price from diminishing by the reproduction of the manufacture. Modern art has, however, in various ways, multiplied the form of this exquisitely proportioned vessel, imitations of which in stucco and other materials are by no means uncommon; but it has failed to imitate the material of which it is constructed. Although it is now nearly a century since the vase was brought to this country, so little is known of the method by which it was fabricated, that we are still left to conjecture what is the substance of which it is made, and the methods by which the beautiful bas-reliefs with which it is adorned have been attached to the surface. Dr. Wollaston supposed that it was formed by first producing an artificial opal, and then blowing it out as is now done with glass vessels; after which, part of the outer layer or surface was cut away, leaving the figures in relief. Wedgewood was of a similar opinion, illustrating his conjecture as to the method of producing the figures, by a reference to the mode adopted in cutting the finest cameos; and hence inferring that the construction and ornamenting of the vase must have been the labour of many years. The explanation is plausible, but not so satisfactory as it would have been, had Wedgewood successfully attempted to follow out the process.

The vase is ten inches high, and its diameter six inches at the broadest part near the centre, whence it diminishes gradually towards the base, and more rapidly upwards into a narrow neck, which again opens towards the lip by a graceful flower-like expansion. Two handles spring from over the broadest and terminate in the narrowest part. The substance of the vessel is vitreous or glassy, and dark-bluish coloured, but translucent. It is upon this dark-blue ground that the figures in bas-relief are laid; and it has been remarked with justice, that they are so firmly united to the ground upon which they are thus fixed, that they seem rather to have grown out of it, and to be a part of itself, than to be fastened on by art. In every view of the supposed method of its fabrication, there are difficulties which render the conjectures hitherto offered on the subject unsatisfactory. If the figures have been placed upon the surface when they were rendered plastic, and the substance of the vase itself adhesive, by means of fire, the only conceivable agent in such a method of uniting them, how is it that the finest lines in these inimitable figures have not suffered in the process, and by what dexterity of manipulation could this be avoided? On the other hand, if the figures were relieved from the surface, as in the production of cameos, by cutting out the surrounding surface, by what process of burnishing could the surface be brought up to its present crystalline smoothness and transparency? Of the figures themselves, as works of art, it is impossible to speak in terms of adequate praise. Their graceful attitudes and picturesque groupings, and the mournfulness and pathos which appear to be the prevailing expression, are as far beyond the reach of modern art, as is the manual skill, which gave the whole its form and symmetry. The emblems are funereal and commemorative, but their precise significance has not been satisfactorily interpreted. Although considerably marred by its misfortune, the vase will ever be prized as a specimen of art unique in its structure, and unrivalled in the classic elegance of its design; and thousands, attracted by the praises of its beauty, the singularity of its history, and its unfortunate fate, hang with admiration — not unmixed with sorrow—

"O'er the fine forms of Portland's mystic Urn."

SEDAN-CHAIRS.

This curious mode of conveyance, which was once in such general use among the rich and fashionable, is now very rarely seen in the streets of London. In the time of Hogarth it was considered as a courtly vehicle, and in one of his plates of the *Modern Rake's Progress*, we see his man of fashion using it to go to St. James's. It continued to be used at a much later period, and does not appear to have been generally laid aside until the beginning of the present century. About five-and-twenty years ago, a sedan was very commonly seen in the hall or lobby of gentlemen's houses, no longer used, but laid up like a ship in ordinary.

It is still used rather extensively in Edinburgh, where the chairmen are all Highlanders born, and a very curious and humorous body. It is pretty commonly seen in the streets of Bath, and not unfrequently in those of Cheltenham, Brighton, and our other watering-places. In Brighton, however, it is being superseded by a vehicle called a "Fly-by-night," which is made in the body like a sedan-chair, but goes upon wheels, and is dragged by one or two men.

It is far from being uninteresting to mark the introduction of these things; as they become curious in after-ages, and give a clue to past habits and manners.

The sedan-chair was first brought into England, from Spain, by Prince Charles, afterwards Charles the First, who, as everybody will remember, went to Madrid for a Spanish wife, whom eventually he did not obtain. On his departure, Olivarez, the prime minister and favourite of Philip the Fourth, gave the Prince a few Italian pictures, some valuable pieces of furniture, and three sedan-chairs of curious workmanship. — (See Mendoza's "Relation of what passed in the Royal Court of the Catholic King, our Lord, on the departure of the Prince of Wales.")

We learn from another contemporary, that, on his return to England, Charles gave two of these sedan-chairs to his favourite the Duke of Buckingham, who raised a great clamour against himself by using them in London. The popular cry was, that the Duke was thus reducing free-born Englishmen and Christians to the offices and condition of beasts of burden. (See Memoirs of Court of England, by Bassompierre, the French Ambassador.)

OLD NAMES WITH NEW FACES.

Those who have duly meditated on the Horatian axiom, *Multa renascentur*, &c., will not be surprised to find the blind Lear an optician in Fetter Lane, while Edgar sells ale in Fenchurch Street; Macbeth and his wife are set up in a fruit-stall in Vinegar Yard, Drury Lane; the melancholy Jacques is established as an apothecary and accoucheur in Warwick Street, Golden Square; Angelo is celebrated as a fencing-master in the Albany; Romeo, having been promoted to a captaincy, is beating up for volunteers in the cause of liberty; Paris is in full practice as a popular physician; and Hamlet himself keeps a silversmith's shop at the corner of Sydney's Alley; Otway is a major-general in the army; Milton breaks in horses in Piccadilly; Rowe and Waller are in partnership as stationers in Fleet Street, and Isaac Newton flourishing as a linen-draper in Leicester Square; Alexander Pope, made straight and fattened up, acts tragedy at Drury Lane; Addison sells globes in Regent Street; Richardson and Swift keep lottery offices in the City; Congreve's pieces (which continue to go off remarkably well) are cannon, not comedies; and Farquhar, instead of a poor author, is a rich banker in St. James's Street; Gay, "in wit a man, simplicity a child," makes dolls in Goswell Street; Cowley is a blacksmith; Phillips is poetical only in his prose; Prior, till very lately, was an ensign in the 12th regiment of foot; Collins, instead of odes, makes glass chandeliers; Butler grinds Greek at Harrow; and Cowper may be seen writing his "task" at the table of the House of Lords any day during the sitting of Parliament.—(Book of Table Talk.)

HOUSE OF COMMONS—THE SPEAKER'S MACE.

There are certain odd forms of proceeding connected with our legislative assemblies, which, it may be presumed, that very few but those acquainted with the details of Parliamentary business have any notion of. Many persons, for instance, may have seen, while standing in the lobby of the House of Commons, Mr. Speaker in his robes, enter, preceded by a tall gentleman with a bag-wig and a sword by his side, carrying on his shoulder a heavy gilt club surmounted by a crown—in short, a *Mace:* but few people are cognizant how important this toy is to the legislative duties of their representatives. Be it known, then, that without it the House of Commons does not exist —and that it is as essential that the mace should be present at the deliberations of our senate, as that Mr Speaker should be there himself:—without a Speaker the House never proceeds to business, and without his mace Mr Speaker cannot take the chair. At the commencement of a session, and before the election of a Speaker, this valuable emblem of his dignity is hidden under the table of the House, while the clerk of the table presides during the election; but no sooner is the Speaker elected, than it is drawn from its hiding-place and deposited on the table, where it ever after remains during the sitting of the House; at its rising, Mr Speaker carries it away with him, and never trusts it out of his keeping. This important question, of the Speaker's duty in retaining constant possession of this, which may be called his gilt walking-stick, was most gravely decided in the year 1763, as appears by the Journals of the House of Commons. On that occasion, Sir John Cust, the Speaker, being taken ill, sent to tell the House by the clerk at the table, that he could not take the chair. It appears that there was considerable discussion whether the mace ought not to have been in the house when this important communication was made. No one, however, presumed to say that it ought to have been *on* the table; but many maintained that it ought, for the dignity of the House, to have been underneath it. It was decided, however, that Mr Speaker had done quite right not to part with his "bauble;" and the House accordingly, as the Journals inform us, "adjourned themselves without the mace."

For a member to cross between the chair and the mace when it is taken from the table by the serjeant-at-arms, is an offence which it is the Speaker's duty to reprimand.

If, however, a prisoner is brought to the bar to give evidence or receive judgment, he is attended by the serjeant-at-arms with the mace on his shoulder, and however desirous any member may be to ask the prisoner a question, he cannot do so, because the mace is not *on* the table: he must therefore write down his questions before the prisoner appears, and propose them through the Speaker, who is the only person allowed to speak when his "bauble" is away.

If the House resolve itself into a committee, the mace is thrust *under* the table; and Mr Speaker leaves his chair. In short, much of the deliberative proceedings of this branch of the legislature are regulated by the position in which this important piece of furniture is placed: to use the words of the learned Hatsell, "When the mace lies *upon* the table, it is a *House;* when *under*, it is a *Committee.* When the mace is *out* of the House, no business can be done: when *from* the table and *upon* the serjeant's shoulder, the Speaker alone manages." The mace, then, may be called the household god of the House of Commons; without the presence of which, good fortune could hardly attend its deliberations: all honour to it!

PLUNDERING A CRYSTAL GROTTO.

The inhabitants of Arta speak with astonishment of an English lady who had visited the cave, and who, contrary to the advice of the guides, rode up the perilous ascent to its entrance on horseback, a thing never done or even attempted by any other person within the memory of man. The exploit of the Englishwoman before-mentioned reminds me of what took place in our country some years ago. There is in a certain western county, and on the estate of a nobleman, a cave in the side of a hill, which is very beautiful; it is coated with the stalactites of arragonite, and, as that mineral is not common, those who visited the cave frequently broke off some of the most ornamental crystals, and carried them away as valuable trophies. The noble Lord to whom the cave belonged, in order to prevent this, built a wall before the entrance, and had a door made with a lock to keep out depredators. An old servant, who lived about a mile off, had charge of the key, and those who wished to see the wonders of the cavern were obliged to have recourse to this man, who thus made a kind of benefice of it. He provided flint and steel, tinder, candles, and all other requisites for exploring, charging for them and his own trouble according to a tariff rather higher, perhaps, than would have been sanctioned by free trade. It happened once that a party of gentlemen, men of rank, learning, and fortune, started on an expedition to explore this cave, and, if possible, to obtain, in despite of the dragon, a few crystals of arragonite. They went to the grasping old janitor, and he, with his usual load, and more than his usual politeness, accompanied them. As the party proceeded, their talk was of geology and chemistry, and all cognate sciences. "See," said an M.D., as he stooped down by the side of a brook, "here is native sulphur; let us see if it is pure enough to burn. Lend me your flint and steel, my good man, and the tinder-box." The materials were produced; but in the act of striking a light, the box was precipitated into the brook. The ill-humour of the door-keeper burst forth at once. "Now I must go back and get some fresh tinder; we are close to the cave, and I have two miles to walk." "No, no," said the doctor; "I have tinder with me;" and, producing some German tinder, he restored good-humour by igniting it by means of a brass cylinder and piston, which acted by the sudden compression of air. When they were fairly within the cave it was found that the German tinder would not act, the doctor having cunningly wetted the piece which he produced for the purpose. "You really must go back to your cottage and get some tinder, but we will take care to remunerate you for your trouble." Thus encouraged, the usher of the crystal chamber departed to his dwelling. As soon as his back was turned dry tinder was found, the piston acted well, the candles were lighted, hammers were brought out, and as many stalactites as could be conveniently disposed of found their way into the pockets of the party. One waited outside as a scout. As soon as the old man was seen approaching, the wax candles were again pocketed, the hammers followed their example, with the piston, and all the gentlemen united in objurgating the guide on account of the time he had taken to go so short a distance. When *his* candles were lighted by *his* tinder and matches, the ravages became evident; but, as he imagined the whole party to have been in the dark, whereas he was the only person in that predicament, he accused some unknown thieves of having obtained entrance by means of a false key, and reported to his lordship accordingly. Lord and servant are now with their forefathers; but I do not feel at liberty to give names.—(The Shores and Islands of the Mediterranean.)

A LEGISLATOR FROM THE PLOUGH.

On this first range is the house and farm of my former travelling companion, Mr. Brown. I paid a short visit to the family in passing; and in front of his house, though on the opposite side of the road, I saw one of the stoniest fields I have ever met with. It was literally paved with huge blocks, and was kept untouched as a monument of what the whole had been. It must, I suppose, have been the industrious perseverance of my friend, Mr. Brown, in making a farm out of such unpromising materials, which caused his neighbours, twenty years ago, to force him from the tail of the plough, and, in spite of opposition, send him to the House of Assembly every year since. "We don't want educated men for legislators, or men specially instructed for them, to fill our public offices," say the democrats of North America; and they point to such men as Mr. Brown. "You see he was taken from the plough-tail, and is still a poor farmer, and yet he does as well, and holds as high a place as any of them."—(Johnstone's Notes on North America.)

A POLYGLOT HOUSEKEEPER IN MEXICO.

This hotel, where we met with great civility and attention, is kept by a Scotchman, very considerably Mexicanized: poor man, he is in very bad health, and the climate seems to be slowly poisoning him. The housekeeper is a German, and she, on the contrary, appears to be more intensified in her nationality by the process of transplantation. She seemed perpetually in a high state of sauer kraut, and utterly Teutonic. She was very kind and good-natured, indeed, to us, although frequently she had declined altogether, we were told, the felicity of lodging ladies in the hotel. She explained to me, in a remarkably intelligent mixture of Mexican-Spanish, English, French, German, Indian, Scotch, and anything else that came into her head, leaving it to me to unravel them, her reasons for this occasional indisposition on her part to receive guests of her own sex. "Mexican ladies mit ther airs muy desagradables. Von Senora, wife of a general, come here, sehr cross, sulky. No canny, I tink, head. Gone, loco. Order comida for she and de general, husband. Muy buena it was; I help cook it. Todos good; when she see it, no taste it, take it all todos up, and trose it all at cook's cabeza! There! wat you tink o' dat? The Senora got no comida, nein, soup, frijoles, chickens, todos she trowed in cook's cara, mit her zwei hands! And dere was dinner, disshes, and todos on floor. De general, husband, poor man, he blind, hear noise, came to mich, say, 'Muy schlecht, me can't help.' He a'most cry, pobrecito! lose him dinner too. Hoot awa, a bonny Senora dat, madame." But, if her languages were wonderful, so were her gesticulations. Impressive indeed they were. While her voice was pitched an unusual height to suit and make up for the Babel of languages in which she was constrained to utter her sentiments, she spoke with great rapidity. Suddenly she changed the scene from Mexico to Hanover, where it appeared she had been housekeeper to a gentleman who was an acquaintance of our late kind Duke of Cambridge. "The English Herzog Cambridge," she exclaimed, "wat von good prince dat! Come von day, all out, tous, madame, come to mich, Cambridge did." (I think the good frau did not intend any disrespect to the royal duke by thus familiarly speaking of him, but, not knowing what herzog was in English, when she did not use the German word, she was quite at fault.) "Well, Cambridge say, tell de family I comes, eh? Ha, ha! he laugh, sehr. Good-nature prince, oui, madame, ja, always smile and laugh. O! how unlike cross lady mit general husband." She then proceeded to tell some wonderful stories about the herzog, and cows and fresh milk, and a party, and a country-house, *hacienda*, but the extraordinary patchwork of languages defied all comprehension. Patchwork! nay, it was more like silks of mixed colours: German, shot with French, and that shot over again with English, and crossed with Spanish. She seized my hands every now and then, as if about to give me a lift to assist the understanding, but I was in a hopeless state. There was a whirl of *haciendas* and Hanoverians, and generals, and chickens, and herzogs, and cows, &c., in one's brain; a human windmill, a living telegraph, making signs at the rate of a million a minute before me, and all was confusion and mental darkness. She continued, however, fast and furious; and the chief actor in this scene was evidently perfectly satisfied: she was exceedingly diverted, and intensely interested by her own tale. Now she seemed on the point of cheering herself with hearty bravos, and now she successfully melted herself almost to tears, speaking, in the most pathetic accents, with clasped and rung hands. We, not having the most remote notion at this juncture what particular form of human grief she was representing, were at a loss to console her. As a housekeeper she was very superior indeed, and most kind and obliging did we find her. She kept the hotel in admirable order, and seemed to be running from morning till night. If any of the *Criadas* or

Mozos neglected their duties, there was the detachment of Hanoverian light horse after them *instanter*, trot trot. She had, however, an unpleasant custom of keeping part of the broad galleries that ran round the house in a perpetually flooded state, from the gigantic scale of washing operations that seemed always going on there. At times the soap-sud breakers ran so high it was a matter of great difficulty to pass them with safety, and a small life-boat was quite a desideratum. — (Lady E. S. Wortley's Travels in the United States in 1849-50.)

ANCIENT ROMAN WATERING-PLACES. BAIÆ AND AVERNUS.

The real watering-place was Baiæ, towards Cape Misenum. It is very remarkable, that at present the district is quite pestilential; if a man were to sleep there one night during the summer, he would be seized with a bilious fever, in consequence of the poisonous air. A French officer, who imagined this to be a mere prejudice, made a bet that he would sleep in the Villa Borghese: he was urgently requested not to do it; but the next morning he was quite swollen, and after a few days he died of a putrid fever. The same is the case at Baiæ; and yet the ancients, as we see from a fragment of Cicero's speech *in Clodium et Curionem*, most commonly staid there in April, when it is already dangerous. I have discovered the explanation of all this, from a conversation with a common man. He said to me that the nature of the Pontine marshes was a very strange thing; that it was not possible for any one in summer to sleep there without fatal consequences, and that it was the same in many parts of Latium; but he added, that to his own knowledge sailors and boatmen, even in the dangerous season, slept in their boats very near the coast without injuring their health. This proves that the poisonous atmosphere does not extend across the water. The man's remarks contain a significant hint. I remembered that the English Ambassador, with whom I often took a walk there—he was not a man of learning—directed my attention to the fact, that beyond Mount Posilipo, in the midst of the sea, ruins of ancient Roman houses were found; and he observed, that the Romans must have had a singular taste in thus building houses in the midst of the water, and connected with the mainland by means of bridges, although there was no beauty to attract them. To abandon such a charming coast, and to build a house in the sea, was, he thought, a strange fancy. When, afterwards, I heard the account of the man I mentioned before, the matter ceased to be a mystery to me. Even at Formiæ, and certainly at Baiæ, the Romans built houses into the sea, in order to isolate themselves from the bad air: these are the *moles jactæ in altum*, and on them people were safe.

The country there is indescribably beautiful and charming; and besides Baiæ, the Lake Avernus, surrounded by very ancient forests, is likewise a spot of great interest. Near it, a road has been cut through the rock leading to Cumæ. Such roads were often constructed for the purpose of shortening the distance and avoiding the heights; for the Romans generally endeavoured by every means to shorten the roads. A similar road leads from Naples to Puzzuoli, likewise made to avoid a hill, which it would be very difficult to cross: hence, the *crypta Pausilippana, Puteolana Neapolitana*. The Avernus was, no doubt originally called ἄορνος, and with the digamma ἄϝορνος. This etymology has been rejected, because it implied the statement that birds could not fly over the lake, which, it is said, is an absurdity. But no bird settles there without dying in consequence, on account of the quantity of carbonic acid which is exhaled by the earth and the lake; dogs, too, are not safe there, but men may pass without any danger. —(Niebuhr.)

GERMAN STUDENTS.

The characteristic marks of the genuine German student, such as the laced velvet coat, the little coloured cap, the long and floating hair, and bare neck, scarcely exist in Berlin; and altogether there is less *esprit de corps* than is found in the smaller universities of Germany. In the latter the students always address each other in the second person singular, *thee* and *thou;* and the neglect of this mode of expression would be considered an insult, sufficient to cause a duel. In Berlin there is more formal ceremony, and the terms *Mein Herr* and *you* are generally adopted. Secret societies, the names of which recal to mind the famous *Burchenshaften* of former days, still exist in Berlin; but instead of having for their object political discussion, they seem to have degenerated into smoking, beer-drinking, and fencing clubs. The Revolution, however, has not been without considerable influence on these societies; and although the Berlin students have not played so conspicuous a part in the political affairs of their country as their fellows of Vienna, nevertheless, towards the end of last year, they formed themselves into a volunteer body, distinguished by its zeal and the good order that reigned among its members. Students generally live two together, in furnished rooms, which are cheaper, more convenient, and cleaner than those of Paris. A room, on an average, costs from five to six dollars per month, inclusive of the servant, a good dinner the same, and supper three dollars a-month. A young man with £50 to £60 a-year may live most comfortably in Berlin, and pursue his studies, while a much greater allowance than this would be injurious to him. The most diligent students are unquestionably the philologists; the poorest, the theologians; the richest, and at the same time the idlest, are the jurists. Those who study medicine have the most work, at least if they follow up the course of study prescribed to them at their matriculation. The lectures are either private or public, and the former cost from one to two dollars half-yearly; while poor students are admitted to attend their professors gratis, on a promise to pay their fees when, in after life, they find themselves in a condition to do so. This custom, however, does not prevail so much in the medical as in the other faculties. Every student must attend, at least, one private teacher in the half-year— or rather, to tell the truth, to pay the fees to one; and the medical student must prove before examination that he has attended the prescribed number. The first medical examination takes place in the second year's study; it is called the *examen philosophicum*, and comprises logic and natural history. At the end of the fourth year's study, a student is allowed to become a candidate for the doctor's degree, having previously deposited about £26 English. The examination—to have passed which does not permit a man to practise his profession—is very slight, the only matter rigorously enforced being, that it is conducted in the Latin language. Then comes the grand and public ceremony in the great aula of the university, at which a dissertation and theses are delivered and defended—the latter being always privately rehearsed beforehand with a friend, and the play acted in public as a species of genteel comedy, the *concedo* and *gratulor* following a desultory altercation of about ten minutes, the insignificance of which is concealed under the veil of a dead language. The candidate then challenges any one present—*è corona*—to break a lance with him; and the comedy is terminated by the dean, generally the only member of the faculty present, putting the oath that he shall do nothing unworthy his art and calling, and presenting the candidate with his diploma.—(Medical Times.)

THE GREENWICH PLANET-WATCHER.

Summer is his time of labour, winter his time of rest. It appears that in our climate the nights, on the whole, are clearer than the days, and evenings less cloudy than mornings. Every assistant takes his turn as an observer, and a chain of duty is kept up night and day; at other periods, the busiest portion of the twenty-four hours at the observatory is between nine in the morning and two in the afternoon. During this time they work in silence, the task being to complete the records of the observations made, by filling in the requisite columns of figures upon printed forms, and then adding and subtracting them as the case requires. Whilst thus engaged, the assistant who has charge of an instrument, looks from time to time at the star-regulated clock, and, when it warns him that his expected planet is nearly due, he leaves his companions and quietly repairs to the room where the telescope is ready. The adjustment of this has previously been arranged with the greatest nicety. The shutter is moved from the slit in the roof, the astronomer sits on an easy chair with a movable back. If the object he seeks is high in the heavens, his chair-back is lowered till he almost lies down; if the star is lower the chair-back is raised in proportion. He has his note-book and metallic pencil in hand. Across the eye-piece of the telescope are stretched seven lines of spider-web, dividing the field of view. If his seat requires change, the least motion arranges it to his satisfaction, for it rests upon a railway of its own. Beside him is one of the star-clocks, and as the moment approaches for the appearance of the planet the excitement of the moment increases. The tremble of impatience for the entrance of the star on the field of view, is like that of a sportsman whose dog has just made a full point, and who awaits the rising of the game. When a star appears, the observer, in technical language, "takes a second from the clock face;" that is, he reads the second with his eye, and counts on by the ear the succeeding beats of the clock, naming the seconds mentally. As the star passes each wire of the transit he marks down in his jotting-book with a metallic pencil the second and the only second of his observation, with such a fraction of a second as corresponds in his judgment to the interval of time between the passage of the star and the beat of the clock which preceded such passage. —(Dickens' Household Words.)

BELLS.

The nearer bells are hung to the surface of the earth, other things being equal, the farther they can be heard. Franklin has remarked that, many years ago, the inhabitants of Philadelphia had a bell imported from England. In order to judge of the sound, it was elevated on a triangle in the great street of the city, and struck, as it happened, on a market-day, when the people coming to market were surprised on hearing the sound of a bell at a greater distance from the city than they had ever heard any bell before. This circumstance excited the attention of the curious; and it was discovered that the sound of the bell, when struck in the street, reached nearly double the distance it did when raised in the air. In the air, sound travels at the rate of from 1130 to 1140 feet per second. In water, 4708 feet per second. Sounds are distinct at twice the distance on water that they are on land.

FOREIGN ORTHOGRAPHY.

In the mineral department of the Museum at Florence, the following label in Italian is affixed to a specimen from Scotland:—"Scolezite, from Hold Kilpatrnk-hill, near Glasgow." We wonder if our friends at Old Kilpatrick are able to inform us what locality is meant.

STUDY.

Logic, however unperverted, is not for boys; argumentation is amongst the most dangerous of early practices, and sends away both fancy and modesty. The young mind should be nourished with simple and grateful food, and not too copiously. It should be little exercised until its nerves and muscles show themselves, and even then rather for air than anything else. Study is the bane of boyhood, the aliment of youth, the indulgence of manhood, and the restorative of age.—(W. S. Landor.)

CURIOUS TEST OF THE NIAGARA SAFETY BRIDGE.

My admiration was much more largely drawn upon by the exquisitely delicate suspension-bridge that spans the rushing waters of the river, which hangs at a distance in mid-air, like the slender threads of the silk-worm, discernible only by the frequent weavings of its tiny wires; and even when approached and surveyed closely, looks rather as if it was intended as a thoroughfare for fairies than a human highway. Our luggage was trundled over in a barrow, but we were not permitted to follow until it reached the other side, which caused me to ask the toll-keeper did he not then consider it safe? "O, yes," he said, "perfectly safe; a *woman* crossed it the day before yesterday; but I must obey my orders." To this conclusive reasoning I made no reply, but waited until the porter reached the opposite side, where I wished I was myself, without the gratification of viewing the foaming river through the wires.—(Kelly's Excursion to California.)

NATURAL COMPASS.

It is a well-known fact, that in the vast prairies of the Texas a little plant is always to be found, which, under all circumstances of climate, change of weather, rain, frost, or sunshine, invariably turns its leaves and flowers to the north. If a solitary traveller were making his way across those trackless wilds, without a star to guide or a compass to direct him, he finds an unerring monitor in a humble plant, and he follows its guidance, certain that it will not mislead him.

AUTOGRAPHS IN THE BRITISH MUSEUM.

During the vast influx of visitors attracted to London by the Great Exhibition, the following autographs were laid out for inspection, along with a collection of books and manuscripts of celebrated individuals, in the British Museum :—

Autograph of Shakspere (*sic*), on a copy of Montaigne's *Essays* translated by Florio, printed in 1603. Autograph of Milton, on a copy of Aratus, printed at Paris, 1559. Autograph of Ben Jonson, on presentation copy of his *Valpone* to John Florio, 1607. Autograph of Lord Bacon on a copy of the works of Fulgentius, 1526. Autograph of Bentley, 1711. Autograph of Martin Luther, 1542, in the first volume of a copy of the German Bible. The same copy was afterwards in the possession of Melancthon, who, in 1557, wrote a long note, still preserved, on the flyleaf of the second volume. Handwritings and letters of Edward IV., V., VI.; Richard III. (application to the Duke of Glo'ster for the loan of a hundred pounds), Richard II. (document concerning the surrender of Brest), Henry VII., Queen Anne Boleyn, John Knox, Calvin, Erasmus, Ridley, Cranmer, Latimer, Queen Mary, Bonner, Sir Thomas More, Sir Walter Raleigh, Sir Isaac Newton, Cardinal Wolsey, Galileo, Hampden, Sidney, Burghley, Tasso, Drake, Hawkins, Oliver Cromwell (the Greek *epsilon*, being used for the letter *e*), Queen Elizabeth (specimen of beautiful writing when a Princess), Lady Jane Grey, Addison, Liebnitz, Dryden, Franklin, Charles I., II., James II., Voltaire, George I., II., III., William III., Queen Anne, Pope, Sully, Marlborough, Gustavus Adolphus, Emperor Charles V., Henry IV. of France, Francis I. of France, Peter the Great, Emperor of Russia, Frederick the Great of Prussia, Napoleon Bonaparte, Catherine de Medici, Mary Queen of Scots (part of her will in her own hand-writing in French), Louis XIV. of France, pen-and-ink sketch of Battle of Aboukir by Nelson, Conde, Turenne, Washington, Wellington, and Sir Walter Scott.

THE FERULA OF THE ANCIENTS.

M. Von Heldriech has presented for the Museum at the Royal Gardens at Kew, a portion, nearly four feet long, and three inches in diameter, of a stem of the *Ferula* of the ancients (*Ferula communis*), and of which it is remarked by Tournefort that it preserves its old name among the modern Greeks, who call it *Nartheca*. It bears a stalk five feet high, and three inches thick. At every ten inches there is a knot, and it is branched at each knot. The bark is hard, two lines thick: the hollow of the stem is filled with a white medulla, which, being well dried, takes fire like a match. The fire holds for a long time, slowly consuming the pith, without injuring the bark, and the stem is therefore much used for carrying fire from place to place. This custom is of the highest antiquity, and may explain a passage in Hesiod, where, speaking of the fire that Prometheus stole from heaven, he says that he brought it in a *Ferula;* the fact being probably, that Prometheus invented the steel that strikes fire from flint, and used the pith of a *Ferula* for a match, teaching men how to preserve the fire of these stalks. The stem is strong enough to be leaned upon, but too light to inflict injury in striking; and therefore Bacchus, one of the greatest legislators of antiquity, commanded that men who drank wine should carry staves of this plant, with which they might, during intoxication, smite each other, and yet not break heads. The priests of this deity supported themselves on sticks of *Ferula* when walking. The plant is now chiefly employed for making low stools; but very different were the uses to which the ancients applied the *Ferula*. Pliny and Strabo relate that Alexander kept Homer's work inclosed in a casket of *Ferula*, because of its lightness. The body of the casket being made of this plant, was covered with rich stuff or skin, adorned with ribs of gold, and studded with pearls and precious stones.—(Journal of Botany.)

THE CHEMIST'S POWER OVER MATTER.

From the power over matter, with which existing progress has already invested man, how wondrously interesting are the results and substances which he can produce at will! One of these substances takes fire, and glows brilliantly when simply exposed to the air—another starts into flame when it is touched with water or with ice—a third shines in the air with a paler and more lambent but almost perpetual light—and the smell of a fourth is too nauseous to be endured. One gas, when diffused through the air, in absolutely inappreciable proportion, affects those who inhale it with violent catarrh—another, when inhaled, exhilarates with a happy but fleeting intoxication—a third, if breathed but once, suddenly arrests the current of life. A single drop of one fluid, if swallowed, will produce instant death —of another, will set in motion the whole contents of the alimentary canal—while the vapour of a third will produce speedy insensibility. One solid substance, if merely touched, will crumble to powder and change its colour—another by gentle friction will explode with a terrific detonation — while others again change by a single gleam of the brilliant sun, and produce the wonderful pictures of Talbot and Daguerre. Again, other substances are enriched with healing, balsamic, and salutary virtues — assuaging, exhilarating, or strengthening at the experimenter's will—realizing, in a somewhat different sense, the aspirations of the latter alchemists after a universal medicine, And then how remarkable are the changes in the sensible properties of an organic compound, and in its relations to animal life, which are produced by a very small alteration in its chemical composition! It is sufficiently striking that the union of combustible hydrogen gas with fire-supporting oxygen should produce the fire-extinguishing fluid, water; and that salutary common salt should contain, mollified and disguised by its combination with a metal, sixty per cent. by weight of suffocating chlorine. But these combinations, water and common salt, consist of equal atoms of each constituent, which may readily be supposed, by their union, greatly to modify the properties of one another. In organic compounds, however, containing many molecules united together, it is more surprising that the addition of a single molecule more should often entirely alter their properties and relations to life. Benzoil, for example, contains twenty-one atoms—fourteen of carbon, five of hydrogen, and two of oxygen—and yet the addition of one of hydrogen to these twenty-one forms the high-flavoured and poisonous oil of bitter almonds; or one of oxygen added in its stead forms the well-known solid benzoic acid, to which our pastilles owe so much of their agreeable odour. In cinnamyle, again, there are present twenty-seven atoms, and yet one of hydrogen added to these forms oil of cinnamon, and one of oxygen, a solid substance called cinnamic acid. How very incomprehensible to us as yet are all such molecular changes!—(Edinburgh Review.)

ILLUSTRATIONS OF HOLY WRIT.

Travelling in this desert of Bayiouda, the pleasantest part of our desert journey, and, as Dairch informed us, the most like the deserts in Syria, we were continually struck with the resemblance to places described in the Bible, or to manners and anecdotes related there. Every day brought some new scene, which explained some passage we had hardly understood, or gave force to some other one, which we had scarcely appreciated. One day we met a Bedouin, rich in herds, who was pursuing a single sheep, or camel, across the sandy wastes, tracking the animal by its footsteps; the next we might come on the ninety and nine left without their shepherd. We have felt the disappointment of arriving at a well and finding the waters bitter. And the cup of cold water cannot be fully appreciated except in a country like this, where the water, rare to get at any time, can hardly ever be obtained, even tepid, and generally has a taste of the skin it is kept in, which would disgust any but the most thirsty. Our Lord's command is still obeyed by these people, indeed, throughout the East, and you may always drink any quantity of water, whoever it may belong to. I was surprised once at seeing a Bedouin walk up to my camel and drink a whole bottle of water, my supply for the day; and I have often, when out shooting, gone into a hut or tent and asked for water, which the poor people have had to carry a great distance. Not only have I never been refused, but my offer of a piastre or two was never accepted; they gave it to me, as a Nubian woman once beautifully expressed it, "for God's sake." One of our guides told us how he was ruined last year; for, intrusting his flocks to a "hireling," they were all eaten by a wolf (hyena), and scattered over the desert, while he was away leading some merchants over the sandy plains. When, after a march of ten days over stony hills and arid plains of deep sand, we came suddenly upon the broad river winding through the rich green of the durra-covered banks, we could exclaim with the Psalmist, "He maketh me to lie down in green pastures; He leadeth me beside still waters;" and, as a Bedouin in advance of us called his servant, who was walking before him with his sandals, that he might put them on before he reached the village, we remembered that John the Baptist did not deem himself worthy to unloose the latchet of our Saviour's shoes.—(Melly's Kkartoum and the Niles.)

ROYAL BOTANIC GARDEN AT KEW—LONDONERS' LOVE OF FLOWERS.

The Royal Botanic Garden at Kew is a favourite resort of all strangers visiting London, and shares with Richmond, Hampton Court, and other suburban attractions, in affording a grateful relief on a summer day from the sweltering heat of its crowded thoroughfares. To the student of science it presents attractions which are not to be found in any other similar institution in Europe or the world. Kew is situated about seven miles above London, and is approached either directly by the South Western Railway, or by the river steamers, the latter being much the pleasanter route, as it gives you an opportunity of leisurely surveying the upper reaches of the river, as you ascend "To where the silver Thames first rural grows,"— and where its banks are skirted with woods and gardens, interspersed with suburban villas, the residences of the magnates of the metropolis, and villages of inviting aspect, frequented by the citizens when holiday-making. Kew was long a favourite residence of the Royal Family, in whose possession it remained for a century. The botanical collection was commenced about the year 1730, and under the auspices of George III., who was a zealous and munificent patron of the object, and aided by the exertions of that distinguished naturalist, Sir Joseph Banks, it speedily acquired importance and celebrity. The Gardens were successively enriched with the contributions of Sir Joseph himself, who accompanied Captain Cooke when he circumnavigated the globe, by those of Captain Flinders and Mr. Robert Brown, and travellers and collectors in Australia, Brazil, the Cape of Good Hope, and other foreign countries. During the reigns of George IV. and William IV. the Gardens were allowed to languish; and the conviction was pressed upon the public mind, about the commencement of the present reign, that the institution should either be abandoned altogether, or rendered commensurate with the advance of science, and placed upon a footing worthy of a great national institution. In the year 1840, her Majesty Queen Victoria, in the most liberal spirit, relinquished her title to the garden and pleasure-grounds, which were accordingly transferred to the care of the commissioners of Woods and Forests, to be by them applied to the public benefit. In the course of improvement which was now resolved upon, the first important step was the appointment to the office of director of Sir Wm. Jackson Hooker, then Professor of Botany in the University of Glasgow. Under the fostering care of the commissioners, and the enlightened zeal of the director, the Gardens have already become unrivalled as a school of horticulture and botany, more especially since the foundation of the Museum of Practical or Economical Botany, to commence which Sir William Hooker generously devoted his own valuable collections. The great Palm-house is without a parallel in the world. The extent of ground, appropriated to scientific purposes is 75 acres, to which are added the pleasure-grounds and arboretum, consisting of 176 acres of wood and lawn. The gates of the Botanic Garden are thrown freely open to the public every day of the week.

An institution so well adapted to gratify the prevailing taste of the Londoners, could not fail to grow in popularity. Their passion for flowers is proverbial, and during the season the market-gardeners drive a profitable business in ministering to it. One is led to wonder where all the roses and posies he sees in the streets can possibly come from; till some fine summer morning he wends his way to Covent Garden market, the centre from which both Flora and Pomona dispense their daily bounties over the ample domain of Cockneydom. The vast quantities of flowers and fruits brought in from the country during the night, exposed for sale, and scattered far and wide amongst the retailers, while the city is sound asleep, is one of the curious sights of the metropolis, but one seldom witnessed by those who prefer "hearing the chimes at midnight," with Master Shallow, to enjoying the "sight so touching in its majesty" described by the meditative Wordsworth, as he took his station, at early dawn, on Westminster Bridge, and saw

"—— The City, like a garment, wear
The beauty of the morning; silent, bare,
Ships, towers, domes, theatres, and temples, lie
Open unto the fields, and to the sky;
All bright and glittering in the smokeless air.
Never did sun more beautifully steep
In his first splendour, valley, rock, or hill;
Ne'er saw I, never felt, a calm so deep!
The river glideth at his own sweet will,
Dear Heaven! the very houses seem asleep,
And all that mighty heart is lying still!"

The most delicate and costly exotics are to be found in the flower-stalls of Covent Garden market; and even some of the rarer and more beautiful of the native wild-flowers, such as the bee-ophrys, not unfrequently appear in the market, to which they are sent by local collectors, to whom the botanist owes a grudge for despoiling the cherished and familiar stations of his favourite plants.

DOCTOR YOUNG.

One day as Dr. Young was walking in his garden at Welwyn, in company with two ladies (one of whom he afterwards married), the servant came to acquaint him that a gentleman wished to speak with him. "Tell him," says the doctor, "I am too happily engaged to change my situation!" The ladies insisted he should go, as his visitor was a man of rank, his patron, and his friend; but, as persuasion had no effect, one took him by the right arm, the other by the left, and led him to the garden gate; when finding resistance in vain, he bowed, laid his hand upon his heart, and spoke the following words in that expressive manner for which he was so remarkable:—

"Thus Adam look'd, when from the garden driven,
And thus disputed orders sent from heaven:
Like him I go, but yet am loth;
Like him I go, for angels drove us both.
Hard was his fate, but mine still more unkind:
His *Eve* went with him, but *mine* stays behind."

BOOK-MAKING.

La Bruyere, many years ago, observed, that "'tis as much a trade to make a book as a clock; c'est un metier que de faire un livre, comme de faire une pendule." But since his day many vast improvements have been made. Solomon said, that "of making many books there is no end;" and Seneca complained, that "as the Romans had more than enough of other things, so they had also of books and book-making." But Solomon and Seneca lived in an age when books were considered as a luxury, and not a necessary of life. The case is now altered; and though, perhaps, as Dr. Johnson observed, no man gets a bellyful of knowledge, every one has a mouthful. What would Solomon say now, could he see our monthly catalogues, or be told that upwards of a dozen critical machines were kept constantly at work, merely to *weigh* and *stamp* publications."

ANCIENT VALUE OF BOOKS.

In the year 1471, when Louis XI. borrowed the works of Rasis, the Arabian physician, from the Faculty of Medicine, in Paris, he not only deposited in pledge a considerable quantity of plate, but was obliged to procure a nobleman to join him as surety in a deed, binding himself under a great forfeiture to restore it. When any person made a present of a book to a church, or a monastery, in which were the only libraries during several ages, it was deemed a donative of such value, that he offered it on the altar, *pro remedia animæ suæ*, in order to obtain the forgiveness of sins.—(Relics of Literature.)

DISCOVERY OF GALVANISM.

The discovery of the effects of electricity on animals, took place from something like accident.
The wife of *Galvani*, at that time professor of anatomy in the University of Bologna, being in a declining state of health, employed as a restorative, according to the custom of the country, a soup made of frogs. A number of these animals, ready skinned for the purpose of cooking, were lying, with

that comfortable negligence common both to French and Italians, which allows them without repugnance to do everything in every place that is at the moment most convenient, in the professor's laboratory, near an electrical machine, it being probably the intention of the lady to cook them there. While the machine was in action, an attendant happened to touch with the point of the scalpel the crural nerve of one of the frogs, that was not far from the prime conductor, when the limbs were thrown into strong convulsions. This experiment was performed in the absence of the professor, but it was noticed by the lady, who was much struck by the appearance, and communicated it to her husband. He repeated the experiment, varied it in different ways, and perceived that the convulsions only took place when a spark was drawn from the prime conductor, while the nerve was at the same time touched with a substance which was a conductor of electricity.—(Eloge de Galvani.)

BOOK COLLECTORS.

A library well chosen cannot be too extensive, but some there are who amass a great quantity of books, which they keep for show, and not for service. Of such persons, Louis XI. of France, aptly enough observed, that "they resembled *hunch-backed* people, who carried a great burden, which *they never saw.*"

SIR THOMAS MORE.

Henry the Eighth, and Francis the First of France, were both princes of a very warm temper, and the former having a design of sending an angry message to the latter, pitched on Sir Thomas More, his chancellor, for the messenger. Sir Thomas having received his instructions, told Henry, that he feared if he carried such a message to so violent a man as Francis, it might cost him his head. "Never fear, man," said the king, "if Francis were to cut off your head, I would make every Frenchman now in my power a head shorter." "I am much obliged to your majesty," replied the facetious chancellor; "but I much doubt whether any of their heads would fit my shoulders."

NEWTON'S ABSENCE OF MIND.

Doctor Stukely one day by appointment paid a visit to Sir Isaac Newton. The servant said he was in his study, and no one was permitted to disturb him there; but as it was near his dinner-time, the visitor sat down to wait for him. In a short time a boiled chicken under cover was brought in for dinner; an hour passed, and Sir Isaac did not appear. The doctor then ate the fowl, and covered up the empty dish, and desired the servant to get another dressed for his master. Before that was ready the great man came down; he apologized for his delay; and added, "Give me but leave to take my short dinner, and I shall be at your service; I am fatigued and faint." Saying this, he lifted up the cover, and without any emotion turned about to Stukely with a smile, "See," he said, "what we studious people are; I forgot that I had dined."

NEWSPAPERS.

Periodical papers were first used by the English during the civil wars of Oliver Cromwell, to disseminate among the people the sentiments of loyalty or rebellion, according as their authors were disposed.

We seem to have been obliged to the Italians for the idea; and perhaps it was their *gazettas*—from *gazzera*, a magpie or chatterer, which have given a name to these papers. Honest Peter Heylin, in the preface to his *Cosmography*, mentions, that "the affairs of each town, or war, were better presented to the reader in the *Weekly News Books*.—(Universal Magazine, 1792.)

ANCIENT GLAZING OF WINDOWS.

Although there are in this country many specimens of painted glass of the twelfth century, that material is not mentioned for ordinary glazing purposes in any document of so early a date hitherto discovered. It seems probable that it was originally confined to ecclesiastical buildings, and that windows in houses were simply closed by wooden shutters, iron stanchions being sometimes introduced for greater safety. That in some cases the method of securing windows was very inefficient, appears by an anecdote related by Matthew Paris. When Henry the Third was staying at the manor of Woodstock, in the year 1238, a person who feigned insanity made his appearance in the hall, and summoned the king to resign his kingdom; the attendants would have beaten and driven him away; but Henry, making light of his conduct, ordered them to desist, and suffer the man to enjoy his delusions. In the nighttime, however, the same individual contrived to enter the royal bedchamber through a window, and made towards the king's bed with a naked dagger in his hand; luckily, the king was in another part of the house, and the intruder was discovered and secured. Where windows were externally mere narrow apertures, widely splayed on the inside, it is probable that there were internal shutters; but it is clear, from early drawings, that shutters frequently opened outwards, being attached by hinges to the head of the window; in such instances they were kept open by props. It would appear that canvas, or a similar material, was occasionally used instead of glass in early times; that it was employed to fill in the windows of churches before they were glazed, as early as the thirteenth century, does not admit of doubt, inasmuch as its application to that purpose is specifically mentioned in the building accounts of Westminster Abbey in the reign of Henry the Third. Whenever purchases of glass are noted in ancient accounts we find that it was bought at so much per foot; indeed, it may be observed, generally, that there has been little variation in the customs of trade in this country since the date of the earliest records existing.—(Turner's Domestic Architecture in England.)

THE MAMMOTH CAVE OF MARTINIQUE.

That the Mammoth Cave is an antiquity of the world before the flood—a city of giants which an earthquake swallowed, and which a chance roof of rocks has protected from being effaced by the deluge, and by the wear of the elements for subsequent ages—is one of the fancies which its strange phenomena force upon the mind. All is so architectural. It is not a vast underground cavity, raw and dirty, but a succession of halls, domes, and corridors, streets, avenues, and arches—all underground, but all telling of the design and proportion of a majestic primeval metropolis. It is not a cave, but a city in ruins —a city from which sun, moon, and stars have been taken away—whose day of judgment has come and passed, and over which a new world has been created and grown old. By what admirable laws of unknown architecture those mammoth roofs and ceilings are upheld, is every traveller's wondering question. In some shape or other, I heard each of my companions express this. No modern builder could throw up such vast vaulted arches, and so unaccountably sustain them. And all else is in keeping. The cornices and columns, aisles and galleries, are gigantically proportionate, and as mysteriously upheld. Streets after streets, miles after miles, seem to have been left only half in ruins; and here and there is an effect as if the basements and lower stories were encumbered with fragments and rubbish, leaving you to walk on a level with the capitals and floors once high above the pavement. It might be described as a mammoth Herculaneum, first sepulchred with over-toppling mountains, but swept and choked afterwards by the waters of the deluge, that found their way to its dark streets on their subsiding. What scenery and machinery all this will be for the poets of the West by and by! Their Parnassus is "a house ready furnished."—(N. P. Willis.)

PROGRESS OF GEOLOGICAL DISCOVERY.

At the close of Sir C. Lyell's address at the anniversary of the Geological Society, there is appended a note respecting an unexpected discovery, the particulars of which became known to him only since this statement of his views was in the press, giving them almost a prophetic character. One of our ablest geologists, Mr. Logan, the director of the Geological Survey of Canada, has brought to England from the lowest fossiliferous beds of the palæozoic rocks in North America, slabs and casts of slabs exhibiting the tracks and trail of a quadruped. These have been minutely examined by Professor Owen, who has determined them to have been made by a reptile, in all probability allied to the tortoise. The position of the rock in which they occur leaves no doubt about their age. Thus, even as when Robinson Crusoe saw the foot-print on the sand, he inferred unhesitatingly the neighbourhood of men, so from these prints in the petrified sand must we accept the conclusion, that air-breathing vertebrata existed during the primeval epoch, when that sandstone was the shore of a sea—and away to the winds are scattered by this single but significant fact, a crowd of ingenious but unfounded theories, and brilliant but hollow hypotheses.—(Literary Gazette.)

JAMES HOGG, THE ETTRICK SHEPHERD.

As it was not entirely suitable for one in the shepherd's circumstances to be contented with praise alone, and, with a slight change, to adopt Sir Egerton Brydges' line,

"Careless of gaining *cash* if I deserve,"

he had taken up the notion, from a scrap-book which lay on my table, of borrowing an original poem from every author of the day, and publishing the collection on his own account. "Annuals" and "Souvenirs" were not known then; and truly if every poet had composed with as much facility as James Hogg, and thought as little as he did about his productions afterwards, the plan might have been realized. One of the first promises he received was from Lord Byron, who often favoured him with long letters, which Hogg usually lost in a day or two after their arrival. From other quarters promises or hopes were held out, but in no instance came to fulfilment, except in that of Mr. Wordsworth, whose poem, however, could not be available by itself alone, and was therefore included by the author in his next publication. This plan being rather inconsistent with Hogg's usual notions of independence, I doubt not he had all along in the back-ground the quizzical plot which he afterwards carried out, namely, that when every brother of the quill failed him, he would keep his own counsel, and would himself quietly compose a poem for every one of the authors who had made half or whole promises and broke them! Accordingly, he began with Byron, writing the "Guerilla Chief," a story in the Spenserian stanza, and followed it by specimens of Scott, Southey, Wordsworth, Wilson, and I forget who more, till at last he made up a volume, which was published under the title of the *Poetic Mirror*. John Ballantyne, who not only loved a joke, but delighted in mystification, made the most of this notable *jeu d'esprit*, bringing his customers into the dilemma of admitting either that the poems were genuine, or else that James Hogg, having produced the whole alone and unassisted, must be the most wonderful shepherd that ever tended a flock. And he managed so well, that within six weeks, he handed over thirty pounds to the author, far more, I suppose, than he ever gained by the first edition of the *Queen's Wake*.—(Memoirs of a Literary Veteran.)

AEROLITES IN THE BRITISH MUSEUM.

One of the first series which attracts attention in the department of minerals in the natural history collection of the Museum, is that of specimens of meteoric bodies discovered in various parts of the world. The origin of these substances, which have received the name of aerolites or meteoric stones, is one of the enigmas of science. They are conjectured to belong to the same class of bodies as shooting-stars and fire-balls, which are supposed to revolve round the sun, in obedience to the laws of gravitation, with the velocity of planets; but coming within range of the influence of the earth, project fragments of their masses through our atmosphere, and which descend with a noise like thunder. This phenomenon has been observed from remote periods, and in all quarters of the globe; and probably it often occurs unseen or unrecorded, in parts of the world which are uninhabited, or tenanted only by uncivilized men, and doubtless also are aerolites are frequently discharged unobserved into the sea. The earliest found of any of the specimens deposited in this curious collection is a portion of a mass of iron which fell at Agram, in Croatia, in 1751. The next in point of time was discovered between ten and twenty years later in Senegal, in Africa; the third is a large fragment of a mass of Siberian iron discovered on the summit of a mountain, and weighing originally about 1680 pounds. There is also a portion of a mass weighing upwards of 3300 pounds found in Rhenish Prussia; a large specimen from Buenos Ayres, sent by Sir Woodbine Parish in 1826; specimens from the Cape of Good Hope, North and South America, including the United States, Brazil, Mexico, and Texas; two specimens from Brandenburg and Bohemia, and one from Tennessee, all three found in 1847. Of meteoric stones, consisting generally of native iron alloyed with nickel, there is a specimen which fell in Alsace in 1492; specimens found in various parts of the Continent from 1723 to 1798; one which fell at Possil, Glasgow, April 5, 1804, and many others. Humboldt mentions that the proportion of native iron contained in specimens of meteoric iron brought by him from Mexico was as high as 96 per cent.; but in other aerolites instanced by him the proportion of pure metal scarcely amounted to 2 per cent. Berzelius discovered, on analysing these meteoric bodies, that they contained fifteen of the chemical elements, which are distributed throughout the crust of the globe, being a third of the entire number known to us. This interesting fact would seem to favour the opinion maintained by Sir Isaac Newton, that all the planetary bodies are composed of the same matter as the earth. Light, heat, and the power of attraction are the ligaments, so to speak, by which our connection is maintained with the other planetary masses. Humboldt suggests that another bond of union, or mode of contact, subsists betwixt our own and the other planets, if we admit shooting-stars and meteoric stones to be planetary asteroids. "Meteoric stones," he remarks in the *Cosmos*, "are the only means by which we can be brought into possible contact with that which is foreign to our own planet. Accustomed to gain our knowledge of what is not telluric solely through measurement, calculations, and the deductions of reason, we experience a sentiment of astonishment at finding that we may examine, weigh, and analyse bodies that appertain to the outer world. This awakens, by the power of the imagination, a meditative spiritual train of thought, where the untutored mind perceives only scintillations of light in the firmament, and sees in the blackened star that falls from the exploded cloud nothing beyond the rough product of a powerful natural force."

THE HOUSE OF LORDS—A VISIT IN THE DUKE'S DAYS.

No description can do justice to the gorgeous appearance of the House of Lords. The length of the house is 91 feet, the breadth 45 feet, and the height 45 feet. A gallery 3 feet wide, having only one row of seats, and accessible alone to the Peers and their families, runs along either side of the house. At the upper end is the throne, at the lower are the galleries for reporters and strangers. The interior of the house is of Riga wainscot, richly and elaborately carved. The throne and other parts are of carved oak, the simple beauty of which is much obscured by gilding. The arrangements for ventilation are concealed in the space (about 30 feet) betwixt the ceiling and the ridge. The ceiling is divided by massive moulded beams into eighteen principal, and these again into smaller compartments, the ground being blue, bordered with red and gold, and blazoned with the royal badges of the United Kingdom. There are six traceried windows on each side— "storied windows richly dight." The piers between the windows are occupied by eighteen canopied niches, intended to receive statues of the chief barons who secured Magna Charta from King John. Around the jambs of the windows is painted the inscription, "Vivat Regina," many times repeated. The wall behind the throne is painted in fresco. One of the paintings, by Mr. Dyce, represents the baptism of Ethelbert, the first Christian king of England; another is Edward III. conferring the Order of the Garter on Edward the Black Prince; a third, Henry, Prince of Wales, committed to prison for assaulting Judge Gascoigne; the latter two painted by Mr. Cope. At the lower end of the house are two frescoes, by Mr. Maclise, representing the spirit of chivalry and the spirit of law; and one by Mr. Horsley,—the spirit of religion. The whole of the carvings and enrichments, with which the walls are profusely studded, bear heraldic or symbolic designs. As for the throne, "it beggars all description." It is exquisite alike in design and workmanship, but its more substantial excellencies are thrown into shade by the extreme prodigality of its gilding. It consists of a canopy in three parts, 18 feet 6 inches wide. The centre rising higher than the sides, is over the Queen's chair, upon and behind which, the Royal arms, with appropriate badges and symbols, are carved and emblazoned. On the upper and projecting part of the central canopy, and in niches surmounted by open tracery, are placed figures of "knights and barons bold," illustrating the orders of knighthood. Under the lower parts of the canopy, on either side of the throne, are the chair of the Prince of Wales and the chair of the Prince Consort, both suitably decorated with heraldic bearings. The chair of the Queen, raised on a dais of three steps, says our architectural cicerone, "is carved and gilt, richly studded with enamels and crystals; the back and arms are covered with velvet, embroidered with the royal arms," &c. The two side chairs (on the second step of the dais) are in the same style, though of smaller dimensions. "The floor of the throne is covered with a velvet pile carpet of deep red ground, powdered with lions (!) and roses." Again—"the floor of the chamber is covered with a carpet of a royal blue colour, dotted with gold. The seats for the peers, five rows on either side, accommodating 235 persons, are covered with red morocco leather, and the woolsacks with red cloth." During the ordinary sittings of their lordships, the three seats of the throne are covered; but they are exhibited to view on the Saturdays, when strangers are admitted to see the house, on which occasions the throne is the great object of attraction to the ladies.

At the lower end of the house, opposite to the throne, is the reporters' gallery, behind which is the gallery for strangers. The front of the former is ornamented with panelling, containing royal badges painted on gilt grounds: in the cove or receding portion, under the front of the gallery, are emblazoned the arms of the different royal lines; and ecclesiastical emblems, mitres, pastoral staffs, and sceptres, occupy panels on each side.

The gas is burned on the plan contrived by Faraday for carrying off the products of combustion. In addition to branch lights springing from the walls, there are two splendid brass candelabra at the upper end, holding each twenty-five lights, and two at the lower end, holding each thirteen lights. They are about thirteen feet in height, and are conspicuous and elegant objects.

Nothing can be more imposing than the *coup d'œil* of this truly palatial chamber, which in all its decorations and appointments reflects the taste and munificence of a great nation, and is worthy of the august body for whom it has been provided. Yet it is to be feared that the eye has been gratified at the expense of the ear. The prevalence of an angular and irregular surface on the walls and roof, produces a reverberation and confusion of sound which shows that, whatever attempts may have been made to introduce a scientific principle of ventilation, every known law of acoustics has been overlooked and set at nought in its construction. It is quite ludicrous to observe the painful efforts of some of the speakers to make themselves heard in the reporters' gallery,—which, by the by, has been advanced several feet into the area of the house, for the purpose of remedying a defect experienced to such an extent as to require the appointment of a Committee of Inquiry. Speakers with an equable voice and distinct articulation stand the best chance of being heard and reported; but even then the speaker must turn away his face from the woolsack, and address himself to the lower part of the house. Should he grow warm as he advances, and elevate his voice beyond a moderate pitch, little else is heard at the distance of the gallery but a succession of inarticulate sounds. This is a serious evil in their lordships' hall of legislation. The new House of Commons suffers from the same defect. There is no apparent method of overcoming the resonance caused by the reflection of the sound from so many unequal surfaces, but that of covering the gorgeously carved and decorated walls with tapestry.

At the upper end of the house, in front of, and at a respectful distance from, the throne, is placed the woolsack, the seat of the Lord-Chancellor, a small plain bench, covered with red. The Ministerial and Bishops' benches are on the right, sloping upwards from the floor; and on the other side are the opposition benches, arranged in a corresponding manner. The space between is occupied by the cross benches and the table. We had not been many minutes in the gallery till we recognized, by sundry unmistakeable indications, one of the two public men we were most anxious to see in London. On the front opposition benches was seated a peer rather above the middle height, of swart complexion, gray hair, bald crown, and a *nez* (to imitate the minuteness of the passports), which it at once occurred to us we had seen portrayed in facetious cartoons, sculptured by nature on the craggy peaks of Goatfell, and which had a few days before been delineated with a graphic power most wonderful to behold, even on the leaves of the caricature plant in the conservatories of Kew. This noble lord, dressed in a rather loose and unstudied style, in a long frock coat and yellow vest, had a notable habit of hitching from side to side on his seat, and rubbing his bald crown with his hand. Seized by a sudden impulse, he would dart across the house, and seating himself on the front treasury bench, would enter earnestly into conversation with one of the ministers; then abruptly glide away to a cross bench, where, after more restless motion and rubbing of the crown, the noble and learned lord would return to his original seat. Presently some question before the house would call him to his feet. He spoke on every topic, and to the purpose. His sentences were long and involved, but perspicuous; he piled epithets—Pelion upon Ossa—with marvellous aptitude and volubility; his voice was clear and sonorous, his accent Scottish; odd historical allusions and piquant personal reminiscences lent an air of vivacity to a commonplace discussion. Their lordships listened — they were compelled to listen, and were diverted, if not instructed. On finishing his speech he would step across to the minister, or other peer whose position he had been combating, and resume the argument with obvious eagerness—aside. A new face or a new fancy would next attract him to some other quarter; for with all the members of the house, and with all parts of the chamber, the noble and learned lord was on the same easy and familiar footing.

When the learned lord addressed the house, he had no more attentive listener than a venerable peer usually seated on a cross bench at the lower part of the chamber, slightly stooping under the weight of years, and who, on such occasions might be observed raising his head, with his hand behind his ear, to catch what the learned lord was saying. To this illustrious individual, it was remarked by the frequenters of the house, Lord Brougham's pleasantries and vivacity of manner always afforded obvious gratification. The Duke of Wellington was himself one of the least obtrusive members of the house, but when he spoke all hearkened in profound silence. A stranger could recognize him amidst the peers by the marked respect they showed to him. The Duke was the best-known and most popular man in London. There were people constantly waiting at the entry to the House of Lords, and not unusually in the vicinity of the Horse Guards, to get a peep at him; and he had been so long accustomed to acknowledge the homage paid to him by all classes, on his appearing in public, that the habit had become mechanical with him. Every well-bred person elevated his hat to the Duke; and the Duke, sitting on horseback in his calm, impassive manner, and looking straight before him, lifted two fingers towards his hat to everybody. It was quite a scene when he chanced to walk along Regent Street, or some of the more frequented thoroughfares in the neighbourhood of the Horse Guards or the Houses of Parliament. A knot of followers instantly fell into his wake, augmenting as he proceeded. Shopkeepers rushed to their doors, or peered out of their windows to catch a glance of him. "The Duke" passed from lip to lip. You could see in the countenance of all sorts of people as they approached and passed — and all sorts of people is a wide word in the streets of London — a pleased expression as they recognized the Duke. It was less striking to observe the respectful greetings of the better-conditioned classes, than the cordial interest which the common people evinced in the great Captain. The omnibus-driver would point him out to his outside passengers; the cad on the steps behind, to his "insides." The butcher's boy, as he dashed along on his poney, drew bridle to look at the Duke. Cabmen, cadgers, costermongers, and *gamins*, gentle and simple, young and old, paused for a moment to gaze at the man whom they delighted to honour.

HEIGHTS AND DEPTHS.

In speaking of the greatest depth within the earth reached by human labour, we must recollect that there is a difference between the *absolute depth* (that is to say, the depth below the earth's surface at that point), and the *relative depth* (or that below the level of the sea). The greatest relative depth that man has hitherto reached is probably the bore at the new salt works at Minden, in Prussia; in June 1844, it was exactly 1993 feet, the absolute depth being 2231 feet. The temperature of the water at the bottom was 91 degrees Fahrenheit, which, assuming the mean temperature of the air at 49 degrees 3 seconds, gives an augmentation of temperature of 1 degree for every 54 feet. If we compare the depth of the old Kuttenberger mine (a depth greater than the height of the Brocken, and only 200 feet less than that of Vesuvius), with the loftiest structure that the hands of man have erected (with the Pyramid of Cheops, and the Cathedral of Strasburg), we find that they stand in the ratio of eight to one. In descending eastward from Jerusalem towards the Dead Sea, a view presents itself to the eye which, according to our present hypsometrical knowledge of our planet, is unrivalled in any country; as we approach the open ravine through which the Jordan takes its course, we tread, with the open sky above us, on rocks which, according to the barometric measurements of Burton and Russeseggar, are 1385 feet below the level of the Mediterranean. Poisson endeavoured, in a singular manner to solve the difficulty attending an assumption of the spontaneous ignition of meteoric stones at an elevation above the earth where the density of the atmosphere is almost null. These are his words:—"It is difficult to attribute, as is usually done, the incandescence of aerolites to friction against the molecules of the atmosphere, at an elevation above the earth where the density of the air is almost null. May we not suppose that the electric fluid, in a neutral condition, forms a kind of atmosphere, extending far beyond the mass of our atmosphere, yet subject to terrestrial attraction, although physically imponderable, and consequently following our globe in its motion? According to this hypothesis, the bodies of which we are speaking would, on entering this imponderable atmosphere, decompose the natural fluid by their unequal action on the two electricities, and they would then be heated, and in a state of incandescence by becoming electrified. —(Humboldt's Cosmos.)

LONDON DOCKS AND WAREHOUSES.

It is nearly a century and a half since Addison wrote—"There is no place in the town which I so much love to frequent as the Royal Exchange. It gives me a secret satisfaction, and in some measure gratifies my vanity, as I am an Englishman, to see so rich an assembly of countrymen and foreigners, consulting together upon the private business of mankind, and making this metropolis a kind of emporium for the whole earth." The Royal Exchange of London still exhibits one of the most remarkable assemblages in the world, if the stranger visiting it is fortunate enough to have the advantage of a city merchant as his cicerone; otherwise there is little in its general aspect differing from what may be seen daily at 'Change hour in Liverpool and Glasgow. But it certainly interests the stranger, on walking into the quadrangle between two and three o'clock, "when merchants most do congregate," to see the representatives of the different nations of the earth, grouped in their respective places under the piazzas, and engaging in negotiations which, more than the councils of Cabinets, influence the policy of States; and to be told, for example, that the thoughtful-looking man, with strongly-marked Jewish features, leaning carelessly against a pillar, is able by a dash of his pen to control the most powerful Governments in Europe. In this quadrangle, too, resides the mysterious susceptibility to the variations in the political and commercial atmosphere, indicated upon the scale of that most sensitive of all barometers, the money market, with its constantly fluctuating prices. Still it is not in the quadrangle of the Royal Exchange that we most readily perceive evidences of the variety and extent of our national commerce, any more than we discover the nature of the operations of a great London merchant by stepping into his small and unpretending office in Mincing Lane. Had Addison lived in the present day he would have resorted to the London Docks and warehouses for proofs of our commercial enterprise, and our national wealth and luxuriance. Nowhere else are we so strikingly reminded of a description which has acquired vastly greater force and significance by the increase of our traffic since it was penned by that graceful writer:— "Our ships are laden with the harvest of every climate. Our tables are stored with spices, and oils, and wines. Our morning's draught comes to us from the remotest corners of the earth. We repair our bodies by the drugs of America, and repose ourselves under Indian canopies. My friend Sir Andrew calls the vineyards of France our gardens; the spice islands our hotbeds; the Persians our silk-weavers; and the Chinese our potters." It is only half a century since the West India docks were completed (in 1802); the London Docks were opened three years after (in 1805); the East India Docks, now combined under the same proprietary with the West India, were finished three years later (in 1808); and St. Katherine's Docks were not constructed for twenty years more (in 1828). According to Mr. M'Culloch, the home and foreign trade of London, taken together, is equal to that of Liverpool or New York, although in foreign trade alone London is greatly surpassed by Liverpool. The produce conveyed into and from London annually is estimated by the same authority at the prodigious value of *sixty-five millions sterling*. A few statements will further illustrate the extent and distribution of the commerce of London. In 1848 the number of vessels entering the port of London with cargoes from foreign parts was—

British, 4636 ships; 830,130 tons.
Foreign, 3050 ships; 427,745 tons.

From our colonial dependencies cargoes were received during the same year by 1843 ships of 546,195 tons. The coasting vessels entering the port of London in 1848 (the number was rather less in 1849) was 22,584, with a tonnage of 3,242,572. At the beginning of the year 1850 the number of sailing and steam vessels belonging to the port of London was 3053; with a tonnage of 667,497; the crews being estimated at 35,000 men and boys. No British port owns an equally large amount of shipping, although it is surpassed by that of New York. The gross amount of customs duty collected upon the cargoes of these vessels in 1849 was little short of twelve millions of money. The extent and capacity of the Docks convey a still more striking idea of the amount of commercial enterprise involved in the foregoing statements.

As we thread our way through the mazes of these vast repositories, where everything seems in a state of transition, and yet every place appears fully occupied—where the ship's cargo of cotton is being hoisted up to one floor, and part of a shipload of tea is being lowered from another on its way to the market,—we see bales of cotton from America, North and South, from India, from Egypt, from the West Indies, and Port Natal;—hemp, Manilla hemp, and jute from three quarters of the globe, for making cordage and matting;—flax for weaving linen, from Egypt and Holland;—China grass, a fibre obtained from a species of nettle, and capable of being woven into fine fabrics;—silks from Italy, China, Syria, India;—horns of the deer and buffalo, from India, for buttons and knife-handles;—ivory, or elephants' teeth, from Africa, and the teeth of a hippopotamus of the west coast, used in making artificial teeth;—horse-hair and cow-hair from Buenos Ayres and Monte Video, for stuffing cushions and weaving hair-cloth;—alpaca and llama wool from Lima;—camel's-hair from Egypt;—goats' wool from Turkey;—sheeps' wool from northern Europe, Iceland, Australia, the Cape, India, Bombay, Syria, Turkey, Egypt, Spain, Portugal, West Indies, South America;—skins and furs from North America, Russia, the United States;—dye-stuffs in the shape of ship-loads of woods, such as Nicaragua wood, camwood, sapan-wood, bar-wood, logwood, fustic, Brazil wood, from India, Africa, the West Indies, Greece, South America; yellow berries from the Levant, and orchella lichens from Valparaiso and the Cape de Verde islands; madder from Holland, France, Spain; tanning bark from the oaks of Holland and Belgium, with various other tanning materials from India, Smyrna, South America;—spices from Ceylon, India, China, and the islands of the Eastern Archipelago; fruits, nuts, seeds, oils, and balsams, vegetable juices and extracts, for food, luxuries, medicines, agricultural and artificial uses. The mammalia send us their skins and furs, for ornament and use, from the frozen north and the sunny south, the buffalo, racoon, and beaver of Canada, the otter of Rio and Bahia, the Polar bear and the African leopard, the Siberian squirrel and the Indian tiger; the whale and the seal yield us oil, and our tallow is supplied by the oxen and sheep of Russia, Australia, India, South America. The birds of South America and the coast of Africa provide our agriculturists with the most valuable of manures, of which 2800 tons were imported in one year into Liverpool alone. The tortoise of the west coast of Africa sent two tons and a half of its shells to Liverpool in one year for combmaking. Fishes supply the isinglass we receive from Manilla, Peru, and Maranham, and the cod-liver oil of Newfoundland, now so frequently and successfully employed in cases of pulmonary disease. The molluscs of the Levant afford cuttle-fish bones for polishing metals and making tooth-powder; those of the Bahamas, the conch shells for cameos; those of the South Pacific, of Manilla, and Panama, the mother-of-pearl; and the elegant little *Cypræa moneta* of the East Indies is the *cowrie*, which is brought to this country, in hundreds of tons every year, both dead and alive, and exported to Africa to be used as money. In the London market, the *cowrie* sells on an average at 70s. to 75s. a cwt. for bright specimens, and 45s. to 48s. for the dead sort, and it forms a regular entry in some London prices current now before us. Our silks are the produce of the worm which ultimately takes its place amongst insects as the *Bombyx mori*, and other insects yield the lac for varnishing and dyeing, and the rich vermillion of the cochineal. Such are some of the commodities imported into the port of London, and stored up in its capacious warehouses, and such the elements of a trade in itself unrivalled in any part of the world, deriving from every country and clime—from men of every colour and condition—from plants and animals—from sea and land, the materials of our clothing, our furniture, our food, our luxuries, our arts and manufactures—a trade which in one year employs for the port of London alone, 3000 ships and steamers of the aggregate burden of 600,000 tons, and 35,000 men and boys. In one year 6400 vessels, foreign and British, with a capacity of a million and a quarter of tons, have entered the port of London; and the gross amount of customs duty derived from their cargoes was £12,000,000 sterling.

Before leaving the warehouses, we must visit the wine-vaults, for which, by the courtesy of a London merchant, we have been provided with what is termed "a tasting order," being the printed form presented at the vault by intending purchasers, and containing the numbers and marks of the barrels from which samples are to be drawn. These orders are often granted to visitors who have no other end to serve than the gratification of their curiosity, by witnessing the greatest quantity of wine accumulated in one place to be seen in the world. In the vaults beneath the warehouses of the London Docks there is cellarage for 65,000 pipes of wine, and the area of the one we now propose to enter measures seven acres!—and this vast space is not only thickly packed with wine-casks, but the casks are in two tiers, one above the other, numbering some 30,000 barrels in the vault at once. On presenting the order at the entrance, the visitor obtains the services of a cooper, who places in his hands a flat piece of stick about a couple of feet in length, with an oil-lamp burning at the extremity, and carries in his own a gimlet and a glass of the larger sort. Following your guide you speedily lose all perception of daylight, except the glimmer of an opening into the roof or wall a great way off, and which only serves to make the darkness visible. The atmosphere is chill, and loaded with the fumes of wine. The roof is supported with rows of stone pillars; and you come unexpectedly upon a huge funnel or chimney-shaft communicating with the upper part of the building, and known by the name of the Queen's Tobacco-pipe, by reason of its being the furnace where the excise incremation of the confiscated "weed" is performed. This is an odd place to botanize in, but the ubiquitous tribe of fungi is represented here, as in wine-vaults of humbler dimensions, by a species named *Racodium cellare*, which occurs in great profusion on the roof, walls, and casks. In its young state, it appears in spreading tufts of snowy whiteness, yielding to the touch, and becoming compressed and pulpy. When more advanced, it extends along the wall in broad patches of a blackish-green hue, soft and dry to the touch, or it festoons the roof in prolonged pendulous masses, more or less dark-coloured. Under the microscope the plant exhibits an inextricably interwoven series of delicate filaments, having a slightly jointed structure. We found the same plant in quantity in the wine-vault connected with the bonded stores in York Street, Glasgow. A paper in the *Records of General Science*, vol. iii., contains an account of an examination and analysis of a specimen of this fungus, taken from a wine-cellar in Mark Lane, London, by Dr. Robert Thomson, who, limiting himself to the early state of the plant, which he describes as a gelatinous-looking stalactite, found it to consist of 97·53 per cent. of water, 2·21 of vegetable matter, and ·25 of carbonate of lime and phosphate of lime. But to return to our *Cellarius*, the cooper, who has by this time discovered the cask we are in quest of. Forthwith he broaches it with his gimlet, and pours out a glass of generous old unadulterated port, or Madeira reposing from the voyage to India, with a flavour such as it will never more possess after its first contact with the market. Strange stories are told of visitors who, having forgotten the necessity of exercising circumspection and forbearance amidst the seductive influences of the place, have become the subjects of an optical illusion, whereby the lights at the end of their flat sticks were seen double, and on emerging from the cool and murky atmosphere of the vault into the warm, clear sunshine, have found their powers of locomotion unaccountably disturbed by an eccentric tendency, requiring the friendly accommodation of a contiguous cab. It was formerly the rule to exclude all visitors after one o'clock, but this is only enforced in the case of ladies, who are not admitted after that hour—no doubt from some inexplicable caprice on the part of the presiding powers of the wine-vaults. *Punch* thought he could unravel the mystery, when visiting the vaults with a "tasting order." After the manner of Mr. Pepys his

Diary, thus wrote the Facetious One:—"After tasting so much, our Party very jolly and noisy, and did begin to dance and sing, and flourish their Lamps; and methought I did see the meaning of the Notice outside, that Ladies could not be admitted after one o'clock. Coming into the open Air, our Company could scarcely stand; and Mr. Goodfellowe did see them into two Cabs, and I home on Foot—I fear not very straight—and my Wife wondering at the Redness of my Nose. Good Lack, to see the Quantity of Goods and Wine in the Docks; and to think what a great and mighty Nation we are, and what Oceans of Liquor we do swill and guzzle."

MEMORIALS OF THE GREAT PLAGUE AND THE GREAT FIRE IN LONDON.

The *Camden Miscellany* recently printed, contains an "Autobiography and Anecdotes by William Taswell, D.D., from 1651 to 1681," a fragment originally written in Latin, from which it has been translated into English by his grandson, the Rev. Henry Taswell. He records that he saw King Charles on the 29th of May proceeding to Whitehall "with a fine red plume in his hat;" and in the January following, "the bodies of Cromwell, Ireton, and Bradshaw, not long before taken out of the Royal depository at Westminster, exposed upon Tyburn gallows." About this time he was admitted into Westminster school.

"In 1666, when the plague commenced in town, Dr. Busby removed his scholars to Chiswick. But it spread its baneful influence even to this place. Upon this Dr. Busby called his scholars together, and in an excellent oration acquainted them that he had presided as headmaster over the school twenty-five years, in which time he never deserted it till now. That the exigency of affairs required every person should go to his respective home. I very greedily laid hold of the opportunity of going to Greenwich, where I remained ten months. It was a custom peculiar to this unhappy time to fasten up the doors of every house in which any person had died, and after having marked it with a red cross, to set up this inscription on them—'The Lord have mercy on them!' The plague at last reached our house, and we sent two maid-servants to the public pest-house. At the time my father and mother lay sick in different beds, and my eldest brother troubled with a tumour in his thigh; but no one of our family dying, I was soon set at liberty. In the month of September, when six thousand were swept away each week, my father commanded me to carry some letters to town. It was not without reluctance I obeyed; but at last my duty got the better of my inclinations, and after he had provided me with the herb called angelica and some aromatics, besides eatables in a bag, my kind and indulgent mother giving me too some Spanish wine, I made the best of my way to town. There a variety of distressed objects presented themselves to me, some under the direct influence of the plague, others lame through swellings, others again beckoning to me, and some carrying away upon biers to be buried. In short, nothing but death stared me in the face; but it pleased God to extricate me from the danger which threatened me."

[He did not return to Westminster school until Easter in the following year, "when the violence of the plague was considerably abated." Here he was witness of the Great Fire of London]:—

"On Sunday, between ten and eleven forenoon, as I was standing upon the steps which lead up to the pulpit in Westminster Abbey, I perceived some people below me running to and fro in a seeming disquietude and consternation; immediately almost, a report reached my ears that London was in a conflagration; without any ceremony I took my leave of the preacher, and having ascended Parliament steps, near the Thames, I soon perceived four boats crowded with objects of distress. These had escaped from the fire scarce under any other covering except that of a blanket. The wind blowing strong eastward, the flames at last reached Westminster; I myself saw great flakes carried up into the air at least three furlongs; these at last pitching upon and uniting themselves to various dry substances, set on fire houses very remote from each other in point of situation. The ignorant and deluded mob, who upon the occasion were hurried away with a kind of phrenzy, vented forth their rage against Roman Catholics and Frenchmen; imagining these incendiaries (as they thought) had thrown red-hot balls into the houses."

[This bitter hostility of the common people towards the French displayed itself in many acts of violence]:—

"On the next day, John Dolben, Bishop of Rochester and Dean of Westminster (who in the civil wars had frequently stood sentinel), collected his scholars together in a company, marching with them on foot, to put a stop if possible to the conflagration. I was a kind of page to him, not being of the number of King's scholars. We were employed many hours in fetching water from the back side of St. Dunstan's Church in the East, where we happily extinguished the fire. The next day, Tuesday, just after sunset at night, I went to the Royal Bridge (King's Bridge) in the New Palace (Yard) at Westminster, to take a fuller view of the fire. The people who lived contiguous to St. Paul's Church raised their expectations greatly concerning the absolute security of that place, upon account of the immense thickness of its walls and its situation; built in a large piece of ground, on every side remote from houses. Upon this account they filled it with all sorts of goods; and besides, in the church of St. Faith, under that of St. Paul's, they deposited libraries of books because it was entirely arched all over; and with great caution and prudence every the least avenue through which the smallest spark might penetrate was stopped up. But this precaution availed them little. As I stood upon the bridge among many others, I could not but observe the gradual approaches of the fire towards that venerable fabric. About eight o'clock it broke out on the top of St. Paul's Church, already scorched up by the violent heat of the air, and lightning too, and before nine blazed so conspicuous as to let me read very clearly a 16mo edition of Terence which I carried in my pocket. On Thursday, soon after sun-rising, I endeavoured to reach St. Paul's; the ground so hot as almost to scorch my shoes; and the air so intensely warm that unless I had stopped some time upon Fleet Bridge, to rest myself, I must have fainted under the extreme languor of my spirits. After giving myself a little time to breathe, I made the best of my way to St. Paul's. . . . . I forgot to mention that near the east walls of St. Paul's a human body presented itself to me, parched up as it were with the flames; whole as to skin, meagre as to flesh, yellow as to colour. This was an old decrepit woman who fled here for safety, imagining the flames would not have reached her there. Her clothes were burnt, and every limb reduced to a coal. In my way home I saw several engines which were bringing up to its assistance all on fire, and those concerned with them escaping with great eagerness from the flames, which spread instantaneous almost like a wild-fire; and at last, accoutred with my sword and helmet, which I picked up among many others in the ruins, I traversed this torrid zone back again. The papers, half burnt, were carried with the wind to Eton. Oxonians observed the rays of the sun tinged with an unusual kind of redness. A black darkness seemed to cover the whole hemisphere; and the bewailings of people were great."

[The great extent of robbery during this time "by certain persons assuming the character of porters," is also referred to; by this means his father lost property to a large amount.]

DESCRIPTION OF AN OCEAN VOLCANO
BY AN EYE-WITNESS.

The eruption of Graham's Island (which soon after sunk to a shoal), off the coast of Sicily, took place as Mrs. Fitz Maurice was returning home; and she had the gratification of seeing that rare sight, a volcanic island in the course of formation:—

"It was on the 5th of August, at 6.30 p.m., smoke was first visible to the many anxious eyes on board the *Melville*, at the supposed distance of about thirty miles. This, as we proceeded, became more apparent, rising to a considerable height above the horizon; at first, as it appeared, from three sources, but further observation showed it to be but from one, divided by the wind, for presently another column arose to windward, whose more rapid ascent showed it originated immediately from the volcano, and which, as it settled over the water in a tardy progress to leeward, assumed a thousand picturesque forms. Bright forked flames were seen to dart upwards; and a loud rumbling noise was heard, compared by a young midshipman on board to the rattling of a chain cable when the anchor is let go.

"At daybreak the following morning I was awoke by a rap at my cabin-door; some one telling me that we were fast approaching the island, and that I had better make haste, as we would soon have passed it if the wind continued in the same direction. I made a rapid toilette, and putting on my bonnet and cloak, ran upon deck; and never shall I forget the sublime sight. In the soft, warm, gray light of a Mediterranean morning, and from the bosom of a perfectly unruffled ocean, the new volcano was exhibiting its mighty operations. From the crater, which appeared in the form of a cone, jagged at the top, a fleecy vapour rose in globular clouds, which, expanding themselves majestically, assumed in their ascent the form of a towering plume—'*si parva licet componere magnis*' — that known as the illustrious decoration of the Prince of Wales. Large stones, carrying with them a quantity of black dust, were thrown up, and as they rose and fell broke into a thousand curious shapes; and the effect of this through the white vapour was magically beautiful. Flashes, like lightning, darted occasionally through the vapour; and noise, as of thunder, was distinctly heard. All this time the white smoke was extending itself, so as to cover the whole island, hanging together like that which issues from Vesuvius, and then ascending in an unbroken column for a much longer period than smoke generally does. The eruption appeared to be most violent at intervals of two hours; and at 11.30 one took place in some respects different from those I have attempted to describe.

It began with a similar burst of white vapour, and similar projections of stones and dust; but immediately after the latter followed a copious mass of black, lurid smoke, which, overpowering the white vapour, covered in its turn the whole island. The effect of this was less beautiful than the former, but more awful. At this time we were sufficiently near for the deck of the vessel to be covered with the black dust, which was thrown up in great quantities, and of which, as well as of some cinders, I have a specimen. It is harsh to the touch, and in colour resembles gunpowder. The latter were gathered in a curious way. The hides of some bullocks which had been killed in the morning for the consumption of the ship, had been as usual fastened to the stern, to be purified by dragging through the water, and in them the cinders were entangled and brought up into the ship. The splash made by the stones, which, during some of the eruptions fell into the sea at the estimated distance of about seventy feet from the island, was greater than that of a shot fired from an eighteen-pounder, and showed they must have been of considerable magnitude.

"The wind was light, and the *Melville* made but little way. At one P.M., however, we passed the east corner of the island; when the immediate source of these eruptions was visible. Here was the mouth of the crater. On this side, the island, which in form resembled a horse-shoe, with the sides somewhat beaten out, did not rise above the level of the sea, but formed a bay; and from this ebbed a boiling bubbling stream, leaving its own tract in the sea for about three-quarters of a mile. Here it seemed as if a continual conflict was waged between the two elements of fire and water. The sea, rushing into the mouth of the crater, was opposed by the fire within, and, partly repelled, formed a whirling steamy Charybdis." — (Recollections of a Rifleman's Wife, by Mrs. Fitz Maurice.)

SHIRT TREE.

The numerous and well-known voyages to the South Sea Islands, &c., have made us well acquainted with what is called the *bread tree*, as well as another kind, known under the name of the *butter tree*. But it remained for the indefatigable Humboldt to discover, in the wilds of South America, a tree which produces ready-made *shirts*. "We saw, on the slope of the Cerra Duida," says M. Humboldt, "*shirt trees* fifty feet high. The Indians cut off cylindrical pieces two feet in diameter, from which they peel the red and fibrous bark, without making any longitudinal incision. This bark affords them a sort of garment, which resembles sacks of a very coarse texture, and without a seam. The upper opening serves for the head, and two lateral holes are cut to admit the arms. The natives wear these shirts of marima in the rainy season; they have the form of the *ponchos* and *ruanos* of cotton, which are so common in New Grenada, at Quito, and in Peru. As in these climates the riches and beneficence of nature are regarded as the primary cause of the indolence of the inhabitants, the missionaries do not fail to say, in showing the shirts of *marima*, 'In the forests of the Oroonoko, garments are found ready-made on the trees.' We may add to this tale of the shirts, the pointed caps, which the spathes of certain palm-trees furnish, and which resemble coarse net-work."

PSALMODY.

I was much pleased with your pamphlet on psalmody, and I cannot think it possible it should give offence. I think psalms, written with great and noble simplicity, and sung in the same manner, friendly to devotion; and it is almost an offence to call in the aid of insensible and inanimate things to praise the Giver of life and reason. A psalm, decently sung by the congregation, always excites my devotion more than the organ. I would employ musical instruments in a pagan temple, but only the voice of man in a Christian church.—(Lady M. W. Montagu to Dr. Beattie.)

PROFESSOR HORSFORD'S MONUMENT EXPERIMENT.

It is wonderful (says an American journal) to think that the Bunker Hill Monument is bending like a bow backward and forward every day by the influence of the sun! As the sun during mid-day shines on the south side of it, that side expands, becomes longer than the north side, and the consequence is that it bends over towards the north. The same must be true of all other tall monuments, and also of tall chimneys—for some of the latter are 500 feet high. This movement is not simply from the south towards the north as at midday, but in the morning it must be westerly—at noon northerly, and in the evening easterly. These results have been unexpectedly ascertained by Professor Horsford with his pendulum. And thus it has ever been in scientific pursuits, while searching carefully after one object, another is unexpectedly found. Herschel, for instance, in trying to find the parallax of the fixed stars was astonished to find them whirling by twos, threes, and fours, around each other. The *Boston Cabinet* thus informs us:— "We learn from good authority that Professor Horsford meets with an unexpected difficulty, in making successful experiments, in reference to the rotation of the earth, on Bunker Hill Monument. The difficulty, not insuperable, is found in the influences of sun light and heat, in changing the centre of gravity in the monument. The stones in the structure follow the universal law of expansion under the influence of the sun, and hence the Monument, during a bright day, is based northward to about three-fourths of an inch, so changing the centre of gravity and the point of oscillation that distance. This natural and curious fact compels the Professor to change the point from which the long pendulum is suspended once or twice each day, more or less according to the length and intenseness of the heat of the day."

TOBACCO.

A tobacco-seller is the only man that finds good in it, which others brag of, but do not; for it is meat, drink, and clothes to him. No man opens his ware with greater seriousness, or challenges your judgment more in the approbation. His shop is the rendezvous of spitting, where men dialogue with their noses, and their communication is smoke. It is the place only where Spain is commended, and preferred before England itself. He should be well experienced in the world, for he has daily trial of men's nostrils, and none is better acquainted with humours. He is the piecing commonly of some other trade, which is bad to his tobacco, and that to his wife, which is the flame that follows his smoke.—(Bishop Earle.)

RESOLUTION OF A DISAPPOINTED FRIEND-HUNTER.

If I be destined to make any progress in the world, it will be by my own individual exertions. As I elbow my way through the crowded vale of life, I will never in any emergency call on my selfish neighbour for assistance. If my strength give way beneath the pressure of calamity, I shall sink without *his* whine of hypocritical condolence; and if I do sink, let him kick me into the ditch, and go about his business. I asked not his assistance while living; it will be of no service to me when dead.—(Henry Kirke White.)

IBRAHIM PASHA'S AUTOGRAPH.

During Ibrahim Pasha's visit to England, in the summer of 1846, his autograph was requested for the royal album. He was obliged to confess that he was unable to write. Yet how could he refuse a request from such a quarter? Various expedients were successively proposed and rejected for compromising matters. At length, however, it was suggested that he should learn to write his name for the occasion. A copy was marked for him, as for a school-boy, and after one or two unsuccessful attempts, he managed to produce a tolerable resemblance of his name; and the royal album can boast the first and last autograph of the great Egyptian warrior. "We have this anecdote," says *Frazer's Magazine*, "from one who witnessed the whole proceeding."

A MADMAN'S ART.

A madman was conveyed from Rye to Bedlam. They slept in the Borough, and he suspected whether they were taking him. He rose before sunrise, went to Bedlam, and told there that the next day he should bring them a patient, "but that, in order to lead him willingly, he had been persuaded that I am mad; accordingly I shall come as the madman. He will be very outrageous when you seize him, but you must clap on a strait waistcoat." Accordingly the sane man was imprisoned, and the lunatic returned home. He entered a room full of his relations and friends, told the story with exceeding glee, and immediately relapsed into his madness. The other man had a strait waistcoat for about four days before he was exchanged.—(Southey's Commonplace Book.)

A FAITHFUL SCRIBE IN THE FIELD OF BATTLE.

I now dismounted from my horse, and asked (without much hope) if any one had pen and paper? "Sahib!" replied a well-known voice behind me; and, turning, I observed Suddah Sookh, the moonshee of my office, pulling out a Cachmere pen-box and paper from his girdle, just as quickly as if he had been in cutcherry. He had no sword, or other implements of war, but merely the writing materials with which it was his duty to be furnished; and, though he looked serious and grave, he was perfectly calm amid the roar of hostile cannon, and men's heads occasionally going off before his eyes. "What are you doing here, Suddah Sookh?" I asked in astonishment. He put up his hands respectfully, and answered, "My place is with my master! I live by his service; and when he dies, I die!" A more striking instance of the quiet endurance of the Hindoo character I never saw.—(Edwardes' Year on the Punjab Frontier.)

LONG SOUNDING LINE.

The United States Government has in process of construction at Plymouth, a line ten thousand yards long. The object is to sound the Atlantic Ocean, and ascertain its depth and the exact shape of its bottom in every part. This is an important point among scientific men. The deepest spot reached as yet, is off the west coast of the Cape of Good Hope. Capt. Ross, of the British navy, found the depth a little more than five miles. At other places no bottom has been touched at that depth. The line now in construction will probably be too short—5 miles and 120 yards. The highest mountains reach upwards of five miles, and thus we know the inequality of the surface of the earth—the distance between its depths and loftiest heights—to be ten miles. Geologists are trying to learn what has caused these elevations and depressions.

A ridge in the bottom of the Atlantic extends eastwardly from the island of Newfoundland, forming the great fishing banks. It is thought to reach all the way across to Ireland, which is in its due direction, for the Gulf Stream is there deflected to the east and south. If such a range exists, it may be available for laying telegraph wires upon it. Behring's Straits are quite shallow, and so are the Straits of Gibraltar. Between Pernambuco, in South America, and Liberia, in Africa, is the narrowest part of the Atlantic south of Greenland. At the rate of the fastest steamers it may be crossed in about three days; and probably it is also shoal for forming future telegraph lines.

BRITISH PLANTS.

The observations of Watson and Forbes lead to the conclusion, that with the exception of *Eriocaulon septangulare* (Jointed Pipewort), the British islands do not contain a single plant which is not found on the continent of Europe. These islands, therefore, cannot be considered as a centre of vegetation, but as having been colonized by successive vegetable migrations. Their opinion as to the origin of British plants is, that these islands have been peopled by many colonies successively leaving the continent of Europe, from the epoch of the middle tertiary formation up to our own. When a vast continent extended from the Mediterranean regions to the British islands, the plants of the Asturias, and those of Armorica, peopled the south of England and Ireland. To this period succeeded the glacial epoch, during which the lands were immerged to the depth of about thirteen hundred or fourteen hundred feet. This is the period of the migration of the Arctic plants, which still inhabit the tops of the Scottish mountains. When these lands emerged anew, England was united to France, the temperature being such as it is at present. At this time, the great German floral invasion took place, absorbing, so to speak, all the rest, and leaving very slight remains of them. Thus, while the Asturian plants, those of the south, are reduced to a small number of species confined to the southwest of Ireland, the hardy vegetables of the north completed their conquest. The colonization being completed, England became separated from the Continent.—(Professor Balfour's Manual of Botany.)

BULWER'S POMPEIAN DRAWING-ROOM.

In 1841, the author of *Pelham* lived in Charles Street, Berkeley Square, in a small house, which he fitted up after his own taste; and an odd *melis* of the classic and the baronial certain of the rooms presented. One of the drawing-rooms, we remember, was in the Elizabethan style, with an imitative oak ceiling, bristled with pendants; and this room opened into another apartment, a fac-simile of a chamber which Bulwer had visited at Pompeii, with vases, candelabra, and other furniture to correspond. James Smith has left a few notes of his visit here:—"Our host," he says, "lighted a perfumed pastille, modelled from Vesuvius. As soon as the cone of the mountain began to blaze, I found myself an inhabitant of the devoted city; and, as Pliny the elder, thus addressed Bulwer, my supposed nephew:— 'Our fate is accomplished, nephew! Hand me yonder volume. I shall die as a student in my vocation. Do thou hasten to take refuge on board the fleet at Misenum. Yonder cloud of hot ashes chides thy longer delay. Feel no alarm for me; I shall live in story. The author of *Pelham* will rescue my name from oblivion.' Pliny the younger made me a low bow, &c." We strongly suspect James of quizzing "our host." He noted, by the way, that in the chamber were the busts of Hebe, Laura, Petrarch, Dante, and other worthies; Laura like our Queen.

TRANSLATIONS AND TRANSLATORS.

LADY BACON.

Lady Bacon displayed at an early age her capacity, application, and industry, by translating, from the Italian of Bernardine Octine, twenty-five sermons on the abstruse doctrines of predestination and election. This performance was published about the year 1550. A circumstance took place, soon after her marriage, which again called forth her talents and zeal. She appeared as the translator into English, from Latin, of Bishop Jewell's *Apology for the Church of England*, in which he retorted upon the Romanists the charges previously preferred by them against the reformers; and with fidelity and elegance she accomplished her task.

She sent a copy of her work to the primate, whom she considered as most interested in the safety of the church; a second copy she presented to the author, lest, inadvertently, she had in any respect done injustice to his sentiments. Her copy was accompanied by an epistle in Greek, to which the bishop replied in the same language. The translation was carefully examined both by the primate and author, who found it so chastely and correctly given, as to stand in no need of the slightest emendation. The translator received on this occasion a letter from the primate, full of high and just compliments to her talents and erudition.

Lady Bacon survived her husband, and died about the beginning of the reign of James I., at Gerhamburg, near St. Albans, in Hertfordshire. She was the mother of the wisest, brightest of mankind.

TOWNLEY'S "HUDIBRAS."

Horace Walpole says of *Hudibras* that it was long esteemed an impossibility to give an adequate translation of that singular work, in any language, still more in French, the idiom of which is very remote from the conciseness of the original. To our astonishment, however, Mr. Townley, an English gentleman, has translated *Hudibras* into French, with the spirit and conciseness of the original.

WILLIAM TYNDALE.

Tyndale was a disciple of Luther. He was born in the year 1500. About the year 1526, he translated the New Testament into English, of which two editions were sold; but he was obliged to perform his work out of the limits of England. He was, however, at length betrayed by Henry VIII., tried, and condemned to be first strangled and then burnt at the stake. His last words were, "Lord, open the King of England's eyes!"

The first translation of the Scriptures was, however, made by Wickliffe, about the year 1382, or nearly a century and a half before the time of Tyndale.

ELIOT AND THE INDIANS.

While Eliot was engaged in translating the Bible into the Indian language, he came to this passage: "The mother of Sisera looked out at the window, and cried through the lattice," &c. Not knowing an Indian word to signify *lattice*, he applied to several of the natives, and endeavoured to describe to them what a lattice resembled. He described it as a framework, netting, wicker, or whatever else occurred to him as illustrative; when they gave him a long, barbarous, and unpronounceable word, as are many of the words in their language.

Some years after, when he had learned their dialect more correctly, he is said to have laughed outright, upon finding that the Indians had given him the true term for *eel-pot*—"The mother of Sisera looked out at the window, and cried through the *eel-pot*."

FRENCH BLUNDERS.

The French make awful havoc of John Bull's English, in their attempts at translation. They seem never to reflect that English words have often many and remote significations. Voltaire translated some of Shakspeare's plays. Shakspeare makes one of his characters renounce all claim to a doubtful inheritance, with an avowed resolution to *carve* for himself a fortune with his sword. Voltaire put it in French, which re-translated reads, "What care I for lands? With my sword I will make a fortune cutting meat." Another, displeased with such blunders, undertook a more correct translation of the great bard. Coming to the following passage—

"Even such a man, so faint, so spiritless,
So dull, so dead in look, *so woe-begone*,"

he translated the Italicized words to read, "So grief—be off with you."

"PARADISE LOST."

In the French translation of *Paradise Lost*, "Hail, horrors, hail!" is rendered thus: "*Comment vous portez vous, les horreurs, comment vous portez vous!*" that is, "How d'ye do, horrors, how d'ye do?"

EXEGI MONUMENTUM.

At an examination of the senior class in a college, a young man construed the following line in Horace, "*Exegi monumentum ære perennius*" (which is, in English, "I have finished a monument more lasting than brass)," thus: "*I have eaten a monument harder than brass.*" One of the trustees immediately replied, "Well, sir, I think you had better sit down and digest it."

ALFIERI AND HIS ASSISTANT.

Alfieri employed a respectable young man at Florence to assist him in his Greek translations; and the manner in which that instruction was received was not a little eccentric. The latter slowly read aloud, and translated, while Alfieri, with his pencil and his tablets in his hand, walked about the room, and put down his version. This he did without speaking a word; and when he found his preceptor reciting too quickly, or when he did not understand the passage, he held up his pencil.

This was the signal for repetition, and the last sentence was slowly recited, or the reading was stopped, until a tap from the poet's pencil upon the table warned the translator that he might continue his lecture.

The lesson began and concluded with a slight and silent obeisance; and during thirteen months thus spent, the count scarcely spoke as many words to the assistant of his studies.

THE CZAR AND THE MONK.

Peter the Great having directed the translation of Puffendorff's *Introduction to the Knowledge of the States of Europe* into the Russian language, a monk to whom this translation was committed, presented it to the emperor when finished, who turned over the leaves, and exclaimed with an indignant air, "Fool! what did I order you to do? Is this a translation?" Then referring to the original, he showed him a paragraph in which the author had spoken with great asperity of the Russians, but the translator had omitted it. "Go instantly," said the czar, "and execute my orders rigidly. It is not to flatter my subjects that I have this book translated and printed, but to instruct and reform them."

THE WELSH CURATE AND TILLOTSON'S SERMONS.

A Welsh curate, being asked how he managed to preach sermons so far above his own powers of composition, replied, "I have a volume of sermons by one Archbishop Tillotson, which I translate into Welsh, and afterwards re-translate into English, after which the archbishop himself would not know his own compositions."

IGNORANCE BETTER PAID THAN KNOWLEDGE.

Sir John Hill contracted to translate Swammerdam's work on Insects for fifty guineas. After the agreement with the bookseller, he recollected that he did not understand a single word of the Dutch language, nor did there exist a French translation.

The work, however, was not the less closely attended to on account of this small obstacle. Sir John bargained with another translator for twenty-five guineas. The second translator was precisely in the same situation as the first—as ignorant, though not so well paid, as the knight.

He re-bargained with a third, who perfectly understood the original, for twelve guineas. So that the translators who could not translate a word feasted on venison and turtle, while the modest drudge, whose name never appeared to the world, broke in patience his daily bread.

"VICAR OF WAKEFIELD" IN FRENCH.

The Vicar of Wakefield has been translated perhaps as many as fifty times into French, but always in a blundering manner, in consequence of the ignorance of the translators of the meaning of certain phrases. In one case, for instance, a translator has completely misunderstood the meaning of the words, "Moses flayed alive," and rendered it, "Moses almost devoured alive by fleas."

Lately, however, the worthy Vicar has had justice done to him by the translation of M. Charles Nodier, who is well acquainted with the idiom of English literature

www.ingramcontent.com/pod-product-compliance
Lightning Source LLC
Chambersburg PA
CBHW021336300426
44114CB00012B/975